HISTORY OF WORLD WAR II

HISTORY OF WORLD WAR II

Editor-in-Chief
A J P Taylor

Compiled by
S L Mayer

Octopus Books

CONTENTS

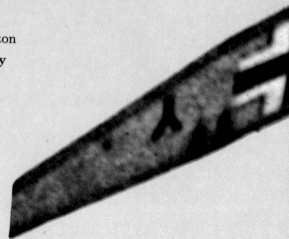

First published 1974 by
Octopus Books Limited
59 Grosvenor Street, London W1

ISBN 0 7064 0399 1

© 1968/69/70 BPC Publishing Ltd.
© 1973/74 Phoebus Publishing Company

This book is adapted from "The History of the 20th Century". It has been produced by Phoebus Publishing Company in co-operation with Octopus Books Limited.

Printed in England by
Jarrold & Sons Limited, Norwich

WORLD WAR II

Introduction

Most people who lived through the Second World War see it in rather simplistic terms. Hitler, Mussolini and Tojo started the war; they attacked the democracies; we gave them better than we got; and Germany, Italy and Japan got exactly what they deserved. Thirty years after the war ended one can afford to take a less emotional look at the greatest war in all history and examine its causes, course and results with a more critical eye. In history there are few genuine villains and even fewer genuine heroes. Interest in the war has increased in recent years, especially among those to whom it is only a distant memory and to those who were born after the war was already part of history. Interest is growing too among historians, for only now are documents being made available which cast new light on the once seemingly simple story of the good guys defeating the bad guys.

It can no longer be argued that Hitler, and Hitler alone, caused the war in Europe, any more than it can be argued that an unprovoked Japan started the war in the Pacific. Both Germany and Japan were provoked by the Western powers. The Germany of the Weimar Republic was a creation of the First World War. Born of defeat and humiliation, it reluctantly commanded the support of its people as long as the economy of Germany maintained its equilibrium. At least twice during the early Weimar years the régime was almost toppled, and was propped up only with the help of those who were yearning for the return of the Kaiser and the stability of Wilhelmine Germany.

By 1933 the Weimar Republic was wholly discredited, blamed both for the Treaty of Versailles, which shackled German ambitions in Europe, and for the Great Depression, neither of which it could have done much to avoid. When Hitler threw off the constitutional bonds of the Weimar régime, he did so with the consent of most people in Germany. Hitler promised jobs and an end to the humiliating terms of Versailles. And Hitler provided jobs, less than five per cent of which had anything to do with arms manufacture or the build-up towards war. He also eradicated civil liberties and most political rights, and soon after his takeover began his active harassment of the Jews, most of whom began to leave Germany in great numbers. All this was viewed with a certain equanimity by the Western powers, Great Britain and France, and with a certain disinterest on the part of the United States. Britain and France did not begin to stir until Hitler's troops re-occupied the Rhineland in March 1936, which was supposed to remain demilitarized according to the terms of the Treaty of Versailles. At this stage France alone had the capability of moving into the Rhineland and if she had done so, Hitler would have withdrawn rather than face a confrontation. But France, without Britain's support, lacked the will. From this moment on Hitler knew that the Western democracies could be pushed. While the newly constructed Luftwaffe and Condor Legion practised against the Spanish in their civil war at the invitation of General Franco, Hitler planned to rewrite the Treaty by force and threats.

As Britain rearmed, at a faster rate than Germany, producing planes such as the Hurricane and Spitfire, France's will to resist German threats crumbled during the years of the Popular Front. Only France believed in upholding the letter of the Treaty, and with her will shaken, Britain had no interest in supporting certain clauses in the Treaty which she no longer believed were just, or those which she had never really supported at all. It was the French in 1919 who insisted that a union or *Anschluss* between Austria and Germany be forbidden. When Hitler marched the Wehrmacht into Austria in March 1938, Britain and France complained but did nothing. The annexation of the Sudetenland of Czechoslovakia was another matter. But Hitler argued that the people there were German-speaking and wanted union with Germany, which was true. Neville Chamberlain, the Prime Minister, had no intention of going to war for the Sudetenland, and the Munich Conference of September 1938 sealed the fate of the Sudeten Germans and Czechoslovakia itself. Britain was unready for war and needed more time to rearm. Although it is now known that if Britain and France had resisted and if Germany had been forced to invade, the German General Staff would have overthrown Hitler, for they knew that in 1938 Germany was equally unready for an all-out conflict. When Czechoslovakian integrity was abandoned, the Western powers relinquished all claim they might have had on influence in Eastern Europe for all time. From 1938 onwards it would be Russia and Germany who would decide the fate of Eastern Europe.

The occupation of the rump of Czechoslovakia in March 1939 was a decisive moment for the West. Now it could no longer be argued that Germany only wanted to bring Germans in Central Europe 'heim ins Reich'. Millions of Slavs were unwillingly wedded to Germany, and Hitler's long-term goal of a German empire in the east was clear. The will of Britain stiffened after the Prague spring of 1939, and with it the resolve of France, who was pledged to defend most of the states of Eastern Europe. Britain allied with Poland, and when Hitler began to ask for German Danzig, then under the League of Nations authority as a free city, Britain began to talk to the nation that she feared as much as Germany, the Soviet Union. Stalin saw at once that Britain's tentative steps towards a Russian alliance were not sincere, and soon began covert negotiations with her bitter ideological enemy, the Third Reich.

The Molotov-Ribbentrop Pact shocked the world and made the partition of Poland possible. It did not necessarily mean that the Second World War was inevitable. Although Britain and France reluctantly declared war against Germany in September 1939 they did not wage it in defence of Poland. Neither did they wage it after Poland fell. The legacy of appeasement which itself was the legacy of the First World War still hung like a pall over the West. That war seemed to have accomplished nothing, and with so many millions of lives lost, it seemed insane to repeat the error. It was this disillusionment and horror of war which blinded the West to the threat Hitler posed. But as long as he confined his activities to Eastern Europe, the West was more or less content to let him have his way. Only when he turned his attentions to Norway and Denmark, and subsequently to the Low Countries and France, did the war begin in earnest.

Even in May 1940 there were still those in Britain who favoured a policy of accommodation with the New Order. The appointment of Churchill rather than Lord Halifax as the replacement for Chamberlain as Prime Minister put an end to any thought of appeasement. Come what may, Britain, if necessary alone, would continue the war despite Hitler's pleas for peace after the fall of France—which would have guaranteed the British Empire against German aggression and, with Russia still at peace with Germany, ended the war. But the appeasement factor was still present in America and in Britain's policy towards Hitler's ally, Imperial Japan.

As the United States withdrew from overseas commitments after the First World War, she sought to contain Japanese ambitions in the Far East through a policy of mutual limitation of arms and the neutralization of the Pacific. As Germany turned to Hitler partly out of the despair of the Great Depression, Japan turned

towards consolidation of her position in Northeast Asia when her greatest market and supplier of raw materials, the United States, sank into the slump. Although Britain and America waxed eloquently about the Japanese takeover of Manchuria in 1931, neither did anything concrete about it. The same was true when Japan expanded into Inner Mongolia, bombed Shanghai and finally, in 1937, invaded China proper. Short of active intervention there was little that either nation could accomplish. Britain was more concerned with rearmament and the containment of Germany. She could not take on Germany and Japan at the same time and hope to win without the support of the United States. Despite Roosevelt's warnings, the United States remained steadfastly isolationist throughout the 1930's. In the election of 1940 both Roosevelt and his Republican opponent, Wendell Willkie, promised not to involve American boys in any foreign wars even after the fall of France. As Japan took over the China coast and moved into French Indo-China, the United States made provisional and thoroughly inconclusive war plans with Britain, Australia and the Dutch, but only took some economic sanctions against Japan. When the Japanese effectively overran what is now South Vietnam in July 1941 the Americans took their most decisive action so far when Japanese assets in the United States were frozen. Britain and the Dutch did the same.

The United States took a bellicose stance against Japan with the full knowledge that this could easily lead to war. True, if Japan attacked Malaya and the Dutch East Indies, which had the natural resources which she required, such as rubber, tin and especially petroleum, without touching the American-owned Philippines, the United States would have been in an awkward position. But, quite deliberately, the Japanese military command, now in charge of the Japanese government when Hideki Tojo became the Premier in October 1941, chose to try to knock out the American Pacific Fleet with one staggering blow. This could not fail to involve America in the war, and of course, the United States declared war against Japan immediately after Pearl Harbour was attacked.

But the United States might have fought in the Pacific alone had it not been for Germany's declaration of war against the United States on 10th December. Hitler did Roosevelt a real favour when he honoured his alliance with Japan. For public opinion in America was all for avenging Pearl Harbour. It did not necessarily follow that isolationist America would support the war in Europe as well. But the decision was taken by Germany. Thus only in December 1941 could it be said that the

Second World War actually began. Until that time several not wholly related wars had been going on: Japan was fighting China, Russia fought Finland, Germany fought Poland, and Britain and (after June 1941) Russia were fighting Germany and Italy. The reluctance born of British appeasement in Eastern Europe and Asia, and American isolationism generally, had allowed Germany and Japan to advance as far as they did. Either power could have been stopped far earlier and defeated far more quickly if the West had not tried to bury its head in the sand when war clouds began to loom in the 1930's. As a result, Western Europe lost the world hegemony which it had held for a century or more. Now the banner was passed to the United States and the Soviet Union.

The Second World War was effectively won by those two powers, since it was primarily Russia which defeated Germany and America which defeated Japan. The British impact on the Axis was peripheral after 1941, apart from the significant role the British Navy played in the Atlantic and the Mediterranean. Although the British 8th Army was chiefly responsible for the defeat of the Afrika Korps in the North African desert, and despite the fact that the British cleared Burma of the Japanese before the war came to an end, she could not hope to reap the benefits of the war, won by Russia and America. Without any doubt, Germany would have been defeated by Russia whether or not the Allies invaded Western Europe. Likewise, and to an even greater extent, the United States would have defeated Japan without British and certainly without Russian assistance, since the Soviet Union chose to declare war against Japan only after Hiroshima had been levelled by the atomic bomb.

There are many lessons to be learned from the Second World War, but perhaps the most important is this: the horrors of cities destroyed, mass murder and genocide, atomic warfare, concentration camps, death marches, starvation, occupation and human degradation of an unparalleled nature, all these could have been avoided. In order to avoid the disappointments and tragedy of the First World War, the Western powers tried to ignore what was happening in Europe and Asia until it was almost too late. By trying to pretend that aggression was not really aggression, that events in far-off countries about which they 'knew nothing' did not concern them, by callously ignoring racism and human suffering, the western democracies themselves were forced to suffer. It can only be hoped that this lesson, lost on the generation who did not want to repeat the First World War, is not lost on the generation which does not want to repeat the tragedy and horror of the Second World War.

1 THE FRAGILE PEACE

Hitler's Germany

Nazi Germany's attempt to win absolute power within Europe was the mainspring of the Second World War. It was, however, on a grander scale, the continuation of that process by which the National Socialists had won power in Germany itself.

Hitler took office on 30th January 1933 not as dictator of Germany but as head of a coalition government in which the Nazis held only three out of eleven ministerial posts. The paradox of his career up to this point had been the combination of a movement built on a revolutionary appeal with the insistence that he meant to come to power by legal means. But once he had got his foot inside the door, Hitler had no intention at all of being bound by the rules of the conventional political game. He very soon showed that it was the façade of legality, not the revolutionary character of the Nazi movement, which was the sham.

The first step was the decree suspending all guarantees of individual liberty on the excuse that the Reichstag Fire on 27th February 1933 was in fact the sign for a Communist rising. Göring, placed in control of the Prussian police, enrolled 40,000 of the Nazis' strong-arm bands, the SA and the SS, as police auxiliaries. This gave them a legal immunity which they used to the full to arrest and beat up political opponents and Jews. The election on 5th March failed to produce the majority the Nazis had hoped for, but by eliminating the Communist deputies (most of whom were already in concentration camps) and pressuring the other parties, they obtained a clear vote for the so-called Enabling Law (23rd March 1933) which set aside the constitution and for four years empowered the

chancellor, Hitler, to enact laws without parliamentary approval.

In the next few months the Nazis proceeded to carry out a political 'take-over' of Germany for which they coined the phrase *Gleichschaltung,* 'co-ordination'. Their political partners were not asked for their agreement but were ignored and elbowed out of the way. Theirs and all other political parties, as well as the trade unions, were abolished.

This was the Nazi revolution, and it was compounded of three elements. The first was the use the Nazis made of the legal authority to command the resources of the state and its administrative machine. This guaranteed to the Nazis control of the police, the neutrality of the armed forces, and the power, which they exercised without scruple, to dismiss any official suspected of opposition or even lukewarmness towards the new regime. The second was terrorism – not the breakdown of law and order, but something more shocking, its deliberate withdrawal. A free hand was given to the Nazi Stormtroopers to seize persons or property and do what they liked with them. The effect of this terrorism extended far beyond the numbers of those who actually suffered death, injury, or loss of property: it created an atmosphere of menace, a pervasive fear of violence which inhibited any thought of opposition. The compulsive power of terrorism was matched by the attractive power of propaganda drummed out by radio, press, and cinema, proclaiming a national rebirth of Germany. This was the third element. Propaganda produced on this scale and directed with the consummate skill of Goebbels was

something new in politics, and it had a great impact on a people which had suffered for fifteen years from a deep sense of national humiliation. Most important of all was the impression of success which Goebbels' propaganda created: the Nazi band-wagon was on the move and anyone eager for power, position, and jobs (in a nation with six million unemployed) rushed to jump on it.

In every move they made, the Nazis showed the advantage enjoyed by a political movement which refused to be bound by any rules, which did not try to avoid but did everything it could to exploit surprise and shock, and instead of repudiating violence in the streets employed the threat of it to break down opposition. The result was that the stability of a society already weakened by the successive experiences of defeat, inflation, economic depression, and mass unemployment was profoundly shaken. But the Nazis' methods, if they repelled many, also attracted many, especially among the younger generation, who felt a great sense of liberation at the promise of action after years of frustration. 1933 produced a feeling that the future held great possibilities.

The question Hitler had to answer in the summer of 1933 was how far he was prepared to let the revolutionary process continue before calling a halt. Was it to extend to the economic as well as the political institutions of the country? There had been a strong element of anti-capitalism in the Nazis' radicalism and there was now a demand to give expression to this in drastic economic reforms. What Hitler saw, however, was that radical economic experi-

*Left: Arresting Communists, Berlin, 1933. The Nazis won popularity as bulwark against Bolshevism. **Right:** Hitler and group of admirers*

ments would destroy any chance of co-operation from industry and business to end the depression, bring down the unemployment figures, and start rearming Germany. In July he told a meeting of Nazi provincial governors: 'The revolution is not a permanent state of affairs and it must not be allowed to develop into such a state . . . The ideas of the programme do not oblige us to act like fools and upset everything . . . Many more revolutions have been successful at the outset than have, when once successful, been arrested and brought to a standstill at the right moment.' By the end of the summer Hitler had made it quite clear that he chose close working relations with big business in preference to the Nazi enthusiasts who talked about 'the corporate development of the national economy' and who were now disowned or pushed into obscure positions.

Hitler's own wish, however, to halt the revolution, at least for the time being, encountered opposition in the Nazi movement, particularly in the brown shirt SA. The SA was a genuine mass movement with strong radical and anti-capitalist leanings, and attracted to it all those dissatisfied elements in the Party who felt they had been left out in the cold and who wanted no end to the revolution until they too had been provided for. And the SA did not lack a leader. Its chief of staff, Ernst Röhm, was the most independent of the Nazi leaders, a man who, having started Hitler on his career in politics in Munich, was not at all afraid to speak his mind.

This quarrel over the so-called 'Second Revolution' was the dominant issue in German politics between the summer of 1933 and the summer of 1934, and threatened to split the Nazi movement. In particular, Röhm and the SA leadership, which contained many who had been through the rough school of the Freikorps and were contemptuous of the conservatism of the German officer corps, were incensed at not being allowed to take over and remodel the German army on revolutionary lines.

Hitler, as his subsequent behaviour showed, was as distrustful of the generals and contemptuous of their conservatism as Röhm, but in 1933 and 1934 he needed their support if he was to rebuild Germany's military strength and, more immediately, if he was to secure the succession to Hindenburg as head of state as well as head of the government. On their side, the generals were determined to resist any attempt by Röhm to incorporate the SA in the army and take it over.

The crisis reached its climax at the end of June 1934 when Hitler suddenly ordered the liquidation of the SA leadership on the pretext that they were planning a putsch. The purge, however, extended far beyond the SA. Amongst those summarily shot besides Röhm — all without any pretence of a trial — were General von Schleicher, Hitler's predecessor as chancellor, and Gregor Strasser, once Hitler's rival for the leadership of the Nazi Party. Hitler had not merely connived at murder, but ordered it to be carried out.

The generals, however, were satisfied to see the threat from the SA removed and when President Hindenburg died on 2nd August, there was no delay in announcing Hitler's succession as head of state, with the new title of Führer (leader) and Reich chancellor. The same day the officers and men of the German army took the oath to their new commander-in-chief, swearing allegiance not to the constitution or to the Fatherland, but to Hitler personally.

June 1934 was a major crisis, a crisis of the regime and the acid test of Hitler's leadership. In the weeks preceding the purge (for example, during his visit to Mussolini at Venice) Hitler gave every impression of being anxious and unsure of himself. This was the characteristic period of hesitation and weighing the odds which so often preceded one of his big decisions: equally characteristically, when the decision was made, it startled everyone by its boldness and brutality. Hitler repudiated the so-called 'Second Revolution' but he

did so in such a radical way as to give no comfort at all to those who wanted to see the rule of law restored and a return to the conservative traditions of the German state.

Nazification

In contrast to the tumultuous days of 1932 and 1933 and the crisis atmosphere of the summer of 1934, the next three and a half years, 1934 through 1937, saw political peace in Germany: no more elections, no more purges. This left the Nazis free to get on with the 're-modelling' of German society. Like other totalitarian creeds, Nazism was unwilling to leave any part of German life unorganized or to allow any group or individual to contract out. German men and women were to be as accountable for their thoughts and feelings as for their actions, and no claim of individual conscience was to be allowed to withstand the demands of the Party and the state.

Practice, of course, as in every form of society, totalitarian as well as democratic, was never so consistent as theory. In the first place, it is necessary to distinguish between the lengths to which the Nazis went in enforcing their style of government in the 1930's, during peace time, and in the 1940's, under war-time conditions. It is to the later period, for example, that the extermination camps, slave labour, and 'the final solution' of the so-called Jewish problem belong. There were concentration camps in Germany from the beginning of the Nazi period, but the total number of prisoners at the beginning of the war was roughly 25,000 compared with ten times that number a few years later.

Up to the outbreak of war, Germany was still open to visitors and foreign correspondents in a way in which the Soviet Union has never been, and the Nazis showed themselves surprisingly sensitive to hostile comment from abroad, for example in their dealings with the Churches. This was an issue on which Hitler several times intervened personally to curb the zeal of those in the Party who wished to push

Left: Burning of 'degenerate' books by Nazi students, 1933. **Right:** *Cartoon showing purified German poetry rising from the flames*

their hostility to the Churches to the limit. Accordingly, Nazi practice towards the Churches was confused and inconsistent, marked by fundamental hostility in outlook and much petty local persecution (such as the expulsion of monks and nuns, the closing of churches, the imprisonment of pastors and priests) but still stopping short of the sweeping measures which some of the Party leaders would have liked.

Even setting aside considerations of expediency, it proved more difficult to translate totalitarian control into practice than is always recognized. It took time for Himmler and Heydrich to create the SS which was eventually to prove the most effective instrument for Hitler's purposes. One important reason for this was the clash of rival authorities which was characteristic of Nazi Germany from the very beginning. Its organization was anything but monolithic. After the summer of 1934 Hitler's authority at the top was uncontested, but right up to the top there was a fierce struggle for power. Hitler himself not only possessed no gift for administration; he was instinctively distrustful of creating settled administrative procedures which would limit his own arbitrary power of decision. Difficulties were to be met by emergency action, by creating special agencies, a method which led almost invariably to overlapping and conflict of authority, between ministries, between Party and state, between different Party organizations. Each minister and Party boss fought for his own hand, a situation which strengthened Hitler's own position —since each sought the Führer's favour against his rivals—but reduced the efficiency of operation and control.

Nonetheless, when all this is said, there is no doubt that between 1933 and 1939 the Nazis went a long way towards remoulding German life, not just German politics, on a totalitarian pattern. The key lay with the younger generation. In a speech on 6th November 1933, Hitler declared: 'When an opponent says, "I will

not come over to your side", I calmly say, "Your child belongs to us already . . . you will pass on. Your descendants, however, now stand in the new camp. In a short time they will know nothing else but this new community." '

To make sure, a start was at once made on the nazification of the schools and universities. All teachers, from kindergarten to university, were compelled to join the National Socialist Teachers' League and to teach what they were told to. German universities, once famous for their scientific research, now became the homes of racist science. Outside the schools, independent youth organizations (including those of the Churches) were banned and all German boys and girls from the age of six were required to join the Hitler Youth. At eighteen boys were conscripted into labour service and the army, girls into farm and household service. Throughout these impressionable years they were subjected to continued indoctrination in the Nazi faith

To make Nazi propaganda doubly effective and allow no independent voice to be heard, Goebbels was made minister of culture as well as propaganda. This gave him control over all the arts, literature, and the cinema, as well as the press. Nothing could be published without the consent of the Propaganda Ministry.

'Jews not wanted here'

A particular object for attack was anybody or anything Jewish. The Jew, according to Nazi teaching, was the source of all corruption and Germany must be purged of this racial poison, if not yet by physical extermination then by the complete exclusion of all Jews from German life. Jews (defined as anyone with a single Jewish grandparent) were excluded from all official posts (with loss of pension rights), from the professions, including teaching, medicine, and the law, from sport, and the arts. Holiday resorts, restaurants, and hotels were decorated with notices, 'Jews not wanted here', and any Nazi hooligan

could beat up, evict, or rob a Jew with impunity. In 1935 the Nuremberg Laws prohibited marriage or any form of sexual intercourse between Jews and German nationals. Those who sought to escape abroad were only allowed to go after they had been deprived of their assets and property. Finally, after a young Polish Jew, driven off balance by the persecution of his people, had assassinated the German legation secretary in Paris, Ernst vom Rath, a deliberately organized attack (represented as a 'spontaneous' outburst of German anger) was made on Jewish synagogues and businesses throughout the country on the night of 9th-10th November 1938. The perpetrators of the attack went scot-free, while the Jews were fined a billion and a quarter marks and saw the insurance payments to which they were entitled confiscated by the state. This so-called 'Crystal Night' was followed by the forced sale of Jewish businesses and property, their eviction from their houses, wholesale arrests, and conscription for forced labour.

No Jew had any hope of protection by the courts. But it was unlikely that any German had more ground for hope if he became suspected of independent views or got involved in a dispute with state or Party officials. Not content with the *Gleichschaltung* of the judiciary and the ordinary courts, the Nazis set up special courts to try offences against the state, a category which could be enlarged at will. The orders and actions of the Gestapo (*Geheime Staatspolizei,* Secret State Police) were in any case not subject to the law. 'Protective custody' was the term cynically employed for those arbitrarily arrested and sent to concentration camps. One of the significant dates in the history of Nazi Germany was 17th June 1936 when Himmler was able to merge control of the two empires which he had built up, the police and the SS. So was created what German historians call 'the illegal executive', an agency with which the Führer, Hitler, responsible to no one but himself, could brush aside any

The Fragile Peace

limitation at all on his power to act outside or contrary to the law.

Terrorism and the secret police, like propaganda and censorship, were essential parts of the totalitarian society the Nazis were seeking to create. And they produced their familiar accompaniments of informers, persecution, and corruption. For those Germans who did not fall into line but stood out against the pressures to conform (and for all Jews) these were years marked by constant fear, often imprisonment and brutal treatment, sometimes death. But these people formed a minority and a small one at that. What counted with the majority was the Nazis' success. In a country which had suffered more severely from the Depression than any other in Europe, the Nazis could claim credit for cutting unemployment from six million to less than a million in four years, for raising national production more than one hundred per cent between 1932 and 1937, and for doubling the national income. This reconciled the millions of Germans who had lost, or feared to lose, their jobs to a regime which might have taken away some of their rights but had given them back security.

In addition to security, the Nazis had given the German people back their pride in Germany as a great power. By the plebiscite of January 1935, Germany recovered the Saar. Two months later (March 1935) Hitler repudiated the military restrictions of the Treaty of Versailles, restored conscription, and announced that the German army would be raised to a peace-time strength of over half a million men. A year later (March 1936) German troops reoccupied the demilitarized Rhineland. The deeply felt national humiliation of the defeat and the 'Diktat' of Versailles had been removed, and there is no reason to doubt that the result of the plebiscite which followed (99 per cent voting and 98.8 of these voting in favour) represented overwhelming gratitude and approval for Hitler's restoration of Germany's status as the leading power of Central Europe.

Finally, it must be said that in abolishing the multiplicity of political parties, which had produced only a series of weak coalitions, and replacing them by a single strong government proclaiming national unity in contrast to sectional interests, the Nazis successfully appealed to the most deeply rooted political tradition in Germany, that of authoritarian government.

Right: Poster urging return of Saar— worker heaves open gates of Saar to Nazi Germany. It was Hitler's last stop before resorting to force to reverse the Treaty of Versailles. Opposite: Nazis march past in snowstorm at political meeting near Saarbrücken on 7th March 1935, the day the Saar plebiscite returned the Saar to Germany

Once his power was established, Hitler showed little interest in the details of domestic administration, except when he had to intervene to settle a dispute. His attention was turned more and more to foreign policy and rearmament. The conquest of political power, even the remoulding of German society, were only stages on the way to his ultimate aim, the recreation of German national power, the reversal of the defeat of 1918.

It suited the Nazis in the early years of their regime when Germany was still unprepared, to conceal this. Hitler never spoke without protesting his love of peace and reproaching the victorious powers of 1918 with the promises they had broken, particularly the promise to disarm. This, however, was the diplomatic equivalent of the tactics of 'legality' which he had practised in Germany before coming to power and was no more reliable a guide than 'legality' to his real aims in foreign policy.

By 1936 there was a change. The re-

Zu Deutschlan

occupation of the Rhineland (March 1936) was a gamble: Hitler later called it the most nerve-wracking forty-eight hours of his life. But it was a gamble that came off and strengthened his belief that, if he played his cards with skill, limiting the issue at stake in each case, the Western powers would always draw back rather than risk a general war. From the summer of 1936 the political balance in Europe moved sharply in Germany's favour. The outbreak of the Spanish Civil War gave Hitler the opportunity to proclaim with redoubled effect Germany's role as the bulwark of Europe against Bolshevism. Italy, quarrelling with the Western powers over Abyssinia, was drawn into the Berlin-Rome Axis. France, divided by the Popular Front and by the Spanish Civil War, no longer had the will to maintain the system of alliances built up to contain Germany. Great Britain was reluctant to face the possibility of another war. The smaller countries began to gravitate to the new centre of power in Berlin and it was of German power that Hitler now began increasingly to speak.

There is no doubt from the evidence now available that accounts of German rearmament before the war were exaggerated. The programme took longer to produce results than was supposed and even in 1939 had not given Germany the military superiority commonly assumed. Most surprising of all is the fact that nothing like the full capacity of the German economy was devoted to war production before 1942. But the type of war for which Germany was preparing was very different from that which she had lost in 1914-18: it was a *Blitzkrieg*, a series of short campaigns in which surprise and an overwhelming initial blow would settle the issue before the victim had time to mobilize his resources or other powers to intervene. This is the sort of war the German army fought in all its campaigns from 1939 to 1941, and it demanded a quite different pattern of rearmament, not long-term rearmament in depth, involving the whole of the economy, but concentration on a short-term superiority and the weapons which would give a quick victory. How nearly the plan worked can be seen from the history of 1939-41 when Germany's 'limited' rearmament pro-

gramme produced an army capable of overrunning the greater part of Europe and very nearly defeating the Russians as well as the French.

It has often been said that Hitler was an opportunist in foreign policy. This is perfectly true, so far as tactics were concerned: he did not proceed by any timetable or 'blueprint of aggression', but kept his options open until the very last moment. Hitler, however, was able to take advantage of the opportunities offered by the mistakes of others because he alone among the European leaders of the 1930's knew what he wanted to achieve: the others only knew what they wanted to avoid.

Hitler set out the Nazi programme in *Mein Kampf*: not simply the restoration of Germany's 1914 frontiers but the conquest of living space *(Lebensraum)* in Eastern Europe from which the existing populations would be cleared by force and a Germanic empire established on a foundation of slave labour. These views have been treated as the fantasy of an unbalanced mind. But they cannot for that reason be dismissed. For not only did Hitler consistently repeat them in private talk for twenty years, but during the war he put them into practice in the most literal way, with the aid of Himmler and the SS, first in Poland, then in Russia.

The 'Blitzkrieg' victories

What Hitler did not know was how he was going to achieve his objective, the order in which he would proceed, what opposition he would encounter. But from late 1937 onwards he was prepared to enlarge the risks he was ready to take. As part of the process he asserted stronger control over the two institutions which had been allowed to escape nazification, the army and the foreign office. Early in 1938 he seized an opportunity to get rid of Blomberg and Fritsch, the minister of war and commander-in-chief of the army, suppressed the office of war minister altogether, and took over the high command of the armed forces (the OKW) as his own personal staff. Schacht, who had protested at the economic risks of the Nazis' rearmament programme, had already been allowed to go, leaving Göring to dominate the economic field, with a clear brief to pre-

pare for war, and Neurath, whom Hindenburg had made foreign minister to safeguard the foreign service against Nazi influence, was replaced by Ribbentrop who for years had been pushing a radical Nazi policy in open rivalry with the more cautious official line of the foreign office.

The annexation of Austria which followed (March 1938) was an improvisation, but an improvisation which fitted in perfectly with Hitler's long-term programme and illustrates the relationship between this and the tactics of opportunism. Throughout the rest of 1938 and 1939, it was Hitler who forced the pace in foreign affairs, both externally by the demands he made on Czechoslovakia and Poland and internally by his determination to take risks which still, in 1938, alarmed the army leaders and led to the resignation of the army's chief-of-staff, General Beck. Neither in 1938 nor in 1939 did Hitler deliberately plan to start a general European war: in August 1939 he was convinced that the masterpiece of Nazi diplomacy, the Nazi-Soviet Pact, would remove any danger of Western intervention and either break the Poles' determination to resist or leave them isolated. But when his bluff failed, he steeled himself to gamble on the chances of a Blitzkrieg victory over Poland before the British and French could bring their forces to bear. The gamble came off and came off again, with the stakes increased, in Norway, the Low Countries, and France in 1940, against Yugoslavia, and almost against Russia the next year. By then the stakes had been raised to the point where failure meant the long-term, two-front war which Hitler had sworn to avoid, and for which Germany was ill-prepared.

The particular war which broke out in September 1939 was not inevitable – what event in history is? But it was no accident either. Nazism glorified force and conflict, and if one thing seemed certain in the later 1930's it was that this movement which had fastened its hold on Germany must, from the necessities of its own nature, seek to expand by force or the threat of force. Once Nazism – a philosophy of dynamism or nothing – came to a standstill and admitted limits to its expansion, it would lose its rationale and its appeal. The only question was whether the other powers would allow this expansion to take place without resistance or would oppose it. The Nazis themselves had always assumed that at some point they would meet opposition and had prepared to overcome it by force of arms. For this reason, while it is right to point to the differences between Nazi Germany up to September 1939 and after the outbreak of war, it is important to see the continuity between the two periods as well. What followed was a logical, if not inevitable, consequence of what went before.

The Brink of War

The international conference at Munich on 29th September 1938 had a practical task: to 'solve' the problem of the three million German-speakers in Czechoslovakia and so to prevent a European war. Apparently it succeeded in this task. The Czechoslovak territory inhabited by the three million Germans was transferred to Germany; the Germans were satisfied; there was no war. The controversy which has raged over the conference from before it met until the present day sprang more from what it symbolized than from what it actually did. Those who welcomed the Munich conference and its outcome represented it as a victory for reason and conciliation in international affairs – appeasement as it was called at the time, 'jaw, not war', as Winston Churchill said of a later occasion. The opponents of Munich saw in it an abdication by the two democratic powers, France and Great Britain; a surrender to fear; or a sinister conspiracy to prepare for a Nazi war of conquest against Soviet Russia. Munich was all these things.

The problem of the German-speakers in Czechoslovakia was real. They had been a privileged people in the old Habsburg monarchy. They were a tolerated minority in Czechoslovakia. They were discontented and grew more so with the resurgence of national pride in Germany. No doubt Hitler encouraged their discontent, but he did not create it. Those in the West who called out, 'Stand by the Czechs', never explained what they would do with the Czechoslovak Germans. Partition seemed the obvious solution. In fact, as later events proved, Bohemia was the one area in Europe where partition would not work. Czechs and Germans were so intermingled that one or other had to dominate. Once Czech prestige was shattered, a German protectorate inevitably followed six months later, to the ruin of the Munich settlement. The Czechs themselves recognized that there was no room in Bohemia for both nationalities. When independent Czechoslovakia was restored at the end of the war, the Germans were expelled – a solution which is likely to prove final.

The timing of the Czech crisis was not determined by the Czechoslovak Germans or by Hitler. It was determined by the British government, and especially by Neville Chamberlain, the British Prime Minister. He wanted to restore tranquillity in Europe and believed that this could be done only if German grievances were met. Moreover they must be met willingly. Concessions must be offered to Germany, not extracted under threat of war. Until 1938 Hitler had been destroying one bit of the 1919 settlement after another, to the accompaniment of protests from the Western powers. This time Chamberlain meant to get in ahead of him. Hitler was to be satisfied almost before he had time to formulate grievances.

Fear not reason

Chamberlain set himself two tasks. First, the French must be induced not to support their ally, Czechoslovakia. Second, the Czech government must be persuaded or compelled to yield to the German demands. He succeeded in both tasks, but not in the way that he intended. He had meant to use the argument of morality: that German grievances were justified and therefore must be redressed. Instead, as the months passed, he came to rely on practical arguments of force and fear. The French were driven to admit, with a reluctance which grew ever weaker, that they were unable to support Czechoslovakia. The Czechs were threatened with the horrors of war unless they gave way. When Chamberlain flew to Munich on his first visit to Hitler, it was not as the emissary of even-handed justice. He came in a desperate effort to avert a war which the Western powers dreaded. Thereafter fear, not reason, was his main argument, and the principal moral which the British drew from Munich was not that conciliation had triumphed, but that they must push on faster with rearmament.

At the Munich conference there was certainly an abdication by the Western powers. France especially had been the dominant power in Eastern Europe since the end of the First World War. Germany was disarmed; Soviet Russia was boycotted; all the new states of Eastern Europe were France's allies. She regarded these alliances as a source of strength. As soon as her allies made demands on her, she turned against them. France had been bled white in the first war, and Frenchmen were determined not to repeat the experience. They believed that they were secure behind their fortified frontier, the Maginot Line. Hence they did not care what happened beyond it. As to the British, they

Left: A poster distributed throughout Czechoslovakia in 1938: 'We will all become soldiers if necessary.'
Czech morale remained high during the war of nerves conducted by Hitler.
Right: Britain's Prime Minister Neville Chamberlain arriving at Heston Airport, London, promising 'Peace in our time'

The Fragile Peace

had always insisted that their interests stopped at the Rhine. Austen Chamberlain had said that no British grenadier would ever die for Danzig – or for anywhere else in Eastern Europe. The British recognized that German predominance would take the place of French. But this did not trouble them. Eastern Europe and the Balkans were no great prize economically. If they absorbed German energies and ambitions, it was all the more likely that Germany would leave Western Europe and the British Empire alone.

Fear of war was also a dominant motive at the Munich conference, but for the Western powers it was war that was feared rather than defeat. The French had confidence in their army, the British in their navy. But while they did not expect the Germans to defeat them, they doubted whether they could defeat Germany – except at a terrible price. There was no way in which the Western powers could give limited aid to the Czechs, as they might have done to the Spanish Republic. The facts of geography stood in the way. It was war on the largest scale or nothing. In those days, everyone believed that aerial bombardment would reduce the cities of Europe to ruin within a few weeks. European civilization would come to an end. This was the peril which Chamberlain sought to avert.

The Czechs themselves shared this fear of war. President Beneš believed that Hitler was bluffing and would give way if faced with a firm united opposition. When Hitler did not give way, even Beneš in the last resort preferred surrender to war. The Czechs, Beneš held, were a small people, who must preserve their lives for a better future. Their country had been occupied before and they had survived. They would survive again. In a sense, his arguments were justified by events. The Czechs were abandoned by the Western powers. Their country fell under German tyranny for six years. But only one or perhaps two hundred thousand of them lost their lives. Prague, their capital was the only great city of Central Europe to remain undamaged in the Second World War, and Czechoslovakia re-emerged with unbroken spirit, at the end. In contrast, Poland was guaranteed by the Western powers, who went to war for her sake. As a result, six million Poles were killed. Warsaw was reduced to a heap of ruins, and Poland, though restored, lost much of her territory and of her independence.

Was Munich a conspiracy?
Did more lie behind? Was the Munich conference not merely a surrender, an abandonment, or even a betrayal of Czechoslovakia? Was it also part of a deliberate attempt to promote a German hegemony and to clear the way for a German attack on Soviet Russia? This is a view strongly held by Soviet and other Communist-inclined historians. The Munich conference was certainly an assertion that Europe could settle its own affairs. Only the purely European powers – France, Germany, Great Britain, and Italy – were represented. The two world powers, Soviet Russia and the United States, were absent. The United States had persistently refused to be involved in European conflicts ever since the end of the First World War. It is likely, too, that the Western powers welcomed the absence of any American representative. If one had attended the conference, he would have preached morality to others without being prepared to act on it himself. Great Britain and France looked forward to a time when there might be a great war and they would need American aid. Even with this in mind, they preferred not to be exposed to American reproaches before the time came for action.

Soviet Russia was a different matter. The Western powers never counted on Soviet aid. They did not believe, and quite rightly, that even if Soviet Russia entered a war against Germany she would be fighting either for democracy as they understood it or for the sanctity of treaties. After all, the settlement of 1919 had been made quite as much against Soviet Russia as against Germany, and the Russians would aim to take Germany's place in Eastern Europe, not to defend the independence of the small states. As well, the Western powers doubted whether Soviet Russia intended to fight Germany seriously or whether she was capable of doing so. They distrusted Soviet Russia quite as much as she distrusted them. Each side suspected the other of pushing it into the front line. Moreover, this was the period of Stalin's great purges. Nearly all the marshals and generals of the Red Army had been murdered or imprisoned. Under such circumstances, it was hard to believe that Soviet Russia could conduct a successful offensive. Geography stood in Russia's way even more than in theirs. Soviet Russia could not strike at Germany without crossing the territory of either Poland or Rumania. Both countries refused to allow the passage of Soviet troops – the Poles more rigorously than the Rumanians. The Western powers were supposed to be defending the rights of small nations and could hardly begin their campaign by trampling on the rights of Poland and Rumania.

On paper, the Soviet government had a position of impregnable righteousness. According to the Czech-Soviet treaty of 1935, Soviet Russia was committed to supporting Czechoslovakia only if France did so first. The Soviet rulers surmised correctly that France would not honour her word. Therefore they were quite safe in declaring that they would honour theirs. Soviet leaders went further. They often hinted that they would be prepared to aid Czechoslovakia even if France did not act. But they would do this only if President Beneš and the Czechoslovak government asked them to do so. Here again the Soviet government was quite safe. The Czechoslovak government was predominantly right-wing, and President Beneš, though less on the Right, was determined not to fight with Soviet Russia as sole ally. This, he thought, would invite the fate of Republican Spain, and he was not far wrong. Hence we cannot tell what the Soviet government really intended to do. They could promise great things in the secure confidence that they would never be called on to fulfil their promises. Similarly, we do not know whether the Soviet government made any serious preparations for war. Most Western observers reported at the time that the Red Army had taken no measures of mobilization. Nowadays the Soviet spokesmen claim that the Red Army had mobilized thirty divisions. This, even if true, was a derisory force to use against Germany, and suggests that the Soviet government were intending only to seize some Polish territory. But as the Soviet government refuses to release evidence, all statements about its policy are guesswork.

We may dismiss one guess the other way round. Soviet writers then and later alleged that the Western powers aimed to switch German aggression eastwards, against Soviet Russia. Many Soviet writers even allege that the Western powers dreamed of joining in this aggression themselves. There is virtually no foundation for their theory. The Communists imagined that everyone in the capitalist world was afraid of them and therefore wanted to destroy 'the workers' state'. In fact, Communism had lost its appeal. Soviet Russia was the best propaganda against Communism – it offered tyranny, starvation, inefficiency. No one in Western Europe feared Soviet Russia any more. Indeed, sensible English people regretted that Soviet Russia was so weak. In the end, German aggression was indeed switched. But it was switched from east to west by the Nazi-Soviet pact. It was not switched from west to east by the conference at Munich.

The Danzig question
The Munich conference was supposed to inaugurate a new era in international relations. The 'slave treaty' of Versailles, as the Germans called it, was dead. A negotiated settlement had taken its place. Greater Germany had at last come into existence, and Hitler himself professed to be satisfied. He declared: 'I have no more

territorial demands to make in Europe.' Nor was this mere pretence. Hitler formulated no plans for aggressive action during the winter of 1938-39. His generals were told to be ready 'to smash the remainder of the Czech state if it adopted an anti-German policy.' But this was no more than a precaution against the counter-offensive which Hitler half-expected from the Western powers. German expenditure on armaments was considerably reduced after Munich and remained at this lower level until the outbreak of war in September 1939 – clear indication that Hitler was not expecting a great war.

There was still one German grievance left over from Versailles which Hitler intended to remove. Danzig, though entirely German in population, was still a Free City, and the Polish Corridor still separated East Prussia from the rest of Germany. But Hitler did not anticipate conflict over these issues. Poland and Germany were on good terms, and Poland had been Germany's faithful jackal during the Czech crisis. Settlement seemed easy. With the creation of Gdynia, Poland was no longer dependent on Danzig as her only outlet to the world. Danzig could remain a free port for Poland and yet return to the Reich, as its inhabitants wanted. It should also be easy to arrange for German extra-territorial roads and railways across the Corridor. Friendship between Poland and Germany would then be secure, and the two could join in conquering the Ukraine from Soviet Russia.

Hitler did not understand Poland's policy of independence. Colonel Beck, the

1938 Czech Communist poster

arrogant foreign minister of Poland, was determined to balance between Germany and Soviet Russia. He would not commit himself to either. He would certainly not enlist Soviet aid against Germany. Equally, he would not co-operate with Germany against Soviet Russia. Hitler wanted to get Danzig out of the way as the only stumbling block between Germany and Poland. For exactly this reason, Beck kept it in the way. Moreover, Beck had learned a lesson from the Czechoslovak affair. He believed that any negotiations or offers of compromise were a slippery slope to ruin. In his view a firm 'no' at the outset was the only safe course. He knew, too, that the Western powers sympathized with Germany over Danzig and would urge concession if they were consulted. He therefore did not consult them. Great Britain and France were assured that Polish relations with Germany were unclouded, while Beck was simultaneously showing a blank and uncomprehending face to Hitler's proposals for compromise.

The limits of appeasement

The Western powers had given up Poland for lost. As Halifax, the British foreign secretary, said: 'Poland can only presumably fall more and more into the German sphere.' British and French statesmen assumed that Soviet Russia and Germany were irreconcilable. Russia would remain as a vague menace on Germany's eastern frontier, and, if Hitler were determined to go somewhere, it were better that he went east. The two Western countries were determined never to be involved again in 'an Eastern quarrel'. The British particularly were anxious to dodge out of the guarantee they had given to Czechoslovakia. Nor had they much faith in their French ally. France, once the advocate of resistance to Germany, now set the pace in appeasement. In December, Ribbentrop came to Paris. He and Bonnet signed a pact of friendship, in which France washed her hands of Eastern Europe – or so it seemed.

The British did not like this. Their idea was to restrain France, not the other way round. Now they needed some other associate who would help to warn Hitler off Western Europe. In January 1939 Chamberlain and Halifax journeyed to Rome. Once more they urged Mussolini to play the moderating part which he had done at Munich. Mussolini was frightened. He knew that Italy was in no state for war and, more wisely than others, recognized that Great Britain might go to war if Hitler pressed too hard. From this moment he importuned Hitler for a firm written alliance – seemingly a move towards Germany. But in Mussolini's eyes, the essential clause of this alliance, finally concluded in May 1939, was that the two powers agreed not

to start a general war before 1942 or 1943, and many things could happen before then.

The early months of 1939 saw everyone in a state of undefined apprehension. The British, alarmed by the deficiencies shown during the Czech crisis, were pushing on with their rearmament, a good deal faster indeed than the Germans were. Hitler snapped at every increase in British arms expenditure and complained that they were incompatible with the trust in his word which Chamberlain had professed at Munich. In his crude way, Hitler imagined that he would shake the British 'warmongers', from Churchill to Eden, if he denounced them. Instead he pushed up their reputation and began to shake Chamberlain's. London ran over with rumours of new German aggressions.

Then one came, though not at all as Hitler intended. Czecho-Slovakia, hyphenated since Munich, broke up. This was not altogether Hitler's doing. The Slovaks had always been discontented and could no longer be restrained when Czech prestige was shattered. They demanded first autonomy and then independence. The Czechs prepared to act against them. The Hungarians prepared to move in on the other side. Hitler could allow neither course. He recognized the independence of Slovakia. Hácha, President of the Czech rump, appealed to Hitler for guidance. He came to Berlin and transformed Bohemia into a German protectorate. On 15th March 1939 German troops occupied Bohemia, and Hitler spent the night in Prague.

Nothing was changed except for the unfortunate Czechs, who received all the blessings of German rule – the secret police, persecution of Jews, and the loss of freedom. The British government rejoiced to be freed from 'the somewhat embarrassing commitment of a guarantee'. But British public opinion was in an uproar. Hitler was supposed to have gone back on his word. He was on the march to the domination of Europe. Neville Chamberlain, much against his will, had to speak words of protest and even of resistance. Secretly, Chamberlain, Halifax, and the rest wanted to settle with Hitler. They believed that war would achieve nothing except the ruin of Europe. But they needed to be stronger if they were to bargain at all and so became the prisoners of public opinion. As for the British people, this was the moment when most of them decided that the only thing to do with Hitler was to 'stop' him.

The British government were in a panic. They thought, quite wrongly, that Hitler was about to overrun the Balkans and Turkey. Any day the Middle East would be in danger. At precisely this moment, Tilea, the Rumanian minister, turned up with the news that German troops were about to enter Rumania. This was a totally false

The Fragile Peace

alarm. The British statesmen believed it. Helter-skelter, they tried to organize a peace front for joint resistance. The French agreed to join. The Russians agreed on condition all the others did. The Poles refused. They were still determined not to take sides. Negotiations over Danzig were becoming tenser as Beck kept up his negatives. But Hitler remained hopeful. As late as 25th March he issued a directive: 'The Führer *does not* wish to solve the Danzig question by force.'

Then came another alarm. There were reports, again unfounded, of German troop movements against Poland. These reports were fed to a British newspaper correspondent by German generals. Why? So that the British would resist Hitler? Or so that they would make the Poles give way? No one knows. At any rate, the correspondent was invited to attend the British cabinet. Chamberlain, convinced, wrote out with his own hand the offer of a British guarantee to Poland. Beck was conversing with the British ambassador when the message from London was brought in. He accepted the guarantee 'between two flicks of the ash from his cigarette'. It seemed to him to be a perfect solution. The British guarantee strengthened his hand against Germany. At the same time, it enabled him to refuse any co-operation with Soviet Russia. The British were entangled in 'an Eastern European quarrel' and yet could not appeal to Russia for aid. Poland would remain the dominant power in Eastern Europe, calling the tune on all sides.

When the British government came to their senses, they did not like what they had done. By giving to Poland an unconditional guarantee, they had committed themselves over Danzig, a cause for which they did not care at all or on which they even agreed with Hitler. Colonel Beck visited London a few days later. The British then tried to modify their guarantee. Beck would not yield. With continued arrogance, he merely offered to make the guarantee mutual. He assured the British that they were in more danger from Hitler than he was. He said not a word of the deadlock over Danzig, and the British were taken in by his self-confidence. They even feared that, unless they stuck by Beck, he would take Poland into the German camp. Besides, British public opinion would not forgive them if they again ran away. Beck departed from London with the assurance that the guarantee would soon be turned into a formal alliance. Actually, this was delayed until 25th August, on the eve of war.

The British guarantee to Poland provoked Hitler instead of restraining him. He was still convinced that his opponents would give way—'they are little worms. I saw them at Munich'—and so raised his bid. On 3rd April he told his generals to be ready for war with Poland in September, though he added an assurance that he would go to war only if Poland were isolated. On 28th April he denounced the Non-Aggression Pact with Poland of 1934 and the Anglo-German Naval Agreement of 1935. He still declared that he wanted agreement over Danzig and looked forward to friendship with the British later, when they too had given way over Danzig. Then, having stated his terms, Hitler withdrew into silence. There were no official exchanges between Germany and Great Britain until the middle of August, and none at all with Poland until the day war broke out.

Alliance without risks?

This was a nerve-racking situation. Hitler had made no precise demands. He had merely stated his dissatisfaction and left others to remedy it. In 1938 the British knew how to do this, or so they thought: concessions from Czechoslovakia would do the trick. Now this road was barred, and Colonel Beck had made it clear that there would be no concessions from Poland. The British government threatened that they would not support him. No good. Beck had their guarantee and knew that they dared not go back on it. The British government had to make the gestures of preparing to resist Hitler, whether they intended to or not. A Ministry of Supply was solemnly instituted, though Chamberlain had earlier dismissed it as a measure of war. It was in fact instituted only in theory and did not operate before war broke out. Compulsory military service was introduced—again an empty gesture. The young conscripts would not make any significant contribution to the British Army until 1942.

The greatest gesture hung over the British government like a hideous black cloud—the proposal for an alliance with Soviet Russia. It would seem to have obvious advantages—a great power enlisted on the side of collective security, aiding Poland, and distracting Germany with an eastern front. The British Opposition clamoured for a Soviet alliance. So did the French, who, having been committed to the Polish guarantee without being consulted, now wanted someone else to fulfil their guarantee for them. But there were grave disadvantages also. The Poles would not make an alliance with Soviet Russia, and Beck insisted that he would reject Soviet assistance even if offered. Some members of the British government believed that Soviet Russia, bled by Stalin's purges, was too weak to fight. Others believed that she would not be a reliable ally. All were shocked at the idea of associating with Bolsheviks and regarded the prospect of Soviet victory, however remote, as even worse than that of a German one. Yet there was no escape. British public opinion wanted the Soviet alliance as the best means of deterring Hitler from war or of winning a war if it came. The French were determined to go forward. The British government therefore timidly set out on the quest for an alliance without risks, much as a man trying to go swimming without getting wet.

The basis of the British proposal, feebly dangled before the Soviet government time after time, was that Soviet Russia should provide aid 'if requested' or 'if desired'. Soviet aid was to be turned on and off like a tap. The Poles were to be allowed to turn the tap. Later the Baltic states were to be allowed to turn the tap. The British were to be allowed to turn the tap. But the Soviets were not to be allowed to turn the tap themselves. They were to stand by patiently, active or inactive according to the will of others. This was not an attractive proposition for the Russians. No one knows the original intentions of Stalin and his associates. Perhaps they hoped for a solid alliance with the Western powers. Perhaps they planned a deal with Hitler all along. Perhaps they intended to play with both sides and see what happened. Speculation is not rewarding and is made less so when the Soviet rulers are denounced for following the path of self-preservation like everyone else. The Bolsheviks lose either way: they are condemned as criminal monsters at one

Above: SA recruits in Memel following the city's return to Germany. Memel's population was predominantly German in origin and many were willing to fight for the Führer. Right: A new mood of resolution was seen in Great Britain after Hitler's move into Prague

May 27, 1939

PICTURE POST

AFS
LONDON

**AN OFFICER OF THE AUXILIARY FIRE SERVICES
PREPARES FOR THE WORST**

(See Inside)

**HULTON'S
NATIONAL
WEEKLY**

In this issue:

BRITAIN PREPARES

3D

MAY 27, 1939

Vol. 3. No. 8

moment and expected to follow a more idealistic course than others at the next.

According to such evidence as exists, the Soviet government was anxious to conclude a firm alliance, and the British, when not evasive, were spinning things out. Each British subterfuge received a prompt Soviet answer. Then the British would take ten days or a fortnight devising another one. By the middle of May, negotiations had reached deadlock. The Russians would look at nothing except a straight defensive alliance. The British inserted the fatal 'if desired' into every draft. When this was rejected, they were ready to break off. Hitler had remained quiet, and perhaps there would be no trouble after all. The French were not so complacent. Failing all else, they would make a simple Franco-Soviet alliance without caring what happened to Poland. To prevent this, the British went reluctantly forward. This time they appeared to offer a pact of mutual security. But there were still problems. The Russians feared that Hitler would attack other countries before attacking them, and a glance at the map suggests that he could do nothing else. The Russians therefore demanded that 'indirect aggression', that is attack on some neighbouring country, should be regarded as attack upon themselves. They even demanded that

peaceful surrender to Hitler by some small country should be treated as indirect aggression on themselves.

The British refused these Soviet proposals. They had made the cause of small countries their own. Besides, they suspected Soviet Russia as an imperialist power, with plans much like Hitler's. In that case, they should not have been seeking a Soviet alliance at all. Finally Molotov, now commissar for foreign affairs, suggested a way out. They should postpone the search for a political agreement and should hold military talks to consider how the alliance could work if it were ever made. The British jumped at this as an excuse for further delay. The French hoped to get military co-operation with Soviet Russia after all. The British and French governments appointed military delegations which departed on a slow boat for Leningrad. By the time they arrived all chance of a united front against Hitler had disappeared.

During the negotiations, both Russians and British had received offers from unofficial German sources. The Russians had indicated their willingness to renew trade relations with Germany. The British had gone further. Chamberlain's agents, though perhaps not Chamberlain himself, had displayed British anxiety to satisfy Hitler

Above: Local police remove customs barrier following Germany's annexation of Danzig, 1st September 1939—the day Poland was invaded. The Free City of Danzig had been under Polish economic domination

over Danzig, if only this could be done in a respectable peaceful way. Once Danzig was settled, Great Britain would forget her guarantee to Poland. She would give Germany a loan of one thousand million pounds. Happy relations would be restored.

By the beginning of August, Hitler knew that negotiations between Soviet Russia and the Western powers were stuck. He knew also that the British government would pay almost any price to avoid a war. He thought that the time had come for him to pull off his great stroke. The British people, he believed, were hoping for a Soviet alliance. If he could show that this hope was vain, the British would back down. He was right, or very nearly, about the British government. He failed to allow for the fact that the British people might have a will of their own. It was a very foolish proposition to suppose that Great Britain and France, without Soviet Russia, could do anything to aid Poland or indeed to deter Hitler in any way. But it was a proposition to which most British people were committed.

The Nazi-Soviet Pact

The Russian view

The Soviet-German Treaty was signed on 23rd August 1939, but to this day the strong feelings it aroused have not calmed down: discussions and intense arguments still go on about the nature of this treaty, about the circumstances in which it was made, and about its consequences.

After the Munich agreement had been signed on 30th September 1938, political events in Europe developed along two different lines. On the one hand, the aggressive behaviour of Germany was intensified. On 15th March 1939 German forces occupied Bohemia-Moravia. A week later Germany seized the Lithuanian port of Klaipeda, and the next day Hitler imposed a shackling economic agreement upon Rumania. On 21st March the German government demanded that Poland hand over Danzig, and shortly afterwards repudiated their pact of non-aggression with Poland. In April Germany's ally Italy grabbed Albania. Thus, the appetite of the Nazis was growing, aggressive deeds were being committed one after another, and the danger of war in Europe was becoming more and more evident.

On the other hand, Great Britain and France continued to follow their policy of appeasing the aggressor, which had culminated in the Munich agreement with Hitler and Mussolini. However, Germany's aggressions, and the increasing alarm caused in Europe by the fascist aggressors, obliged the British and French governments to take certain measures during the first half of 1939. Great Britain announced on 31st March that she guaranteed the independence of Poland, and this was

Below: Molotov signs the non-aggression pact with Nazi Germany on 23rd August 1939, while von Ribbentrop and Stalin look on

The Fragile Peace

followed by guarantees to Greece and Rumania on 13th April and to Turkey on 12th May. France endorsed these British guarantees. At the same time, Great Britain and France agreed to begin negotiations with the Soviet Union for joint resistance to Hitler's aggression.

On 18th March the Soviet government handed a special note to Schulenburg, the German ambassador in Moscow, stating that it did not recognize the inclusion of Czechoslovakia in the German Reich. On the same day the USSR proposed that a conference of the states concerned be convened to discuss the situation caused by the German threat to Rumania. The British government said it considered such a conference to be premature, and in mid-April proposed that the USSR guarantee Poland and Rumania against possible German aggression.

Later, Great Britain repeated her proposal, with the aim of binding the USSR to go immediately to the aid of Poland and Rumania if Hitler should decide to attack these countries, and also in case Hitler were to turn westward. But the British government did not want to give similar guarantees against possible German attacks on Latvia, Estonia, or Finland, although from the point of view of the USSR attacks on the Baltic countries would represent no less danger than attacks on Rumania or Poland.

The calculation made by the leaders of British and French foreign policy became clear. They wished to make sure of Soviet aid in the event of attacks by Germany on those countries in which Great Britain and France were interested, but they had no intention of undertaking similar obligations towards the USSR.

The USSR put forward counter-proposals for the formation of a powerful coalition capable of resisting any aggression by Germany. For three weeks the British government left these Soviet proposals unanswered. It then tabled its own plan, which again provided only for Soviet guarantees to Poland and Rumania.

In June the Soviet government invited Halifax, the British foreign secretary, to come to Moscow; but he was unable to find the time for this visit. On 23rd July the Soviet government proposed that negotiations begin in Moscow between military representatives of the three powers, so as to agree on possible joint military action against the aggressor. Again, however, London and Paris did not hasten to answer. Nineteen days elapsed between this proposal by the Soviet government and the arrival in Moscow of the British and French missions.

The talks began in Moscow on 12th August. The Soviet delegation was headed by the people's commissar for defence,

Marshal K.E.Voroshilov, and included the commissar for the navy, the chief of General Staff of the Red Army, and his deputy, who commanded the Soviet air force. The British and French missions were headed by men of only secondary rank, without the necessary authority.

The course taken by the talks further showed that the Anglo-French side did not wish to discuss definite military plans, the conditions for allowing Soviet troops to traverse Polish and Rumanian territory, the number of divisions to be committed, and so on. The talks arrived at an impasse when Poland announced that she would not agree to allow Soviet troops to cross her territory.

Anglo-French plan

About the same time, reports appeared in the press about talks going on between Great Britain and Germany. Though the details did not become known until much later, the USSR was obviously threatened by the possibility of another Munich.

It was in this situation that the German government offered the Soviet Union a pact of non-aggression. Actually, the Germans had begun sounding the USSR about the possibility of an agreement as early as the beginning of 1939. At that time the Soviet government had left these German approaches unanswered and entered into talks with Great Britain and France. When, however, in mid-August, it became more and more obvious that no agreement could be reached with Great Britain and France, the Soviet government consented to the visit by Ribbentrop to Moscow which had been proposed by the Germans.

The Anglo-French plan was to direct Germany's appetite towards the East and involve Hitler in conflict with the Soviet Union. The USSR was faced with the immediate danger of finding herself facing Hitler on her own. Munich and the subsequent negotiations provided clear proof of the unwillingness of the British and French governments to form an anti-Hitler alliance. And in these same months Soviet-Japanese relations became strained. Japanese troops invaded the territory of the Mongolian People's Republic in the area of the River Khalkhin Gol. The Soviet Union, acting in accordance with the mutual aid treaty of 1936, sent forces to help the MPR. At the very moment when fruitless negotiations were going on with the British and French in Moscow, the Red Army was engaged in battle with substantial Japanese forces.

In these circumstances the USSR was confronted with the prospect of a war on two fronts, without any allies. To ensure the country's security, the Soviet government accepted the German proposals. On 22nd August 1939 Ribbentrop arrived in

Moscow, and on the 23rd the Soviet-German Treaty of non-aggression was signed.

In signing this treaty the Soviet Union followed one of the principles of its foreign policy, namely, to make use of the contradictions between the capitalist countries. It was not easy for the Soviet Union to sign this treaty. There had to be taken into account, in the first place, the effect on public opinion of an agreement made between the land of socialism and fascist Germany, against whose policy the USSR had fought for many years. The problem was further complicated because the general public did not know about all the vagaries of the Anglo-Franco-Soviet negotiations.

In the second place, it was clear to everyone, including the USSR, that the treaty meant only a temporary postponement, that sooner or later Hitler would proceed to carry out his programme of struggle against Communism and the USSR.

The treaty with Germany was a step which the USSR was forced to take in the difficult situation that had come about in the summer of 1939. The Soviet government did not deceive itself regarding Hitler's aims. It understood that the treaty would not bring the USSR lasting peace but only a more or less lengthy breathing-space. When it signed the treaty with Germany the Soviet government undertook the task of using the time thus gained to carry through the political and military measures needed in order to ensure the country's security and strengthen its capacity for defence.

THE PACT

'The Government of the German Reich and the Government of the Union of Soviet Socialist Republics, desirous of strengthening the cause of peace between Germany and the USSR, and proceeding from the fundamental provisions of the Neutrality Agreement concluded in April 1926 between Germany and the USSR, have reached the following agreement:

'Article I. Both High Contracting Parties obligate themselves to desist from any act of violence, any aggressive action, and any attack on each other, either individually or jointly with other powers.

'Article II. Should one of the High Contracting Parties become the object of belligerent action by a third power, the other High Contracting Party shall in no manner lend its support to this third party.

'Article III. The Governments of the two High Contracting Parties shall in the future maintain continual contact with one another for the purpose of consultation in order to exchange information on problems affecting their common interests.

'Article IV. Neither of the two High Contracting Parties shall participate in

Left: Soviet cartoon, 1936, sees Western capitalists as Hitler's guardian angels. Criticism stopped abruptly with signing of Nazi-Soviet Pact. *Right:* Japanese soldiers captured by Russians in Mongolia. Committed to aid Mongolia, Russia wanted to avoid war in the West

any grouping of powers whatsoever that is directly or indirectly aimed at the other party.

'*Article V.* Should disputes or conflicts arise between the High Contracting Parties over problems of one kind or another, both parties shall settle these disputes or conflicts exclusively through friendly exchange of opinion, or, if necessary, through the establishment of arbitration commissions.

'*Article VI.* The present treaty is concluded for a period of ten years, with the proviso that, in so far as one of the High Contracting Parties does not denounce it one year prior to the expiration of this period, the validity of this treaty shall automatically be extended for another five years.

'*Article VII.* The present treaty shall be ratified within the shortest possible time. The ratification shall be exchanged in Berlin. The agreement shall enter into force as soon as it is signed.'

'**Secret Additional Protocol**
'On the occasion of the signature of the Nonaggression Pact between the German Reich and the Union of Soviet Socialist Republics the undersigned plenipotentiaries of each of the two parties discussed in strictly confidential conversations the question of the boundary of their respective spheres of influence in Eastern Europe. These conversations led to the following conclusions:

'1. In the event of a territorial and political rearrangement in the areas belonging to the Baltic States (Finland, Estonia, Latvia, Lithuania), the northern boundary of Lithuania shall represent the boundary of the spheres of influence of Germany and the USSR ...

'2. In the event of a territorial and political rearrangement of the areas belonging to the Polish state the spheres of influence of Germany and the USSR shall be bounded approximately by the line of the rivers Narew, Vistula, and San.

'The question of whether the interests of both parties make desirable the maintenance of an independent Polish state and how such a state should be bounded can only be definitely determined in the course of further political developments. . . .'

The division of Poland
'Further political developments' were provided by the Germans themselves when they invaded Poland. Four weeks later, on 28th September, Germany and the USSR carried their co-operation a step further with a treaty dividing Poland:

'The government of the German Reich and the government of the USSR consider it as exclusively their task, after the collapse of the former Polish state, to re-establish peace and order in these territories and to assure to the peoples living there a peaceful life in keeping with their national character. To this end, they have agreed upon the following:

'The government of the German Reich

and the government of the USSR determine . . . the boundary of their respective national interests in the territory of the former Polish state . . .

'. . . the territory of the Lithuanian state falls into the sphere of influence of the USSR, while, on the other hand, the province of Lublin and parts of the province of Warsaw fall to the sphere of influence of Germany . . .

'Both parties will tolerate in their territories no Polish agitation which affects the territories of the other party. They will suppress in their territories all beginnings of such agitation and inform each other concerning suitable measures.'

The American view

Any Soviet historian dealing with the history of the events leading to the outbreak of the Second World War and the subsequent Soviet involvement in it starts with four great difficulties.

Firstly, despite a quite substantial degree of de-Stalinization among Soviet military historians, who now feel free to discuss Stalin's errors as a military commander, Soviet diplomatic historians are unable to admit that Stalin's and Molotov's conduct of foreign policy could in any way have been influenced by misjudgment or misinformation. Secondly, although the British, Italian, American, German, and even the Hungarian diplomatic archives have been published *in extenso,* we still have no idea what the various Soviet ambassadors were reporting, or the instructions that were going out from Moscow to them. Thirdly, despite the implications heavily underlined by Soviet historians that the British government would have preferred to find a way of avoiding war with Germany, the fact remains that Great Britain chose to fight Hitler in 1939 and the Soviet Union chose to make an agreement with him that made it possible for him to conquer all Europe between the Channel and the Soviet frontier the following summer. Fourthly, whatever else the Soviet government did during the years 1939-41, it did not 'carry through the political and military measures needed in order to secure the country's security and strengthen its capacity for defence', or at least not with any great energy, efficiency, or enthusiasm. The Soviet government dismissed the warnings that reached them, even from their own intelligence sources such as Richard Sorge in Tokyo, of imminent German attack. The German forces that attacked in June 1941 achieved complete tactical surprise; they found no fortifications to oppose them, and they virtually obliterated the Soviet armies in the west. Only the innate heroism of the Soviet people saved the Soviet Union from conquest by those with

whom a non-aggression pact had been signed two years earlier.

The inadequacies of the Soviet interpretation of the period January to August 1939 are evident, for example, on the subject of the development of British policy against Hitler. In January 1939, *before* the German invasion of Prague, the British authorities had already both expressed their anxieties lest Hitler seek new adventures in the Ukraine, and asked for concerted staff action with the French to face a possible German attack westwards. They had also begun to mend their fences with the Soviet Union, in the face of much Soviet suspicion. The British answer to the occupation of Prague and the reports of an economic ultimatum to Rumania was an immediate approach to the Soviet Union. The Soviet proposal of 18th March was in answer to this. The British proposals that the Soviet Union guarantee Rumania and Poland were, after all, only that the Soviets should follow the British example. The reason why Great Britain was reluctant to give guarantees to the Baltic states and Finland was that these states flatly refused to ask for them, and Great Britain did not wish to drive them into Germany's arms. The Baltic states also turned down the Soviet offer of a non-aggression pact preferring to conclude one with Germany. Great Britain had constantly to labour, as her published documents make clear, with the absolute refusal of the states between Germany and the Soviet Union to commit themselves in any way to contacts with the Soviet Union.

Nor does the Soviet view account for the evidence on German-Soviet relations. The German approach to the Soviet Union in January is not reflected in the German diplomatic documents (unless this is a reference to Hitler's talk at a New Year's reception with the Soviet diplomatic representative). At the end of January 1939, when Ribbentrop recalled the German trade mission to Moscow in his eagerness to obtain an agreement with Poland, German-Soviet relations were at a very low ebb. They continued that way until the reopening of contacts ostensibly *from* the Soviet side in April. (We have, of course, no way of knowing whether the Soviet representative was acting on his own, or even if the German report, prompted by the wish for better German-Soviet relations, misrepresented this initiative as coming from the Soviet side. Soviet historians who deal with this episode at all simply dismiss the German record as a forgery.) The real signal was, however, the replacement as commissar of foreign affairs of Litvinov, a Jew, by Molotov on 3rd May, an event which struck Hitler as so important that the German ambassador in Moscow was

immediately recalled to report. He advised an approach to Molotov beginning with economic affairs, and it was Molotov's remark that good economic relations were impossible unless political relations improved which encouraged the Germans to proceed. The truth is that through Sorge in Tokyo and their agents in Germany, the Soviet authorities knew that Hitler was preparing to attack the West if he could not frighten them off – and he expected the signing of the Nazi-Soviet Pact to do this. Yet no serious evidence has been produced which would show that British policy was directed to attempting to procure a German attack on the Soviet Union. If the Soviet leadership believed this to be the aim of British policy, they would appear to have been influenced by a major misjudgment.

The real defence of Soviet policy in 1939 is that the British were casting them in a role which if it succeeded in restraining Hitler would redound to the credit of Great Britain, whereas if it failed, the Soviet Union would have to bear the burden of fighting on land. Great Britain had no forces available for a major land offensive in Europe and the French saw no point in abandoning their fortifications. The Soviets thus had every reason for rejecting the early British proposals. The later ones, however, gave them everything they had originally asked for. It is the difficulties that Molotov made in the negotiations in June and July which make British historians suspect that Molotov was holding the option of an agreement with Germany open all the time and that the decision to conclude the agreement with Germany was not the last minute affair it is so often represented as being by Soviet historians. It is clear that despite their intelligence in the West, the Soviet military had no idea actually how weak Great Britain and France were. Otherwise the revelations made by Admiral Drax, and General Doumenc, heads of the British and French missions, would not have struck them with such suspicion.

British policy in this period is a record of misordered priorities and misunderstood information. Great Britain was much weaker than even her leaders believed; and they were attempting to create a deterrent bloc in Eastern Europe without properly considering who was to provide the real element of deterrence behind that bloc. British intelligence, partly from ideological conviction, possibly from awareness of the Soviet-German exchanges (the Americans knew of them through the German embassy in Moscow) was dominated by suspicion of the Soviet Union. Yet in the end Great Britain was not deterred by the Nazi-Soviet Pact and went to war against the Nazi menace in September 1939.

The Storm Breaks

The war crisis of 1939 began on 21st August, with the announcement that Ribbentrop, German foreign minister, had been invited to Moscow by the Soviet government. Though the Nazi-Soviet Pact was not formally concluded until 23rd August, it was obvious that Ribbentrop would not go to Moscow unless agreement had already been reached in principle. Hence it was certain that the negotiations for an alliance between France, Great Britain, and Soviet Russia had broken down. This is what Hitler wished to establish. Soviet neutrality in itself was not enough for him. What he needed was public news of this neutrality so that he could shake the nerves of the British and French governments. Stalin, the Soviet dictator, exacted his price in return. Though he, too, like Hitler, probably expected British and French resolution to collapse, he wanted to keep the Germans far from the Soviet frontier if war occurred after all. Hence the Nazi-Soviet Pact drew a barrier in Eastern Europe which the Germans were not to cross.

The pact was neither an alliance nor a partition agreement. The Soviet government merely promised to stay neutral which is what the Poles had always asked them to do, and in addition they set a limit to German expansion. However, the immediate effect was certainly discouraging for the Western powers. Until the last moment they had gone on dreaming either that Hitler would be frightened by the Soviet bogeyman or that Soviet Russia would do their fighting for them. Now they had to decide for themselves, and Hitler was convinced that they would run away. On 22nd August he delivered to his generals a wild oration: 'Close your hearts to pity. Act brutally.' He boasted: 'I have got Poland where I wanted her,' and added cheerfully: 'The probability is great that the West will not intervene.' Hitler was play-acting in order to impress the German generals. He guessed that some of them would leak to the British, and sure enough some did. Almost at once the British embassy received an exaggerated version of Hitler's speech and was correspondingly alarmed.

On 23rd August Hitler went a step further. He moved forward the attack on Poland, fixed for 1st September, to 4.40 a.m. on 26th August. This, too, was play-acting. The German preparations could not be complete before 1st September. Attack on Poland before then was possible only if she had already surrendered. Thus Hitler counted confidently on the collapse of the Western powers.

The French almost came up to his expectations. Georges Bonnet, the foreign minister, had always wanted to desert the Poles. He accepted the German case over Danzig. He had no faith in the Polish army. On 23rd August Daladier, the Premier, summoned the Committee of National Defence at Bonnet's request. Bonnet asked: should they push Poland into a compromise and postpone the war until they were stronger? Gamelin, the French commander-in-chief, would not admit the weakness of his army. He asserted that the Poles could hold out until the spring. By then, France would be 'impregnable'. There was no suggestion that France could aid Poland in any way. Nor did the French attempt to discuss the situation with the British. There were no Anglo-French meetings of ministers such as had marked the Czech crisis. Ideally, the French would have liked the British to force surrender on them. But they would not take the lead in abdication themselves. There was a choice between abandoning Poland and fighting a great war in which France would carry most of the burden. The French refused to choose. They sat helplessly by throughout the week when others decided the fate of Europe and of France.

British obstinacy

The British government were apparently more resolute. On 22nd August they issued a statement that the coming Nazi-Soviet Pact 'would in no way affect their obligation to Poland'. There was nothing else to do. The British ministers were proud and obstinate. They were not going to have the Opposition crowing that their policy was in ruins. Besides, they feared to be swept away in a storm of public opinion if they showed weakness. Conservative backbenchers had disliked the negotiations with Soviet Russia. But many of them had fought in the First World War. They could not imagine that Great Britain was unable to impose her will on Germany if she determined to do so. As for the Opposition, they had championed the Soviet alliance. Now they were resolved to show that, unlike Stalin, they stuck to their principles.

In secret, the British ministers wanted to

Right: *In contrast to the scenes of August 1914, Britain and France went to war in September 1939 with a sense of weary foreboding, although their resolution to fight for Poland had not collapsed as Hitler had expected; appeasement had run its course. This newsvendor in London's Trafalgar Square tells his own story*

The Fragile Peace

give way. Chamberlain told Kennedy, the American ambassador: 'The futility of it all is frightful; we cannot save the Poles; we can only carry on a war of revenge that will mean the destruction of all Europe.' Chamberlain said he could not put pressure on Poland himself. Would President Roosevelt do it for him? Roosevelt refused. The only hope was to warn Hitler, or rather to plead with him. On 23rd August Nevile Henderson flew to Berchtesgaden. He delivered a warning that Great Britain would stand by Poland. But he also asserted that Hitler could get Danzig peacefully, and he spread out the delights of an Anglo-German alliance. Hitler appeared to be unimpressed. He stormed and ranted. When Henderson left, Hitler slapped his thigh and exclaimed: 'Chamberlain will not survive that conversation. His government will fall tonight.' Back in Berlin, Henderson told Lipski, the Polish ambassador, that the only chance was for Poland to start negotiations immediately. Lipski took no notice.

On 24th August the British Parliament met. It unanimously applauded what it supposed to be the government's firm stand. Hitler began to doubt whether the British government had yet reached the point of surrender. He flew to Berlin and held a conference with Ribbentrop and his leading generals. He asked: should they stick to 26th August as the date for the attack on Poland? He decided that he would make a further attempt to detach the Western powers from their alliance with Poland. This took the form of a 'last offer' which Hitler made to Henderson soon after midday on 25th August. He declared that the problems of Danzig and the Corridor must be 'solved' – though he did not say how. Once this was done, he would guarantee the British Empire, accept an agreed limitation of armaments, and renew his assurance that Germany's western frontier was fixed for ever. Henderson was impressed as usual and thought that Hitler spoke 'with apparent sincerity'. Henderson promised to take Hitler's offer to London the next morning. Hitler approved. What was he up to? By the time Henderson left Berlin the German attack on Poland would presumably have begun. Did Hitler think that the British would abandon the Polish alliance on sight of his offer? Had he forgotten his own time-table? Or was advancing the date of attack to 26th August a bluff all along?

The last seems the most probable explanation. All afternoon on 25th August Hitler raged round the Chancellery. At 3 p.m. he ordered the attack to proceed. Three hours later Attolico, the Italian ambassador, brought the news that Italy could not enter the war unless she received vast quantities of raw materials

Henderson (second from left), escorted by German officials, arrives to see Hitler on night of 30th-31st August. He had come to ask for time to start talks – but time had run out

which Germany was in no position to supply. Immediately afterwards Ribbentrop reported that the Anglo-Polish treaty had been formally signed in London. Hitler pulled back. He summoned Keitel, the chief-of-staff, and said: 'Stop everything at once. I need time for negotiations.' The attack on Poland was called off at the last moment.

The British government seemed to have committed themselves for good when they signed the alliance with Poland, particularly as it included a guarantee of Danzig. Their real attitude was quite different: they were still eager to sell out. The Foreign Office drafted terms for an offer to Hitler which stated that Danzig should have 'the right to determine its political allegiance', and Halifax, the foreign secretary, told the Polish ambassador that the Polish government would make a great mistake if they ruled out 'peaceful modifications of the status of Danzig'. Hitler and the British government thus agreed how negotiations should end – with a Polish surrender. The problem was how to get negotiations started. The two sides circled round each other like wrestlers before a clinch. The British offered to arrange direct negotiations between Germany and Poland if Hitler promised to behave peacefully. Hitler answered that there would be no war if he got his way over Danzig.

Göring, who did not want war, now

called in an unofficial intermediary, a Swedish businessman called Dahlerus. Dahlerus flew to London on 25th August and back to Berlin on 26th August; to London and back on 27th August; and the same again on 30th August. In Berlin he saw Göring and sometimes Hitler. In London he saw Chamberlain and Halifax. Each side got the impression that the other was weakening. Both wanted another Munich, but on favourable terms, and neither side knew how to push the Poles over the brink.

On 28th August Henderson delivered the British reply to Hitler's last offer. The British government urged that there should be direct negotiations between Germany and Poland. If these reached agreement, the way would be open for 'a wider and more complete agreement between Germany and Great Britain'. Hitler had repeatedly declared that, as his offers to Poland had been rejected in the spring, he would never negotiate directly with the Poles again. On the other hand, Henderson made no objection when Hitler said that negotiations must involve a Polish surrender over Danzig and the Corridor. Thus Hitler thought he would succeed either way. If the Poles yielded, he would get Danzig and the Corridor. If they refused, the British government would repudiate them. He decided to accept direct negotiations, but to do it in such a way that Germany would still seem to be dictating to both Great Britain and Poland.

On 29th August Hitler saw Henderson again and delivered his answer. He agreed to direct negotiations, but a Polish representative, with full powers, must arrive in Berlin within the next twenty-four hours. Henderson objected that this was an ultimatum. Hitler and Ribbentrop answered, with typical German pedantry, that the word 'ultimatum' nowhere appeared in the German note. Ultimatum or not, Henderson was eager to accept it. Hitler's offer, he telegraphed to London, was 'the sole chance of preventing war'. Henderson urged acceptance on everybody – on his own government, on the French, on the Poles. He hurried round to Lipski and urged immediate acceptance. Lipski was unmoved and did not even report Hitler's offer to Warsaw. The French were as resolute in the opposite direction. Bonnet telegraphed to Beck that he should go to Berlin at once.

Decision rested with the British government. Here was the proposal they had always wanted: direct negotiations between Germany and Poland. Hitler had agreed. Now they could not deliver the Poles. Chamberlain told Kennedy that he was 'more worried about getting the Poles to be reasonable than the Germans'. And with reason. Beck replied firmly: 'If invited to Berlin of course he would not go, as he had no intention of being treated like President Hácha.' (President Emil Hácha of Czechoslovakia had, five months before on 15th March, been forced by Hitler, Göring, and Ribbentrop to sign away his country's independence.) The British government had to make a temporizing reply, which Henderson delivered only twenty-five minutes after midnight on 30th August, that is after the German 'ultimatum' had run out. The British welcomed Hitler's proposal, but they asked him to wait a bit – they could not produce a Polish representative at such short notice.

Hitler meanwhile had prepared terms which he would present to the Poles. They were for him moderate: immediate return of Danzig and a plebiscite in the Corridor. Henderson thought that these terms were 'not unreasonable'. Back at the British embassy, he summoned Lipski and urged him to seek an interview with Ribbentrop at once. Lipski refused and went back to bed. The next morning Göring sent Dahlerus to Henderson with the German terms in writing. Henderson again summoned Lipski, and when he refused to come, sent Dahlerus round to him. Lipski was still obstinate. He declared that 'German morale was weakening and that the present regime would soon crack'. Dahlerus reported his failure to London and added that the German terms were 'extremely

reasonable'. The British agreed. Henderson telegraphed to London that 'on German offer war should be completely unjustifiable', and Halifax telegraphed to Warsaw: 'I do not see why Polish government should feel difficulty about authorising Polish Ambassador to accept a document from the German government.'

Hitler's manoeuvre was succeeding. A breach was opening between Poland and her Western allies. But Hitler was trapped by his own time-table. He had repeatedly declared to his generals that he would either produce a Polish surrender by 1st September or go to war. He dared not face their contempt if he confessed failure. Besides, military action could not be improvised at a moment's notice. If the attack planned for 1st September were called off, it would have to be postponed for many weeks or even months. All the British messages had been intercepted, and Hitler knew how anxious the British government were to surrender. He had to gamble that they would surrender even if war against Poland had started. In this tight situation he had no choice if he were to maintain his prestige. Maybe too, he liked gambling. As he told Göring: 'I always call *va banque*. It is the only call I know.' At 12.40 p.m. on 31st August he ordered that the attack on Poland should proceed.

At 1 p.m. Lipski asked to see Ribbentrop. He was asked whether he was coming as a plenipotentiary. He replied: 'No, as ambassador.' This was enough for Hitler. The Poles were still obstinate. At 4 p.m. Hitler confirmed the order for war. At 6.30 p.m. Lipski at last saw Ribbentrop. Lipski said that the Poles were 'favourably considering' the idea of direct negotiations. Ribbentrop again asked whether he was a plenipotentiary. Lipski again said no. Ribbentrop did not communicate the German terms. If he had tried to do so, Lipski would have refused to receive them. The Poles had kept their nerve unbroken to the last moment. At 4.45 a.m. on 1st September the German forces attacked Poland without warning or pretext. At 6 a.m. German aeroplanes bombed Warsaw.

Trapped into war

The ally of Great Britain and France had been wantonly attacked. It only remained for them to declare war on the aggressor. They did nothing of the kind. The two governments merely 'warned' Hitler that they might have to go to war unless he desisted. Meanwhile they hoped that Mussolini would save them as he had done during the Czech crisis, and he duly did his best. He proposed a European conference to survey all causes of conflict, with the condition that Danzig should return to Germany at once. Hitler replied that he would answer on 3rd September.

The British and French governments were therefore desperate to postpone any action until that day. But they, too, were trapped – by the indignation of British opinion. The French remained supine. The British were in an uproar. At the very least, German troops must be withdrawn from Poland before the proposal for a conference was accepted. Mussolini knew that this was hopeless and dropped his proposal. The British and French governments went on hoping for a conference which was already dead.

On the evening of 2nd September Chamberlain addressed the House of Commons. MP's expected to hear that war had been declared. Instead Chamberlain said that, if the German government would agree to withdraw their troops from Poland (not actually to withdraw them), the British government would forget everything that had happened, and diplomacy could start again. Chamberlain sat down in dead silence. Greenwood, rising to speak for Labour, was greeted with a shout from Amery: 'Speak for England, Arthur.' Afterwards Greenwood warned Chamberlain that there would be no holding the House if war were not declared. The cabinet met late at night and resolved that an ultimatum should be sent to Germany at once. Halifax, who regretted this decision, put off the ultimatum until the next morning.

The British ultimatum was delivered in Berlin at 9 a.m. on 3rd September. The German government made no reply, and the ultimatum expired at 11 a.m. The French trailed after their ally and declared war at 5 p.m. The Second World War had begun. It is possible that Hitler intended to conquer Europe at some time. It is also possible, though less likely, that the British government intended at some time to resist him. Neither of these intentions caused the actual outbreak of war. Then Hitler merely wanted Danzig and the Corridor, and the British government wanted to give them to him. These plans were wrecked first by Polish obstinacy and then by the indignation of Conservative backbenchers. The very men who had applauded Munich now insisted on war.

There was much talk later about a crusade against fascism. In fact most countries were pushed into war. The Poles had no choice. The French were dragged along by the British. Russians and Americans, mighty boasters both, waited supinely until Hitler chose to attack them. Only the British people and their dominions went to war of their own free will. They were not concerned about fascism. They did not even save Poland. They went to war out of national pride and for the sake of national honour. Ultimately they brought Hitler down, and this was something to be proud of.

The Balance of
Power, 1939

Relative strength of all major belligerents in Second World War. The number increased after the first blows: Italy entered in 1940 and Russia, Japan, and the USA the following year. Russia's apparent dominance was offset by the obsolescence of her land forces

		Great Britain	France	USSR	USA	Poland	Germany	Italy	Japan
	Population (thousands)*	47,692	41,600	167,300	129,825	34,662	68,424	43,779	70,590
	National income ($m)*	23,550	10,296	31,410	67,600	3,189	33,347	6,895	5,700
	Reserves (millions)	0.4	4.6	12.0†	**	1.5	2.2	4.8	2.4†
	Peacetime armies (millions)	0.22	0.8	1.7†	0.19	0.29	0.8	0.8	0.32†
	Aircraft (first line)	2,075	600	5,000†	800	390	4,500†	1,500††	1,980
	Destroyers	184	28	28	181	4	17	60	113
	Submarines	58	70	150	99	5	56	100	53

*1938   **not available   †approximate   ††1940

The Military Balance

Germany, from a population a little under sixty-five millions, lost in the First World War just under two millions killed. Despite their support for Hitler and their enthusiasm for the successful outcome of his early military adventures, the German people dreaded another war no less than those of other nations. The generals and admirals, while willing to contemplate war to redress what they saw as the iniquities of the Versailles Treaty, knew in 1939 the work of rearmament and expansion to be far from complete. Yet events were to show the Germans better equipped psychologically, technically, and materially to fight again

than the other nations of the world who watched the re-appearance of German power with fascinated alarm and growing—if supine—horror.

The Versailles Treaty limited the German army to 100,000 and forbade Germany tanks, heavy artillery, aircraft, gas, submarines, and a general staff. General Hans von Seeckt, head of the Reichswehr from 1920 to 1926, rigorously selected officers and men, re-established discipline and professionalism, and sought to combine the old Prussian tradition with a more modern and flexible spirit. Against the day of expansion, officers and men were prepared for

German pilots before their Henschel Hs 123s strap on parachutes, 1937. These aircraft were to give tactical support to the army in the early months of the war

higher rank and secret arrangements enabled the training of personnel and development of the forbidden weapons to be carried out abroad.

When expansion came Seeckt would have preferred an élite striking force of some 2-300,000 backed by a national militia – de Gaulle advocated something similar for France. Hitler, however, demanded a modernized version of the old mass Imperial Army. In October 1934 he announced the expansion of the Reichswehr to 300,000, then in March 1935 denounced the Versailles Treaty, proclaimed conscription, and set the strength of the army at 600,000 and thirty-six divisions. By 1939 it had reached a peace-time strength of 730,000 with 1,100,000 in the reserves.

An increase in strength by eighteen times in seven years was far greater than anything contemplated by Seeckt, and only a minority of the officers and experts needed could be found in the Reichswehr. Every possible source was tapped for the rest – police, Party organizations, former officers of the Imperial Army, and, of course, mass intake and training of the young. The Nazi philosophy lent itself to rigorous training and discipline, and a combination of extreme standardization in training and equipment, on the one hand, with encouragement of initiative and flexibility in action, on the other, was remarkably successful in the rapid production of highly effective forces.

Although he failed to appreciate the full potential of the tank, Seeckt had believed in the traditional Prussian strategy of dynamic mobility. Heinz Guderian, a young infantry captain appointed in 1922 to the motor transport staff, became the leading German proponent of armoured warfare. As chief of staff to the director of motorized troops in 1931, pressing for armoured divisions, he met the same sort of opposition that had appeared in other armies, but Hitler, when he came to power, took up the idea. 'That's what I need,' he exclaimed when he first saw Guderian's armour, 'that's what I want to have!'

An experimental armoured division took part in the summer exercises of 1935, and that autumn the first three armoured divisions were formed. Next year they were

Top left: Battle simulation in the Nuremberg stadium, 1938. Amid smoke effects, infantry and Panzer II tanks cavort for a capacity crowd. Top right: Refuelling Stuka dive-bombers, January 1939. The dreaded gull-winged Ju 87 was to win easy victories in Poland and France in the absence of adequate fighter opposition. Left: Battleship Bismarck, 1940. Her fifteen-inch guns, massive armour, and high power made her the pride of Hitler's navy and the strongest battleship of the day

formed into an armoured corps, while three light divisions – a throwback to earlier doctrine – and four motorized divisions were formed. Massed armour appeared in the manoeuvres of 1937 and again in 1938. In March 1937, under Guderian, one armoured and one SS motorized division entered Vienna, having driven 420 miles in forty-eight hours. The Panzers of the Second World War had appeared.

When the army mobilized in September 1939 there were six armoured, four light (later converted to armoured), four motorized, and eighty-four infantry divisions. There was, however, a shortage of the later types of tanks – even in May 1940 only some 600 of the new Panzerkampfwagen (armoured fighting vehicle) III and IV had reached the armoured divisions, which had over 300 modern Czech tanks and about 1,500 of the older, lightly armoured and armed, Pzkw I and II. The superiority of the forceful, energetic Panzer groups lay in their organization into self-contained divisions and corps, and in their insistence on using these forces massed for a breakthrough in depth.

At the head of the army, generals such as Brauchitsch, Halder, Rundstedt and Bock were orthodox, able, and more forceful, though little younger, than their French opponents. It was at the next level that the architects of victory were to be found: Guderian, 51, commanding XIX Panzer Corps, Manstein, 52, who devised the plan that routed the French, and Rommel, 46, a divisional commander in France.

Limited under the Versailles Treaty to warships of 10,000 tons, Germany had built three 'pocket battleships'. Planned as commerce raiders, more powerful than any cruiser and faster than most battleships, these caused anxiety in Great Britain. The new German submarine force that began to appear under Admiral Dönitz caused less, for it was believed that the new sound-echo system Asdic (later Sonar) would deal with submarine attack. By September 1939 two new 31,000-ton fast battle-cruisers, the *Gneisenau* and *Scharnhorst,* had been completed, and, in addition to the pocket battleships, there were one new heavy cruiser, five light cruisers, seventeen destroyers, and fifty-six submarines.

Grand-Admiral Raeder had counted on a much stronger navy for war against Great Britain, for under his Plan Z four 42,000-ton battleships were being built or projected, besides an aircraft-carrier, two more heavy cruisers, and a large ocean-going submarine force. Now all work on surface ships was stopped, except on the battleships *Bismarck* and *Tirpitz* and the cruisers *Blücher* and *Prinz Eugen,* and transferred to submarines.

It was, however, fear of German air-power, rather than of Panzers and U-boats,

that kept the statesmen and peoples of Europe awake at night. Forbidden military aircraft were being built. Germany had become very air-minded. Flying and gliding clubs flourished. Aircraft factories were established abroad. The Reichswehr secretly trained military pilots in Russia and Italy. The state airline Lufthansa held men and operating resources that could be transferred to the Luftwaffe when it was formed. In December 1933, four months before its existence was announced, Göring had assembled 1,888 aircraft for it, 584 of them operational types.

By September 1939 the first-line strength of the Luftwaffe was between 4,000 and 4,700 aircraft: some 700 Me 109 fighters, 1,100 Ju 88 and He 111 day-bombers, 350 Ju 87 (Stuka) dive-bombers—all new and successful types—400 Me 110 two-seater fighters—an unsuccessful new type —and 550 transport aircraft. The remainder were army and naval co-operation aircraft and a few older fighters and bombers.

Despite the cold-blooded destruction of Guernica by the Condor Legion in the Spanish Civil War, the Luftwaffe was not primarily an anti-city or strategic bombing force. It was planned for army support, and paid little attention to the development of a long-range heavy bomber, concentrating instead on medium day-bombers and dive-bombers. These latter, although very vulnerable to fighters, could be highly effective in support of the Panzers.

Maginot Line and Maginot-mind

Although for France, victory had in 1918 avenged the defeat of 1870, the nation's confidence in itself and in the army had been deeply eroded by the frightful years of the more recent war—the shattering miscalculations of 1914, the repeated failures in the offensives from 1915 to 1917, and, etched in memory, Verdun in 1916. A

Left: Life on the Maginot Line, the French fortification system built in the 1930's along the eastern frontier. The fortresses proved practically useless: Germany's fast-moving armour bypassed them in the 1940 invasion. 1 Troops in an underground gallery. They were quartered in air-conditioned compartments and typical forts had underground recreation areas and railways. 2 Food for the garrison. 3 Artillery casemate, gun, and crew. Soldier in foreground is fusing shells. Right: British weaponry. 1 British Vickers Mark 6 light tanks on manoeuvres, October 1939. These obsolescent tanks operated in France and the desert in a scouting role. 2 Practice scramble. RAF pilots race for their Spitfires, May 1939. 3 Aircraft-carrier, HMS Ark Royal. Completed in 1938, she was sunk by a German submarine in 1941

△1

△2   ▽3

The Fragile Peace

population of under forty million had lost 1,385,000 men killed, and large areas had been occupied or devastated. The price of victory was remembered with bitterness that turned to cynical despair when, after what France saw as the undue leniency of Versailles and the culpable failure to enforce reparations, Germany rearmed and threatened war.

In the years between the wars, the mass army was retained, but its effectiveness was sapped by financial stringency, by successive reductions in the length of military service, and by distrust of its usefulness to do anything but bring about another bloodbath. The doctrine of offensive à outrance was abandoned for one of slow, heavily prepared infantry advance, and the Maginot Line was built. The generals of 1918 stayed on, in the words of de Gaulle, 'growing old at their posts, wedded to errors that had once constituted their glory'.

Alsace and Lorraine, lost in 1870 and now returned, lay vulnerable to a German war of revenge. Along the Rhine the Alsatian frontier is easily defensible, but the Lorraine frontier, running westwards from the Rhine to the southernmost point of Belgium, is much less so. André Maginot, renowned for his gallant war record and subsequent work as minister of pensions, forced through financial provision for the line that bears his name, sited primarily to guard the Lorraine frontier, with an extension along the Rhine.

To the obvious criticism that the line did nothing to guard against a repetition of the German advance through Belgium of 1914, the French General Staff gave several answers. Germany was the potential enemy, not Belgium. The ground was low lying and unsuitable for Maginot-type fortifications and the Lille industrial complex too close to the frontier to be protected. In the north a field force would advance to the rescue of Belgium, while further south the Ardennes were impracticable to large armies. Much of this, though certainly not the last point, was sound enough, but the Maginot Line soon began to absorb far too much of the material resources and moral commitment of the nation, diverting them from the developing concept of mobile, armoured warfare.

The French generals, indeed, paid lip service to the tank, and, as war drew near, large numbers were provided for the army. But neither Pétain, nor Weygand, who followed him as the head of the army in 1931, nor Gamelin, who followed Weygand in 1935, would accept the idea of self-contained armoured divisions concentrated for breakthrough in depth. Infantry, they insisted, was the dominant arm. The tank should support it.

In September 1939, after mobilization, some sixty infantry divisions, two cavalry divisions, two light armoured divisions (divisions légères mécanisées, DLM) and two heavier armoured brigades faced the Germans in north-eastern France. Nine infantry divisions faced the Italians in the south-east. There were, in addition, fortress units on both fronts and training units and new units forming in reserve. In the colonies there were about ten infantry divisions and some cavalry brigades. By May 1940 one more DLM would be formed and the armoured brigades would be expanded to armoured divisions (divisions cuirassées), while a third armoured brigade would be forming. This was, however, from a total of some 2,250 reasonably modern tanks, roughly equivalent to the German and Czech tanks, and 440 First World War Renault FTs, completely obsolete and out of place on a 1940 battlefield.

Gamelin, 67, aide to Joffre in 1914, imperturbable, colourless, complacent, held the supreme command, and his pale orthodoxy set the tone for lower commanders. 'We need tanks, of course,' he had written to Reynaud, '. . . but you cannot hope to achieve a real breakthrough with tanks. . . . As to the air, it will not play the part you expect. . . . It'll be a flash in the pan.'

The French navy was relatively more formidable than in 1914. As well as five reconstructed older battleships, there were seven modern 10,000-ton cruisers, ten slightly smaller ones, sixty flotilla leaders and destroyers, seventy submarines and an aircraft-carrier as well as two fine new 26,500-ton battle-cruisers, the Dunkerque and Strasbourg. Four 35,000-ton battleships and two aircraft-carriers were building or about to be laid down.

The air force, an independent service, had stagnated both in doctrine and material. The vital factors of aircraft performance and industrial capacity had been neglected and continued to be even after rearmament had started in the other services. In September 1939 the first-line strength of the French air force was some 600 fighters, 170 bombers and 360 reconnaissance aircraft. Of these 520 were modern fighters but outclassed by the Me 109; most of the remainder were obsolete. The warning system was rudimentary. By May 1940 improvements would have been made, but France would still be fatally weak in the air.

Great Britain – weak on land

Great Britain, traditionally a sea power, was confirmed in her distrust of continental commitment by the experiences of her armies on the Western Front. There and elsewhere on land she had lost 700,000 dead. Yet in the First World War the Royal Navy had not come up to expectations. The stranglehold of blockade, though effective in the long run, had been far too slow to rescue France and Russia, let alone Belgium, from invasion. German submarines had brought Great Britain close to defeat. Perhaps independent air-power, to which Lloyd George and Smuts had looked hopefully in 1917 when all attempts to break the German line in France seemed doomed to failure, might offer something better than the two older modes of warfare.

The vulnerability of Great Britain to sea blockade, however, continued to demand adequate naval strength, and imperial commitments seemed to require conventional land forces. Painting a lurid picture of cities under air attack, proponents of air-power raised ethical problems, and also, by making defence appear hopeless, strengthened the hands of the appeasers who would condone aggression at any price. Under these influences British strategic policy developed much as might be expected. In another war Great Britain would fight at sea and in the air, it was decided, rather than commit an army to the continent, but, until well into the 'thirties, most of the limited funds available for defence went to the two older services and was spent by them on traditional arms.

Great Britain had led the way with the tank in the First World War, and for a while continued to hold her lead in its postwar development. Liddell Hart and Fuller developed the concept of the armoured breakthrough, and their writings were avidly studied in Germany and Russia. An experimental mechanized force was set up rather half-heartedly in 1927, but a tide of reaction was setting in. The British Army, small in size, long-serviced, based on a fully-developed industry, was singularly well-adapted to the armoured concept, but Great Britain, having given birth to the idea, now turned away from it to the compromise of restricted armoured support for an infantry army and to nostalgic horse-worship. Tank design faltered, and production failed to get into its stride when rearmament began.

At almost the last moment, in the spring of 1939, Great Britain woke to the reality that France dared not face Germany without British assistance in the defence of her land frontier. In quick succession the doubling of the Territorial Army and the imposition of conscription were announced in a belated attempt to provide an army adequate to the need, but shortage of weapons and outmoded leadership went near to stultifying the effort.

Thus in the autumn of 1939 Great Britain was able to send to France only four regular infantry divisions with fifty cavalry light tanks. By May 1940 one more regular and five more divisions from the Territorial Army had arrived, and tank strength had grown to a two-battalion infantry tank brigade (100 tanks) and two cavalry light tank brigades (200 tanks). One—largely regular—armoured division was about to cross for final training in France. Three other Territorial Army divisions, for whom there were only rifles and no artillery, had spent the winter building airfields in France. The equivalent of one division had fought in Norway. Other divisions were arming and training in Great Britain.

In contrast the Royal Navy was a major world force. Under the Washington Treaty the navies of Great Britain, the USA, and Japan had been set at the ratio of 5:5:3 for battleships and aircraft-carriers. British battleships were on the whole rather older than those of the other two powers, and her carriers, like theirs, a mixed collection. Denounced by Japan, the Washington Treaty ended in 1935, and now nine new British battleships of 35,000 tons or over and six excellent new carriers were building or projected, as well as cruisers and smaller ships, but only the carrier *Ark Royal* had joined the fleet, which in September 1939 comprised: twelve battleships, three battle-cruisers, seven aircraft-carriers, sixty-four cruisers, 184 destroyers, and fifty-eight submarines.

Naval aviation remained a weakness owing mainly to the poor performance of carrier-borne aircraft. Reliance was placed on the gun against air attack and on the Asdic against submarines. In general, the navy was surface-ship minded, regarding the air and submarines as ancillaries, but in spirit and confidence nothing was lacking.

When in July 1934 Mr Churchill had warned Parliament that Germany possessed a rapidly expanding secret air force, the Royal Air Force at home amounted to 488 first-line bombers and fighters in forty-two squadrons, with nine squadrons for naval and army co-operation, and twenty-four overseas. The programme then announced to raise forty-one new squadrons in five years soon gave way to new and more ambitious programmes, each overtaken by its successor before completion. As radio location (later Radar) was developed and the high-performance eight-gun fighter appeared, fighters began to get priority over bombers. The four-engine heavy strategic bombers under development would not be ready for several years.

By September 1939 first-line strength had reached a total of 2,075 aircraft, of which 415 were overseas and 1,660 at home, which included 530 bombers, 608 fighters and 516 reconnaissance and co-operation. 500 fighters were modern, Hurricanes and some Spitfires, but the bombers, intended for day-bombing, were highly vulnerable to fighters. An advance air striking force was to leave for France, so as to bring bombers closer to German industrial targets.

Poland — an easy victim

Cut off from Great Britain and France on the eastern frontier of Germany, Poland after mobilization had an army of thirty-nine infantry divisions and eleven horsed cavalry brigades, but only one tank and two motorized brigades totalling together 225 modern and 88 obsolescent tanks in addition to armoured cars and reconnaissance vehicles. First-line air-strength, mostly obsolescent, amounted to 150 fighters, 120 reconnaissance bombers, 36 medium bombers and 84 army co-operation aircraft. In the navy there were four destroyers, five submarines, and some light craft. Including frontier defence the whole amounted to a peace strength of 370,000 with 2,800,000 in reserves.

Failing a land offensive in the West against Germany, for which as we have seen the French army was neither trained nor organized, or strategic air bombardment, for which at the time Great Britain was neither technically capable nor ethically prepared, help for Poland could only come from Russia. By signing the non-aggression pact with Germany on 23rd August 1939 Russia declared that no help would be given. For the present Poland was on her own against Hitler.

Force of a vanished era: Polish cavalry, 1939. During the German invasion of Poland a cavalry unit charged Panzers

2 GERMANY'S TRIUMPH

Blitzkrieg on Poland

The Polish Campaign opened in the early morning of 1st September 1939, when German forces crossed the Polish frontier shortly before 0600, preceded by air attacks which had begun an hour earlier. It was of great significance in the history of warfare because it was the first exposition of the theory, originated in Great Britain in the 1920's, of fast-moving mechanized warfare by armoured forces and aircraft in combination.

Britain's early protagonists of the theory depicted its action in terms of the play of 'lightning'. From now on, aptly if ironically, that simile came into world-wide currency under the German title of Blitzkrieg (lightning war).

Poland, with its far-stretching frontiers — 3,500 miles in extent — was well fitted, all too well fitted, for the practice and demonstration of the Blitzkrieg theory. The stretch of 1,250 miles adjoining German territory had recently been extended to 1,750 miles by the occupation of Czecho-Slovakia. This also meant that Poland's southern flank had become exposed to invasion — even more than the northern flank, facing East Prussia, already was.

The Polish plain offered flat and fairly easy going for a mobile invader, though not so easy as France would offer because of the scarcity of good roads in the country, the deep sand often met off the roads, and the frequency of lakes and forests in some

The Panzer Mk IV. Cutting edge of the Panzer Divisions and the forefront of tank design in the period of Germany's early victories. The commander's black uniform with the soft beret changed after Poland

areas. But the time chosen for the invasion — when the terrain was dry and hard-surfaced — minimized these drawbacks.

In view of the geographical and strategical conditions, it would have been wiser if the Polish army had assembled farther back, behind the Vistula and the San. That, however, would have meant abandoning some of the most important industrial areas. The Silesian coalfields lay close to the frontier, and most of the main industrial area, although farther back, lay west of these river-lines.

The economic argument for delaying the enemy's advance was reinforced by national pride and military over-confidence, as well as an unrealistic idea of what Poland's allies in the West could do to relieve the pressure. A third of the Polish forces were concentrated in or near the 'Corridor', where they were exposed to a double envelopment from East Prussia and the west combined. This indulgence of national pride — in opposing Germany's re-entry into the piece of her pre-1918 territory for which she had been agitating — seriously reduced the forces available to cover the areas more vital to Poland's defence. Nearly another third of Poland's forces lay in reserve north of the central axis, between Łódź and Warsaw, under the Commander-in-Chief of the Polish Army, Marshal Smigly-Rydz.

The Poles' forward concentration in general forfeited their chance of fighting a series of delaying actions, since their foot marching army was unable to get back to man rear positions before they were overrun by the invader's mechanized columns. Lack of mobility was more fatal than incomplete mobilization.

On the other side the forty German infantry divisions used in the invasion counted for much less than their fourteen mechanized or partially mechanized divisions. These included six armoured divisions, four light divisions (motorized infantry with two armoured units), and four motorized divisions. Their deep and rapid thrusts decided the issue, in combination with the attacks of the Luftwaffe — which smashed the Polish railway system, besides knocking out most of the Polish air force before it was able to come into action.

The Luftwaffe operated in a very dispersed way, instead of in large formations, but it thereby spread a creeping paralysis over the widest possible area. Another weighty factor was the German radio bombardment, disguised as Polish transmissions, which did much to increase the confusion and demoralization of the Polish rear. All these factors were given a multiplied effect by the way that Polish over-confidence in the power of their men to defeat machines led, on the rebound, to disillusionment and disintegration.

In the north, the invasion was carried out by Bock's Army Group, which comprised the III Army (under Küchler) and the IV Army (under Kluge). The former thrust southward from its flanking position in East Prussia, while the latter pushed eastward across the Polish Corridor to join it in enveloping the Poles' right flank.

The principal role was given to Rundstedt's Army Group in the south. This was nearly twice as strong in infantry, and more in armour. It comprised the VIII Army (under Blaskowitz), the X (under Reichenau), and the XIV (under List). Blaskowitz, on the left wing, was to push towards

the great manufacturing centre of Lódź, and help to isolate the Polish forces in the Poznań salient, while covering Reichenau's flank. On the right wing, List was to push for Kraków and simultaneously turn the Poles' Carpathian flank, using Kleist's armoured corps to drive through the mountain passes. The decisive stroke was delivered by Reichenau, in the centre, who had the largest part of the armoured forces.

By 3rd September—the date Great Britain and France declared war—Kluge's advance had cut the Corridor and reached the lower Vistula, while Küchler's pressure from East Prussia towards the Narew was developing. More important, Reichenau's armoured forces had penetrated to the Warta, and forced the crossings there. Meanwhile List's army was converging from both flanks on Kraków, forcing the Poles in that sector to abandon the city and fall back to the Nida and the Dunajec.

On the following day Reichenau's leading forces had reached and crossed the Pilica, fifty miles east of the frontier. By 6th September his left wing was well in rear of Lódź, and his right wing had driven into Kielce. The other German armies had all gone far towards fulfilling their part in the vast enveloping operation planned by Halder, the Chief of the Army General Staff, under the direction of Brauchitsch, Commander-in-Chief of the Army. The Polish armies had begun to split up into unco-ordinated fractions, some of which were in retreat while others were delivering disjointed attacks on the enemy columns nearest to them.

Exploiting a gap, one of Reichenau's armoured corps drove through to the edge of Warsaw on 8th September—having covered 140 miles in the week. The next day the light divisions on his right wing reached the Vistula farther south, between Warsaw and Sandomierz, and turned north.

Near the Carpathians, List's mobile forces had swept across the Dunajec, and a series of other rivers in turn, to the San

Left: 1 Russian tanks move into Poland. 2 Motorized German infantry advances. The leading car carries insignia plundered from a Polish frontier post. **Right: 1** *Sarcastic German comment on Paderewski playing while Warsaw burns. The famous pianist and former Prime Minister was invited to succeed Moscicki as President of Poland after the latter fled to Rumania. He declined because of ill health. 2 Cavalry—the pride of the Polish army but hopelessly obsolete. 3 The campaign, showing subsequent Russo-German boundary. 4 'Luftwaffe' by the Polish artist B.W.Linke portrays horror felt by those who experienced the Blitzkrieg. 5 Hitler on a visit to the Polish front stands before the bust of Pilsudski*

on either flank of the famous fortress of Przemyśl. In the north Guderian's armoured corps (which was in Küchler's army) had driven across the Narew and was attacking the line of the Bug, in rear of Warsaw. Thus a second and wider pincer-movement developed outside the inner pincers that were closing on the Polish forces in the bend of the Vistula near Warsaw.

This stage of the invasion had seen an important variation of plan on the Germans' side. Their view of the situation was momentarily obscured by the extraordinary state of confusion on the Poles' side, where columns appeared to be moving in many different directions, raising clouds of dust that obscured aerial observation. Under these circumstances the German High Command thought that the bulk of the Polish forces in the north had already escaped across the Vistula. On that assumption it gave orders that Reichenau's army was to cross the Vistula between Warsaw and Sandomierz, with the aim of intercepting the Poles' anticipated withdrawal into south-eastern Poland. But Rundstedt demurred, being convinced that the bulk of the Polish forces were still west of the Vistula. After some argument his view prevailed, and Reichenau's army was wheeled north to establish a blocking position along the Bzura west of Warsaw.

As a result the largest remaining part of the Polish forces was trapped before it could withdraw over the Vistula. To the advantage which the Germans had gained by their strategic penetration along the line of least resistance was now added the advantage of tactical defence. To complete the victory it had merely to hold its ground – in face of the hurried assaults of an army which was fighting in reverse, cut off from its bases, with its supplies running short, and increasingly pressed from the flank and behind by the converging eastward advance of Blaskowitz's and Kluge's armies. Although the Poles fought fiercely, with a bravery that greatly impressed their opponents, only a small proportion ultimately managed to break out, by night, and join troops of the Warsaw garrison.

On 10th September the Polish commander-in-chief, Marshal Smigly-Rydz, ordered a general retreat into the south-east of Poland and put General Sosnkowski in charge there, in the hope of developing a defensive position for prolonged resistance on a comparatively narrow front. By now the Germans were already penetrating deeply into the country beyond the Vistula, while they had also outflanked the line of the Bug in the north, and that of the San in the south. On the northern flank Guderian, with his armoured corps, swept southward to Brest Litovsk, while on the southern flank Kleist's armoured corps

reached Lwów on 12th September. These mechanized spearheads were running short of fuel, after their deep drives, but the Polish command system was so badly disjointed that it was unable to take advantage of the Germans' diminishing pace, and increasing tiredness.

Guerrilla resistance

Then on 17th September the forces of Soviet Russia advanced, and invaded Poland from the east, at a moment when there were scarcely any Polish troops left to oppose them. On the following day the Polish government and the Commander-in-Chief of the Army left Polish soil and took shelter in Rumania. Even after that, the garrison of Warsaw held out for a further ten days, under heavy bombardment both from the ground and the air. Indeed, the last large fraction of the Polish army fought on until 5th October before it surrendered, and many fragments continued resistance in a guerrilla manner throughout the winter.

The Russian forces met the Germans on a line mid-way through Poland, running south from East Prussia past Brest Litovsk, to the Carpathians. The fresh partition of Poland that followed was short-lived. It did not cement their temporary partnership but increased the friction that arose once the two countries were in close contact along a common frontier.

Meantime the French had merely made a small dent in Germany's western front. It looked, and was, a feeble effort to relieve the pressure on their ally. In view of the weakness of the German forces and defences it was natural to feel that they could have done more. But deeper analysis tends to correct the obvious conclusion suggested by the comparative figures of the opposing forces.

Although the French northern frontier was 500 miles long, in attempting an offensive the French were confined to the narrow ninety-mile sector from the Rhine to the Moselle – unless they violated the neutrality of Belgium and Luxembourg. The Germans, however, were able to concentrate the best part of their available forces on this narrow sector, and they sowed the approaches to their Siegfried Line with a thick belt of minefields, thus imposing delay on the attackers.

The conscript mass

Worse still, the French were unable to start their offensive until about 17th September – except for some preliminary probing attacks. By that date, Poland was so obviously collapsing that they had a good excuse for countermanding it. Their incapacity to strike earlier arose from their mobilization system, which was inherently out of date. It was the fatal product of their

reliance on a conscript army – which could not come effectively into action until the mass of 'trained reserves' had been called up from their civil jobs, and the formations

Marshal Smigly-Rydz, C-in-C of the Polish Army. He was quite unable to defend his country against the German Blitzkrieg

had been made ready to operate. But the delay was increased by the French command's persistent belief in old tactical ideas – particularly the view that any offensive must be prepared by a massive artillery bombardment on the lines of the First World War. They still regarded heavy artillery as the essential 'tin-opener' in dealing with any defended position. But the bulk of their heavy artillery had to be brought out of storage, and could not be available until the last stage of mobilization. That condition governed their preparations to deliver an offensive.

For several years past one of France's political leaders, Paul Reynaud, had constantly argued that these conceptions were out of date, and had urged the necessity of creating a swift-moving mechanized force of professional soldiers ready for instant action – instead of relying on the old and slow-mobilizing conscript mass. But he had been a voice crying in the wilderness. French statesmen, like most French soldiers, placed their trust in conscription, and numbers.

The military issue in 1939 can be summed up in two sentences. In the East a hopelessly out-of-date army was quickly disintegrated by a small tank force, in combination with a superior air force, which put into practice a novel technique. At the same time, in the West, a slow-motion army could not develop any effective pressure before it was too late.

The Winter War

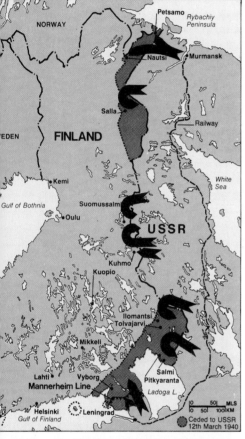

Finland first came within the orbit of Russia in 1808, when, following a rather sordid 'sphere of influence' agreement with Napoleon, Tsar Alexander I was enabled to forcibly incorporate Finland into the Russian Empire as a semi-independent duchy. One hundred and thirty years later, following another sordid agreement with Hitler, Russian troops again invaded Finland. In the intervening years Finland had seen its privileges gradually reduced but never entirely eliminated under the Tsars and then, from 1917, enjoyed two decades of independence.

It was Stalin, the commissar for nationalities of Russia's new Bolshevik government, who granted independence to the Finns. This accorded with Lenin's principle of offering freedom to non-Russian peoples formerly subject to the Tsar. However, Finland was soon immersed in a brutal civil war as local Communists tried to seize power. The Communists had some help from Russian soldiers while the 'National' forces, led by the talented General Mannerheim, had some German help. The Communists lost, and those who did not escape over the frontier were rounded up, ill-treated, and shot or sent to concentration camps. The brutality and wanton bloodshed of this period were to be divisive factors in Finnish society for many years. Despite this, Finland muddled through by a combination of hard work and last-minute common sense. Internationally, Finland was strictly neutral, while strengthening ties with her Scandinavian neighbours.

But the rise of Hitler's Germany and geographical circumstances were to deny Finland the right to be neutral. After the Munich settlement it seemed clear to the Soviet government that an attack on the USSR could be expected sooner rather than later. Russia began to look to her defences, and concluded that her most vulnerable city was Leningrad. Situated at the eastern end of the narrow Gulf of Finland, Leningrad could easily be attacked by a naval power commanding the Baltic. Alternatively, or simultaneously, an enemy might attack by land through Finland, for the Russo-Finnish frontier was only twenty

*Above left: Pattern of the war, 30th November 1939-12th March 1940. After resisting the Russian colossus for some months, the Finns finally signed a peace treaty by which they lost some territory but not their independence. **Left:** Mannerheim (centre), Finnish commander-in-chief, with two senior officers*

miles from Leningrad (which meant that Leningrad could, in theory, be shelled from Finnish soil). In August 1939 the Soviet Union, to gain time and space, concluded the Nazi-Soviet Pact, and this enabled her to mend some of her fences around Leningrad. By acquiring bases in Estonia and Latvia she was able to command the southern shore of the Gulf of Finland and, being more or less assured of Nazi goodwill, felt able to take strong action on the Finnish northern shore without running the risk of German intervention.

Unofficially, as early as 1938 the Soviet government had informed Helsinki that it was anxious for an exchange of territory, but the Finns had not been accommodating. Pressure was renewed in the autumn of 1939, and a Finnish delegation was invited to Moscow to discuss 'outstanding issues'. When the delegation opened the discussion with Molotov and Stalin it discovered that the USSR expected Finland to sacrifice parts of its territory regarded as crucial to Russian defence. In return, the USSR offered to recompense Finland with territory amounting to double the area in a non-vital part of the Russo-Finnish frontier. In brief, the Soviet Union wanted the frontier moved back in the Karelian Isthmus area, so as to make Leningrad more secure; some islands in this area would also be transferred to Russia. Then, at the narrow entrance to the Gulf of Finland, Russia required a long-term lease of the port of Hanko, situated in the south-west corner of Finland; with Hanko fortified and a corresponding base on the southern shore in Estonia, Russia could command the entrance to the gulf. Finally, Russia required territory near the Finnish port of Petsamo, so as to forestall an enemy annexing the same area and thereby threatening the sea route to Murmansk.

Red Army attacks

The Finnish government could not accept these suggestions. To move the frontier back in the isthmus would mean abandoning the best defensive line which the terrain offered, as well as a half-completed line of elementary fortifications. But it was the Hanko lease which was the main obstacle, for with Hanko fortified by the Russians, Finland would be very much at the mercy of Moscow. The Finnish delegation left Moscow with no agreement reached, and two more delegations got no further. Neither the Finns nor the Russians could make significant compromises, although both recognized the force of the other's arguments. Moreover, the Finns did not believe that Russia, with whom they had a treaty, would make war on the issue, while knowing quite well that the Finnish Diet would oppose territorial concessions to the USSR.

The last Finnish delegation arrived back in Helsinki on 15th November 1939. Already the Soviet press was attacking the Finnish government and on the 26th Molotov accused the Finnish army of bombarding Russian territory just beyond the frontier. Seven shells had in fact landed in Russia, but they came from the Russians' own guns. Soon the Soviet government claimed that Finnish troops were making attacks along the frontier. On the 29th the USSR broke off diplomatic relations and on the 30th, without warning, Russian aircraft bombed Helsinki and the Red Army advanced over the frontier.

Thus Finland stood alone against her giant neighbour. And she seemed likely to continue alone. Her natural ally, Germany, had through the Nazi-Soviet Pact assured Moscow of a sympathetic attitude. France and Great Britain were preoccupied with their own war and had poor access to Finland. Sweden, with whose foreign policy Finland had been carefully aligned, offered warm words in private and a cold shoulder in public. All of these countries had great sympathy for Finland, but none believed that that small nation could resist the Red Army for more than a few days.

The Red Army was evidently of the same opinion. The Finnish army was one of the weakest in Europe; it was small, had no tanks, disposed of little artillery and in any case only had three weeks' stock of shells. Its air force had less than one hundred aircraft. The invading Red Army could call on one million men, 3,000 tanks, and about 2,500 aircraft.

On the outbreak of war the Finnish government was reformed so as to include more of the political parties, and transferred its meetings to the vaults of the Bank of Finland—the Soviet news agency claiming that the government had fled the capital. Meanwhile the Soviet government installed a so-called Finnish Peoples' Government in a recently-captured town on the Finnish side of the frontier; this substitute government, composed of Finnish Communists living in the USSR, was not taken by the Finns or the outside world as seriously as had been hoped, largely because it never sat in Helsinki.

Mannerheim was appointed commander-in-chief of the Finnish forces. Earlier he had been one of the few who urged his government to concede the Soviet territorial demands so as to avoid a war which Finland could not hope to win. Now he threw himself into the task of doing the impossible. The war was fought on four fronts: in the far north around Petsamo; in the centre of the Russo-Finnish frontier, where the Russians hoped to cut through Finland's narrow waist and reach the Gulf of Bothnia; around the northern edge of Lake Ladoga; and in the Karelian Isthmus. It was on the latter two fronts that the heaviest and most vital fighting took place.

To the surprise of the whole world the 'Russian steamroller' failed to roll. The Red Army, and especially its officers (recently thinned by a drastic purge), proved quite unsuited for the war on which it had so optimistically embarked. The land of forests, marshes, and lakes did not favour the tactics of mass attack which the Russians employed. Although the Finns had few anti-tank guns (in fact until the war few Finnish infantry men had ever seen a tank) they were able to destroy whole columns of tanks simply by picking them off one by one as they milled around in an unfamiliar terrain. Later lone Finnish infantrymen would attack tanks with 'Molotov cocktails'—bottles of inflammable liquid with primitive detonators. The Finnish ski troops likewise captured the attention of the world's press with their swift and unexpected attacks on unwary Soviet units. There were instances of single companies of Finns holding off whole divisions of Russians.

Gallant little Finland

Thus in this war of 105 days the first month was unquestionably an amazing Finnish victory. Despite some tactical errors, poor training of reserves, and lack of modern equipment, the Finns had made only minor withdrawals and inflicted enormous losses on the attackers. During the war as a whole, Finnish casualties were almost exactly one tenth of the Russian, they captured or destroyed 1,600 Russian tanks and over 700 aircraft. But it was evident that without outside help Finland could not continue the battle.

The moribund League of Nations had already expelled the Soviet Union for invading Finland, its eagerness in this contrasting sadly with its earlier reluctance to take a strong line against fascist aggression. Elsewhere on the diplomatic front, Finland made unsuccessful peace overtures throughout the war. She also tried to persuade Sweden and Norway to allow the passage of troops from France and Great Britain. The Western Allies meanwhile were planning an expeditionary force designed to kill two birds with one stone: public opinion in the West, stirred up by the press and unable to resist the spectacle of a small nation gallantly defending itself against a bigger (and Bolshevik) neighbour, was clamouring for action; while the strategists were saying that if troops were sent to Finland across Norway and Sweden they could cut off en route the Swedish iron-ore supplies on which Hitler depended.

At the front winter was setting in, which meant that the lakes and marshes (and later the sea) were freezing over and providing an easier passage for tanks and men. Learning from their defeats, the Russians were by January better trained and led, and one of their better generals, Timoshenko, had been placed in command on the isthmus front. Their attacks were becoming better co-ordinated and were preceded by intense artillery barrages. Their aircraft were so plentiful that behind the Finnish lines it was not safe for even an individual soldier to move in daylight. By the beginning of March the Finns had been forced to make significant withdrawals—a Russian success which the Soviet press hailed as 'a deed without parallel in the history of war'. The army was worn out and without reserves. Supplies and 'volunteer' soldiers were beginning to trickle in from abroad (especially from Sweden), but they were too few and too late. On the other hand, London and Paris had promised that they would send their expeditionary force as soon as the Finns made a request for it, and that it would be sent through Norway and Sweden even though the governments of the latter, wishing to preserve their neutrality, still refused transit permission.

Russian peace terms were now higher than before, but the Finnish government realized that it was a case of now or never—it was better to make peace while the Finnish army was still undefeated and while there still existed the threat of Western intervention. So Helsinki decided not to call on Great Britain and France (thus preventing, incidentally, these two countries coming into open conflict with the USSR). On 12th March 1940, the Treaty of Moscow was signed in which Finland conceded not only the original Soviet requests but extensive areas in addition, including the city of Vyborg. Moscow however abandoned its Finnish Peoples' Government. Finland had lost territory and industry but not its independence or its honour.

By the standards of that time, the USSR had not behaved especially badly. Its original requests had not been outrageous, and it had tried hard to negotiate what it wanted. However, the recourse to force proved a mistake: the humiliation of the Red Army (which encouraged Hitler to attack Russia later), and the loss of moral standing in the outside world were a heavy price to pay. Moreover, Moscow's treatment of Finland ensured that when Hitler did attack in 1941 he was aided by a vengeful Finnish army, which overran in a matter of days the territory so expensively won by the Red Army a year before.

The Invasion of Norway

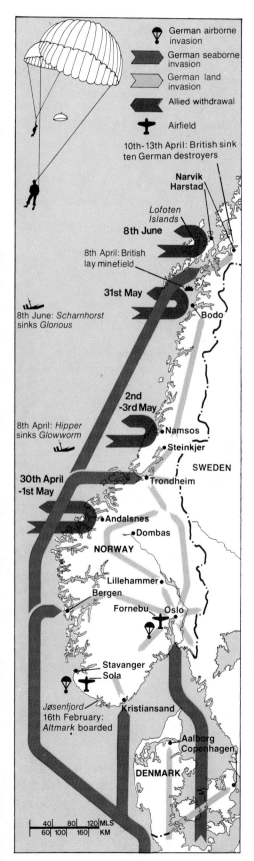

German airborne invasion

German seaborne invasion

German land invasion

Allied withdrawal

Airfield

10th-13th April: British sink ten German destroyers

Narvik
Harstad

Lofoten Islands

8th June

8th April: British lay minefield

31st May

8th June: *Scharnhorst* sinks *Glorious*

Bodo

8th April: *Hipper* sinks *Glowworm*

2nd -3rd May

Namsos

Steinkjer

SWEDEN

30th April -1st May

Trondheim

Andalsnes

Dombas

NORWAY

Lillehammer

Bergen

Fornebu

Oslo

Stavanger
Sola

Jøsenfjord
16th February: *Altmark* boarded

Kristiansand

Aalborg
Copenhagen

DENMARK

40 80 120 MLS
60 100 160 KM

Left: The campaign: by evening on 9th April all Norway's main cities, ports, and airfields were in German hands. The first Allied landings were not until 14th April. They proved ineffective

Neither Norway nor Denmark, avowedly pacifist and neutral, had done anything to provoke German aggression. Yet the plan for the invasion and occupation of the two Scandinavian states, innocuously code-named *Weserübung* or 'Exercise Weser', was dictated by the need to prevent possible British encroachment on Scandinavia and the Baltic, to safeguard vital iron-ore supplies from Sweden which passed through Narvik when the Gulf of Bothnia was frozen, and in order to provide the navy with bases from where submarines and surface raiders might be able to elude the British naval cordon and then break out onto the high seas.

The Commander-in-Chief of the Navy, Grand Admiral Erich Raeder, had impressed Hitler with the importance of obtaining naval bases in Norway, and the value of airfields in both countries had not been lost on the Luftwaffe. But Hitler did not show any real enthusiasm for the Norwegian operation until after 16th February when it became clear that Great Britain no longer intended to respect Norway's neutrality. As soon as the Allies began to organize an expeditionary force to aid the Finns in their struggle against the Soviet Union, German invasion plans took on a new urgency for it was realized that while crossing Norway and Sweden on their way to Finland the Allies could easily sever Germany's supply of Swedish iron-ore. On 12th March the Russo-Finnish war ended and General Jodl gloomily noted in his diary 'Conclusion of peace between Finland and Russia deprives England, but us too, of any political basis to occupy Norway.' But Hitler and Ribbentrop were at no loss for a pretext to invade. On 9th April 1940 Denmark was occupied and Norway invaded ostensibly to protect them from Anglo-French occupation. The two countries had been conferred with the 'protection of the Reich'.

Early the previous day, eight British destroyers entered Norwegian waters south of the Lofoten Islands and laid mines in the Leads on the approaches to the Arctic iron-ore port of Narvik. Four hundred miles to the south, two others marked a dummy minefield off Molde. A few hours later the British destroyer *Glowworm*, a hundred miles west of Trondheim, sighted German destroyers, and, giving chase in heavy seas and poor visibility, met the heavy cruiser

Hipper. Damaged and hopelessly outmatched, the *Glowworm* rammed the *Hipper,* then dropped astern burning and sinking. Still further south that morning, near the southern tip of Norway, villagers heard a dull explosion at sea. Later fishing boats brought in German soldiers from the transport *Rio de Janeiro,* who told them that they had been torpedoed on their way to Bergen to protect the Norwegians against the British.

In Oslo a distracted cabinet met. Norwegian sympathies lay with the Allies and against Hitler, but, hopelessly exposed to overwhelming German land and air strength, Norway longed to stay neutral. When on 16th February Captain Vian in the destroyer *Cossack* had defied Norwegian protests and boarded the German supply ship *Altmark* in Jøsenfjord to rescue three hundred captured British merchant seamen, from ships sunk by the *Graf Spee* and bound for German prison camps, German propaganda had raged against the British 'crime'. How would Hitler take this new violation of Norwegian neutrality?

Since the 3rd April reports had been coming in of ships and troops concentrating in north German ports, and more warnings came on the 8th. At 3 a.m. on the 9th the Norwegian cabinet ordered mobilization, but only 'silent' mobilization by post instead of by proclamation. By then the Norwegian coastal defences, manned only at one-third strength, were in contact with warships of unknown nationality entering the country's main ports.

The first ships of the German invasion, unescorted merchant ships carrying follow-up troops and equipment, had in fact sailed from Germany on the 3rd. On the morning of the 7th the fast battle-cruisers *Gneisenau* and *Scharnhorst* left the Schillig Roads escorting the *Hipper* and fourteen destroyers with mountain troops on board to seize Narvik and Trondheim. Other warships followed later with troops for the more southerly Norwegian ports and for Copenhagen.

Norway fights on

Invaded by land and sea, Denmark surrendered early on the 9th, but Norway decided to fight on. Narvik, Trondheim, Bergen, and Kristiansand fell quickly, but, two-thirds of the way up Oslofjord, the heavy guns and torpedoes of the old fort, Oscarsborg, set ablaze and sank the new German heavy cruiser *Blücher*, and turned back the German seaborne invasion of the capital. Aircraft carrying parachutists to seize Fornebu, the Oslo airport, met low

cloud and were recalled, but ten Me 110 fighters, their petrol exhausted, were forced to land at Fornebu, and were followed by a squadron of Junkers 52s carrying infantry, which had failed to obey the recall. Oslo, the vital key-point of the German plan, fell that afternoon, and the ships came up the fjord next day. Stavanger with the main west coast airfield, Sola, fell early on the 9th to German parachutists and air-transported troops respectively. Thus by the evening all the main cities, ports, and airfields of Norway were in German hands.

For the next few days the Germans built up strength in Oslo, and the Norwegians mobilized as best they could in the hope of containing the Germans in the cities. Then on the 14th the Germans struck out, first to the south-east and west, then on the 15th north and north-west for Trondheim and Bergen. By the 20th they were close to Lillehammer and Rena, 120 miles from Trondheim, at the entrance to the Gudbrandsdal and Østerdal valleys.

Having failed to intercept the Germans at sea on the 9th, or, under air attack, to follow them into the Norwegian ports, the British Home Fleet had turned north to Narvik. There, on the 10th, Captain Warburton-Lee had led five British destroyers up the fjord to attack ten larger German destroyers, sinking two for the loss of two of his vessels. On the 13th the British destroyers returned accompanied by the battleship *Warspite,* and finished off the German ships, isolating the Germans in Narvik.

Although the British, foreseeing some German reaction to the mining, had held a small land force ready in Scottish ports for Norway, the speed and daring of the German landings threw their plans into confusion. The first Allied troops landed at Harstad, forty miles from Narvik, on 14th April. Weaker detachments also landed at Namsos in central Norway on the same day and troops who landed at Åndalsnes on the 17th, moved south to join the Norwegians at Lillehammer. British plans to enter Trondheimfjord, land near the small airfield at Vaernes, and re-capture Trondheim were, in the face of dominant German air power, finally abandoned on the 19th.

A mishandled campaign

On the 21st the Germans attacked in strength up the Gudbrandsdal and Østerdal, driving back the Norwegians and British, and, eight days later, linking up with elements pushing south from Trondheim. By then the British had decided to withdraw from central Norway. The last soldier re-embarked from Åndalsnes under heavy air attack early on the 1st May, and from Namsos on the 2nd. Deserted by their allies, the Norwegians in central Norway capitulated on the 3rd.

Deep snow in the north had held up operations around Narvik, and it was not until the 28th May that a British, Norwegian, and French force together with a brigade of Poles recaptured the port, while the British delayed the German relief force coming north from Trondheim. By then disastrous events in France had forced Churchill to order withdrawal from north Norway. The last convoys left Harstad on the 8th June, and the Norwegians, who had fought a gallant campaign in the mountains, capitulated.

The *Gneisenau* and *Scharnhorst* had returned to Germany after the April landings. Early in June they came north again undetected by the British, and on the 8th June met the aircraft carrier *Glorious* and two escorting destroyers off Harstad, sinking all three with heavy loss of life. However, a last torpedo from the destroyer *Acasta* struck the *Scharnhorst* and seriously damaged her, forcing both ships to return to Trondheim and so saving the troop convoys. Off Trondheim the British submarine *Clyde* torpedoed and damaged the *Gneisenau*.

The Norwegian campaign was for the Allies, and especially for the British, muddled both in concept and execution. As first lord of the Admiralty, Churchill had since September 1939 pressed for action against the winter iron-ore trade through Narvik, but Chamberlain and Halifax had wisely restrained him. The German invasion, almost simultaneous with the British mining of the Leads, revealed the extent of Churchill's misjudgment of the strategic position. Yet there were moments when Hitler was on the point of losing his nerve, first over Narvik, then over Trondheim. Had the British acted then with comparable skill and daring they might have inflicted serious reverses on the Germans. That the fall of France would, in the end, almost certainly have forced the British to evacuate Norway, is little excuse for the mishandling of the campaign.

Right: As dusk gathers over the Norwegian fjords, a German anti-aircraft unit keeps watch over this outpost in the north, a new bastion in Hitler's Fortress Europe. The date: 15th June 1940, six days after the Norwegian capitulation. Churchill eloquently expressed this new Allied defeat when he said: 'For many generations Norway, with its homely, rugged population engaged in trade, shipping, fishing, and agriculture, had stood outside the turmoil of world politics. . . . A tiny army and a population with no desires except to live peaceably in their own mountainous and semi-Arctic country now fell victims to the new German aggression'

Victory in the West

At the end of the Polish campaign, on 27th September 1939, Hitler ordered his generals to prepare for an offensive in the West that same autumn. At that moment the German army was quite unready. Its armoured and motorized divisions needed re-equipping and the line divisions needed officer reinforcements and further training.

Hitler insisted, against his generals' advice, that the offensive should be launched on 12th November. The army command produced a plan of attack on 19th October code-named *Fall Gelb* or 'Plan Yellow'. It was a half-hearted scheme, so conservative and uninspiring that it might well have been thought up by a British or French general staff of the inter-war years, with objectives far less ambitious even than those of the Schlieffen Plan of 1914. Its main effort was directed through Belgium towards the Ghent–Bruges area, with the object of covering the Ruhr against any Allied attack, and providing air and sea bases nearer Great Britain. There was no thought of striking a decisive blow against the Allied forces.

Hitler's natural ingenuity now came into play. He had already ordered that aircraft and tanks were to be used on a broad front for the offensive, the latter operating in open country and in massed formations to achieve surprise. Now he introduced the idea of parachutists and gliders to facilitate the crossing of the Meuse north of Liège; and he was also thinking of an attack on the Meuse south of Liège, followed through with an advance in the direction of Rheims and Amiens. Thus by 29th October the army's objective was 'to destroy the Allied forces in the sector north of the Somme and to break through to the Channel coast.'

The weight of the offensive still lay in north Belgium, with the German Army Group B under General von Bock. Hitler, however, produced a 'new idea' which required the utilization of the east–west gap in the Belgian Ardennes (along a line from Arlon through Tintigny to Florenville), which was guarded only by neutral Luxembourg, to reach the French frontier town of Sedan on the upper Meuse.

The commander of the German Army Group A on the southern sector, facing the Ardennes, was General von Rundstedt. He and his brilliant chief-of-staff, General von Manstein, saw the weaknesses and hesitations in the army's directives for 'Plan Yellow', which did not provide for the rapid and complete destruction of all the enemy's forces. They proposed that Army Group A should be made strong enough to cross the Meuse south of Namur and roll round south of the Allied armies (which were expected to have moved up into Belgium) and then sweep through in the direction of Arras and Boulogne. The commander-in-chief, Field-Marshal von Brauchitsch, was not interested in these proposals, and so Hitler did not hear of them; neither Rundstedt nor Manstein were aware of Hitler's simultaneous 'new idea.'

'Plan Yellow' compromised

Bad weather early in November compelled Hitler to agree to a series of postponements, and gave the generals time to elaborate his ideas. The task of leading Hitler's proposed thrust through the Ardennes to Sedan, was entrusted to XIX Panzer Corps under the command of Germany's chief exponent of tank warfare, General Heinz Guderian. This thrust would open up the possibility of expanding the offensive on the heights beyond Sedan; but Brauchitsch still turned a deaf ear to Manstein's plea for the strengthening of Army Group A to enable it to drive through to the lower Somme.

By the end of December, Hitler and Brauchitsch had still not decided where the main weight of the offensive was to fall. Rundstedt and Manstein, however, were continuing their private campaign on behalf of Army Group A in the south, with detailed plans for a crossing of the Meuse from Dinant, in Belgium, southwards–the main effort being directed initially at Sedan.

The prospect of a period of bright weather brought the German forces into readiness for the launching of the offensive in the middle of January. The Luftwaffe had now persuaded Hitler to concentrate the landing of parachutists and airborne troops in Holland, where they feared the British might obtain air bases for the bombing of the Ruhr.

The weather again changed for the worse. Furthermore the German command had been made uneasy by the forced land-

Left: German anti-tank gunners cover a road during the attack on Northern France. Mobile and hard-hitting German anti-tank guns could not deal with the heaviest Allied armour, but the French frittered their advantage away in penny-packets.
Right: Hitler breaks into a jig of joy on hearing the French offer of an armistice

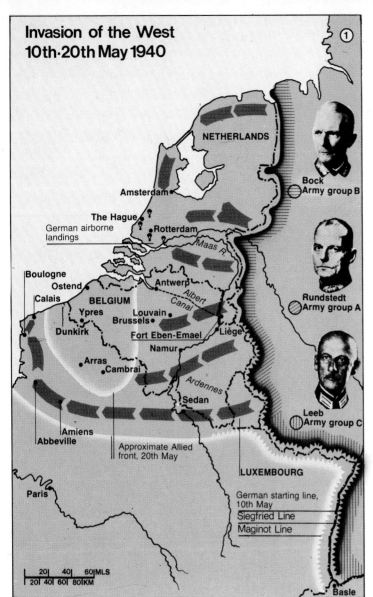

Invasion of the West 10th-20th May 1940

NETHERLANDS
Amsterdam
The Hague
German airborne landings
Rotterdam
Maas R.
Boulogne
Ostend
Antwerp
Albert Canal
Calais
BELGIUM
Ypres
Louvain
Brussels
Dunkirk
Fort Eben-Emael
Liège
Arras
Namur
Cambrai
Ardennes
Sedan
Amiens
Abbeville
Approximate Allied front, 20th May
Paris
LUXEMBOURG
German starting line, 10th May
Siegfried Line
Maginot Line
Basle

Bock Army group B
Rundstedt Army group A
Leeb Army group C

20 40 60 MLS
20 40 60 80 KM

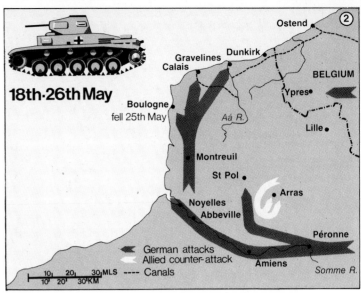

18th-26th May

Ostend
Gravelines
Dunkirk
Calais
BELGIUM
Boulogne
fell 25th May
Aa R.
Ypres
Lille
Montreuil
St Pol
Arras
Noyelles
Abbeville
Péronne
Amiens
Somme R.

German attacks
Allied counter-attack
Canals

10 20 30 MLS
10 20 30 KM

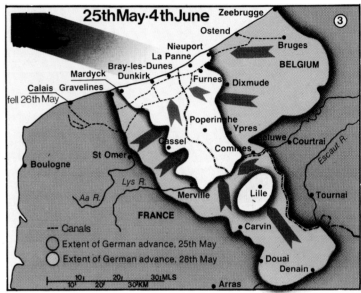

25th May-4th June

Zeebrugge
Ostend
Bruges
BELGIUM
Nieuport
La Panne
Bray-les-Dunes
Dunkirk
Mardyck
Furnes
Dixmude
Calais Gravelines
fell 26th May
St Omer
Poperinghe
Ypres
Cassel
Comines
Courtrai
Boulogne
Lys R.
Lille
Tournai
Aa R.
Merville
Escaut R.
FRANCE
Carvin
Canals
Extent of German advance, 25th May
Douai
Extent of German advance, 28th May
Denain
Arras

10 20 30 MLS
10 20 30 KM

ing in Belgium of two senior German air force officers carrying documents describing aspects of 'Plan Yellow'. It was now postponed indefinitely. Although the German officers partially destroyed the documents, enough information filtered back to French Intelligence to convince the Allied High Command that, as in 1914, the main German blow was going to come through the north of Belgium.

Manstein had meanwhile crystallized his ideas in a memorandum which Rundstedt sent to Brauchitsch on 12th January but the commander-in-chief, sensitive of his authority, refused to forward it to Hitler. However, two sets of map exercises in February made General Halder, Brauchitsch's chief-of-staff, realize that Army Group A needed reinforcement in any case. In the next few days Hitler's staff officers brought Manstein's plan to his attention and in it he saw his own un-schooled ideas set out with professional clarity and detail. Brauchitsch also had by now come round to shifting the offensive's centre of gravity away from Bock's Army Group B in the north to Rundstedt's Army Group A in the south. There was agreement all round.

Brauchitsch and Halder now put these general proposals into precise form. Manstein's contribution had been his insistence on the use of Army Group A to swing round south of the Allied armies in Belgium and

trap them there. Hitler's contribution had been the exploitation of the Ardennes gap and the choice of Sedan for the crucial crossing of the Meuse, and the use of special air operations to secure vital objectives. The perfected plan, in masterly working detail, was Brauchitsch's and Halder's contribution; and to effect the Meuse crossings between Dinant and Sedan they now capped the operation with a spearhead of seven out of the Wehrmacht's ten Panzer divisions. From its original twenty-two divisions, Rundstedt's Army Group A had escalated to $45\frac{1}{3}$ divisions; while von Bock's Army Group B had dwindled from 43 to $29\frac{1}{3}$ divisions. On 24th February the new directive was ready, under the appropriate name of *Sichelschnitt* – or 'the sweep of a scythe'.

Patchy morale

Now at last the generals were ready. But because the invasion of Denmark and Norway had acquired priority, the attack in the west was postponed into May.

When *Sichelschnitt* came into action at dawn on 10th May the skill and balance of the German planning in themselves ensured a measure of success. The generals' obstinate delaying tactics in the face of Hitler's impatience in the autumn had been justified: the winter had been spent in perfecting their plans, and in training their troops for the precise and demanding

requirements of the Blitzkrieg, which had tightened morale and whipped up considerable enthusiasm.

The picture was very different on the Allied side. After the first few weeks of war, all pretence of offensive action on land had been given up. French and British troops were subjected to a hard and unending winter, waiting for an enemy who never came, despite the many alarms during which they stood to in wet or icy weather, while Hitler and his generals, oblivious of the good they were doing their own cause, battled over their dates for the offensive. In the French army, and particularly in those units in the Sedan sector where the main weight of the German attack was due to descend, morale was extremely patchy.

The French High Command, in charge of Allied land operations, thought only of defence. But the Maginot Line, to which their faith was pinned, guarded nothing more than Alsace and Lorraine in the east. It ended opposite the south-eastern corner of neutral Belgium, and French and British troops spent much of the winter navvying, in a poorly co-ordinated attempt to extend the French frontier fortifications, north-westwards to the Channel. Even this measure held contradictions, since General Gamelin, the French commander-in-chief, had decided to rush the Allied forces for-

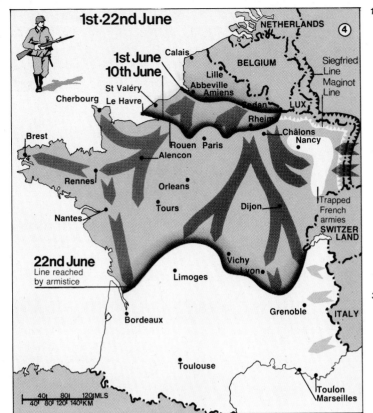

1st·22nd June

1st June
10th June

Calais
NETHERLANDS ④
BELGIUM
Lille
Abbeville
Amiens
LUX
Sedan
Rheims
Siegfried Line
Maginot Line

St Valéry
Le Havre
Cherbourg
Brest
Rouen Paris
Alencon
Châlons
Nancy

Rennes
Orleans
Tours
Dijon
Trapped French armies
SWITZERLAND

Nantes

22nd June
Line reached by armistice

Limoges
Vichy
Lyon

Bordeaux
Grenoble
ITALY

Toulouse
Toulon
Marseilles

40┃ 80┃ 120┃MLS
40┃ 80┃ 120┃ 140┃KM

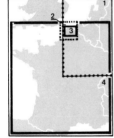

Left and above: 1 While Bock's Army Group B struck into Holland and Belgium in what appeared to be the main thrust, Rundstedt's Army Group A headed by Kleist's Panzers emerged from the Ardennes to the south and raced for the Channel in what was, in fact, the main thrust of the offensive. 2 Eleven days after breaking through at Sedan, Kleist's armour reaches the Channel. 3 The Allied perimeter at Dunkirk shrinks before the encircling German armies. 4 Extent of German advance on signing of armistice, 22nd June

ward into central and northern Belgium as soon as the German offensive started.

The French army was powerful on paper; it had more tanks than the Germans, and some that were better, but it had no conception of massing them for a breakthrough in the way the Germans had already tried out in Poland. The French tank strength was instead spread out thinly and ineffectually, ready, like a lot of small corks, to plug holes in the line. The few really mobile armoured units were earmarked for the Allied defensive line in Belgium.

The British contribution in France amounted to nine divisions, and in its smallness became the butt of German propaganda broadcasts. A modest support air force was also sent to France, but the valuable Spitfire fighter, which had suffered from production delays, was held back for the defence of Great Britain.

It was in the air that the Allies were at their greatest disadvantage. French aircraft production had been doubly hit by strikes and nationalization, and the French air force was largely filled out with obsolete machines. Gamelin, to whom it was theoretically subordinate, had little use for aircraft in battle, and the air crews' efforts were to be fruitlessly dissipated.

The German air force, under the vainglorious leadership of Göring and the energetic administration of his secretary of state, Milch, had been built up into a fearsome weapon, tested and hardened in the earlier Spanish Civil War and the Polish campaign, and supplied with an extra gloss of terror by German propaganda. It was designed and trained, too, for a single clear-cut purpose – to be an integral part of the German offensive machine. Its fleets of medium bombers were ready to wreak havoc behind the enemy's lines while its dreaded dive-bombers – the Stukas or Junkers 87s – gave direct support to the advancing tanks and infantry.

The Breakthrough

Germany's intended victims in the West had expected terror from the air, and it arrived at dawn on Friday, 10th May. Troop-carrying gliders descended silently beside the crossings of the lower Meuse in south-eastern Holland, and landed on the very roof of the key Belgian fort of Eben-Emael near by; paratroops rained down from the sky round Rotterdam and The Hague; air transport planes unloaded fresh troops onto the half-captured airfield at Waalhaven; and formation after formation of bombers blasted railway junctions and air bases in north-eastern France.

The paratroops and gliders, though not numerous, served to focus the Allied attention on this northern sector, and the cream of the French army and the whole of Lord

1 Field-Marshal Walther von Brauchitsch. Initially he showed no interest in the winning stroke. 2 General von Rundstedt. He saw the weaknesses of 'Plan Yellow'. 3 General Ewald von Kleist. His Panzers led the dashing southerly thrust. 4 General Erich von Manstein. He insisted Army Group A swing south of the Allies.

Gort's British Expeditionary Force, under the overall command of the French general, Billotte, went racing forward into Belgium to meet and hold what they considered to be the main German thrust. Not only that, for the French 7th Army, under its dashing general, Giraud, was sent headlong up through Belgium into southern Holland. Giraud took with him the most valuable mobile reserves of the French army and he was protected, through some curious decision, by the main weight of the French fighter force – although he was moving up on the flank furthest from the main German effort.

When Hitler heard that Gamelin had sent forward the bulk of his forces into the Belgian trap to counter the secondary effort of the German Army Group B, he 'could have wept for joy'.

Army Group A, providing the principal thrust, had started its advance through Luxembourg into the wooded hills of the Belgian Ardennes at the same time, but it

53

was virtually ignored by the French command. It had become an axiom of the French defence planning that armoured forces could not negotiate the restricted roads of the Ardennes in any appreciable strength, and air reconnaissance reports of a build-up on this sector were treated as irrelevant.

German organization, however, was equal to the challenge of the Ardennes. The spearhead of its two armoured corps, which had been put under the command of General von Kleist, crossed Luxembourg and moved forward steadily along parallel forest roads, meeting almost no opposition from the Belgians, and only startled French cavalry groups on reconnaissance, emerging on their horses as if from another age of warfare. The worst problems confronting the Germans in their approach were the vehicle jams occurring on the inadequate roads of the Ardennes. Stretching back fifty miles east of the Rhine, the advancing columns were protected by a massive and constant umbrella of fighters, for a few well-placed bombs on these roads would have impeded the onslaught of the armour for mile upon mile; but the eyes of the Allies were focused on the attack they had expected, in the north.

Guderian's XIX Panzer Corps, making for the Meuse at Sedan, formed the southern wing of Kleist's armoured group. They were through the Ardennes and into France by 1200 on 12th May, Whit Sunday, and in the afternoon I and X Panzer Divisions reached the Meuse on either side of Sedan. During the evening the French troops, fearing a German outflanking movement, evacuated the town; and there was a general withdrawal from the east bank of the Meuse all the way northward to Dinant in Belgium, in the face of the advancing German armour.

While in the south the Germans were already drawing up along the Meuse, the Allies were still advancing through central Belgium to their planned holding positions on the line of the little River Dyle. The advance guard, consisting of France's fine armoured Cavalry Corps under General Prioux, was managing to cover the Dyle line against the first German tank attacks on 12th May, while behind it the French 1st Army, under General Blanchard, moved forward, albeit too slowly, to positions which proved to be virtually unprepared.

An all-out tank battle between Prioux's Cavalry Corps and the German XVI Panzer Corps developed on 13th May and lasted into 14th May. The French tanks fought tenaciously and enabled 1st Army to reach its position; but German training, leadership, and mobility had their effect, and the Germans' ancillary weapon, the Stuka dive-bomber, against which the French had

no defence, was hurled in at crucial stages of the battle. The Cavalry Corps withdrew and its units were dispersed by Billotte along 1st Army's front; the courageous Prioux saw one of the few modern instruments the French possessed broken up into useless fragments.

On 1st Army's right flank, the French 9th Army under General Corap had also moved forward into Belgium, to take up their positions on the Meuse southwards from Namur. In the north they were therefore opposed to the German XV Panzer Corps, under Hoth and approaching Dinant, further south in French territory, to Reinhardt's XLI Panzer Corps, the right wing of Kleist's armoured group which was attacking the Meuse bends at Monthermé. Reinhardt's troops were successfully pinned down at Monthermé for three days by the French 102nd Fortress Division. On the north side of Dinant, however, the Germans were able to establish bridgeheads across the Meuse on the 13th and 14th of May, as much through French carelessness in defending the west bank as through the energy and courage of the German VII Panzer Division's young and unknown general, Erwin Rommel.

But it was in the south, at Sedan, that the decisive battle was being fought. So blind had the French command been to any serious threat through the Ardennes that the skilled and massive thrust by the three armoured divisions of Guderian's XIX Panzer Corps against the Meuse at Sedan, was opposed only by two divisions of flabby, reluctant reservists, who made up the left wing of Huntziger's 2nd French Army. Unfortunately for the French, Sedan also happened to be right on the hinge between two armies, Huntziger's 2nd and Corap's 9th – a situation which greatly increased the difficulties of command for the French. Furthermore their concrete emplacements on the left bank of the Meuse, which should have enabled them to direct a withering fire on any Germans attempting to cross the river were far from complete, as the sharp eyes of a German photographic interpreter had noticed. Many of the French guns, massed on the Marfée Heights opposite Sedan, had not been properly dug in.

Guderian breaks through

Encouraged by his successful advance on Sedan, Guderian agreed with his superior, Kleist, on the evening of 12th May that he would attack at once, even though one of his three Panzer divisions had not yet emerged from the forest. Guderian was promised maximum air support, in particular from the dive-bombers of Richthofen's VIII Flying Corps, and the attempt to cross the Meuse was ordered for 1600 next day, 13th May. The French commanders, however, were estimating that the Germans would need several more days to bring up artillery and infantry for a crossing of the river, and they were summoning up their reserves with little urgency.

The German dive-bombing attacks on the French positions on the left bank, which started in the morning of 13th May and continued with ever increasing force, reached their climax in the half-hour before the German assault and met with only the slightest opposition in the air. On the ground, the French gunners, who should have found the Stukas easy targets, cowered in their shallow trenches beneath this appalling new method of attack; the howling, diving aircraft, and the screaming bombs seemingly aimed at each individual Frenchman. The material damage the bombers did was not important, but by 1600 they had demoralized these civilian soldiers and garrison troops, trained during the past tedious winter to little more than concrete-mixing.

It was the assault troops of the German I Panzer Division, attacking immediately downstream from Sedan against the base of the vulnerable Iges peninsula, that made the first usable bridgehead in the afternoon of 13th May. On their left, above Sedan, X Panzer Division only managed to establish a small foothold across the river with difficulty; and on their right, at Donchery, II Panzer Division would not be assembled in sufficient strength until the following day.

By nightfall on 13th May I Panzer Division troops had fought their way up the Meuse's southern escarpment, through the French main and secondary defence lines, to the dominating height of Marfée Wood. The division now held a bridgehead on the south bank three miles wide and four to six miles deep. During the night they were busy throwing a pontoon bridge across the river and pushing their tanks forward into the bridgehead.

Everything the French tried to do on 14th May to neutralize this dangerous pocket opposite Sedan was too slow and too late. A dawn counter-attack by two light tank battalions and an infantry regiment – there had been no thought of a counter-attack the previous evening – eventually got partly under way at 0700, in time for the French 7th Tank Battalion to be caught on the flank by a newly arrived wave of German tanks, and the counter-attack quickly petered out. And in the afternoon, when there was still an opportunity to drive a powerful wedge into the exposed eastern flank of the German I Panzer Division, before X Panzer Division had broken out of its own small bridgehead, the French threw away their 3rd Armoured Division, full of spirit and eager to attack, with delayed orders and slow refuelling arrangements. When the division could still have attacked with some effect, the order was suddenly countermanded and its precious armour was utterly and finally dispersed by the new local corps commander, who strung it out in a series of weak defensive positions.

On 14th May the Allies despatched all available tactical bombers, the greater part of them British, to attempt the destruction of I Panzer Division's pontoon bridge. They pressed home their attack heroically in obsolete planes, but never concentrated in sufficient numbers to overwhelm the excellent anti-aircraft defences. Their losses were disastrous, and the bridge remained intact. This was the day that broke Allied offensive air-power in the Battle of France.

To Guderian, the Channel coast far away to the west was now his clear objective. Early in the afternoon of 14th May, though X Panzer Division was still struggling up from the Meuse to the east of Marfée Wood, he swung I and II Panzer Divisions sharply westwards, their wheeling southern flank only tenuously protected by the Waffen-SS Infantry Regiment Grossdeutschland against any French counter-attack. This was a risk Guderian rightly took, for the French wasted the whole of 15th May in preparing and then abandoning a counter-attack by the dispersed 3rd Armoured Division; and by then the German XIV Motorized Corps had crossed the Meuse as a much-needed reinforcement.

Having dealt a crippling blow to Huntziger's 2nd Army, Guderian's tanks were now pushing westward into the territory of Corap's 9th Army. But already, to the north, behind the Belgian Meuse, this army was in complete disarray.

As in the south, the French, faced with Rommel's small bridgeheads to the north of Dinant, had muffed all arrangements for a counter-attack, and Rommel's VII Panzer Division had been able to complete a bridge by dawn on 14th May and to start sending its tanks across. On this day, too, the German dive-bombing effort, which had lacerated French nerves opposite Sedan the previous day, was concentrated on 9th Army, and its formation headquarters, its lines of communication, and its artillery. Its supply lines were, moreover, disrupted by incessant bombing and machine-gun fire from low-flying fighters.

By nightfall on 14th May, Rommel's tanks were four miles west of the Meuse, and their companion formation, V Panzer Division, was crossing the river. Corap himself was extremely dejected, and during the night informed Billotte, his army group commander, that his units were withdrawing everywhere. But there was confusion over where the new line was to be; communications were seriously disturbed; and in the darkness, with memories

Tanks of General Erwin Rommel's VII Panzer Division pause during the lunge across France. Rommel's inspired use of armour prompted Hitler to appoint him Afrika Korps commander in February 1941

of the day's bombing and the threat of German tanks already in their rear, 9th Army's withdrawal became a disorderly retreat.

The dash to the sea

A French armoured counter-attack, which could still have restored the situation on the 13th and 14th of May proved to be a repetition of the missed opportunities opposite Sedan. When, after many delays, the French 1st Armoured Division, coming from Charleroi, was refuelling at dawn on 15th May, halfway between Philippeville and the Meuse, with 9th Army retreating rapidly to its rear, it was caught and fiercely attacked on two sides near Flavion by strong elements of VII Panzer Division on its southern flank and of V Panzer Division to the north. After a bitter fight, the French had only seventeen tanks left.

In the meantime, the main body of VII Panzer Division had by-passed the battle on the south: at noon Rommel was in Philippeville, and at the end of 15th May he was well on his way towards the French frontier.

By the end of 15th May Giraud, brought over to replace Corap at the head of 9th Army, found nothing to command, just an open gate for the enemy, sixty-two miles wide. Even the French 41st Corps, on 9th Army's right wing, which had been holding the Meuse line resolutely on the Monthermé and Mézières reaches, was caught out by Corap's withdrawal order. Their attempt at a fighting retreat was rapidly demolished by the unleashed forces of Reinhardt's XLI Panzer Corps, and by the end of the day Reinhardt's tanks were in Montcornet, thirty-seven miles west of the Meuse, and only eleven miles from 9th Army's HQ at Vervins. This alarming news was the first positive indication Gamelin had received in the rarefied fastness of his HQ of the disasters which were overtaking his armies.

On the boundary between the French 9th Army and 2nd Army, west of Sedan, units from both armies had been offering poorly organized though occasionally stiff resistance to Guderian's westward-plunging armour. But, coincidental with Corap's withdrawal order to 9th Army, Huntziger's 2nd Army units, unable to hold their own, had fatally pulled back southwards and eastwards—thus increasing the width of the gap rent in the French defences. Tearing through the hole opening in front of him, Guderian's II Panzer Division was also well on its way to Montcornet by the evening of 15th May.

Although that day it seemed to the German corps and divisional commanders that the road to the west lay open to them, matters looked less assured to the German higher command. Hard fighting during 14th

May at Stonne, on Guderian's left flank as he wheeled westward, had revived old fears of a massive French counter-attack from the south. The Germans were not yet aware that, out of the strong French armoured reserve, 1st and 3rd Armoured Divisions had already frittered away their strength, and 2nd Armoured Division, while deploying, had been cut in two by Guderian's sudden advance towards Signy-l'Abbaye. Nor did they know that on the evening of 15th May Gamelin was admitting to Daladier, minister of national defence, that he had no reserves left, and that this was the end of the French army.

To the German generals who had not themselves come face to face with the wilting enemy, the French collapse and the brilliant success of their own daring operational plan were hard to believe; all had bitter memories of the French army's powers of resistance in the First World War. Hitler particularly, who had realized better than most that France, with its weak leadership and divided political loyalties, was no longer a formidable military power, was extremely nervous.

So it was that Kleist, commanding this spectacular armoured force, and anxious to keep personal control of its advance, called a halt on the evening of 15th May to permit the infantry to catch up and consolidate before the tanks moved on. Guderian was furious at this denial of the new principles of armoured warfare, and managed to gain a twenty-four-hour extension. But on the morning of 17th May he was still pushing forward, and Kleist descended on him in a towering rage, insisting that he halt. Guderian offered his resignation. A compromise was reached, and Guderian, reinstated, was allowed to continue a 'reconnaissance in force'—an arrangement which he was to interpret very liberally.

Summoned by Paul Reynaud, the French Prime Minister, Churchill arrived in Paris on 16th May amid an atmosphere bordering on panic. It was his first visit since becoming Prime Minister the day the German Blitzkrieg had begun. To some extent he managed to restore French government morale by promising to send to France additional RAF fighter squadrons; much against the wishes of Air Chief Marshal Dowding of Fighter Command. But, not for the last time in the war, it was to be a case of 'too little, too late'.

The following day the French attempted one more offensive action, towards Montcornet with a hastily agglomerated 4th Armoured Division under Colonel de Gaulle. But unsupported to its rear and unprotected in the air, it was soon repulsed by the incessant Stuka attacks and by German tanks of XIX Panzer Corps infiltrating behind it.

Now began the German dash to the sea. On 16th May Rommel was through the French frontier defences south of Maubeuge and had advanced another fifty miles, reaching Avesnes in the night; by the evening Reinhardt's XLI Panzer Corps was on the river Oise beyond Vervins; and south of Vervins, Guderian's XIX Panzer Corps had reached the river Serre. On the morning of 17th May French resistance on the upper Oise collapsed, and the road seemed clear, either to Paris, or to the Channel coast in the rear of the Allied armies in Belgium. The French command still had no idea what the objective of *Sichelschnitt* was to be.

On 18th May the Germans were again driving furiously westwards, their advance always many miles and several townships ahead of the fumbling French orders. Billotte, withdrawing the Allied forces south-westwards out of central Belgium, started to establish a line facing south, roughly along the Belgian frontier, attempting to contain the quickly forming Panzer corridor on its north side, while the main French command set up a defensive line along the Somme on the corridor's southern flank, defending Paris, which of course was not Hitler's immediate goal.

On 20th May the German I Panzer Division captured Amiens, while II Panzer Division reached Abbeville in the evening and the Channel coast at dusk after an advance of over sixty miles that day. The Allied forces were cut in two. Reinhardt's corps was heading for St Omer, and Rommel, to the north, had reached the area of Arras. After a brief delay, while the German command took breath, the order was given for Guderian's divisions to swing northward up the coast to Boulogne and Calais, in order to complete the envelopment of the Allied armies in Belgium.

The German armour was now far ahead of even the motorized infantry, and their southern flank was very vulnerable. The French command was aware of the enemy's present weakness and knew that a counterattack undertaken simultaneously from the south and the north, cutting through the middle of the corridor, might entirely sever the cream of the German armour. But the Allies no longer had the ability to coordinate such an action. Gamelin's replacement as commander-in-chief by Weygand on the evening of 19th May contributed nothing except two days' delay in ordering a pincer movement. By then, Allied communications were as confused as their troop movements, and a limited British tank attack southwards from Arras on 21st May with French support on its flank, was carried out with no corresponding French attack from the south. The British achieved a fine local success and made a strong impression upon Rommel; but then, seeing

no French follow-up, withdrew and proceeded to concentrate their plans on the evacuation of the British Expeditionary Force across the Channel.

The northern armies now suffered from the additional disarray caused by the death of their commander, Billotte, in a motor accident, and tension between the Allies in Belgium quickly came to a head. Gort had become disillusioned by the weakness and incompetence of the French command and by the poor resistance of its troops; the French felt that the British were thinking of nothing except saving their own skins across the Channel; and the Belgians, their country almost entirely overrun, were considering surrender. It was in this atmosphere that the retreat to Dunkirk and the evacuation to England took place.

Once the German thrust had reached the Channel and isolated the élite of the Allied armies in the north, the outcome of the campaign had been virtually decided. After Dunkirk it became largely a matter of marching for the Germans, now wheeling southwards to face the French forces which had dug themselves in on the line of the Somme and the Aisne—the so-called 'Weygand Line'. Fighting with often greater tenacity than they had shown on the Meuse, though against hopeless odds, the French resisted the first German onslaught on 5th June. But the 'Weygand Line' was a line in little more than name, and once the Germans had broken through it—Hoth's armour to Rouen, Kleist's to Burgundy, and Guderian's to the Swiss frontier—there was nothing to stop them. On 14th June Paris fell, undefended. The French armies holding the redundant fortifications of the Maginot Line were taken in the rear, Italy administered her infamous 'stab in the back', and on 22nd June France was forced to agree to a humiliating armistice—signed in the same railway carriage where Foch accompanied, among others, by Weygand had accepted the German surrender in 1918.

The brilliantly improvised German operational plan for the attack in the west had succeeded beyond all dreams. France had been utterly defeated in six weeks. But Great Britain, strangely, was not yet seeking terms. The plan had made no further provision; and while the Germans gorged themselves on their triumph and the delights of Paris, the RAF was spending the unexpected respite in bracing itself for the defence of Britain—in which it was to rob Germany of final victory.

Right: France 'in extremis'. Two German soldiers watch Rouen burn after attack from the turret of a knocked-out Renault FT 17, a relic of the First World War

Deliverance at Dunkirk

'Dunkirk,' A.J.P.Taylor has written, 'was a great deliverance and a great disaster.' Yet it might simply have been a great disaster.

The German Blitzkrieg offensive in the West had whirled into the Low Countries on 10th May 1940 with its customary surprise, violence, ruthlessness, and treachery. As a counter-measure three days later 1st, 7th, and 9th French Armies together with the nine divisions of the British Expeditionary Force under Field-Marshal Lord Gort raced to join the Belgian army in defensive positions running along the River Dyle from Antwerp to Namur and south along the Meuse to Sedan. It was a trap. While General von Bock's Army Group B struck into Holland and Belgium in what seemed the primary German thrust, General von Rundstedt's Army Group A, its formidable armour to the fore, emerged from the Ardennes between Dinant and Montmédy in what was in fact the main German assault, and advanced against a front lacking permanent fortifications and manned by only two divisions of professional troops. On 14th May the avalanche broke. Preceded by waves of Stukas, General von Kleist's Panzer Group, comprising the armoured corps of Guderian and Reinhardt, forced a crossing of the Meuse at Mézières, Monthermé, and Sedan. Cutting a swath through the weak and ill-prepared 9th and 2nd Armies the mass of armour, unopposed by any French reserves, plunged towards the Channel threatening to isolate the British, Belgian and French armies in the north. On 21st May Kleist's Panzer Group reached the mouth of the Somme at Abbeville, captured Boulogne, enveloped Calais, and advanced within twelve miles of Dunkirk.

Thus between a formidable wedge of seven armoured divisions and Bock's advancing Army Group B lay the Belgian army, ten divisions of the French 1st Army, and the bulk of the BEF. They were trapped and Kleist was poised to hammer them against the anvil of the advancing VI and XVIII Armies which had just crossed the River Schelde after breaching the Dyle line. For the dazed Allied forces annihilation seemed inevitable. The final phase of the great encirclement battle appeared to be at hand. But suddenly, on 24th May, the bounding armour stopped dead in its tracks. For the reeling Allied armies disaster was about to be mitigated.

On Hitler's orders Kleist's Panzers were halted west and south of Dunkirk on a line from Lens, through Béthune, Aire, St Omer to Gravelines. It was the first of the German High Command's major mistakes in the Second World War. It reprieved the Allies and made possible the 'miracle' of Dunkirk.

The only hope the Allies had of extricating themselves from encircling German forces was for the armies in Belgium to disengage from VI Army attacking them there, turn south-west and fight their way through the German armoured wedge and link up with French forces pushing northwards from the Somme. But by 25th May Lord Gort realized that with the forces at his disposal such a break-out, with Belgian resistance crumbling fast and no evidence of a French attack northwards, stood little chance of success.

The British, French, and Belgian armies were by now confined to a triangle of territory with its base along the Channel coast from Gravelines to Terneuzen and its apex at Valenciennes. There could be no escape but by sea. On 27th May the British government, which on 19th May had insisted Gort attack southwards to Amiens, informed the Commander-in-Chief of the BEF that his sole task was 'to evacuate the maximum force possible'. It was a measure he had foreseen and for which contingency plans had been prepared.

Seven days earlier in the deep galleries below Dover Castle Vice-Admiral Bertram Ramsay had inaugurated a discussion on 'emergency evacuation across the Channel of a very large force'. In the following days the Admiralty began to amass shipping for a possible evacuation of the BEF and Allied forces from France. The desperate venture code-named 'Operation Dynamo' was in large part to be facilitated by the interruption of the German Panzer onslaught.

What was the reason for this apparently inexplicable order to arrest the progress of the armour on the threshold of what could have been one of the worst disasters in military history? Who was responsible for it? The generals led by Halder, the Chief of the Army General Staff and Rundstedt, commander of Army group A, have since put the blame exclusively on Hitler. The peremptory order, although emanating from the Führer in his capacity as Supreme Commander of the Armed Forces did, however, enjoy the support of both Rundstedt and Göring.

The Führer visited the former's headquarters at Charleville on the morning of 24th May where he listened to a report of the fighting and heard the intentions of Army Group Command. Rundstedt suggested that the infantry should attack to the east of Arras, where on 21st May the British had shown they were still capable of vigorous action, while Kleist's armour, which he knew had suffered serious losses, stood on a line west and south of Dunkirk in order to pounce on the Allied forces withdrawing before Army Group B. Hitler expressed com-

Above: British soldier replies to German aircraft strafing him on Dunkirk's beaches. Though the British troops were dangerously exposed, the sand partially muffled the blasts of the German bombs. Left: Relics of a defeated army. German soldiers examine the debris of the BEF's hasty exit strewn along Dunkirk's promenade. The British Army lost most of its heavy equipment, tanks and artillery in the evacuation. All the soldiers could carry back were their rifles

plete agreement with the Army Group commander and underlined the need to husband the armour for the coming operations south of the Somme. Hitler and Rundstedt were thus in agreement in their judgement of the situation.

Göring makes an offer

But the Führer had other reasons for issuing the apparently inexplicable order to restrain the armour. He recalled how in 1914 the low-lying Flanders plains between Bruges, Nieuport, and Dixmude had flooded and bogged down the German northern flank. The low-lying terrain to the west and south of Dunkirk was similarly intersected by thousands of waterways and was, Hitler believed, clearly unsuited for large-scale armoured operations. In view of Hitler's concern for Kleist's armour, Göring's characteristically flamboyant offer to the Führer on 23rd May was received enthusiastically.

From his mobile HQ in the Eifel mountains the Commander-in-Chief of the Luftwaffe telephoned Hitler to propose that 'his' air fleets which, after all, were 'to settle the fate of the German nation for the next thousand years' should destroy the British Army in northern France. After this had been accomplished Göring claimed the German army would only have to 'occupy the territory'. He further urged acceptance of his proposal by remarking that the final destruction of the enemy should be left to the 'National Socialist' Luftwaffe as Hitler would lose prestige to the army generals if they were permitted to deliver the coup de grâce.

It is clear that Hitler's plan, prompted by Göring and Rundstedt, was to let the Luftwaffe and Army Group B, which with very little armour was slowly driving back the Belgians and British south-west to the Channel, eliminate the troops in the Dunkirk pocket. It would, of course, be essential to halt Kleist's armour for fear of hampering Luftwaffe operations in the area. But neither the Luftwaffe nor Bock's Army Group were to prove capable of achieving their objectives.

Hitler, however, had yet further reason to impose his own military leadership on the army for on 24th May a crisis of leadership had occurred. From 2000 on that day Field-Marshal von Brauchitsch, the Commander-in-Chief of the Army who was determined to see that Army Group B fought the last act of the encirclement battle, decided that Rundstedt should surrender tactical control of Kluge's IV Army and that together with all mobile units it should pass under the command of Army Group B. Whether Brauchitsch preferred to make the transfer rather than restore harmony between the two Army Groups and confront the organizational problems that their conjunction

would pose or whether he was dissatisfied with the less dynamic Rundstedt is not clear. Knowledge of the transfer may have led Rundstedt to propose measures he knew the Führer would support when they met at Charleville, but what is clear, however, is that neither Hitler nor OKW, which had replaced the War Ministry and become Hitler's personal staff, knew anything about this Army High Command (OKH) transfer order. Hitler was highly indignant that Brauchitsch and Halder had reorganized command responsibilities without informing him. He promptly cancelled the order.

Thus in halting the armour Hitler sanctioned Rundstedt's proposal besides demonstrating that on the battlefield his position as Supreme Commander of the Wehrmacht was no mere formality. But Halder was not prepared to accept the Führer's order and on the same night issued a wireless message to both Army Groups stating that the continuation of the attack up to Dunkirk on the one hand and Ostend on the other was permissible. In an act unprecedented in German military history Rundstedt decided not to pass on the communication from his superiors to IV Army. Supported by Hitler, and assuming his observations on the morning of the 24th represented his own opinions, he could afford to hold a different view of the situation from that of OKH. In his opinion Army Group B would sooner or later subdue resistance in Flanders and it therefore appeared wiser to preserve the armoured forces for later use.

Although Hitler may have genuinely taken political objectives into consideration when he restrained the armour it is patently obvious that he did not intend to spare Great Britain a bitter humiliation and thereby facilitate a peace settlement by such action. Both the Luftwaffe and the German army had clear and definite instructions to destroy the entrapped enemy in Flanders and this was made unmistakably apparent in Führer Directive No. 13, signed by Hitler on the evening of 24th May 1940. Halder has since claimed that Hitler expressed his determination to fight the decisive battle in northern France rather than on Flemish soil for political reasons. The Führer, Halder maintains, explained that his plans to create a National Socialist region out of the territory inhabited by the 'German-descended' Flemish would be compromised if war was permitted to ravage the region. Therefore although Hitler was partially responsible for the decision to halt the armour he has undoubtedly been unjustly credited with the sole responsibility for the fatal error.

The perimeter shrinks

'Operation Dynamo' was based on the assumption that three ports would be avail-

able but the fall of Boulogne, followed on 26th May by the collapse of British resistance in Calais left only Dunkirk. Yet the defence of Calais termed by Guderian 'heroic, worthy of the highest praise' gave Lord Gort time in which to elaborate his plan for evacuation. The Allies' predicament grew steadily worse. On 25th May the Belgians expended their last reserves and their front broke. On the following day Hitler rescinded the halt order in view of Bock's slow advance in Belgium and the movement of transports off the coast, authorizing the resumption of Rundstedt's advance by 'armoured groups and infantry divisions in the direction of Dunkirk'. However, for technical reasons sixteen hours were to pass before the armoured units were ready to move forward and assail the town. By 28th May the Allies had organized a tighter perimeter defence around Dunkirk stretching from Nieuport along the canals through Furnes and Bergues to Gravelines. Repeatedly assaulted by German tanks and without the support of the Belgian army which had capitulated the same day, the perimeter shrank. South-west of Lille, however, the Germans encountered spirited resistance from the French 1st Army which detained seven of their divisions from 29th May to 1st June thus preventing their participation in the assault on the Dunkirk pocket. The exhausted and bewildered Allies often fragmented into separate battalions or separate companies retreated steadily along congested roads into the perimeter and by midnight on the 29th the greater part of the BEF and nearly half of the French 1st Army lay behind the canal line, by which time the naval measures for evacuation had begun to demonstrate their effectiveness.

At 1857 on 26th May the Admiralty launched Operation Dynamo. Besides an inspiring example of gallantry and self-sacrifice it was to display what Hitler had always held to be one of Great Britain's greatest strengths—the genius for improvisation.

The first day of the evacuation, 27th May, proved disappointing. Only 7,669 troops were brought out by a motley assortment of destroyers, passenger ferry steamers, paddle steamers, self-propelled barges, and Dutch *schuiten* which Vice-Admiral Ramsay had collected. But after the loss of Boulogne and Calais only Dunkirk with its adjacent beaches remained in Allied hands. For the intrepid rescuers, entering the harbour, when not impossible, was a hazardous task. Not only had they to contend with fire from shore batteries and ferocious air attack but they had to negotiate the many wrecks that lay between them and the blazing town.

It became clear that the hungry, exhausted troops would have to be embarked from the sandy beaches on either side of the

An orderly line of British troops wading out to a rescue steamer. The evacuation by larger boats was mostly well-ordered, though there was some panic in the rush to smaller vessels

town, but as yet Ramsay had few small craft capable of embarking men in shallow water. He signalled urgently for more. The next day, 28th May, utilizing the beaches together with the surviving but precarious East Mole of the harbour 17,804 men were embarked for Britain. The losses in craft on that day, however, were very heavy. Ships that left the congested mole unscathed were frequently damaged or sunk by bombing as they steamed down the narrow offshore channel unable to manœuvre adequately for wrecks, debris, and corpses.

Despite the fact that 47,310 men were snatched from Dunkirk and its neighbouring beaches the following day, as soon as the wind had blown aside the pall of smoke obscuring the harbour and roadstead, the Luftwaffe wreaked fearful havoc with a concentrated bombardment of the mole, sinking three destroyers and twenty-one other vessels.

On 30th May smoother seas, smoke, and low cloud ceiling enabled the rescuers to remove 13,823 men to safety. Although a number of small craft had arrived off Dunkirk on 29th May they were only the vanguard of a volunteer armada of some 400 yachts, lifeboats, dockyard launches, river tugs, cockle boats, pleasure craft, French and Belgian fishing boats, oyster dredgers, and Thames barges which, with small craft called into service by the Royal Navy, ferried 100,000 men from the beaches to the deeper draught vessels from the following day. Moved by the desperate plight of the Allies, the seafaring population of south and south-eastern England had set out in a spontaneous movement for the beaches of Dunkirk where in innumerable acts of heroism they fulfilled a crucial role in the evacuation.

On 31st May despite intense bombing and shelling, 68,014 troops were removed to safety but on the following day a furious artillery bombardment and strafing of the whole length of the beaches together with resolute dive-bombing of shipping out at sea and in the harbour effectively halted daylight operations.

The climax of the evacuation had taken place on 31st May and 1st June when over 132,000 men were landed in England. At dawn on 2nd June only 4,000 men of the BEF remained in the perimeter, shielded by 100,000 French troops. On the nights of 2nd and 3rd June they were evacuated along with 60,000 of the Frenchmen. Dunkirk was still defended stubbornly by the remainder who resisted until the morning of 4th June. When the town fell 40,000 French troops who had fought tenaciously to cover the evacuation of their Allied comrades marched into captivity.

'Let us remember,' wrote Churchill, 'that but for the endurance of the Dunkirk rearguard the re-creation of an army in Britain for home defence and final victory would have been gravely prejudiced.'

The British with French and Belgian assistance had evacuated 338,226 troops, of whom 139,097 were French, from a small battered port and exposed beaches right under the noses of the Germans. They had extracted every possible advantage from the valuable respite accorded them when the armour was halted, consolidating defensive positions in the west, east, and on the Channel front. Moreover they had fought tenaciously, upholding traditions that had so impressed the Germans in the First World War.

The primary German error was to regard the Dunkirk pocket as a subordinate front. In fact its strategic importance was not recognized until too late largely because it was not clear until almost the last moment how many Allied troops were actually in the pocket.

Moreover, for the nine days of Operation Dynamo, the Luftwaffe, due to adverse weather conditions only succeeded in seriously interfering with it for two-and-a-half days—on 27th May, the afternoon of 29th May, and on 1st June. The Luftwaffe's mission, readily shouldered by the vain, ambitious Göring proved too much for it. If Rundstedt had made a mistake, Göring fatally miscalculated. His aircraft had failed to prevent the Allied evacuation because the necessary conditions for success —good weather, advanced airfields, training in pin-point bombing—were all lacking. Bombers and dive-bombers for the first time suffered heavy losses at the hands of British Spitfires and Hurricanes now operating from their relatively near home bases.

For Germany's military leadership Dunkirk was the first great turning point in the Second World War, for it was during the campaign that Hitler first forced OKH to accept his own military views, by short-circuiting it at a critical juncture of the fighting and transferring a decision of far-reaching importance to a subordinate command whose views happened to coincide with his own. OKH, the actual military instrument of leadership, was in future to be undermined, overruled, and with terrible consequences for the German people, finally abolished altogether.

The grim realities

At Dunkirk instead of winning a battle of annihilation the German army had to content itself with an ordinary victory. Great Britain on the other hand could console itself with the knowledge that almost its entire expeditionary force had been saved. 'In the midst of our defeat,' Churchill later wrote, 'glory came to the Island people, united and unconquerable . . . there was a white glow, overpowering, sublime, which ran through our Island from end to end . . . and the tale of the Dunkirk beaches will shine in whatever records are preserved of our affairs.'

If the British people felt they had won a great victory the grim realities belied their euphoria. The BEF, no longer in any condition to defend the country had suffered 68,111 killed, wounded, and taken prisoner. It had been compelled to abandon 2,472 guns, 90,000 rifles, 63,879 vehicles, 20,548 motorcycles and well over 500,000 tons of stores and ammunition. Of the 243 ships sunk at Dunkirk, out of 860 engaged, six were British destroyers. A further nineteen British destroyers were damaged. In addition the RAF had lost 474 aircraft.

Dunkirk had been a catastrophe alleviated, not by a miracle, but by German miscalculation and Allied tenacity and improvisation. Yet the elation of victory pervaded Britain. A supreme effort had cheated Hitler of his prey and a little self-congratulation seemed appropriate. The British had been the first to confound the German military juggernaut and after Dunkirk they resolved with a wholehearted determination to defeat it.

Italy: The Achilles Heel

Italy in June 1940 was in no condition to fight a major war. The Italian army simply did not possess the kind of equipment which had made possible the German successes in the West. Anti-aircraft guns were virtually non-existent, only half the motor vehicles required by the army could be supplied, and there was only fuel enough for seven to eight months. In the event of general mobilization, the troops could not even have been properly clothed. The navy and air force were only slightly better off, and underlying everything was the weakness of the Italian war economy. Italy was desperately short of such strategic raw materials as copper, nickel, aluminium, and rubber, and these shortages were accentuated when, after the declaration of war, the Royal Navy closed both the Suez Canal and the Straits of Gibraltar to Italian shipping.

Mussolini was well aware of these unpleasant facts, but in his view the war was as good as won already, and it was imperative to enter the conflict before it was too late.

But, unfortunately for the Duce, things did not quite go according to plan. After the conclusion of the Battle of France—in which the Italian forces failed to penetrate more than a few miles into French territory—Great Britain gave little evidence for the widespread view that she was finished, and failed to come to terms with Germany in spite of Hitler's apparently sincere appeal. The Germans began to prepare seriously for an invasion of the British Isles, and Mussolini offered Italian troops to participate in the landings. When Hitler somewhat disdainfully rejected this offer, Mussolini was left to obtain his military glory elsewhere. This prospect was by no means uncongenial to him, for even before Italy's entry into the war, he had repeatedly spoken of the need to wage what he called a 'parallel war': a war alongside Germany and against the same opponents, but in different theatres and for specifically Italian objectives. He now had the chance to put this conception into practice.

Africa was the obvious arena for the 'parallel war'. The Italians had some fourteen divisions (215,000 men) in Libya, excluding air force personnel, and the fall of France meant that they were now free to concentrate all their strength against the British in Egypt without having to bother about the French in Tunisia. Some twelve hundred miles to the south-east, in Italian East Africa, there were two divisions and twenty-nine colonial brigades, totalling

255,000 men exclusive of naval and air force units. This was a large force, strategically concentrated on the flank of the main British supply route to Egypt via the Red Sea. It was Mussolini's ambition to break out of the Mediterranean 'prison' in which the British had confined him: a concerted Italian attack from Libya and East Africa in the direction of Egypt and the Sudan would serve this purpose, and seriously embarrass the British.

But things were not so easy as that. In spite of repeated prodding from Rome, the Italian commander in Libya, Marshal Rodolfo Graziani, argued that his forces were in no state to take on the British without large-scale reinforcements, and it was not until 13th September 1940 that his army finally lumbered across the Egyptian frontier, only to come to a prolonged halt some four days and sixty-odd miles later.

A paper tiger

It should be emphasized at this point that it was not the 'parallel war' strategy as such which was at fault, but Italy's capacity to carry it out unaided. Some of Hitler's military advisers, particularly in the navy, saw the advantages of concentrating upon Great Britain's power position in the Middle East if the proposed invasion of the home islands failed to take place, or even as an alternative strategy altogether. They were well aware, however, that the Italians could accomplish little or nothing on their own, and it was as a result of this awareness that proposals were put forward in the autumn of 1940 to send German armoured units to North Africa. But for prestige and other reasons Mussolini would have none of it. 'If they set foot among us,' he told the Armed Forces Chief of Staff, Marshal Pietro Badoglio, 'we will never get rid of them.'

If, in view of Italy's weakness, Mussolini was rash to turn down the offer of German assistance in North Africa, he was mad to contemplate expanding his commitments still further by engaging in military operations on the continent of Europe. Yet, in the summer of 1940, we find him planning more or less simultaneous invasions of Switzerland, Yugoslavia, and Greece. All were the object of long-standing Italian ambitions. The desire to attack them at this stage can be explained partly by the desire to stake out a claim in time for the peace conference, and partly to guard against the threat of a German hegemony over areas which Italy considered vital to her security. However, Mussolini was com-

Top: Poster after the election of March 1934 'Year XII of the fascist era'. The approved list of fascist candidates were overwhelmingly voted in. **Above:** *Mussolini watches with delight the collapse of the League of Nations after the invasion of Ethiopia.* **Left:** *'Il Duce'*

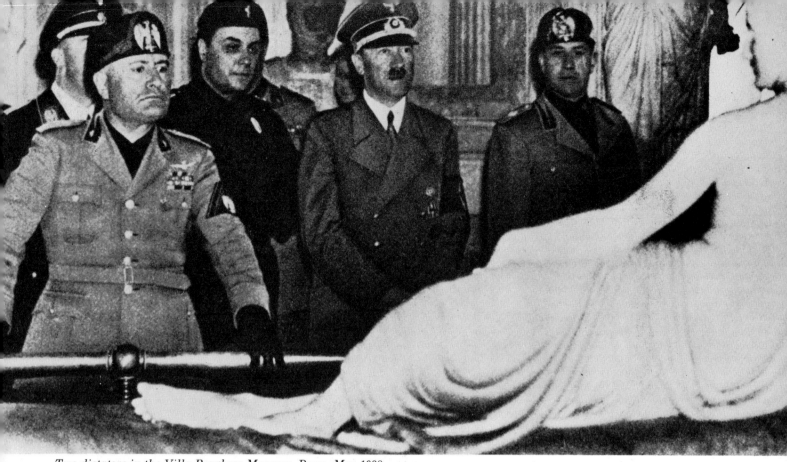

Two dictators in the Villa Borghese Museum, Rome, May 1938

pelled to drop the plan for the invasion of Switzerland because the troops for it were also needed to invade Yugoslavia, and he was compelled to drop the plan for the invasion of Yugoslavia because of opposition from his military advisers. Hitler was also anxious for stability in the Balkans on account of Germany's vital oil supplies from Rumania and because he wished to preserve—at least temporarily—his alliance with Russia. He had tried to veto the invasion of Yugoslavia, and would undoubtedly have tried to veto the invasion of Greece had he taken rumours of the invasion seriously; but he did not.

Italy invaded Greece on 28th October 1940 from Italian-occupied Albania. 'I shall send in my resignation as an Italian if anyone objects to our fighting the Greeks', Mussolini told his son-in-law and foreign minister, Count Ciano, a fortnight before the invasion, thereby indicating his belief that the operation would be a walkover. Although this belief was shared by many others, and not least by Ciano and the Italian civil and military authorities in Albania, the Greeks soon expelled the invading forces and pressed on into Albanian territory. At one point, early in December, Mussolini was faced with the humiliating prospect of having to ask for an armistice through Hitler but, fortunately for him, the Italian forces managed to hold their ground. Shortly before, a daring raid by torpedo bombers of the Royal Navy had disabled a large portion of the Italian battle fleet in Taranto harbour (11th–12th November) and shortly afterwards (9th December), O'Connor launched the British counter-offensive in the Western Desert which was to drive Graziani not only out of Egypt, but out of Cyrenaica as well.

This series of disasters had far-reaching effects. There was a thorough shake-up in the Italian High Command, which included the dismissal of the Chief of Staff of the Armed Forces, Marshal Badoglio, and the Chief-of-Staff of the Navy, Admiral Domenico Cavagnari, as well as that of certain lesser lights. But the situation might well not have been saved had not Hitler responded favourably to his fellow-dictator's belated calls for help. At the end of 1940 and the beginning of 1941, Hitler decided first to support the Italians in Albania with a German attack on Greece from Bulgaria; second, to send units of the German air force to Sicily to help the Italians attack the British Mediterranean Fleet; third, to despatch German forces, including armoured units, to North Africa to prevent the loss of Tripolitania, and fourth, to increase German economic assistance to Italy. These decisions may have saved the Fascist regime from early extinction, but they also sounded the death-knell of Italy's autonomous 'parallel war'. From the beginning of 1941 onwards, Nazi Germany exercised ever greater control over the activities of her weaker partner, much to the latter's annoyance.

On the face of it, things went extremely well for the Axis during the first six months of 1941. Thanks largely to General Rommel and the Afrika Korps, the British were driven out of Libya, except for Tobruk, by the beginning of April. Greece was overcome in the same month, although the Italian forces were not able to do much more than hold the line in Albania. Moreover, an additional Blitzkrieg campaign was added to the list when, at the end of March, Yugoslavia finally spurned Axis offers of an alliance. Hitler resolved to 'smash Yugoslavia' and, after a brief campaign in which Italian forces also participated, the Yugoslavs were forced to

sign an armistice on 17th April 1941.

Only in East Africa, where Germany was unable to come to the aid of Italy, was the Axis defeated. Attacking from Kenya, the Sudan, and from across the Gulf of Aden, British forces occupied Italian Somaliland and Eritrea, recaptured British Somaliland, and thrust deep into Ethiopia. Addis Ababa fell on 6th April, and the Duke of Aosta himself was compelled to surrender at Amba Alagi on 16th May. Two sizeable concentrations of Italian troops remained in Ethiopia—one, under General Gazzera, in the south-west, and the other, under General Nasi, in the north-west—but both were eventually forced to surrender, the former in July and the latter in November. The empire which Mussolini had defied the League of Nations to create in 1935 was no more.

But Axis successes elsewhere were not nearly so impressive as they seemed at first sight. The German plans for an invasion of the British Isles had long since been abandoned, and the British power position in the Middle East remained intact, in spite of the Rashid Ali revolt in Iraq in April. It was true that the Axis intended to exploit Arab nationalism against the British, and the German army had worked out an elaborate timetable which involved simultaneous offensives against Egypt along the North African coast and, via Turkey, down through Syria and Palestine at the turn of the year 1941-42. But all this was to follow upon what was confidently expected to be the early defeat of the Soviet Union, an eventuality which never materialized. On the grounds that the Italians could not afford to stay out of the decisive struggle against Bolshevism, Mussolini initially contributed three divisions to the German invasion of Russia in June 1941. These troops would have been much better employed in North Africa, a theatre which, as a result of the Russian campaign, was inevitably down-graded in Hitler's eyes, with serious consequences for Italy.

The resultant withdrawal to the Balkans of the bulk of the German air force units which Hitler had sent to Sicily at the end of 1940 greatly reduced the pressure upon Malta, the British island base which lay athwart the main supply route from Italy to North Africa. In the autumn of 1941, as a result, Italian convoy losses increased to an intolerable degree. So, on 2nd December, Hitler issued a directive appointing Field-Marshal Albert Kesselring as Commander-in-Chief South, in charge of an entire air corps and with the threefold mission of protecting the supply route between Italy and North Africa, co-operating with the Italo-German ground forces in North Africa, and stopping enemy traffic through the Mediterranean. Kesselring's appointment, which was regarded with mixed feelings by the Italians, marked a further stage in the subordination of Italy to Germany.

Not long after Kesselring's arrival in Italy, the Second World War was transformed into a truly global conflict by the Japanese attack on Pearl Harbour and British and Dutch possessions in the Far East. Mussolini, together with Hitler, gratuitously linked his fate with that of the Land of the Rising Sun by declaring war upon the USA on 11th December 1941. Initially American intervention did not provide much relief for the British position in the Mediterranean and the Middle East, whereas Japanese intervention seemed to offer alluring prospects to the Axis powers. 'The Japanese admirals have informed us that they intend to proceed towards India,' Ciano noted in his diary on 7th March 1942. 'The Axis must move towards them in the Persian Gulf.'

Before this could happen, however, the Italo-German base in North Africa had to be made secure. The key to this was supply, and the key to supply was the elimination of Malta. Kesselring had set himself the task of 'neutralizing' the island from the air, but the Italians had come to the conclusion that nothing less than its seizure would suffice. In this they were surely right, for whatever the short-term success of an aerial assault, it could not be maintained indefinitely, particularly when it depended almost entirely upon German aircraft which were always liable to recall to the Russian front. As early as October 1941, the Armed Forces Chief of Staff, General Ugo Cavallero (who replaced Badoglio in December 1940), had instructed the army to plan the invasion of Malta. By the beginning of 1942, the other services were involved and the Germans were

also drawn in. At a meeting between Hitler and Mussolini at the end of April, it was decided to recapture Tobruk and advance as far as the Egyptian frontier by the middle of June, and then to take Malta before any further advance in North Africa.

Unfortunately for the Italians, however, they were dependent upon German help for the success of the Malta invasion, and it soon became clear that Hitler was not very enthusiastic about the operation. In a meeting with his military advisers on 21st May, he argued that the Italians were really incapable of carrying out such a complex manoeuvre and that, in any case, their security was so bad that the British would soon know as much about the plans as their own commanders. In these circumstances, it was not surprising that, after the Italo-German forces had captured Tobruk on 21st June and Rommel, confident in the belief that he could be in Cairo by the end of the month, had pressed for the restrictions upon his advance to be lifted, Hitler urged Mussolini to let him have his way. 'Destiny has offered us a chance which will never occur twice in the same theatre of war,' he wrote. 'The goddess of battles visits warriors only once. He who does not grasp her at such a moment never reaches her again.' But the Duce did not need such lyrical prose to persuade him. He was as mesmerized by the prospect of conquering Egypt as Hitler or Rommel and, in spite of the reasoned objections of Cavallero and Kesselring, he gladly gave the German field commander his head. The Malta invasion was postponed – indefinitely as it turned out – and the Duce even went to North Africa to preside personally over the fall of Egypt.

But Egypt did not fall. Auchinleck held Rommel's offensive and the initiative passed to the British with the second Battle of El Alamein in October. The following month, the Anglo-American landings in French North Africa (Operation Torch) put the Italo-German forces in a vice, and when they were finally expelled from Tunisia in May 1943, the way was clear for a direct assault upon *Festung Europa* ('Fortress Europe') itself – by way of Italy.

Was Italy a liability?

Later in the war Adolf Hitler pondered upon the effects of his partnership with Italy. 'When I pass judgement, objectively and without emotion, on events,' he wrote, 'I must admit that my unshakeable friendship for Italy and the Duce may well be held to be an error on my part. It is in fact quite obvious that our Italian alliance has been of more service to our enemies than to ourselves. Italian intervention has conferred benefits which are modest in the extreme in comparison with the numerous difficulties to which it has given

rise. If, in spite of all our efforts, we fail to win this war, the Italian alliance will have contributed to our defeat.'

Italy's presence at Germany's side, he claimed, prevented him from mobilizing the Muslim peoples in his support, 'for the Italians in these parts of the world are more bitterly hated, of course, than either the British or the French.' On a more purely military level, the Italian defeats in Greece 'compelled us, contrary to all our plans, to intervene in the Balkans, and that in its turn led to a catastrophic delay in the launching of our attack on Russia. We were compelled to expend some of our best divisions there. And as a net result we were then forced to occupy vast territories in which, but for this stupid show, the presence of any of our troops would have been quite unnecessary . . . Ah! if only the Italians had remained aloof from this war!'

When reflections such as these are placed alongside the actual record of Italian performance during the Second World War, it is easy to see the basis for the belief that Italy was Germany's Achilles heel. But is this belief justified? After all, it was not the Italian alliance which prevented Hitler from exploiting Arab nationalism, but his preoccupation with Barbarossa (the offensive against Russia). And even if that operation could have been launched a few weeks earlier but for the German campaigns in Greece and Yugoslavia (which is very doubtful), would it have made all that much difference to the final outcome? As for the German troops allegedly tied down in the Balkans, these amounted to seven divisions in June 1941 compared with the 153 massed for Barbarossa. It is hard to see how they would have had much effect upon the balance of forces on the Eastern Front.

It was not so much Hitler's support for Mussolini which contributed to his losing the Second World War, as his failure to give him adequate support by according the Mediterranean a higher priority in his overall strategy, as, for example, his naval advisers constantly urged. The Middle East was of great strategic importance to the British Empire, and a small increase in German resources devoted to the area could have resulted in proportionately large rewards. As it was, the main burden of Axis operations in the Mediterranean fell upon the Italians, who were totally incapable of shouldering it. The brilliant tactical successes of a commander like Rommel could obscure the harsh realities for a while, but by the end of 1942 they were plainly there for all to see, and Mussolini had cause to reflect upon the words of his fellow-Italian, Niccolò Machiavelli: 'Everyone may begin a war at his pleasure, but cannot so finish it.'

The Battle of Britain

Of all the innumerable battles fought during the last 2,500 years, no more than fifteen have been generally regarded as decisive. A decisive battle has been defined as one in which 'a contrary event would have essentially varied the drama of the world in all its subsequent stages'. By this reckoning, the Battle of Britain was certainly decisive.

To find another decisive battle fought so close to British homes we have to go back to the defeat of the Armada in 1588, when Drake's well-handled little ships, with some assistance from the weather, destroyed a vast array of Spanish warships. But a closer parallel is with the Battle of Trafalgar.

In 1805 Napoleon controlled the whole of Europe west of the Russian frontier, with the exception of Great Britain and some parts of the Iberian peninsula. He understood very well that if he could destroy British sea power he could invade and conquer that stubborn island kingdom, and the whole of Western Europe would fall under his sway. But at Trafalgar his own sea power was destroyed by Nelson's fleet, and with it disappeared his hopes of subduing Great Britain. The narrow waters of the Channel were an insuperable barrier to his invading armies. Thwarted in the west, he turned against Russia, and his Grande Armée was all but destroyed amid the ice and snow during the terrible retreat from Moscow in the winter of 1812.

In August 1940 Hitler had mastered all Western Europe, apart from Great Britain, Spain, and Portugal. Although most of the men of the British Expeditionary Force had been brought home—the miracle of Dunkirk—they had lost almost all their weapons and equipment. This disaster had left Great Britain without any effective land forces, for in the whole country it

Germany's Triumph

was scarcely possible to put into the field one division, fully armed and equipped.

Things had changed since the days of Napoleon. This time the Royal Navy could not save Great Britain, for its ships could not operate in the southern North Sea and the Channel against concentrated German air and submarine attacks. And many of its warships were absent, fully employed in guarding the convoys that brought in the vital supplies of food and raw materials.

The Germans knew that if they could destroy the Royal Air Force, they could invade and conquer Great Britain, and all military resistance in Western Europe would end. Hitler had every reason to feel confident of success. The German air force (Luftwaffe) had destroyed the Polish, Dutch, Belgian, and French air forces. Its Commander-in-chief, Reichsmarschall Hermann Göring, had no doubt that his powerful air fleets would make short work of the much smaller RAF.

In 1805 and again in 1940, Great Britain stood alone against a large continental army, flushed with success, and on both occasions, by a brilliant and decisive victory, she saved herself from invasion and Western Europe from complete military subjection.

But there the similarity ends. Trafalgar was fought and won in a day, but the Battle of Britain, the first decisive battle in the air, was a long drawn out battle of attrition. The daylight battle began in early August, and continued through a long fine autumn until the middle of October. After the day battle had died down, the struggle was carried on by night, through the winter of 1940-41. It ended only when Hitler, despairing of conquering Great Britain, turned, as Napoleon had done before him, against Russia. And, like Napoleon, Hitler was to see his great armies all but annihilated battling against the illimitable spaces and the bitter winter climate of Russia.

Looking back, the people of Great Britain may wonder why the battle had to be fought in their skies, over their heads, and why it was their towns and cities that were bombed and devastated by fire. The answer to this is to be found in the sequence of events between the two world wars.

After the Armistice in November 1918 the greatly expanded armed forces of the Allies were hastily and clumsily demobilized. Improvised war organizations were dismantled, and the watchwords of the British government were economy and retrenchment. The war had been won, there was no visible threat to Allied security, and Great Britain and France were swept by a wave of anti-war feeling, largely induced by the terrible casualties and intolerable conditions of trench warfare.

In 1925 the League of Nations had set up a Preparatory Commission to explore the ground for a general disarmament conference. Progress in this field is never rapid, and for many years the commission was involved in interminable difficulties and arguments. Eventually a Disarmament Conference was convened in Geneva in 1932, at which proposals for outlawing air bombardment and drastically limiting the loaded weight of military aircraft were discussed. Hoping for success in these negotiations, the British government declined to authorize the design and construction of any effective bomber aircraft. In addition, it had introduced in 1924 what became known as the 'Ten-year Rule', which postulated that there would be no major war for ten years. Unfortunately each successive year was deemed to be the starting point of this tranquil epoch, and so the period always remained at ten years.

The Disarmament Conference finally broke up in May 1934 without achieving any result whatsoever. But, meanwhile Hitler had come to power in Germany, and was clearly bent on a massive programme of rearmament. In 1933 the British government at last permitted the issue of Air Staff requirements for a high-performance multi-gun fighter, which in due course produced the Hurricane and Spitfire. It is often asserted that these two aircraft, and especially the Spitfire, were forced on a reluctant Air Ministry by a far-sighted aircraft industry and its capable designers. There is not a word of truth in this. Both aircraft were designed, ordered, and built to Air Ministry specifications.

Even after the collapse of the Disarmament Conference in 1934 the British government was reluctant to rearm. Alone

The aces. 1 Squadron Leader 'Sailor' Malan. He was the third highest RAF scorer with thirty-five enemy aircraft shot down. The RAF's top scorers were M.T.St John Pattle with forty-one kills, and Johnny Johnson (thirty-eight). 2 Squadron Leader Stanford Tuck. Between May 1940 and January 1942 he shot down twenty-nine German aircraft making him the eighth highest RAF scorer for the war. In 1942 he was shot down over France and captured. 3 Major Adolf Galland, top German scorer in the Battle of Britain with fifty-seven kills. Although he was grounded for three years he shot down 103 aircraft in the West and was the Luftwaffe's fourth highest scorer in that theatre. Top German scorer in the West, Captain Hans-Joachim Marseille, shot down 158 aircraft. 4 Lieutenant Colonel Werner Mölders. In the Battle of Britain he scored fifty-five kills. He was shot down and killed in 1941. 5 and 6 Spitfires seen from the nose gun position of Heinkel 111 bombers

5 △ 6 ▽

among nations the British seem to think that if they rearm it will bring about an arms race. The result of this curious delusion is that they usually start when the other competitors are half-way round the course. The bomber force was therefore given a very low priority, but development of the fighters was allowed to proceed, though without any undue haste.

In 1935 two British ministers, Mr Anthony Eden and Sir John Simon, visited Germany. They reported that Hitler's rearmament in the air had proceeded much farther and faster than the British government had believed possible. This was because the Germans had made a secret agreement to train the Soviet air force, an agreement enabling them to keep in being a sizeable corps of expert pilots and technicians. The government was alarmed, and ordered quantity production of the Hurricanes and Spitfires before the prototype had even flown—the so-called 'ordering off the drawing-board'.

Lord Trenchard, chief of the Air Staff from 1919 to 1928, had always believed that in air defence the bomber was as important as the fighter. He maintained that the air war should be fought in the skies over the enemy's territory, and he therefore advocated a bomber force powerful enough to take the offensive, and attack an enemy's vital centres from the outset. He argued that this would rob an enemy of the initiative and throw his air force on to the defensive.

Eventually Trenchard's views were accepted by the British government, and in the air defence of Great Britain two-thirds of the squadrons were to be bombers and one-third fighters. But because it was thought that the bombers were offensive while the fighters were defensive in character, it was judged that the building up of fighter strength would not be liable to trigger off an arms race. The seventeen authorized fighter squadrons were in existence by 1930, but at that date no more than twelve of the thirty-five authorized bomber squadrons had been formed, most of them

1 German air reconnaissance photograph of oil installations at Purfleet on the Thames after the heavy air raid on London on 7th September 1940. 2 Poster issued by Ministry of Home Security calling for national solidarity against incendiary attacks. The first heavy incendiary attack was on 15th October 1940. To meet the new threat, the minister of home security, Herbert Morrison, organized a compulsory fire-watching service and consolidated local fire brigades into a single National Fire Service. 3 German fighter pilots relaxing but ready to 'scramble'. 4 Remains of a German bomber brought down in an English farmyard

equipped with small short-range day bombers. In 1935 the alarm caused by German rearmament in the air occasioned a further shift of emphasis in favour of the fighters. A system of radio-location, later called radar, which would provide invaluable early warning and make it possible to track incoming raids, was pioneered by Robert Watson-Watt, and given all possible encouragement.

The Munich crisis of 1938, when for a time war seemed unavoidable, brought home to the British government, though not to the British people, their appalling military weakness and almost total unreadiness for war. France, which was in no better shape, and Great Britain had to make the best bargain they could with Hitler. The British government now realized that war was likely in the near future, with no possibility of building up a bomber force that could carry the war into the enemy's skies. The opening phase of the war was therefore bound to be defensive, to gain the time needed to modernize and build up the armed forces. The Air Ministry had to switch all remaining priorities to the expansion and equipment of Fighter Command, at the expense of the development of the bomber force. It was also necessary to build, with great urgency, a chain of radar stations to provide early warning and controlled interception of incoming enemy raids. The most that could be hoped for was to foil any attempt at invasion, and survive the opening defensive phase in good enough shape to begin to build an offensive capacity. For it must be remembered that even the most successful defensive action cannot win a war; it can stave off defeat and buy time to create the right conditions for an offensive, but no more.

At the outbreak of war in September 1939 the odds against the RAF, in terms of modern aircraft, were about four to one. Although money had been poured out like water during the years since the Munich crisis, it had been too late to redress the balance. It was only time—as much

1 Battle of Britain poster emphasizes importance of fighter aircraft for national survival. 2 Member of the Women's Voluntary Service carrying some of the aluminium pots and pans given in response to Lord Beaverbrook's appeal. The WVS drove mobile canteens, cared for the bombed-out, staffed rest centres and clothing depots, and helped with evacuation. 3 London street after an air raid in September 1940. 4 Ack-ack girls practise air raid drill. Women from the Auxiliary Territorial Service worked in anti-aircraft units and performed non-combatant duties, like plotting and ranging enemy aircraft, releasing men for active service

Germany's Triumph

time as possible—would be able to do that.

Hitler's assault on the West began on 10th May 1940, and within two months Belgium, Holland, and France were defeated and prostrate, with Denmark and Norway already occupied by German troops and air forces. During these two months the RAF operated at maximum intensity, in a vain effort to stave off disaster, and later to give protective cover to the evacuation from the continent. Losses were very heavy, and in some ways these operations put just as great a strain upon Fighter Command as did the Battle of Britain.

At the beginning of July Great Britain stood alone, with no more than a narrow strip of sea separating her from the victorious armed forces of Hitler's Germany. The strategy and assumptions with which the Allies had begun the war lay in ruins all around them. Had the Germans been able to follow up their success by an immediate invasion across the Channel they might have succeeded, for Fighter Command was exhausted, and Great Britain's land forces were so disarmed and disorganized that effective resistance would scarcely have been possible. But fortunately the Germans were also in need of a breathing space. They needed time to regroup their armies, collect barges and stores, re-deploy their air forces on new airfields in captured territories, build up stocks of bombs, ammunition, fuel, and spare parts, and to give their aircrews a much needed rest.

It is sometimes forgotten that the object of the RAF in the Battle of Britain was not simply to defeat the German air attacks, but the destruction of Hitler's plan, code-named 'Sea Lion', for the invasion and conquest of Great Britain. This was to involve not only Fighter Command, but the whole of Bomber Command too.

The battle began on 8th August 1940. Rising production of fighter aircraft and intensive training of pilots had by this time reduced the odds against the RAF to about three to one. On the very day that Hitler launched his assault against the West, a new Ministry of Aircraft Production was set up, with Lord Beaverbrook at its head. He was especially charged with doing everything possible to increase the production of fighter aircraft and all of the equipment needed for air defence. He was a man of boundless energy, whose administrative methods were ruthless, improvised, and fluid rather than methodical or orderly. He spared no effort to make the people of Great Britain realize the vital importance of fighter production. Householders were asked to give every aluminium saucepan they could spare, and many did so in the belief that in the twinkling of an eye their household utensils would be turned into Hurricanes and Spitfires.

In sober fact there were only three ways in which the planned production of fighters could be accelerated during the next three months. Firstly, by convincing the aircraft industry and the trade unions of the vital need to increase production; secondly, by concentrating every available priority on air defence; and thirdly, by reducing the production of spare parts and using the capacity thus released to build aircraft instead. Beaverbrook used all three methods. The first two had only a marginal effect, and the third produced the most obvious result, though largely at the expense of serviceability in the field. It compelled squadrons to 'cannibalize'; that is, to rob unserviceable aircraft of spare parts to keep the others going. Though Beaverbrook assumed office too late to achieve much genuine increase in production until the day battle was over, it was generally believed that he had done so. In addition, his iconoclastic activities and dramatic personality had a salutary moral effect, both on the RAF and the British public.

The German plan for the invasion of Great Britain required the destruction of the RAF, followed by the transport across the Channel of some 200,000 German troops and their impedimenta, conveyed in the huge barges used commercially on the Rhine and other great European rivers and canals. It was the task of Fighter Command to avoid destruction and to win the air battle, and that of Bomber Command to destroy the barges and dumps of war material collecting in the Channel ports.

At the beginning of the battle, Fighter Command consisted of fifty-four regular and auxiliary squadrons, of which twenty-seven were equipped with Hurricanes, nineteen with Spitfires, six with Blenheim night-fighters, and two with Defiants, a two-seater fighter which proved unsatisfactory in operations. Thus there was a total of forty-six effective day fighter squadrons, giving a front-line strength of about 820 aircraft. Against this, the Germans had deployed a total of some 2,600 aircraft, of which about 1,000 were day fighters, and the remainder bombers of various kinds.

The German fighters were the single-engined Messerschmitt 109, and the twin-engined Messerschmitt 110. The performance of the Me 109 was slightly better than that of the Hurricane, but not as good as the Spitfire. The Me 110 was regarded by the Luftwaffe as a destroyer rather than a fighter. It combined long range and a powerful armament, but was relatively unmanoeuvrable, and no match for the British interceptor fighters.

The 1,200 long-range bombers were mainly Dornier 17s and Heinkel 111s, both good fast aircraft, but with inadequate defensive armament. The normal bomb load of the Dornier was 2,205 lb, and that of the Heinkel about 3,000 lb, with provision in the latter for a maximum of 5,512 lb for short ranges. They flew in well-drilled formations, with the Me 110s as close escort, and the Me 109s providing high cover.

Göring was confident that he could achieve his aim by smashing the fighter defences around London, and then extending his assault northwards and westwards until all effective resistance ceased.

Fighter Command

Fighter Command, however, had immense confidence in its aircrews, its aircraft, and its well-developed system of ground-controlled interception. Its aircrews were as well-trained as any in the world, and second to none in courage and determination. They had inherited the great traditions of the gallant fighter pilots of the Royal Flying Corps in the First World War, and their morale was very high. They knew very well how much depended on their efforts, and they were obviously defending their homeland from a monstrous assault. Moreover, they had their parachutes and friendly territory beneath them. The Hurricanes and Spitfires were reliable and had an excellent performance. With their eight machine-guns they were superior in armament to any other fighter in the world. And there had been time to build the chain of radar stations, and accustom the pilots and operations rooms staffs to the new techniques of interception. Finally, a simplified and very effective system of battle tactics had been worked out.

Fighter Command was ready—but only just ready—for battle.

Air Marshal Sir Hugh Dowding, the Commander-in-Chief of Fighter Command, was a shrewd and very experienced commander. He was generally held in more respect than affection, for he had a sharp tongue and a gruff and somewhat ungracious manner, which had earned him the nickname of 'Stuffy'. But those who knew him well realized that this manner concealed a humane and rather shy personality.

Dowding understood very well the magnitude and importance of his task. He also realized that the battle would be one of attrition and that, while the most vigorous and resolute tactical offensive against the Luftwaffe was essential, he would have to husband his resources. He had to guard against exhausting his pilots and ground crews by asking too much of them. Except for short spells in an emergency, he must keep his operations at a level that could be maintained for a long period.

The command, group, and sector operations rooms, placed underground, each had

a large map in the form of a table. All incoming raids were plotted by radar, and counters were immediately placed on the map, indicating position, altitude, direction of flight, and approximate strength. Large numbers of officers and airwomen of the Women's Auxiliary Air Force were employed in the operations rooms on these duties, and in intelligence and codes and cyphers. The controller, in a gallery, could see all the information on the map at a glance, and issue orders to the appropriate squadrons. Once airborne, they could be given a course which would bring about an interception. Controllers had to be cool and experienced, to avoid being deceived by feints and to ensure that the main attacks were intercepted with maximum force. While delegating much to the group commanders, the command operations room retained general over-all control of the battle.

The first phase opened with a very intense attack on British shipping in the Channel. This was, however, a probing attack, involving but slight penetration of the defences. A few days later, on 12th August, orders were given for the full-scale offensive. On 15th August the pattern changed, and a widespread attack by 1,800 German aircraft was carried out against all sorts of objectives. That evening Göring gave orders that all further attacks were to be directed solely against the RAF — its bases and communications, and especially against the main strength of Fighter Command deployed in a ring of airfields around London.

This second phase was, from the British point of view, the most dangerous of the whole battle. Concentrated attacks severely damaged airfields at North Weald, Hornchurch, and Debden, and Biggin Hill was so wrecked as to be temporarily out of action. All the fighter airfields suffered varying degrees of damage. The defence of these airfields was vital, and so intense were the operations that the pilots and airmen were near to exhaustion. The worst hit squadrons were sent north to quieter sectors to recuperate, but all too soon the 'rested' squadrons would have to return to the south-east. The situation was becoming desperate, and had the Germans persisted in their policy for another fortnight the

Seen from behind the undercarriage of a British Hawker Hurricane, an RAF pilot adjusts his parachute before going into action. Hanging from the face mask are the oxygen line and the lead for the pilot's radio-telephone, which fed information from the chain of radar stations and plotting-rooms, and rapidly vectored the eight-gun Hurricanes and Spitfires on to the incoming enemy bomber streams

result might well have been disastrous for Fighter Command.

Soon, however, affairs were to take a new turn. On the night of 23rd August the Germans bombed London, and the Prime Minister ordered a retaliatory attack on factories in Berlin. The night was almost too short for such an operation, but Bomber Command successfully carried it out. Hitler reacted promptly. He ordered that German air attacks should in future be directed against British industrial cities and towns, with London as the primary objective. Göring had told him that the air battle was all but won, and that the RAF was at its last gasp. Hitler believed that these new attacks would shatter British morale and pave the way for his invasion.

Invasion imminent

In fact, this change of emphasis in the third phase relieved the pressure on Fighter Command. Damaged runways and other airfield facilities were repaired, broken communications were quickly made good, and the Command's fighting capacity rapidly restored. On 7th September the Germans launched a tremendous attack, involving almost their whole strength. Wave after wave of bombers, escorted by hordes of fighters, crossed the coast. Many great fires were caused, especially in the London docks. Guided by the flames, the bombers continued the attacks through the hours of darkness. The damage and loss of life were grievous, but the British people were undaunted, and the over-all effect was far less catastrophic than the attack on the fighter airfields. An attempt to follow up these attacks on 8th September was repulsed with heavy losses.

There could be no doubt, however, that Operation Sea Lion was imminent, and on 7th September the British government issued a warning that invasion was probable during the next few days. That night the whole strength of Bomber Command was concentrated against the barges and military dumps in the Channel ports. The weather was good, and these attacks were highly successful. Night after night the bombers pounded the invasion ports. On 11th September Hitler postponed the date of Sea Lion to 24th September. But on the night of 13th September an especially successful bombing attack did enormous damage, sinking no less than eighty huge barges in the port of Ostend alone.

Göring remained optimistic. He assured Hitler that 'given four or five more days of good weather, the results would be decisive'. But another tremendous air assault on 15th September, which raged from dawn to dusk, suffered a severe defeat at the hands of Fighter Command. This day is generally regarded as the climax of the Battle of Britain.

On 17th September Hitler resolved to postpone Operation Sea Lion indefinitely. He realized, more clearly than did Göring, that the Luftwaffe had failed to defeat Fighter Command, and that he could no longer maintain his vast concentrations of barges, troops, and military stores in the Channel ports in the face of Bomber Command's devastating attacks. He gave orders for the remaining barges and stores to be dispersed, and the troops moved away from the danger areas around the ports.

Air reconnaissance soon confirmed that these German concentrations were melting away, and it was clear that the danger of immediate invasion was over. The supply of trained pilots had proved to be just sufficient, while the production of fighter aircraft just managed to cope with the wastage.

The German air force had failed utterly to achieve its aim of breaking Fighter Command, and had suffered severe losses in the attempt. It was not easy to assess these losses accurately. No doubt, at the time, the German losses were exaggerated, but this is inevitable in large-scale fighting in the air. But whatever the actual losses were, they were enough to call a halt to Göring's air attacks, while Bomber Command had destroyed a great part of the shipping and war material on which the invasion depended.

On 13th October Hitler postponed Operation Sea Lion until the spring of 1941, but in reality the plan was dead.

The Blitz continues

As the battle by day slowly died away, the fourth phase began and the German bombers were switched to night operations. There had been a fair number of night attacks during the day battle period, but these were not very heavy and were usually follow-up attacks of targets bombed during the preceding day.

The problems confronting aircraft operating in darkness were at that time largely unsolved. The bomber's problems were those of navigation by night, often in poor weather conditions over a blacked-out countryside, of target identification, and bomb-aiming. For the fighter there were the problems of finding the bomber in the dark, and making an effective attack on it.

The German bomber crews were not well trained or experienced in night operations. Hence they used a radio beam technique, called 'Knickebein' (crooked leg), which enabled a pilot to navigate by radio signals. The system had the disadvantage of being vulnerable to radio counter-measures. It could be interfered with by jamming, but the most successful method was to bend or deflect the beam.

By day the fighters could be vectored on to incoming enemy formations located by radar, and interception made relatively easy. By night, against a swarm of individual bombers, such methods failed. A means of interception had to be carried in the fighter itself. This was the AI (aircraft interception), which was at first fitted to the Blenheim, a fast bomber aircraft converted, in default of anything better, to a night-fighter. After many initial set-backs and failures, it was found possible to vector a night-fighter close enough to a bomber to pick it up on its AI, and a sighting made. But progress was slow. The Blenheim was not fast enough or well enough armed to be very successful.

Later in the period a new night-fighter, the Beaufighter, appeared. This was an adaptation of a sea-reconnaissance aircraft, the Beaufort. With improved AI, and armed with four 20-mm cannon and four machine-guns, it proved a most useful night-fighter. But it was not available in sufficient numbers until the night-blitz was almost over.

Considerable success was in fact achieved by the night air defences, but not enough to provide a deterrent.

The attacks on British towns and cities killed and wounded many civilians, and caused serious, if temporary, losses of industrial output. Indeed these losses, due not so much to the actual destruction of factories as to the disruption of gas, electricity, and water supplies, communications, and above all to absenteeism caused by the destruction of workers' dwellings, gave the British a somewhat exaggerated idea of the effectiveness of such operations.

For centuries, except for a few civil wars long ago, the British people had been used to the idea that battles were fought on the high seas, or far away in other countries and were exclusively the business of the armed forces. The First World War disturbed, but did not destroy, these beliefs.

The direct attack from the air on their homes and places of work shocked and angered the British people, but they were not dismayed. A new spirit of neighbourly friendship and concern developed. Little had been known, in the absence of actual experience, of the behaviour of a civilized population under air attack, and on the whole the courage and endurance of the British people exceeded most official expectations.

With the coming of the shorter summer nights the night bombing attacks died down, and when in June 1941 Hitler began the invasion of Russia, his bombers were moved to the Eastern Front.

The Battle of Britain had been fought and won. But it was not the beginning of the end of the war, but the end of the beginning.

The Battle of the Atlantic

The Second World War was only a few hours old when the British passenger liner *Athenia* was sunk in the Atlantic without warning by a torpedo from the German submarine U30. The loss of the liner, carrying a number of children, sent a wave of indignation through the country and persuaded the Admiralty to institute a convoy system for the protection of Allied merchant shipping.

The two main convoy systems were the east-west transatlantic convoys to and from North America and the north-south convoys to and from the South Atlantic, the Mediterranean, and West Africa. Although the very act of concentrating shipping into compact bodies in this way gave them a measure of immunity from attack by making them harder for an enemy to locate, warship escort was obviously essential. However, Admiralty policy had been to organize shipping into convoy only if the enemy resorted to unrestricted submarine warfare, believing that Hitler's navy would abide by the conditions for submarine warfare laid down by the Hague Convention, and no steps had been taken to acquire ships suitable for anti-submarine escort. The anti-submarine force available in September 1939 consisted of 150 destroyers (including those required to operate with the Fleet), six coastal patrol vessels, and twenty-four sloops.

With this number it was only usually possible to give convoys an escort of two ships. Fortunately the Germans entered the war possessing only forty-eight operational submarines, though a programme for rapid expansion was put in hand at the end of 1939. For the first eight months of the war, therefore, the scale of attack was small, almost ceased during the Norwegian campaign when the U-boats were recalled to take part in it, and was concentrated almost entirely on ships sailing independently.

U-boat commanders who did attack convoys, using the conventional method of approaching and firing submerged, came up against the combination in the escorts of the 'asdic' which could detect and locate them and the depth charge which, if accurately placed, could sink them. Asdic, details of which had been kept secret, was a device with which the range and bearing of an object under water could be determined, by transmitting a narrow sound beam of very high frequency and measuring the time taken for an echo from it to return.

Near the end of the Norwegian campaign in May 1940 the U-boats reverted to attacks on merchant shipping and, when the fall of France gave them bases from which the Atlantic trade routes could be easily reached, the Battle of the Atlantic began. The sinking of eleven German submarines in the first six months of the war by destroyers had induced a respect for the asdic among U-boat commanders. They therefore concentrated on unescorted ships whenever possible. These consisted not only of independently routed ships, of which there was still a large number, but also ships which had, for one reason or another, 'straggled' from their convoys, and ships from outward-bound Atlantic convoys which had been dispersed when the escorts left them to meet homeward-bound convoys. This took place at first some 200 miles west of Ireland, and extended a further 200 miles by the autumn of 1940, the limit imposed by the fuel endurance of the escorting destroyers.

Beyond this no anti-submarine protection for our merchant shipping could be given. Coupled with the desperate shortage of destroyers as a result of the number sunk or damaged in the Dunkirk operations and the need for others to be deployed on anti-invasion duties, this provided the U-boats with what their commanders were to call the first 'Happy Time'. In the period July to October 1940, 144 unescorted ships were sent to the bottom. Such convoys as were located were so meagerly escorted that they could be attacked with near impunity. From them seventy-three more ships were sunk. Only two U-boats were destroyed in reply by convoy escorts. The majority of the U-boats' attacks were made by night, operating on the surface where they enjoyed high speed and manoeuvrability. The U-boats' night attacks not only confirmed that their low silhouette made them virtually invisible against the dark background of the sea from the bridge of a ship high above them; they also discovered a fatal flaw in the asdic. Its performance against a surfaced submarine was almost negligible. Until the development of an effective ship-borne radar at the end of 1941, the advantage in a night-encounter, even with a destroyer, lay with the U-boat.

It was at this time, too, that another main feature of the tactics of the U-boats was first developed, the deployment of a number

Top: Commander F.J.Walker, the most successful U-boat killer of the war.
Centre: Otto Kretschmer, the top-scoring U-boat commander. He was taken prisoner when his U99 was destroyed in March 1941. Bottom: Günther Prien, another U-boat ace. In 1939 his U47 penetrated Scapa Flow and sank HMS Royal Oak. U47 was lost in March 1941 with all hands

Germany's Triumph

of them on a patrol line across the convoy route and their concentration into a 'wolf-pack' as soon as the convoy was located. It was immediately spectacularly successful.

The slow, homeward-bound convoy SC7 of thirty-four ships, which left Nova Scotia on 5th October 1940 with the solitary escort of a slow, lightly-armed sloop, had plugged through heavy seas to 500 miles west of Ireland by the 16th. There it was met by two more escorts – another sloop and one of the new Flower-class corvettes.

There, too, it was located by a lone U-boat which signalled its position, course, and speed to headquarters before attacking in the moonlight that night and sinking two ships. The escorts, engaged in picking up survivors and hunting vainly for the attacker, left the convoy to steam on without even their meagre support until the following evening when two of them were able to rejoin in time to suffer attack by another solitary U-boat. It achieved only a single torpedo hit which damaged but did not sink a freighter. Another sloop and a corvette now joined the escort, the corvette being directed to stand by the crippled ship.

There were thus two sloops and a corvette with the convoy when darkness fell on the evening of the 18th.

Just over the horizon ahead six U-boats of a patrol line, alerted by the sighting report, had been concentrating. Among them were two top-scoring 'aces', Joachim Schepke of U100 and Otto Kretschmer of U99. During the night that followed fourteen ships were sunk, seven of them by U99. The distracted escorts, unable to locate the attackers, could do nothing but pick up the crews of the sunken ships. By the morning the dwindling convoy had virtually disintegrated. Including three stragglers, which suffered the usual fate of such ships, twenty had been sunk and two more damaged out of the thirty-four which had set out. The remainder made their way individually to port, saved from further attack by the discovery of a fresh convoy for the wolves, the fast HX79 following two days behind SC7.

There the same scenes of destruction, the same failure by the escorts, either to defend their charges or exact any retribution, re-enacted themselves, twelve ships being sunk and two more damaged out of a convoy of forty-nine.

Another small pack attack mounted against a convoy in December 1940 sank eleven ships and the escorting armed merchant cruiser. Such shocking losses led to a searching enquiry to seek a solution.

One of the shortcomings in the defence was the lack of fast escort destroyers which had been held back in the anti-invasion forces. They were now released for trade protection duties. Strengthening of the convoy escorts in this way paid an encouraging dividend, three U-boats being destroyed by them in November 1940, the first success for five months. There were still too few destroyers to do more than add a leavening to the inexperienced and ill-equipped corvettes, however.

The prime antidote to the wolf-pack tactics – air escort – was in fact available but denied to the navy by priority decisions. The only long-range aircraft available to Coastal Command for support of the convoys were a few Sunderland flying-boats. Twin-engined planes of the Command came to join them when the onset of winter released them from anti-invasion reconnaissance duties.

In conjunction with much foul weather, these factors caused something of a lull in the battle during the winter of 1940-41, following the holocaust of October. But while escort numbers were slowly growing, so were those of the U-boat fleet which numbered under thirty in 1940. None was lost between November 1940 and March 1941 and meanwhile the numbers were growing. An ominous feature of this period, also, was the first appearance of U-boats on

the convoy route between Britain and Freetown, Sierra Leone, the assembly port for the large and vital trade with the Orient which, until the entry of Italy into the war, had passed through the Mediterranean and the Suez Canal. The spring of 1941 therefore saw a large upsurge of activity.

Although the Battle of the Atlantic refers primarily to the long struggle waged between the German U-boats and convoy escorts for control of the vital Atlantic lifelines, other forms of attack were also developed, each calling for specialized efforts to counter them.

First in point of time came the commerce-raiding cruise of the pocket-battleship *Admiral Graf Spee*. Her interception by a group of three British cruisers off the River Plate in December 1939, and her subsequent scuttling outside Montevideo harbour had all the elements of high drama. Her depredations had only amounted to nine ships sunk in three months, however. Her sister ship *Deutschland*, operating in the North Atlantic, accounted for only two merchantmen in two months before returning to Germany.

In October 1940 the Germans once again

Above: From a U-boat's conning-tower, German officers scan the horizon for the telltale smoke signals of a convoy. Left: Crew of a torpedoed merchant ship being picked up by an escort vessel. Right: On the bridge of an escorting destroyer on convoy duty in the Atlantic. As convoy escort improved the U-boats moved to new hunting grounds

loosed a major warship on the Atlantic trade routes. This was the pocket-battle-ship *Admiral Scheer*. Almost her first en-counter was with a convoy of thirty-seven ships, escorted only by the armed merchant cruiser *Jervis Bay* which steamed out against her in gallant defiance. By the time the *Jervis Bay* had been sunk, the convoy had been able to scatter to such an extent that the *Scheer* was only able to catch and sink five of the merchantmen. The pocket-battleship went on to make a five-months' cruise in the South Atlantic and Indian Ocean during which she sank sixteen ships before returning to Germany.

A greater menace were the battlecruisers *Scharnhorst* and *Gneisenau* which broke out into the Atlantic on the 7th February 1941. They sank twenty-two independently steaming ships before the two ships re-

turned safely to Brest on 22nd March.

The last and potentially the most serious attempt to use major warships against Allied convoys was the famous foray of the giant battleship *Bismarck* in company with the cruiser *Prinz Eugen* in May 1941. Intercepted by the battleships *Hood* and *Prince of Wales*, the *Bismarck* sank the *Hood*; but, damaged by the *Prince of Wales*, and by a torpedo attack by aircraft from the carrier *Victorious*, she was forced to make for Brest for repairs, only to be again tor-pedoed and crippled by aircraft from the *Ark Royal*, and finally overwhelmed by the massed power of the Home Fleet. The *Prinz Eugen* escaped to Brest having accom-plished nothing.

Alarming as these various forays by surface warships were, the sum of their achievements were small compared to those

of the U-boat fleet whose head, Admiral Karl Dönitz, never ceased to press for priority to be given to the one arm which he rightly believed could bring victory to Ger-many. That he was never listened to or given a free hand is perhaps the principal cause of his ultimate failure.

The other main threat to Atlantic con-voys was that of long-range Focke-Wulf Condors, adaptations of civil aircraft. Operating from Bordeaux from August 1940, they caused serious shipping losses, some convoys having U-boats homed on to them while others were attacked by groups of Condors directed on to them by shadowing U-boats.

Steps to combat the new menace were taken. Surface escorts were reinforced as much as possible, long-range fighter escorts were provided from bases in Northern Ire-

Germany's Triumph

land and anti-aircraft guns, manned by army crews, were mounted in merchantmen. On other ships a catapult was mounted from which a Hurricane fighter could be launched, the pilot baling out or 'ditching' his aircraft on completion of his mission. Deterred from bombing by these measures, the Condors reverted to their original task, reconnoitring the north-south convoy routes to and from Gibraltar and Sierra Leone.

U-boat war—measure and counter-measure

Meanwhile, on the transatlantic convoy routes, the battle had been a straight fight between the U-boats and the surface escorts supported by the slowly increasing but still scanty reconnaissance aircraft of Coastal Command. The majority of these were of medium endurance and their chief effect was to push the area of operations westwards, beyond their range. It was thus in an area south of Iceland that the first major encounters of the spring of 1941 took place.

During the winter lull, the steps taken to improve the quantity and quality of the convoy escorts under the control of the newly-established Western Approaches Command at Liverpool had borne fruit. Dönitz's 'aces' found much tougher opposition when they attacked an outward convoy in the first days of March. Sinking two freighters and damaging two more, they lost one of their own number and two others were forced to withdraw damaged. Continuing to shadow the convoy, Günther Prien's U47, in which he had achieved a hero's reputation by penetrating Scapa Flow in October 1939 to sink the battleship *Royal Oak*, was caught and sunk with all hands.

A week later the wolf-pack was directed on to a homeward convoy in the same area. Five ships were sunk in a single night; but before dawn two more U-boat 'aces' had been eliminated. Schepke had gone down with U100; Otto Kretschmer and the crew of U99 were prisoners in the escort commander's ship.

During this month it cost the Germans five U-boats to sink nineteen ships in convoy. They were shifted farther west again so as to catch the convoys before they joined their anti-submarine escorts. The result was the massacre of a slow convoy intercepted south-east of Greenland before its anti-submarine escort had joined. In reply the Admiralty based groups and aircraft in Iceland which could give escort as far as longitude 35° west (roughly 1,200 miles west of Ireland).

The ocean wastes to the south and south-east of Cape Farewell, Greenland, now became the U-boats' chosen field. At the end of May an unescorted convoy south of Greenland lost nine ships. On the other hand when the wolf-packs tried their luck

in June with a convoy which had picked up its escort, they lost two of their number in sinking five merchantmen. The total number of ships sunk by U-boats was steadily rising—from forty-two in April to sixty-one in June. But only twenty per cent of these were in convoy where escorts destroyed five U-boats in reply.

The lesson was plain to see and in July 1941 the Admiralty at last had the resources to benefit from it. Besides the over-age 'four-stacker' destroyers, acquired from the USA under Lend-Lease, and the large number of Flower-class corvettes coming from British shipyards, other corvettes built in Canada were being manned by the Royal Canadian Navy as well as seven of the 'four-stackers'. A Newfoundland Escort Force was formed in May, based at St John's, Newfoundland, which gave escort—weak at first but slowly growing—over the western portion of the convoy route. Thus end-to-end escort was now effective over the east-west trade route.

Frustrated in their search for easy prey on the transatlantic route, Dönitz sent U-boats south to the Freetown area. A rich harvest was reaped for a while, no less than eighty-one unescorted ships being sunk. Then end-to-end escort was extended to this route also. There were no soft spots now left. The U-boats would have to face the escorts to reach their prey.

For a while they concentrated in the Western and South-Western Approaches against the Freetown and Gibraltar convoys where it was hoped that in co-operation with the Condor aircraft the earlier successes might be repeated. But this brought the encounters inside the range of Coastal Command's long and medium range aircraft and into an area in which it was possible to give the convoys a large escort. The German move proved a failure and once again Dönitz sought a weak spot on the far side of the Atlantic where the escort groups provided by the Royal Canadian Navy were weak in numbers and experience. In September he found it when a slow, homeward-bound convoy was beset by a group of seventeen U-boats and in two days lost sixteen ships before an escort group from Iceland came to the rescue.

No way of strengthening the defence of the western portion of the convoy route was open to the Admiralty at this time. Dönitz prepared to take advantage of the fact; the disasters of a year earlier might have been repeated. But at this moment Hitler stepped in with an order for the entire force of operational U-boats to be transferred to the Mediterranean, where the fate of Rommel's Afrika Korps was being put in jeopardy by British domination of his sea supply routes, and to the approaches to the Straits of Gibraltar.

Although this greatly eased the situa-

tion on the transatlantic route at a critical moment, it brought the Gibraltar convoys once again under concentrated attacks. A combination of air and U-boat attack inflicted heavy losses on two of them. Two of the factors which were eventually to decide the Battle of the Atlantic in favour of the Allies were now, however, introduced.

A victory for the escorts

An escort group permanently organized and intensively trained under its own regular leader, such as had already been deployed on the transatlantic route, was allocated to the Gibraltar run. Its leader, Commander F.J.Walker, RN, was to become the most successful U-boat killer of the war. At the same time the first escort aircraft carrier, *HMS Audacity*, was also put into service.

A combination of these two factors inflicted the heaviest defeat so far suffered by the U-boats, when a wolf-pack supported by Condor aircraft concentrated on a homeward bound Gibraltar convoy in December 1941. Four U-boats were sunk, two Condors were destroyed, another two damaged. Two of the convoy, an escort and the *Audacity* herself were sunk.

In spite of the calamitous loss of the only British escort carrier as yet in existence, both sides saw this encounter as a notable victory for the escorts. The use of the long-range aircraft was abandoned, the Condor squadron being dispersed to other functions. The swing of the pendulum was clearly moving towards Allied superiority. Escorts were increasing in numerical strength and efficiency.

Up to this time, since the beginning of the war, shipping losses had exceeded replacements by nearly 7,000,000 tons, the great majority of the casualties being ships which for one reason or another were not sailing in convoy. These figures meant that the Allies had been slowly but steadily losing the battle along the trade routes. Now, however, with nearly all but the fastest ships absorbed into the convoy system and with the convoy defences being at last perfected, it could be expected with some confidence that the trend would be halted or reversed.

Then, on 7th December 1941, the whole situation was changed. Following the Japanese attack on Pearl Harbour, Hitler declared war on the United States. Immediately the stream of merchant shipping passing along the eastern seaboard of the United States, which had been immune to attack since the American declaration of a Security Zone covering those waters, became exposed to attack. A new 'Happy Time' for the U-boat commanders began, marked by a veritable holocaust of Allied merchant ships.

America, the Arsenal of Democracy

When war broke out in 1939 an overwhelming majority of the American people favoured neutrality for the United States. This was the natural outcome of almost two decades of isolationist sentiment. President Harding's call for a 'return to normalcy' in the 1920's first enshrined the doctrine. His successors continued it. When war broke out in Spain in 1936, President Franklin Roosevelt declared: 'We shun political commitments which might entangle us in foreign wars. . . . We seek to isolate ourselves completely from war.' In March 1937 a Gallup poll showed that ninety-four per cent of the American people wished the United States to keep out of all foreign wars. By 1939, this had risen to ninety-nine per cent. If Great Britain and France looked to the United States for assistance against Germany, therefore, the American mood was not auspicious.

On 3rd September 1939 President Roosevelt broadcast to the American people: 'This nation will remain a neutral nation, but I cannot ask that every American remain neutral in thought as well. . . .' Roosevelt's words provide a clue to his private thoughts. When war came to Europe, Roosevelt had two main aims for the United States: he wished to keep America out of the war, and he wished to prevent further Nazi aggression. These two aims were to prove mutually exclusive. Privately, Roosevelt favoured the cause of Great Britain, France, and the democracies, but neutrality was already built into American statutes. The Neutrality Act of 1937 prohibited the export of arms and munitions to all belligerent powers. Apart from this, powerful members of the Congress were determined that the United States should have no part in the European war.

Yet as Hitler's armies marched through Poland in September 1939, crushing all resistance in a matter of weeks, Roosevelt was faced with an uncomfortable truth. The American arms embargo favoured the Nazis—efficiently prepared and already geared for war. The United States was denying the unprepared democracies the arms and munitions they desperately needed to face Hitler's war machine.

Roosevelt acted quickly. In a message to Congress on 21st September he called for a repeal of the arms embargo. At the end of a fierce debate in Congress, the Neutrality Act of 1939 was passed on 4th November. This act repealed the arms embargo and allowed the belligerents to buy munitions and supplies from the United States provided they paid cash and provided they transported all such supplies in non-American ships. This 'cash and carry'

policy undoubtedly favoured Great Britain and France, who had command of the seas. Their interests were further served by another American proclamation which excluded submarines from American territorial waters while allowing armed merchant vessels to use the same waters.

Despite the new 'cash and carry' policy, however, there were severe limitations on the amount of munitions and supplies Great Britain and France could hope for from the United States. The American economy was not adapted to war production. During the New Deal era the nation's resources had been devoted to peaceful, domestic programmes. In 1939, as in 1914, the United States was unprepared for war. Moreover, although the conflagration in Europe was now uppermost in Roosevelt's mind, the United States faced dangers in the Far East, where Japan's mounting ambitions showed clearly that the United States could not afford to distribute all its available munitions and supplies to the European democracies, however desperate their need.

By spring, 1940, however, President Roosevelt was faced with the disagreeable —and dangerous—possibility that Hitler might indeed become master of Europe. April brought the invasion of Norway and Denmark. May saw the fall of Belgium and the Netherlands. When Italy declared war on France, President Roosevelt cast aside all pretence of impartiality, saying: 'The hand that held the dagger has struck it in the back of its neighbour.'

In his annual budget message of January 1940 President Roosevelt requested $1,800 million for national defence. In May he requested additional expenditure of more than $1,000 million. Both requests were granted. Roosevelt could now turn more hopefully to Winston Churchill's urgent requests for arms and supplies. In June the United States War Department sold to Great Britain more than $43 million worth of arms, munitions, and aircraft. These were valuable, though most were drawn from outdated stocks and supplies. For Great Britain, the most urgent need was for warships, to help fight the submarine menace and retain mastery of the seas.

In May 1940 Churchill made a direct request to Roosevelt for fifty old American destroyers to help repair British losses

Two currents in American feeling, 1940.
Above: *Comment on reluctance to face reality of Nazi threat—an attitude fast losing ground.* ***Below:*** *Preparing for war—Boeing works, Seattle, building Flying Fortresses*

Germany's Triumph

and protect the merchant fleets. American law prohibited the sale or loan of American warships, yet to deny or even to delay this assistance might mean defeat for both Great Britain and France. The German armies were already penetrating deep into France. When France fell, the Battle of Britain began and the Battle of the Atlantic continued with renewed ferocity.

Roosevelt was acutely anxious to help Great Britain in her plight, but he could not move too far ahead of American public opinion. Powerful members of the Senate were watching his movements and the direction of his policies. Many members of Congress had vivid memories of America's part in the First World War, and were bitterly opposed to any American participation in another European war. Moreover, 1940 was a presidential election year, and Roosevelt had to decide whether he should relinquish office or stand again for election. He had already served two four-year terms, and tradition and convention decreed that he should not seek a third term. But this was a time of crisis, and Roosevelt was convinced that it was his duty to serve if the nation wished him to. He declared his availability and meanwhile continued to give his unremitting attention to events in Europe.

As the Battle of Britain developed, Churchill bombarded Roosevelt with requests for help. Roosevelt knew that his critics would seize on any action calculated to involve the United States in war with Germany. Churchill's request for fifty destroyers was thus a delicate affair. By a shrewd political stroke, Roosevelt arranged to 'trade' the destroyers for ninety-nine year leases on a number of British bases in the American hemisphere, from Newfoundland to the Caribbean. Roosevelt could thus claim that the deal not only

provided for American security but was an excellent bargain for the price of fifty outdated destroyers.

American public opinion applauded the President's action, even though members of Congress grumbled at this use of executive power without the consent of Congress. For Winston Churchill, the occasion marked a new phase in Anglo-American co-operation. In the best Churchillian style he observed:

'These two great organizations of the English-speaking democracies, the British Empire and the United States, will have to be somewhat mixed up together in some of their affairs for mutual and general advantage. For my part . . . I do not view the process with any misgivings. No one can stop it. Like the Mississippi, it just keeps rolling along. Let it roll. Let it roll on full flood, inexorable, irresistible, to broader land and better days.'

In the November 1940 elections, Roosevelt defeated the Republican candidate Wendell Willkie. He could now claim another four-year mandate for his conduct of affairs. Churchill had already told Roosevelt in a long, secret memorandum that Great Britain's financial resources were rapidly running out and that she could no longer afford to pay for munitions on the 'cash and carry' basis. With his re-election confirmed, Roosevelt now devised a bold and imaginative policy to assist Great Britain. This policy was a 'Lend-Lease' programme, whereby the President was empowered to sell, transfer, exchange, lease, or lend war supplies to any nation whose defence was deemed by the President to be 'vital to the defence of the United States'. Roosevelt prepared the ground in a dramatic speech on 30th December 1940, calling for 'all out aid' to Great Britain and her allies. The United States, Roosevelt declared, must become the 'arsenal of democracy'.

The Lend-Lease Bill was introduced into Congress in January 1941. A prolonged and bitter debate followed. Isolationist senators such as Senator Burton K. Wheeler of Montana suspected a covert plan to bring the United States into the war. Others resented these new additions to the President's executive powers. But the President was assisted by his fresh mandate, and the favourable public reaction to his broadcast 'fireside chats' in which he brought home to the people the full extent of the Nazi menace. In March 1941 the Lend-Lease Bill became law. From now on the United States could indeed become the arsenal of democracy.

Such was the intention, though practical problems remained. An initial appropriation of $7,000 million was granted by Congress, but the American economy was not yet geared to war production. Nevertheless the capacity was there, if government and

industry combined to plan; and fortunately the experience of the New Deal, together with the planning expertise it bequeathed, helped to ease the transition.

Again, Roosevelt demonstrated his knack of picking the right men for the right job, for in Henry L. Stimson as secretary for war, Cordell Hull as secretary of state, and General George C. Marshall as Chief of the Army General Staff, he had advisers fully alive both to the urgency of the hour and also to the requirements of American policy. These men knew that in modern warfare, military strategy must be firmly linked to the world of science and technology. To take one example, air power

*Left: US Army poster, produced after the United States entered the war, extols her new tanks. **Below:** Reporters watch one of 50 US destroyers the Allies were given in exchange for bases before lend-lease opened the way to all-out US aid*

Joker from pack of war-time cards depicts Hitler being burned by the flame from the torch of Liberty

must be given a central role in all strategic thinking and planning, and not merely a peripheral role as hitherto. American logistical planning followed these determinants. Between 1940 and the end of 1944, the production of military aircraft rose from 23,000 per annum to 96,000. Military advisers also took note of the vital part played by Panzer divisions in the German victories. Accordingly, tank production was increased from 4,000 in 1940-41 to almost 30,000 in 1943.

Innovation and invention went hand in hand with greater efficiency in production. The assembly lines of the vast Detroit automobile factories were re-tooled and given over to the mass production of planes, armoured vehicles, and the engines of war. New methods of ship construction were devised and exploited, until American yards could claim to be launching a warship every day. The combination of American engineering and technology with boundless resources of coal, iron, and steel soon tipped the economic balance of power, even though Hitler's military successes in Europe and North Africa still made the outcome of the war uncertain.

Meanwhile, as Great Britain faced Hitler alone in Western Europe, Churchill took pains to further the Anglo-American alliance. British military secrets were passed to United States political and military experts in London, and joint consultation at the level of strategic planning became one of the less publicized aspects of Churchill's

direction of the war. In August 1941 Roosevelt and Churchill held secret meetings aboard the US cruiser *Augusta* off Newfoundland. From these meetings the two leaders issued the Atlantic Charter, a declaration of common aims and purposes. Among them were opposition to all forms of territorial aggrandizement, support for the right of all peoples to choose their own form of government, freedom from want and fear, freedom of the seas, and the disarmament of aggressor nations until a permanent peace-keeping organization was securely established.

By now, the United States was firmly on the side of the Allies, though Hitler was prudently avoiding a direct confrontation with the United States. Events moved a step nearer war with Germany when a U-boat attacked the *USS Greer* and brought American naval strength into direct conflict with German naval vessels. From then on, American warships had the President's orders to 'shoot first'.

On 7th December, when Japan perpetrated its 'day of infamy' by its attack on the American fleet at Pearl Harbour, the remaining vestiges of isolationist sentiment in the United States vanished. America now had a common cause with the democracies against the Axis powers. On 8th December, with only one dissenting voice in Congress, the United States declared war on Japan. Three days later Germany and Italy declared war on the United States, and the President and Congress recognized a state of war with these nations. The 'arsenal of democracy' now brought its army, its navy, and its air force to the task of defeating the Axis powers. The final result of the war was no longer in doubt.

America's economy is geared to war

American industry turned to full-scale wartime production. New plants were constructed in a matter of days. Six million women were added to the labour force as selective service took labour away from factory and farm. Older men returned to work and the unemployed were quickly drawn into the national effort. Between 1940 and 1943 the total labour force increased by eight million, from forty-seven to fifty-five million. The working week was increased from forty to forty-eight hours. By 1942, more fighter planes were being produced in one month than had been produced in the whole of 1939. Between Pearl Harbour and the end of the war the United States produced more than 295,000 aeroplanes. Germany's production was less than a third of this, a fact which made it certain that Germany would lose the mastery of the skies.

Not all of American expertise was given to the production and development of conventional weapons. As early as the autumn

of 1939, when Albert Einstein warned President Roosevelt that Germany was seeking to develop an atom bomb, federal funds were channelled into an atomic energy programme. Research and development proceeded with the utmost secrecy at Oak Ridge, Tennessee, and Los Alamos, New Mexico. In December 1942 physicists produced a controlled chain reaction in an atomic pile at the University of Chicago. Following this, federal funds of more than $2,000 million were poured into the development of an atomic bomb, although the first successful test did not take place until after the defeat of Germany in 1945.

By the autumn of 1943 Churchill, Roosevelt, and Stalin realized that the defeat of Germany was only a matter of time. The 'Big Three' discussed plans for a post-war settlement in conferences at Tehran and later at Yalta. Roosevelt and Churchill developed a close personal friendship in Anglo-American discussions at Casablanca and at Washington in 1943. Two further meetings at Cairo that same year cemented their friendship. Their common language, and the fact that both Roosevelt and Churchill found Stalin a somewhat impenetrable figure, inevitably brought the two English-speaking allies into closer counsel. Churchill, needless to say, was entirely happy at this development, even though the American President had doubts about Great Britain's apparent aim of preserving her Empire after the war.

In the field, military commanders did not always see eye to eye on strategy or tactics. When General Dwight D. Eisenhower was made Supreme Commander for the invasion of Western Europe, his commander in the field, General Montgomery, was a loyal but not an altogether uncritical colleague. Nevertheless, combined operations worked remarkably smoothly on land, sea, and in the air.

The final victory over Germany owed something to a common language, but much more to a common set of ideals. If Franklin Roosevelt had not declared the United States the 'arsenal of democracy' in December 1940; if he had not used his presidential power to hurry the Lend-Lease Bill through Congress, we may doubt—as Churchill doubted—that Great Britain could have survived her 'darkest hour'. It would be easy for Europeans to underestimate the skill and determination required by Roosevelt to bring the United States into the war on the side of the Allies. It is worth recalling that on the eve of the presidential election of 1940 Roosevelt's opponent wrung from him a categorical promise to the American people that: 'Your boys are not going to be sent into any foreign wars.' Fortunately for Great Britain, fortunately for Europe, President Roosevelt did not keep this promise.

The Desert War

In the months before the outbreak of war the importance of the Middle East in British grand strategical planning gradually increased. As early as spring 1939 the British and French staffs decided that in the event of war ,Italy rather than Germany would offer the best prospects for Allied offensive action in the early years. The Italian colony of Libya was sandwiched between the French in Tunisia and the British in Egypt, while Italian East Africa would be a wasting asset cut off from home. At the same time British and French forces in Palestine, Iraq, and Syria were well placed to support Turkey.

The fall of France in June 1940 obliterated these happy prospects. At once the balance of naval and military power swung in Italy's favour – indeed it was only the certainty that France was already beaten that induced Mussolini, the Italian dictator, to declare war. Now it was the British whose position in the Middle East was precarious. Against some 500,000 Italian troops, the Commander-in-Chief Middle East Land Forces, General Sir Archibald Wavell, could muster only some 60,000 to defend a theatre of war 1,700 miles by 2,000 miles, a theatre which encompassed nine countries from Iraq to Somaliland.

The importance of the Middle East to the British no longer lay in the Suez Canal route to the East, because the neutralization of the French fleet left the Royal Navy alone too weak to command the whole Mediterranean sea-route from Gibraltar to Egypt. The importance lay in the oil of the Persian Gulf. Its loss would throw Great Britain into dependence on dollar oil from the Americas, while on the other hand its possession by the Axis powers would solve their chronic fuel problems.

The most direct and serious threat to the oil was posed by the Italian army in Libya, some 300,000 men; and the most suitable place to parry the threat was Egypt. From a naval standpoint, the Egyptian port of Alexandria was the base for British sea-power in the eastern Mediterranean, while the Suez Canal was its emergency exit. From a military point of view Egypt

simultaneously blocked the invasion routes up the Nile into the Sudan, eastwards to the Persian Gulf, and northwards into Syria towards Turkey. Retention of Egypt would also hold enemy heavy bombers out of effective range of the Gulf oilfields. Lastly Egypt offered many advantages as a main theatre base – good ports and communications, abundant water and labour.

Thus the whole North African campaign from 1940 to 1943 arose from the need to defend the Persian Gulf oilfields from Egypt – and Egypt from the Western Desert. The area of desert where the battles of 1940-42 were fought stretches nearly 400 miles from El Alamein in the east to Derna in the west. The only road follows the coast. The railway from the Nile Delta ended at Mersa Matruh until extended by the army. The one dominating physical feature is a 500-ft escarpment facing north to the coastal plain, and descending from the limestone plateau where the armies manoeuvred. The desert is a featureless waste of gravel and scrub, dotted with ancient cisterns and tombs of sheiks. Armies therefore moved almost with the freedom of fleets, navigating by compass and the stars. However all supplies and water had to be imported. Long columns of trucks from horizon to horizon sustained the fighting troops, while dumps and water pipelines were the jugular veins exposed to enemy armour. The Desert Campaign constituted a unique episode in the history of warfare – war in its purest form, unencumbered by civilians and habitations except along the coast, or by natural obstacles other than the escarpment.

Wavell appointed Major-General R.N. O'Connor to command Western Desert Force. O'Connor, a small, immensely alert and alive man, had a reputation for high intelligence and unorthodoxy. He soon won and always retained the complete confidence of his officers and men. Immediately Italy entered the war on 11th June 1940, raids and ambushes on Italian territory established British moral superiority. However, Wavell's great weakness forced him to stand everywhere on the defensive for the time being, and so Western Desert Force was withdrawn to Mersa Matruh to await the expected Italian invasion of Egypt. This materialized only on 15th September after Mussolini had repeatedly prodded his reluctant commander, Marshal Rodolpho Graziani. Graziani halted after advancing some sixty miles and proceeded to organize his army in a series of defended camps stretching some fifteen miles inland from the coast at Sidi Barrani.

Left: Supply and defence for the Afrika Korps: Junkers 52 transports and Me 110 fighters on a Luftwaffe base in the desert. **Right:** *The Campaign generals.* **Top:** *Graziani, the Italian commander.* **Centre:** *An immaculately attired Wavell (right), talks to his Western Desert Force Commander O'Connor, January 1941.* **Bottom:** *Auchinleck (right), with New Zealand General Bernard Freyberg*

Italians surrendering at Bardia. Their strength of numbers was not enough to counter superior British leadership and equipment. O'Connor's 36,000-strong force had already taken 38,000 prisoners in its December offensive, and then in January took another 40,000 in Bardia. The Italians often showed immense individual heroism, but consistently failed where large-scale organization was demanded

It was his intention to march on the Nile Delta once he had built up supplies, metalled the coast road, and laid water pipelines. O'Connor on his part had prepared a model defensive battle at Matruh for Graziani's reception, to culminate with a counter-stroke by all the British armour. But Graziani never came. Instead the British prepared their own offensive.

Although Great Britain herself was threatened by invasion, and her home defence forces were terrifyingly weak, the Prime Minister, Winston Churchill, took the great risk of shipping 150 tanks to the Middle East. For it was the Middle East that was now the only place where there was contact between British and enemy ground forces, and attacking the Italians offered the best hope of a resounding victory to set against the catastrophes of the year. This belief was shared by the c-in-c, General Wavell, whose selected victim was the Duke of Aosta and his garrison of Italian East Africa, cut off from aid and reinforcements from Italy. However, before Wavell could open a campaign so far from Egypt, the threat from Graziani had to be neutralized. He therefore ordered O'Connor to plan a spoiling attack to last five days, after which O'Connor's infantry division would be wanted for Eritrea. O'Connor instead aimed at a decisive victory.

There were two groups of Italian fortified camps, separated by a gap in the centre, the Tummars and Nibeiwa near the coast, and the Rabia and Sofafi camps further inland, garrisoned by three divisions with tanks in support. Well to the rear and widely separated were another six divisions. No one could foretell how the army of Fascist Italy would fight. Although Italian tanks were known to be poor, their artillery outnumbered the British by two to one.

O'Connor's own forces numbered 36,000 men, organized in two divisions, 4th Indian (infantry) and 7th Armoured, together with a mixed group called Selby Force after its brigadier. 4th Indian Division, together with fifty-seven heavily armoured 'I' (infantry co-operation) tanks, was to assault, while 7th Armoured, with its cruiser-tanks, was to protect the British flank and then exploit and pursue. Western Desert Force was thoroughly well-trained, with a high proportion of professional soldiers. O'Connor's plan was bold and unorthodox. The assault force penetrated through the gap in the centre of the Italian camps and assaulted from the west, the Italian rear. At the same time British artillery, without waiting to register, opened heavy surprise fire from the east to demoralize and confuse the Italians. The British force had thus to assemble within the enemy's defence zone and make an approach march through his defences. The risks paid splendidly. On the first day of the offensive (9th December 1940), the Italians were taken completely by surprise, and although they fought stoutly, their camps fell one by one, Nibeiwa first, then the Tummars, while the British armour cut the coast road between Sidi Barrani and Buq Buq. The remaining camps were abandoned and the armour pursued the routed enemy towards the Libyan frontier.

In two days' fighting O'Connor had ended the threat to Egypt, smashed two Italian corps, taken 38,000 prisoners (including four generals), 73 tanks, and 37 guns at the cost of only 624 killed, wounded and missing. It was exactly the kind of victory the British at home needed in the grim winter of the Blitz. It also fulfilled Wavell's purpose and enabled him to withdraw the Indian division for use in Eritrea.

This was one of the decisive moments of the whole North African campaign. Wavell's strategic intention in the desert was defensive; O'Connor was expected now to halt, although not specifically ordered to do so. However, O'Connor pressed on with the forces remaining to him. By 16th December he had closely invested the fortress of Bardia, just inside Libya. His continued success induced Wavell to send him the understrength 6th Australian Division in place of the Indians. Thus the strategy of the campaign changed from the defensive to the offensive, and the consequences were to be far-reaching.

On 3rd January 1941 13th Corps (as Western Desert Force had been renamed) attacked Bardia and captured it in one day. The bag included 40,000 prisoners, 13 medium and 115 light tanks, 400 guns, and 706 trucks (a windfall for O'Connor). The British armour pressed on to cut off Tobruk, the next port and fortress along the coast. Like Bardia, Tobruk fell in a single day, on 22nd January 1941. This time the bag comprised 25,000 prisoners, 208 guns, 23 medium tanks, and 200 trucks.

In front of O'Connor now was the bulge of Cyrenaica, the Jabal Akhdar, a fertile region of hills colonized by Italian settlers, and beyond it the city of Benghazi. The remnants of Italian X Army were seeking to escape into Tripolitania along the coast road, which wound round the Jabal Akhdar to the Gulf of Syrte. Although O'Connor's force was now almost worn out mechanically, he flung it along appalling and unreconnoitred desert tracks south of the Jabal to try to reach the coast road ahead of the Italians and bar their retreat. On 5th February 1941 his trap closed with half an hour to spare. For two days the Italians strove desperately to break through, but

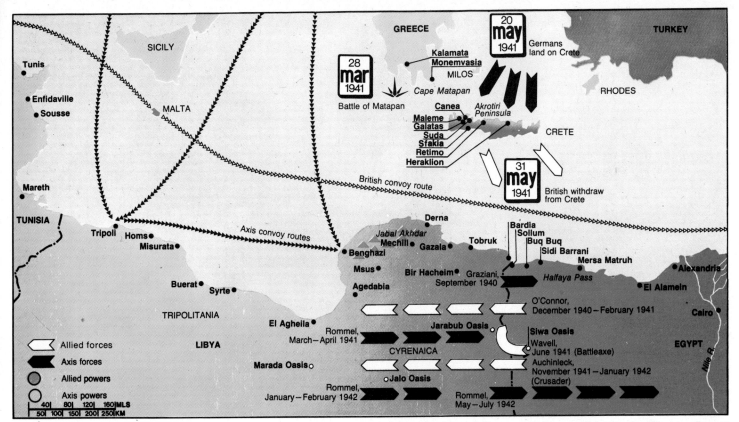

The war in the Mediterranean and North Africa from 1940 to 1942, showing the loss of Crete and the struggle for the Western Desert. O'Connor's devastating successes against the Italians were not followed through because of the need to help Greece. Rommel had his chance. After a year-long duel, during which he was thrown back by Auchinleck's offensive, Rommel finally broke through into Egypt

failed. In this Battle of Beda Fomm O'Connor achieved that rare military phenomenon, a complete victory, for the X Army had been utterly destroyed. In ten weeks O'Connor had taken 130,000 prisoners, 400 tanks, and 1,290 guns.

It seemed to O'Connor that Tripolitania, now almost defenceless, might also fall to a swift advance, and the whole of Italian North Africa be cleared. Thus a campaign that had begun with the defence of Egypt was now pointing towards the destruction of Italian power, first in Africa, later perhaps at home. However, the British government decided that instead of striking at Tripoli, the bulk of O'Connor's veterans should be made available to aid the Greeks against an expected German invasion. O'Connor went on sick leave and 13th Corps was broken up. The British never recovered the professionalism and cohesion of this matured formation.

There is little question that the decision not to drive on to Tripoli at the beginning of February 1941 was one of the most unfortunate of the war. The aid to the Greeks achieved nothing in the event, while on 12th February Lieutenant-General Erwin Rommel arrived in Tripoli with an advance party of German troops. O'Connor's victories, by being halted in mid-career, had only served to draw the Germans into North Africa, a vastly more potent danger to Egypt than the Italians could ever have been.

The Germans in North Africa

The danger became swiftly manifest. On 31st March 1941, long before either Wavell or the German High Command itself believed he could be ready, Rommel attacked the British round El Agheila. The bewildering speed and agility of Rommel's advance brought about the collapse of the green formations that had replaced O'Connor's veterans. O'Connor himself, sent up to advise his successor Neame, was captured along with Neame. The whole of Cyrenaica was lost except for Tobruk which was cut off and besieged, and Rommel only halted, just over the Egyptian frontier, because he had outrun his supplies.

Henceforth the duel with Rommel in the Western Desert was more and more to fascinate the British, especially the Prime Minister, Winston Churchill. The Western Desert was the only place where the British Empire could fight Germany on land. It was now therefore less of a case of defending Egypt than of winning a great victory over Rommel's Panzer Group Africa; of, in fact, attempting again in very different circumstances to carry out O'Connor's intention of completely clearing North Africa.

British prospects were not good. The British Army had begun to prepare for modern tank warfare at least five years later than the Germans, and lacked German operational experience. The British Empire forces had been hastily and recently expanded. British military doctrine and staff methods did not equal those of Germany. These weaknesses were compounded again and again when half-raw divisions had to be committed to battle in haste because of the hunger at home for victories, or at least offensive action. British equipment, too, bore the signs of late and hasty rearmament. The British cruiser-tanks were highly unreliable mechanically, while the four-gallon petrol can wasted untold quantities of fuel because of its flimsiness. These British qualitative inferiorities in skill and equipment were never understood or accepted by the Prime Minister, who repeatedly urged his commanders-in-chief in the Middle East to attack before they felt ready. The consequences of such attacks were demonstrated in June 1941, when an offensive (Battleaxe) was heavily defeated. It was Battleaxe that finally doomed Wavell, already in disfavour.

His successor was General Sir Claude Auchinleck, of the Indian Army, a big man with a strong but warm personality. He too was immediately pressed for an offensive, but remained adamant that 1st November was the earliest that the green reinforcements and untried equipment now pouring into Egypt could be shaped into an army fit to meet Germans in battle. In the event, the offensive, code-named Crusader, was launched on 18th November, and its course was to bear out all Auchinleck's misgivings. Except in dogged courage, 8th Army (as the desert forces had now become) showed itself generally inferior in operational skill at every level to XV and XXI Panzer Divisions (the Afrika Korps), and 90th Light Division (trucked infantry). German tanks proved themselves superior mechanically and German tank recovery services were also better organized.

According to the British plan, the infantry divisions of 13th Corps would make an attack on the fixed Axis defences round the Halfaya Pass (leading up the escarpment from the coastal plain), while the armour of 30th Corps would swing wide through the desert, fight and beat the German armour, and relieve Tobruk. 8th Army fielded in an augmented 7th Armoured Division 453 gun-armed tanks against fewer than 200 German tanks in XV and XXI Panzer Divisions, and some 130 Italian. The British plan soon fell apart into sprawling actions all over eastern Cyrenaica, with

both sides mixed up in a way unprecedented in war. A sheik's tomb, Sidi Rezegh, was the focus for repeated encounters, and gave the alternative name to the Crusader battles.

At first it seemed that the British had won the armoured battle. Then news seeped back of appalling losses and stalled attacks. It was a proof of the superiority of German tactics and of British inexperience. While the British tried to charge home, cavalry-style, the Germans fought defensively, drawing the British on to their anti-tank guns, especially the deadly 88-mm guns adapted from an anti-aircraft role.

The 8th Army commander, Lieutenant-General Sir Alan Cunningham, who had never commanded such masses of armour or troops in battle before (what British soldier had?), was near a breakdown. He believed that the offensive had failed, and that unless the army fell back into Egypt, it would be destroyed and the Nile Delta endangered. Auchinleck relieved him and ordered the offensive to go on. In Cunningham's place, Auchinleck temporarily appointed Major-General Neil Ritchie, his Deputy Chief of the General Staff in Cairo, a burly, phlegmatic man who loyally carried out Auchinleck's order to grip Rommel and wear him down.

Rommel's reserves of tanks were smaller than the British and he was denied supplies from Italy. Gradually the stubborn British dominated the battlefield. Tobruk was relieved. The Germans slowly fell back to El Agheila (5th-6th January 1942). Despite its rawness 8th Army had taken 36,000 prisoners and reduced the German tank strength to thirty. Crusader was the first British victory over the Germans in the Second World War.

It now proved no more possible for Auchinleck to push swiftly on into Tripolitania than for Wavell a year earlier. Whereas Greece had competed with the desert for resources in 1941, it was now to the Far East, under heavy Japanese attack, that Auchinleck lost two divisions and much equipment. Once again Rommel took advantage of the British pause in front of the Agheila position. On 21st January 1942 he emerged from his defences to give one of his most brilliant displays of op-

Above left: Worthless medals used by the Italians as rewards to local population in North Africa. Above: German airmen resting in the desert. Left: British troops captured by Germans in North Africa. The conditions of desert fighting far from the parade ground and the supply depot bred a spirit of improvisation in uniforms and equipment. The British wear a mixture of battle-dress and tropical kit, and the armoured-car mounts a collection of infantry weapons

portunism and agility – 1st Armoured Division in the forward area, fresh from England, was routed. In the ensuing confusion Ritchie incorrectly read the situation and proved indecisive and slow to act; only round Gazala, on the Cyrenaican coast was the situation stabilized.

Auchinleck was now advised that there was lack of confidence in Ritchie among 8th Army commanders, and that he was not up to the job of commanding an army. Auchinleck nevertheless confirmed Ritchie's hitherto temporary appointment instead of asking for a more experienced and senior general from Great Britain; a decision partly owing to Auchinleck's lack of personal ruthlessness and partly to his belief that it would be bad for public opinion to sack another general so soon.

In spring 1942 both sides were preparing for major offensives. There were sharp contrasts. For Hitler the Mediterranean and North Africa were sideshows compared with Russia and deserved only minimal German support of Italy. Rommel's command therefore still numbered only two under-strength Panzer divisions (the Afrika Korps) and 90th Light Division plus one Italian armoured division and five infantry. This force, now designated Panzer Army Africa, and Rommel himself were supposed to be under Italian supreme command. Owing to British naval action and Italian incompetence, Panzer Army Africa was always short of supplies, reinforcements, and fuel. Thus for Rommel the only hope of keeping the North African campaign alive lay in bluff and risk. He brilliantly succeeded, not only in the field but through his own personality. The British – and again particularly the Prime Minister – had by 1942 become really obsessed with the duel in the desert. On the British side therefore North Africa was no sideshow. Sustained by an immense base in Egypt, it was the focus for the greatest single military effort of the British Empire – a miniature war economy. The ration strength of Middle East Command rose to over half a million men.

For both sides Malta was the key to the campaign. It served as a base for British interruption of Rommel's seaborne supplies and the Axis High Commands therefore decided that Malta must be taken before Rommel could hope to attack the Nile Delta itself. From the British point of view Malta itself could only survive if supplies were run in by sea. This required air cover; and this in turn required airfields in Cyrenaica further west than Gazala. Air cover was the more urgent in spring 1942 because of the collapse of British naval power in the Mediterranean. Here was the immediate spur to British offensive action.

However, Auchinleck was now the more cautious about 8th Army's chances because

of the experiences of the winter battle. Like Haig in 1916 he knew he had less of an army than a collection of divisions untrained (to a greater or lesser extent) for the field. Nor was 8th Army a 'British' army. Its infantry formations were largely imperial – at one time or another, Australian, New Zealand, South African, and Indian – and the dominion divisional commanders had the right of appeal to their own governments if they thought dominion interests imperilled by British orders. In addition there were Greek, Polish, and Free French contingents. The 8th Army commanders and the c-in-c's Middle East were in fact Allied commanders, with all the difficulties therein traditionally involved.

It was Auchinleck's belief that inferiority of weapons and skill must be compensated for by numbers and careful preparation. The consequent long delay displeased the Prime Minister, who eventually ordered Auchinleck to attack in June 1942.

Rommel attacks

Instead Rommel attacked first, on 26th May. He fielded 561 tanks, of which only the 280 German mediums really counted, against some 850 tanks with 8th Army, of which the 167 American Grants, with a 75-mm gun, outshot all German tanks except 19 Mark III Specials. Unfortunately the Grant's gun was mounted in the hull and had only a limited traverse. Rommel's anti-tank guns were greatly superior to the British: 50-, 76-, and 88-mm as against 2-pounders.

Ritchie's defensive dispositions were faulty. His infantry were placed in static field defences ('boxes') inside minefields, a European-style defence system stretching from Gazala to Bir Hacheim but ending in an open desert flank. Behind lay the British armour, dispersed in brigades and much too far forward. Rommel, sweeping south of Bir Hacheim in a great column of tanks, trucks, and guns in a swing aimed at cutting the coast road behind the British, at first trampled through the British brigades one by one, taking them by surprise. Then British numbers and the powerful Grants began to tell. Rommel's offensive stalled in confused and bitter struggles and the problem of supply became acute. Rommel averted defeat by one of his most imaginative improvisations. He breached the centre of Ritchie's line of minefields from the east, or British rear, opening up direct communications with his base and covering his bridgehead with anti-tank guns.

Against this bridgehead through the British centre Ritchie belatedly launched ill-coordinated attacks which foundered miserably. Rommel then took the lynchpin of the whole Gazala Line, Bir Hacheim, garrisoned by the Free French, on 11th

June. The Gazala Line thus demolished, Rommel swept again towards Tobruk. Ritchie had drawn on the large British reserves of tanks, so that 8th Army could still field 250 cruisers and 80 heavy 'I' tanks against some 160 German and 70 Italian tanks. However the precarious skill and cohesion of the British armoured divisions were disintegrating. In a great tank battle on 11th and 12th June 8th Army lost 200 cruisers and 60 'I' tanks. The virtual destruction of the British armour exposed 8th Army to disaster.

The defences of Tobruk were derelict, for the last siege had proved so costly and difficult to maintain that Middle East Command had decided it should never again be held in isolation. This decision had been communicated to London in the winter. Now, however, the Prime Minister signalled that he expected it to be held as in 1941. Following a series of equivocal signals between Auchinleck, London, and Ritchie, the Prime Minister was satisfied and Tobruk was allowed to be 'temporarily' invested, with 1st South African Division as the main part of the garrison.

Rommel first lunged after the main body of 8th Army as it retreated precipitately ('the Gazala Gallop') towards Egypt, and then pounced back on Tobruk. Its hastily improvised and feeble defence collapsed in a single day, on 21st June 1942, yielding 30,000 prisoners and much booty. Rommel, now a field-marshal, took the road for Egypt. It was the climax of his career. However, the Axis supreme commands in the Mediterranean had earlier agreed that Rommel should halt on the Egyptian frontier to allow Malta to be taken, so that adequate seaborne supplies could be assured for the final offensive against the Nile Delta. Nevertheless, because the British seemed so totally routed, Rommel persuaded his superiors to allow him to gamble on thrusting his way into the Delta before the British could recover.

On 23rd June Rommel crossed into Egypt, and by 25th June was in front of the old Mersa Matruh defences of 1940. Here Ritchie hoped to make a last stand with survivors of the Gazala defeat and new formations sent up by Auchinleck. Since 26th May 8th Army had lost 80,000 men, mostly in prisoners – a mark of the extent of the victory of the ruthless German professionals against superior numbers of British imperial troops.

Egypt and the entire British position in the Middle East were now exposed to catastrophe. On 25th June Auchinleck flew up from Cairo to take over personal command of 8th Army from Ritchie. He took command of a battered, retreating army. With Rommel still attacking, to give his forces time to reform, he planned withdrawal – to a place called El Alamein.

The Balkan Campaign

Throughout the first twelve months of the Second World War neither the British nor the Germans wished to disturb the peace of South-Eastern Europe. In London the War Office, notoriously unsympathetic to Balkan ventures, feared that extension of the conflict would pose taxing problems of aid and supply; and in Berlin it was felt that the Reich could gain far more from peaceful exploitation of the region's economic resources than by a war of conquest. Hitler was particularly concerned to safeguard the oilfields of Rumania from destruction by invaders or by bombing from bases in other Balkan states; and early in October 1940 he secured from a pliant Rumanian government the right to station German troops in the country so as to preserve its 'neutrality' and 'independence' from an increasingly menacing attitude by the Soviet Union to the north.

This assertion of German primacy in Eastern Europe irritated Hitler's Axis partner Mussolini. Fascist diplomacy habitually regarded the Balkans as an area designed by nature for the greater glory of Italian arms; and in the spring of 1939 Mussolini had made this clear to an unimpressed Europe by annexing Albania (which was already economically dependent on Rome) to the Italian crown. The Duce would have liked to have followed up this paper triumph by invading Yugoslavia; his foreign minister, Count Ciano, preferred a march on Athens; but Hitler, with a sounder sense of general strategy, persistently vetoed either project, and the Italians watched sulkily as Ger-

man units carried the swastika flag eastwards until on 8th October 1940 they reached the Rumanian Black Sea coast.

It was at this point that Mussolini decided to act. For once he would take a military decision without consulting the Germans. On 15th October preparations were hurriedly begun for a campaign against Greece from the Italian bases in southern Albania. Hitler, belatedly realizing that the Italians were about to bring war to the Balkans, hastened southwards in a last effort to hold his partner back. It was too late. He was greeted at Florence station on the morning of 28th October by an exultant Mussolini boasting that 'victorious Italian troops crossed the Graeco-Albanian frontier at dawn today'. The Führer did not offer his congratulations at the news.

The Albanian expedition was a disaster. Near the coast the invaders advanced some twenty-five miles in three days to the Kalamas river, but they were soon repulsed and farther west they ran into early difficulties. The Italian armoured divisions moved slowly through the valleys of Epirus towards the plains. Greek mountain regiments, holding heights above the columns, waited until they had reached the bleak Pindus gorges and fell on them from the rear. An Alpini division was wiped out. Within eleven days the Greeks had taken 5,000 prisoners and forced the invaders to pull back towards the frontier. The German military attaché sent gloomy reports to Berlin: rain and snow made the front an impassable morass; and there seemed no

Left: Hitler bails out his Italian ally. The Germans cross into Yugoslavia on the first stage of their Balkan conquest. **Below left:** *An Italian 'Alpini' colonel and his Greek captors.* **Below right:** *Italian prisoners march to a brief captivity*

ΟΙ ΗΡΩΙΔΕΣ ΤΟΥ 1940

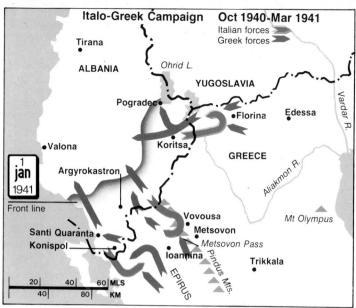

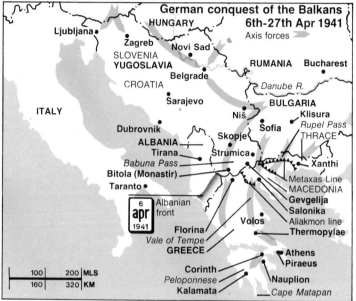

Left: Greek poster shows 'the heroines of 1940'. Peasant women head for the mountains with guns and ammunition to fight the Italians.
Right: Maps show the failure of the Italians and the sweeping success of the Germans in their campaigns against the Greeks, 1940—41

hope of transporting fresh divisions to prevent a rout. On 21st November Koritsa, the third largest town in Albania, fell to General Papagos's army. Before the wintry conditions halted all operations the Greeks had penetrated to a distance of thirty miles along the whole front. They inflicted 30,000 casualties and accumulated an impressive list of prizes—the town of Pogradec, upon Lake Ohrid; the fortress of Argyrokastron; and the naval base of Santi Quaranta, which sycophantic Italians had re-named 'Porto Edda' in honour of Mussolini's daughter, the Countess Ciano. The Duce thus suffered military defeat and political humiliation at the hands of the Greeks. Nor was this all. On 11th November three Italian battleships and a cruiser were put out of action in a raid on Taranto by torpedo-bombers from *HMS Illustrious*. Italian morale rapidly sank to a low ebb.

Hitler was furious with his ally, especially as the British began to establish bases in Crete and other Greek islands which brought the vital supply route from Rumania within range of the RAF. It was clear that the Italians would have to be rescued by German arms. As early as 12th November Hitler signed an order instruct-

ing the High Command to prepare a Balkan campaign. Mussolini continued to ask that the Greeks should receive 'a first correction' from the Italians, although he accepted a proposal for the despatch of a German military mission to the front.

The Germans themselves had no intention of striking prematurely. Hitler was willing to wait until the spring, first making certain that the other states of South-Eastern Europe would render diplomatic support to the Axis. He was already sure of the Rumanians and he began to put pressure on the Bulgars. On 8th February an agreement was duly signed in Sofia permitting the German XII Army to concentrate in southern Bulgaria, along the Greek frontier. There remained only Yugoslavia; and throughout the winter months the Germans alternated threats and blandishments to draw the Yugoslav government into the Axis camp.

Yugoslavia and the 'New Order'

Yugoslavia was more directly concerned with the outcome of the Italo-Greek campaign than any other Balkan state. For twenty years the Yugoslavs had enjoyed special treaty rights in the Greek port of

Salonika; they had no wish to see the city in the hands of their old rivals, the Italians. Hitler hoped to tempt the Yugoslavs by a promise to cede Salonika once Greece had fallen. But Prince Paul, the Regent of Yugoslavia, and his ministers were in a difficult position. They were unpopular with almost every section of opinion in the country, for they had tried to please too many conflicting groups. They knew that the sympathies of the Serbs, the largest of the nationalities in the kingdom, were with their old allies in Greece and collusion with Germany might precipitate an internal revolt. The Regent himself favoured the British cause, but he was a realist. He was certain that Germany could overrun Yugoslavia within a fortnight of the start of any campaign and he was bitterly conscious of Yugoslavia's isolation. When the American minister tried to strengthen his resolve, he replied with justice: 'You big nations are hard. You talk of our honour but you are far away.' He therefore chose a policy of strict neutrality.

This, however, was not enough for Hitler. By now the General Staff was planning not only Operation Marita against Greece, but Operation Barbarossa against Russia. It

German Dornier 17 bombers flying over Athens. The occupation of the Greek capital on 27th April 1941 was the culmination of Germany's three-week Balkan campaign. Athens fell with no resistance after the precipitate withdrawal of the Allied troops to Crete and Egypt

would be dangerous to leave an uncommitted Yugoslavia on the German flank during these forthcoming campaigns. Gradually Hitler increased pressure on the Yugoslavs to join the Tripartite Pact between Italy, Germany, and Japan, the charter of co-operation in the 'New Order' to which the Hungarians, the Rumanians, and the Bulgars had already adhered. Reluctantly Prince Paul authorized his Prime Minister and foreign minister to travel to Vienna and there, on 25th March, they duly signed the pact. At last Hitler was ready to rescue Mussolini from his Greek entanglement. Operation Marita was fixed for early April.

The Italians, for their part, were still making desperate efforts to administer that 'first correction' to the Greeks. They assembled no less than twenty-eight divisions, twice as many as their opponents. For the final Italian offensive, on 9th March, Mussolini even crossed to Albania in person; but though the Duce struck splendidly martial attitudes, his mere presence failed somehow to ensure success. Although under severe strain, the Greeks held their positions; and from 7th March onwards small groups of British and Common-

wealth troops began to arrive at the Piraeus and Volos so as to meet the threat from the German army in Bulgaria. At the same time the Royal Navy prevented any movement of the Italian fleet towards the Aegean and on 28th March gained a striking victory against two Italian squadrons off Cape Matapan. Mussolini's prestige remained low: there was even a music-hall song in Great Britain mocking his failure to 'put it over the Greeks'.

Yugoslavia finds her soul

Yet, as the snow-line began to recede along the mountains, both sides waited for the Balkan Front to erupt. The Germans were confident of an easy victory; but on 27th March their self-assurance was shaken by unexpected news from Belgrade – a revolt, headed by General Bora Mirković of the Yugoslav air force, had overthrown the government. The streets of the capital filled with cheering crowds ostentatiously supporting the British and Greeks. It was, as the *New York Times* wrote next day, 'a lightning flash illuminating a dark background'; and in London Churchill rejoiced that Yugoslavia had 'found her soul'.

Hitler regarded the Belgrade coup as both a personal affront and a military threat. That same day he issued a crisp directive: 'The Führer is determined, without waiting for possible loyalty declarations of the new government, to make all preparations to destroy Yugoslavia militarily and as a national unit.' Assistance would be sought from Italy, Hungary, and Bulgaria and every attempt made to turn the various nationalities of Yugoslavia against the dominant Serbs. No ultimatum would be issued; war would come with a massive aerial chastisement of the impudent city of Belgrade. The attack would coincide with the opening of Operation Marita against Greece; Operation Barbarossa would be delayed until order was restored in the Balkans.

Had Hitler waited he would have found the new government, which was headed by General Dušan Simović, far less hostile to the Axis than either he or the people of Belgrade supposed. Simović would do nothing to provoke the Germans; and secret talks between Yugoslav representatives and senior British and Greek commanders produced no real accord. If the Germans attacked, the Yugoslavs asked for fifteen

Germany's Triumph

British divisions to be rushed to Salonika. But most of the troops which could be spared from the Desert War in Africa were already in Greece: two Australian divisions, a New Zealand division, a Polish brigade and an armoured brigade from Great Britain. This army, which numbered no more than 58,000 men, was required to strengthen the Greek lines, for the winter campaign in Albania had sadly depleted General Papagos's reserves. It was hard to see how these limited reinforcements could afford succour to the Yugoslavs as well as the Greeks. There was never much hope that the British and their Balkan allies could stem the German tide.

Operation Marita: a triumph of planning

Operation Marita proved a triumph of staff-planning. The campaign duly began with the bombardment of Belgrade by squadrons of Stukas soon after dawn on 6th April. German raiders continued to dive on the city for more than two days until its centre was reduced to rubble and 17,000 of its citizens lay dead. At precisely the same moment as the first bombs fell on Belgrade, Field Marshal List's XII Army crossed the Bulgaro-Yugoslav frontier in Macedonia, thus opening the operations on land. This German gambit was unexpected, for the Yugoslavs were guarding their northern frontiers more closely than those in the south. But List's move had a double advantage: it struck deeply into Yugoslavia while, at the same time, providing for a southward thrust down the Vardar valley towards the vital Greek port of Salonika. List's deployment of troops virtually won the Balkan campaign for Germany within fifty hours of the first shots being fired.

Yugoslav resistance lasted for only twelve days. Some units fought bravely, especially to the east of Niš where two divisions which had no anti-tank guns at all sought to delay three armoured brigades of General von Kleist's XIV Corps. There was, however, little will to fight for Yugoslavia among the Croatian regiments, and the German-speaking minority carried out numerous acts of sabotage in the north. The first territorial losses came in the south: Skopje fell to List on 7th April and Niš to Kleist on 8th April. The German II Army in the north did not begin its main advance until 10th April but it encountered far less opposition and covered the seventy miles from the frontier-crossing at Gyékényes to the Croatian capital of Zagreb in under twelve hours. A 'Croatian State' was proclaimed under Axis patronage.

With Yugoslavia disintegrating, the Italians and Hungarians moved in for the kill and Bulgarian infantry divisions followed the German armour across the Macedonian frontier. On 11th April Italian troops cautiously approached the Slovene capital of Ljubljana, only to find it already under German control. The Hungarians reached Novi Sad on the Danube but their preparations lacked German efficiency and one Hungarian armoured unit ran out of petrol thirty miles south of the frontier. The military successes of the campaign were exclusively German and were gained at a cost of only 151 men killed in action. It was a German column which received the surrender of Belgrade on 12th April and it was German staff-officers who negotiated an armistice with a Yugoslav general on 17th April. That same day an Italian regimental band marched triumphantly into Dubrovnik — Mussolini's army, though magnificently warlike in time of peace, at heart owed less to the tradition of Caesar than to Verdi.

The vanguard of the German XII Army moved on to Greece in three columns: one made for Štip, crossed the Vardar river on 7th April and headed over the Babuna Pass towards Bitola (Monastir) and the mountains running from southern Albania into north-western Greece; a second column moved from Strumica on to Gevgelija and the main railway to Salonika; while a third column crossed the Rupel Pass and headed for Salonika from the north-east. By 0800 hrs on 8th April the first German tanks were rumbling into the Greek port, which had served as a base for the Allies for three years in the First World War. The German advance effectively cut all links between Yugoslavia and Greece. It also ensured that the Greek divisions which were manning the defences of Thrace, the so-called 'Metaxas Line', were isolated just as the garrisons of the French Maginot Line had been in the campaign on the Western Front a year before.

The commander of the British forces in Macedonia, General Sir Henry Maitland Wilson, had never liked the Greek plan to hold the Metaxas Line. He favoured a defensive position along the loop of the River Aliakmon, from the solid bastion of the Albanian mountains to the natural ramparts north of Olympus. When List's army struck at Greece, Wilson's troops were north-west of this line, guarding the broad corridor from Bitola to Kenali and Florina, the scene of fierce battles in the First World War. This time, however, the weight of German armour was too strong for the defenders. List's tanks thrust Wilson back to the Aliakmon on 12th April. Two days later the Germans began to turn his left flank, breaking through in the wild mountains around Klisura and heading south-westwards towards the Pindus gorges so as to cut off the Greek army on the Albanian front. Ironically it was in the Metsovon Pass, where the Greeks had destroyed an Alpini division

only five months previously, that crack SS troops finally broke Greek resistance in the west. With his line of retreat cut the local commander, General George Tsolakoglou, opened negotiations with List's advance troops and on 20th April all Greek forces in Albania, Epirus, and Macedonia capitulated to the Germans. A general Graeco-German armistice was concluded on the following day but Mussolini insisted on a separate act of surrender to the Italians on 23rd April.

Meanwhile Wilson's forward troops sought to delay the German advance on Athens so as to enable the evacuation of the main British and Commonwealth army and those Greeks and Yugoslavs who wished to continue the fight. Australian and New Zealand units held the vital passes around Olympus and through the Vale of Tempe for three days before falling back on 20th April to the historic pass at Thermopylae, where British forces were already in defensive positions. List massed six divisions against the Thermopylae Line which became untenable on 24th April. It was impossible to use the port facilities of the Piraeus, for the town was devastated on the night of 6th April when an ammunition ship received a direct hit in an air-raid. Commonwealth troops made for the inhospitable open beaches of the Peloponnese, at Nauplion, Kalamata and Monemvasia. But on 26th April the Germans struck again: parachute troops seized the town and isthmus of Corinth so as to cut the British retreat. A series of moonless nights aided the last stage of the evacuation and by 1st May nearly 50,000 Allied troops had been got away to Crete and Egypt. But it had proved a costly expedition; many thousands had passed into captivity.

Swastika on the Acropolis

By mid-day on 27th April the Germans were in Athens and the swastika flag shaming the heights of the Acropolis. Although in the mountains of both Greece and Yugoslavia men were preparing to resist the occupation forces, there was no doubt that the Germans had gained a striking victory, of which the spoils were undeservedly shared by their Italian ally. Yet in retrospect it could be argued that the Balkan campaigns were a disastrous diversion of effort for the Axis armies. In order to deal with the Yugoslavs and Greeks the German High Command had postponed Operation Barbarossa from 15th May to 22nd June. It is anyone's guess what would have happened in the autumn of 1941 if the Red Army had been forced to hold the approaches to Moscow for another five weeks before the Russian winter came to its rescue. Inevitably the imponderable remains unacknowledged.

The Battle of Crete

The British evacuation of Greece began on 25th April 1941. That same day Hitler authorized the invasion of Crete. This was a logical sequel. Crete's central position in the eastern Mediterranean made it of great strategic importance: in British hands its excellent harbour, Suda Bay, might still be of use as a naval base and the RAF could reach the Balkans, and especially the Rumanian oil centre, Ploesti, from the airfields at Heraklion, Retimo, and Maleme.

Since October 1940, when the Italians invaded Greece, General Sir Archibald Wavell had been able to spare little in the way of troops and materials to garrison the island. And the chief increases now were in troops evacuated from Greece between 25th and 29th May, 6th Australian Division, and 4th and 5th Brigades of 2nd New Zealand Division being the main elements. General Bernard Freyberg was

given over-all command. All the evidence indicated that invasion would come soon and Freyberg addressed himself to organizing the defences and extracting all the material he could from Middle East Command.

What guns and tanks he was able to get were inadequate in number and mostly obsolescent. The troops from Greece had had to leave behind all their heavy equipment. Supply from Alexandria was a long and dangerous haul for shipping and by the time battle began three weeks later the troops were still short of everything, especially of wireless and signals equipment. Air support was totally absent.

The Germans, on the other hand, had available about 500 transport aircraft, 70 to 80 gliders, 280 bombers, 150 dive-bombers, 180 fighters, and 40 reconnaissance aircraft. They planned to

A small success before withdrawal: Allied fire brings down German Junkers 52 dropping paratroops over Crete, May 1941

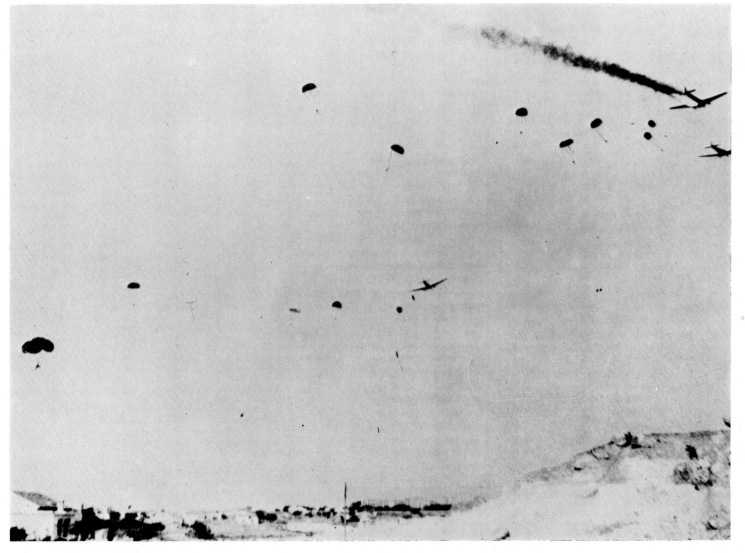

German paratroops take their first British prisoners after landing on Crete. Paratroops played a dominant role in Germany's rapid occupation of the island: the attack was the greatest airborne offensive mounted by the Germans during the whole of the Second World War

invade with a total of 22,750 men—750 by glider, 10,000 by parachute, 5,000 by air transport, and 7,000 by sea.

The British forces totalled about 30,000 with 11,000 poorly-armed Greek troops in support. But these had to be organized around widely separated defence areas connected by one vulnerable road along the north coast closest to the German air bases. These areas were Heraklion, Retimo, and Maleme airfields, Suda Bay, and Canea, the island's capital.

These were indeed the German objectives. The attack was planned in two waves: a dawn attack by Group West against Maleme and by Group Centre against Canea and its environs; and an afternoon attack by Group East against Heraklion and Retimo.

Just after first light on 20th May, the sky was full of the sound and fury of hundreds of aircraft. The blitz was particularly heavy on Point 107, the hill which commanded Maleme airfield and which was held by 22nd NZ Battalion. Three glider detachments landed first: one destroyed the anti-aircraft positions at the mouth of the Tavronitis River; the second seized the main road bridge over that river; and the third was virtually destroyed by the defence. The bridge lodgement was vital and the glider troops held on long enough for a battalion of paratroops landed in an undefended area to the west to come up in support.

Lieutenant-Colonel Andrew VC, commanding 22nd NZ Battalion, lost touch with his forward companies almost at once. Telephone lines were cut, runners could not get through, and the only wireless was to Brigadier Hargest at 5th Brigade HQ. Heavy fighting began and continued without break. Calls to 5th Brigade for help were refused, because the other battalions were themselves engaged. In the middle of the afternoon Andrew counter-attacked with his reserve platoon and two obsolete tanks. The tanks broke down and the infantry had to fall back, the few survivors mostly wounded.

By nightfall Andrew believed three of his companies were destroyed. A reinforcing company from 23rd Battalion arrived but did not seem enough to counterbalance his losses. He decided to withdraw to the areas of 21st and 23rd Battalions. By daylight he had done so. The missing companies, finding he had withdrawn, followed; and he realized, too late, that the position was better than he had believed.

21st and 23rd Battalions had meanwhile destroyed a battalion or more of paratroops in their own areas. Elsewhere on the 5th Brigade front the story was similar: dead paratroops lay everywhere among the olive trees.

The German Group Centre had also had a bad day. The glider detachment landed on Akrotiri Peninsula had been wiped out

by 1st Northumberland Hussars. The groups' commander, General Suessmann, had been killed in a crash. The survivors and stragglers filtered through to the main body, General Heidrich's III Parachute Regiment, which had landed south west of Galatas, largely out of range of the defence. This consisted of 10th NZ Brigade, improvised mainly from drivers without trucks and artillerymen without guns, under the command of Lieutenant-Colonel H.K.Kippenberger. The paratroops had attacked as soon as they could and there were some desperate encounters: at one point the line was saved only by a wild charge of Greek soldiers and villagers organized by Captain Michael Forrester of the Queen's Regiment.

At Heraklion and Retimo, in spite of some initial local successes, the Germans had also failed. By the end of the day General Freyberg, unaware of the withdrawal from Maleme, was soberly confident. And General Student in Athens, the apostle of air invasion and commander of German airborne forces, was close to despair.

Air reconnaissance at dawn on 21st May, however, revealed to him that Maleme was in German hands. He decided to stake everything on this foothold, sending in all his remaining paratroops and flying in a mountain battalion that afternoon.

Painting shows the hair-raising method of assault used by Italians on 26th March 1941 when they penetrated Suda Bay harbour to sink the British cruiser York *and three supply ships. The pilot ejected himself after ensuring his explosive boat was on target*

Days of bitter fighting were to follow but possession of Maleme was decisive. The defence could not move large counter-attacking forces in daylight because the Germans controlled the air. The knowledge that there was to be a sea invasion as well forced Freyberg to keep troops in reserve along the coast. So the counter-attack could not begin until late that night. The forces that carried it out, 20th NZ Battalion and the Maori Battalion, fought their way to the fringes of the airfield and Point 107 but daylight found them there and made further progress impossible. Meanwhile the Royal Navy had found the invading sea forces in the dark and smashed them.

By hampering the counter-attack, however, the threat of sea invasion had succeeded in spite of failure. In the following days, German aircraft poured out their battalions of mountain troops and heavy equipment. General Ringel, the local commander, began to push these battalions round the south flank of the defence and would have been even more swiftly successful if it had not been for the stout resistance of badly-armed Greek troops inland. But this steady envelopment from the flank and a heavily supported thrust down the coast road drove the New Zealanders back. Eventually Group West joined with Heidrich's troops and there was a single front from the sea to south of Galatas.

By 25th May the Germans were able to mount a full-scale attack and in the late afternoon they took Galatas. The defence was about to have a hole torn right through it when Kippenberger sent 23rd Battalion and everyone else available into a counter-attack which retook Galatas in ferocious hand-to-hand fighting.

Further withdrawal before an ever-strengthening opposition was inevitable. Freyberg could now see that the island was lost. On the night of 26th May the New Zealanders and Australians who now held the front had to withdraw once more. By a tragic misunderstanding Force Reserve (1st Welsh, 1st Rangers, and 1st Northumberland Hussars) failed to get their orders to do likewise and, in spite of an heroic stand, were cut off by paratroops driving down the coast road. A second thrust by two mountain battalions under Colonel Jais surprised the New Zealanders and Australians at 42nd Street but was routed by a counter-attack with rifle and bayonet.

Canea and Suda Bay could no longer be held, however, and a reinforcement from Alexandria of Commandos under Colonel Laycock could do no more than assist in the series of arduous rearguard actions that covered the withdrawal of the main body over the difficult White Mountains to Sfakia, a fishing port on the south coast.

Meanwhile a message had been got through to the garrison at Heraklion and they were embarked by the Royal Navy in the early hours of 29th May. But all efforts to get the orders to Retimo failed and the Australians there, about to triumph in their own local battle, could not be got away and had to disperse or surrender.

At Sfakia the defenders held back the pursuit while evacuation went on each night between 28th and 31st May. One last disaster marred the melancholy success of the embarkation. The companies of 2nd/7th Australian Battalion, which had fought so well and never better than in the rearguard, were unable to reach the beaches in time and had to be left behind.

Desperate as the battle was and tragic its immediate outcome, its consequences were less disastrous for the war than at first seemed likely. The Germans did not have the ships to exploit Crete's naval potentialities though it was a useful stepping stone for the reinforcement of Rommel in North Africa. And their losses in victory had been so severe that they never again used paratroops in an airborne role. Dreams of going on to Cyprus and attacking Egypt from the east evaporated. And the experience of Crete made them flinch from the airborne invasion of Malta which might have been a serious blow to the British. In the words of General Student: 'Crete was the grave of the German paratroops.'

Barbarossa

On 22nd June 1941 Nazi Germany attacked the Soviet Union. The eastern horizon had hardly begun to lighten when thousands of German guns opened fire across the Soviet border. Without warning German aircraft attacked airfields of the Soviet air force situated near the border, and German assault groups opened the way for the main forces of the Wehrmacht.

Hitler and his generals had not the slightest doubt that Germany would rapidly vanquish the Soviet state. They had carried out prolonged preparation, secretly concentrating on the Soviet frontiers a huge army, three million strong, which had experienced no defeat during two years of war and which had confirmed on the battlefields of Europe its doctrine of Blitzkrieg. They had worked out in detail a war-plan (Barbarossa) according to which the main forces of the Red Army were to be wiped out in a single gigantic operation, and Soviet territory right up to the Volga occupied by the autumn of 1941.

When the invasion began the Soviet forces guarding the 2,000-kilometre frontier were not ready. On 22nd June the Red Army in the western border districts of the Soviet Union were being deployed, and the only forces that faced the German tanks and infantry as they crossed the border were frontier guards and a small part of the covering force which had succeeded in getting to the frontier in response to the alarm. The principal forces guarding the western frontier were scattered over a large area up to 280 miles from the front. Despite all the indications that war with Germany was approaching neither the Soviet people nor the Red Army were expecting the German attack when it came. In the summer of 1941 everyone hoped that war might be avoided for a little longer.

Apart from the complete surprise of their attack the Germans had great superiority of forces in the areas where the main blows were struck.

The German armies broke through deep into Soviet territory, trying to surround and destroy concentrations of Soviet forces and prevent a retirement by the effective forces of the Red Army towards the east, behind the Dnieper and Dvina.

At 0715, Marshal Timoshenko, people's commissar for defence, ordered retaliation. Air attacks were to destroy German

Left: After the Luftwaffe's raids the Panzer spearheads thrust through the Russian towns. Right: German troops move into the Ukraine

planes on the ground, and land forces were to throw back the German army to the frontier, without, however, crossing it. But the order was impossible to fulfil. Deep penetration by German tank units, supported by aircraft, frequently resulted in the enemy appearing in the rear of Soviet troops, who were then surrounded.

The German armies were divided into Army Groups North, Centre, and South under the command of Field Marshals Leeb, Bock, and Rundstedt. Facing them were the Soviet troops of the north-western, western, and south-western fronts under Generals Kuznetsov, Pavlov, and Kirponos.

The situation became especially critical on the western front, in Belorussia. German Army Group Centre surrounded the principal forces of 3rd and 10th Armies of the western front near Białystok, broke through to Minsk with II and III Panzer Groups commanded by Generals Guderian and Hoth, captured Minsk (after it had first been largely destroyed by bombing), and then began to move towards the Dnieper. By the beginning of July there were wide gaps in the line of the western front, through which the German tank columns poured farther and farther eastwards. Meanwhile Army Group North invading from East Prussia had penetrated about 450 kilometres into the Baltic region by 10th July, and Army Group South was moving its main forces towards Kiev.

At Hitler's headquarters, the *Wolfsschanze* (wolf's lair), set in strong bunkers of reinforced concrete amid the forests of East Prussia, near Rastenburg, a triumphant atmosphere reigned. In a report to Hitler on 3rd July, General Halder, Chief of Army General Staff, concluded: 'The main forces of the Russian army in front of the Dnieper and Dvina rivers have been largely destroyed . . . it will be no exaggeration if I say that the campaign against Russia has succeeded in a single fortnight' – a view with which Hitler entirely agreed. There were even plans for the withdrawal of troops to concentrate on the conquest of Great Britain and the Near East.

Hitler's war on the Soviet Union had not finished, however; it had only just begun. The Soviet government and the Supreme Command of the Armed Forces carried out far-reaching mobilization of the country's resources for the fight against the invaders. On 30th June the State Defence Committee (GKO) was set up, with Stalin at its head. The GKO concentrated all power in its hands. The national economy

was reorganized and wholly geared to the production of war materials. Civilian factories were turned over to the production of weapons and equipment and more than 1,500 factories, with their entire plant and personnel, were moved bodily to eastern areas away from the western part of the country, where they were in danger of falling into enemy hands. This was a very large-scale operation, unprecedented in its complexity. All through the summer and autumn of 1941 trains ran in endless streams along all the main railway lines, carrying machine-tools and other factory machinery. On these same trains, some in carriages and some in open trucks, travelled the engineers and workers of these factories with their families and belongings. It was as though entire towns had been plucked up and were moving in a great migration to new lands. Having arrived at their new locations in the Urals, in Siberia, or in Central Asia, the war factories began production without delay. Often the workers and engineers got down to work on sites under the open sky, in rain and foul weather. In the opposite direction, towards the front, flowed another stream, carrying troops, tanks, guns, ammunition.

The Supreme Command of the Red Army did much to form fresh reserves. In the course of the summer of 1941 more than 324 divisions were sent to the front. It is interesting to note that, before the invasion, the German command estimated that the Soviet Union was capable of mobilizing a maximum of 140 divisions in the event of war.

In July 1941 the whole front was split into three strategic sectors: north-western, western, and south-western. Several fronts (army groups) came under the authority of each sector. Of decisive importance was the western sector commanded by Marshal Timoshenko, the Smolensk-Moscow axis. There, between 10th July and 10th September, the greatest battle of the summer and autumn of 1941 took place—the battle for Smolensk.

At the start of the battle the Germans outnumbered the Soviet forces on the western sector in men by 1.6 to 1, in guns by 1.8 to 1, in tanks by 1.5 to 1, in aircraft by 4 to 1. The Soviet reserves which had just arrived from the interior of the country

Top: German motorized infantry streams eastwards at the opening of Barbarossa. By the evening of 22nd June the forward units of the German armies had penetrated far into Soviet territory. Centre: Germans shell a Russian village. Bottom: Soviet supply train carrying guns to the front. Right: Two sequences from the German attack on Zhitomir—the artillery in action, and its effects

could not be fully deployed. The gigantic battle at first went in the enemy's favour. Between 10th and 20th July II, IX, and IV German Armies and their II and III Panzer Groups strove, along a 500-kilometre front, to break the forces of the western front into isolated sections, to surround 19th, 20th, and 16th Armies protecting Smolensk, and to seize the city which had long since been marked down by the invaders as the 'key to Moscow'.

The Germans, using powerful tank groups which they concentrated on narrow sectors of the front, and with massive air support, achieved a number of deep breakthroughs in the areas of Polotsk, Vitebsk, and Mogilev. Hoth's III Panzer Group succeeded in breaking through in the Yartsevo area and cutting the chief line of communication of the western front, the motor road between Minsk and Moscow. Farther south, Guderian's II Panzer Group penetrated the outskirts of Smolensk. On the right flank of the western front the Germans forced the Soviet troops to fall back on Velikiye Luki and Nevel, while on the left flank they captured Yelnya, establishing a salient extending far to the east. The German command began to consider this as the jumping off area for the next offensive, against Moscow.

The Soviet troops put up resistance all along the line. Step by step they slowed down the offensive of Army Group Centre and steadily counter-attacked. In order to divert the German forces from the Smolensk sector, an offensive by General Kuznetsov's 21st Army was launched in the direction of Bobruysk. The 20th Army, led by General Kurochkin, deeply enveloped on both flanks in front of Smolensk, tied down a number of German formations for several weeks.

The battle for Smolensk reached its climax between 21st July and 7th August. During this struggle the Red Army Supreme Command deployed several dozen additional fresh formations in three echelons in the western sector and established a new front, called the reserve front, in the rear of the western front.

The principal centres of fighting in this desperate battle were Smolensk, Yelnya, and Yartsevo. For several days troops of the 16th Army, led by General Lukin,

Top: Russian prisoners. Trapped by the German advance, 3,000,000 were captured in 1941—few survived. In their camps they were just left to die of starvation and disease. Knowing their fate if captured, the Russians fought fanatically.
Centre: German soldiers survey the ruins of a Russian village. Bottom: SS troops resting. The speed of their advance exhausted the German troops

Barbarossa:
the campaign

Barbarossa was intended to occupy Russia well beyond Moscow by the autumn. But within two months it was clear that the plan was not going to succeed.

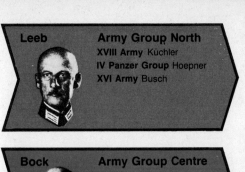

Leeb — **Army Group North**
XVIII Army Küchler
IV Panzer Group Hoepner
XVI Army Busch

Bock — **Army Group Centre**
III Panzer Group Hoth
IX Army Strauss
IV Army Kluge
II Panzer Group Guderian

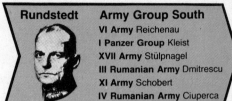

Rundstedt — **Army Group South**
VI Army Reichenau
I Panzer Group Kleist
XVII Army Stülpnagel
III Rumanian Army Dmitrescu
XI Army Schobert
IV Rumanian Army Ciuperca

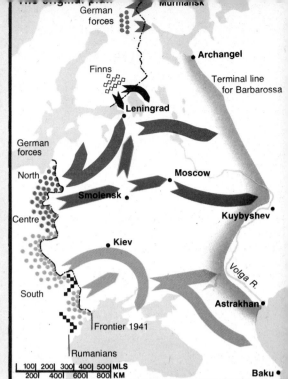

Army Group North: the first major obstacle was the Dvina River, but by 2nd July all of Leeb's armour was across, ready to tackle the next problem: the northern strongpoints of the Stalin Line. Smashing a Soviet armoured challenge, Leeb's Panzer units pressed on to the Luga, under 100 miles from Leningrad itself, which they reached on 14th July. Trapping 20,000 prisoners in the Luga pocket, the Panzers cleared out Estonia by the end of August and were preparing to storm Leningrad. But Hitler had already decided to fence off the city, and to concentrate on Moscow. On 17th September all of Army Group North's armour except for one Panzer corps was switched to the centre under Hoepner and the siege of Leningrad was taken over by infantry.

Army Group Centre had two Panzer Groups poised north and south of the Bialystok salient. The Soviet frontier forces were surrounded in large pockets around Bialystok on 30th June, and Minsk on 9th July. Fending off counter-attacks from the south by Timoshenko, the Panzer forces loosely roped off another huge pocket of over 300,000 Russians by taking Smolensk on 16th July. Then Hitler switched Guderian's armour to the Ukraine to smash Budenny at Kiev, reprieving Moscow, and losing vital campaigning weeks. Operation Typhoon, the offensive against Moscow, began on 2nd October, with spectacular successes in the double battle of Vyazma/Bryansk. But within a week the mud of the Russian autumn and ever-stiffening Soviet resistance halted operations. A new offensive in mid-November, when the early frosts restored movement to the Panzers, took the Germans to within nineteen miles of Moscow, but they could do no more. Exhausted and badly equipped for the Russian winter, Army Group Centre now had to face Zhukov's counter-offensive which began on 5th December.

Army Group South: the target was Kiev and the Ukraine. Spearheaded by Kleist's Panzers, Army Group South battered through the southern Stalin Line forts by 9th July and the Rumanians moved on Odessa. Budenny, Soviet commander in the south-west, planned to concentrate at Uman and Kiev after the failure of his first counter-offensives. But Russian plans to defend the western Ukraine were shattered by the speed of the two German claws which pushed south-east between the Dniester and the Dnieper, sealing off the Uman concentration on 4th August and taking 100,000 prisoners. In the next three weeks Kleist pushed into the Dnieper bend. Then came the southward switch of Guderian's Panzers from Army Group Centre, which joined up with Kleist on 16th September. After the annihilation of the Kiev pocket in late September, in which over 500,000 were killed or captured, Rundstedt's forces drove for Kharkov and the Donets, trapping another 100,000 on 6th October. XI Army, now under Manstein, sealed off the Crimea and Kharkov fell on 24th October. The Moscow offensive by Army Group Centre was mirrored in the south by a drive on Roştov, which fell on 21st November; within a week the Wehrmacht suffered its first major defeat when the Russians recovered it.

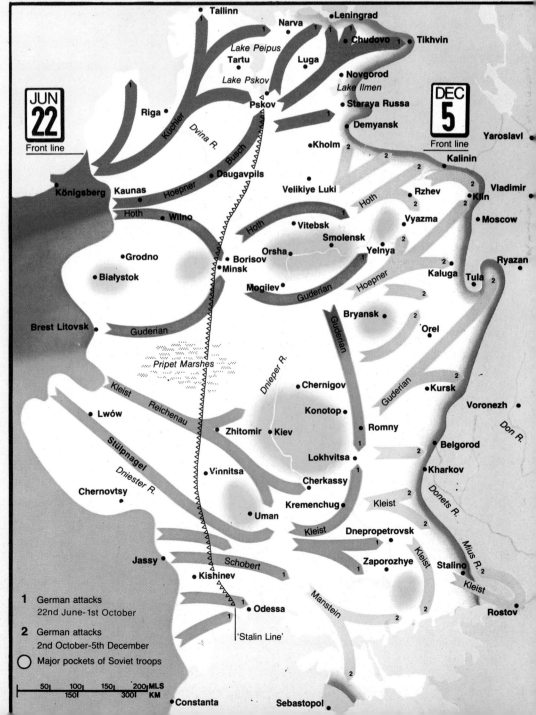

JUN **22** Front line

DEC **5** Front line

1 German attacks 22nd June–1st October

2 German attacks 2nd October–5th December

○ Major pockets of Soviet troops

50 — 100 — 150 — 200 MLS
150 — 300 KM

put up a stubborn resistance in Smolensk. An extremely intense struggle went on for many weeks without a break around Yelnya. Here the Nazis suffered such heavy losses that they called it 'the bloody furnace'. The battle for Yelnya was crowned with success for the Soviet troops, who drove the Germans out of the town and occupied it themselves. Near Yartsevo, tanks and infantry of Hoth's III Panzer Group were halted by General Rokossovsky's troops. Yartsevo, burning and in ruins, changed hands several times. German reports from the front commented on the fanatical Russian resistance; Halder was even beginning to doubt whether decisive victory was possible.

At the beginning of August a balance of forces was achieved on the western sector. The German armies were pinned down and obliged to go over to the defensive.

Within two months Army Group Centre had penetrated 170-200 kilometres to the east of the Dnieper, but this was not the progress that the German High Command had expected. Whereas in the first days of the war the German troops had advanced

on the average thirty kilometres in twenty-four hours, in July they had slowed down to six or seven kilometres. Smolensk, at the very centre of gravity of the German advance, had delayed the Blitzkrieg for two months and upset the schedule of Operation Barbarossa. Hitler was forced to change his plans, and, on 23rd August, rejected his generals' proposal to launch a concentrated attack on Moscow and made up his mind to attack the Ukraine and the Crimea. Economic factors obsessed Hitler; the wheatlands and industries of the Ukraine were of more importance than Moscow. And the Crimea, according to Hitler, was 'a Soviet aircraft-carrier for attacking the Rumanian oilfields'. Guderian's II Panzer Group was therefore transferred from the Smolensk-Moscow sector to the Ukraine.

At the same time there was fierce fighting in the other sectors of the Soviet-German front as well, namely, the north-western and the south-western sectors.

The Nazi leaders calculated that the capture of Leningrad, Kronstadt, and the Murmansk railway would result in the

Soviet Union losing the Baltic region and the far north, together with the Baltic Fleet. They also counted on acquiring a suitable area for a blow from the north-west at the rear of the Soviet forces protecting Moscow. Simultaneously, the Finnish army was to attack on the Karelian Isthmus and in the direction of Petrozavodsk. To the south of this they were to join up with the Germans who were attacking round Lake Ilmen, also in the Petrozavodsk direction. The XVIII Army was to occupy Estonia.

The Soviet people were determined to defend Leningrad. As early as the end of June a plan was drawn up for making defensive fortifications round the city, and this task was put in hand at the beginning of July. Around Leningrad a system of defences was established, comprising several zones. The city's inhabitants worked on these fortifications alongside the soldiers. No fewer than 500,000 people went out every day during July and August to take part in the digging. Weapons for the front were being forged in the works and factories of the city. Home guard battalions were formed.

On 10th July the Germans attacked Novgorod. In a stubborn battle lasting four days, near the town of Soltsy, Soviet troops annihilated part of the German Panzer corps commanded by General Manstein. Field Marshal Leeb, commanding Army Group North, found himself obliged to halt the offensive of IV Panzer Group for a time.

After re-grouping, the Germans reached Krasnogvardeysk, a town situated less than ten kilometres from Leningrad. Their XVIII Army occupied Estonia and arrived on the shores of the Gulf of Finland.

Before beginning to attack the defensive positions in front of Leningrad, the Germans subjected the city to a heavy artillery and air bombardment. Facing stiff opposition German troops got as far as the suburbs. From 8th September the city's communications with the outside world had to be kept up exclusively by air and across Lake Ladoga. However, the Germans' attempt to break into the city and link up with the Finnish army advancing over the Karelian Isthmus was decisively rebuffed by the Soviet forces directly defending Leningrad and those deployed along the northern bank of the Neva. The Germans were unable to move one step further forward. Army Group North was forced to abandon the offensive. Hitler decided to take the city by blockade.

In the Ukraine in July 1941 the Soviet troops of the south-western front waged great defensive battles to the south of Polesye and before Kiev and Korosten. The southern front held the invading Germans and Rumanians in check in Moldavia.

Having great superiority of forces, German I Panzer Group, followed by VI Army, pressed towards Kiev, where they were halted. For seventy-two days the brave garrison of the Ukrainian capital defended the city, while to the south-west 5th Army, led by General Potapov, carried on a stubborn struggle, pinning down twelve German divisions and thereby easing the task of Kiev's defenders.

Farther south, the main forces of the south-western front were absorbed in great battles in right-bank Ukraine (the part of Ukraine to the west of the River Dnieper), which carried on until the first days of August 1941. Soviet 6th, 12th,

Soviet painting of an incident in the Crimea in 1941. A Black Sea sailor arms himself with grenades before throwing himself at a German tank

and 26th Armies inflicted heavy losses on German Army Group South. Kleist's I Panzer Group lost fifty per cent of its tanks. But by means of a deep turning movement at the beginning of August the Germans surrounded 6th and 12th Armies near Uman and thereby changed the general course of the battle in their favour.

In view of the grave situation, the Red Army Supreme Command ordered the armies of the south-western and southern fronts, commanded by Generals Kirponos and Tyulenev, to retire behind the Dnieper and stand on its left bank, while holding Kiev, Dnepropetrovsk, and a number of bridgeheads on the right bank of the river. The Soviet forces carried out this retirement in the last days of August, and military operations were transferred to left-bank Ukraine (Ukraine to the east of the Dnieper).

Now Guderian's II Panzer Group and II

Army were transferred from Army Group Centre near Smolensk to the Ukraine to help Army Group South encircle the Soviet armies near Kiev. Guderian's tank formations broke through the defence lines of the Soviet forces near Konotop and moved from the north into the rear of the main forces of the Soviet south-western front. Kleist's tank divisions pushed up from the south to meet Guderian, coming from the bridge-head on the Dnieper at Kremenchug. The two tank wedges met at Lokhvitsa. The four Soviet armies of the south-western front were now surrounded to the east of Kiev. On 18th September the Germans began to close in on the Kiev pocket of half a million trapped Red Army soldiers. On the next day the capital of the Ukraine fell to Hitler's armies. The battle of Kiev was the greatest disaster in the Red Army's history. The German forces advanced to the approaches to the Crimea.

At the same time Rumanian and German forces were blockading and besieging Odessa, one of the chief bases of the Black Sea Fleet. The city's inhabitants had constructed some defence lines around Odessa by the beginning of September. The enemy's attack on Odessa began on 10th August. The troops of the Special Black Sea Army and sailors of the Black Sea Fleet who were defending the city threw back the onslaught. Marine light infantry, supported by naval artillery, counter-attacked and smashed several Rumanian units.

On 20th August the enemy renewed the attack, with a five-fold superiority of forces over the defenders of the city. A bloody battle raged for a whole month. Very slowly, and with heavy losses, the attackers drew near the outskirts. Since the overall situation of the Soviet forces in the Ukraine and the Crimea in the autumn of 1941 had become extremely critical, the Supreme Command decided to evacuate the defenders of Odessa by sea and use them to strengthen the garrison of Sebastopol, the principal base of the Black Sea Fleet, which was also threatened.

By throwing in fresh reserves, the Soviet Supreme Command halted the German armies in the south in the late autumn. The Germans had suffered heavy losses. Nevertheless they were able, at the beginning of November, to get as far as Rostov, regarded as 'the gate to the Caucasus'. As a result, however, of transfers of Soviet troops to this area and a counter-offensive near Rostov, the shock force of Army Group South was smashed and thrown back from the town.

By the autumn of 1941 Hitler's plan for a

*Left: A man lies crushed in the wake of the advance. **Top right:** Reprisals. **Bottom right:** German machine-gunners*

On 5th December 1941 the Red Army counter-attacked the German armies threatening Moscow. Warmly-clad, well-equipped fresh troops from Siberia pounded the exhausted, ill-clad Germans in temperatures far below zero. The Germans retreated and Moscow was saved

Blitzkrieg against the Soviet Union had failed. Despite some resounding victories, Hitler and his strategists had proved unable to complete their eastern campaign before the autumn as they had hoped. The war was dragging on. The Soviet Union was still standing. The Red Army had repulsed the first and strongest blow of the aggressor, and had created the conditions for a turning point in the course of the war. This determined everything that followed. The main forces of Hitler's Wehrmacht were tied down for a long time on the Soviet-German front, and the danger of a Nazi invasion of Great Britain and of the Near East was finally dissipated.

Hitler and his generals had not achieved the victory they had expected. But the situation of the Soviet Union remained critical. The invaders were before the walls of Leningrad, were threatening Moscow, had occupied the greater part of the Ukraine, and held some of the most important economic areas of the country.

Hitler thought that victory over the Soviet Union was near. He now ordered the final blow against Moscow, so as to capture the Soviet capital and thereby terminate the eastern campaign.

The drive on Moscow was assigned to Army Group Centre, headed by Field Marshal Bock. Operation Typhoon, as it was called, envisaged the striking of three blows by tank and infantry groups in order to break up and surround the Soviet forces defending Moscow. After opening the road to the capital, Bock's forces were then to capture it by means of a headlong attack.

An army of a million men, comprising seventy-seven divisions (including fourteen tank divisions and eight motorized divisions with 1,700 tanks and assault guns) and 950 fighter aircraft assembled near Moscow. The preparations for the 'final blow' took more than a month.

The Soviet command entrusted the task of defending the approaches to Moscow to the troops of the western, reserve, and Bryansk fronts under the command of General Konev, Marshal Budenny, and General Yeremenko. The Nazis had twice as many tanks and guns as the defenders of the capital and three times as many aircraft.

The offensive began on 2nd October. The defenders were unable to repulse the attack. By 7th October the main forces of the western and reserve fronts were surrounded near Vyazma. The roads to Moscow were open.

Extraordinary efforts now had to be made and measures taken by the Soviet command in order to prevent the fall of the capital. Above all it was necessary to gain time. By their stubborn resistance the surrounded troops tied down twenty-eight German divisions for over a week. The Supreme Command and the new commander of the western front, General Zhukov, began to concentrate all available forces in the Moscow area. First, a rapid redeployment of the troops stationed nearby succeeded in covering the main roads leading to the capital from the west and in holding the German units which were advancing from Vyazma. Meanwhile, from Siberia, the Volga region, the Far East, and Kazakhstan troop-trains flowed in bringing fresh forces. Soon it was possible to throw another fourteen divisions, sixteen tank brigades, forty artillery regiments, and other units into the battle for Moscow. A new defensive front was formed, along the Mozhaysk defensive line prepared by the people of Moscow.

On 10th October the Germans reached this line and attacked it. Desperate fighting went on for many days and nights without a break. The Germans succeeded in breaking through on a few sectors, capturing Kalinin, Mozhaysk, and Volokolamsk. They reached the close approaches of the capital.

At the end of October and the beginning of November the German advance was halted, thanks to the tremendous efforts of the Soviet troops. The German armies, which had made a 250-kilometre dash in October 1941, were forced to go over to the

Russian peasants fleeing before the German advance on Moscow. By December 1941 70,000,000 people were living under German rule in Russia. The Nazi exploitation of occupied Russia was brutal. Millions were deported for slave labour, millions were arbitrarily executed

defensive along a line 70 to 120 kilometres from Moscow. There was a pause in the battle. The Soviet command had gained time for further strengthening of the approaches to the capital. The pause before Moscow enabled the Red Army Supreme Command to reinforce the western front with fresh troops and an anti-tank defence system was constructed in depth along the principal lines of approach to Moscow. In the first half of November the western front received an additional 100,000 men, 300 tanks, and 2,000 guns. The Muscovites dug defence-works in front of the entrances to their city.

The German command, after concentrating forces along the main roads leading to Moscow, began their second attack on the Soviet capital on 15th and 16th November. Again there was fierce and bloody fighting. Slowly, suffering heavy losses, the Germans drew nearer to Moscow, the capture of which they saw as their single and final aim, and their salvation. But the defences in depth held by the Soviet forces prevented them from penetrating the front. Guderian's II Panzer Army broke through to Tula, an important industrial centre and hub of communications. Numerous attempts to capture the town were successfully resisted by the troops under General Boldin, aided by detachments of Tula workers. Tula stood its ground, trans-

formed into the southern defence bastion of the western front. Then Guderian, leaving part of his forces to cover his right and left flanks, pushed on northwards with his main tank group, in order to come out to the east of Moscow and there join up with II and III Panzer Groups which were advancing from the north-west. The Germans were within a few kilometres of Moscow.

But the crisis of the German offensive had already come to a head. The staunch defence put up by the Soviet forces had worn out the shock troops of Army Group Centre. Having failed on the northern and southern approaches to Moscow, they tried to break through the defences in the centre of the western front. On 1st December the enemy succeeded in doing this in the sector to the north of Narofominsk (forty miles south-west of Moscow). Tanks and motorized infantry streamed along the highway as far as Kubinka, sixty kilometres from Moscow. But their further advance was held up by formations of 5th Army, commanded by General Govorov. After losing nearly half their tanks, the Germans turned eastwards into the area of Golitsyno station. Here the counter-blows of 33rd and 5th Armies descended upon them. The enemy's attempt to get through to Moscow had been frustrated. On 4th December, formations of these armies routed the Germans in fierce fighting and managed to

restore the front on the River Nara.

Thus concluded the last Nazi offensive against Moscow. The Soviet armed forces had won the defensive battle. The German shock groups had been bled white and deprived of power to continue their attack. Between 16th November and 5th December alone the enemy lost 55,000 dead and over 100,000 wounded and frostbitten.

The success of the defensive battle in front of Moscow was largely due to the fact that, at the most difficult period in the defence of the capital, Soviet forces went over to the counter-offensive south-west of Leningrad and in the Rostov area. The enemy was therefore unable to transfer forces from these areas to the Moscow sector. At the same time fresh Red Army reserves were assembled in the capital. The 1st and 20th Armies were deployed to the north of Moscow, and 10th Army to the south-west. The balance of forces gradually changed to the advantage of the Soviets.

On 5th December the Red Army began its counter-offensive before Moscow. The Germans were pushed back from the capital and were forced to assume the defensive, and were never again able to mount an offensive simultaneously along the entire strategic Soviet-German front. Their defeat at the walls of Moscow showed how much Hitler had under-estimated Soviet resistance.

3 THE RISING SUN

Challenge in the Pacific

The Japanese attack on the American fleet at Pearl Harbour was less an attempt to provoke the United States into a declaration of war than a final admission that war between the United States and Japan was bound to come. It signalled the end of a long period of increasingly embittered relations between the two powers. The struggle centred on Japan's ambitions for an unchallenged hegemony in the Far East, and these cannot be understood without at least a glance at the astonishing rise of Japanese power in the 20th century.

Unlike China, Japan did not resist the imported Western civilization introduced by the American Commodore Matthew Perry and his successors in the 19th century. Indeed, the Japanese showed an acute ability to adopt or to adapt all the inventive genius of America and Europe, and by the First World War her industrial revolution was well under way. She was greatly assisted by a sharply rising population and low wage scales—so much so that after the First World War other nations found it necessary to introduce trade barriers against unrestricted Japanese competition.

Although under the constitution of 1889 the Emperor, as a constitutional monarch, was to reign rather than rule, the military continued to occupy a place of unique privilege, beyond ordinary democratic controls familiar to Western democracies. Eleven years later an Imperial Ordinance stated that the ministers of war and navy must be serving officers. There was no civilian control over their departments

Left: Italian postcard shows Japan smashing the Allied Pacific fleets

and if either minister resigned over a disagreement with the government the service he represented could refuse to appoint a successor. In 1925 universal manhood suffrage was introduced but the government also introduced and saw enacted a bill enforcing a Peace Preservation Law providing ten years' imprisonment for those who sought to alter the national constitution or repudiate the system of private property. It helped break up and drive underground the Japanese Communist Party. By 1931 the rising tide of ultra-nationalism was manifesting itself in murderous conspiracy at home and unchecked aggression abroad. The Japanese occupation of Manchuria was inspired and carried out solely by the army. The government and cabinet were not so much defied as ignored.

American reactions to the seizure of Manchuria, which inspired a wave of patriotism among Japanese, might have been more forceful had not the United States embarked on an isolationist phase, with a consequent unwillingness to risk entanglements overseas. Nevertheless Japan's invasion of Manchuria presented a direct threat to the 'open door' policy which the United States, along with the other trading nations, had maintained towards China since the beginning of the century. This policy required that no power should claim any special or favourable commercial relationship with the vast Chinese market—least of all by territorial conquest. Japan had clearly offended this policy and the United States accordingly was bound to take notice. In the end, however, she did nothing positive, apart from

issuing public statements deploring the Japanese action and refusing to recognize the state of Manchukuo which Japan set up to replace Manchuria.

Emboldened by the seizure of Manchuria, Japan's ambition and adventurism soon turned to naval matters. The Washington Conference of 1921-22 had fixed the tonnage of capital ships among the three leading naval powers—Great Britain, the United States, and Japan—at a 5:5:3 ratio. Other treaties signed between the great powers, Japan among them, placed further restrictions upon Japan's naval construction programmes, as they also restricted the other powers. In December 1934, however, Japan demanded naval parity with the United States and when this was refused under the terms of existing treaties she abrogated the agreements and withdrew from the London Naval Conference in January 1936. Within a year, Japanese naval construction considerably exceeded that of France, Italy, Germany, or Russia, and building programmes promised to make her a formidable rival to the United States fleet in the Pacific.

Already Japan's leaders were declaring a policy of Japanese hegemony over Eastern Asia, and often alluded to a 'Japanese Monroe Doctrine'. They were aware of the new opportunities created in Asia as rumours of war occupied the attention of the colonial powers.

USS Panay is sunk
American policy was in a dilemma. The after-effects of the Depression and the initiation of the New Deal in consuming the national effort, coupled with the con-

tinued mood of isolationism in foreign affairs, were calculated to encourage Japanese ambitions. Although primarily designed to keep America out of European wars, the Neutrality Acts passed by Congress in 1935, 1936, and 1937 suited Japan's expansionists, just as President Roosevelt's declaration 'I hate war' in a speech in August 1936 must have fallen pleasantly on their ears.

Japan now sought to extend her interests on the Chinese mainland. In July 1937 Japanese forces extended her control over Inner Mongolia and northern China. Key ports on the coast of central and southern China were also seized and occupied. The American people sympathized with the Chinese, and public opinion called for something stronger than the moral gestures put forward by President Roosevelt. However, the President replied with no-

thing more forceful than his famous 'Quarantine' speech of October 1937. Observing that war was a disease and that the best thing would be to stop the contagion spreading, President Roosevelt suggested 'a quarantine of the patients in order to protect the health of the community against the spread of the disease.'

This was one of Roosevelt's least inspired addresses in the field of foreign affairs. In Great Britain, Neville Chamberlain, the Prime Minister, remarked of it: 'I read Roosevelt's speech with mixed feelings . . . seeing that patients suffering from epidemic diseases do not usually go about fully armed, there is something lacking in his analogy.'

In 1932 the League of Nations had condemned Japan for violating the Nine-Power Treaty and the Kellogg Pact in its invasion of China and proposed a meeting

of the signatories of the Nine-Power Treaty to discuss the situation. Japan had refused to attend the conference at Brussels which consequently had achieved nothing.

Thereafter the United States arranged to evacuate its nationals from Chinese territory. Once more, in 1937, Japanese militarists reacted to what they took to be a sign of weakness, and within a matter of weeks, on 12th December, the US gunboat *Panay* was bombed and sunk in the Yangtze River. The United States immediately protested, demanding reparations. Japan apologized promptly and paid indemnities. Whatever her territorial ambitions, at this stage Japan had no wish to find herself at war with the United States. But she did continue to expand her dominion over the Chinese mainland,

Emperor Hirohito inspects defences

bombing innocent civilians in a new and barbaric type of warfare which Europe was also to suffer during the next six years. By 1938, Japan had seized much of northern and central China: the only real opposition to her further control over the whole mainland came from Chinese Communists in the northern provinces and the Nationalist forces at Chungking.

Public opinion in the United States became more and more incensed at the Japanese methods of warfare and demanded at the very least an embargo on trade with Japan. In the summer of 1938 the American government urged manufacturers to place a 'moral embargo' on the shipment of aircraft and other engines of war. But in fact Japan's main purchases from the United States were oil, petrol, and huge quantities of scrap iron, so the 'moral embargo' hardly threatened her war potential.

Not surprisingly, perhaps, Japan's militarist leaders seized every opportunity to exploit the deepening crisis in Europe, and when Great Britain and France were drawn into war with Germany, Japan acted swiftly in the Far East. As Hitler marched into Prague in March 1939, Japan occupied the island of Hainan, controlling the Gulf of Tonkin. Then in 1940 she moved into French Indo-China, wringing concessions from the Vichy government as soon as France fell. The next step was to deny China supplies via the Burma Road by insisting that the British stop supplies to China along this vital route. Unable to gain any formal gesture of support from the United States, Great Britain was forced to close the road.

By now, there was sharp disagreement on United States policy towards Japan in American government circles, with the cabinet itself divided. Experienced diplomats and statesmen such as the secretary of the treasury, Henry Morgenthau, and the secretary for war, Henry L. Stimson, favoured some form of ultimatum to Japan. They were convinced that at all costs Japan was anxious to avoid a direct conflict with the United States but that, equally, her leaders were immune to the ordinary language of diplomacy. Others among President Roosevelt's advisers, however, urged caution, anxious not to provoke Japan into even wilder actions, such as an attack on the Dutch East Indies, now that the Netherlands were overrun.

In response to mounting pressure for some sort of deliberate action, President Roosevelt issued an order restricting the supply of strategic materials, especially petroleum products, and also ordered the United States fleet to Hawaii. This move met with strong opposition from the US Navy, who much preferred the home anchorage of San Diego in southern Cali-fornia. Admiral Richardson, the fleet commander, protested that it was logistically unwise to have the fleet stationed at Pearl Harbour, so far from a home base. The admiral was overruled, however, and relieved of his command. The United States fleet was renamed the Pacific Fleet, and its main base became Pearl Harbour.

Greater East Asia Co-Prosperity Sphere

Japanese policy towards the United States had become double-edged. The diplomatic programme was to avoid provoking war with the United States whilst seeking to gain maximum concessions for Japanese expansionist aims in China and South-East Asia. At the same time, however, Japanese military experts were laying plans for an offensive war against the United States if the diplomatic programme failed.

On 27th January 1941 Joseph Grew, the American ambassador in Tokyo, sent a remarkable despatch to Washington which was ignored by State Department officials:

'My Peruvian colleague told a member of my staff that he had heard from many sources including a Japanese source that the Japanese military forces planned, in the event of trouble with the United States, to attempt a surprise mass attack on Pearl Harbour using all their military facilities. He added that although the project seemed fantastic the fact that he had heard it from many sources prompted him to pass on the information.'

The Chief of Naval Operations insisted that according to all the known data on Japanese naval forces, such a move could be discounted both then and in the foreseeable future. Nevertheless Japanese records show that in January 1941 Admiral Yamamoto began to prepare a careful study of the Pearl Harbour fortifications and stated that if war between Japan and the United States were to come, 'we will have no hope of winning unless the US fleet in Hawaiian waters can be destroyed.'

But there were also divided opinions within the Japanese government. The Prime Minister, Prince Konoye, favoured some sort of détente with the United States. On the other hand Yosuke Matsuoka, the headstrong nationalist foreign minister, favoured further expansion, including an attack on the Soviet Union now that Germany was engaging Russian armies in the west. Matsuoka's proposals were rejected in order to conserve Japanese forces for the thrusts into South-East Asia and the consolidation of Japanese gains there. Matsuoka continued to press his grandiose schemes on his colleagues, freely citing the German successes in Europe as the model for an expansionist Japan. But his belligerency eventually proved too much even for his cabinet colleagues and in July 1941 Prince Konoye reconstructed his cabinet without including Matsuoka.

The US State Department still hoped for some agreement with Japan and took heart at this development. Moreover, Grew in Tokyo became more optimistic. But their optimism was short-lived, however, for it soon became clear that Japan intended to press on with her territorial ambitions, especially towards Indo-China now that France had fallen. President Roosevelt now recognized that positive action was needed from the American side if Japan was to be dissuaded. On 24th July the President made another attempt to reach an agreement when he proposed the neutralization of Indo-China. But Japanese forces were already on the move, and on 26th July Roosevelt issued an executive order freezing Japanese assets in the United States. Admiral Nomura, the Japanese ambassador in Washington, urgently telegrammed his government that the Americans 'meant business', and advised that some appeasement gestures be made promptly. The American action had, however, merely strengthened the convictions of the militarists, who urged that Japan must press on towards hegemony in Eastern Asia with all speed. Moreover Japan was now in acute need of oil and petrol for her war machine, and the rich deposits of the Dutch East Indies were ripe for pillage.

Prince Konoye, the Prime Minister, still hoped to avoid a direct confrontation with the United States, insisting that the overall policy of Japan was to set up a peaceful condominium of states, to be known as the Greater East Asia Co-Prosperity Sphere. Unfortunately for this pretence, American intelligence experts had succeeded in cracking the Japanese diplomatic code and knew a great deal more of Japan's expansionist aims than Prince Konoye realized. Nevertheless the wish to avoid war with the United States was genuine enough – if only because it was dictated by prudence and self-interest. Accordingly, Nomura in Washington sought to arrange a meeting between President Roosevelt and Prince Konoye – a proposal which Grew in Tokyo also favoured as he felt it would help strengthen the moderate elements in the Konoye cabinet, who were in danger of being overwhelmed by the militarists. On 29th September 1941 Grew sent a long despatch to Roosevelt urging a meeting and adding that failure to meet Konoye might well result in the fall of the government and its replacement by 'a military dictatorship with neither the temperament nor the disposition to avoid a head-on collision with the United States.'

Roosevelt's advisers differed sharply on the proposal. Some experts detected clear signs of Japan's willingness to scale down her territorial ambitions if American insistence were accompanied by a display

of military strength. Navy experts argued that Japan would not run the risk of engaging the Pacific Fleet. Other military experts pointed out that Japan was dangerously over-extended in Asia, and 'already more than half beaten'.

Roosevelt's diplomatic advisers, on the other hand, included those who strongly urged that a meeting with Konoye was the only way to avoid war with Japan, for the military leaders were pressing on with war plans in the event of a failure of diplomacy. One report stated that war plans were now being prepared for possible conflict at the end of October.

Faced with contradictory advice, Roosevelt played for time. In exchanges between the secretary of state, Cordell Hull, and Nomura, the American government asked for clear assurances that Japan would withdraw all military, naval, air, and police forces from China and Indo-China. Prince Konoye, caught between his own policies and those of the war leaders who watched his every move, was unable to supply the assurances demanded by Roosevelt.

The die is cast

When hopes of a meeting between Roosevelt and Prince Konoye vanished, the Konoye government soon collapsed. An assassination attempt on the Prime Minister failed, but by mid-October the cabinet submitted its resignation and General Tojo, war minister and army officer on the active list, took over with a new cabinet containing many military leaders. Although the Tojo cabinet continued diplomatic negotiations with the American government, reports from US Navy Intelligence pointed out that Japan's manpower was now being placed on a war footing, and that her naval forces were now fully mobilized 'for imminent action'.

A final effort at a modus vivendi was attempted on 20th November. Japanese diplomats presented a number of proposals whereby Japan would agree to withdraw her troops from Indo-China once peace had been restored in the Pacific area and normal trade had been re-established between the United States and Japan. A further requirement added that the United States should provide Japan with a required quantity of oil, and that the United States should refrain from any action 'prejudicial to the endeavours for the restoration of general peace between Japan and China.'

Not surprisingly, perhaps, the United

Left: Tojo, Prime Minister and army officer on the active list, addresses the House of Representatives in November 1941, the month before Pearl Harbour. Even after the war, he insisted: 'I believe firmly that it was a war of self-defence'

States found these proposals unacceptable. But intelligence sources also confirmed that Japan was now poised for war, and that these proposals were in fact Japan's final ultimatum. Roosevelt and Cordell Hull conferred carefully and decided once more to play for time. The American reply proposed a three months' period during which a certain amount of trade would be permitted in return for an end to Japanese hostilities in China and Indo-China. Messages intercepted by American intelligence disclosed that Tojo was not disposed to adopt the American proposals. The deadline for accepting the Japanese proposals was 29th November. 'After that,' the Japanese foreign minister informed his ambassador in Washington, 'things are automatically going to happen'.

Lulled by a decade of isolationist sentiment, neither America's leaders nor her people seemed able to accept that Japan would actually risk war with the United States. Certainly the balance of Roosevelt's policies implied that a conflict could be avoided and that reason and good sense would prevail in the Japanese cabinet. When, in late November 1941, the American cabinet accepted that war was now inevitable, secretary of war Stimson noted in his diary that the cabinet was now preoccupied with the question of 'how we should manoeuvre them [the Japanese] into the position of firing the first shot without too much danger to ourselves.' Rarely can a nation have approached a conflict so reluctantly.

Again, despite the hard evidence coming in from decoded cables and wireless messages in the Pacific, American military strategists seemed loath to take note of warnings that the first blow might come at Pearl Harbour.

With the American rejection of Japan's final proposals, and Japan's refusal to take up the American modus vivendi, the die was cast. On 5th December, Tokyo ordered members of the Japanese embassy staff to leave Washington. An intercepted message from Ambassador Nomura to his superiors in Tokyo read: 'We have completed destruction of codes . . .' On the morning of 7th December, even as Japanese diplomats kept up the farce of parleying in Washington, bombers took off from Japanese aircraft-carriers and swooped on Pearl Harbour, destroying a major part of the Pacific Fleet and killing over 2,300 American servicemen. Next day Congress declared war on Japan. The war which followed on sea and on land in the Pacific featured the ugliest and bloodiest fighting ever experienced by American forces. In calling for a declaration of war, President Roosevelt said of the attack on Pearl Harbour on 7th December 1941 that it was 'a date which will live in infamy'.

Pearl Harbour

America's decision to position her Pacific Fleet at a point covering Japanese lines of expansion was an event of great significance. Near Honolulu in the Hawaiian Islands, United States military authorities had dredged out a lagoon called Pearl Harbour, on which they located America's strongest outlying naval base before the Second World War and set up army and army air installations to protect it and the Pacific Fleet. Because of its location, Pearl Harbour came to be variously viewed as the Gibraltar of the Pacific, the defensive outpost of continental United States, a deterrent to Japanese aggressive intentions, or an encouraging inducement to Japanese to attack American forces and supplies situated in the East.

Launch edges up to blazing West Virginia *to snatch a survivor from the water. In fact, most ships damaged and even sunk were restored to fighting condition*

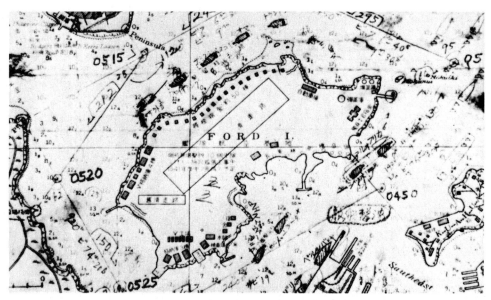

Japanese chart supplied to Pearl Harbour strike pilots marks the supposed position of US Navy vessels in the base. It was not very accurate

Pearl Harbour's destiny inevitably became involved in relations between Japan and the United States. These had been deteriorating badly since the previous year, as disagreements arose over Japan's southward expansion on the Asiatic continent. During the 1930's the United States had limited its objections to efforts to impose moral sanctions.

By 1940 both countries began to examine their relationships in the light of the war in Europe. The Japanese took advantage of Nazi successes to make new advances down the coast of China. The hard pressures of war forced the French to acquiesce in the movement of Japanese troops into northern Indo-China and the British to agree to close the Burma Road, the last important supply line into China from Lashio to Kunming. By imposing a limited check on the export of war materials to Japan, the United States emerged as the principal obstacle to Japanese advance.

In May 1940 President Roosevelt changed the Pacific Fleet's main base from San Diego, California to Pearl Harbour despite the opposition of its commander, thus making the force a pawn in the diplomatic manoeuvring between Japan and the United States.

But the Japanese had been making moves as well and in September 1940 secured a new alliance with Germany and Italy, known as the Tripartite Pact, which established spheres of influence, in effect giving Germany Europe, and Japan the Far East. In an obvious reference to the United States, the pact guaranteed mutual aid 'if attacked by a power at present not involved in the European war or in the Sino-Japanese conflict'.

Early in 1941, Japan fatefully started a dual course of action, one diplomatic and the other military, both aimed at removing American obstacles to Japanese expansion. The diplomats hoped to gain these ends peacefully by persuading the United States to stand aside. Meanwhile the militarists planned on war should the diplomats fail.

In January 1941 the American ambassador to Japan Joseph C.Grew reported a rumoured Japanese plan for a surprise attack on Pearl Harbour, but the report was discounted as 'fantastic'. Actually Admiral Isoroku Yamamoto was starting a study of the Pearl Harbour operation, convinced that the Pacific Fleet's destruction was essential to Japanese victory. In July, military and civilian leaders meeting before the Emperor decided to work for the 'establishment of the Greater East Asia Co-Prosperity Sphere and World Power', and declared that they would 'not be deterred by the possibility of being involved in a war with England and America'. The United States, too, hardened its position by freezing Japanese assets in the United States on 26th July 1941.

By this time the Washington government was being assisted greatly by intercepted and decoded messages. This 'Magic', as the decoding system was called, made it possible for the Americans, unknown to the Japanese, to be aware of Japanese diplomatic communications throughout the world. While it had limitations, including the fact that the information was diplomatic rather than military, the 'Magic' intercepts gave the American government at least an important diplomatic preview of things to come.

Another Japanese resolution on 6th September set in operation the advance to war. Only the successful achievement by diplomacy of three principal demands could halt the move. The United States and Great Britain should neither interfere with the settlement of the 'China Incident' nor strengthen their own forces in the Far East. Moreover, they should co-operate with Japanese efforts to obtain raw materials.

When a new, more militaristic government came into power in mid-October, the Japanese ambassador to the United States Kichisaburu Nomura felt out of touch and requested recall. Instead, the Japanese government sent Saburu Kurusu to Washington as a special emissary to work with Nomura.

On 5th November another Imperial Conference ordered one more diplomatic effort. If it failed, the question of war would go to the Emperor. Unable to persuade Tokyo to wait, its diplomats presented a new memorandum to Washington. Cordell Hull, the secretary of state, had no intention of accepting this proposal, which would have meant a reversal of the American position, but since he was under pressure from the military to delay, he and Roosevelt drafted a counter-proposal, including a short truce. They also learned through 'Magic' that Tokyo had set a final deadline for the diplomats—29th November. 'After that, things are automatically going to happen,' said the message.

Discouraged by British and Chinese opposition to the temporary proposal, Washington dropped it and presented a ten-point memorandum to the Japanese, restating its original position. Nomura and Kurusu 'argued back furiously' against the proposal but had to forward it when Hull remained 'solid as a rock'. Two days later Tokyo told Nomura that the memorandum was unacceptable and that negotiations would be 'de facto ruptured', although Nomura was instructed not to reveal this fact to the Americans.

Diplomatic efforts fail

After the war, Japanese leaders claimed that the American note forced Japan into war. True, the memorandum threatened Japanese expansion, but it did not menace Japan, its people, or its right to trade in the Far East. It challenged Japan's right to hold lands she had seized on the mainland but it did not threaten Japan in the sense that if Japan rejected the proposals the United States would declare war. The United States was not following a policy of dual initiative; it was not even planning

Right: Detail of illustration from American magazine Fortune, *published after Pearl Harbour, depicting (from left) a Japanese soldier, Prime Minister Tojo, Admiral Nagumo, who delivered the raid, and Emperor Hirohito*

The Rising Sun

to sever diplomatic relations. Nevertheless, Hull realized that the Japanese would not accept the proposals and that diplomacy was virtually at an end. On the 27th he told the secretary of war: 'I have washed my hands of it and it is now in the hands of . . . the Army and the Navy.'

Warnings had already been going out from time to time to outlying military commands. On 25th November, for example, Admiral Husband E. Kimmel in Hawaii heard that neither Roosevelt nor Hull 'would be surprised over a Japanese surprise attack'. On 27th November, military authorities decided to send new warnings to Admiral Kimmel and General Walter C.Short, the navy and army commanders in Hawaii. The note to Kimmel was the more explicit: 'Consider this dispatch a war warning.' It stated that diplomatic efforts had failed and that Japan might make an aggressive move 'within a few days'. Another message to Short on the same day, unfortunately, indicated sabotage as the principal threat, and he responded by issuing an alert, bunching aircraft against sabotage rather than dispersing them against air attack. Fortunately, no American aircraft-carriers were in Pearl Harbour on 7th December as the *Enterprise* and *Lexington* had been despatched to carry Marine fighter aircraft to Wake and Midway Islands.

Acting as if negotiations were still possible, the Japanese diplomats continued the farce, even while receiving orders to destroy codes and prepare to leave. On 6th December they received word that a fourteen-part memorandum was on the way, but were told, 'the situation is extremely delicate, and when you receive it I want you to keep it secret'.

The first thirteen parts of the memorandum were received first and, decoded by 'Magic', were ready for distribution about 9 p.m. on 6th December. When Roosevelt saw them, he reportedly said 'this means war', and discussed the matter with his confidential assistant Harry Hopkins, without mentioning Pearl Harbour. Knox, the secretary of the navy, and some high military officials also saw the message but acted as if it had no military significance. Moreover, the despatch was not sent to General George C.Marshall, Chief-of-Staff, although he was at his home.

The fourteenth part was available by 7.30 or 8 a.m. on 7th December. Seeing it about 10 a.m., President Roosevelt commented that it looked as if Japan would sever diplomatic relations, for this part stated that it was 'impossible to reach an agreement through further negotiations'.

Meanwhile, another intercepted message from Tokyo was ready for distribution about 9 a.m. Referring to the longer memorandum, it asked: 'Will the ambas-

sador please submit to the United States government (if possible to the secretary of state) our reply to the United States at 1 p.m. on the 7th your time.'

The officer in charge saw that the message was significant and got it to a presidential aide within twenty minutes. General Marshall returned late from a morning ride and did not read the message until almost 11.30 a.m. He immediately went into action and in longhand prepared a warning to key commands, including the Hawaiian Command:

'The Japanese are presenting at 1 p.m., Eastern Standard Time, today what amounts to an ultimatum. Also they are under orders to destroy their code machine immediately. Just what significance the hour set may have we do not know, but be on the alert accordingly.'

The message which went to Pearl Harbour met obstacles that appear almost comic in retrospect and did not arrive until after the bombs began to fall.

Target Pearl Harbour

In Washington, the diplomatic game came to an anticlimactic end. The Americans decoded the Japanese messages faster than did the Japanese embassy, which had to ask for a delay in meeting Secretary Hull, and the diplomats did not arrive until shortly after 2 p.m. On his way to meet them, Hull received a telephone call from President Roosevelt, who said, 'there's a report that the Japanese have attacked Pearl Harbour'. He added that the report

Pearl Harbour seen on Japanese film.
Top: *Still shows hilarity with which pilots of Pearl Harbour Task Force, en route for their objective, greeted a broadcast by the unsuspecting Americans on Oahu.*
Above: *Carrier deck crews hold Zero fighters bound for Pearl Harbour until their engines have been revved up to take-off speed.* **Right:** Oklahoma *and* West Virginia *gush oil after the attack.* **Below right:** *Ford Island as the raid begins. A Kate peels off after scoring a direct hit on* Oklahoma*; the torpedoed* Utah *(arrowed) lists to port*

had not been confirmed. Hull then went to meet the ambassador and Kurusu and read quickly through the fourteen-point memorandum which, unknown to the Japanese, he had already seen. Coldly furious, he told them that in his fifty years of public life he had never seen a document 'more crowded with infamous falsehoods and distortions on a scale so huge that I never imagined until today that any government on this planet was capable of uttering them'. He dismissed the diplomats and a few minutes later received confirmation of the Pearl Harbour attack.

All nations at this time had plans for possible war, and the United States was no exception. In 1924, American military planners prepared an 'Orange' plan in case of war with Japan. In the 1930's they replaced this with 'Rainbow 5' which envisaged war with the Axis, seeking particularly to enforce the Monroe Doctrine and protect the United States, its possessions, and its sea trade. By 1941 the United States had held discussions about the Far East with the British and the Dutch, but had not reached agreement. When war came each nation began fighting according to its own plan.

As war neared, American military leaders became increasingly concerned with fighting a defensive struggle in the Pacific against Japan and making the major effort in the Atlantic against Germany. Transfer of vessels from the Atlantic to the Pacific might 'well cause the United States to lose the battle of the Atlantic in the near future'. Consequently, the only plans recommended by General Marshall and Admiral Stark were 'to conduct defensive war, in co-operation with the British and the Dutch, for the defence of the Philippines and the Dutch East Indies'. Knowing that preparations were inadequate, they asked for more time.

Meanwhile, as we have noted, the Japanese had been carrying on their own war plans, in line with the policy of dual initiative. The nature of the nation's resources dictated a short conflict. Plans included early capture of oilfields in the East Indies, seizure of Singapore and the Philippines, and disabling the United States Pacific Fleet to keep it from interfering. Planners developed three phases of attack. First would be a blow at Pearl Harbour and an advance south in the Far East to seize lands and establish a perimeter extending from Wake Island through the Gilbert Islands, New Guinea, and the Dutch East Indies to Burma and the border of India. Second would be strengthening the perimeter, and third would be beating off attacks until the enemy tired of the effort. From the standpoint of the amount of territory to be occupied, the plan was aggressive and greatly expansionist. On the other hand, Japan apparently had no designs on either the United States or Great Britain.

Actual preparations for the Pearl Harbour attack began in August. The striking force consisted of six aircraft-carriers, screened by nine destroyers. A supporting force included two battleships, two cruisers, three submarines, tankers, and supply ships. Of the advance force of some twenty submarines, eleven bore small planes, and five were equipped with midget submarines, carrying two men and powered by storage batteries.

The battleships devastated

Leaving Japan in mid-November, the Pearl Harbour task-force rendezvoused in utmost secrecy at Tankan Bay in the Kurile Islands. On 26th November, it left the Kuriles to approach the Hawaiian Islands from the north. The weather probably would be rough and refuelling difficult, but the chances of avoiding detection were best by this route. On the morning of 7th December, the force reached its predetermined launching site, some 230 miles north of Pearl Harbour, and at 6 a.m. the first aircraft took off: forty Nakajima B5N2 ('Kate') torpedo-bombers equipped with torpedoes adapted for dropping in shallow water, fifty more Kates for high-level bombing, fifty Aichi D3A2 ('Val') dive-bombers, and fifty Zero fighters (Mitsubishi Zero-Sens, officially code-named 'Zekes' by the Allies). The second wave consisted of fifty Kates, eighty Vals, and forty Zeros.

There was no significant advance warning. In the fleet a so-called 'Condition 3' of readiness was in effect, in which one machine gun in four was manned, but it was a peacetime 'Condition 3' in which main and 5-inch batteries were not manned and even manned machine guns had their ammunition in locked boxes to which officers of the deck had the keys.

The raid begins

At 7.30 a.m. a boatswain's mate saw twenty to twenty-five aircraft circling, but he did not identify them as enemy machines. At about 7.55 a.m. the Commander, Mine Force Pacific, on a mine-layer in the harbour, saw an aircraft drop a bomb but thought it was an accident until he saw the crimson sun insignia on the machine. He immediately called General Quarters and had the signal hoisted: 'All ships in harbour sortie.' A few minutes later Admiral Kimmel heard of the attack, and Rear-Admiral Bellinger broadcast: '*Air raid, Pearl Harbour—this is no drill.*'

Earlier, at 6.45 a.m., a midget submarine was detected and sunk, but the sole reaction was to send another destroyer to the area. Radar protection was primitive, poorly understood, and underrated. The one detection that was made by men practising on a radar set was disregarded by the watch officer as blips of approaching American bombers from the mainland.

Escaping detection and initial opposition, therefore, the Japanese aircraft swept in from over the sea. The first attack, starting at about 7.55 a.m., lasted for approximately half an hour. There were four separate torpedo-bomber attacks, with the first two directed at the main objectives, the battleships lined up in 'Battleship Row' on the south-east shore of Ford Island. The third attack was by a single aircraft on the

cruiser *Helena,* and the fourth struck at ships on the north side of the island.

The second major attack came at about 8.40 a.m., after a brief lull, and consisted of a series of high-level bombing runs across the targets. Dive-bombers and fighters followed with a half-hour attack, and at 9.45 a.m. the aircraft withdrew.

The results were devastating. Among the battleships, *West Virginia* was hit by six or seven torpedoes, and quick counter-flooding alone prevented the vessel from capsizing. *Tennessee,* moored inboard of *West Virginia,* was protected by it from torpedoes and suffered relatively little damage or loss of life from bombings and fires. *Arizona* was the hardest hit. Torpedoes and bombs caused explosions and fires, and the vessel sank rapidly, carrying to their deaths over a thousand men trapped below decks. Although sustaining at least five bomb hits and one torpedo, *Nevada* managed to get clear and avoid sinking or capsizing. *Oklahoma* took three torpedoes and capsized until her masts stuck in the mud of the harbour bottom. *Maryland* was saved from torpedoes by *Oklahoma* and suffered the least damage of the battleships. *California,* struck by torpedoes, sank into the water and mud until only the superstructure showed. Aircraft attacking the north-west shore inflicted heavy damage on the light cruiser *Raleigh,* damaged the seaplane tender *Curtiss* and capsized the old battleship *Utah* which had been converted to a target ship. Another light cruiser *Helena* was heavily damaged and *Oglala,* the minelayer alongside it, was sunk. Other vessels damaged included the light cruiser *Honolulu,* the destroyers *Cassin, Downes,* and *Shaw,* and the repair ship *Vestal.* The battleship *Pennsylvania,* in drydock, was hit but received no serious damage.

Although the battleships and other vessels were the prime targets, the Japanese did not forget airfields, and, relatively speaking, American airpower suffered more heavily than did sea power. The attackers strafed and bombed land-based aircraft and practically eliminated the seaplanes. Army Air Force aircraft at

Above left: At the height of the attack on Pearl Harbour. **West Virginia** *lies sunk but upright as a result of prompt counter-flooding. Inboard is the* Tennessee *which she protected from torpedoes and which consequently suffered relatively little damage.*
Above right: Marines at Ewa Field fire at attacking Japanese aircraft. Men fought back against hopeless odds, at great personal danger and sacrifice, and with insufficient weapons. **Below:** *A scene of devastation at Pearl Harbour's Naval Air Station after the attack*

Hickam Field, bunched against sabotage, proved a perfect target for Japanese attackers.

By the end of the day, 'a date which will live in infamy' as President Roosevelt called it, the Americans had suffered 2,403 deaths, of which, 2,008 were from the navy. Three battleships sank, and other vessels took varying degrees of punishment. The Japanese destroyed two-thirds of American naval aircraft and left only sixteen serviceable Army Air Force bombers. In contrast, Japanese losses were slight: besides five midget submarines only nine Zeros, fifteen Vals, and five Kates were lost out of an attacking force of 360 aircraft.

American reactions on the island ranged from an initial incomprehension through disbelief, shock, frustration, to displays of the utmost courage. Men fought back with all they had, in some cases successfully, as the twenty-nine downed planes attest, but more often against hopeless odds, at great personal danger or sacrifice, and with insufficient weapons.

A tremendous blunder

Nearby Honolulu suffered little damage. The fires which started were determined later to have stemmed mainly from misdirected anti-aircraft fire from Pearl Harbour. Over a local radio, the governor proclaimed a state of emergency, and at 11.41 a.m. the army ordered commercial broadcasting stations off the air. Radio silence and the suddenness of the attack gave rise to uncertainties among the civilian population and the spreading of many unfounded rumours. Radio stations occasionally broadcast important messages, such as the announcement at 4.25 p.m. that the island had been placed under martial law.

Viewed from the level of high political policy, the Pearl Harbour attack was a tremendous blunder. It is difficult to conceive of any other act which could have rallied the American people more solidly behind a declaration of war on Japan. Generally speaking, Americans were not neutral; they favoured and gave aid to the nations fighting the Axis. However, without an incident such as Pearl Harbour, there would have been strong opposition to open participation in the war. Many people remembered the unsatisfactory aftermath of the First World War and they questioned what the Second World War could accomplish. The Pearl Harbour attack ended all significant debate on such matters. The nation, in the eyes of Americans, had been attacked ruthlessly and without warning, and the only way out was to declare war on Japan.

The Japanese predicted American reactions but reasoned that strategic results would be worth it. Strategically, however,

Pearl Harbour

the Pearl Harbour attack was a blunder in that it was unnecessary. The Pacific Fleet could not have stopped or even checked the initial planned advance of the Japanese. American war plans envisaged defensive action by a slow penetration into the Pacific. The fleet would not have dared move within range of land-based enemy aircraft without the most careful preparations. The fate of the British ships *Repulse* and *Prince of Wales* early in the war is an indication of what would have happened.

Even tactically the Pearl Harbour attack was a blunder. Capital ships were no longer as effective a means of exercising sea power as aircraft-carriers, and the two carriers *Lexington* and *Enterprise* were out of harbour when the Japanese attacked. In fact, most of the ships that were damaged and even sunk were later restored to fighting condition. *Nevada*, for example, participated in the Normandy invasion and later helped bombard Iwo Jima. *California, Maryland, Pennsylvania, Tennessee,* and *West Virginia* all took part in the Philippines campaigns. It would have been more effective to blast permanent installations and oil supplies than ships. Destruction of the oil tanks would have delayed advance across the Pacific longer than damage to ships and aircraft. In fact, one of the reasons for surprise was the belief that the Japanese also recognized that such an attack would be unnecessary.

Pearl Harbour might have been more effective had it not been followed by a colossal blunder by Hitler. After the attack, Japan called on Germany to join in the fight against the United States. Had Hitler refused, the American administration would have been in a most difficult position. Its leaders viewed Germany as the principal enemy, but without any specific incident in the Atlantic they might have had difficulty gaining support for a declaration of war on Germany while launching into a struggle with Japan. Pressure would have been strong to fight the visible and open enemy and not deliberately to seek another foe. It is difficult to know what would have been the result in the Atlantic. One recalls that Marshall and Stark earlier had warned that withdrawal of American ships from the Atlantic might cause Great Britain to lose the Battle of the Atlantic. Fortunately for the American government, Germany forced the United States with a declaration of war. This action made it possible for the Allies to plan a coalition war that was world-wide.

Painting by Japanese artist M.Susuki of newly qualified pilots at a passing-out ceremony – part of the militaristic ritual which reinforced the self-sacrificial fighting spirit of the Japanese

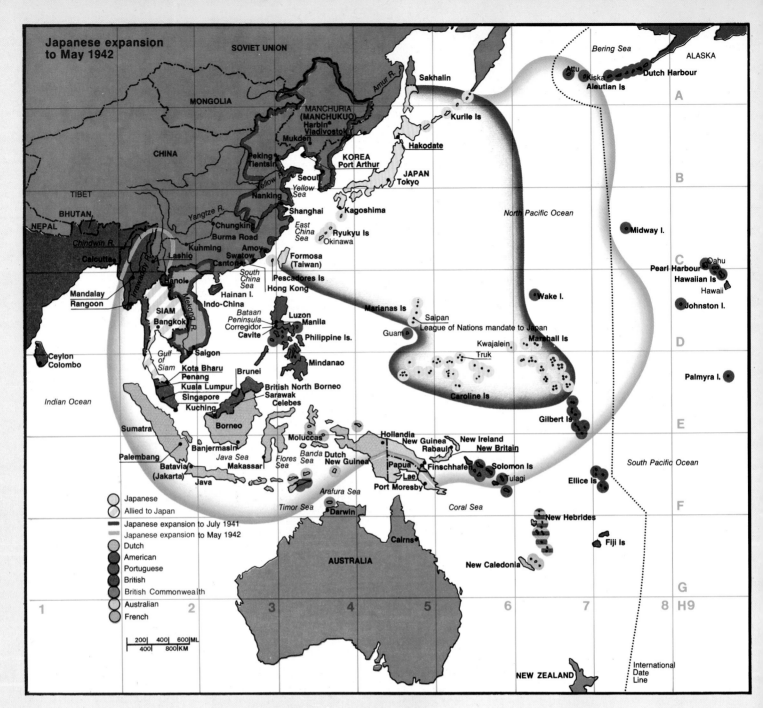

Japanese expansion to May 1942

Legend	
◯ Japanese	
◯ Allied to Japan	
Japanese expansion to July 1941	
Japanese expansion to May 1942	
Dutch	
American	
Portuguese	
British	
British Commonwealth	
Australian	
French	

Scale: 200 400 600 ML / 400 800 KM

The Risen Sun

America's introduction to total war came on 7th December 1941, with the greatest naval defeat suffered by a first-class power since the Battle of Trafalgar. In an age in which the battleship was still the index of maritime power, nothing experienced by the Germans in the First World War or by the Italians in the Second World War compared with the blows delivered on the United States Pacific Fleet by Admiral Chuichi Nagumo's naval aviators.

The catastrophe of Pearl Harbour was made possible on the Japanese side by a combination of superb training and re-markable duplicity, and on the American by culpable negligence in both Hawaii and Washington, aggravated by unsatisfactory communication between them. Perhaps it could be said that the Americans had made an even more direct contribution to their own defeat, as Nagumo's airmen followed a plan of attack based on that executed successfully against the same target by Vice-Admiral Ernest J.King during manoeuvres carried out by the Pacific Fleet in 1938. But there was some excuse for American negligence. All parties concerned fully appreciated in the last months

Japanese boys ape their soldier fathers. Young and old held the victorious military in great esteem in the early stages of the Pacific War

of 1941 that the Japanese were planning to attack the British and Dutch colonial empires in the Pacific. Few considered it rationally conceivable that they would add immeasurably to their difficulties by an attack on the United States at the same time.

Nor indeed did it prove to have been a rational decision. But there were certainly few signs during the first six months of the Pacific War that the Japanese had over-extended themselves. The assault on Pearl Harbour itself did not nearly exhaust their offensive capacity. Seven other attacks were launched almost simultaneously against British, Dutch, and American positions in the Pacific. These developed into an enveloping march of conquest unmatched in military history. No soldiers or sailors had ever before won such victories against such enemies. In terms of human achievement, nothing compares with Japanese triumphs in the Second World War except Japanese economic recovery after it. On 8th December forty-two American aircraft were destroyed on the ground in the Philippines, for the loss of only seven Japanese. Two days later, *HMS Prince of Wales* and *HMS Repulse,* observed rather than escorted by one antique and two veteran destroyers, and under the command of an admiral resolutely disbelieving in air power, made history by becoming the first capital ships to be sunk in open sea by aerial bombardment. But the Japanese were to establish a number of records at British expense during the next few months. Hong Kong surrendered on Christmas Day 1941 after a resistance which cost the attackers some 2,754 casualties but involved the total loss of its uselessly exposed garrison of 12,000 British and Commonwealth troops. Meanwhile a numerically superior Commonwealth army, inadequately trained and inappropriately deployed, was hustled through Malaya into Singapore by a Japanese force less than half its size, and forced to capitulate on 15th February 1942. 138,708 British troops had become prisoners or battle casualties in the greatest defeat and most humiliating surrender in British history. General Yamashita's invaders had lost only 9,824 killed or wounded. The catalogue of disaster rolled on. In two days of fighting in the Java Sea on 27th-28th February, a combined American, British, Dutch, and Australian fleet lost eleven of its fourteen vessels, without managing to sink a single Japanese warship. And in four dreadful days in the Indian Ocean Admiral Nagumo's veteran fliers sank a British aircraft-carrier, two cruisers, two destroyers, and a corvette, and drove British naval power helplessly back to the Arabian Sea. Even the RAF itself was unable to match the attackers.

In wild air battles over and around Ceylon, the British lost some forty-three aircraft, not counting those sunk with the carrier *Hermes,* against seventeen Japanese. And on 20th May the last British forces withdrew from Burma across the Indian border, after the longest retreat in British history, having suffered 13,463 casualties, against 4,597 Japanese.

The conquest of the Dutch East Indies presented the invader with even fewer problems. Borneo and Celebes were effectively overrun by 24th January; Ambon by the end of the month; Sumatra, Bali, and Timor by the third week of February; and Java by 9th March. The American colonies presented a rather different prospect, however. Almost undefended, Guam was overrun easily on 10th December. But Wake Island repelled a first attack and held out until 23rd December, by which time its garrison of 520 Marines had sunk two Japanese destroyers and killed or wounded about 1,150 of the enemy. And American resistance in the Bataan Peninsula and Corregidor Island actually set back the Japanese time-table for the conquest of the Philippines by a whole four months, and resulted in the disgrace of the unfortunate Japanese commander, General Homma. The heroic tenacity of his fighting men managed to obscure the fact that MacArthur's generalship in the Philippines was distinguished by errors of optimism at least as serious as those which General Percival had been guilty of in Malaya, and that the number of American and Filipino troops put out of action by General Homma was about the same as that of the British and Commonwealth forces routed by Yamashita. But due to the fact that Wake, Bataan, and Corregidor held out for longer than anybody expected they have entered American mythology as symbols of defiant and inspiring resistance, while Singapore has become associated with disgrace, and Hong Kong with tragic futility.

'Victory disease'

There was no disputing the sweep and rapidity of the Japanese conquests or the relatively slight losses with which they were gained. But they were not without features ominous for the victors themselves. The most serious one was that they had clearly not achieved their basic purpose. Japanese grand strategy required the establishment of an island barrier behind which the conquerors could enjoy the fruits of their conquest while meeting the inevitable American counter-attack. But this required that American offensive capacity should first have been effectively destroyed. And this had not been done at Pearl Harbour. The battleship force of the Pacific Fleet had certainly been put out of action. But the fast aircraft-carriers had

completely escaped the Japanese attack. *Saratoga* was still in California; *Lexington* was delivering Marine fighter aircraft reinforcements to Midway; and *Enterprise* was returning to Pearl Harbour from Wake Island having completed an identical mission there. This meant that the United States still possessed the means of striking against Japan with the same weapon of naval aviation which had been used so devastatingly against herself. Elementary prudence would thus have suggested that all the resources of the Imperial Navy should have been devoted to bringing the American carrier squadron to battle and destruction. But elementary prudence was the last quality to be considered in the Japanese plan of action. They, of course, had sufficient reason to be confident. Their fighting men had undoubtedly earned a reputation for invincibility; their only naval losses had been the five submarines lost at Pearl Harbour and the two destroyers sunk at Wake Island; and they still possessed a great numerical superiority in the air over the Americans, as well as in all classes of surface ships. But there was reason to believe that this invincibility was incomplete, and that the numerical advantage could easily be lost. Air losses had turned out to be about equal at the end of the Burma campaign, but in the brief air battles over Rangoon the Japanese had shown a disquieting inferiority to the veterans of the American Volunteer Group, who were shooting them down for a time at the rate of four or five to one. This at least suggested that the Japanese might need all the air supremacy they could get. And it was clear that Japanese strategic planning seemed to discount the basic principle of the concentration of force.

It was not merely the case that the Japanese and their supposed German allies were fighting totally separate and unrelated wars. So, frequently, were individual Japanese commanders in the field. Their tendency to go off on wild hunts after easy conquests unrelated to any overall strategic plan was categorized by the Japanese themselves as the 'victory disease'. It was accompanied and aggravated by what might

Right: 1 Lieutenant-General Sakai heads triumphant Japanese entry into Hong Kong, Christmas Day, 1941. 2 Japanese troops on a British gun emplacement in Hong Kong cheer news of the garrison's surrender. 3 Japanese paratroops are dropped to seize oil installations near Palembang, Sumatra, 14th February 1942. 4 Sinking of small British aircraft-carrier Hermes off Ceylon, 9th April 1942. Attacked by ninety bombers and fighters, she was sunk in twenty minutes. Orders to British fighters to give her cover failed to get through

similarly be termed the 'octopus complex'. This took the form of a predilection for enormously ambitious and complex plans of campaign which merely compounded the possibilities for human error in situations where rational military direction should surely have sought to minimize them.

The victory disease and octopus complex appeared in full bloom in the crucial campaigns of May and June 1942. Conflicting factions in the Imperial Navy were unable to agree either with themselves or with the army whether immediate priority should be assigned to seizing Port Moresby, so as to neutralize Australia; to attacking the Aleutian Islands, to divert American strength from the central Pacific; or to a thrust at Midway Island, to force the remainder of the Pacific Fleet to accept battle, as should have been done as soon as possible after Pearl Harbour. It was effectively decided to proceed with all three. Even this did not satisfy the determination of the Japanese High Command to make things difficult for themselves. The ships assigned to the Port Moresby campaign were divided into no less than six separate forces, performing two quite distinct operations. By contrast Admiral Chester W. Nimitz, Commander-in-Chief of the US Pacific Fleet, boldly concentrated every available ship to meet the Japanese in the Coral Sea. The result was that the opposing forces were not too disproportionate. When battle was actually joined on 7th May, two American aircraft-carriers with 121 aircraft and seven cruisers faced three Japanese carriers with about 180 aircraft and six cruisers. The odds were soon shortened in any case when bombers from both *Lexington* and *Yorktown* blew the carrier *Shoho* out of the water. *Lexington* was itself lost the following day, but in the meantime the Americans had put a further carrier, *Shokaku*, out of action.

The action in the Coral Sea might have seemed inconclusive as shipping losses were about equal and both fleets withdrew from the area, but in fact every advantage lay with the Americans. They had lost only eighty-one aircraft against 105 Japanese; the assault on Port Moresby was countermanded; and all the Japanese carriers had been immobilized, as the third, *Zuikaku*, had lost too many aircraft to be fit for action until its losses had been replaced. This weakening of the Japanese carrier strength at the Battle of the Coral Sea may well have determined the course of the Second World War.

It was not that the Japanese were even then seriously short of carriers. The enormous fleet available to Admiral Isoroku Yamamoto must have guaranteed him victory in any single enterprise he had committed it to. But Japanese naval power was dissipated in a futile attempt to confuse an enemy who could have been overwhelmed by a direct and concentrated attack. Yamamoto decided to proceed with the diversionary raid on the Aleutian Islands as well as the frontal assault on Midway, despite the failure of the Port Moresby bid. His plan of campaign resulted in the Japanese armada being scattered in ten separate groups all over the north and central Pacific. Two carriers were detached to cover the attack on the Aleutians, leaving the Midway force actually deficient in air power, although excessively strong in surface ships. Seven battleships, six heavy and light carriers, thirteen cruisers, and fifty destroyers challenged Nimitz's three carriers, eight cruisers, and fourteen destroyers. But Yamamoto brought with him only 325 aircraft, while Nimitz could assemble a motley collection of 348 land and sea-based machines. The Americans obviously could not offer battle at sea. Everything depended upon the prowess of the United States Naval Air Service— a glamourized body of fighting men, with their swashbuckling airborne admirals, their huge wooden-decked carriers, and years of experience in dive-bombing techniques.

And here two Japanese errors helped Nimitz decisively. The first was that Yamamoto still thought that two American carriers had been sunk in the Coral Sea engagement, and consequently quite underestimated the strike capacity of his opponent. The other was that the Japanese had not yet been forced to learn how to integrate their carrier squadrons with the rest of their fleet. The Americans had learned the hard way. Bereft of battleships, they had of necessity adopted their carriers as capital ships, and deployed their other craft as escorts around them. But the battle force which should have been in attendance to shield Nagumo's carriers with its anti-aircraft batteries was 400 miles distant when the assault on Midway commenced.

However the Japanese nearly won. The initial air battles between their naval aircraft and American land-based planes were wholly in their favour. They wrecked everything above ground on Midway and shot down thirty-three American aircraft for a loss of only six of their own. Then retribution came. Rear Admiral Raymond A. Spruance on board *Enterprise* ordered strikes by his torpedo and dive-bombers at a time deliberately calculated to reach the Japanese carriers while they were still refuelling their aircraft. The torpedo bombers arrived first and flew on to destruction, losing three-quarters of their number without scoring a single hit. But the death-flight of the old Douglas Devastators drew the attention of the Japanese away from the upper air where Spruance's Douglas Dauntless dive-bombers were assembling.

In less than five minutes three Japanese carriers, the *Kaga, Akagi* and *Soryu,* were on fire and out of action, and the great Pacific War had been won and lost. The surviving carrier *Hiryu* struck back, crippling *Yorktown,* but was itself destroyed by a further strike from *Enterprise.* By the end of the day, Yamamoto's air arm had been virtually eliminated. Twice on the following nights, he belatedly deployed his battle force in attempts to sink Spruance's carriers by gunfire. However, the Americans skilfully drew away at evening, returning with daylight to deliver more strikes, as a result of which a Japanese heavy cruiser was sunk.

Final casualty figures were four carriers, a cruiser, and 322 aircraft for the Japanese, against a carrier, a destroyer, and 147 aircraft for the Americans. The battle had been won on the American side by Spruance's almost faultless judgment and by the courage and technical skill of his aviators. It had been lost on the Japanese by the now familiar vices of over-confidence, over-complexity of planning, and unwillingness to concentrate on one objective at a time. This time they had been fatal. The margin of strength so brilliantly gained at Pearl Harbour had been squandered. The siege of the Japanese Empire had begun.

Victims of success
There can be little doubt that at any time between 7th December 1941 and 4th June 1942 the Japanese might have secured the victory of the Axis powers, if only they had got their priorities right and been content to do one thing at a time. An all-out search-and-destroy operation against American naval power after Pearl Harbour, culminating in an air and sea bombardment of California, would have made it virtually impossible for the Roosevelt administration to have maintained its policy of 'Germany First'. It would have certainly inhibited the transfer of American tanks and artillery to Africa which made possible the British victories at El Alamein, and thereby prevented the Germans from outflanking the Russian defences from the south. Even a headlong drive across India might have achieved the same end result. But the Japanese were the victims of their own military prowess. They had triumphed beyond all expectation. It was accordingly not surprising if they neglected the precautions necessary in a combat with an adversary whose economic capacity was some sixteen times as great as their own. But one need not be too critical of Japanese strategy. The outcome of the Pacific War, and effectively of the Second World War as a whole, was decided after all in less than five minutes over Midway. And there are many ways in which those minutes might never have happened.

Japanese arms in action

In the wave of conquest which followed Japan's strike southward, four actions were of special significance. A detailed examination of these is important for an understanding of the nature of the Japanese successes and why they should have had such a stunning effect on the world. Two of these were British disasters: the loss of *Prince of Wales* and *Repulse*, and the fall of Singapore; two were tough, fruitless defensive actions by Americans in Wake Island and the Philippines.

The nature of the Japanese offensive which disguised its central objective and dazed ill-prepared opponents was dictated by a number of important considerations. The need to continue the war against China and protect Manchuria from Soviet incursions together with the shortage of merchant shipping necessitated the employment of the same units in successive operations and precluded protracted fighting. Fast moving, surprise attacks, moreover, were essential if the considerable oil, rubber, tin, and bauxite (aluminium ore) resources of South-East Asia and the southwest Pacific were to be seized undamaged at an early stage in the hostilities, which Japan's Naval and General Staffs had timed to avoid the north-east monsoon in the South China Sea and the violent gales in the north Pacific.

Force Z detected

The first American possession to fall to a Japanese invasion force was Guam which capitulated on 10th December after half an hour's resistance. On the same day, the third of the Pacific war, the Japanese invaded the Philippines and seventy-five of their bombers from Saigon sunk the British capital ships *Prince of Wales* and *Repulse* seventy nautical miles south-east of Kuantan in eastern Malaya. At 1755 on 8th December the vessels, in company with the destroyers *Electra*, *Express*, *Vampire* and *Tenedos* under the command of Admiral Sir Tom Phillips, had slipped out of Singapore into the misty sunset to forestall further Japanese landings on the north-east coast of Malaya.

Later that evening at 2253, Phillips received a signal from Singapore informing him that fighter cover would not be available when he reached the area. The Japanese

Above: Seven of Wake Island's twelve Grumman Wildcats lie destroyed after a Japanese bombing raid on 8th December 1941. Left: An American soldier gives a dying Japanese captive a drink during bitter fighting on the Bataan Peninsula in the Philippines, March 1942. American and Filipino forces had withdrawn into the peninsula on Luzon for a last ditch stand

Survivors scrambling over the sides of HMS Repulse *as she settles into the waters of the South China Sea after being bombed by Japanese aircraft off Malaya on 10th December 1941*

had taken Kota Bharu airfield, thus depriving the fleet (code-named Force Z) of one of the basic conditions on which the successful execution of its mission depended. But the British force had the advantage of surprise and Phillips decided to proceed. The following day driving rain and thick, low cloud shrouded Force Z from Japanese air reconnaissance. But at 1700 the weather suddenly cleared to reveal three aircraft observing the fleet and Phillips, who had planned to alter course for Singora at nightfall to shell Japanese transports, was now robbed even of the advantage of surprise.

Although he was unaware that his ships had also been sighted by the Japanese submarine I 65 south of Poulo Condore at 1340, he promptly decided to abandon the mission and turn back. But to confuse the enemy he ordered Force Z, with the exception of *Tenedos*, to continue north until nightfall before altering course south. The heavy guns of the fleet, it appeared, would not be brought to bear on the vulnerable Japanese transports. But at 2400 as the fleet steamed for Singapore, *Prince of Wales* received a message which read: 'Enemy reported landing Kuantan, latitude 03 degrees 50 north.' Force Z, its commander hoped, would still have an opportunity of disrupting the Japanese landings in Malaya and fearful of sacrificing the element of surprise he once more enjoyed, Phillips maintained strict radio silence, assuming incorrectly that fighter cover would be provided when he reached his new objective.

At 0220 the following day, 10th December, a Japanese submarine, I 58, sighted Force Z and between dawn and 0930, seventy-five aircraft took off from Saigon in pursuit of the British fleet which had arrived off Kuantan at 0800 to discover it had answered a false alarm. The detonation of a number of mines in the vicinity of the town by straying water buffaloes had apparently prompted Indian troops to pass the information to Singapore that a Japanese landing was taking place.

Disappointed, Admiral Phillips ordered his fleet back onto a north-easterly course and proceeded to search for a suspicious tug and barges sighted earlier. Half an hour later *Tenedos*, which Phillips had ordered to Singapore when Force Z was discovered by Japanese reconnaissance aircraft, radioed that she was under air attack. Increasing their speed to twenty-five knots the ships of Force Z assumed first degree readiness and raced for base. But a patrolling Japanese reconnaissance aircraft sighted them and put out a general call.

At 1107 aircraft of the Japanese XXII Air Flotilla, which had strayed almost within sight of Singapore in quest of Force Z and which had bombed *Tenedos*, were sighted and at 1119 precisely the high angle guns throughout the fleet began firing at the attackers. Under a barrage of bombs and torpedoes *Repulse* sank at 1233 and as the eleven Buffalo fighters charged with the protection of Force Z arrived at 1320 in response to a belated distress call from Captain W.G.Tennant, commander of *Repulse*, *Prince of Wales* rolled over ponderously to port and sank with Admiral Phillips still on the bridge.

The loss of the two ships with 840 men on board sealed the fate of Malaya and confirmed Japan's command of the Pacific and Indian Oceans for the loss of three

aircraft. 'Over all this vast expanse of water Japan was supreme, and we everywhere were weak and naked,' wrote Churchill. On the day after the action, a Japanese aircraft dropped a large bouquet of flowers over the sea in honour of the men who had died.

Wake spits back

There was no respite for the Allies. The exultant Japanese kept on hitting. But for two weeks the defenders of a lonely, treeless atoll in the central Pacific held a powerful invasion fleet at bay, subjecting the victory-flushed Japanese navy to its only defeat in the opening months of the war. Wake Island, annexed by the United States in 1899 and later developed as an aircraft staging post, belonged with Makin and Tarawa in the Gilbert Islands to a group of objectives Japan required if she was to secure the eastern boundary of her defence perimeter. On the outbreak of war, the island's occupants comprised seventy civilian employees of Pan American Airways, 1,146 civilians employed by contractors and a garrison of 449 marines, sixty-eight sailors, and five soldiers. Major James Devereux of the United States Marine Corps who effectively commanded the garrison had at his disposal six 5-inch coast defence guns, twelve 3-inch anti-aircraft guns, a number of machine-guns, besides twelve obsolete Grumman Wildcats of Marine Fighting Squadron 211 flown in from the *Enterprise* on 4th December. Not only did the island lack two-thirds of its garrison, it had no radar, fighter control centre, or fire control equipment. There were, moreover, no mines, no barbed wire, and no revetments for aircraft.

On 8th December, under cover of rain squalls, thirty-six Japanese bombers swept in over Wake and destroyed seven Wildcats on the ground. Air attacks continued on the following two days and on the 11th at 0500 the invasion forces composed of the light cruisers *Yubari*, *Tenryu*, and *Tatsuta* with six destroyers and accompanying vessels under the command of Rear-Admiral Sadamichi Kajioka steamed in, guns blazing to assault the island. Major Devereux held his fire. Contemptuous of the atoll's defences, Kajioka took his invasion fleet to within 4,500 yards of the shore. Suddenly, Devereux's 5-inch guns opened up and with their second salvo damaged the flagship *Yubari*. Within the first few minutes the island's 5-inch batteries sank the destroyer *Hayate* and damaged several other ships. Four of the five surviving Wildcats then took off to bomb and strafe the fleet, damaging the light cruisers *Tenryu* and *Tatsuta* and sinking the destroyer *Kisavagi*. It was one of the most humiliating reverses the Japanese navy had ever suffered and soon after 0700 Kajioka retreated to Kwajalein six hundred miles away to lick his wounds. Wake Island's few guns and aircraft had repulsed a powerful amphibious attack, sunk two destroyers, damaged several other vessels and inflicted some 700 fatalities on the invaders for the loss of two Wildcats.

Alarmed by this ignominious rebuff at Wake, Admiral Yamamoto, Commander-in-Chief of the Combined Fleet, ordered reinforcements to assemble for a second landing attempt and on 15th December Rear-Admiral Tamon Yamaguchi's II Carrier Division with the aircraft carriers *Soryu* and *Hiryu* escorted by four destroyers proceeded to a position north of the island. Accompanying the carrier force was Rear-Admiral Abe's VIII Cruiser Division with the heavy cruisers *Tone* and *Chikuma*. While the powerful invasion fleet assembled off Wake, the island was subjected to a series of attacks by land-based bombers and on the 21st aircraft from the carriers lent their weight to the bombardments. On the same day Kajioka again sailed from Kwajalein and before dawn on 23rd December, with no preliminary bombardment, substantially reinforced troops of the naval landing force began to pour ashore at points on which the American 5-inch guns could not be brought to bear. The only gun trained on the two antiquated destroyers, which had been beached with companies of the landing force, put fifteen shells into the nearest one, breaking its back. Without air support, its last two Wildcats having been shot down the previous day, the island's defences were pounded by aircraft and naval guns and at 0730, heavily outnumbered, the garrison surrendered. Fifty-two American servicemen, seventy civilians and 820 Japanese soldiers were killed during the bitterly contested landings, and 470 officers and men and 1,146 civilians were captured. The navy had vindicated itself for its initial failure to take the island and the gallant American defenders, despite their defeat, earned the admiration of the world.

Singapore surrenders

Yet Wake might have been saved and a naval victory scored had Rear-Admiral Frank Fletcher's carrier-borne aircraft intervened while the Japanese invasion force was still disembarking equipment and supplies. Fletcher, who left Pearl Harbour for Wake on 17th December with a relief force which included the aircraft-carrier *Saratoga*, lost his chance of preventing the Japanese landings by pausing to refuel his destroyers. Although he could have caught the invasion fleet at a disadvantage he was ordered back to base for fear of risking his vessels in an encounter with those units detached from the Pearl Harbour Striking Force which were believed to contain two battleships.

While Wake defied the wrath of the Japanese navy, and American and Filipino troops were being driven into the Bataan Peninsula, the Japanese invasion of Malaya was proceeding swiftly. Its extent, once appreciated, spread demoralization among the confused British and Commonwealth forces. Without either command of the sea or air they fell back down the west coast of Malaya before Lieutenant-General Yamashita's XXV Army until they reeled into Singapore on 31st January. At 1810 on 15th February 1942, Lieutenant-General Arthur Percival, GOC Malaya, surrendered the town to Yamashita in a room in the Ford factory at Bukit Timah. It was the greatest disaster inflicted on the British Empire since Cornwallis surrendered Yorktown in the American War of Independence, and Churchill termed the fall of what was considered to be an impregnable fortress, 'the worst disaster and largest capitulation in British history'.

In the Malayan campaign, lost by the failure to provide adequate defence in the north, British, Indian and Australian forces lost a total of 138,708 soldiers of whom more than 130,000 were taken prisoner. The Japanese casualties in the seventy-three day campaign were 3,507 dead and 6,150 wounded.

It had been General Percival's misfortune, as James Leasor has written in *Singapore*, *The Battle That Changed The World*, to 'direct an ill-equipped and wrongly-trained army in a hopeless campaign; to defend a country for whose defence pre-war politicians influenced and activated by blind, petty motivations and crass ignorance, by indifference on the part of the voters who had elected them, had neglected to pay the insurance premium.' The humiliation of Great Britain at the hands of a numerically inferior Asiatic army that rode on bicycles and lived on rice was to have fateful consequences for the Far East.

The capture of Singapore, 'the bastion of the Empire' and the consequent premature collapse of Europe's hegemony in South East Asia after the war created a power vacuum which Communism struggled desperately to fill.

Bataan Death March

The fall of Malaya and Singapore led directly to the collapse of the Dutch East Indies. Burma was overrun within weeks and the Japanese tide swept on to the Indian frontier. For the United States, the military outlook was as bleak and on 6th May, after a desperate defence of the Bataan Peninsula and Corregidor Island, which humiliated General Homma's XIV Army and delayed Japanese victory for four months, American and Filipino resistance ended. Morale among the diseased, under-nourished men had slumped when with the departure of General MacArthur, Commander-in-Chief United States Army Forces in the Far East, on 12th March, it became evident that reinforcements could not be expected. However, before handing over his command and leaving for Australia at Roosevelt's insistence, MacArthur promised the Filipinos that one day he would return to redeem the pledge of complete independence by 1946 which the American government had given eight years earlier. Just over a month after he left, the 64,000 Filipinos and 12,000 Americans who had surrendered on Bataan, began a fifty-five mile march from Mariveles to San Fernando. Because the Japanese had only expected to take some 25,000 prisoners, their arrangements for transporting and feeding the captives broke down. Between 7,000 and 10,000 men, including 2,330 Americans died of disease, starvation, exhaustion or brutality on what became known as the Bataan Death March.

It revealed the contempt the Japanese reserved for enemy soldiers who had not fallen in battle and foreshadowed the barbarous treatment Allied prisoners would receive at Japanese hands throughout the Pacific War.

Japan was everywhere victorious and the Allies everywhere in defeat or disarray. Yet prior to the outbreak of the Pacific War the strength of Japan's armed forces had been gravely underrated, ignored or even disbelieved. It was popularly supposed that, preoccupied with China, she was unable to mount military operations elsewhere. But although the allocation of forty divisions and 800 aircraft to the defence of Japan, Korea, Manchuria, and occupied China only left eleven divisions and some 700 first-line aircraft for the other theatres of war, Japan was able to reduce the whole vast south seas region. The myth of Japanese inferiority was promptly replaced by the myth of Japanese invincibility.

4 THE TIDE TURNS

Alamein

General Sir Claude Auchinleck, Commander-in-Chief Middle East Land Forces, took over personal command of 8th Army from Lieutenant-General Neil Ritchie on 25th June 1942. There is little doubt that Auchinleck had been ill-judged in February 1942 when he confirmed Ritchie in what had been a temporary command, despite evidence and advice that Ritchie lacked the experience and capacity to command an army. Equally it would have been well if Auchinleck, as Prime Minister Churchill had urged, had taken personal charge of the Gazala battles at an early stage. However, the Western Desert was only one among the commander-in-chief's several cares. It was not so simple a matter to go off and look after a single front. For although the Middle East Command had shed East Africa since Wavell's time, it was still responsible for support of Turkey, a neutral state, and for the defence of the Persian Gulf oilfields from attack from the north, through the Caucasus. Auchinleck had lived with this latter danger ever since the German invasion of Russia had reached the Don the previous autumn.

Auchinleck, therefore, unlike his predecessors or his successor, bore the double burden of an army commander and of a theatre commander-in-chief.

For this reason it was Auchinleck's belief as commander-in-chief that 8th Army must not be exposed to the risk of a final defeat, but must at all cost be kept in being,

Left: A German Hanomag half-track of the Afrika Korps rolls across the soft sand of the desert. The number plate prefix means 'Wehrmacht Heer', indicating an Army vehicle

in order to continue to defend the Gulf oil from Rommel. Whereas Ritchie had planned a do-or-die battle at Mersa Matruh, Auchinleck wished to retreat to El Alamein which would give him a little time to reorganize his forces and plan his own battle instead of fighting Ritchie's. But Rommel struck the day after Auchinleck assumed personal command. The Battle of Mersa Matruh (26th-28th June 1942), fought in decayed defences according to Ritchie's deployment, marked the climax of German moral domination in the desert. With handfuls of exhausted troops Rommel bluffed the British (including fresh, strong formations) into thinking they were broken through, surrounded, and beaten, while poor communications virtually cut Auchinleck off from the battle. As soon as he saw the compromised battle was lost, Auchinleck ordered the army back to Alamein. Both armies, units all mixed up, raced each other for the forty-mile-wide neck between the sea at Alamein and the impassable Qattara Depression. Alexandria lay only sixty miles beyond.

Although 8th Army narrowly won the race, the British still faced the possibility, in Auchinleck's words, of 'complete catastrophe'. 'No one,' he wrote later, 'least of all I, could say whether the Army could be rallied and re-formed soon enough to hold Rommel and save Egypt.' Auchinleck thus faced the greatest test of a general — the rallying of a beaten army and the redemption of a lost battle. Behind him in Egypt there was panic and defeatism. He told his soldiers: 'The enemy is stretching to his limit and thinks we are a broken army . . . He hopes to take Egypt by bluff. Show him where he gets off.'

In fact this was an accurate military appreciation. By failing to halt after Tobruk to allow Malta to be attacked, as agreed, Rommel had taken an immense gamble. For unless he managed to break through to the Delta very quickly, his army would be increasingly starved of supplies, reinforcements, and fuel, owing both to British naval action based on Malta and the length of his own communications. On 1st July, three days after Matruh, Rommel attacked 8th Army at Alamein.

The essential unity of all the fighting at Alamein from July to November 1942 has been obscured by the changes in the British command that took place in mid-August, when General Sir Harold Alexander replaced Auchinleck as commander-in-chief and Lieutenant-General B.L.Montgomery became the new 8th Army commander. It was one extended battle with pauses between the actions. It opened with Rommel's desperate attempts to shoulder his way past Auchinleck, his failure, and the failure in turn of Auchinleck to force him into retreat. This was the First Battle of Alamein (1st-26th July 1942). There followed a period of stalemate broken only by an unrealistic and vain second attempt by Rommel to break through: the Battle of Alam Halfa (31st August-3rd September). Finally came the British counter-stroke with massive fresh forces that swept Rommel out of Egypt. This was Montgomery's victory in the Second Battle of Alamein (23rd October-4th November 1942).

The commanding natural features of the Alamein battlefield (although so slight as to be discernible only to the military eye) were two east-west ridges, the Ruweisat

Ridge, and farther to the south and well to the east, the Alam Halfa Ridge. These were the tactical keys to the neck of land between the sea and the Qattara Depression. At no time in the Alamein battles was this neck solidly held by the British. In July Auchinleck had lacked the troops, and later he (and after him Montgomery) preferred to form a south-facing left wing that might entice Rommel into a trap.

Auchinleck's army at First Alamein was made up of survivors of the Gazala battles like 1st South African and 50th Divisions, survivors of Matruh like the New Zealand divisions and 9th Indian Brigade, together with fresh troops like 18th Indian Brigade from Iraq. Auchinleck was weakest in armour, for although 1st Armoured Division possessed 150 tanks, only two squadrons were Grants, and the division's skill, cohesion, and morale were not high. Nevertheless 8th Army heavily outnumbered Panzer Army Africa, now reduced to 60 German and 30 Italian tanks, some 5,000 Germans, and a similar number of Italians.

As a personal adviser and acting chief of staff in the field Auchinleck had brought with him from Cairo Major-General E.Dorman-Smith. He was not a member of the British army 'establishment' who had muddled the Gazala battles, but a man fertile in unorthodox ideas. These were reflected in some of the reforms Auchinleck attempted to carry out in the army's organization and tactics during First Ala-

mein. Auchinleck believed that the standard British infantry division was too large, cumbersome, and lacking in hitting power for mobile desert warfare. He therefore extemporized brigade-groups or smaller 'battle-groups' on the German pattern—trucked infantry escorting guns. Instead of manning the static defences of the Alamein perimeter, he kept the brigade-groups of 1st South African Division mobile in the open desert to the south. After the first day's fighting he also evacuated two 'boxes' in the centre and extreme south of the Alamein neck, in order to keep his army mobile and concentrated. (Boxes were strongpoints surrounded by wire and minefields.) At the same time the heavy and medium artillery was transferred from corps to army command to provide massed firepower. Auchinleck also tried to diminish the sluggishness and rigidity of the stratified British command organization by demanding the energetic local initiative and flexibility evinced by the enemy. The course of the First Battle of Alamein was to show that orders or instructions in this spirit failed to have much effect on minds habituated to another military tradition.

Although First Alamein was a highly complicated and shifting battle on the ground, it was essentially a struggle of will between the opposing generals. The struggle lasted for the first two weeks of July and ended with Rommel's surrender of the initiative to Auchinleck.

On 1st July Rommel tried to repeat his triumph at Mersa Matruh with a similar plan and similar audacity. He proposed to drive through Auchinleck's centre and turn outwards in a double envelopment of Auchinleck's wings. Both envelopments stuck under heavy flanking-fire from British battle-groups. On 2nd July Rommel reduced his plan to a single envelopment of the Alamein perimeter. This too failed. On 3rd July he tried again in the centre, made some progress, and stuck again, despite his own personal leadership of the attack. On 2nd and again on 5th July Auchinleck counter-attacked elsewhere, forcing Rommel to re-group, but 8th Army proved a slow and hesitant instrument. However, Rommel was forced to deploy Italian infantry for the first time since he attacked at Gazala. Nevertheless he decided to attack again on 10th July, after a brief respite, and try to break straight through eastwards into the Delta. Instead, on 9th July Auchinleck launched a major-counterstroke in the coastal sector: a bombardment that reminded some Germans of the Western Front in 1917, followed by an assault by Auchinleck's personal reserve, the fresh 9th Australian Division. The Italians collapsed, the hill of Tel el Eisa fell, and Rommel had to abandon his own

Wreckage of a German Junkers 52. Rommel's supply planes were shot down in droves crossing the Mediterranean

offensive in order to succour the Italians.

It was Auchinleck's plan (suggested by Dorman-Smith) to go for the Italians in one sector after another, thus forcing Rommel to run to and fro to their aid with his Germans. It worked brilliantly. Between 9th and 16th July six such attacks on Italians were launched, and Rommel only prevented the total collapse of his front by using his last German reserves.

On 21st-22nd July and 26th July Auchinleck attempted to turn Rommel's defeat into his destruction or retreat. These counter-strokes were a total failure. The cause lay yet again in the gulf of misunderstanding between British armour and infantry, which were incapable of the supple and intimate co-operation of the German troops who were trained together on common lines. A further cause lay in a breakdown of radio communication. Either the infantry was massacred by German armour because the British armour failed to come up in time; or the armour was massacred trying to 'charge' German defences that should have been carefully assaulted in conjunction with infantry.

Although Rommel had not been forced to retreat, First Alamein saved Egypt and the Middle East. It was one of the decisive battles of the Second World War.

It was Dorman-Smith's prediction, expressed in a strategic appreciation of 27th July accepted by Auchinleck, that Rommel even after reinforcement would not be strong enough to launch another offensive except as a gamble. Auchinleck therefore looked ahead to a set-piece British offensive in strength some time in September.

Meanwhile the British and American governments had taken a major strategical decision. Instead of an invasion of France in 1942, deemed a hopeless undertaking with the available troops and landing craft, the Allies were to invade French North Africa in the autumn, and, in conjunction with 8th Army, clear the entire North African coast. This operation would both re-open the Mediterranean to through sea traffic and appease Stalin with some kind of a 'second front' at not too great a risk of failure. The decision was made on 24th July, after Auchinleck had halted Rommel's offensive. It entirely changed the context of the war in the desert, for occupation of Algeria and Tunisia would directly threaten Rommel's own base at Tripoli and squeeze him between two armies.

Churchill visits the front
On 3rd August Churchill and the Chief of the Imperial General Staff arrived in Cairo. On 6th August, after visiting Auchinleck at 8th Army Headquarters, Churchill decided to replace Auchinleck and his immediate staff. General Sir Harold Alexander was appointed commander-in-chief, and Major-General W.H.E. Gott, a corps commander with a legendary though not altogether justified reputation, was appointed to command 8th Army. In these decisions personal political considerations undoubtedly played a large part. There was mounting public criticism of Churchill's leadership in Great Britain, and by-elections had gone heavily against the government. There had been a long run of disaster: the loss of the *Prince of Wales* and *Repulse,* the fall of Singapore, the loss of Burma, the loss of Tobruk, the Gazala battles. Churchill needed a resounding victory as quickly as possible to preserve his own position. There can be little doubt that Auchinleck therefore sealed his fate when he stubbornly refused to promise to attack before mid-September, arguing that this was the earliest that 8th Army could be re-organized and re-trained, and the new equipment run in.

Churchill instructed the new Commander-in-Chief Middle East, General Alexander, that his primary task was 'to take and destroy the German-Italian army commanded by Field-Marshal Rommel.' The commander-in-chief was relieved of anxiety about the German threat from the Caucasus (the German offensive in Russia poured across the Don into the Caucasus on 24th July, in the last days of First Alamein), for Iraq and Persia were transferred to a new command. Thus in the end all the vast existing resources of the Middle East base, and the immense reinforcements and supplies now flowing into Egypt had come to be devoted to the single purpose of fighting four somewhat neglected German divisions and their Italian allies. It was a measure of the success of the German diversion in North Africa, and also of the usefulness of the British Empire's contribution to ground fighting in the third year of the war. The Red Army was currently engaging some 180 German divisions, including twenty Panzer divisions.

Alexander's sole responsibility was therefore to support his 8th Army commander. On 7th August, however, Gott was killed, when the aircraft flying him to Cairo was shot down, and Lieutenant-General Montgomery was appointed commander of 8th Army. Montgomery was a man of legendary eccentricity and ruthless professionalism. He had not commanded in the field since 1940, had never commanded large masses of armour in battle, and was new to the desert. He compensated for these initial handicaps by a brilliant clarity of mind, iron willpower, and a bleak realism about the potentialities of individuals and units alike. He had an unrivalled power of piercing complex matters to the underlying simplicities. In August 1942 he enjoyed the advantage of the new broom, and he swept very clean indeed.

His first task was to meet the renewed German offensive which was expected soon. His plan, like that evolved by Auchinleck and Dorman-Smith, depended on forming a south-facing left wing along the Alam Halfa Ridge, and his main dispositions followed the existing defences and minefields. However, he brought up 44th Division, now available, to strengthen Alam Halfa. Although his general plan so closely resembled Auchinleck's, his style of fighting the battle was very different. He accurately took the measure of 8th Army's capabilities and enforced his own direct control right down to division level. It would be in his own words 'an army battle'. There would be no loose fighting, but a tight defence of tactical ground.

Rommel launched his offensive on 31st August 1942. It was, as Dorman-Smith had predicted in July, a gamble without much chance. Rommel had 203 tanks against 767 British; he himself and several senior officers were sick; and his army was so short of fuel that it had to make a tight turn up to the Alam Halfa Ridge instead of outflanking it to the east. After four days of vain effort to pierce the British defences while under violent air attack he slowly withdrew. An attempt by the New Zealand Division to endanger his retreat broke down in the usual 8th Army muddles and misunderstandings. Except for this failure Montgomery's first battle had been entirely successful. He was free to continue preparing his own offensive.

Alexander like Auchinleck was strongly pressed by the Prime Minister for an early offensive. He and Montgomery, with the advantage of being new men who could not be sacked, also refused. They, like Auchinleck, realized that an immense amount of training and preparation was needed before 8th Army would be fit to attack. In fact the Second Battle of Alamein opened on 23rd October, and even then 8th Army was by no means up to German standards.

The chronic problem lay in the inability of the British armour and infantry to work closely together. It originated in peacetime, when the British failed to evolve a coherent doctrine of tank warfare, but instead divided ground war into two separate compartments—the infantry battle of positions, and the (almost) all-tank mobile battle. Just before his departure Auchinleck had proposed to re-model the whole 8th Army into German-style mixed tank-infantry divisions. Co-operation would be secured under a single divisional command. Montgomery and his advisers instead decided to form a special wholly armoured corps (10th) in addition to the existing 30th and 13th Corps, charged with fighting a tank battle and then exploiting in pursuit. Thus co-ordination of armour and infantry would not now be secured by

The Tide Turns

divisional commanders, or corps commanders as hitherto, but by the army commander himself. The course of Second Alamein was to show that Montgomery also failed even by this scheme to solve the problem of armour and infantry.

Second Battle of Alamein

In planning his offensive Montgomery faced what was for the desert a novel problem. Rommel had created a continuous defence system across the forty-mile-wide neck between the sea and the Qattara Depression. It was of the standard German pattern dating back to 1917 – a maze of strongpoints and switchlines, protected by belts of wire, in minefields some 2½ to 4½ miles deep, and garrisoned by intermingled German and Italian infantry. Close behind lay the Panzer divisions. To this Western Front problem Montgomery produced a Western Front answer – a deliberate infantry attack under cover of a massive bombardment to drive a gap right through both the forward and main battle zones of the enemy defence system. The 10th Corps (armour) would then pass through this gap on to the enemy communications and fight and defeat the Panzer divisions. Montgomery recognized however that the skill and training of 8th Army was such that any 'mixing it' with the Panzer Army in the open would be risky. He therefore altered his plan to make it even more deliberate and methodical. The armour would merely defend the gap made in the enemy defences against counter-strokes, while behind its shield the defence system and its infantry garrison would be 'crumbled' away piecemeal. This Montgomery hoped would force the Panzer divisions to attack to try to save the infantry and expose themselves to defeat by British tanks and anti-tank guns fighting defensively.

For the battle Montgomery fielded 1,029 tanks against 496 (220 German); 1,451 anti-tank guns against 550 German and 300 Italian; 908 field and medium guns against 200 German and 300 Italian (plus 18 heavy howitzers); 85 infantry battalions against 31 German and 40 Italian. The overall odds were about two to one: 195,000 men against just over 100,000. For the first time the British anti-tank artillery was principally composed of powerful six-pounders, while the armour included 252 American Shermans, tanks at last really the equal of German equipment. The British enjoyed complete air superiority.

The Second Battle of Alamein fell into three phases. During 23rd-25th October the original plan of breaking clean through the German left centre failed. The infantry assault, instead of piercing the German defence system in one bound as ordered, spent its force in the German forward zone and stalled in the battle zone. Mont-

gomery ordered 10th Corps (armour) to force its own breakthrough, then modified his order to one armoured regiment; but the armour too became bogged down in the German defences. The super-imposition of two corps (10th and 30th) on the same sector caused much confusion. In the second phase of the battle (26th-31st October) Montgomery re-made his plan of operations and got a stalled offensive on the move again by sheer force of will. In this phase divisional attacks 'crumbled' the Axis defences away, while Rommel's counter-strokes (he had returned from a hospital bed in Austria to take command) foundered under air attack and anti-tank fire. In the third phase (1st-4th November) Montgomery (who had patiently re-created a reserve) launched a second massive breakthrough attempt. After fierce fighting and heavy loss the British this time succeeded. An order from Hitler to stand fast delayed the Axis retreat for twenty-four hours, and then the Panzer Army streamed west in defeat.

Second Alamein, like the battles of 1917, had turned on the size of reserves available to both sides. Although the Panzer Army had consistently inflicted a higher rate of loss on the British throughout the battle (the British lost more tanks than the original total German strength), the British superiority in resources proved just too great. Yet it had been a near-run battle for the exhaustion and confusion of 8th Army prevented immediate and effective pursuit.

Nevertheless the Panzer Army had been shattered: most of the Italian infantry were captured (some 26,000) and only 36 German tanks remained in action.

Because of the late pursuit, the British failed to cut off and destroy the remnants of Rommel's army. There followed a long pursuit and retreat back to Rommel's old bolt-hole of El Agheila characterized by bluff on Rommel's part and caution on Montgomery's—perhaps understandable in view of Rommel's reputation.

Meanwhile the Anglo-American landings in North Africa (Operation Torch) had taken place on 8th November. 'This,' wrote Rommel, 'spelt the end of the army in Africa.'

Left: 1 Montgomery, wearing Australian hat, discusses military situation with officers of 22nd Armoured Brigade in August 1942, soon after taking command of 8th Army. 2 Painting by British war artist Anthony Gross of desert casualties. 3 A barbed-wire fence is lifted to enable Rommel (striding ahead) to pass through to inspect units of the Afrika Korps. Rommel acquired a legendary reputation extending far beyond North Africa, among Germans and Allies alike

1

3

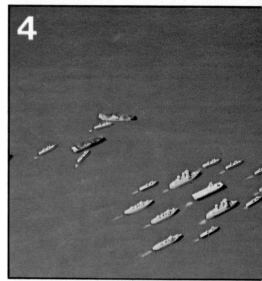

2

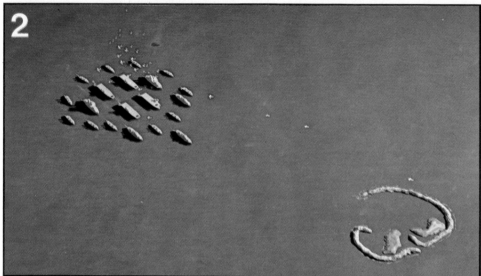

4

The course of the fleets

The Battle of Midway, 4th-5th June 1942

Ⓐ 1022 *Kaga, Akagi* crippled
Ⓑ 1025 *Soryu* crippled
Ⓒ 1435 *Yorktown* crippled
Ⓓ 1705 *Hiryu* crippled

Task-Force 17
Fletcher
Task-Force 16
Spruance

Main Body
Yamamoto

I Carrier Striking Force
Nagumo

Ⓓ

Ⓐ Ⓑ   Ⓒ

II Fleet **Kondo**
Destroyer Squadron **Tanaka**

Cruiser Division **Kurita**

400 miles   300   200   100

•• *Midway I.*

Midway I.

5

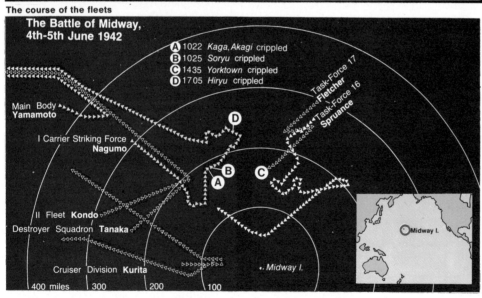

For many years Japanese naval strategists had prepared for a 'decisive fleet action' with the Americans in the Pacific and at Midway in early June 1942 they hoped to destroy the surviving vessels of the US Pacific Fleet in such an encounter. Admiral Yamamoto, Commander-in-Chief of the Combined Fleet, was convinced that a threat to Midway, and therefore to Hawaii, would compel the weak enemy fleet to challenge overwhelming Japanese forces under whose guns and bombs, he imagined, it could not survive. He also planned to seize Midway as an advance air base and assault the western Aleutians to distract American forces from his central objective, that of eliminating US naval power in the Pacific.

But the Japanese were arrogant and over-confident, scattering their forces in a defective, diffuse, and over-complicated operational plan which, through a singular feat of code-breaking, was known to the US Navy. Moreover, they reckoned without the skill and self-sacrifice of a handful of American pilots.

1: At 0430, 107 Japanese torpedo-bombers, dive-bombers, and fighters are launched from the carriers *Kaga, Akagi, Soryu,* and *Hiryu* of I Carrier Striking Force. At 0634 they attack Midway. Of twenty-five fighters sent up to oppose them, only two survive.

2: Twenty-six Midway-based dive-bombers, torpedo-bombers, and bombers swoop on the Japanese carriers at 0705. They fail to score a single hit. Only nine aircraft return. A strike by eleven slower dive-bombers at 0817 proves similarly ineffective and costly.

3: Thirty-five dive-bombers led by Lieutenant-Commanders Leslie and McClusky from Task Forces 16 and 17 *(Yorktown* and *Enterprise)* pounce on *Akagi, Soryu,* and *Kaga* at 1025 and cripple them. The carriers, their decks crowded with aircraft, had not detected the approaching Americans as they had been pre-occupied with mauling a force of forty-one unescorted American torpedo-bombers.

4: At 1435 sixteen Japanese dive-bombers and fighters from *Hiryu* launch a second strike on *Yorktown* (Task Force 17), dooming it. Only seven aircraft survive the raid. Fire-racked *Akagi* and *Soryu* drift aimlessly.

5: Shortly after 1700 twenty-four dive-bombers from

Midway

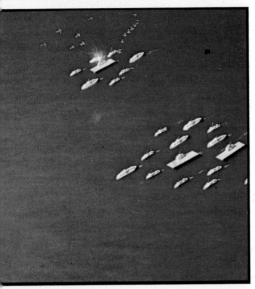

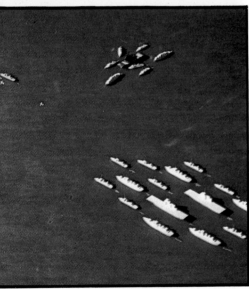

Task Force 16 attack *Hiryu*. Four bombs land near the bridge and cripple the carrier. *Yorktown*, dead in the water, is attended by her screening force.

The course of the fleets: fleet movement between 2400 on 3rd June and 2400 on 4th June. Apart from *Mikuma* of Kurita's Cruiser Division which was attacked by Midway-based bombers on 5th June, the remaining forces took no part in the action. Yamamoto's Main Body cruised hundreds of miles from the carriers, depriving them of anti-aircraft protection and him of any opportunity for night action. *Soryu* sank at 1913 and *Kaga* at 1925. *Akagi* was scuttled at 0455 on 5th June and at approximately 0915 *Hiryu* went down. *Yorktown*, which remained afloat, was torpedoed by a Japanese submarine on 6th June

After 1918 the Japanese navy regarded the United States as its most probable enemy, and consequently maintained an up-to-date and highly trained fleet. To a dispassionate observer, however, it was clear that Japan's geographical position, the size of her armed forces, and above all the disparity between her total resources and those of the United States gave her a poor chance of victory in any war with America.

But when war between the two countries became inevitable in 1941 the Japanese navy, for all its slender hopes of success, found itself in the front rank confronting the American navy.

The dilemma facing the strategists of the Imperial Japanese Headquarters was that until the occupation of the southern territories with their vast resources was completed they neither wanted to face an attack from the American fleet, nor entanglement in a protracted war. Although the Japanese navy and US Pacific Fleet were more or less evenly balanced in 1941, the Japanese had a greater number of aircraft-carriers, and because of the demands of the 'China Incident', the JNAF possessed pilots who were both experienced and highly trained. But it was certain that these advantages would promptly be nullified if America mobilized her massive productive strength and directed it to wartime production. What would happen, it was asked, if America was to wait until her crushingly superior forces were fully equipped, and then attempt to decide the issue with a single attack on Japan? To eliminate this possibility it was necessary, by a positive and continuous offensive, to force America into decisive battles at an early date, to destroy the main strength of her fleet, and to build up 'conditions for protracted warfare from an invincible position' by turning the resources of the southern territories to military purposes.

It was from this standpoint, too, that Admiral Isoroku Yamamoto, Commander-in-Chief of the Combined Fleet, planned the attack on Pearl Harbour in December 1941, and persuaded the Naval General Staff, who had opposed the plan as being too risky, to accept it.

Yamamoto stands firm

Possible future objectives the following year included Australia, Ceylon, Hawaii, Fiji, and Samoa but opinions differed as to the advisability of selecting targets among

Left: The course of the fleets during the Battle of Midway. The battle restored the balance between the American and Japanese navies in the Pacific

them. Moreover, the army was inclined to favour a withdrawal of land forces to Manchuria after the operations in the south in order to take the opportunity of combining with the German army in a double attack on Russia. Since it showed no enthusiasm for expanding the war on the Pacific front, and was hesitant about providing troops, plans for the second phase of the war had to be kept within the bounds of what naval forces alone could accomplish.

Yamamoto's plan for the Midway operation was put before the General Staff at the beginning of April, when discussions about strategy for the second phase of the war were already in their final stages. The primary object of the operation was to lure out and then destroy the US Pacific Fleet. This was to be achieved by attacking and occupying the solitary Pacific island of Midway, which served as an outpost for Hawaii, thus quickly forcing America into a major battle. At the same time it was planned to extend the defence perimeter in anticipation of American air attacks on the Japanese mainland by occupying the Aleutian Islands.

The Naval General Staff also accepted that it was desirable to involve the United States in a decisive battle as soon as possible, but it did not consider Midway, so close to Hawaii, an advantageous location for a major battle, or a suitable area into which to lure the American aircraft-carriers. It strongly advocated cutting the lines of communication between the United States and Australia by advancing on Fiji and Samoa which were about the same distance away as the Japanese outpost of Truk in the Caroline Islands. Nor were the Naval General Staff the only opponents of the Midway operation. II Fleet, which was to support the occupation forces, was opposed to it on the grounds that it was not ready; IV Fleet, which was to look after the logistical problems following the occupation, objected to it on the grounds that it could not be confident of fulfilling this role even if the operation was successful. In particular, I Air Fleet, which had arrived back in Japan in the middle of April following operations in the Indian Ocean, was anxious to postpone the operation so as to allow some time for rest and re-equipment.

But Admiral Yamamoto was firm in his resolution and the Naval General Staff eventually gave in to the Combined Fleet, as it had done before.

Just at this point, on 18th April, sixteen B-25 Mitchell bombers, led by Lieutenant-Colonel James Doolittle, took off from Vice-

1 Japanese Mitsubishi Zero fighter. During the Battle of Midway Zeros swept away attacks on their aircraft-carriers, slaughtering the lumbering Devastators of Torpedo Squadron 8. In the early part of the war the Zero was faster and more manoeuvrable than any opposing Allied aircraft. 2 Admiral Chester W.Nimitz, Commander-in-Chief US Pacific Fleet. He concluded correctly that Japan's objectives were Midway and the Aleutians and he decided to concentrate all his forces on the defence of Midway. 3 Devastators of Torpedo Squadron 6

Admiral Halsey's aircraft-carriers *Enterprise* and *Hornet* and carried out a surprise bombing attack on Tokyo. Damage was slight, but the psychological shock of this first air-raid on Japan itself was very great, and when the case for extending the defence perimeter to Midway and the Aleutians was again proposed, this time much more strongly, opposition to it melted away at once. Preparations for a major assault by almost the whole of the Japanese navy went forward with all speed, and the army, until now a mere onlooker, contributed one infantry regiment.

The second phase of the war was to proceed with the occupation of Port Moresby in early May, the occupation of Midway and the Aleutians in early June, and the occupation of New Caledonia, Fiji, and Samoa in July. On the 5th May Imperial General Headquarters ordered the occupation of Midway and the Aleutians.

Unlearned lessons

The forces taking part were almost the full strength of the Combined Fleet, including eleven battleships, eight aircraft-carriers, twenty-one cruisers and more than 200 other ships, together with 500 planes and 6,000 marines and soldiers. The plan was for this vast fleet to set out at different times and from different places in either nine or eleven groups with the object of attacking and occupying Midway and the Aleutians.

From some points of view this plan was a subtle and artistic one, but at the same time it revealed characteristic shortcomings in the Japanese navy, and Admiral Chester Nimitz, Commander-in-Chief of the US Pacific Fleet, later criticized it for both attempting to lure the US Pacific Fleet into a decisive battle and seeking the occupation of Midway. He also criticized the multiplicity of divisions within the forces needed to execute it. Admiral Yamamoto, Commander-in-Chief of the Combined Fleet, who had overall command of the operation, was to be aboard the newly-constructed Combined Fleet flagship *Yamato,* the world's biggest battleship, in company with eight battleships drawn from the Main Body of the Main Force, the Main Force's Guard Force, and Rear-Admiral Abe's Support Group. They were to advance 600 nautical miles (this was later revised to 300 nautical miles) behind Nagumo's I Carrier Striking Force. As *Yamato* was obliged to maintain strict radio silence, it was hardly to be expected that there could be adequate leadership. Yamamoto was well-known as the foster-father of the Naval Air Corps, and had been quick to attach great importance to aircraft and aircraft-carriers. His foresight had already been proved by Japanese successes in the opening days of the war. But now Yamamoto was compromising with the conservative advocates of the big ships and the big guns, possibly with the idea of letting the battleship fleet have some of the glory for the expected victory.

The main striking power undoubtedly lay with Vice-Admiral Nagumo's I Carrier Striking Force consisting of the aircraft-carriers *Akagi, Kaga, Soryu,* and *Hiryu* and whether or not the task-force was successful it seemed unlikely that there would be any opportunity to use the battleships' big guns, with their maximum range of forty nautical miles. In fact the young officers of Nagumo's force suggested sarcastically that the battleship fleet was going to hold a naval review in the Pacific. It is now accepted that, mainly due to the relaxed atmosphere resulting from Japan's string of initial victories and an underestimation of the enemy's strength, secrecy was not strictly maintained, intelligence reports were inadequate, instructions were not followed as carefully as they should have been, and tactical preparations in general were insufficient and left too late.

April's operations in the Indian Ocean together with the Battle of the Coral Sea in May had provided a number of valuable lessons about the weaknesses of reconnaissance work and aircraft-carrier vulnerability which should have been taken

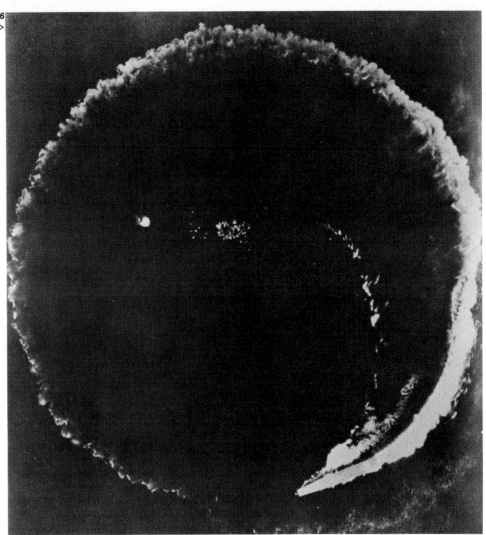

prepare to take off from Enterprise. *Only four came back. But the torpedo squadrons from* Yorktown *and* Hornet *suffered even greater losses. 4 Rear-Admiral Raymond A.Spruance, commander of Task Force 16. He decided to time his attack for the moment when the Japanese aircraft would have returned from Midway. 5 Admiral Isoroku Yamamoto, Commander-in-Chief Combined Fleet. By attacking Midway he wanted to lure out and destroy the US Pacific Fleet. 6* Soryu *makes a full circle at high speed in an attempt to evade attack*

into consideration as a matter of course when the Midway operation was planned, but which, in fact, were largely ignored. A particularly interesting point was that the Battle of the Coral Sea was the first ever important battle in naval history in which aircraft-carriers opposed aircraft-carriers. The opposing forces, the Japanese V Carrier Division under Rear-Admiral Chuichi Hara containing the aircraft-carriers *Shokaku* and *Zuikaku,* and Task Force 17 containing the two American carriers *Lexington* and *Yorktown,* under the command of Rear-Admiral Frank Fletcher, were more or less evenly matched. Tactically speaking, it could be called a Japanese victory since the *Lexington* was sunk and the *Yorktown* damaged, but the Americans achieved their aim in preventing the occupation of Port Moresby. Moreover, although the Japanese carriers did make their way back to Japan, they had suffered such severe losses in combat-ready pilots that they were unable to take part in the battle of Midway, whereas the *Yorktown* returned quickly to Hawaii, underwent emergency repairs, and left again for the battle area. The Combined Fleet put down the 'unsatisfactory result' of the battle to the imperfect discipline of the recently-formed V Carrier Division, and did not attempt to analyse the nature of engagements between aircraft-carriers.

The US Navy had lost most of its battleship fleet at Pearl Harbour, but two large, fast aircraft-carriers had escaped. The traditional notion of battleship supremacy was no less firmly rooted in the US Navy than in the Japanese navy, but the former had lost their battleships and had been obliged to alter their tactics to make the aircraft-carriers the centrepieces of their strategy. From the beginning of 1942 two aircraft-carrier groups, under the command of Admirals Halsey and Fletcher, had carried out bold surprise hit and run attacks on Japan's peripheral defence-line timed to avoid confrontation with Nagumo's task-force. In February they had struck at the Marshall Islands, in March at Lae in Papua, and in May at Tulagi in the Solomon Islands.

The code-breakers

But the only aircraft-carriers Admiral Nimitz could muster for the defence of Midway were *Enterprise, Hornet,* and *Yorktown.* Their chances of successfully resisting a direct confrontation with the six large and four small Japanese aircraft-carriers, superior both in the power of their aircraft and the training of their crews, seemed slight. However, at the same time the US Navy had in its hands an invaluable weapon, which proved the key to victory—namely the expertise of their

intelligence service, and especially of their cryptographers. Before the outbreak of war the American code-breaking experts using their so-called 'Magic' system had succeeded in decoding the Japanese Foreign Ministry machine cypher, which proved of advantage to the Americans in conducting negotiations with Japan. In the spring of 1942 the code-breaking group from the Pacific Fleet, under the direction of Commander Rochefort, gradually, by dint of hard work, managed to break the main strategic code used by the Japanese navy. As a result they were able to alert Task Forces 11 and 17 just in time to frustrate the occupation of Port Moresby in the Coral Sea.

The first hints of the Midway operation began to appear in code messages in late April and early May, but until about 10th May Nimitz's headquarters were still tending to think that the next Japanese objective would probably be Fiji and Samoa. On 14th May Nimitz collated all his reports, which were based mainly on the decoded messages, and concluded correctly that Japan's objectives were Midway and the Aleutians. He decided to concentrate all his forces on the defence of Midway, and hurriedly ordered the strengthening of the island's garrison and additions to its defence facilities and fortifications. In addition, three submarine patrol arcs were set up at a distance of 100, 150, and 200 miles from Midway, with a total of twenty submarines on stations by 4th June. Moreover, Pacific Fleet Headquarters urgently ordered Task Forces 16 (grouped around *Hornet* and *Enterprise)* and 17 (including damaged *Yorktown*) to return at once to Pearl Harbour from the south-west Pacific. The defence of Dutch Harbour was to be the responsibility of a new fleet under Rear-Admiral Theobald.

Vice-Admiral William Halsey was now in hospital, and Rear-Admiral Raymond Spruance had replaced him as commander of Task Force 16, composed of *Enterprise, Hornet,* six cruisers, and nine destroyers, which sailed from Pearl Harbour on 28th May. Task Force 17, comprising *Yorktown,* whose damage was actually repaired in three days rather than in the estimated three months, plus two cruisers and five destroyers under the command of Rear-Admiral Frank Fletcher, left Pearl Harbour on 30th May. The two fleets met at 'Point Luck', about 325 nautical miles north-east of Midway, on the evening of 2nd June, and waited for the Japanese to attack. Since the end of May Catalina flying-boats, deployed at Midway, had been spreading a fine net of observation flights over a 700-mile radius around the island.

The attacking Japanese navy was also doing its best to collect reports. On 18th May a patrolling flying-boat spotted Halsey's two aircraft-carriers to the east of the Solomons archipelago, but thereafter no further reports of US aircraft-carriers were made. However, it was thought highly probable that they were in port at Pearl Harbour. On the basis of this supposition a second flying-boat reconnaissance was planned. An 'Emily' flying-boat, with its vaunted range of 4,000 nautical miles, was to take off from its base in the Marshall Islands, and, after stopping to refuel from a submarine at French Frigate Shoals, was to arrive over Hawaii during the night of 30th May. The mission had to be abandoned, however, when it was discovered that the shoals were already being used by the US Navy as a seaplane base. Moreover, submarines arriving at the north and south ends of the Hawaiian archipelago on 3rd June were too late to sight the two US aircraft-carriers.

On 26th May Nagumo's I Carrier Striking Force left the Bungo Strait and two days later the Main Body, the Midway invasion force Main Body, and the Guard Force followed. On 27th May the Transport Group sailed from Saipan towards the battle-area in the central Pacific. The whole fleet had maintained absolute radio silence, but immediately signs appeared which augured ill for its hopes of achieving a surprise attack. US submarines off the Bungo Strait and Saipan sent long radio code messages directly after the Japanese fleets had left these points, which were intercepted. Furthermore, two Japanese ships lost their way in fog and broke the radio silence, and it was assumed that their messages must have been picked up by the Americans. On 1st June the number of messages sent to the Hawaii area, including a good many urgent messages, increased sharply, and the commanding officers of the Combined Fleet decided that their movements were already known to the Americans. Rear-Admiral Ugaki, Combined Fleet Chief of Staff, noted in his diary: 'This should do us no harm. It will give us a bigger prize to fight for'. On the evening of the 3rd the cruiser *Tone* spotted 'enemy flying-boats', but the fighter aircraft sent up from the *Akagi* to intercept lost them in the clouds.

All these alarms were in fact no more than groundless fears originating with the Japanese themselves. The Americans had not in fact made any contact, and Nagumo's I Carrier Striking Force, which was hidden in the sense that it was out in front, was not spotted by American reconnaissance aircraft until early on the 4th June, the first day of the battle. Luck had not yet deserted the Japanese navy in the war.

The electrifying message

The final, decisive warning was sounded on 2nd June. On that date VI Fleet's interception unit on Kwajalein atoll detected messages being passed between what appeared to be two US aircraft-carriers, which suggested that the ships were at sea to the north-west of Midway Island. This information was passed on immediately to the whole fleet, but Nagumo's force, out in front, paid no attention. It, moreover, decided that the 'flying-boats' supposed to have been sighted on the evening of the 3rd had in fact been birds. I Carrier Striking Force still had confidence in its surprise attack scheduled for the following day.

The operation began on the morning of 3rd June with an aerial attack on Dutch Harbour by aircraft from II Carrier Striking Force under the command of Rear-Admiral Kakuta. To create a diversion and distract attention from Midway the Japanese navy arranged a simultaneous surprise attack on Sydney and Diego Suarez in Madagascar with special midget submarines, but as a result of reports extracted from decoded messages Admiral Nimitz was able to grasp almost every aspect of the Japanese plan.

On the same day a section of the Transport Group which had proceeded ahead of schedule was spotted by a patrolling Catalina plane, and the upshot was that one tanker was damaged in a torpedo attack the same evening.

At 0430 the following day, the 4th, Nagumo's I Carrier Striking Force arrived on schedule at a point 240 nautical miles north-west of Midway Island and the first attack wave, made up of thirty-six Nakajima B5N2s ('Kates'), thirty-six Aichi D3A2s ('Vals'), and thirty-six Zeros, took off to attack the island. The second attack wave, composed as the first, waited on the carriers' flight decks prepared for the appearance of enemy forces on the horizon.

As has already been stated, the chief purpose of the operation was to lure the American Pacific Fleet to destruction. But although I Carrier Division carried out a reconnaissance sweep that morning, there was a conviction that it would reveal no cause for uneasiness. This attitude of the General Staff, reflected in the movements of the reconnaissance planes, was a fatal weakness in the operation. At the same time as the first Midway attack set out, seven search aircraft took off to make a 300 nautical mile fan-shaped reconnaissance, but the heavy cruiser *Chikuma*'s seaplane which must have come close to passing directly above the US task-force at about 0630, not only failed to spot it, but also failed to report the important fact, indicating as it did the presence of an enemy aircraft-carrier, that the aircraft had encountered and engaged a Dauntless dive-bomber from the *Yorktown*. The *Tone*'s machine was assigned a course south of the *Chikuma*'s seaplane but because of a catapult fault its take-off was delayed for thirty minutes. However, at 0728 on its return flight it reported sighting 'what appears to be ten enemy surface ships'. This was Task Force 16, which had sent up aircraft at 0700 for an attack on Nagumo's I Carrier Striking Force after a Catalina plane had spotted it at 0534. But because of the clear visibility and the presence of enemy aircraft the *Tone*'s seaplane at first hesitated to move in close above the enemy fleet. It turned away, but at 0747 the General Staff of I Carrier Division demanded: 'Ascertain types of ships'. The seaplane flew in close and at 0807 radioed 'five cruisers and five destroyers'. Thirteen minutes later it sent the electrifying message: 'Enemy force accompanied by what appears to be aircraft-carrier bringing up the rear.'

But when the first message came in from the seaplane, Nagumo's force was being attacked by aircraft from Midway. However, without fighter cover the series of attacks by B-17s, B-26s, Avengers, Vindicators, and Dauntlesses of the army, navy, and marine corps were in vain. The aircraft were swept away by Zeros and failed to score a single hit.

Further evidence of the manoeuvrability of the Zeros was provided during the Midway strike between 0630 and 0710. The US defences, alerted by radar an hour before, sent up twenty-six Grumman Wildcats and Brewster Buffaloes to intercept the Japanese attackers. However, seventeen of the defenders were shot down, and a further seven damaged beyond repair. Japanese losses in the first wave attack were negligible. Three Kates and one Val were shot down by enemy anti-aircraft fire, and only two fighters failed to return. But Lieutenant Tomonaga, the leader of the attack, realized that the defences had been strengthened beyond what they had been led to expect and at 0700 radioed Admiral Nagumo: 'There is need for a second attack.'

There had been no report so far from the reconnaissance aircraft, so the General Staff, confident that there was no US fleet in the vicinity, decided that the second attack wave, which was waiting on the flight decks, should head for Midway, and at 0715 gave the order that the torpedo-laden Kates on *Akagi* and *Kaga* should be de-armed and re-loaded with bombs. After the seaplane's sighting of a US carrier a

Moment of impact on Yorktown. *The blast of a torpedo which has just crashed into her side hurls the port side catwalk into the air as a crewman crossed the deck*

message came by blinker signal from Rear-Admiral Yamaguchi, commander of II Carrier Division: 'Consider it advisable to launch attack force immediately'. Even though the torpedo-bombers were not yet ready, he wanted the dive-bombers dispatched immediately to bomb the US carrier. But Nagumo, who had witnessed the slaughter of the unescorted US bombers and torpedo-planes, decided on the advice of Commander Minoru Genda, of the aviation staff, to follow the orthodox line of recovering both the Midway strike aircraft and the second wave fighters which were now on combat air patrol and sending them as escort for the Kates and Vals.

Slaughter of the Devastators

At 0745 Nagumo ordered that the aircraft which had already taken on bomb loads should start exchanging them once again for torpedoes. In the small hangars maintenance crews worked desperately. If Nagumo had realized it would take two hours before the strike-force was ready, no doubt he would unhesitatingly have followed the timely advice given him by Rear-Admiral Yamaguchi. But misfortunes occurred one after another to retard the preparations. At 0830 the first attack wave

returned from Midway and began circling, waiting for permission to land. The landings were completed by 0918, and it was calculated that it would be 1030 before the attack squadron, now re-equipped with torpedoes, would have replaced the incoming aircraft on the flight decks and be ready for take-off.

At 0905 a message from the *Tone's* seaplane stated that a large fleet of US torpedo aircraft was on its way towards Nagumo's fleet. All the commanding officers of the I Air Fleet were on edge, but by now there was no time to regret taking the wrong decision. The only possible thing to be done was urgently to press on preparing the aircraft for take-off in time to meet the large fleet of US aircraft. The commanders turned their ships from a south-easterly course to a north-easterly one to meet the oncoming attack, and officers fiercely urged on their men.

When the news came through from a Catalina on the same morning that Nagumo's I Carrier Striking Force had been spotted, the two US task forces were 240 nautical miles east-north-east of the Japanese fleet. At that time the radius of activity of the US torpedo aircraft was not more than 175 nautical miles, so that 0900

The Tide Turns

Yorktown *listing heavily to port after attack by Japanese aircraft from* Hiryu. *She was finished off by a Japanese submarine, I-68*

was the earliest that the ships could reach their launching point. Rear-Admiral Spruance, however, knew that the Japanese had begun their bombing attack on Midway, and decided to time his attack for the moment when the Japanese aircraft would have just returned from their raid and would therefore be at their most vulnerable. He therefore launched his attack planes at 0700, two hours ahead of schedule. 116 aircraft took off from *Enterprise* and *Hornet* and an hour later an attack fleet of thirty-five aircraft took off from *Yorktown*.

The first to reach the target was Torpedo Squadron 8, from *Hornet,* led by the intrepid Lieutenant-Commander John Waldron. But his old-fashioned and unescorted Douglas Devastators were surrounded by a large number of Zeros and one after another they were shot down in flames. Every one of the fifteen aircraft was lost, and Ensign George H.Gay, who was picked up from the sea the next day by a navy Catalina, was the only man to be rescued.

The torpedo squadrons from *Enterprise* and *Yorktown* plunged into the attack after them, and they too were roughly handled. In the end only six aircraft survived out of the total force of forty-one, and they did not achieve a single hit. Nevertheless, their blood was not shed in vain. The low-altitude Devastators drew the Zeros down after them, and thus made possible a surprise attack by the Dauntless dive-bombers, which attacked from a high altitude.

Lieutenant-Commander Clarence McClusky, of *Enterprise,* leading eighteen Dauntless dive-bombers, made straight for the estimated position of the fleet. He failed to find it, however, and after flying on westward for a short time, surmising correctly that Nagumo's task-force had altered

course, he turned north and continued the search. This was one of the most significant decisions of the battle. The thirty-four dive-bombers from *Hornet* found themselves in a similar position, but they turned south and did not find their target.

McClusky was extremely lucky. At 0955 he spotted the destroyer *Arashi*, followed it, and ten minutes later spotted Nagumo's fleet through a break in the clouds. At about the same time *Yorktown*'s dive-bomber squadron led by Lieutenant-Commander Maxwell F. Leslie, which had arrived by a different route, spotted their target. McClusky's aircraft began dive-bombing attacks on three of the Japanese aircraft-carriers at 1022. Three minutes later, when Leslie's squadron began their dive-bombing attack on the *Soryu*, the four carriers of Nagumo's task-force had almost completed their preparations, and were heading directly into the wind, ready for their aircraft to take off. Rear-Admiral Kusaka later bewailed the fact that, given just five more minutes, the aircraft would probably all have been in the air and moving in a great mass to attack the US aircraft-carriers. The whole shape of the battle altered in those few minutes. Four bombs struck *Kaga,* and as soon as it had gone up in flames, McClusky's squadron scored three direct hits on the *Soryu* and another on the *Akagi,* and a great cloud of black smoke went up from these three aircraft-carriers. In the normal course of events, bombs of between 550 and 1,100 pounds would damage the flight deck of an aircraft-carrier, but would hardly destroy the whole ship. In this case, however, the three carriers each had a full complement of aircraft loaded with fuel, torpedoes, and bombs, so that fires once started spread in a rapid series of explosions, and these, exacerbated by the fact that the damage control units were caught unprepared, were fatal to the three huge ships.

Hiryu *hits back*

Initially the *Hiryu* escaped damage and in a spirit of furious revenge sent up eighteen escorted Vals, seven of which eluded *Yorktown*'s combat air patrol and penetrated the anti-aircraft fire from the carrier's screening cruisers and destroyers to severely damage the vessel with three bombs. A second strike by ten escorted Kates scored two torpedo hits and doomed the carrier. Within fifteen minutes of the torpedoes crashing into her port side Captain Buckmaster ordered the crew to abandon ship, but the carrier was still afloat two days later when the Japanese submarine I-68 found her in the afternoon of 6th June and, penetrating her screen, sunk her. Meanwhile dive-bombers from Task Force 16 had crippled *Hiryu*.

Following the news of the destruction of

Nagumo's task force the staff of the Combined Fleet ordered all their forces to proceed to an attack on Midway Island. Kurita's Close Support Group of four heavy cruisers and two destroyers in the van was within ninety nautical miles of the island by the middle of the night and was preparing for battle on the following morning, but Rear-Admiral Spruance, wary of being caught in a night battle, for the Japanese navy specialized in night fighting, had begun to retreat eastwards in the evening. When Yamamoto learned of this he called off the whole operation, and ordered the withdrawal of the fleet.

The Battle of Midway is of particular interest in the history of naval warfare in that it marked the end of the transition period between the era of battleship domination and that of the aircraft-carrier. But the Battle of Midway, unlike Salamis, did not decide the outcome of the entire war in a moment. Unlike Jutland, Midway did not bring together the opposing forces in their entirety; unlike the battle of the Japan Sea it was not a conflict ending in the utter destruction of one of the two sides. If one considers the battles of the Pacific War from the point of view of their scale, then the Battle of the Philippine Sea and the Battle of Leyte Gulf were both greater than Midway. It can be said, indeed, that the Battle of Midway was the point in the Pacific War where the tide turned but, contrary to what is often stated, it was not the decisive battle determining the course of the entire war. Japan did lose four of her major aircraft-carriers, it is true, but this left *Zuikaku* and *Shokaku* besides six smaller carriers, which more or less matched America's fleet of three large carriers and a smaller one. At the same time Japan retained her superiority in battleships and heavy cruisers. In other words it can be said that the Battle of Midway broke Japan's superiority in the Pacific and restored the balance between the Japanese and American navies.

As is amply demonstrated by statistics, what really wore down the fighting power of the Japanese navy was the exhausting struggle for the Solomon Islands which began in August 1942. As compared to the Battle of Midway, where Japan lost 296 aircraft and 114 airmen, representing twenty per cent of the total number attached to Nagumo's task-force, in the battle for the Solomons the figures were as high as some 3,000 aircraft and 6,200 men.

No doubt the primary significance of the Battle of Midway lay in its psychological aspect. In the words of the naval historian Rear-Admiral Samuel Eliot Morison 'Midway was the first really smashing defeat inflicted on the Japanese navy in modern times.' But it had by no means been a foregone conclusion.

Stalingrad

It has often been said that Stalingrad was the decisive battle, and the turning point, of the eastern campaign. And indeed a glance at the map, with some hindsight of the German plans for the summer of 1942, would seem to make this the obvious site. Yet the irony is that neither side intended, or foresaw, that the fight to the death should be there.

At the beginning of 1942 both the German Armed Forces High Command (OKW) and the Stavka (the Supreme Command of the Red Army) projected planning for the summer that grossly over-estimated their own capabilities. In spite of the punishment they had sustained during the Soviet winter offensives of 1941 the Germans were confident that they could master the Red Army when the weather no longer impeded their mobility. And indeed there was some substance in this, for the terrible battles of the deep winter had been fought by a quite small proportion of the German strength which the extreme temperatures had isolated from manoeuvre or relief. More than sixty-five per cent of

Russians contest a few yards of rubble in the shattered streets of Stalingrad

the infantry had never been engaged in the winter fighting, and had spent the winter in training and re-equipment.

At the nadir of German fortunes there had been voices in the German Army High Command (OKH) which had favoured retreat to the line of the Dnieper and a suspension of offensive operations for a whole twelve-month period. But with the milder weather this caution evaporated (helped, no doubt, by the wholesale dismissals which Hitler had implemented in the new year) and planning proceeded apace for the summer campaign.

In fact it was the Red Army which got off the line first, staging three separate offensives immediately after the spring thaw. The Soviet intention was to relieve Leningrad and Sebastopol, and to recapture Kharkov—objectives more ambitious even than those of mid-winter, and set, moreover, in a context of German recovery and Russian exhaustion. In the result all three failed, and with crippling casualties. The Kharkov offensive in particular had most serious consequences as it ran head-on into a strong enemy concentration deployed to eliminate the Lozovaya salient, which had been established by the Red Army in January. The Russians lost over 600 tanks and in this critical area, where the Germans had decided to concentrate their summer offensive, the ratio of armour swung dramatically from five to one in the Russian favour to nearly ten to one against them.

For the Germans then, an initial domination of the battlefield was a certainty. How they would exploit this was less definite. At least three separate operational plans existed. The most conservative, naturally, was that formulated by the OKH staff, which envisaged advancing as far east as was necessary to safeguard the mineral resources of the Donets Basin. Stalingrad was suggested as a final objective but with the escape clause that if its seizure was not possible it would be enough to 'expose it to our heavy fire, so that it loses its importance as a centre of communications'. The OKW toyed with two schemes; the first anticipated swallowing Stalingrad in the opening weeks, wheeling north up the left bank of the Volga and outflanking Moscow; the second, only slightly less grandiose, also presumed the city's early fall followed by its tenure as a 'blocking point' to cover a *southward* wheel into the Caucasus where the Soviet oilfields lay. General von Kleist, commanding I Panzer Group, had been personally told by Hitler as early as April that '. . . I and my Panzers were to be the instruments whereby the Reich would be assured of its oil supplies in perpetuity. Stalingrad was no more than a name on the map to us.'

The southern offensive

Army Group South, commanded by Field-Marshal von Bock, launched its attack on 28th June. Three armies split the Russian front into fragments on either side of Kursk, and Hoth's eleven Panzer divisions fanned out across hundreds of miles of open rolling corn and steppe grass, towards Voronezh and the Don. Two days later the southern half of the army group went over to the attack below Kharkov, and Kleist took I Panzer Group across the Donets.

The Russians were outnumbered and outgunned from the start, and their shortage of armour made it difficult to mount even local counter-attacks. With each day the Russian disorder multiplied, their command structure degenerating into independent combat at divisional, then at brigade, finally at regimental level. Without even the protection of mass, which had characterized the Red Army's deployment in the Ukraine in 1941, or of swamp and forest, which had allowed small groups to delay the enemy in the battle of Moscow, these formations were at the German's mercy. Polarizing around the meagre cover of some shallow ravine or the wooden hutments of a *kolkhoz*, they fought out their last battle under a deluge of firepower against which they could oppose little save their own bravery. '. . . quite different from last year [wrote a sergeant in III Panzer Division]. It's more like Poland. The Russians aren't nearly so thick on the ground. They fire their guns like madmen, but they don't hurt us.'

Within a fortnight the Soviet command structure had disintegrated and on 12th July the Stavka promulgated a new 'Stalingrad front'. The title of this force (front was roughly equivalent administratively, though not necessarily in strength, to a German army group) showed that the Stavka, at least, appreciated where they must make their stand, and it was here that they were now directing their last reserves, which had been concentrated around Moscow. General Chuykov, who was to emerge as one of the vital personalities who inspired and directed the battle of Stalingrad, brought his reserve army of four infantry divisions, two motorized and two armoured brigades from Tula, a distance of 700 miles south-east. On his arrival Chuykov was given instructions so vague as to convince him that 'front HQ obviously possessed extremely limited information about the enemy, who was mentioned only in general terms'.

Chuykov has described how on his first day he was on a personal reconnaissance: 'I came across two divisional staffs . . . they consisted of a number of officers travelling in some three to five trucks filled to overflowing with cans of fuel. When I asked them where the Germans were, and where

they were going, they could not give me a sensible reply. It was clear that to restore to these men the faith they had lost in their own powers and to improve the fighting quality of the retreating units would not be easy.'

This was the moment which offered the Germans the best prospect of 'swallowing' Stalingrad as postulated in the wide outflanking plans of the OKW. In fact the Russian troops, though thrown into battle piecemeal as they arrived, proved just adequate to slow the German advance guard, now outrunning its supplies after an advance of 300 miles in three weeks. It took Paulus's VI Army five days to clear the Don bend, and he did not have the strength to eliminate every Soviet position in the loop of the west bank—an omission which was to have catastrophic consequences in November.

Stalingrad now began to exercise its magnetism over the whole of Army Group B (the northern section of Army Group South) and up along the chain of command to the Führer himself who moved his headquarters from Rastenburg to Vinnitsa (120 miles south-west of Kiev) on 25th August, where it remained until the end of the year. The Germans were committing themselves to the one kind of battle where their adversary held the advantage, forsaking their own enormous superiorities in firepower and mobility for a mincing machine of close combat. Hoth's Panzers were swung north, out of the steppe into the brick and concrete of the Stalingrad suburbs, and for nearly four months the city was wracked by continuous hand-to-hand fighting.

The nearest historical parallel is with the Battle of Verdun in 1916. But there are significant differences. At Verdun the contestants rarely saw one another face to face; they were battered to death by high explosives or cut down at long range by machine-gun fire. At Stalingrad each separate battle resolved itself into a combat between individuals. Soldiers would jeer and curse at their enemy across the street; often they could hear his breathing in the next room while they reloaded; hand-to-hand duels were finished in the dark twilight of smoke and brick dust with knives and pickaxes, with clubs of rubble and twisted steel. General Doerr has described how 'the time for conducting large-scale operations was gone for ever; from the wide expanses of steppe-land the war moved into the jagged gullies of the Volga hills with their copses and ravines, into the factory area of Stalingrad, spread out over uneven, pitted, rugged country, covered with iron, concrete, and stone buildings. The mile, as a measure of distance, was replaced by the yard. GHQ's map was the map of the city.

'For every house, workshop, water tower, railway embankment, wall, cellar, and every pile of ruins, a bitter battle was waged, without equal even in the First World War with its vast expenditure of munitions. The distance between the enemy's army and ours was as small as it could possibly be. Despite the concentrated activity of aircraft and artillery, it was impossible to break out of the area of close fighting. The Russians surpassed the Germans in their use of the terrain and in camouflage and were more experienced in barricade warfare for individual buildings.'

In the first week of September Hoth's tanks, operating in the southern sector, broke through to the Volga bank and split the Russians into two. A critical four-day period followed, with the defenders of the northern half outnumbered three to one, and the Germans got close enough to bring the central landing stage (where the Volga ferries landed supplies for the defending forces) under machine-gun fire. But the sheer tenacity and individual courage of the Russian foot-soldier was the deciding factor. General Paulus's offensive subsided, fought to a standstill.

It was now plain that a major strategic revision was called for. But the Germans were prisoners of their own propaganda, which had steadily been building up the importance of the battle. Any misgivings that Paulus himself may have felt were quietened by a visit from General Schmundt, formerly Hitler's adjutant and now chief of the Army Personnel Office. Schmundt strongly hinted that Paulus was being considered for 'a most senior post' (in fact the succession to Jodl as Chief of the Armed Forces Operational Staff), but that the Führer was most anxious first to see the Stalingrad operations 'brought to a successful conclusion'. Paulus's awareness of his own interests was, at all times, keener than his tactical abilities. This time he decided to strike head-on at his enemy's strongest point—the three giant edifices of the Tractor Factory, the Barrikady (Barricades) ordnance plant, and the Krasny Oktyabr (Red October) steel works, which lay in the northern half of the city, ranged one after another a few hundred yards from the Volga bank. This was to be the fiercest, and the longest, of the five battles which were fought in the ruined town, and that which finally drained the offensive strength from the German armies in south Russia. It started on 4th October and raged for nearly three weeks. Paulus had been reinforced by a variety of different specialist troops, including police batta-

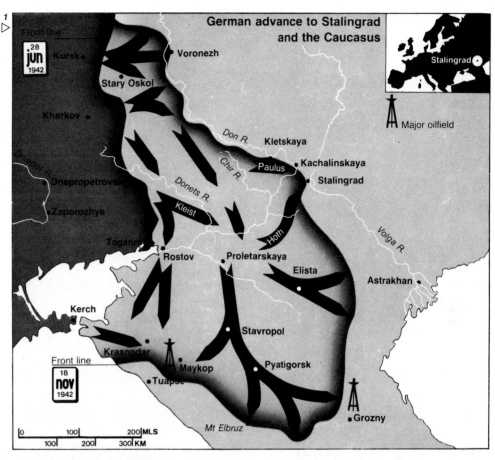

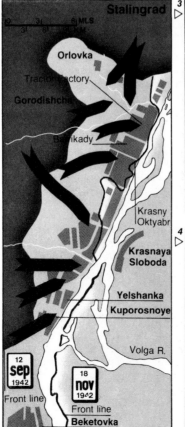

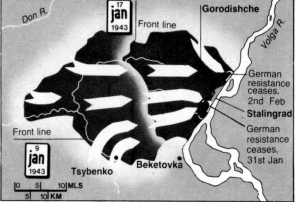

1 The German advance. 2 The German assault on Stalingrad. 3 Red Army counter-attacks. 4 The crushing of VI Army

The Tide Turns

lions and engineers skilled in street fighting and demolition work. But the Russians, though still heavily outnumbered, remained their masters in the technique of house-to-house fighting. They had perfected the use of 'shock groups', small bodies of mixed arms – light and heavy machine-gunners, tommy gunners, and grenadiers usually with anti-tank guns, who gave one another support in lightning counter-attacks; and they had developed the creation of 'killing zones', houses and squares heavily mined, to which the defenders knew all the approach routes, where the German advance could be canalized.

Slowly and at a tremendous price the Germans inched their way into the great buildings, across factory floors; around and over the inert machinery, through the foundries, the assembly shops, the offices. 'My God, why have you forsaken us?' wrote a lieutenant of XXIV Panzer Division. 'We have fought during fifteen days for a single house, with mortars, grenades, machine-guns, and bayonets. Already by the third day fifty-four German corpses lay strewn in the cellars, on the landings, and the staircases. The front is a corridor between burnt-out rooms; it is the thin ceiling between two floors. Help comes from neighbouring houses by fire escapes and chimneys. There is a ceaseless struggle from noon till night. From storey to storey, faces black with sweat, we bombard each other with grenades in the middle of explosions, clouds of dust and smoke, heaps of mortar, floods of blood, fragments of furniture and human beings. Ask any soldier what half an hour of hand-to-hand struggle means in such a fight. And imagine Stalingrad; eighty days and eighty nights of hand-to-hand struggles. The street is no longer measured by metres but by corpses . . . Stalingrad is no longer a town. By day it is an enormous cloud of burning blinding smoke; it is a vast furnace, lit by the reflection of the flames. And when the night arrives, one of those scorching, howling, bleeding nights, the dogs plunge into the Volga and swim desperately to gain the other bank. The nights of Stalingrad are a terror for them. Animals flee this hell; the hardest stones cannot bear it for long; only men endure.'

By the end of October the Russian positions at Stalingrad had been reduced to a few pockets of stone, seldom more than three hundred yards deep, bordering on the right bank of the Volga. The Krasny Oktyabr had fallen to the Germans who had paved every metre of the factory floor with their dead. The Barrikady was half lost, with Germans at one end of the foundry facing Russian machine-guns in the extinct ovens at the other. The defenders of the Tractor Factory had been split into three.

Zhukov counter-attacks

But these last islets of resistance, hardened in the furnace of repeated attacks, were irreducible. Paulus's VI Army was spent, as exhausted as Haig's divisions at Passchendaele had been exactly a quarter of a century before. And all the time, to the north and west, a terrible storm was gathering. Early in September the Stavka had sent Zhukov – architect of their winter victory at Moscow – to the southern theatre and with him Zhukov had brought his colleagues Novikov and Voronov, the artillery specialist. For two months Zhukov carefully built up his reserves on the German flank and reinforced the Don bridgeheads against the Rumanians defending the German northern flank. Of twenty-two fresh infantry divisions created during this period only two were committed in Stalingrad itself. Virtually the entire autumn tank production was held back for use in the counter-offensive.

Paulus's Intelligence had warned him that something was afoot, but both Luftwaffe and army had grossly under-estimated its scale. The XLVIII Panzer Corps, VI Army's sole mobile reserve, consisted of ninety-two Czech light tanks, with Rumanian crews, and the remains of XIV Panzer Division refitting after five weeks continuous action in the rubble of Stalingrad. Against this, on 19th November, Zhukov threw six fresh armies, 450 new T34 tanks, and an artillery barrage from over 2,000 guns, in a pincer movement that converged on either side of the German salient whose tip was at Stalingrad.

The staff of VI Army went sleepless for two nights as they struggled to regroup the precious Panzers and pull back their infantry from the smoking maze of Stalingrad to protect the collapsing flanks. In the rear confusion was absolute: the western railway from Kalach had already been cut by Russian cavalry in several places; the sound of firing came from every direction, and periodically broke out between Germans going up to the front and ragged groups of Rumanians in leaderless retreat. The huge bridge at Kalach over which every pound of rations and every bullet for VI Army passed, had been prepared for demolition, and a platoon of engineers was on duty there all day on 23rd November in case the order to destroy the bridge should come through. At half past four that afternoon tanks could be heard approaching from the west. The lieutenant in charge of the engineers thought at first that they might be Russians but was reassured when the first three vehicles were identified as Horch personnel carriers with XXII Panzer Division markings; assuming that it was a reinforcement column for Stalingrad he instructed his men to lift the barrier. The personnel carriers halted on the bridge and

disgorged sixty Russian tommy-gunners who killed most of the engineer platoon and took the survivors prisoner. They removed the demolition charges and twenty-five tanks from the column passed over the bridge and drove south-east, where that evening they made contact with the southern claw of the pincer, 14th Independent Tank Brigade from Trufanov's 51st Army. The first tenuous link in a chain that was to throttle a quarter of a million German soldiers had been forged, and the turning point in the Second World War had arrived.

In the three days following their penetration of the Rumanian corps, the Russians had moved thirty-four divisions across the Don, twelve from Beketonskaya bridgehead and twenty-two from Kremenskaya. Their tanks had turned westward, defeating XLVIII Panzer Corps and probing dangerously into the confusion of stragglers, service and training units, and mutinous satellites who milled about in the German rear. Their infantry had turned east, digging with feverish energy to build an iron ring around VI Army. Zhukov kept the whole of the Stalingrad pocket under bombardment from heavy guns sited on the far bank of the Volga, but for the first few days he had exerted only a gentle pressure upon the surrounded Germans.

The Soviets' intention was to probe in sufficient strength to be able to detect the first signs of their enemy's actually striking camp, but to avoid any action which might precipitate this. For them, as for Paulus, these first hours were vital. All night on 23rd and during the morning of 24th November, men and tractors hauled and struggled with battery after battery of 76-mm guns across the frozen earth. By that evening Russian firepower on the west side of the pocket had trebled. Over a thousand anti-tank guns were in position in an arc from Vertyatchy, in the north, around to Kalach, then eastwards below Marinovka, joining the Volga at the old Beketonskaya bridgehead.

Field-Marshal von Manstein, the newly appointed commander of the German army group, set about preparing a relief operation, using the rump of Hoth's Panzers that had been left out of the encirclement, and some mobile units pulled back from the Caucasus. However, Russian pressure and administrative difficulties delayed the counter-attack (Operation Winter Tempest) until 12th December. Hoth's column was never strong enough to penetrate the Soviet ring on its own, and a simultaneous full-scale sortie by Paulus's force on the code signal Donnerschlag – 'Thunderclap' – was to be vital to its success. When it came to the point Paulus refused to move, making a succession of excuses and finally referring Manstein to Hitler. Hitler, over the telephone, said he had to leave it to

Paulus. With the overall position deteriorating daily it was impossible to keep Hoth's column poised in the steppe for long and over Christmas it withdrew, carrying with it the last prospects of relief for the beleaguered army.

Stalingrad was the greatest single defeat suffered by German arms since the Napoleonic Wars. To this day it is impossible to make a final assessment of the failure to relieve the surrounded army because all the surviving participants are inhibited, for one or another reason, from giving an impartial account. Russian strength was, of course, a primary factor. Also contributory was the misrepresentation by the Luftwaffe of its ability to supply VI Army (incredibly Göring assumed that the He 111, which could carry 2,000 kilogrammes of *explosive* could as easily load 2,000 kilogrammes of *cargo*). But the real mystery is a strategic one. There was a widespread conviction that the Stalingrad garrison must stay where it was in order to cover the retreat of the rest of the army. Manstein himself is on record with the view that 'if the enemy siege forces had been released . . . the fate of the whole southern wing of the German forces in the East would have been sealed.' It was impossible to recommend that Paulus should be *sacrificed* to this end – easy to take comfort (as Paulus himself was doing) from the fact that many, weaker 'pockets' had held out through the previous winter until the thaw had brought relief.

At all events, the revictualling of so large a garrison was quite beyond the powers of the Luftwaffe even while its forward airfields were safe. Once these were lost to the Russian advance the garrison's life could be measured in weeks. VI Army rejected a surrender demand on 10th January and defeated the last Russian attack. On 2nd February the last remnants of the garrison were obliged by shortage of food and ammunition to surrender. Over 130,000 men went into the prison cages and German strength in the East was never to recover.

Russian soldiers emerge from hiding in a ruined house, October 1942. The stubbornness of the Russian defence baffled the Germans—and as they became tied down in the savage hand-to-hand fighting, they chose to regard it as a 'battle of attrition' in which the Red Army would be bled white. But it was the Wehrmacht which had failed to understand tactics as well as strategic reality; it was the German Army which was being exhausted and forced to throw in all its reserves, while the Russians built up their strength, committing only enough troops to deny the Germans any chance of a breakthrough

5 THE NEW ORDER

SS: The Empire Within

The SS (Schutzstaffel meaning protection squads) first showed their strength in the Night of the Long Knives, the moment chosen by Hitler to eliminate the SA. With their violent and rowdy demonstrations the Brownshirts had dominated the streets of Germany and, indeed, Germany's political life, throughout the 1920's. They were to do so no longer. On 30th June 1934 the main leaders of the SA were arrested, executed on the spot, or handed over to improvised execution squads. The instrument of this savage purge was the SS, which now became the custodian of Party values.

Although created in 1923, the SS had less than 300 members when Himmler was appointed Reichsführer-SS in 1929. Under his leadership the SS greatly increased in size and importance but it remained, until 1934, a force within a force, nominally subordinate to the general organization of the SA. 'Made up of men at the peak of physical fitness, the most trustworthy and the most faithful to the Nazi movement', its role was to keep an eye on the Party and to guarantee the Führer's personal safety. The latter task was entrusted to a guard of 120 select men of absolute reliability under the command of Sepp Dietrich, a Bavarian ex-sergeant, former waiter and butcher's boy, who had made a veritable cult of the person of Hitler. At the end of 1933, the Führer gave his personal guard the official title of Leibstandarte (bodyguard regiment) SS Adolf Hitler.

The SS, in their elegant black uniforms, were the evil guardian angels of the Nazi

Left: Dutch civilians in a Gestapo jail

regime. Recruited from a higher social class than the SA, they were more discreet and avoided rowdy demonstrations; they had other means of proving their terrible efficiency. Completely dominated by Nazi ideals their prime characteristic was absolute fidelity and blind obedience to Hitler's orders: 'On 30th June 1934,' Himmler said later, 'we did not hesitate to do the duty laid down for us and put guilty friends up against the wall and shoot them . . . . . . Each of us found it appalling, yet we are all sure that if such orders were ever necessary again, we would carry them out as we did then.'

On the eve of the war, the SS, with its 250,000 members, constituted the élite of the Party and of the Third Reich. Already the formidable organization created by Himmler was taking on its definitive form with its three main branches: the intelligence service of the Party, or SD (Sicherheitsdienst), which towards the end of the war absorbed the armed forces intelligence services (Abwehr); the police, including the regular police (Ordnungspolizei or Orpo) and the security police (Sicherheitspolizei or Sipo), itself composed of the state criminal police (Kripo) and the state secret police (Geheimestaatspolizei or Gestapo); and finally the military section of the SS. When war broke out the latter consisted of four regiments: Leibstandarte Adolf Hitler, Deutschland, Germania, and Der Führer. Deutschland and Germania had been formed in 1936, and Der Führer in 1938 after the Anschluss. These four regiments were known as the Verfügungstruppe (troops at Hitler's disposal). After the Polish campaign, Deutschland, Ger-

mania, and Der Führer were brought together in the Verfügungsdivision, and two other divisions were raised: Totenkopf, from the concentration camp guard units, and Polizei, from the police. These three divisions, together with the Leibstandarte which remained an independent regiment until 1941 when it was raised to division strength, became known as the Waffen-SS (armed SS) in 1940. Together they constituted an autonomous branch of Himmler's organization.

Himmler planned to expand the military SS into a group of shock troops which would attract the greater part of German youth, become an army in its own right, and constitute the 'racial' élite of the Third Reich. But from 1938 onwards Hitler resisted these ambitions and the Waffen-SS thus remained a militarized police force, though very well armed. Its main task was to quell any attempts at a coup d'état and maintain law and order in occupied territories. To acquire the necessary prestige in the eyes of the German population, Waffen-SS members shed blood on the battlefield—in compliance with Hitler's orders—alongside regular army units. Limited to five per cent of the army's total strength, the Waffen-SS acted as a model, embodying the ideals which National Socialism intended to instil into the army.

In 1940 the SS organization already had its own characteristics: it was, for instance, independent as far as administration and recruitment were concerned. Until 1942 it only accepted volunteers who fulfilled strict moral and physical conditions, though as the Third Reich's 'stud' became

149

weaker under the blows of the Allies and the Red Army, the requirements became less demanding. 'Up until 1936,' Himmler was to write, 'we never took on anyone with the least physical defect, even if it was just a filled tooth. We were able to bring together in the SS the most superb elements of our race.'

The Waffen-SS cadres, recruited with the greatest care, were trained in special officer-schools—*Junkerschulen*—in Brunswick and Bad Tölz. Instruction was ideological, physical, and military. The future officers had to be convinced of the value of the Nazi racial theories. Did not they make up the ethnic élite of the Third Reich, destined to dominate a Europe no longer encumbered with the racial problem and to integrate within its frontiers all the peoples of Germanic origin? They had to show themselves hard, pitiless, scorning their own lives and those of others. It was not in good taste to declare oneself an atheist, Protestant, or Catholic; the future officers were advised to be theistic. The whole liberal and Christian heritage of Western civilization was ruthlessly rejected. The training of the future Waffen-SS leaders adhered to the very roots of National Socialist doctrine: the cult of will, the attachment to 'blood and soil', the scorn of so-called 'inferior' peoples.

A very important place was given to sport as a means of toughening the body and mind of the volunteers. Finally, there was intensive military training: tank and infantry exercises of the greatest possible realism. There was one particularly demanding test: to prove his self-control, the future officer had to prime a grenade, balance it on his helmet, and stand to attention until it exploded.

At the end of their ruthless training, the young Waffen-SS members had to take an oath of absolute obedience to Hitler: 'I swear to you, Adolf Hitler, as Führer and Reich Chancellor, loyalty and bravery. I vow to you, and to those you have named to command me, obedience unto death, so help me God.'

By 1942 the Waffen-SS had won a reputation for 'cold daring . . . , spirit in action . . . , unshakeable fortitude in tough moments . . . , comradeship,' and even for 'modesty', in the words of General von Mackensen.

But in 1942 the Waffen-SS was on the brink of profound changes. After Stalingrad, it underwent development in two directions. Its total forces doubled annually, reaching 300,000 at the end of 1943 and almost 600,000 in 1944-45. At the same time, foreign members were taken on until they made up more than half the total strength. These sudden changes followed from Hitler's realization that German forces would have to be reconstituted to undertake a longer war. The

Waffen-SS was now to become a powerful army, able to mount the most vigorous possible counterattack.

Revolution in recruitment

The enormous jump in membership naturally led to a revolution in its recruiting programme, which had scarcely been able to fulfil Himmler's demands. From the end of 1942, Himmler was authorized to draw on the Wehrmacht intake, despite its protests. Thenceforth, the majority of the SS recruits were members of the Hitler Youth and of the *Volksdeutsche*—foreign nationals of German race. This influx of new blood undoubtedly lowered

the ideological level of the intake. There was no longer the time to devote to political indoctrination, but on the whole, the new Waffen-SS, at least the German formations, preserved their National Socialist 'purity', their intransigence, their scorn of life, and their effectiveness.

The Waffen-SS were military shock troops, but time and again they showed their importance as a political force. As the custodians of the regime, they had to prevent any attempt at internal subversion or at a putsch by generals sceptical of the outcome of the war. The Waffen-SS were also responsible for maintaining the dependence of Germany's allies on the

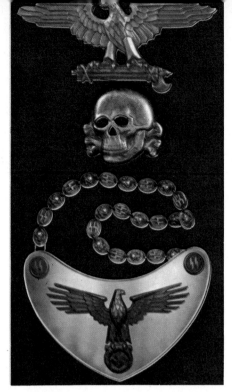

Initially a German élite force, the SS was transformed to include men of numerous nationalities and races. The need for man-power and a desire to strengthen the Nazi hold over occupied Europe led to large-scale foreign recruitment. In 1943 only fifteen of the thirty-eight large SS units had a German or Volksdeutsch *origin.* **Above left:** *Léon Degrelle, Belgian collaborator, whose volunteer unit was integrated into the Waffen-SS.* **Above right:** *Italian officer's cap badge, death's head badge (common to all SS divisions), standard-bearer's gorget.* **Left:** *Belgian SS division recruiting poster*

Reich. One method of ensuring this was the massive intake of foreign volunteers. In 1943, of thirty-eight large SS units, some fifteen only had a German or *Volksdeutsch* origin. All the other units were composed of foreigners from Eastern or Western Europe. In 1944, the Waffen-SS presented the most extraordinary ethnic mixture that one could imagine: there were 'Westerners' – Scandinavians, Dutch, Walloons, Flemings, and French, together with 'Easterners' – Balts, Ukrainians, Bosnians, Croats, Serbs, Albanians, Hungarians, Rumanians, Bulgarians, Russians, not to mention British and Indian legions.

Only military necessity and ulterior political motives could have justified recruitment in such blatant contradiction of the ethnic principles which were the basis of the Waffen-SS. By appealing in particular to Eastern volunteers – a far remove from the pure Nordic ideal – Himmler played on the ethnic and religious antagonism which periodically embroiled Eastern Europe and the Balkans. Thus, to support the Prinz Eugen SS Division in action against Tito's partisans, the Handschar Division was created out of Muslim Bosnians, who nourished a more than secular hatred towards the Serbs. Wearing fezes, receiving special rations, and accompanied by their Imams, the Bosnian battalions received the blessing of the Grand Mufti in

Jerusalem. This gave a considerable twist to Himmler's atheism and he was later to tell Goebbels that 'he had nothing against Islam because this religion assumes the task of instructing men, promising them heaven if they fight with courage and get themselves killed on the battlefield; in short, it is a very practical and attractive religion for a soldier!' The creation of the Handschar Division was followed by other Muslim formations; the Skanderbeg Mountain Division, recruited in Albania, and the Kama Division of Croats.

The call for a Galician SS division met with extraordinary success; some one hundred thousand volunteers came forward, mostly Ukrainians. Two other divisions composed of Russians fought with the Germans or were set against General Vlasov's so-called Liberation Army. During the last months of the war, there appeared many other more or less bizarre formations of Serbs, Hungarians, Rumanians, Bulgarians, even Caucasians and Cossacks. And from 1942 each of the Baltic states undertook to provide one foot-division.

What motives could have prompted such diverse people to join the SS? Traditional hatreds certainly played a part: Muslims against Serbs, Ukrainians and Balts against Russians. Enrolment in the SS also meant for many – especially Russians – an escape from forced labour and the hell of prison camps ravaged by famine and typhus. There was in addition a higher motive among the Balts and Ukrainians: 'The volunteers from the East fought above all for the liberation and independence of their countries,' wrote Felix Steiner, a senior Waffen-SS leader. Most of the volunteers from the East did not join to defend Western civilization, still less to be part of the future of a Greater Germany.

There was no shortage of volunteers in the West either. There, the Waffen-SS recruitment drive had undeniable success, and more than 125,000 young people applied for membership. The Dutch headed the list with 50,000, followed by the Flemings and Walloons with 40,000; the

French provided 20,000; the Danish and Norwegian contingents amounted to 12,000; there were 1,200 Swiss, Swedes, and Luxembourgers. Many were very close to the ethnic ideal of the SS. The avowed motive was to participate in a crusade against Bolshevism. The Waffen-SS might have been a multi-national, European army, the forerunner of a united Europe. This theme was developed copiously by Léon Degrelle, commander of the SS unit Wallonie, in his book *The Russian Campaign:* 'Whatever our views on the way in which the war has been waged, whatever regrets we have for the past, whatever bitterness there has been for our countries in foreign occupation, each of us knows that, above the satisfaction or disagreements experienced between 1939 and 1941 by the European nations, the fate of all Europe was in the balance. It is this which explains the extraordinary mood which has spurred countless young people to action, from Oslo, to Seville, from Antwerp to Budapest. They did not leave their homes . . . just to serve Germany's special interests. They were taking a part in defending 2,000 years of the highest form of civilization.'

A Greater German Reich

The ideal of a Greater German Reich was the guiding light of the *Junkerschulen*. Himmler in 1943 told the officers of the SS armoured divisions: 'The Reich, the German Reich – nay, the German Reich within the German nation – will rightly find confirmation of its destiny in the fact that henceforth we have an outlet to the East . . . Then, centuries hence perhaps, it will be possible to constitute a world-wide German Empire, which will be politically German . . . In this operation all the peoples which were formerly part of Germany, of the German Empire, and which belonged to us from 1606 or even 1648, that is, Flanders, Wallonia, the Low Countries, must be and will be incorporated into the German Reich. Furthermore, we must have the power to bring into our ranks by a second operation all the Germanic peoples and states which have not yet been part of the German Reich: Denmark and Norway, and their populations.'

The Reichsführer-SS envisaged the creation of a Western area called Burgundia, grouping the Netherlands, Belgium, and the north and east of France, which was to be the prototype SS state. In this new satrapy, Himmler intended to put his organizational talent to work. Whatever the appeal of this, there were many other reasons than the struggle against Bolshevism which dictated the entry of the young people into the SS. Many of the young – disorientated and out-of-work – were conscious of the prestige of the Waffen-SS, of a need for adventure, of the

rewards of high office. In some measure, the Waffen-SS perhaps played the same role as the Foreign Legion before the war. The scorn for the Western regimes which had broken down in 1940 impelled a large number of men to don the SS uniform and to adhere to a system which had proved its superiority.

Certainly, political considerations were not far from their minds. Many had decided to back totalitarian style regimes in their own countries, subservient to Germany. Léon Degrelle admitted in 1943, when his volunteer unit was integrated into the Waffen-SS: 'An identical will united us all: to represent with brilliance our people among the twenty nations who had come running to the battle; to fulfil, without subservience, our duty as Europeans fighting against Europe's mortal enemy; to obtain for our country a choice place in the continental community which would result from the war . . .' This ideal of a European union was common among foreign members of the Waffen-SS. It envisaged a union of free and independent states with a common army, held together by the desire to ensure the survival of Western civilization and of a 'common country, Europe', as Degrelle called it.

But there was no question of a Europe of 'free states' nor of a European army. Himmler made this quite clear: 'From the start I told the volunteers: you can do what you want, but be certain of this: the SS will be organized in your country and there is in all Europe just one SS—the Germanic SS under the command of the Reichsführer-SS. You can resist, but that is a matter of indifference to me, for we will create it in any case . . . We do not ask you to turn against your country nor to do anything repugnant to anyone proud of his country, who loves it, and has his self-respect. Neither do we ask you to become Germans out of opportunism. But what we do expect of you is that you subordinate your national ideal to a superior racial and historical ideal, that of the German Reich.' In short, in the minds of the Nazi leaders, the foreign Waffen-SS in occupied and satellite countries was to constitute a catalyst for the German cause.

A way of life

How did this 300,000-strong mass of foreigners perform? On the whole, the Eastern volunteers were mediocre. Those from the Balkans, the Russians, even the Ukrainians were disappointments. Among the Balts, only the Letts displayed fortitude under fire. The Indians had a talent for making Hitler angry; he had never been favourable to the unlimited extension of the foreign Waffen-SS. 'The Indian Legion is a joke!' he once said. 'There are Indians who can't kill a louse, who would rather

let themselves be eaten up. They won't kill an Englishman either. I consider it nonsense to put them opposite the English . . .'

The behaviour of the Western volunteers was on the whole better; they fought to the end with more desperation than many Germans. The Wallonie Division showed exceptional courage: of 6,000 volunteers, 2,500 died in the east. It was the same with the Viking Division, in which Germans, Dutch, and Scandinavians fought side by side. The French volunteers, first placed in the Wehrmacht, then, in 1944, in the Charlemagne SS Division with 2,000 militiamen and other Frenchmen of diverse origin, fought with gallantry near Moscow, in White Russia against the partisans, in Minsk and on the Vistula in 1944. The survivors took part in the last defence of the Reich Chancellery during the battle of Berlin.

Although SS units were under the tactical command of the Wehrmacht, they preserved administrative and legal independence and there was certainly no question of them applying the Wehrmacht code of honour. Their reputation for callousness and savagery could scarcely be surpassed. From May 1940, during the French campaign, a detachment of the Totenkopf unit distinguished itself by the summary execution at Paradis-Finistère of 100 British soldiers who had put up a particularly tough resistance. During the battle of Normandy, the Hitler Jugend units time and again slaughtered groups of Canadian or British prisoners in cold blood. Finally, during the Ardennes offensive, the Peiper group of the Leibstandarte unit machine-gunned seventy-one American prisoners. If the SS took great liberties in the West with normally accepted conventions, on the Eastern Front their excesses were far more numerous, though many of the atrocities imputed to them were committed by the regular army. At Taganrog, as a reprisal for the execution of six German soldiers, the SS killed in the course of three days all the soldiers who had fallen into their hands—more than 4,000 in all. When the SS fought against the partisans, they lost all restraint. During a 'pacification operation' in the Pripet region in 1941 the cavalry brigade Florian Geyer killed 259 Russian soldiers and 6,504 civilians. In northern Italy, in the antipartisan struggle, the Leibstandarte destroyed the town of Voves and massacred its inhabitants. As it crossed the Massif Central to reach Normandy, the Das Reich Division left the hangings of Tulle and the bloody ruins of Oradour in its wake. The operation figures in the division records gives the balance as '548 enemy dead' at the price of 'two wounded'.

In the Balkans, where the war took on an unheard-of savagery, SS units like the

SS: The Empire Within

Prinz Eugen Division won a notorious name for infamy. There too, where all the refinements of cruelty were practised, the German and Italian troops took reprisal for assassinations, sabotage, or the defeat of some of their units with atrocities. Specialized groups of the Waffen-SS undertook the extermination of racial minorities on a massive scale. The Polizei Division, composed mainly of policemen who in peace time were in control of traffic and noise abatement, was used in Russia in 1941 but not in the front line. It was mainly used against the partisans, with exemplary brutality. Most of the atrocities committed in the East by the SS were due to its activities. Transferred to Greece, it again committed heinous crimes, like the massacre of the inhabitants of a village of Klissoura. In certain cases SS units helped the Einsatzgruppen — Special Action units — charged with the mass execution of Jews in the Eastern territories — in their sinister task. Near Minsk, a company of Das Reich helped one of these Special Action units to shoot 920 Jews. The destruction of the Warsaw ghetto was in part the work of SS recruits.

Although Waffen-SS participation in the racial extermination policy was limited and often accidental, and although its members fought bravely on the battlefield as ordinary soldiers, it is impossible to forget their sinister ideology and the horrors they undoubtedly perpetrated. Himmler and his clique always claimed responsibility for these atrocities. The Waffen-SS became symbolic of an attitude, of a way of life, of policies against which the whole of the rest of the free world was fighting.

These 'soldiers like any others' — as Guderian once called the SS — may be exonerated by some, but nothing can ever change the significance of their double flash emblem as a symbol of the worst danger to life and civilization that humanity has ever faced.

Opposite top: SS prisoners taken by British paratroopers, Normandy 1944. Opposite centre: Sauberzweig, commander of the Muslim SS Handschar Division. Political expediency caused Nazi views on race and religion to be relaxed. Himmler, an atheist, even regarded Islam, with its stress on courage, as a 'very practical and attractive religion for a soldier'. Opposite bottom: Sepp Dietrich, brutal commander of Hitler's bodyguard regiment. In 1946, he received twenty-five years for complicity in the murder of American prisoners-of-war. He was released after ten years. Left: Members of Der Führer SS regiment, predominantly Austrian, created after the Nazi invasion of Austria in March 1938

Europe under the swastika
Hitler's hegemony in November 1942

Hitler's dreams of European domination had once been dismissed as the ravings of a madman. In 1942 the dream was almost reality. As the map shows, German domination had spread across the face of Europe from the Atlantic coast to the heartland of Soviet Russia. In the darkened areas, in Greater Germany and the areas occupied by Germany, the New Order reigned supreme. This was a Nazi-ruled Europe whose resources were plundered for the profit of Germany, whose peoples became slaves of the German 'master race', and whose 'undesirable elements'—above all the Jews, but also the Slavs—were in the process of extermination.

Himmler, as head of the SS, held the power of life or death over 80 million Germans and twice as many conquered peoples. It was a power he used ruthlessly and arbitrarily. 'Whether 10,000 Russian females fall down from exhaustion while digging an anti-tank ditch interests me only in so far as the anti-tank ditch for Germany is finished,' he said. In labour camps all over occupied Europe the subject peoples suffered and died in the service of the Reich. At the great Krupp arms works, for example, 600 Jewish women were quartered in a bombed-out work camp. A doctor who visited the camp described how he found 'these females suffering from open festering wounds and other diseases . . . One could not enter the barracks without being attacked by fleas . . . I got large boils on my arms and the rest of my body from them.' Forced labour was the fate of millions, but millions more were tortured in concentration camps or simply killed. Between five and six million Jews alone were massacred during the

Below: The map shows how Europe's national boundaries, as of September 1938, were overrun by Nazi Germany

war. Naturally opposition to such policies was to be expected but there were ways to deal with this. Hitler suggested that the police should be equipped with armoured cars, but Göring assured him that aircraft could 'drop bombs in case of riots'. Everywhere the rule of fear replaced the rule of law.

⬤ Greater Germany
Certain territories of particular interest to Germany were directly incorporated into the Reich. In defiance of the Treaty of Versailles Germany burst her boundaries and became Greater Germany. Austria was the first victim, in the Anschluss of March 1938. A year later it was the turn of the Czechs. Their homeland was given a special status: called the Protectorate of Bohemia-Moravia it was placed under 'Hangman' Heydrich, the ruthless head of the SD (SS security service). It is shown here with pre-Munich frontiers. In the case of Poland, Germany annexed her former provinces and some additional territory including the free city of Danzig. In the West, the Belgian provinces of Eupen, Malmédy, and Moresnet, between the toe of Holland and the tip of Luxembourg, Luxembourg itself, and the French provinces of Alsace and Lorraine were all incorporated, as also were three northern provinces of Yugoslavia.

⬤ Occupied by Germany
Western Europe succumbed to Nazi occupation in just over two months. From the summer of 1940 Great Britain stood alone off the coast of a hostile continent. Its subject countries were governed in various ways: some were controlled by a civilian Reich commissioner, minister, or governor-general, such as Denmark. In Norway the puppet government of the collaborator

Quisling held power for a time, and Marshal Pétain's regime remained at Vichy until all France was occupied in November 1942 (as shown here). Belgium was placed directly under the control of a military commandant. In Eastern Europe, occupied Poland, under the General Government headed by the cold-blooded killer Dr Hans Frank, was nothing more than a reserve of unskilled labour for Germany. In the Balkans Yugoslavia was technically partitioned between Germany, Italy, Bulgaria, Hungary, and Albania, although in fact German hegemony was supreme. Greece was also jointly occupied. It was in the East that the savagery of German occupation was greatest. 20 million Russians lost their lives in the war, a great many of them civilians and prisoners of war.

⬤ Allied to Germany
The Tripartite Pact between Germany, Italy, and Japan was signed on 27th September 1940. Other countries which joined the Axis did so by adhering to the pact. Hungary, Rumania, and Slovakia signed in November 1940. Bulgaria followed in March 1941. By April when the invasion of Yugoslavia was complete, South-East Europe was firmly under Hitler's control for, although Hungary remained relatively free under Regent Horthy and Bulgaria was free to the extent that she did not declare war on Russia, these were satellite states mesmerized by Germany's power. (Finland had no formal alliance with Germany but was a co-belligerent. Albania and Corsica were occupied by Italy. The boundaries shown here are the pre-war ones. There were small boundary changes between wartime Hungary, Rumania, and Bulgaria.)

The only neutral countries remaining in Europe were Switzerland, Sweden, Spain, Portugal, Turkey, and Eire.

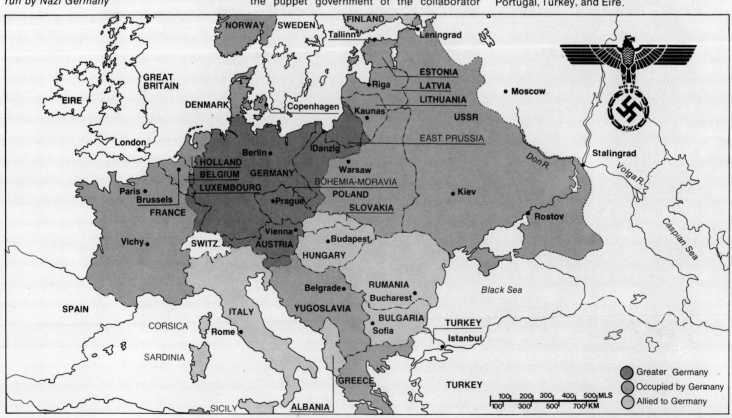

Greater Germany
Occupied by Germany
Allied to Germany

The Nazis at War

When Hitler ordered the attack on Poland on 1st September 1939, he thought he had only a localized campaign before him, yet he consciously risked its extension into world war. War for Hitler and the Nazi regime was not only a means to an end; with it was bound up the whole philosophy of Nazism. The Nazi dogma of the 'iron law' of struggle between races was nothing more than the naked spirit of warfare. And the preparation for the battle for 'Lebensraum' had defined all Nazi policy in Germany since 1933.

The First World War had shown what levels such a national fighting spirit was capable of reaching. Hitler consciously seized on this model. The desire to raise Germany from the 'disgrace' of 1918, the conviction that only treachery, stupidity and weakness had caused defeat in the First World War, and the fanatical determination to resume once again—and this time more resolutely—the fight for Germany's greatness and her place in the world: all this was part of the special gospel of National Socialism. The Second World War was the decisive act of Hitler's regime. The total strength and the true nature of Nazism only came out fully in war, but so did its great weakness—its fanatical egocentricity, which was eventually to bring about its destruction.

Hitler's enormous military successes in the first years of the war—the eighteen-day war against Poland, the daring naval and air action to occupy Norway, and, above all, the swift victory over France which inspired Mussolini to come into the war on Hitler's side—spread Germany's hegemony over almost the whole continent and created a readiness practically everywhere for the creation of a 'new Fascist order in Europe'.

The sensational triumphs in the military field and in foreign policy also strengthened the Nazi position in internal affairs and lent conviction to the belief that Hitler was not a dangerous gambler but a divinely endowed genius. Now National Socialist propaganda in Germany itself, conducted by its talented leader Joseph Goebbels, could pull out all the stops in the creation of national euphoria. This included special radio broadcasts linked by resounding military marches, newsreels glorifying German successes put out by the army's propaganda unit, the composition and broadcasting of more and more new battle songs, the award of higher and higher decorations for bravery, and the popularization of individual war-heroes. Hitler himself contributed to the creation of this

mood with fifteen big speeches in the first two years of the war and so successful was Nazi 'education' that apparently only a minority in Germany preserved enough critical capacity to see the mania which spoke through Hitler's uncontrolled attacks.

It was true, however, that there was in the German population, as the confidential security service reports for 1940-41 show, an enduring and lively fear that Germany would, by over-extending her forces, run the risk of 'conquering herself to death'. But the full extent of Hitler's miscalculations, already visible in 1940, remained largely hidden. Thus only a few realized the importance of the RAF's success in the Battle of Britain and that Great Britain had by this time received the first reliable indication of active military support from the United States in the form of fifty destroyers.

But it was not only propaganda which served to conceal the seriousness of the situation. Food rationing, instituted in August 1939, guaranteed the nation a sufficient amount to eat in the first years of the war. Trusting in Hitler's Blitzkrieg strategy and the economic preparations for war which had been going forward since 1934, the Nazi regime thought that even in 1942 no radical switch in the economy to arms production was necessary and that it would be possible to preserve a relatively high standard of living for the civilian population. Nor did the military situation cause immediate alarm. The number of Germans killed in action up to the end of 1941 remained relatively low (about 200,000) and the RAF's night attacks, which had increased during 1940-41, did not at first cause great damage.

Military developments and Nazi propaganda also largely hid the changes in the state's power structure which were to have serious consequences in the future.

Although the army was potentially an important power-factor it had for some time shown itself to have feet of clay. The clearest signs of this were the forced resignations of Fritsch, the Commander-in-Chief of the Army, and General Beck, the Chief of the General Staff, and Hitler's

LA BELLE SIBERIE VOUS APPELLE!

Premier départ 3 semaines après la libération

Mobilizing mass support for Nazism.
Above: One of a series of slides shown to women in the Nazi Labour Service, stressing the joys of working for Germany.
Right: 'Come to lovely Siberia': Nazi poster issued in Belgium equates Allied 'liberation' with terrors of Bolshevism—deportation and death

setting up in February 1938 of the High Command of the Armed Forces (Oberkommando der Wehrmacht, OKW) which was directly answerable to him under the command of General Keitel. These developments showed that after the consolidation of Nazi power Hitler was not prepared to allow the armed forces any significant influence in making political decisions. After the outbreak of war he pursued the suppression of the forces' political influence even more rigorously (for instance, by strangling the truth about the sinking of the *Athenia*). From the first day of the war, it was not the military commanders but the highest-ranking Gauleiters who were appointed Reich defence commissioners and entrusted with making the top decisions in all cases of civil emergency.

The army leaders took another fall — not without protests from individual generals — when in the autumn of 1939 commanding officers in occupied Poland tolerated the first systematic mass shooting of Poles and Jews by Special Action Units of the SS which claimed that they were acting under special secret orders from above.

The appointment of the Waffen-SS, under Himmler's supreme command, in the winter of 1939-40 also ended the army's monopoly as the only element allowed to bear arms, the monopoly which had been defended so successfully against the SA in 1934. The Waffen-SS, a direct rival to the army, amounted to only one division at the beginning of 1940, but towards the end of the war its numerous volunteer units comprised some 600,000 men.

As he had done on many different occasions since 1937 when he presented his expansionist aims, Hitler reproached the army leadership for being far too cautious and hesitant in applying his plan for the campaign in the West. This plan, which foresaw the violation of Dutch and Belgian neutrality, led to further deterioration in his relations with top officers on the Army General Staff (for example with Halder, Chief of the General Staff, and Canaris, head of the Abwehr, the OKW counter-intelligence department). The first cells of military opposition formed.

The success of the campaign in the West, however, once again justified Hitler's judgement and increased his prestige to the detriment of that of the army leadership. In December 1941, after the first failures in Russia, Field-Marshal Brauchitsch resigned as Commander-in-Chief of the Army and Hitler took over this position himself.

As in Poland, moreover, Hitler took care to force the commanding army generals out of the administration of those occupied territories in which the Nazi regime was especially interested as soon as they had been overrun. Everywhere civilian rulers were installed. They were always high Party functionaries, usually Gauleiters, and all directly responsible to Hitler. There arose autocratically ruled satrapies in which control was wielded by Party favourites, the officials responsible for the carrying out of Göring's Four-Year Plan, and the security police and other SS organs under Himmler. It was this type of administrative irregularity that provided the basis for mass shooting, mass deportation, concentration camps, and ghettos, and finally, from 1941, the extermination camps — the means of achieving the 'final solution to the Jewish problem'.

Revolutionizing the law

The shift of power in the occupied territories into the hands of Party officials and the security police had its effect on the constitution of the Nazi regime itself. A variety of measures, caused directly by the war, but which were principally ideological and political, altered the division of power between the Nazi leaders to the advantage of the extremists.

This was particularly true of the law. Demands by Hitler and other Party leaders for stiff war-time penal laws led in the autumn of 1939 to the passing of a mass of new laws covering, for example, listening in to enemy radio broadcasts, economic sabotage of the war effort, 'disrupting the armed forces', and 'crimes of violence'. Crimes which carried the death sentence rose to forty-six by 1944. Statistics on death sentences passed by the civil courts rose from 43 in 1938, to 2,015 from January to August 1944. Hitler was however not content with the draconian increase in the severity of legal sentences. In the autumn of 1939 he had already authorized Himmler to use the security police for immediate execution without a court death sentence in cases of anti-national acts and sabotage which seemed particularly serious. The

The Nazis and German Youth.

Left: *A poster of the 1930's expressing the National Socialist ideal of the young Nazi. The rival youth organizations of the pre-Hitler years, the red-scarved communists and the socialists in berets flee with their decadent mentors from the vision of Aryan heroism. Goebbel's propaganda reached to the cradle.* **Right:** *A Hitler Youth at a hero commemoration ceremony. The Nazi grip on the young was total, from the Adolf Hitler Schools through the ranks of the Hitler Youth, training was for total obedience. Drafted into the Civil Defence early in the war, by 1945 twelve-year-olds went into the front line to face the advancing Russian tanks*

The New Order

executions were mostly carried out in concentration camps. The SS and security police officials who undertook these killings received formal protection from inquiries by the state prosecutors by the introduction of special SS and police tribunals in October 1939. The total number of concentration camp prisoners in Germany between 1934 and 1938, when the Nazi regime was relatively moderate, was around 7,000 to 10,000, but after the beginning of the war the imprisonment of those from occupied countries suspected of opposition and the erection of new camps pushed the figure up to some 100,000 by 1942. But the highest numbers are to be found in the last war years (1944-45) when, under the forced labour scheme for armaments production, some half a million prisoners of all nationalities were crammed together in twenty main camps and 165 subsidiary camps.

From the start of the war, Hitler sought to link his fight against external enemies with the eradication of internal enemies and 'inferior' national elements. His aim was made quite explicit by his secret order of September 1939 to kill all the mentally ill. Under the euthanasia programme, for which a secretly selected commission of doctors was responsible, about 70,000 mentally ill were killed in hospitals in Bernburg, Hadamar, Hartheim, and elsewhere, until, in 1941, Hitler felt himself obliged to call a halt in response to various protests, especially from clergy.

Calculation and hate

The more extreme nature of the Nazi regime in 1941-42 was directly connected with the critical military situation. The combination of rational calculation and pathological hate, which increasingly dominated Hitler's decisions the more he was dominated by the idea of his role in history, was especially apparent in his decision to attack Russia.

This decision had no necessity other than as an escape from the military dead-end Hitler had reached in the West over Great Britain. It was also, however, an attempt to wage his own war, the war he had planned two decades before with the intention of conquering the Lebensraum of the East and destroying 'Jewish Bolshevism'.

His decision linked many elements: an obstinate determination to keep the initiative, if not against Great Britain, then against the last potentially dominant power on the continent, an impatient, half-blind impulse to take action (always a characteristic of Hitler and the Nazi movement as a whole), bitterness and anger that the Blitzkrieg strategy had not brought victory, increasing hate of the world-wide enemy, Jewry, on which he blamed his own

miscalculations, and an increasingly fanatical desire for destruction.

Thus, significantly, it was in connection with the preparations for the Russian campaign that Hitler issued the brutal secret orders which were later to acquire such terrible infamy in the Nazi war crimes trials: the order for the 'final solution of the Jewish problem', the order that captured Soviet commissars should be shot (an order which the Wehrmacht did not oppose), and the 'Night and Fog' decree of September 1941, which as a deterrent against sabotage in the Western occupied territories laid down that those suspected of opposition should be seized by police and whisked away to German prisons without any information being given to their families as to their fate.

At the same time, the German police introduced a mass of oppressive new measures against the churches, mostly the Catholic Church, with tighter bans on church demonstrations and the seizure of some 100 monasteries.

Failure and forced labour

The battle for Moscow during the winter of 1941-42 and the long drawn-out attacks of 1942 revealed what the battle of Stalingrad (October 1942 to February 1943) then confirmed: that victory in the East was no longer within reach. In the West, too, the initiative passed to the other side after the United States entered the war (December 1941). From 1942, 'area bombing' by the British and American air forces, which from 1943 possessed undisputed mastery of the air over Germany, had a disastrous effect on Germany's war economy and on the German population. Bombs killed some 400,000 civilians, and destroyed countless towns and industrial plants. The Anglo-American landing in Morocco and Algeria in November 1942 forced the capitulation of the Afrika Korps in May 1943. The Allied invasion of southern Italy in July 1943 also led to a German retreat. Mussolini's subsequent fall and the withdrawal of Italy from the Axis in August 1943 – which also brought into question the reliability of Germany's smaller allies (Hungary and Rumania) – threw the Nazi regime into its most severe political crisis to date.

This string of failures accelerated the growing extremism of Nazi policy inside Germany and caused further lasting changes in the Party's power structure in accordance with the 'total warfare' which had now been instituted. Symptomatic of this were the innovations in armaments production and labour allocation in March 1942. Particularly successful was the appointment of Albert Speer as Reich minister for armaments and production; the energetic and talented direction of

German cartoon of 1940 accuses Churchill of sinking the Athenia *to arouse anti-German feeling. The British liner was sunk a few hours after war started by a German U-boat, drowning 112 people, twenty-eight of them Americans. Mindful of how the sinking of the* Lusitania *helped bring America into the First World War, Hitler ordered a denial that a U-boat was involved and in October the official Nazi newspaper proclaimed: 'Churchill sank the* Athenia'. *The naval leaders who knew the truth were ordered to keep silent. Hitler had taken a further step towards total control of Germany and her people*

the former architect put Germany's armaments economy into high gear, and made possible a three-fold increase in arms production in 1943-44 compared with 1941, despite the Allied bombing raids. This brilliant technical and organizational feat was, however, closely bound up with the simultaneous massive extension of forced labour, for which responsibility was borne by Gauleiter Fritz Sauckel, named plenipotentiary general for the allocation of labour in March 1942, and – in the control of concentration camps – by Himmler. Millions of Russians – referred to derogatorily as *Ostarbeiter* (Eastern workers) – and Poles were forcibly brought to work in the Reich (as were French, Belgians, Dutch, Serbs, Czechs, Italians, and others). The building of the underground V-weapon production plant in the Harz mountains (transferred from Peenemünde after the RAF attack in 1943) was largely the work of 30,000 concentration camp prisoners. At least a quarter of them died of exhaustion before the end of the war.

Instruments of the police state

The fact that the regime had become more markedly a police state was also shown by the appointment of the former president of the Nazi People's Court, Otto Georg Thierack, as minister of justice in August 1942. Until then the department had been under the control of Franz Gürtner, of the German National People's Party (DNVP), and after his death in January 1941, of his state secretary, Schlegelberger. Both had repeatedly intervened to uphold fundamental legal principles and at least partly preserve the competence of the law, even if they were unable to prevent the law adapting in some form to Hitler's political and ideological standards. Thierack sought from the first a close understanding with Himmler and undertook on his behalf the sell-out of the legal system, for instance by his readiness to transfer some 10,000 state prisoners into SS concentration camps and to allow the prosecution of certain groups (Jews, Poles, Eastern workers) to be pursued wholly by the security police. His successor as president of the People's Court was Roland Freisler, who took office in the summer of 1942. Under his direction, this tribunal became an exemplary dispenser of Party justice after the manner of Stalin's show trials, most notably in the sentencing of the July Plot conspirators in 1944. In fact Freisler had become a fanatical Bolshevik as a prisoner of war in Russia in the First World War; he turned Nazi in 1924 but remained a warm admirer of Soviet terror. 'Freisler is our Vishinsky' (who was prosecutor during the Purge) exclaimed Hitler in one of the first conferences after Stauffenberg's attempt on his life.

An exotic Eastern court

Apart from Speer, who after 1942 replaced Göring as the leading power in economic policy (the Reichsmarschall's credit largely ran out with Hitler after the failure of the Luftwaffe), it was Goebbels, Himmler, and Bormann who held the most power and were the decisive influences from 1942-43. As Speer, the ablest and least corrupted member of Hitler's entourage, said: 'Relations between the various high leaders can only be understood if their aspirations are interpreted as a struggle for the succession to Adolf Hitler'. Hitler's last years reveal the steadily quickening breakdown of the machinery of government until his cabinet resembled an exotic Eastern court, with each vying with the other for the ruler's favours.

From 1942 onwards, Hitler tended to avoid public speeches and gatherings and seldom left his headquarters in East Prussia; the responsibility for the whole field of propaganda in the second half of the war thus fell increasingly on Goebbels. In contrast to the other Nazi officials, the propaganda minister, with an instinctive feeling for his job, saw that the turn of events after the first euphoric phase of the war demanded a completely new approach to propaganda. He knew that in the case of dire necessity, appeal to the suppressed readiness for self-sacrifice and participation, and to defiant national solidarity could be even more effective than delirious rapture. Thus Goebbels, in the famous demonstration in the Berlin Sportpalast on 18th February 1943, shortly after the Battle of Stalingrad was able even so to carry his listeners away into a fanatical affirmation of his own total commitment to sacrifice, an affirmation which later seemed merely to be an expression of mass hysteria.

In fact the attitude of a large part of the German population at this stage would be hard to understand without a knowledge of the psychological state of mind so successfully controlled by Goebbels. Certainly there was now growing doubt and criticism, and the war had brought considerable hardship – two million German soldiers dead by 1945. But recognition of the one who was truly responsible became more difficult the longer Hitler was relied upon and applauded. People managed to convince themselves that it was a precept of loyalty to hold out in the face of difficulties; they no longer really believed in 'final victory', but no-one dared think of defeat since in the present situation this would mean Russian victory and domination. This psychological mixture of panic, loyalty, self-pity, and self-deception also created a moral blindness to the spreading oppressiveness of the regime and the sufferings of the persecuted Jews, with whom contact had long been lost by discrimination and imprisonment in ghettos, even before the secret, but not unnoticed, deportations in 1941-42. It was the greatest failure that at this time those guardians of the nation who still held their posts – clergy, university professors, high-ranking officers – remained almost completely silent.

Goebbels' indispensability as propagandist of the total war effort greatly extended his influence in the last years. He remained true to the myth which he had served faithfully for so many years. At the end he had no thought of escape. He planned his death to mirror Hitler's. The high standing Goebbels won with the Führer was shown when Hitler appointed him future chancellor of the now non-existent Reich in his political testament dated 29th April 1945.

Himmler, too, had continually acquired new powers and responsibilities since the beginning of the war. Since 1936 joint SS-chief and head of the police, he was appointed Reich commissioner for the consolidation of German nationhood on 7th October 1939 and was given responsibility for the direction of the whole policy of deportation and Germanization of the East. Himmler's influence and that of individual SS departments spread increasingly to foreign policy through Himmler's control of relations with Germans living abroad, the enrolment of Germanic volunteers for the SS, and above all through his contacts with the security police and the intelligence services of allied and neutral countries. In addition, Himmler assumed control of the Reich Interior Ministry in 1943, and of the Reserve Army at home after the July Plot. Göring, Ribbentrop, Frick, and other formerly very influential ministers were unequivocally outmanoeuvred by Himmler from 1941 onwards.

Byzantine absolutism

Himmler's only competitor in the last years of the war was Martin Bormann, who was largely unknown even in 1939 but assumed the direction of the Party Chancery in May 1941 when Hitler's deputy Rudolph Hess flew to Great Britain on his peace bid. But what was more decisive for Bormann's rise was his position of confidence as Hitler's permanent attendant and secretary. He became the vital intermediary between Hitler and the outside world. He matched his master's eccentric hours and became the sole channel for his orders.

The more Hitler absented himself from Berlin, the more absolute his rule became. And, as it was impossible for his ministers to penetrate his headquarters for months on end, the more important became Bormann's position as king of the lobby, as executor and interpreter of Hitler's orders.

This Byzantine consequence of Hitler's absolutism was characteristic of the last phase of Hitler's rule; it meant that even Hitler's adjutants and the permanent representatives of the ministers in Hitler's headquarters became decisive figures. The almost permanent power struggle between personalities and groups for Hitler's favour and the increasing chaos in the definition of responsibilities – all this led to a process of growing self-destruction in the regime, which was only held together by more orders from the Führer. In the end, everyone who had the power to do so was playing the petty Führer to the full extent of his influence. With Hitler's suicide, dissolution was complete. Colossal energies had been unleashed, colossal crimes begun, colossal destruction risked – and nothing remained.

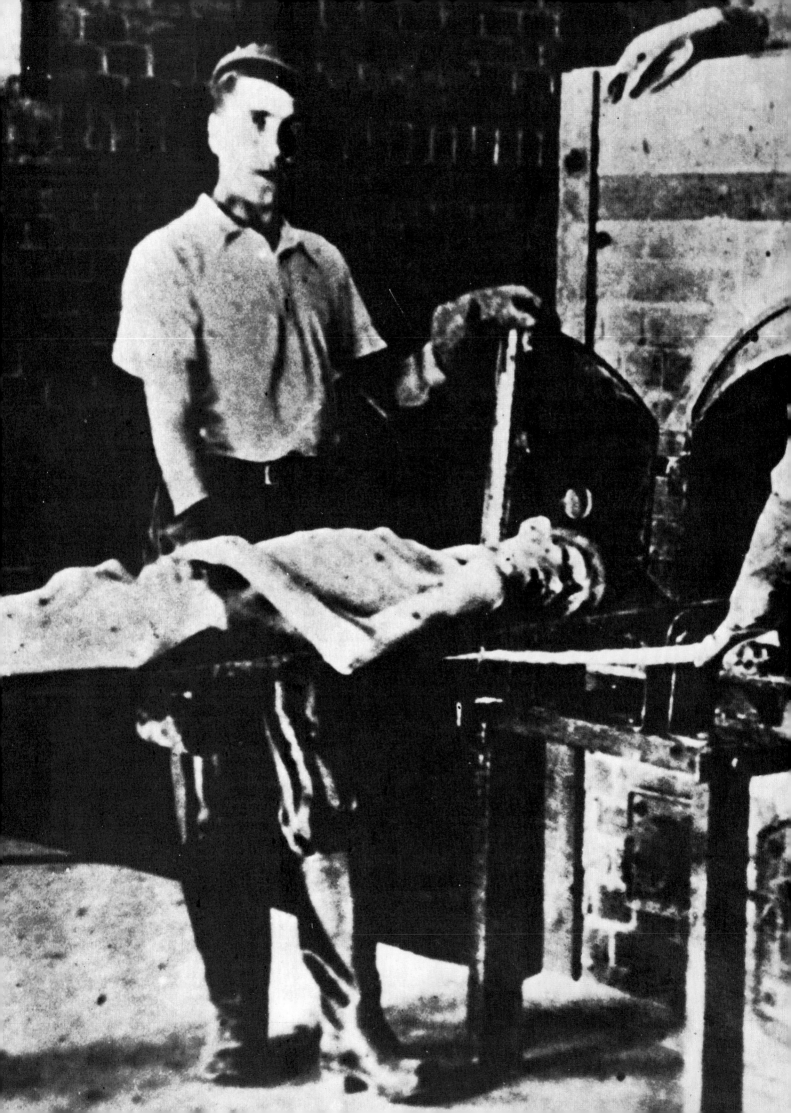

The Final Solution

Before the beginning of the war in Europe, the measures taken by Hitler against the Jews seemed essentially to be aimed at excluding them from all functions within German society. The result of this progressive isolation was that the majority of Jews decided to leave first Germany itself, and then post-Anschluss Austria, and the Protectorate of Bohemia-Moravia. But after the conquest of Poland more than three million Jews found themselves under German control and their number exceeded seven million after the extension of the Nazi hegemony of Western Europe, the Balkans, the Baltic countries, White Russia, and the Ukraine. Until October 1941 Jews were theoretically allowed to emigrate, but in fact only a few thousand privileged ones managed to escape those regions controlled by the forces of the Reich.

Three weeks after the German invasion of Poland, on 21st September 1939, the head of the Central Security Office of the Reich, Reinhard Heydrich, issued an order to keep the Polish Jews closely grouped together 'as a means to the final aim' *(als erste Voraussetzung für das Endziel)*. This enigmatic phrase did not prove that the Nazi leaders were already envisaging the physical extermination of the Jews. On 23rd November 1939, the Polish Jews received the order to wear a distinctive sign — the yellow star. In April 1940, the Jews at Lódź were confined in a ghetto and in October of the same year it was the turn of the Jews at Warsaw to suffer the same fate. Soon, nearly all Polish Jews were imprisoned in ghettos containing populations ranging from several thousand to half a million in the Warsaw ghetto. The ghettos were separated from 'Aryan' quarters by high walls or barbed wire, guarded by both local and German police.

In the ghettos the administration of community affairs was allotted to 'Jewish councils', the *Judenräte,* whose authority was often considerable, backed up by an auxiliary Jewish police force. The role of the *Judenräte* has often been criticized, but the majority did what they could to alleviate the sufferings of the inhabitants of the ghettos. Nevertheless, from the winter of 1940-41, famine, cold, and epidemics caused tens of thousands of deaths.

After the beginning of the war, the fate of the Polish Jews was harshest, but that of the Jews who remained in the Reich was scarcely better. They were systematically submitted to the most humiliating and

Auschwitz camp oven for disposal of bodies. The Nazis saw the 'final solution' as an industrial problem, to be solved by industrial means

sadistic rules: they were forbidden to use public transport, to sit on park benches, to use public telephones, to own domestic animals, furs, or woollen clothes, typewriters, bicycles, spectacles, or electrical appliances. Converted Jews no longer had the right to attend religious services at the same time as 'Aryan' Christians. In the meantime, in the offices of the Wilhelmstrasse they were considering the possibility of deporting all European Jews to the island of Madagascar, which would become a sort of Jewish 'reserve' under the control of the German police. In fact the Madagascar plan came to nothing.

The fate of Jews in the Nazi-occupied countries of Western Europe differed vastly from one to another. In Denmark and Norway they were treated no differently from the rest of the community, but in Vichy France anti-Semitic laws were passed in 1941. Before long, thousands of foreign Jews were interned in special camps in both zones. In Holland, also, the plight of the Jews deteriorated rapidly: thus at the beginning of 1941 several hundred Jewish hostages were deported to the camp of Mauthausen where they were tortured to death: of the 618 who arrived in the spring of 1941, only eight survived to the beginning of 1942.

But a dramatic change in the Jewish situation took place with the preparations for the German attack on the Soviet Union.

When Adolf Hitler took the final decision to attack the Soviet Union, the conflict, within the sphere of political and strategic machinations, undoubtedly appeared to him as an apocalyptic struggle between the forces of good led by National-Socialist Germany and the forces of evil of which 'Jewish Bolshevism' was the supreme manifestation. It was then that Hitler decided to carry out what he had prophesied in a speech to the Reichstag on 30th January 1939: that a new world war would mark the extermination of the Jewish race in Europe....

It is not known exactly when Hitler gave the official order to exterminate all Jews under Nazi control, but he certainly gave this order orally to Göring and Himmler in March or April 1941. The commanders of the Special Action Units *(Einsatzgruppen),* who were made responsible for the liquidation of the Jews in occupied Russia, stated after the war that they had been informed of their mission by word of mouth in May 1941. On 31st July 1941, Göring gave Heydrich a written order charging him to take any steps necessary towards a 'general solution to the Jewish problem in the areas of German influence in Europe'. On 20th January 1942, Heyd-

rich put forward his plan at the so-called Wannsee Conference which brought together the leading functionaries of the principal German ministries: 'The final solution *(Endlösung)* to the Jewish problem in Europe', he declared, 'will be applied to about eleven million people . . . The Jews must be transferred to the East under close surveillance and there assigned to forced labour . . . It goes without saying that a great many of them will be naturally eliminated by physical deficiency. The remainder who survive this — and who must be regarded as the most resistant group — must be dealt with accordingly. Indeed, history has shown us that this natural élite carries within itself the seeds of a new Jewish renaissance . . .'

Mass-execution of the Jews began in Russia with the beginnings of the German occupation. The Special Action Units, mostly supported by the local militia and often aided by Wehrmacht units, sometimes organized temporary ghettos where the inmates were not liquidated until several months later. But their most frequent method was immediate mass-execution. During the first five months of the Russian campaign the Special Action Units massacred more than 100,000 Jews a month. Machine-gun executions were supplemented with executions by means of the carbon monoxide fumes of lorries. In all, nearly 1,400,000 Jews were executed in Russia by 3,000 members of the Special Action Units.

The deportation of German Jews to the ghettos and camps in the East began at the end of 1941. In the course of 1942 the Nazis systematically deported Jews from the various occupied and controlled countries in Western Europe. Depending on the country and the attitude of local authorities, the German action met with varying degrees of success. In Poland itself, where, in spite of famine and disease, more than two and a half million Jews were still living early in 1942, nothing could be done to halt the massacre.

The extermination of the Jews in Wartheland (that part of Poland which was annexed to the Reich) began in March 1942 at the Chełmno camp. There the gas chamber was most frequently used. Soon after it was the turn of the Jews from Lublin and Lwów who were taken to the Bełżec camp, where carbon monoxide was the usual method. Systematic liquidation

Top: Himmler (left) is shown Mauthausen concentration camp. When he watched the extermination of Jews at Auschwitz it made him feel physically sick. **Centre:** *Gestapo search for weapons during Warsaw ghetto raid.* **Bottom:** *Inspection of Warsaw Ordnungsdienst, those Jews responsible to the Germans for maintaining order in the ghetto*

in the Warsaw ghetto began in July: hundreds of thousands of Jews from the ghetto in the capital were transferred in groups to the Treblinka camp. 'Operation Reinhard', so-called after Reinhard Heydrich, killed in June 1942 by Czech agents, swiftly engulfed the whole of Poland. Soon the immense installations of the Auschwitz-Birkenau camp (in German-controlled Upper Silesia) became the main execution site. Inspired by the 'experience' gained in 1940 and 1941 when euthanasia had been practised on the mentally ill, new methods of extermination were perfected, and from then on prussic acid (Zyklon B) replaced carbon monoxide from diesel engines. Extermination by means of Zyklon B took place in large gas chambers, each capable of holding up to 2,000 people, disguised as showers or disinfectant rooms. Those deportees who were not directly selected for the gas chambers soon died as a result of the forced labour to which they were submitted for the vast enterprises run by the SS within the camps or set up in close proximity by German industry (notably I.G.Farben). Others died by 'medical experiments' which included exposure to high-pressure, freezing, and vaccination with infectious diseases. The organization of deportation, forced labour, and immediate extermination of millions of people required the setting-up of a vast bureaucratic machine. This was primarily inspired by Hitler himself, but the actual responsibility fell to the Reichsführer SS, Heinrich Himmler. Himmler set the work in motion through many channels but primarily through the Central Security Office of the Reich, under the direction of Reinhard Heydrich and later Ernst Kaltenbrunner, and the Central Office of Economic Organization of the SS under the direction of Oswald Pohl. The hunt for Jews and their deportation to the camps was mainly carried out by the Central Security Office and particularly by Adolf Eichmann's office IV B4, while the actual supervision of the camps fell to Pohl's office. But the responsibilities in each of these domains remained imprecise, a situation which was further complicated by the delegation of special powers to the 'heads of police and of the SS' in certain zones.

The 'final solution' was only incidentally exploited to further the German 'war effort'. Certainly those who were forced to do hard labour contributed, but the essen-

Above: Member of a Judenrat, or Jewish council which administered community affairs in the Warsaw ghetto, counting the victims of starvation and disease whose emaciated corpses were piled into handcarts for removal and burial. Right: A pile of human bones and skulls at Maidanek extermination camp in Poland

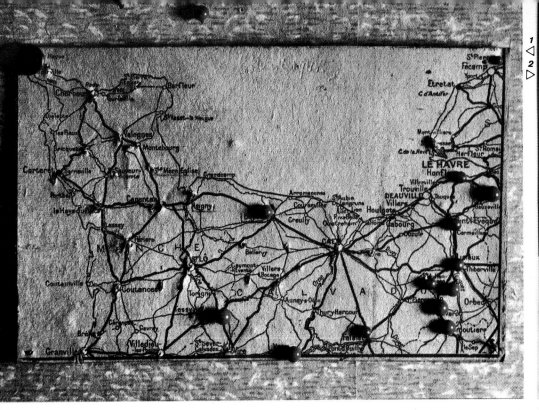

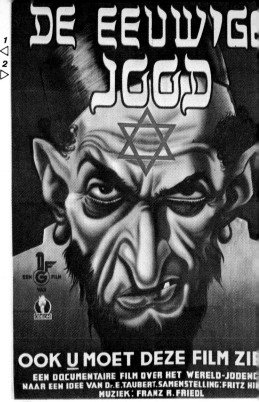

DE EEUWIGE JOOD

1F EEN FILM VAN G

OOK U MOET DEZE FILM ZIE

EEN DOCUMENTAIRE FILM OVER HET WERELD-JODENG
NAAR EEN IDEE VAN Dr. E. TAUBERT. SAMENSTELLING: FRITZ HI
MUZIEK: FRANZ R. FRIEDL

tial aim of the operation was to kill the Jews. Indeed during the last two years of the war, deportation hindered the war effort because the vehicles used to transport the Jews to camps were badly needed on the Eastern Front.

When at the beginning of 1945, this programme was about to end between five and six million Jews had died. (Himmler seems to have ordered an end to the 'final solution' in November 1944, but it was not followed.)

From 1943 the large-scale extermination of the Jews was a well-known fact in Germany, the neutral countries, and among the Allies. But protests were only sporadic and nothing was done to try to save those who still could be saved. In the occupied countries of the East, those Jews who managed to escape the Germans for a time were often killed by partisans or handed over to the Nazis by civilians.

When one takes this into consideration, it is easier to understand the strange 'passivity' of the Jews in Europe in the face of this massacre. The majority could not and would not believe that the Nazis had decided to kill them all. Others—who had understood—were exhausted both morally and physically to such an extent that they no longer had the strength to put up a resistance that was without hope. Many realized that they were in a hopeless position, caught between the barbarity of the Nazis and the general indifference of the 'spectators'. Only a few insignificant groups organized armed revolts in some ghettos and camps. The revolt in the Warsaw ghetto which flared up on 18th April 1943 is the best known. For several weeks, a few thousand Jews practically without arms and entirely without outside assistance held out against several German battalions. From the German point of view it was nothing but a minor anti-partisan affair and only a few dozen Germans were killed. But the revolt in the Warsaw ghetto became a symbolic turning point in the history of the Jews: 'It was,' as Reitlinger points out, 'the first national military combat undertaken by the Jews since the Bar Kochba revolt under the reign of the Emperor Hadrian, 1,800 years before.'

Left: 1 Map showing advancing Allies found in home of the Franks, a Jewish family in Amsterdam. In her diary Anne Frank left a moving account of Nazi persecution. 2 Dutch poster advertises The Eternal Jew, *a pre-war film shown widely in occupied Europe. 3 The gaolers confronted with their crime. SS wardresses transfer bodies to a mass grave after the British liberation of Belsen, April 1945.*
Right: 'The Prayer of the Killed' by Polish artist Bronisław Linke. A Jew, depicted surrealistically, prays amid the rubble of Warsaw

6 CLOSING THE RING

Russia Strikes Back

By November 1942 German forces were fighting on the banks of the Volga at Stalingrad, and in the foothills of the Caucasus. Hitler had not yet given up his plan to cut off central European Russia from the Caucasus and Central Asia and to seize the former's oilfields. In fact, by seizing this very rich and strategically important region he calculated on eliminating the Soviet Union the following summer, thus threatening the Middle East and India.

The predicament of the Soviet Union and its armed forces remained perilous. Leningrad was under blockade by German and Finnish troops and large forces of the enemy were still operating in the outer approaches to Moscow; the protracted and ferocious battle at Stalingrad was absorbing more and more forces; the main lines of communication with the Caucasus were cut and the Baltic Fleet was blockaded in the eastern end of the Gulf of Finland. But events had now passed out of German control. All those factors and circumstances which German Blitzkrieg strategy had failed to take adequately into account were making themselves increasingly felt. The turning point had been brought gradually nearer during the stubborn battles fought by the Red Army in 1941 and the summer of 1942, and as a result of the intense effort made by the entire country. The victory of the Soviet forces before Moscow between December 1941 and March 1942 served as a terrible warning to the enemy. Moreover, the failures suffered in the summer campaign of 1942 did not destroy the Red Army as a fighting force. By the autumn of that year it had made good its

Left: German painting shows a grenadier priming his weapon

losses and was no longer inferior to the enemy in strength. The front was stable along its whole length, from the Barents Sea to the foothills of the Caucasus.

The southern grouping of the enemy's armed forces was the most active and dangerous and it was necessary first and foremost to destroy this concentration. The very idea of a counter-offensive was conceived in the midst of defensive battles and as early as 13th September Marshal Zhukov wrote 'after studying all possible variants, Marshal Vasilyevsky and I decided to propose the following plan of action to Stalin: firstly to continue active defence in order to wear the enemy down and secondly to prepare a counter-offensive in order to deal such a blow to the enemy in the Stalingrad area as would radically change the strategic situation in the south of the country to our advantage.'

As a result of the Red Army's victory at Stalingrad, VI Army was annihilated and the strategic initiative passed, for good, to the Soviet Union. Soviet strategy was now faced with the question of how and in what order it should exploit the new opportunities arising out of victory on the Volga. At that time the Red Army had already achieved a certain numerical preponderance over the enemy, but this was not so significant that the simultaneous fulfilment of several strategic tasks could be contemplated. The Soviet Supreme Command wanted first and foremost to take advantage of the fact that the Voronezh, south-western, and southern fronts had achieved an ascendancy over the enemy. They could develop offensives in the direction of Rostov, into the rear of Army Group A in the northern Caucasus and towards the north-west into the rear of

Army Group B. Defeat of these forces would enable the Red Army to liberate important economic areas—the North Caucasus, the Donbas, Kharkov, Orel, Kursk, and other regions. The main forces of the Red Army were directed to these two objectives. In addition, the Supreme Command decided to lift the enemy blockade of Leningrad, and to destroy the Demyansk and Rzhev-Vyazma salients, from which the German forces might renew their offensive against Moscow if favourable circumstances should offer themselves.

After the destruction of German forces in Kotelnikovo the southern front command sent units towards the Donbas, and two armies towards Rostov. On 28th December Hitler was obliged to order Army Group A to fall back, destroying as it did so all railway lines and rolling stock. In mid-January two armies of the southern front reached the River Manych, where they encountered stubborn resistance from Army Group Don. On 3rd January the northern group of the trans-Caucasian front and the 11th Black Sea Group began offensive operations; but these Soviet forces lacked sufficient men, resources, and motor transport to make the pace of their offensive a rapid one. This fact enabled I Panzer Group to evade Soviet forces pursuing it, and one part fell back to Rostov while another joined XVII Army in the Taman Peninsula. On 12th February Soviet troops took Krasnodar and two days later Rostov. Although the offensive against the German XVII Army continued until the beginning of April, by mid-February the Red Army had liberated nearly all the north Caucasus, with its population of ten million.

In the second half of January the Voronezh front launched an offensive against Army Group B, resulting in the defeat, in the Ostrogozhsk and Rossosh areas, of the Hungarian II Army and the left wing of the Italian VIII Army.

At the end of January and the beginning of February 1943, a new and violent conflict erupted on the southern wing of the Soviet-German front. The Stavka (Soviet equivalent of Combined Chiefs of Staff) and the General Staff drew up a plan for a non-stop offensive by forces of the Voronezh, south-western and southern fronts in left-bank Ukraine (Ukraine to the east of the Dnieper), calculating that before the melting of the winter snows they would have reached the Dnieper along a front stretching from Chernigov to Kherson. In addition, it was planned to launch an offensive by the armies of the Kalinin, western and Bryansk fronts against Army Group Centre in mid-February.

The enemy strove to halt the Red Army's advance and, if unable to throw the Soviet forces back to the Don, then to stabilize the front and prepare to turn the tables when summer came. Hitler wanted, in any event, to hold on to the Donbas because of the importance of this area from the standpoint of war production. The reserves which had been concentrated in the south for the purpose of liberating Paulus's army were now assigned a different task, that of halting Red Army forces on the approaches to the Donbas and Kharkov and hurling them back. The forces of both sides exhausted themselves in ceaseless battles. With extremely extended lines of communication Soviet troops undertook a fresh offensive without adequate reserves, and without re-grouping. The Supreme Command had assumed that the enemy would retire. 'This idea,' General Shtemenko has written, 'which arose from an incorrect evaluation of the enemy's behaviour only seemed to correspond to the real situation. At that time, however, the General Staff and the Stavka were convinced of the correctness of their appreciations and calculations. The triumphant despatches from the fronts lulled the vigilance of both the Stavka and General Staff.'

At first the offensive on all fronts proceeded successfully. Voronezh front captured Kursk on 8th February and Kharkov on 16th February. Other centres of population followed. By mid-February the south-western front had cleared the enemy from the north-eastern Donbas and its forward divisions had reached the Dnieper at Dnepropetrovsk. The southern front had pushed between 90 and 150 kilometres to the west and arrived at the River Mius. By this time, however, the enemy possessed substantial advantages over the advancing Soviet troops. Owing to extremely extended lines of communication

both Soviet fronts were experiencing interruptions in the supply of munitions, fuel, and even food, whereas the enemy, in falling back, drew nearer to his main supply base.

The front stabilizes

While the Soviet forces were continuing their offensive towards the Dnieper, Manstein launched a counter-offensive towards Pavlodar with XLVIII Panzer Corps and towards Barvenkovo with XL Panzer Corps. Ferocious battles began in conditions unfavourable to the Soviet forces who continued to receive orders to advance. At last General Vatutin gave up trying to continue the offensive and began organizing defensive positions. The troops withdrew with heavy losses to the north part of the River Donets and at the beginning of March took up a firm defence line. At the same time, Manstein sent his Panzer Corps against the left flank of the Voronezh front which was still moving towards the Dnieper. The Soviet troops put up a determined resistance, but had to fall back under pressure of the superior German forces, abandoning Belgorod and Kharkov. Fighting continued in this sector until the end of March but the Germans were unable to advance any further and the front was stabilized, forming the Kursk bulge.

In order to stabilize the front in the south-western sector the Soviet Supreme Command was obliged in March to draw largely upon its strategic reserve. This meant that the offensive against Army Group Centre in the Smolensk sector had to be undertaken solely by troops of the Kalinin and western fronts. Within a fortnight they had smashed the Rzhev-Vyazma salient and advanced to the outer approaches of Smolensk.

In March 1943, after the siege of Leningrad had been partially lifted, a lull fell on the front. Every day for the next three months stereotyped communiqués reported that 'nothing important had happened at the front'. Behind this outward calm, however, intense preparations for the summer campaign were under way on both sides. The Soviet Union had achieved definite advantages over the enemy and during the year production of arms and military equipment increased considerably: the average monthly output of aircraft, for example, rose to 3,000 and that of tanks and self-propelled guns to 2,000. By the summer the strength of the operational army had grown to 6,442,000 while the enemy's comparable strength was 5,325,000. The operational section of the Red Army was equipped with 103,085 artillery pieces and mortars, the enemy with 56,250; our forces had 9,918 tanks and self-propelled guns as against the enemy's 5,850, and 8,357

fighter aircraft as against his 2,980. Inspired by their victories, the morale of the Red Army had risen, whereas that of the enemy had fallen. The Soviet troops had acquired a tremendous amount of battle experience and now knew both the enemy's strong and weak points. By the summer, the Soviet ground forces, the air force, the anti-aircraft defences, and the rear services of the Red Army had all been completely reorganized and in consequence the armed forces as a whole now possessed an organizational structure which was more flexible and better adapted to war conditions so that their striking power and mobility were enhanced. Besides restoring and reorganizing the front-line armies, the Supreme Command increased the number of reserve armies to ten.

At the end of March and beginning of April 1943 the problem on which the Stavka and the General Staff were working was where, when, and how to concentrate the forces they possessed so as to accomplish the main strategic tasks set for the summer. The views of the commanders who represented the Stavka in the operational armies were sought, and also those of some of the front commanders. After a thorough study had been made of intelligence about the state and disposition of the enemy's forces, all agreed that the centre of strategic operations during the summer should be the area of the Kursk salient. As regards the method to be followed, the first to express himself definitely on this question was Marshal Zhukov. In a letter he sent to Stalin on 8th April he wrote: 'I consider it inadvisable for our forces to go over to the offensive in the very first days of the campaign in order to forestall the enemy. It would be better to make the enemy first exhaust himself against our defences, and knock out his tanks and then, bringing up fresh reserves, to go over to a general offensive which would finally finish off his main force.' Four days later, Stalin convened a special conference at Supreme Headquarters to discuss the plan for the summer campaign. It was decided to concentrate the main effort in the Kursk area.

For operations along the 550-kilometre Kursk salient twenty-six per cent of the total manpower of the operational Red Army, twenty-six per cent of its artillery and mortars, thirty-five and a half per cent of its fighter aircraft, and over forty-six per cent of its tanks were concentrated. Meanwhile intensive operations for the summer campaign were also going on at Hitler's headquarters, the Wolfsschanze (Wolf's Lair) in East Prussia, in the German General Staff, and in the staffs of their armies and army groups. Hitler insisted that the positions won must be held. After careful inquiries and discussions, it was

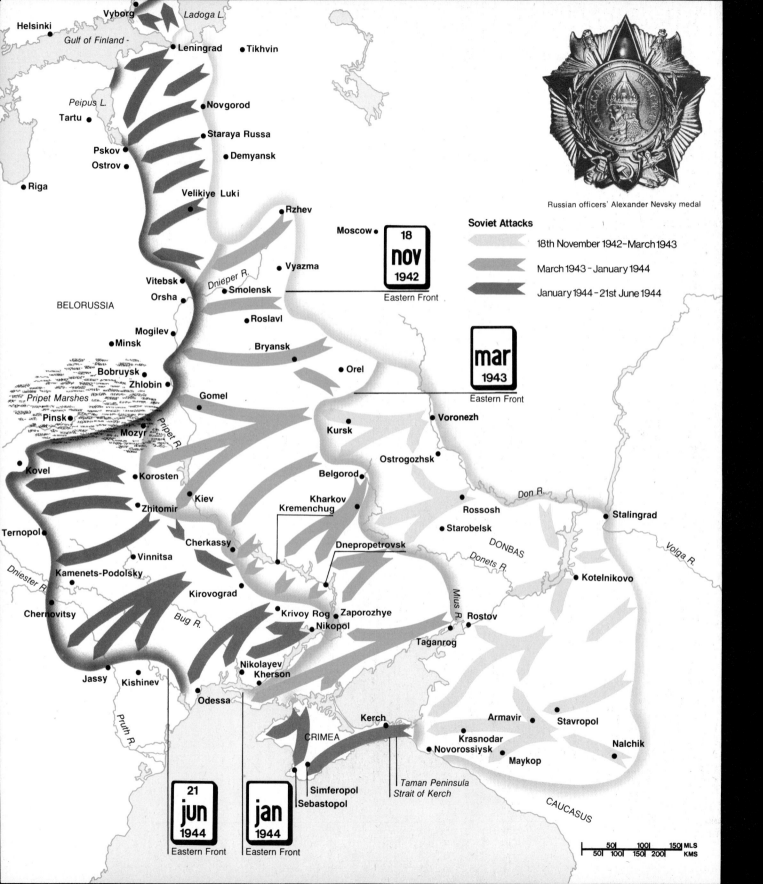

Helsinki
Vyborg
Ladoga L.
Gulf of Finland
Leningrad
Tikhvin
Peipus L.
Novgorod
Tartu
Staraya Russa
Pskov
Demyansk
Ostrov
Riga
Velikiye Luki
Rzhev
Moscow
18
NOV
1942
Eastern Front

Soviet Attacks

18th November 1942–March 1943

March 1943 – January 1944

January 1944 – 21st June 1944

Russian officers' Alexander Nevsky medal

Vyazma
Dnieper R.
Vitebsk
Smolensk
BELORUSSIA
Orsha
Roslavl
Mogilev
Minsk
Bryansk
Bobruysk
Orel
Zhlobin
Pripet Marshes
Gomel
mar
1943
Eastern Front
Pinsk
Mozyr
Pripet R.
Voronezh
Kovel
Kursk
Korosten
Belgorod
Ostrogozhsk
Kiev
Kharkov
Zhitomir
Kremenchug
Rossosh
Don R.
Ternopol
Starobelsk
Stalingrad
Cherkassy
Dnepropetrovsk
Vinnitsa
DONBAS
Kamenets-Podolsky
Donets R.
Kirovograd
Volga R.
Chernovitsy
Krivoy Rog
Zaporozhye
Kotelnikovo
Nikopol
Bug R.
Rostov
Mius R.
Jassy
Kishinev
Nikolayev
Taganrog
Kherson
Odessa
Kerch
Armavir
Stavropol
CRIMEA
Krasnodar
21
jun
1944
Eastern Front
jan
1944
Eastern Front
Simferopol
Novorossiysk
Nalchik
Sebastopol
Maykop
Taman Peninsula
Strait of Kerch
CAUCASUS

| 50 | 100 | 150 | MLS |
| 50 | 100 | 150 | 200 | KMS |

decided in mid-March to prepare and carry out during the summer an offensive code-named Operation Citadel, which should have the aim of surrounding and destroying the Soviet forces in the Kursk salient. After that, it was proposed to launch Operation Panther into the rear of the south-western front, which lay along the northern section of the River Donets. Hitler hesitated. Several times he put off the launching of the offensive. On 21st June he ordered its launching on 3rd July, later changing this date to 5th July.

The German offensive was tensely awaited in the Soviet camp. Stalin showed some irritation; Zhukov and Vasilyevsky stayed with the troops. All ranks at the front were kept in constant readiness for battle. And when on the morning of 5th July seventeen enemy Panzer divisions, with three motorized divisions and eighteen infantry divisions, moved from Orel and Belgorod towards Kursk, they met stubborn resistance from the central and Voronezh fronts. In five days the enemy's Orel force advanced only some nine to twelve kilometres and soon spent its offensive power. In the Belgorod-Kursk sector German forces did better, advancing between fifteen and thirty-five kilometres. Stalin approved the proposal made by Vasilyevsky and Vatutin to begin the Voronezh front's counter-offensive without waiting for the enemy forces to be brought to a halt. On 12th July five armies of this front, reinforced by one tank army and one general purposes army from the strategic reserve, delivered a counter-attack on the Germans while they were still continuing their advance. A bitter struggle began, especially in the Prokhorovka area, where about 1,100 tanks of both sides joined battle. The Soviet and German forces alike suffered great losses, but the German offensive was finally halted on the southern section of the Kursk salient.

On 12th July the western and Bryansk fronts launched Operation Kutuzov aimed at destroying the enemy's Orel forces. With difficulty they broke the long-sustained defence put up by the enemy on the edges of the Orel salient. Three days later the forces of the central front joined

Left: 1 January 1943 — village children near Stalingrad play with abandoned German weapons. The Germans were on the retreat, and in Stalingrad itself the remnants of VI Army were being bombarded, starved, and frozen into surrender. 2 Soviet infantry attacking. 3 Red Army patrol on the Volkhov front. 4 German soldiers captured by the Russians. The losses in manpower on the Eastern Front were enormous. By now young and old alike were drafted to fill the ranks

in the offensive. On 26th July the German commander, General Model, gave the order for his troops to withdraw from the Orel salient so as to avoid forming another cauldron. The Soviet forces pursuing them captured Orel on 5th August and within two days completely wiped out the Orel salient. As they retreated, the German forces burned down towns and villages, shot or drove away the local inhabitants, and destroyed the crops.

On 16th July, German troops in the Belgorod-Kharkov sector began to pull back to their start line. The troops of the Voronezh front, together with General Konev's troops of the steppe front, brought into the battle from the Stavka's reserve, reached the line held by the Soviet troops before the beginning of the defensive battle within a week and after re-grouping launched Operation Rumyantsev to smash German units in the Belgorod-Kharkov area on 3rd August. Belgorod was taken on 5th August,

and on 23rd August, Kharkov capitulated. Now Soviet forces began to advance towards the Dnieper. With the destruction of German forces at Kharkov the Battle of Kursk came to an end.

Having won the strategic initiative, the Red Army advanced along a 2,000-kilometre front from Velikiye Luki to the Black Sea. The troops taking part in this advance were carrying out an operation which has become known as the battle for the Dnieper.

On 13th August, the forces of the southwestern front, commanded by General Malinovsky, resumed the battle for the Donbas and forced their way across the northern section of the River Donets. Five days later, the southern front, commanded by General Tolbukhin, began to advance on Taganrog. The two fronts enveloped Army Group South from the flanks. In order to avoid encirclement, Manstein ordered his forces to retire across the Dnieper, applying scorched earth tactics as they went. Vigor-

ous pursuit by the Soviet forces prevented this plan from being fully realized, though the Donbas did suffer enormous damage.

In the second half of September, Soviet troops arrived on the banks of the Dnieper along a 700-kilometre front from the mouth of the River Sozh to Zaporozhye. After reaching the river they forced crossings at a number of points, besides utilizing those crossing places which had been captured and held by the partisans. Owing to the rapidity of the advance, the rear services had not been able to keep up the supply of engineering materials for bridging the river. By the end of the month, Soviet forces had won twenty-three bridgeheads on the right bank of the river, many of these being merely narrow strips of the

German prisoners with shaved heads being paraded through the streets of a Russian town—a ritual which underlined Russia's growing ability to seize the initiative

bank which were held until reinforcements could come up. Gradually, these bridgeheads were enlarged, and men and equipment assembled in them.

The offensive also proceeded in other directions. In August the Kalinin and western fronts undertook active operations in the direction of Smolensk, throwing back German forces and occupying the city. Although this offensive was not so successful as the southern one, it tied down fifty-five enemy divisions. Further south, the Bryansk and central fronts moved forward. By the beginning of October they had reached the borders of Belorussia and were fighting on the approaches to Vitebsk, Orsha, and Mogilev. On 10th September the forces of the North Caucasian front, commanded by General Petrov, began to advance on the Taman Peninsula. They destroyed this last German bridgehead'in Caucasia, forced a crossing of the Strait of Kerch and seized a bridgehead for themselves in the Crimea.

In October the Soviet fronts were reorganized and renamed. On the foundation of the Bryansk front the 2nd Baltic front was formed, while the Kalinin front was renamed the 1st Baltic front, the central front became the Belorussian front and the Voronezh, steppe, south-western, and southern fronts were now called, respectively, the 1st, 2nd, 3rd and 4th Ukrainian fronts. The Ukrainian fronts waged an uninterrupted offensive battle right down to the end of the year. On 3rd November, two armies of the 1st Ukrainian front struck at the Lyutezh bridgehead, broke through the enemy front and on the evening of 5th November reached Kiev. By the next morning the city had been cleared of the enemy, and the troops of this front began to move on Zhitomir and Korosten. By the end of November they had established a strategic bridgehead extending 230 kilometres along the front and 150 kilometres in depth. The forces of the 2nd and 3rd Ukrainian fronts resumed their offensive from the bridgeheads they had won, captured the towns of Cherkassy, Dneprodzerzhinsk and Zaporozhye, and established a wide strategic bridgehead on the middle and lower course of the Dnieper. In September the 4th Ukrainian front smashed the German front on the River Molochnaya and came out on the lower reaches of the Dnieper and the Crimean Isthmus. Only at Nikopol did the Germans manage to retain a bridgehead on the left bank of the Dnieper.

The offensive continues

The onset of winter did not stop the Red Army's offensive in the Ukraine. And although the losses suffered by our operational forces were such as to make it impossible to restore and keep their strength at the level of summer 1943, an overall superiority over the enemy was maintained. As for the enemy, he had to fall back on the strategic defensive, hoping to be able to gain time to prepare to recover the initiative later on.

But the Stavka planned not only to continue the offensive but also to extend its front to the Baltic Sea. The main blow was to be struck in the south-western sector, in order to smash Army Group South and Army Group A in right-bank Ukraine and the Crimea. The Soviet forces operating in the north-western sector were assigned the tasks of smashing Army Group North, finally raising the blockade of Leningrad, and entering the approaches of the Baltic region. In the centre the task was to defeat Army Group Centre and clear a substantial part of the enemy from Belorussia. The implementation of this plan resulted in the liberation of nearly all Soviet territory.

On 14th January 1944 the forces of the Leningrad and Volkhov fronts went over to the offensive and within a week compelled the enemy's XVIII Army to begin withdrawing south-westward from its positions before Leningrad. In the other sector, troops of the Volkhov front smashed German forces before Novgorod and on 20th January recaptured this ancient Russian city. Subsequently the Leningrad front to which the greater part of the Volkhov front was subordinated, continued its advance, halting at the end of the winter on the approaches to Pskov and Ostrov. Meanwhile the 2nd Baltic front took Staraya Russa and an important road junction at Dno station. The result of the one-and-a-half-month offensive by the Soviet forces in the north-western sector was an advance of 220-280 kilometres and the complete raising of the blockade of Leningrad.

In the Ukraine, the Stavka planned an offensive along the entire front, from the River Pripet to the Black Sea. The first stage of this offensive was to finish finally with the enemy defences of the Dnieper and reach the southern section of the River Bug, and the second to cut the enemy's front in two, advance towards the Carpathians and reach a line from Lutsk through Mogilev Podolsky to the River Dniester. The four Ukrainian fronts were opposed by Army Group South under Field-Marshal Manstein and Army Group A under Field-Marshal Kleist. The German command thought that the Red Army would be unable to continue its advance immediately after the intense battle for the Dnieper.

The enemy's calculations were not confirmed by events. At the end of December 1943 and in the following January, the 1st Ukrainian front continued its advance towards Vinnitsa and the 2nd Ukrainian front its advance towards Kiro-vograd, deeply enveloping the flanks of the German VIII Army. At the end of January the forces of these two fronts surrounded the main German forces in the Korsun-Shevchenkovsky area and by the middle of February had annihilated them. The 3rd and 4th Ukrainian fronts, resuming their advance at the end of January, liberated Nikopol and Krivoy Rog, important industrial centres of the Ukraine.

By the beginning of March the Ukrainian fronts had been reinforced with men and equipment and possessed two and a half times as many tanks as the enemy. The Germans had also been reinforced and were strengthened by the arrival of fresh divisions transferred to the Soviet-German front from Germany, Yugoslavia, France, and Belgium. Nevertheless, overall superiority in men and material remained with the Soviet side. The Soviet forces continued their advance along the whole front from Polesye to the Black Sea. The offensive did not stop by day or by night. On 26th March the 2nd Ukrainian front arrived at the River Prut along an eighty-five kilometre stretch of bank and crossed into Rumanian territory. The 1st Ukrainian front advanced up to 350 kilometres westward and occupied Vinnitsa, Kamenets-Podolsky, Ternopol, and Chernovitsy. After forcing their way across the southern Bug, troops of the 3rd Ukrainian front took Nikolayev and Odessa. In mid-April they reached the Dniester. The 4th Ukrainian front and the Special Maritime Army, supported by the Black Sea Fleet and the Azov Naval Flotilla, began the liberation of the Crimea on 8th April. The operation proceeded successfully. Within only five days the administrative centre, Simferopol, was taken. By 12th May the Crimea had been completely liberated by the Red Army. The main forces of the 200,000-strong German XVII Army had been routed.

The advance proceeded less fortunately in Belorussia and the Baltic region. Down to the spring of 1944 battles continued along the whole front from Velikiye Luki to the River Pripet, but their outcome was successful only in the Kovel direction, where the Soviet forces reached Kovel and turned the southern flank of Army Group Centre.

The beginning of May saw a lull in the fighting. The Red Army had marched hundreds of kilometres, fighting fierce battles in which it had smashed dozens of enemy divisions. In the winter and spring it had freed 329,000 square kilometres of Soviet territory, inhabited by nineteen million people, re-established the state frontier of the USSR along 400 kilometres of its length, and entered Rumania. Favourable conditions had been created for the complete liberation of the Soviet Union and the final defeat of Hitler's Wehrmacht, the following year.

Resistance

Wherever men have exercised power there have been others to offer resistance. A greater number are usually prepared to collaborate, even in war. But in the Second World War collaboration became a dirty word and resistance acquired a new dimension, a new sense of tragic dedication. Hitler's conquest of Europe was no simple matter of armies crossing national boundaries. As the peculiar atrocities of the Nazis and the vicious doctrines of their perverted ideology became evident, they provided an indisputable reason against collaboration. It was the argument against selling one's soul to the devil. Those who aided their Nazi overlords soon reaped the scorn of all self-respecting men and, when liberation came, the most violent reprisals. It was not only patriotism but the need to defend human decency which impelled many men and women to risk capture by the Gestapo, to suffer brutal torture, and to give their lives in the cause of a free Europe.

As Hitler's Panzers rolled up to the western coast of Europe in the fateful summer of 1940, representatives of the governments of eight defeated nations withdrew across the Channel to Europe's last bastion of democracy, Great Britain. There they provided a focus for the loyalty of their now subject peoples and a base for continuing the fight against Nazism. Already in the lands they had left spontaneous resistance was growing. In Holland, for example, the introduction of anti-Jewish legislation led to long queues outside Jewish shops and crowded waiting-rooms in the surgeries of Jewish doctors. Clandestine newspapers and pamphlets began to play an important role in psychological warfare. The underground Press in Belgium became so highly organized that in November 1943 100,000 copies of a fake edition of the German-controlled *Le Soir* were sold on newstands throughout the country. But in the ultimate aim of freeing national territory the resistance was helpless without Allied aid.

In Western Europe this aid came from Great Britain, together with the émigré governments. Churchill showed an immediate interest in the European underground and, in keeping with his resolve 'to set Europe ablaze', he established in July 1940 the Special Operations Executive (SOE). Directed from a secret address in London, bankers, dons, lawyers, journalists, film directors, schoolmasters, wine merchants, and even women were trained to harass the enemy. This was to be done by setting up intelligence networks, organizing sabotage on a large scale, and training secret armies which would emerge when the Allied invasion of Europe was mounted. New per-

sonalities were carefully fabricated, forged documents prepared, and special kits assembled. A whole new industry arose supplying false-bottomed suitcases and toothpaste tubes with special compartments. In 'Operation Lavatory' agents hid their radio sets in the cistern, set up a special chain as the aerial, and transmitted using codes in invisible ink written on men's shirt-tails and on women's pants and petticoats. There were new developments in sabotage: explosive 'coal lumps' destined for Gestapo offices, hand-painted explosive 'horse droppings' to be dropped in the path of German staff cars, and incendiary 'cigarettes'. Finally there was the 'L' pill which contained potassium cyanide. Held in the mouth during torture, its insoluble coating could be crushed between the teeth if the pain became too much for the agent to bear. Death would be almost instantaneous.

Agents were despatched to Hitler's Europe by parachute, by Lysander aircraft, submarine, or small fishing boat. The moment when they set off on their missions was likely to be the most solitary they had ever experienced. In the early days this was not purely subjective. The first agents were entirely on their own and 'parachuted blind', for British secret service links with all the occupied countries of Europe had virtually broken down. SOE therefore started from scratch, and by June 1941 little had been achieved and many lives tragically lost. It was the 'heroic' period of the resistance, characterized by lack of co-ordination, inexperience, and successful infiltration by V-men, informers working for the Nazis. But on 22nd June there was a turning point, for when Hitler attacked Soviet Russia Communists all over Europe ranged themselves wholeheartedly behind the Allies in a 'holy' war against Nazism. By the end of 1941 resistance was better organized and more efficient.

In Western Europe the Nazi tyranny never became as harsh as it was in Eastern Europe. Though exploiting to the full the occupied territories in the West, the Germans also attempted to win the allegiance of their new subjects. But even in partly German-speaking Luxembourg this policy failed. Everywhere resistance became the norm and in most countries proved its value in the struggle against Nazism. It was

Top: Fake issue of the Nazi military magazine Signal *printed by Belgian resistance, entitled: 'An outrage against humanity; after the Munich Putsch Mr Hitler was arrested.'* **Right:** *Fruits of resistance in Czechoslovakia. Freight train derailed by partisans in Moravia*

resistance which removed the possibility of a Nazi nuclear bomb. In March 1943 the Norwegian secret army, Milorg, co-operated with SOE in destroying the heavy water plant at Rjukan upon which the Nazi nuclear research programme depended. In Belgium, a vital staging-post for escape routes to Switzerland and Spain, underground engineers put all the high-tension lines in the country out of action simultaneously in January 1944, costing the Nazis vital man hours in repairs. In Denmark, however, resistance was slower to mature since the government, not officially at war with Germany, remained in Copenhagen. Until 1943, therefore, when the Nazis imposed direct rule, underground activity was hindered by the stigma of treason. And in Holland resistance suffered a catastrophe. The early capture by the Nazis of an SOE radio operator and the use of the secret code to deceive London condemned many Dutch agents to death and, by crippling the Dutch resistance, was ultimately responsible for the delayed liberation of the country after D-Day.

Radio, as the case of Holland suggests, was a vital element in resistance activities. It was underground Europe's chief contact with the outside world. On average two million words a week passed through SOE signals stations and on 5th June, the eve of D-Day, 500 signals were sent to alert agents and their secret armies. The German counter-measure was the Funkpeil Dienst (radio direction finding service) whose 'detection' vans constantly toured the darkened streets of occupied Europe in search of underground transmitters. The BBC had its own special war effort, broadcasting messages of hope and providing news for clandestine publications. Apparently meaningless sentences heard on overseas programmes, such as 'the cow will jump over the moon tonight', were in fact prearranged signals to herald the arrival of a new agent from London or to convince a sympathetic foreign banker of the *bona fides* of an agent in need of money.

Resistance was not only a revolt against Nazism; it was also a political movement. This was particularly true in France where the shattering of the Third Republic created a constitutional desert in which new institutions would have to be set up. As the dust settled, two architects appeared among the ruins. The first was the right-wing Marshal Pétain, victor of Verdun. To begin with the population rallied to his French State based on Vichy and collaboration became the order of the day. But as the Nazi tyranny became more oppressive the French turned to resistance—and therefore to Charles de Gaulle who as an unknown general had arrived in London in June 1940 as the self-appointed representative of the Free French. Progressively he established

himself as the leader of the new republic which was to be constructed.

The road to victory was not an easy one. It was marred by bad relations between the general's BCRA (Bureau Central de Renseignements et d'Action), established with British credits, and SOE whose French section under Colonel Maurice Buckmaster played a major part in organizing the resistance. In addition the Nazis infiltrated several important circuits. Through one such coup they were able to make full preparations to repulse the ill-fated Dieppe Raid in August 1943. However, after the union of disparate resistance groups under the National Resistance Council in November 1942, sabotage increased and by early 1944 100,000 underground fighters were organized to take part in the fight for liberation. With the founding of the French Forces of the Interior (FFI) the resistance war effort was linked directly to SHAEF (Supreme Headquarters, Allied Expeditionary Force) and played an important part behind the lines during the Allied landings in Normandy (Overlord) and Provence (Anvil). Alone the resistance could never have defeated the Nazis, but together with the Allied armies General Eisenhower considered that it 'played a very considerable part in our victory'.

Bearing the brunt of the worst Nazi barbarism, the peoples of Eastern Europe were quick to organize resistance. Help came from two sources, Soviet Russia and Great Britain, and it was to be politically motivated: once the Red Army was bearing down on Berlin, Stalin used the Communist elements of the resistance to install regimes congenial to himself. This pattern became evident in Czechoslovakia. President Beneš and his government in exile at first directed resistance operations from London. It was from London that the murder of 'Hangman' Heydrich, protector of Bohemia-Moravia, was arranged in co-operation with SOE in May 1942. But when Beneš saw that the Red Army would reach Prague before the Western powers, he established closer relations with Soviet Russia. Increasingly control passed from London to Moscow. The same occurred in Poland where the resistance, which ran the best radio communications system in occupied Europe, was at first directed by General Sikorski in London. But after the Warsaw Rising in August 1944, when Stalin stood by while the Germans ruthlessly crushed the uprising of the Polish Home Army and razed Warsaw to the ground, Poland fell under a Russian-directed Communist regime based on Lublin.

Resistance also brought Yugoslavia into the Communist camp, but for the less sinister reason that here the British supported the Communist partisans under Tito. But in Greece, where antagonism between the two

wings of the resistance verged on civil war, monarchist elements triumphed—because Churchill sent British troops to crush the Communists.

Resistance in the Axis countries and their satellites was by far the weakest. In these countries it was resistance by citizens against their own governments and therefore treason. Against traitors the Reich proved to have all the trump cards, and since the Allies seemed not to believe in the possibility of 'good Germans', resistance in Germany was deprived of outside help. It was therefore condemned to failure as the July Plot demonstrated, but it is as well to remember the words of Moltke, leader of the Kreisau circle, in a letter to an English friend: 'Never forget that for us there will be a bitter, bitter end to all this. When you are through with us, try to remember, however, that there are still a few who earnestly want to help you win the war and the peace.' In Italy the anti-Fascists succeeded in toppling Mussolini from power in July 1943, but this was more a matter of coincidental rather than concerted action. Once Mussolini was re-established at Salò, resistance was no longer treason for he was merely the puppet of an external power. In German-occupied Italy, therefore, resistance took much the same form as elsewhere in Europe: sabotage and assassinations. It was at the hands of Italian partisans that Mussolini met his death in April 1945.

Was resistance worth it? Compared with the victories of the Allied armies its achievements were modest. It could never have played more than a supporting role but as an ancillary force it had many successes. As an instrument of destruction it rivalled and on occasion surpassed Bomber Command. The continuous strain imposed by sabotage and assassination in the interior tied down many divisions that could otherwise have been employed on the front lines against Allied troops. As a medium of intelligence the resistance performed a vital service. And in France FFI units liberated five departments unaided.

But the achievements of the resistance were won at great cost. The murder of Heydrich was avenged by the destruction of Lidice and the massacre of 3,000 hostages in Prague and Brno. In France the disabling by FFI units of the SS Division Das Reich on its way to Normandy in June 1944 led to the murder of ninety-nine hostages in Tulle and the massacre of the entire population of Oradour-sur-Glane. In Russia anti-partisan operations often turned into orgies of murder and destruction.

For the many unsung heroes who fought in the secret war the reward was to know that they had played their part in the destruction of National Socialism. For those in Eastern Europe it was to see a new tyranny imposed. And for a great many it was death.

Victory in the Atlantic

By December 1941 the stage had been set for a decisive encounter on the Atlantic convoy routes between the convoy escorts, both surface and airborne, and the U-boats. The declaration of war on the United States by Germany on 11th December might, at first sight, have seemed to spell a huge access of strength to the escort forces, one which could tip the balance decisively in their favour. It was to prove, initially, quite the contrary.

Successive acts by the United States government since the President's declaration in July 1940 of a policy of 'all aid (to Great Britain) short of war' and the transfer of fifty over-age destroyers had clearly shown where American sympathies lay. In March 1941 'Lend-Lease' had been authorized and ten US coastguard cutters transferred to the Royal Navy. In July, when American troops relieved the British garrison in Iceland, US destroyers had begun to escort convoys to and from the island —convoys which ships of any nationality and ultimate destination could join. Two months later the US Navy had begun to take part in escort of transatlantic convoys during the western part of their voyages, on the grounds that ships for Iceland were included, and when five US destroyers were sent from Iceland to the aid of a convoy under attack in October, one of them, *USS Kearney,* had been torpedoed. A fortnight later *USS Reuben James,* escorting a convoy, was sunk with the loss of all but a handful of her crew.

Nevertheless, so long as the United States remained officially neutral, it had been German policy to avoid provocation. American declaration of a Defence Zone in the western half of the Atlantic had been respected to the extent that the great volume of merchant traffic thronging the sea route up the American east coast from the Caribbean and the Gulf of Mexico had been unmolested. Now, suddenly, it was open to attack.

This would not have been of vital consequence if effective protection for it had been prepared. Unfortunately, in spite of their own experience in the First World War and of more recent British experience, the fruits of which had been made freely available to them, the US Navy had taken no steps whatever to organize a convoy system. Shortage of escorts and the accepted dogma that inadequately escorted convoys were worse than none were given as the reasons, although in fact, some fifty per cent more surface craft and five or six times more aircraft were available than had been available to the British at the outbreak of the war.

An equally potent influence, as with the British in 1916 and, to some extent, in 1939 and 1940, was the unquestioning cult of the offensive, which demanded the employment of such forces as there were on 'search and patrol'. Leaving the stream of freighters and tankers to steam independently, warships and aircraft patrolled the route and dashed hither and thither in search of U-boats which betrayed their position by sinking merchantmen. They were, uniformly unsuccessful. Not one U-boat was destroyed off the American coast until April 1942, by which time more than 200 merchant ships and one of the patrolling destroyers had been sunk, many of them in sight of the shore.

Holocaust in American waters

The U-boat offensive began with only five boats, joined by three more before the end of January. Between 13th January and the end of the month they accounted for forty ships. Their easy success made Dönitz, the German Commander of Submarines, decide to deploy his whole available strength in American waters. Though frustrated by Hitler's insistence on retaining a number of U-boats in Norwegian waters and in the Mediterranean, he was able, by the use of supply U-boats, known as 'milch-cows', to loose his smaller, 750-ton boats, as well as the longer range 1,000 tonners in a simultaneous attack along the whole sea route from the Caribbean to New York.

The result was a holocaust. During February, sixty-five ships were sunk in American waters; in March eighty-six; a slight drop to sixty-nine in April was followed by a new 'high' in May of 111 ships. The Americans tried everything—except convoy—to stem the flow of Allied lifeblood. Ships were routed close in shore, the only result of which was to present an even denser stream of traffic to the attackers. Movements were restricted to daylight hours, ships sheltering in protected anchorages by night. Yet shipping losses continued to mount.

In May, at last, the Americans were convinced. A convoy system was instituted along their east coast. Sinkings in that area immediately ceased. The U-boats moved

Grand-Admiral Karl Dönitz, Commander of Submarines throughout the war and Commander-in-Chief of the German Navy from 1943. He succeeded Admiral Raeder, the exponent of surface ships. Nominated as Hitler's successor, Dönitz was head of the German state at the time of Germany's surrender

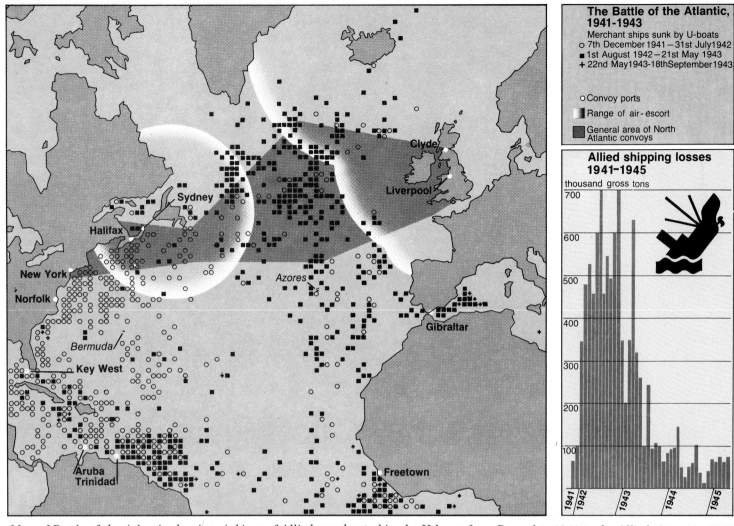

The Battle of the Atlantic, 1941-1943
Merchant ships sunk by U-boats
○ 7th December 1941 – 31st July 1942
■ 1st August 1942 – 21st May 1943
✚ 22nd May 1943 – 18th September 1943

○ Convoy ports
▨ Range of air-escort
▨ General area of North Atlantic convoys

Allied shipping losses 1941–1945
thousand gross tons

Map of Battle of the Atlantic showing sinkings of Allied merchant ships by U-boats from December 1941 to the Allied victory in 1943. The area in mid-Atlantic not covered by air-escort is the 'Black Gap'. The table of Allied shipping losses shows the U-boats' 'Happy Time' from December 1941 to June 1942. The heavy losses of November 1942 were during the Allied Torch landings in North Africa

south to the Gulf of Mexico and the Caribbean, however, where the stream of 'independents', many of them valuable tankers, continued to flow. June saw the highest score of all, with 121 ships sunk in those waters. Nevertheless, conversion of US naval thought when it came was nothing if not whole-hearted. The Commander-in-Chief of the US Navy, Admiral King, had stated the view in March that 'inadequately escorted convoys were worse than none'. Now he went on record as saying that 'escort is not just one way of handling the submarine menace; it is the *only* way that gives any promise of success. The so-called patrol and hunting operations have time and again proved futile.'

By the end of June the Gulf of Mexico and the Caribbean were being incorporated into a comprehensive convoy system with sea and air escort. Sinkings there likewise ceased. In July five U-boats were destroyed in American waters. The second 'Happy Time' for U-boats was over. Once again the U-boat commanders sought for the weakest portion of the convoy chain. They found it in the 'Black Gap' in mid-Atlantic where air escort was still almost non-existent.

In the meantime both sides had grown stronger. U-boat losses had been few during the previous six months; the construction programme was in full swing. But the escorts had also greatly increased in numbers and efficiency. They had been formed into regular groups composed usually of

two destroyers and four corvettes, the former having been modified to give them more anti-submarine weapons and devices at the expense of gun armament. The majority had received intensive individual and group training. Except for one or two groups in which American coastguard cutters led a mixed flotilla of American, British, and Canadian escorts, about half the groups were British and half Canadian.

Improved equipment

Most escorts and anti-submarine aircraft had received the new ten-centimetre radar which enabled them to detect surfaced submarines at considerable ranges. Some ships were equipped with High Frequency Direction Finders (HFDF) by means of which the bearing and to some extent the range of a unit transmitting on short wave radio could be determined. The existence of these two devices was unknown to the Germans. The latter enabled the escort commander to send an escort ship or aircraft probing for any U-boat making the signals essential to the concentration of a wolf-pack. The former could then cause the U-boat to be surprised on the surface at night or in low visibility. When they then submerged they were hunted with greatly improved asdics and attacked with larger salvos of more powerful depth-charges.

So that escorts could remain with their convoys for the whole of the long voyage,

tankers from which they could refuel under way were included in the convoys. To avoid the need to distract escorts from the task of driving off and hunting down the attackers, rescue ships specially equipped to pick up and give medical aid to survivors of sunken merchant ships were also attached.

Where the improved equipment and well-led and trained groups combined, the U-boats were detected and foiled. Either for this reason or because of skilful diversions based on the information gathered in the U-boat tracking room in the Admiralty, the majority of convoys got through without loss. But in the rapid expansion of the escort force, particularly the Canadian element which had grown out of a tiny pre-war navy, there were bound to be groups lacking experience and ships in which provision of up-to-date equipment had been delayed. When convoys with such less effective escorts were located by the U-boats, scenes of earlier times were repeated with the defence swamped by the concentrated attack.

The primary antidote to such massed attacks was close air escort which, either by patrolling round the convoy or by flying along the bearings obtained by HFDF in the surface escorts, could force the U-boats to dive and so virtually immobilize them until the convoy had passed. Equipped with radar and, after more than two years of war, with effective depth-charges, these aircraft were the greatest dread of the U-

A U-boat surfaces after being hit by a depth-charge fired by a British convoy escort vessel in the North Atlantic. Oil painting by Norman Wilkinson. On the deck of the escort in the foreground are torpedoes, usually used against enemy surface vessels but sometimes for sinking a torpedoed and burning merchant vessel which might give away the location of a convoy to a prowling U-boat

boat commanders, allowing them no relaxation or opportunity to surface and recharge their batteries in peace by day or night. It was in the mid-Atlantic gap, therefore, that they preferred to operate, where so long as Coastal Command of the RAF was denied the very long-range Liberator aircraft they needed, only scanty air escort could be given.

It was to fill this 'Black Gap' in air cover that escort aircraft carriers, converted from merchant ships, were being constructed in American and British yards. The first four were in commission by the late summer of 1942; but it was then decided that they were required to give fighter cover to the forthcoming Anglo-American landings in North Africa. None could yet be spared for Atlantic convoy protection, though one of them, *HMS Avenger,* played a decisive part in fighting a convoy through to north Russia against a concentrated air and submarine attack in September.

So it was principally between the surface escorts and the U-boats in the 'Black Gap' that the battles round the Atlantic convoys were fought out. German ability to read coded messages between the Admiralty and the escorts enabled them to place U-boat patrol lines across the convoy routes. Where wolf-packs were able to concentrate, they inflicted some heavy losses. In August a slow convoy with a make-shift escort-force lost eleven ships in a six-day running

fight. Two of the U-boats were destroyed. In the next month the U-boats sank nine ships from an outward-bound convoy without loss to themselves. Similar disasters to convoys continued to occur at intervals during the autumn and winter months.

In October an outward-bound convoy lost seven of its number as well as the destroyer *Ottawa* of its Canadian escort, and four more freighters were torpedoed and damaged without any loss to the wolf-pack. But in another convoy similarly beset, the loss of seven ships was offset by the destruction of two U-boats and several more damaged—a rate of exchange the U-boats could not afford. Had Dönitz been given his head to deploy his whole force in the Atlantic, the crisis in the Battle of the Atlantic would probably have developed at this time, perhaps with fatal consequences to the Allies; fortunately Hitler still insisted on maintaining a large U-boat strength in the Mediterranean and the Arctic. So the outcome hung in the balance while in the savage North Atlantic winter each side was as much occupied in fighting the wild weather as the enemy.

Climax of the battle

It was true that merchant ships were still being sunk, worldwide, at a rate greater than they could be replaced; but the American shipyards were swinging into full production. Furthermore the majority of merchant ship casualties were among

the independently-sailing vessels; these would get fewer and harder to find as the convoy system was being steadily extended. U-boat losses were by no means insupportable as yet and the number of operational boats was growing fast. But their opponents were gaining daily also in numbers and efficiency. Thus a climax in the Atlantic was approaching.

From the Allied point of view, as the storm-imposed winter lull was passing, three features of the situation made prospects for the spring of 1943 bright. At long last the Prime Minister's Anti-U-boat Committee, delivering a judgment of Solomon between the rival claimants for allocation of very long-range Liberator aircraft, reached a compromise which raised the number in Coastal Command from ten to forty, allowing about thirteen to be operational at any one time. By increasing the size of individual convoys and so reducing their frequency, enough escorts would be released to form independent support groups which could be used to reinforce threatened convoys. And, finally, the long-awaited escort carriers were at last to be employed in the task for which they had been conceived.

Yet March 1943 was to prove one of the most disastrous of the war in terms of merchant shipping lost. The more experienced escort groups had a well-founded confidence that they were a match for the wolf-packs; U-boats which encountered them paid

heavily for any sinkings they achieved. But it was not always possible to give convoys top quality protection; then disaster set in. Thus, while the well-trained veteran escorts of the mixed British, Polish, and Free French group were fighting a homeward-bound convoy through a dense U-boat concentration, destroying two of the enemy at the cost of four ships of the convoy and the escort commander's ship, another inexperienced group lost thirteen of their convoy without exacting any retribution.

Then two convoys, a fast and a slow, homeward bound, each beset by a large wolf-pack, came together to make one huge, widespread chaotic struggle in which twenty-one merchantmen were lost and, though one U-boat was finally sunk and Dönitz was to record that 'nearly all the other boats suffered from depth-charges or bombs and two were severely damaged', viewed from the Admiralty the scale of disaster was appalling. For a while the validity of the convoy system came in question.

The loss of morale was brief, however, being restored by the safe arrival of the next two convoys in spite of their being similarly threatened by several wolf-packs. In fact the elements which were to ensure the defeat of the U-boat were now present for the first time. The escort carrier, *USS Bogue,* and a support group of British destroyers gave these convoys cover through the danger area. By the end of March five British support groups were ready for operations, one of them centred on the escort carrier *HMS Biter.*

U-boats checked

At the same time a stream of fresh U-boats from Germany and the Biscay bases, no less than ninety-eight during April, was setting out for mid-Atlantic for what was to be the decisive battle. Convoys were duly located; yet somehow, inexplicably to the Germans, the well-tried techniques for gathering the wolf-packs failed. Hardly had the U-boat making contact flashed his radio message to headquarters when there would be seen the sharp stem and frothing bow wave of a racing destroyer following up the bearing obtained by her HFDF set or a Liberator plane directed by the escorts diving to the attack. Often it was the last object in the outside world the U-boat crew would see. The first signal would be the last; at U-boat headquarters another U-boat lost would be chalked up. At best, the submarine would be forced to stay submerged, blind and reduced to a crawl,

Left: Allied convoy in the North Atlantic
Right: German propaganda designed for Holland shows torpedo-boat and Dutch man-of-war sailing against England

STEEDS DEZELFDE VIJAND

1673
1943

while the convoy slipped through the patrol line to safety.

In the last week of April five U-boats were destroyed round the convoys for an almost negligible loss of merchant ships. However Dönitz did not yet concede victory. During May his force was deployed in massed attacks against the convoys. Sixty U-boats fought an eight-day battle with the escorts of an outward-bound convoy in the first week of that month. By the end of the month twelve merchant ships had been sunk; but it had cost the attackers eight of their number with many others severely damaged.

As the losses became known and the tales of narrow escapes by the survivors spread through the U-boat fleet, the nerves of the submarine crews cracked. Redirected on to other convoys they refused to press home their attacks and even so they were detected and surprised on the surface by air and surface escorts. A number were sunk; the convoys steamed on unscathed. During May forty-one U-boats were sunk, twenty-five of them by the air and surface escorts, seven more, on passage in the Bay of Biscay, were surprised on the surface by aircraft equipped with new radar. At last Dönitz accepted defeat, at least for the time being, and withdrew all U-boats from the North Atlantic convoy routes.

Allied victory

It is generally accepted that May 1943 marked Allied victory in the Battle of the Atlantic. To quote from Captain Roskill's official history, *The War at Sea*: 'After forty-five months of unceasing battle of a more exacting and arduous nature than posterity may easily realise, our convoy escorts had won the triumph they so richly merited.'

Nevertheless, though Dönitz was forced to abandon his efforts against the transatlantic convoys, he has recorded in his memoirs his conclusion at that time that 'the U-boat campaign must be continued with the forces available. Losses, which bear no relation to the success achieved, must be accepted, bitter though they are.' Furthermore, new weapons were under development which could tip the balance back in his favour.

Having started the war equipped with a torpedo which was unreliable in its depth-keeping, his U-boats had been forced to limit their attacks to deep-draught vessels and could not strike back at the escorts. Now, however, a torpedo was under trial which, by means of an acoustic device in its head, would 'home' on to the propeller noises of a ship. With this, a hunted submarine could turn the tables on its attacker.

When Holland was overrun, Dutch submarines had been captured which had an ingenious device, a *Schnörkel* or breathing tube through which a submerged submarine could draw air to enable it to run its diesel engines to propel it, as well as to recharge its electric storage batteries. The Germans now adopted this; U-boats when fitted with it would no longer need to come to the surface, exposing themselves to radar detection. The menace from the air would then be largely overcome. Finally a new U-boat with greatly increased battery power, the Type XXI which would be able to make as much as 18 knots submerged, was being designed.

U-boats' last hope

The knowledge that these several improvements were in the offing kept hope alive. Meanwhile the U-boats were redeployed in the hope of finding more profitable and less dangerous areas. In the Caribbean and off the coast of Brazil there were still some independently sailing ships to be found; but there were convoys, too, and in attacking them eight U-boats were destroyed by the air escorts. Once again the survivors were withdrawn.

Another group had been sent to an area south-west of the Azores to intercept United States to Mediterranean convoys. They found themselves harried by aircraft from American escort carriers. In June *USS Bogue*'s group sank two U-boats. In the next month the *Bogue, Core,* and *Santee* destroyed six more; not a single merchant ship was sunk.

But in the meantime the work of re-equipping the U-boats had pressed ahead – acoustic torpedoes to strike back at surface escorts, increased anti-aircraft armament, an improved radar search receiver, and a radar decoy to reduce the threat from the air. On 13th September Dönitz announced 'all the essentials for a successful campaign are to hand'. Once again they were launched against the main transatlantic convoys. They found them even more effectively guarded than before.

The target they first assailed comprised a conjunction of two convoys, a fast and a slow, which being fairly close to one another when the threat developed, had been ordered to unite. The total of sixty-five merchant ships thus had no less than fifteen escorts as well as a merchant aircraft carrier (MAC-ship), one of a number of tankers and grain ships which had been equipped with a flight deck from which four Swordfish aircraft could operate.

Emboldened by the possession of acoustic torpedoes, the U-boats fought their way through the screen by night, sinking three escorts in the process. Heavy casualties resulted from the loss of one of these which had embarked the survivors from another. Six merchant ships were torpedoed; two U-boats were destroyed and two more severely damaged. The Germans believed they had sunk many more escorts and were pleased with their new offensive tactics.

The sudden revelation of the new weapon was certainly a blow to the morale of the escort crews; but it was quickly countered by towing a noise-maker at a distance astern – a device known as a 'foxer' – which diverted the acoustic torpedo away from its target. With this, the escorts' ascendancy was re-established. A second massacre of U-boats round the North Atlantic convoys followed, and by November the U-boat command was seeking fresh remedies, including a renewal of co-operation by long-range aircraft.

In the face of the combined air and surface escort now available to convoys and of support groups, often operating with escort carriers, ever poised to intervene when a convoy was threatened, nothing availed. In February 1944 the most successful of the support groups, 2nd Escort Group commanded by Captain F.J.Walker, during a three-week patrol accounted for six U-boats in the vicinity of the three convoys it assisted. At the end of March the Germans again conceded victory on the North Atlantic convoy routes; U-boats were transferred to independent cruises in southern waters.

The submarine dominated

A feature of these was the necessity to refuel in mid-Atlantic from milch-cows. And here, time and again, US escort carrier groups, aided by good intelligence, surprised and destroyed them. Compelled to abandon mid-ocean refuelling, the U-boats' time on patrol became so restricted that their operations were uneconomical and ineffective. The submarine had been completely dominated.

The Battle of the Atlantic could finally be seen to have been won by the Allies. The fruits of the victory gained in May 1943 were now to be gathered as the anti-submarine forces went over to the offensive. Although the U-boats continued to fight with a dogged and desperate courage, their expectation of survival was reduced to one and a half sorties each; though equipment with the *Schnörkel* device greatly reduced the danger from air attack and of being surprised on the surface by night while re-charging their batteries, the U-boat threat was nevertheless reduced to negligible proportions from this time onwards. Never again were they seriously to threaten the vital life-line between Europe and America.

How near the campaign had come to achieving victory for the Germans can perhaps best be judged from the wry admission by Winston Churchill: 'The only thing that ever really frightened me during the war was the U-boat peril.'

Malta: The Island Fortress

The two-and-a-half-year struggle for the Mediterranean from the fall of France in June 1940 to the Allied landings in North Africa in November 1942 was an increasingly desperate one, for on it depended the safety of the convoy routes to North Africa and thus the outcome of the North African campaign. The action increasingly centred on Malta as both Axis and Allies came to see the importance of the island as the key to control of the Mediterranean. The conflict reached a climax in the first months of 1942 with the concentrated bombing attacks by the Axis on Malta and the convoys, all but starving the island into surrender. Its endurance and ability to hit back played a major role in Allied victory.

On Italy's declaration of war on 10th June 1940, Mussolini with typical flamboyance called for 'an offensive at all points in the Mediterranean and outside'. Within hours, Italian aircraft dropped their first loads of bombs on Malta.

For the first three weeks, Malta's only protection came from three Gloster Gladiators which had been removed from their crates and assembled on the island. The three, known as Faith, Hope and Charity, won a permanent name as symbols of Malta's resistance, forcing the Italians to bomb from a higher level and thus lose accuracy, but they could scarcely hope to hold off full-scale bombardment.

The poor state of Malta's defences was the result of pre-war decisions that Malta was indefensible, and should not be defended. Now, reinforcement had to start almost from scratch. By the end of the year, Malta had only fifteen Hurricanes and twenty-eight bombers. It was hardly surprising that Italy lost less than three per cent of the 690,000 tons of shipping running the convoy route to North Africa in 1940.

In the wider context of the Mediterranean war, both sides were evenly matched in surface vessels. But Italy had a huge advantage in submarines and aircraft, and the British suffered from having to cover both the Suez Canal (with the Mediterranean Fleet under Admiral Sir Andrew Cunningham) and Gibraltar (with Force H under Vice-Admiral Sir James Somerville).

They were helped by the timidity of the Italian naval leaders, who held to the need to maintain 'a fleet in being'. This meant attacking only when circumstances were clearly favourable. They appeared never favourable enough: this uncertainty led to Italy's failure to seize the initiative even in 1940 when her fleet could have gained Malta and control of the Mediterranean.

With the Italians unwilling to engage, it was clear that air-power was going to be the decisive factor, and its importance was brought home dramatically to the Italians by two actions—in Taranto and off Cape Matapan—before the Allied withdrawal from Crete in April 1941 focused Axis attention finally on Malta.

In October 1940 three Glen Martin Maryland reconnaissance planes arrived in Malta. They allowed Cunningham to keep watch on the Italian fleet and gave him a chance to realize a plan he had long dreamed of: an attack on that fleet in harbour.

All six Italian battleships were together in Taranto as the British approached on the night of 11th November. Italian reconnaissance reports had been so confused that the Italian commander, Campioni, remained in harbour, vainly waiting for information. In a very short space of time, the twenty-one Swordfish torpedo-bombers, dipping and weaving to avoid the hawsers of barrage balloons and the storm of tracer shells, reduced Italy's serviceable battleships to two, the Vittorio Veneto and the Cesare, for the loss of two aircraft. After Taranto, the mere presence of a carrier was enough to make an Italian naval commander nervous of any engagement.

Four months later, on the night of 27th-28th March, the Italian navy, under German pressure, set out to break the British convoy route to Greece. Iachino, who had replaced Campioni after Taranto, expected Luftwaffe support. None came. Instead, he was taken by surprise by aircraft from the carrier Formidable. The cruiser Pola was damaged, and two other cruisers returning to help her were picked up on British radar and sunk within five minutes. The crew of the Pola, meanwhile, having abandoned ship, found she was not sinking after all, climbed back on board and set about warming themselves—with alcohol. When the British boarded, the Italians were in no state to offer any resistance. They were taken prisoner and the Pola too was sunk.

By this time the Germans had already seen the need for full-scale support in the Mediterranean. By January, about 100 bombers and 25 fighters of X Fliegerkorps had arrived in Sicily from Norway to bring the Axis forces there up to 150 bombers and 100 fighters. The Germans signalled their arrival on 10th January with a dive-bomber attack on the carrier Illustrious.

The Illustrious limped into Malta, and over the next fortnight the Germans launched what are still known as the 'Illustrious raids' to knock out the carrier and the airfields. The exhausted ground crews on Malta were only able to put some ten fighters in the air at any one time against perhaps eighty German aircraft, but the

Clearing the streets of rubble in Valletta after the Opera House had been hit by German bombs

One of Malta's rock-shelters; people would sometimes stay underground for days on end

Illustrious was hit only once. She sailed on the 23rd bound for America for repairs.

Malta now stood in immediate peril of subjection by the Luftwaffe. From February to May 1941 only thirteen ships got through, with some 100,000 tons of supplies.

There was little Malta's bombers could do to prevent the Italian supplies for the Afrika Korps getting through. The Italians even got one of their few congratulatory messages from the Germans for their efforts. With Rommel's successes in March and the German advance down Greece and into Crete, Malta's position seemed more and more hopeless.

Reprieve

But in June Hitler removed aircraft from the Mediterranean to strengthen his attack on Russia, and Malta was given a chance to recover. By mid-August aircraft strength rose to about 130, including 69 Hurricanes.

The second half of 1941 saw an immense improvement in the Allied position. The Axis forces in North Africa needed some 50,000 tons of supplies a month, but in September they lost a quarter en route and in November a staggering sixty per cent. The speed of Auchinleck's Crusader offensive in November was due largely to Malta's domination of the Mediterranean.

But Malta's real test was still to come, and the end of 1941 saw the pendulum swing once more against the Allies. In November, the carrier *Ark Royal* was torpedoed. In December, Force K, a four-vessel reinforcement from Force H, was almost totally destroyed by mines off Malta.

Also in December Hitler redeployed II Fliegerkorps from the Russian front to Sicily and North Africa. Together with X Fliegerkorps, which was responsible for the eastern Mediterranean, it formed Luftflotte 2 under Field-Marshal Kesselring, who could soon call on 500 Stukas, up to 300 Me 109s, and a mass of heavy bombers.

George Cross Island

The Axis once more had a free hand from Crete, Libya, and Sicily to bomb the Allied convoys, and Italian vessels could provide Rommel with the supplies he needed to take the offensive and press on into Egypt.

In February, Malta's serviceable aircraft were down to eleven and the island was reeling under the impact of ten raids a day. Malta had to have more fighter cover and supplies if it was not to be starved into surrender. But any success seemed to call forth increased Axis efforts.

On 23rd March, two freighters, *Talabot* and *Pampas*, the survivors of a four-vessel convoy, came steaming through bomb splashes to a delirious welcome from Malta's inhabitants thronging the harbour walls. Kesselring, however, had assured Hitler he would 'wipe Malta off the map' and he

directed over 300 bombers to destroy the two freighters. In three days of ceaseless attack, they succeeded. Only 5,000 of the 20,000 tons which had left Alexandria with the convoy was unloaded before the *Talabot* and *Pampas* were sunk in harbour.

The idea of reinforcement seemed hopeless, and Malta was slowly starving. A soldier on active service was supposed to get 4,000 calories a day; in Malta the average was now half that, with a bread ration of ten ounces. Communal—or 'Victory'—kitchens were set up in which goat stew became the staple diet.

It was in recognition of the island's spirit of endurance and defiance that on 15th April a simple message arrived for the governor of Malta: 'To honour her brave People I award the George Cross to the Island Fortress of Malta to bear witness to a Heroism and Devotion that will long be famous in History. George R.I.'

The pendulum began to swing finally against the Axis on 9th May when sixty Spitfires landed from the carriers *Wasp* and *Eagle*. The next day, just when Kesselring was reporting the neutralization of Malta, his raiders were met by a superior force for the first time in months.

But there had to be aid from outside. In June a massive double operation from both ends of the Mediterranean set out to end Malta's permanent fuel and food crisis. Five freighters and a tanker were to come from the west (Operation Harpoon) and eleven freighters from the east (Operation Vigorous). Its tragic results showed how hopeless was the task of running convoys with inadequate air cover.

The convoy from the east was an utter failure. Movement and counter-movement in 'Bomb Alley' between Crete and Africa took their toll of ammunition, and the whole convoy had to turn about and return to base, with the loss of several freighters and warships. But the Italian admiral, da Zara, misjudged the path of the western convoy and two freighters escaped the devastating Axis air attacks to deliver their 15,000 tons of supplies to Malta. Without them, Malta would undoubtedly have fallen. Of the seventeen supply ships loaded for Malta, covered by eighty-two warships, just two had got through and six had been lost.

But by July, the siege was nearing its end. Fighters shot down sixty-five Axis aircraft for the loss of only thirty-six Spitfires. The submarines returned, and seven Axis supply ships were sunk.

The failure of the Axis powers in the siege can be ascribed to lack of consistent planning. It was never clear whether the island was to be subdued by bombardment, by assault, or by starvation. Too frequently policies were changed and other demands intervened allowing the Allies to recover.

A landing had in fact been tentatively

planned for July by the Axis, but by this time the operation would have involved enormous losses. Malta's coasts were defended with thickets of barbed wire and three lines of concrete strong points had been built inland. Rommel's successes in North Africa seemed to make a landing unnecessary and it was postponed.

By August, the Allies were beginning to dominate the Mediterranean theatre. Thirty-eight per cent of all Rommel's supplies were being lost en route. But Malta had only enough fuel and food to last a month; the time had come for a final effort to raise the siege. By 10th August, Operation Pedestal was ready: fifty-nine warships were to escort fourteen merchant ships from Gibraltar to Malta. Lying in wait for the convoy were twenty-one Axis submarines and some 800 aircraft.

The first blow was the torpedoing of the carrier *Eagle*, which sank within eight minutes taking 200 of her crew with her. The heavy ships turned back as planned on the 12th, and immediately a night of chaos began. Axis MTBs surged to within fifty yards of their prey, sweeping decks with automatic fire, while Allied vessels steamed in all directions to avoid torpedoes as best they could. By morning on the 13th there were just seven merchantmen left. One of them was the tanker *Ohio*, lying dead in the water with her vital 11,000 tons of fuel, awaiting a tow over the last ninety miles to Valletta. The following day two more freighters were sunk, but four of the scattered fleet arrived in Malta. The Italian navy, deprived of air cover by the German demand that fighters should accompany the Luftwaffe bombers, was deterred from any attacks by a massive display of air strength from Malta.

It took forty-eight hours to tow the sinking *Ohio* to Grand Harbour, and having discharged her cargo she lay immovable in the harbour until she was expended as an RAF gunnery target in 1946.

Stocktaking after Pedestal showed that Malta could hold out until December, at a pinch. But even with the Allied victories of October and November in North Africa, there was no sign of relief, and discussion started on how the island's surrender was to be made known. It was not until 17th November that the last convoy, codenamed Stoneage, sailed from Port Said. It entered Malta on the night of 19th-20th November without interference, and the siege was finally over. The balance of power had passed to the Allies, now pouring troops into the western Mediterranean following the Torch landings, and Malta was free to back the invasion of Sicily in July 1943.

Rommel had prophesied in February 1941: 'Without Malta, the Axis will end by losing control of North Africa.' He had now been proved right.

Desert Victory

Even before Italy entered the war in June 1940, the Mediterranean and the Balkans to the north had loomed large in British strategic thinking. In addition to the great importance of keeping the Mediterranean open as a route to India and the Far East, it was recognized that a hold on the Middle East was vital to the retention of Persian oil; while the Balkans, which provided an important part of German oil imports, was an area which should be denied to the enemy as soon as possible. Thus the encouragement of subversion in the Balkans and the retention, at the least, of Turkish neutrality were among the first objectives of British policy. On the American entry into the war, this strategy was confirmed at a conference at Washington in December 1941, code-named 'Arcadia', when it was decided that one of the primary aims should be to 'close and tighten the ring around Germany', the southern sector of which was to run along the North African coast, from where attacks across the Mediterranean were to be launched. While the American military authorities agreed with this strategy, they were critical of what they believed to be a leisurely British

approach to the ultimate invasion of north-western Europe and the defeat of Germany, and they looked upon operations such as those projected in the Mediterranean as politically motivated diversions from the main objective. Possibly the British, with memories both of the Somme and Passchendaele and of defeat in France in 1940, were slow and unenthusiastic, but they were realists and the American suspicions were not fully justified.

In November 1942 the first effective steps to occupy the whole of the North African shore and thus complete the southern sector of the ring around Germany were taken, in the east by 8th Army under Montgomery, which after ten days hard fighting broke through the Axis lines at El Alamein on 4th November and in the west by 'Operation Torch', the Allied invasion of north-west Africa which was launched on 8th November. In the centre, Malta still hung on precariously—four ships out of a convoy of fourteen (Operation Pedestal) had reached the island in August—while the bases in Egypt and Gibraltar were secure. There were fears of a German attack on Spain as a result of Operation

Men of US 1st Division disembark in Morocco from Royal Navy landing craft. All Allied forces landed quickly in the face of only slight Vichy French resistance

Torch and the ensuing neutralization of Gibraltar, but General Franco preserved his neutrality and Gibraltar was able to handle the vast mass of ships, stores, and aircraft needed for the operation.

Operation Torch had been forced on the reluctant Combined Chiefs of Staff by Roosevelt and Churchill who were determined that their pledge to Stalin of a 'second front in 1942' would be redeemed. The US Joint Chiefs of Staff never lost their dislike for the operation which they regarded, rightly, as likely to delay the invasion of north-west Europe until 1944; the British chiefs of staff, however, soon became enthusiastic supporters. An American, Lieutenant-General Dwight D. Eisenhower, was placed in supreme command with a British naval commander, Admiral Sir Andrew Cunningham, under him. The air forces, contrary to all experience up to date, were split into national components, each under its own commander, while the commanders of the land forces for all three initial landings were to be American generals until their forces, once ashore, combined to form 1st Army under Lieutenant-General Sir Kenneth Anderson. Major-General Mark Clark, an American, was appointed deputy commander.

An American task force was to attack Casablanca, while combined Anglo-American task forces were to attack Algiers and Oran. At the latter American troops were to land first as it was thought that the French would welcome the Americans and resist the British. The British chiefs of staff believed that the Bône-Bougie area should have been the target of one of the task forces rather than Casablanca, but caution prevailed; indeed, at one stage, the American planners envisaged landing only in Morocco and fighting their way eastwards overland, because of the dangers of passing the Straits of Gibraltar.

In the event French resistance was spasmodic, the chance presence of Admiral Darlan, the Commander-in-Chief of the French Armed Forces, proving a strong influence in favour of capitulation. All three task forces landed quickly with few casualties or material losses, despite the lack of training and experience of many of those engaged, and by 11th November an armistice had been signed and preparations for the move east towards Bizerta and Tunis under way.

The landings came as a complete surprise. Only one submarine attack was made on the vast fleets and the Italian surface ships were 'grounded' by lack of fuel, but the German reaction was quick and effective. Troops moved into the unoccupied zone of France early on 11th November and simultaneously strong forces were flown to Bizerta where the airfield had been occupied on 9th November while Italian

troops advanced from Tripolitania. So, despite the landing of a British brigade at Bougie on 11th November and the capture of Bône airfield by British paratroops the following day, the Germans with remarkable efficiency and flexibility, and, aided by the weather and the terrain, were able to stabilize a line in the mountains west of the Tunisian plains in early December. Allied hopes of capturing Tunis and Bizerta by Christmas were thus frustrated.

The Mareth Line

The stalemate was doubly disappointing as 1st Army had been so close to victory. But much had gone well. The intricate organization required had been effective and it had proved possible to form integrated staffs of American and British officers. Spain had not interfered, and French troops, re-armed with Allied equipment, were fighting the Germans. That a little more boldness in the original concept of the operation would almost certainly have allowed the capture of Tunisia by the new year must not mask the quick and competent German reaction to the landings which surprised the intelligence experts. One unexpected side effect had been the scuttling of the French fleet at Toulon on 27th November 1942, but this tragedy at least ensured, as Darlan had always promised, that the ships would not fall into the hands of the Germans.

Meanwhile Rommel had been conducting a well organized fighting retreat from Alamein, harried by impossible directives from Hitler which if obeyed would have meant the destruction of his army. A succession of well-known names filled the newspaper headlines, places which had often changed hands more than once such as Mersa Matruh, Sidi Barrani, Bardia, Tobruk, Derna, Benghazi, Agedabia, and finally El Agheila, where Rommel made his first serious stand on 12th December. All attempts to cut off the Afrika Korps during the long chase across the desert failed and Rommel's skilful disengagements retained his forces almost intact. The pursuit was vigorous, but most of the British, Australian, New Zealand, and Indian troops had been there before and some were looking over their shoulders for the Rommel magic which would cut them off and send them reeling back. But when Montgomery broke through at El Agheila, it was clear that this time there would be no recovery. Logistical problems made the pursuit difficult and the whole of one corps had to be withdrawn from the line to help with the transport of supplies. Ports were quickly reopened and supplies started to flow by sea, but the pace of the advance was determined as much by logistics as by enemy resistance. Rommel withdrew from El Agheila on 18th December and the

retreat continued, with checks at Buerat, on the Homs-Taruna line, and outside Tripoli, which fell to Montgomery on 23rd January 1943. By 24th February the Afrika Korps had withdrawn behind the formidable Mareth Line on the boundary between Tunisia and Tripolitania, detaching some formations to counter-attack successfully the American troops that were threatening its rear.

Throughout January and February 1943, the Germans in Tunisia under the command of Colonel-General Dietloff Jürgen von Arnim were building up to a strength of 100,000 men and continued doggedly to counter-attack the Allied forces. The Allied command was unsatisfactory; the French refused to take orders from the British, and Anglo-American co-operation was not good. None of the lessons of the use of tactical aircraft in the land battle which had been learned at such cost in the desert were being applied in Tunisia and it was only when 8th Army and the desert air force joined in that land-air co-operation became satisfactory. Moreover, the training and experience of most of the troops was inferior to that of the Germans. By early February, Rommel, with his main force behind the Mareth Line, took a hand in the Tunisian battle, bringing with him a strong detachment of the Afrika Korps. On 14th February Rommel and Arnim launched a major attack, from the southeast and east respectively. It had considerable initial success, capturing a number of important features, including the Kasserine Pass. On 19th February, General Alexander, who had been placed in command of both 8th and 1st Armies, found a most confused situation and took over personal command of all the Allied forces in Tunisia. After some bitter fighting, the Allied line held and Rommel's dream of cutting off 1st Army by a thrust to the coast faded. But the battle had been close and had shattered Allied complacency.

The end in North Africa was now inevitable. Between 20th and 28th March, 8th Army fought the Battle of Mareth against tenacious opponents who managed to withdraw in good order. On 6th April, 8th Army crossed the Wadi Akarit after another tough fight and by 28th April it had attacked the Afrika Korps at Enfidaville without success. It had now joined up with 1st Army and the ring around Tunis and Bizerta was complete. Alexander had been watching a series of unco-ordinated attacks by both armies and now stepped in, halting the attack at Enfidaville and then, on 30th April, transferring two of the best divisions in

Right: General George Patton, the brash American tank expert who broke on to the scene after the landings in North Africa

Closing the Ring

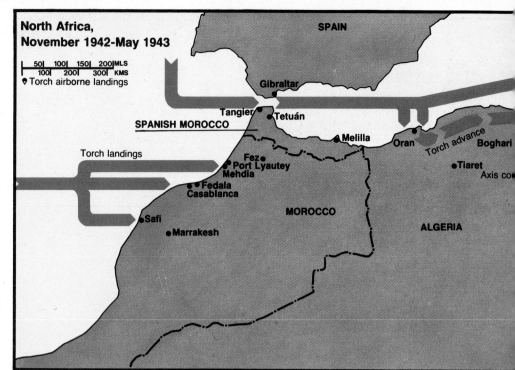

North Africa, November 1942–May 1943

50 100 150 200 MLS
100 200 300 KMS
Torch airborne landings

SPAIN
Gibraltar
Tangier
SPANISH MOROCCO
Tetuán
Melilla
Oran
Torch advance
Boghari
Torch landings
Fez
Port Lyautey
Mehdia
Fedala
Casablanca
Tiaret
Axis co
Safi
MOROCCO
Marrakesh
ALGERIA
Axis col

8th Army to join in the attack from the centre of the line opposite Bizerta and Tunis. The effect of this concentration was immediate. On 7th May, Tunis and Bizerta were captured and with the end of Axis resistance on 13th May, Alexander was able to report to Churchill: 'We are masters of the North African shore.' The Germans who had fought so bitterly to the end now surrendered meekly, most of those who escaped being destroyed at sea by the Royal Navy which obeyed its task of executing Cunningham's signal: 'Sink, burn, and destroy. Let nothing pass.' Some 240,000 German and Italian prisoners had been taken with great stores of weapons and equipment. On 20th May, a convoy reached Alexandria and one of the main Allied objectives, that of opening the Mediterranean, had been achieved.

The next move

Since the autumn of 1942, a continual debate had been carried on between the British and American planners on the next step after the capture of the North African shore. Many possibilities had been canvassed—ranging from landings in the south of France, the capture of Crete and the Dodecanese, landings in the Balkans, to the establishment of a stabilized 'defensive encircling line' and the transfer of the main forces to Great Britain to prepare for an invasion of north-west Europe in 1943. Generally, the Americans, supported by Churchill, who wanted to keep up the pressure in the Mediterranean and Middle East, were pressing for invasion in 1943 while the British chiefs of staff believed that it would not be possible to mount a successful invasion that year and that momentum in the Mediterranean must be maintained by further attacks to the northwards. The differences were serious and there was a danger that the Americans would divert forces to the Pacific, thus ignoring the 'Germany first' principle. Indeed, fifteen groups of aircraft destined for the British theatre of war were sent to the Pacific and the build-up of land forces in Great Britain slowed down.

However, at the Casablanca Conference in January 1943 it was agreed to attack Sicily in the summer and from then on, although nothing else was agreed and the Allied chiefs of staff did not want to land on the mainland, the Italian campaign became inevitable.

Above: The end in North Africa. Allied forces advancing from Morocco, Algeria, and Egypt roll up the Axis. But final victory was not gained until bitter German resistance in Tunisia had been overwhelmed. Below: Operation Torch. In a painting by Richard Eurich the vast invasion fleet steams for its objectives

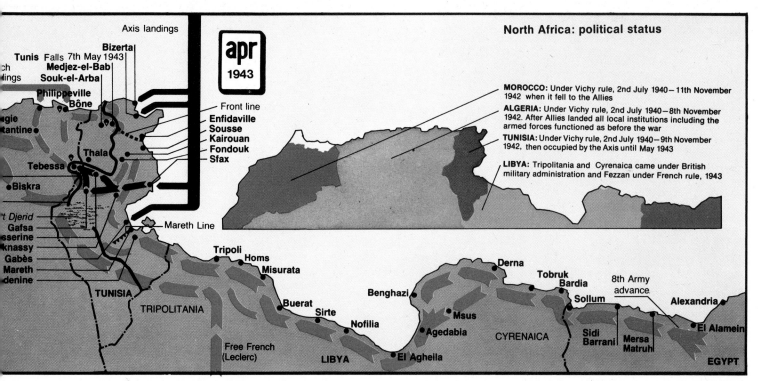

Axis landings

Bizerta
Tunis Falls 7th May 1943
Medjez-el-Bab
Souk-el-Arba
Philippeville
Bône

ch
dings

gie
tantine

Thala

Tebessa

Biskra

t Djerid
Gafsa
sserine
knassy
Gabès
Mareth
denine

TUNISIA

Mareth Line

Front line
Enfidaville
Sousse
Kairouan
Fondouk
Sfax

apr
1943

North Africa: political status

MOROCCO: Under Vichy rule, 2nd July 1940—11th November 1942 when it fell to the Allies
ALGERIA: Under Vichy rule, 2nd July 1940—8th November 1942. After Allies landed all local institutions including the armed forces functioned as before the war
TUNISIA: Under Vichy rule, 2nd July 1940—9th November 1942, then occupied by the Axis until May 1943
LIBYA: Tripolitania and Cyrenaica came under British military administration and Fezzan under French rule, 1943

Tripoli
Homs
Misurata

TRIPOLITANIA

Buerat
Sirte
Nofilia

Free French
(Leclerc)

LIBYA

Benghazi

Msus

Agedabia

El Agheila

Derna

Tobruk
Bardia

Sollum

CYRENAICA

Sidi
Barrani

8th Army
advance

Alexandria

El Alamein

Mersa
Matruh

EGYPT

Italy: The Hard Underbelly

The Italian campaign was born of compromise, continued in discord, and ended in controversy. From its beginning in July 1943 to its end in May 1945, it was the pawn between opposing British and American concepts of war. The Americans, confident in their immense material resources and true to their own military tradition, favoured frontal attack. If war was the science of military victory, then Germany should be attacked by the shortest and most direct route: across the Channel. Overlord therefore came first on the list of American priorities in Europe; Italy was regarded as a tiresome division.

The British, forced to rely on smaller resources and schooled by long experience as a naval power, preferred a more indirect approach. Churchill believed that Italy, the 'soft underbelly of the Axis', was the ideal target. An Allied military presence there would be the best way of maintaining a threat to the Balkans and causing Hitler to disperse his forces. But there is evidence Churchill also looked beyond the moment of victory for the direction which military planning should take during the war. Fearing post-war Soviet domination of South-East Europe, he saw Austria and the Balkans as the ultimate objectives of the Italian campaign.

These strategic differences at the highest level dictated the course of the whole campaign. They became clear at the Casablanca Conference between Churchill and Roosevelt and their staffs which began on 14th January 1943. This has become celebrated as the moment when the words 'unconditional surrender' entered the Allied war vocabulary. More significant were its strategic decisions. Now that victory in North Africa was in sight, an answer had to be found to the question: what next? The answer was to invade Sicily. This was no easy decision. The Americans were brought to it unwillingly, and then only as a strategic conclusion to the North African campaign, with the aim of clearing the Mediterranean sea route. Eisenhower argued that if the aim was to invade Italy in strength, the proper objectives were Sardinia and Corsica. But no agreement could be reached about Italy, and therefore no commitment was made to move beyond Sicily for the time being. However, while the Americans intended to stop there, the British, on the other hand, hoped to go on.

The invasion of Sicily (Operation Husky) was a thoroughly well-planned operation. The planning began in February, but without the direct supervision of the commanders, who were still engaged in North Africa. The Supreme Commander was to be an American, General Eisenhower, but direct conduct of the fighting was assigned to the British. General Alexander became commander of 15th Army Group, consisting of 7th US Army and 8th British Army; Admiral Cunningham was the naval commander, and Air Chief Marshal Tedder the air commander. When they were finally able to pay more attention to Husky in April, a number of changes were made to the provisional plan. There were two reasons for this. First General Montgomery, commander of 8th Army, buttonholed General Bedell Smith, Eisenhower's chief of staff (in a lavatory), and persuaded him of the superiority of his own plan. Second, and more decisive, was the emergence of the DUKW, a six-wheeled amphibious lorry, and the LST (landing ship for tanks). These were now available for the first time, and their specifications convinced Alexander that he could rely on maintenance over open beaches—in defiance of the orthodox doctrine of amphibious warfare. He therefore adopted a plan which he had originally favoured himself and which was the same plan as that proposed so assiduously by Montgomery. This envisaged a concentrated attack by 7th and 8th Armies on the south-eastern end of the island.

Husky was the largest amphibious attack mounted by the Allies in the Second World War. Eight divisions were put ashore during the initial assault compared with only five during the same phase of the Normandy landings eleven months later. Nearly 3,000 ships and landing-craft took part, starting from places as far away as Suez, Tunisia, Algiers, and even Scotland. One division came direct from the United States, staging only at Oran. Malta served admirably as army and navy headquarters, and its airfields were packed with as many aircraft as they could absorb. On the night of the invasion, 10th July 1943, a storm blew up and seemed to threaten the success of the operation. In fact, apart from making them seasick, it proved a positive advantage to the seaborne invaders, for it caused the Italian coastal divisions to relax their vigil. The troops achieved complete surprise and mostly landed unopposed. But the airborne assault, intended to capture certain key road junctions and bridges, suffered considerably from the bad weather. More than a third of the gliders landed in the sea,

Left: Americans in Tunis with their prisoner, a Luftwaffe officer. Victory in North Africa was the jumping-off stage for the invasion of southern Italy. Right: Troops of the British 8th Army wade ashore in Sicily

189

and American parachute troops were scattered all over southern Sicily.

The plan now was for Montgomery to drive to Messina at top speed in order to cut off the two German and nine Italian divisions on the island from their escape route into the toe of Italy. This danger was not lost on the Axis garrison, and although he quickly captured Syracuse, Montgomery was soon held up in the malarial plain of Catania by strong German reinforcements. He therefore transferred his main thrust to a left hook round Mount Etna, the active volcano which dominates the eastern end of the island. Meanwhile, US 7th Army was making good progress further west. Palermo fell on 22nd July and by the beginning of August General Patton was advancing along the northern coastal road towards Messina at high speed. This, combined with Montgomery's left hook round Mount Etna, quickly led to the evacuation of the German garrison (most of the Italians had surrendered by the end of July) and on 17th August Patton's forces entered Messina. Montgomery arrived from the south shortly afterwards. The island had been taken in only thirty-eight days.

Italy knocked out of the war

Further up the Italian peninsula these dramatic events had been having repercussions. Plots against Mussolini had begun to hatch as early as November 1942. Now they gathered momentum. On 24th July, at an extraordinary meeting of the Fascist Grand Council, the Duce received a stunning vote of no confidence. The next day the King had him arrested and driven away in an ambulance. Marshal Badoglio, one of the chief conspirators, took over the government and declared his intention to continue the war. Few people took him seriously. Already on 15th August the first official peace feeler was extended. Unfortunately for the new government, the Germans had moved in quickly to take control of the country, and a capitulation augured ill for their own safety. The negotiations therefore centred on the arrangement of an Allied attack to coincide with the announcement of surrender.

The successful operations in Sicily and the fall of Mussolini encouraged those who favoured an all-out campaign in Italy. At the Quebec Conference (code-named 'Quadrant') in August the Americans agreed to a landing in Italy, but at a price. The priority of Overlord was re-affirmed and the British were forced to agree to a landing in southern France. Soon after the conquest of Sicily, the hard realities of life in a secondary

High in the Apennines, two German soldiers watch an Italian farmhouse burn. The mountain ranges of Italy provided defensive positions of great strength

theatre began to dawn. Eight of the best divisions, four American, four British, were ordered back to Great Britain in preparation for Overlord, and Eisenhower was informed that he could expect the number of landing craft at his disposal to dwindle. The forces remaining in the theatre were assigned the role of containing the maximum number of German divisions. In fulfilment of this aim, the next objectives were to be the airfields of Foggia, from which the bombing of Germany could be stepped up, and the port of Naples.

On 3rd September an entirely new phase of the Italian campaign opened. Operation Baytown was launched and Montgomery slipped unobtrusively across the Straits of Messina to Reggio on the toe of Italy. This was the first time an Allied army had set foot on the continent since Dunkirk. 'It is a great day,' wrote Montgomery to Sir Alan Brooke. But privately he was less enthusiastic. He had been told of no master plan for Italy, and indeed there was none. From now on, in comparison with Husky, operations were conducted off the cuff. Montgomery began to push on up the mountainous toe of Italy.

Meanwhile, negotiations with the Italians had been maturing, though for a moment there seemed to be danger of a hitch. On 8th September at 6.30 p.m. General Eisenhower announced the surrender of Italy over Algiers radio. Badoglio was due to broadcast at the same time, but Rome radio continued to play operatic selections. There were fears of a double-cross, but finally about an hour later the expected announcement was made and Italy was out of the war. However, the Germans in Italy quickly took over control, disarmed the Italians, and prepared for a defensive campaign.

The Allies now staged their part of the surrender agreement: Operation Avalanche. On 8th-9th September US 5th Army under General Mark Clark landed on the beaches of Salerno. Having just heard the news of the armistice, the troops expected little resistance. But Field-Marshal Kesselring, the German commander, deployed his forces with lightning rapidity. For eight days the Allied army fought with its back to the sea against heavy counter-attacks. Reinforcements were hurriedly brought in, but the most notable part of the Allied recovery was the success of naval gunfire against troops. Admiral Cunningham ordered in the battleships *Warspite* and *Valiant*, and their 16-inch salvoes proved highly effective against the Germans. By the 15th the leading elements of Montgomery's 8th Army were only fifty miles away and the Allied bridgehead was firmly secured. The Germans fell back.

Simultaneously with Avalanche another operation had been launched against the heel of Italy. This was Slapstick, the in-vasion of Taranto. British 1st Airborne Division was transported in Admiral Cunningham's battle fleet straight into Taranto harbour. This unorthodox action was a success, though a cruiser with more than 200 men aboard was sunk by a mine. The Allies were now firmly ashore at three points in southern Italy: Reggio, Salerno, and Taranto. By 1st October both Foggia and Naples were in Allied hands and the first major objectives of the Italian campaign had been achieved. Corsica and Sardinia had been evacuated. The Italian fleet had surrendered and Admiral Cunningham had sent his famous signal to the Admiralty: 'Be pleased to inform their Lordships that the Italian fleet is anchored under the guns of the fortress of Malta.'

On 12th September there occurred a dramatic event. Mussolini was rescued from the hotel which served as his prison in the Gran Sasso d'Italia. On Hitler's orders Captain Otto Skorzeny of the Waffen SS landed by glider with a force of shock-troops and after a daring escape flew the Duce to Munich. Here Mussolini received his orders from Hitler and returned to Italy as the ineffective puppet leader of the Salò Republic. Although a few Italian divisions continued to serve by the side of Germany, Mussolini's rump Fascist state posed no real threat to the Allies.

Hitler reacts

The consensus of opinion at the Cairo Conference in November was that only modest objectives should now be attempted in Italy. The desirability of reaching the Po during the winter was acknowledged, but to achieve this, it was agreed, would mean withholding so many troops and so much equipment that the cross-Channel operation would not be possible in the spring of 1944. Therefore the shipment of troops and equipment to England continued.

At about this time, apart from the onset of winter, another event occurred which ensured a slower pace in Italy. This was Hitler's sudden decision to appoint Kesselring rather than Rommel Commander-in-Chief South-West and to stop withdrawing up the leg of Italy. Instead Kesselring was to make a stand south of Rome.

The German's winter position, the Gustav Line, was a formidable barrier, and the most formidable part of its defences was Monte Cassino, crowned with a famous sixth-century Benedictine monastery. Until Cassino had been forced, the Liri valley which was the key to Rome was denied to the Allies, and Cassino defied every attempt to blast it into submission. While Clark's US 5th Army struggled across the Volturno and moved up towards Cassino, the western bastion of the Gustav Line, Montgomery's British 8th Army prepared to assault the eastern defences on the River Sangro. In late

Closing the Ring

November he pushed across the river against fierce resistance and in bad weather. Heavy rain turned streams into torrents, roads into mud. The cold became intense. Montgomery's assault was soon held up and by Christmas Day 1943 the Allies were halted along the length of the Gustav Line.

At that time a new amphibious operation came under discussion. Rather than crawl up the leg of Italy 'like a harvest bug', in Churchill's phrase, the obvious tactic was to mount amphibious hooks along the vulnerable flanks of the peninsula. Here a direct conflict arose with Overlord, for such operations depended on landing craft earmarked for the Normandy landings. However, a landing at Anzio was now proposed and in Tunis Churchill managed to persuade Eisenhower, newly appointed to command the Normandy landings, to postpone the departure of this shipping.

At Anzio, complete tactical surprise was achieved. The first the Germans knew of the operation was the report on 22nd January from a fighter pilot that a full-scale invasion was in progress. This was six hours after the first landings by 6th Corps. However, this initial advantage was lost by the failure of the commander, General Lucas, to strike out of the bridgehead. Equally, Kesselring was once again quick in throwing together reinforcements. When Lucas eventually did strike out, he was held up, and on 3rd February subjected to a heavy counter-attack. Anzio convinced Hitler that the Allies meant business in Italy. His reaction, to send two new divisions to eliminate the bridgehead, was a success for the official Allied intention to tie down as many German forces as possible in Italy. General Truscott replaced General Lucas just in time to parry a major counter-offensive, imposing a heavy defeat on the Germans. However, this was not until 6th March, more than six weeks and 19,000 Allied dead after the first landings. Even then there was no breakout until 23rd May.

Meanwhile, renewed attacks on Cassino had failed. The Air Force now offered to help out by dropping 1,100 tons of high explosives on the monastery which was wrongly believed to be occupied by the Germans. In fact it was still occupied by the abbot and his monks who were inside when bombing began. The monastery was reduced

Right: Three stages in the Italian campaign. 1 Salerno, 9th September. Infantry of US 5th Army dash onto the beaches during Operation Avalanche. A tough, bitter fight awaited them. 2 Cassino, end of May. Allied mopping-up patrol clears all that remains of the town. 3 Rome, 5th June: Lieutenant-General Clark (left), commander US 5th Army, and Major-General Truscott, Commander US 6th Corps, arrive at the Capitol to take over the city

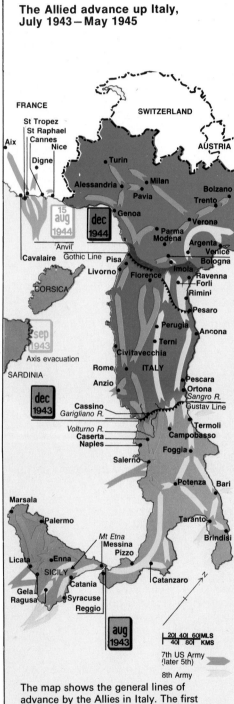

The Allied advance up Italy, July 1943 – May 1945

The map shows the general lines of advance by the Allies in Italy. The first two rounds ended with winter stalemates, and the third in victory. In the first, the Allies captured Sicily and drove the Germans back to their winter position south of Rome, the Gustav Line. By this time Corsica and Sardinia had been evacuated. In the second round the Allies broke the Gustav Line, took Rome, and drove swiftly on until the loss of forces to Anvil and the onset of winter halted their advance half-way across the Gothic Line. The third round saw the rapid pursuit and defeat of the German armies

to powder, but Cassino still held out.

It was impossible to break out from Anzio because there were no longer any landing craft available to bring in necessary reinforcements. They had returned to England for Overlord. Another attempt had to be made in the Cassino area. Alexander therefore thinned out the forces on the Adriatic front, bringing the bulk of 8th Army temporarily over to the west, and built up formidable forces between Cassino and the sea. Their presence was carefully camouflaged. After successfully persuading Kesselring that he intended to launch an amphibious attack on Civitavecchia, on 11th May Alexander threw thirteen divisions, consisting of both 8th and 5th Armies, against the unsuspecting Germans. On 17th May Monte Cassino was finally evacuated and 8th Army rolled forward up the Liri valley. On the 23rd Truscott broke out of the Anzio bridgehead and joined up with 5th Army two days later. X and XIV German Armies, retreating before 8th Army, were now threatened with envelopment, but instead of attempting to cut them off, Clark drove straight for Rome which he entered triumphantly on 4th June, two days before the D-Day landings.

For the Allies there seemed to be every chance of driving over the Apennines and across the Po before the summer was out. Alexander hoped to be into Hungary or Austria by autumn, an achievement which would have had profound effects on postwar Europe. However, it was now time for the Allies to fulfil their pledge to mount an invasion of southern France. This was Anvil, later named Dragoon. Seven divisions, three American and four French, were withdrawn from Alexander's Italian front at a time when operations there held out every promise of success. Kesselring was given a vital breathing space. Anvil went in on 15th August, meeting very little resistance. Strategically it had little effect, except to accelerate the arrival of the German Riviera garrison in front of Eisenhower's forces attacking from Normandy.

At the same time that Alexander was losing seven divisions Kesselring was gaining eight. Soon the Allied advance beyond Rome would have to slow down. Once established in the formidable Gothic Line, astride the Apennines, Kesselring could look south with confidence.

The Allied plan for assaulting the Gothic Line demanded that 5th Army should strike in the centre towards Bologna while 8th Army would make for the flat ground on the other side of the Apennines. The attack opened on 25th August. Four days later 8th Army was sweeping through the eastern defences. But Kesselring, as always, acted swiftly, bringing up reinforcements from the centre. He was aided by two days of torrential rain. On 8th September, however,

5th Army mounted an attack in the denuded centre simultaneously with a further attack by 8th Army on the right. 8th Indian Division succeeded in breaking the line and came within ten miles of Imola. 8th Army also broke the line and debouched on to the plain of the Romagna, entering Rimini on 20th September.

On the 20th the rains began. Rivers turned into brown torrents, roads and bridges disappeared. Infantry and armour foundered in a sea of mud. In addition, ammunition became scarce. The Allied armies had lost momentum, and once more faced a winter stalemate. 5th Army came to halt in the mountains just south of Bologna at the end of October, 8th Army in December with the capture of Ravenna and Forli.

The winter stalemate lasted until April 1945. The final battles in Italy were a fine example of strategic skill. During the winter Alexander had lost five more divisions to northern Europe and now had only seventeen against twenty-three German and four Italian. Yet on 9th April 8th Army launched an attack in amphibious vehicles across Lake Comacchio, to the east of Argenta, and by 23rd April both 5th and 8th Armies were across the Po and pursuing the remnants of Vietinghoff's X Army northwards. Two days later the Italian partisans rose in general insurrection but the Germans were already beaten. On 28th April Mussolini was executed and the following day the German forces in Italy signed an instrument of unconditional surrender at Caserta. Resistance ceased on 2nd May. This unilateral capitulation is generally considered to have shortened the war in Europe by several weeks.

But this was only a minor contribution to the Allied victory in Europe. Was there also a more significant contribution? It is often believed that because the Western powers did not beat the Russians to Vienna—Churchill's dream—the Italian campaign failed. This is not so. Such an outcome would have been a bonus to what was essentially a holding operation. The most that can be claimed for the Italian campaign is that had it not taken place German strength on the Channel front would have been even greater. On a broader perspective, of the 127 German divisions covering the long arc from Norway to Greece twenty-two, scarcely more than a sixth, were directly held down by operations in Italy at the time of D-Day. The thirty Allied divisions employed to do this represented an expensive investment with a relatively poor return.

But this should not obscure the achievement of the Allied armies which fought with such determination during the long struggle in Italy, receiving the first surrender of a great German army group on the continent.

D-Day

To uninitiated Frenchmen the second half of a verse by Verlaine transmitted by the BBC at 2115 on Monday 5th June 1944 meant nothing. But to the resistance *'Blessent mon coeur d'une langueur monotone'* concealed a message they had longed to hear: more than three and a half million Allied troops were poised to invade and liberate France in one of the greatest amphibious operations in history.

Although Stalin had urged the creation of a second front in France ever since the German invasion of the Soviet Union, proposals for an attack on Brest or Cherbourg in 1942 and the liberation of France in 1943 never developed. In fact planning for a mighty cross-Channel assault on Hitler's *Festung Europa* (Fortress Europe) did not begin until the Casablanca Conference in January 1943 when it was resolved to set up a joint Anglo-American staff to attend to the multiplicity of problems involved in such a massive and hazardous venture. The conception of a full-scale invasion of France was confirmed at the Washington Conference in May 1943 and code-named 'Operation Overlord', it was set for 1st May 1944.

Three months later Lieutenant-General Sir Frederick Morgan, who led the Allied team with the designation Chief of Staff to the Supreme Allied Commander (COSSAC), submitted a tentative plan to the Quebec Conference, and although Churchill suggested a twenty-five per cent increase in the forces employed, its proposals were approved. At the end of the year the appointment of General Dwight D. Eisenhower as Supreme Allied Commander for Operation Overlord was announced. Within the space of one year a relatively unknown chief of staff of an American army training in Texas, whose promotion had been consistently slow, had become the Allied commander-in-chief of a daunting military array charged with striking into the heartland of Germany and destroying her armed forces. It was an inspired choice. The Supreme Commander may not have been a great soldier but the great soldiers of his day willingly served him. Universally trusted, he won the affection, respect, and loyalty not only of his men but of political and military leaders alike. But his greatest contribution to victory undoubtedly lay in his very real ability to allay inter-Service rivalry and

Men of the 1st South Lancashire Battalion help wounded comrades ashore during their comparatively easy landing on Sword beach, 6th June 1944

international prejudice among the forces under his command. It was a gift that enabled him to weld together the Allied armies in the field and forge a weapon which the Germans, distracted by their mortal struggle in the east, were unable to deflect.

The remainder of Eisenhower's team was speedily selected. Air Chief Marshal Sir Arthur Tedder was appointed as his deputy, and General Walter Bedell Smith became his chief of staff, with General Sir Frederick Morgan as his deputy. Admiral Sir Bertram Ramsay, the mastermind of Dunkirk and Air Chief Marshal Sir Trafford Leigh-Mallory had been appointed earlier as the commanders-in-chief of the Allied naval and air forces respectively. There was no parallel appointment of commander-in-chief for Allied land forces and although Eisenhower expressed a preference for General Alexander, 'a friendly and companionable type', Churchill felt he could not be spared as Commander in Chief Allied Armies in Italy and consequently Sir Bernard Montgomery handed over command of the 8th Army to assume command of the British 21st Army Group with operational control of all land forces during the initial phase of Operation Overlord. When he was first shown the COSSAC plan for the invasion of France and asked for his comments by Churchill, Montgomery replied that he considered the initial assault forces too weak and the proposed frontage of assault too narrow. The Supreme Commander thus requested the dynamic, and supremely confident general to make his first task the revision of the plan in co-operation with Ramsay, Leigh-Mallory, and Bedell Smith.

COSSAC had proposed the area between Grandcamp and Caen in the Bay of the Seine for the assault. The choice of location, confined by the effective range of the Spitfire to the coast between Flushing and Cherbourg, had to possess harbours capable of handling an immense concentration of men and matériel besides beaches across which the assault forces could be reinforced before ports could be captured. Although the Pas de Calais area offered many obvious advantages such as good air support and a quick turn round for shipping it was formidably defended and offered poor opportunities for an expansion out of the lodgement area. On the other hand, the relatively lightly defended Caen sector afforded a sheltered coastline and offered good terrain for airfield construction. In addition the region was suitable for the consolidation of the initial bridgehead and discouraged the development of

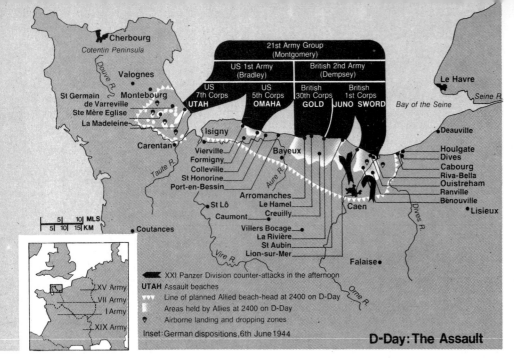

Map labels:

Cherbourg
Cotentin Peninsula
Valognes
St Germain de Varreville
Montebourg
Ste Mère Eglise
La Madeleine
Carentan
Isigny
Vierville
Formigny
Colleville
St Honorine
Port-en-Bessin
Arromanches
Le Hamel
Creuilly
Villers Bocage
La Rivière
St Aubin
Lion-sur-Mer
St Lô
Caumont
St Lô
Coutances
Bayeux
Caen
Falaise
Le Havre
Seine R.
Bay of the Seine
Deauville
Houlgate
Dives
Cabourg
Riva-Bella
Ouistreham
Ranville
Bénouville
Lisieux
Douve R.
Taute R.
Aure R.
Vire R.
Orne R.
Dives R.

21st Army Group (Montgomery)
US 1st Army (Bradley)
British 2nd Army (Dempsey)
US 7th Corps — UTAH
US 5th Corps — OMAHA
British 30th Corps — GOLD
British 1st Corps — JUNO SWORD

5 | 10 MLS
5 | 10 | 15 KM

XXI Panzer Division counter-attacks in the afternoon
UTAH Assault beaches
Line of planned Allied beach-head at 2400 on D-Day
Areas held by Allies at 2400 on D-Day
Airborne landing and dropping zones
Inset: German dispositions, 6th June 1944

Inset: XV Army, VII Army, I Army, XIX Army

D-Day: The Assault

armoured counter-attacks. COSSAC's plan, limited as it was by resources, proposed the invasion of Normandy with three seaborne divisions and two airborne brigades in the assault, and although Montgomery accepted its proposals, he considered that the assault should be mounted in greater strength and on a wider front.

He therefore recommended the dropping of two, or, if possible, three airborne divisions before a seaborne assault on a five-divisional frontage. But it was easier to recommend these increases than to find the means of implementing them. While Air Chief Marshal Leigh-Mallory envisaged no difficulties, Admiral Ramsay reported that the Admiralty was uncertain whether it could even meet COSSAC's demands for 'Operation Neptune' (the cross-Channel assault phase of Overlord) which called for 3,323 landing-craft (a generic term embracing landing-ships), 467 warships, and 150 minesweepers. Montgomery's amended plan would double the number of minesweepers and require a further 240 warships and 1,000 landing craft. The central problem was the provision of these craft and although a quantity could be obtained from other theatres of war, Ramsay and Montgomery proposed that the invasion should be postponed until early June to enable an additional month's factory production to be utilized. However, even with this extra production it was discovered that there would still be insufficient craft for the undertaking and it was suggested that additional resources be apportioned Overlord from the Mediterranean. Ever since the Casablanca Conference an invasion of southern France code-named 'Operation Anvil' had been under consideration. By the end of 1943 the Combined Chiefs of Staff decided that both assaults on France were to be 'the supreme operations for 1944'. But although Eisenhower regarded Anvil as an important adjunct to Overlord he advised the Combined Chiefs of Staff that he regarded Overlord as the first priority and that if insufficient naval resources were available for both operations, Anvil should be postponed or reduced. Therefore, despite the fact that he would have preferred to launch the invasion of Normandy in May, to obtain the longest campaigning season, he recommended to the Combined Chiefs of Staff

Left top: The Normandy landings, 6th June 1944. With the exception of Omaha, where the Americans were delayed at the cost of 1,000 dead and 2,000 wounded, the Allies landed swiftly. *Centre:* Rommel (left) inspects the Atlantic Wall, January 1944. He was given command of the two armies holding the most important sector of the invasion coast. *Bottom:* Eisenhower briefs paratroopers before take-off

that Overlord should be postponed for a month. They agreed to this on 1st February and at the same time General Eisenhower informed them that the exact date of the assault would depend on a detailed study of moonlight and tidal conditions prevailing during the first week of June. On 24th March the American chiefs of staff, who had opposed any interference with Anvil, agreed to its postponement so that the landing craft of one division could be used for the invasion of Normandy. The craft for a further division would be obtained by the postponement of Overlord. As for the additional forces, Great Britain and the United States would each contribute one division to bring the total to five.

Apart from the question of shipping, the postponement of Operation Overlord afforded a longer period for the strategic bombing of Germany which had been accorded highest priority at the Quebec Conference and for the destruction of bridges and railways which had to be severed if German communications into the invasion area were to be disrupted. Moreover, weather conditions at the end of May would be more likely to favour the launching of a large-scale Russian offensive in conjunction with Operation Overlord.

The broadening and strengthening of the assault was only a partial solution to the problem of breaching the German Atlantic Wall. It was to take specialized equipment and new techniques to break out from the beaches and establish a lodgement. Fortunately the COSSAC planners and the War Office had paid close attention to lessons of the disastrous Dieppe raid which taught that a far stronger and closer fire support for the assaulting troops together with tank support from the moment of disembarking would be required of any future attempt to land in France.

The débâcle had a profound effect on the planning of Overlord and in March 1943 General Sir Alan Brooke, Chief of the Imperial General Staff, ordered the conversion of 79th Armoured Division into Specialized Armour and ordered its commander, Major-General Sir Percy Hobart, to devise and develop specialized armour and equipment for the invasion of France. As a brigadier, Hobart had commanded 1st Tank Brigade, evolv-

Right top: Picture by Robert Capa, who went in with the first wave of troops, shows a GI struggling through the surf to land on Omaha, the bloodiest of the landing-areas. Assault troops landed cold, sodden, cramped, and weakened by seasickness. Centre: American forces land on Omaha after dogged assaults and naval bombardment had breached the defences. Bottom: Survivors of a wrecked landing-craft are helped ashore on Utah

ing tactics and doctrines of armoured warfare which the Germans had eagerly assimilated. In 1938 he had created the celebrated 7th Armoured Division (the 'Desert Rats') but in the process so outraged orthodox thinkers with his pioneering concepts that he was relieved of his command and, driven into premature retirement in 1940, he became a corporal in the Home Guard. Happily he was rescued from oblivion on Churchill's personal intervention but it was not until Brooke became convinced of the need for specialized armour to eliminate beach obstacles that his exceptional ingenuity received full rein. By early 1944, despite numerous frustrations, he was able to reveal a range of vehicles to his brother-inlaw, General Montgomery, and to the Supreme Commander, General Eisenhower. Tagged 'The Funnies', Hobart's creations presented a bizarre spectacle. There were Crabs, Sherman tanks fitted with flails to beat pathways through minefields; Bobbins, track-laying Churchill tanks; Churchill AVREs (Armoured Vehicles, Royal Engineers), bridge-laying tanks; Churchill Crocodiles, flame-throwing Churchill tanks; Churchill AVREs which could hurl explosive charges against blockhouses; armoured bulldozers, and most significantly of all, amphibious or Duplex-Drive (DD) tanks which could swim ashore

under their own power. Although the latter were the brainchild of Nicholas Straussler, a Hungarian-born engineer, Hobart's contribution was to adapt the canvas screen attachment, which enabled the tanks to swim, from obsolete British Valentines to American Shermans. Montgomery immediately recognized the significance of Hobart's 'Funnies' and while Eisenhower appreciated the value of the DD tanks, requesting a brigade's worth, he left the choice of other vehicles to General Omar Bradley, commander of the American assault forces. With fateful consequences, Bradley rejected the devices.

'Occupied England'

The Dieppe raid had made it clear that no major port could be captured quickly or intact and before Cherbourg could be cleared of mines and repaired, Overlord forces would have to be supplied across open beaches. The upshot was the production of two prefabricated harbours known by their code names as Mulberry A and Mulberry B which would be towed across the Channel and sunk or anchored in position off the Normandy coast northwest and north-east of Bayeux. However, only one was brought into use as the harbour on the American sector near Vierville was destroyed in a violent storm from the 19th-22nd of June.

Faced with the inevitable destruction of port facilities, the provision of adequate fuel for vehicles and aircraft was another problem that had confronted COSSAC planners. Their solution was 'PLUTO' or Pipe-Line-Under-The-Ocean along which fuel was pumped first from the Isle of Wight to Cherbourg and later from Dungeness to Ambleteuse near Boulogne. But the pipeline only began functioning forty-one days after the invasion and by that time the Allies were moving through Belgium.

By the spring of 1944 all southern England had become a gigantic air base, workshop, storage depot, and mobilization camp. On 1st January American forces in Great Britain numbered three quarters of a million and in the following five months they increased to over one and a half million. While British and Canadian troops assembled in south-eastern England, the Americans gathered in the western and south-western coastal belt. Between Dorset and Cornwall, Sir Basil Liddell Hart observed wryly, lay 'occupied England'.

While the massive invasion force trained and rehearsed its tasks, constant reconnaissance, often involving daring landings

Flail tank for clearing minefields. Had General Bradley provided such tanks on Omaha, assaulting American forces would not have suffered so grievously

on the enemy beaches, provided vital information on off-shore rocks, the geological formation of the beaches, beach obstacles, tidal conditions, and changes in the sea-bed. Great pains were moreover taken to persuade the enemy that the blow was to fall in the Pas de Calais. This was done by simulating concentrations of troops in Kent and Sussex, assembling fleets of dummy ships in south-eastern ports, staging landing exercises on nearby beaches, stepping-up wireless activity, and dropping more bombs on the Pas de Calais than in Normandy. Furthermore, the SD and Abwehr were deliberately swamped with 'secret information' which convinced them that the invasion was scheduled for July in the Pas de Calais. And they were no better served by the Luftwaffe. Its reconnaissance aircraft seldom managed to penetrate the formidable defences which ringed southern England from Falmouth to Harwich. The Germans were almost completely deceived – only Hitler guessed the correct location for the invasion and he was reluctant to back his hunch. The larger part of the German forces were thus deployed east of the Seine and even after D-Day, the Germans believed that the real attack was still to come.

In the last few months before the invasion, security dictated a severe restriction on civilian movement. Coastal areas from the Wash to Land's End were banned to visitors and innumerable ammunition dumps, airfields, camps, and vehicle parks became prohibited areas. Nothing was left to chance. The delivery of letters was postponed and foreign embassies were forbidden to send cipher telegrams. Even their diplomatic bags were delayed.

'The whole mighty host was tense as a coiled spring,' wrote Eisenhower in *Crusade in Europe*, 'and indeed that is exactly what it was – a great human spring, coiled for the moment when its energy should be released and it would vault the English Channel in the greatest amphibious assault ever attempted.' Immense force had been assembled: 1,200 warships, 4,000 assault craft, 1,600 merchant vessels, 13,000 aircraft, and over three and a half million men. They would shortly be pitted against the Atlantic Wall.

For several years the Germans had been developing this coastal defence complex, primarily concentrating on the defence of ports and the Pas de Calais, and although by the end of 1943 a quarter of a million men, conscript workers, and garrison troops were toiling at its construction, it was only approaching completion between Antwerp and Le Havre. Field Marshal Gerd von Rundstedt, Commander in Chief West, had no faith in forts. He was acutely aware of the wall's weaknesses, observing after the war that it had been nothing but

'an illusion fostered by propaganda to fool the Germans as well as the Allies'. Committed to defending 2,000 miles of French coastline, Rundstedt believed that an actual landing could not be prevented and he planned, therefore, to hold strongly only key ports and the most vulnerable sections of the coast. By these tactics the Commander-in-Chief West hoped to delay any Allied build-up long enough for counter attacks to drive small bridgeheads back into the sea.

Throughout the winter of 1943 Rundstedt had appealed repeatedly to OKW for reinforcements; but instead of the men he badly needed, Hitler sent him the hero of North Africa, Field Marshal Erwin Rommel. Initially appointed to inspect defences between Denmark and the Spanish border in November 1943, he was given command of the two armies holding the most important sector of the invasion coast from the Zuider Zee to the River Loire – VII and XV Armies – three months later. Rommel predicted that Allied air power would disrupt the movements of Rundstedt's reserve and that once Allied forces had secured a lodgement they would inevitably break out. He therefore insisted that the invasion would have to be broken on the beaches if it was to be broken at all.

The differing theories of how best to counter the invasion were to lead to a fatal compromise. While the armoured reserves were generally kept well back, the majority of the infantry divisions were committed to strengthening the coastline. In the event the Panzer divisions were forced into action prematurely and found it impossible to concentrate in order to deliver a co-ordinated blow until too late.

In February 1944 Rommel, who had come to share Hitler's view that Normandy would be the main Allied target, instituted an elaborate scheme for obstructing the coastline with underwater obstacles. It was hoped that the 'Czech hedgehogs', concrete tetrahedrons, and mined stakes would impale, cripple, or destroy landing-craft before they reached the beach minefields and that steel 'Belgian grilles' and 'Maginot portcullises' would disable any tanks that landed. To obstruct airborne assaults all open areas within seven miles of the coast were to be sown with booby-trapped stakes. In addition, low-lying areas were to be flooded and gaps between them mined. It was Rommel's intention that heavy coastal batteries immune to air attack should engage the Allied armada at sea. As they raced for the beaches the assault waves would be met by direct fire from fortified machine and anti-tank gun emplacements and from the indirect fire of inland mortars and artillery. Rommel believed that those craft which survived such a devastating concentration of fire

and the forest of lethal underwater obstacles would shatter themselves on the mined beaches. Any troops or tanks which landed would have to contend with additional minefields, barbed-wire, anti-tank ditches, and the withering blast of flame-throwers. Immediately behind this belt Rommel proposed to deploy all armoured divisions so that they could pour their fire onto the foreshore. It was imperative, he maintained, that the maximum force should oppose the invasion on the very day of the landings. 'The first twenty-four hours,' Rommel averred, 'will be decisive.'

The considerable variation in the quality of the sixty German divisions in the West gave Rommel further cause for concern, for while the equipment, training, and morale of the SS and Panzer divisions was superb, the infantry formations contained many low-quality, static, coast-defence troops. Many were too young or too old and many more were Armenian, Georgian, Azerbaijanese, and Tartar 'volunteers' who had elected to wear a German army uniform rather than face a slow death in a prison camp. Rommel had few illusions about his task. The German armies in the West, deprived of training, transport, and their essential radar installations and harassed continually from the air, could only wait for the blow to fall. It was perhaps fortunate for the Allies that the dynamic hero of North Africa had not been appointed earlier and that his plans were neither wholeheartedly supported by his superiors nor thoroughly executed by his subordinates.

In essence, Allied mastery of the air (won by the introduction of the Mustang long-range escort fighter in December 1943) ensured the success of Operation Overlord, but the interdiction of road and rail communications into the battle area was not achieved without prolonged and acute inter-Allied wrangling. The 'Transportation Plan', as the massive air offensive was code-named, concentrated on the scientific destruction of those control, repair, and maintenance facilities which were vitally necessary for the operation of railways in northern and western France, the Low Countries, and western Germany. By mid-May the German armies in France were cut in two for lack of communications.

On 17th May Eisenhower selected Monday 5th June as the tentative D-Day. A final decision would depend on the weather. But the weather was not favourable. Gales and high seas lashed the fog-bound Normandy beaches on Sunday 4th June and the Supreme Commander decided that the invasion would have to be postponed. At 4 a.m. the following day, promised a short period of good weather, Eisenhower announced 'OK, we'll go', and within two hours a mighty armada began emerging into a stormy Channel from Falmouth,

Closing the Ring

Fowey, Plymouth, Salcombe, Dartmouth, Brixham, Torbay, Portland, Weymouth, Poole, Southampton, Shoreham, New-haven, and Harwich. It was almost four years to the day that the BEF had escaped by the skin of its teeth at Dunkirk. Now with powerful Allies the British were going back to avenge their humiliation and liberate France.

Meanwhile Allied aircraft had been maintaining diversionary attacks on gun emplacements and beaches in the Pas de Calais and that evening the impression created by these attacks was reinforced. It was essential that the enemy should not discover the course of the invasion fleet and accordingly those radar stations between Cherbourg and Le Havre which had survived air attacks were jammed, while those between Le Havre and Calais were persuaded that the fleet was moving towards this section of the coast. As ships of the Royal Navy towed barrage balloons and produced 'big ship echoes' on the operative German radar sets, bombers circled nearer and nearer the French coast jettisoning bundles of metal foil known as 'Window' which appeared to German radar operators as a large convoy crossing the Channel.

On D-Day, 6th June 1944, the long months of preparation and planning for the most momentous amphibious operation in history came to an end. As the silent column of ships surged towards the Bay of the Seine through ten swept channels, waves of aircraft roared over them and at 0020 the first Allied troops to reach French soil, a *coup de main* force of the British 6th Airborne Division, landed by glider with extreme accuracy near Bénouville to seize the bridges over the Canal de Caen and the River Orne. Half an hour later 3rd and 5th Brigades began to drop east of the Orne to silence the Merville battery, destroy the bridges over the River Dives, and clear an area north of Ranville so that seventy-two gliders carrying guns, transport, and heavy equipment could land at 0330. While 6th Airborne Division was securing the eastern flank of the beach-head, the US 101st and 82nd Airborne Divisions had landed in the south east corner of the Cotentin Peninsula near Ste Mère Eglise and Vierville to carry out the same task on the western flank. Despite losses and confusion arising out of the scattered nature of the landings they forced the enemy on the defensive and succeeded in capturing the causeways across the inundated areas behind the western-most landing area.

While the airborne landings were in progress, over 1,100 British and Canadian bombers attacked coastal batteries between Le Havre and Cherbourg and at daybreak, during the half hour before the first waves hit the beaches, a massive naval and air bombardment was delivered against coastal defences in the target area. The Germans were confident they could not be surprised, but blinded by the bombing and jamming of their radar installations they failed to intercept the airborne forces and only detected the invasion fleet when it was close enough to be heard.

At 0630 Force U, comprising the US 4th Infantry Division of the 7th Corps of the US 1st Army spearheaded by 8th Regimental Combat Team, made a swift and painless landing at the eastern base of the Cotentin Peninsula near the village of La Madeleine, on a beach code-named Utah. Through a navigational error the force had been deposited a mile too far south in a surprisingly weakly defended area and this fortunate error, together with the fact that late launching of the DD tanks ensured the survival of twenty-eight out of thirty-two, accounted for the ease of the landing achieved at the cost of only twelve dead.

Bloody Omaha

Force O, however, landing between Vierville and Colleville on Omaha beach, was not to breach the Atlantic Wall with similar impunity. The plan on this beach provided for the US 1st Infantry Division of 5th Corps of the US 1st Army to assault with two regimental combat teams, supported by two battalions of the DD tanks and two special brigades of engineers. At 0300 the force boarded its assault craft and was lowered into heavy seas twelve miles offshore. Almost at once ten small craft were swamped and others were only kept afloat by troops who baled vigorously with their helmets. As the assault battalions lurched towards the shore beneath a protective barrage, limited in its effectiveness by poor visibility, twenty-seven prematurely-launched DD tanks foundered. There were no dry landings. The apprehensive men, cold, sodden, cramped, and weakened by sea-sickness, disembarked awkwardly to be raked with mortar shell and machine-gun fire. Three hours later the foreshore was littered with burning vehicles, shattered craft, dead, exhausted, and terrified men. For some hours the position on Omaha hung in the balance. Yet the outcome need never have given rise to such anxiety or the battle claimed so many lives had the commander of the American assault forces, Lieutenant-General Omar Bradley, utilized more of Hobart's menagerie of specialized armour. As a consequence of his rejection of the Crabs, Crocodiles, and AVREs, Omaha rapidly became a bloodbath where the Americans suffered 1,000 dead and 2,000 wounded. Although they met a degree of resistance from a spirited infantry division whose presence they had discounted, their cruel losses from gunfire and mines would have been infinitely fewer had Crabs been available to flail the necessary exits. The failure to land the DD tanks—which Bradley had only grudgingly accepted—in advance of the infantry and the ineffectiveness of the naval and air bombardment left the infantry at the mercy of strongpoints they were expected to storm. Only a combination of sustained and accurate naval bombardment and dogged assaults broke the crust of the defences and prevented a local disaster from becoming a major crisis.

If it had not been for the specialized armour and the policy of preceding all British units by special assault teams of Hobart's 79th Armoured Division, progress on the British beaches, code-named Gold, Juno, and Sword, might have been as agonizingly slow and costly as it was on Omaha. But Forces G, J, and S, comprising British and Canadian troops of 1st and 30th Corps of the British 2nd Army under the command of Lieutenant-General Sir Miles Dempsey, landed swiftly between Le Hamel and St Aubin, and Lion-sur-Mer and Riva-Bella.

'Apart from the factor of tactical surprise, the comparatively light casualties which we sustained on all beaches, except Omaha, were in large measure due to the success of the novel mechanical contrivances which we employed and to the staggering moral and material effect of the mass of armour landed in the leading waves of the assault,' the Supreme Commander stated in his report, adding, 'it is doubtful if the assault forces could have firmly established themselves without the assistance of these weapons.'

By nightfall on 6th June 1944, 156,000 Allied troops had landed in Normandy and, although Caen had not been carried in the first onslaught as was planned, the vaunted Atlantic Wall had been breached on a front of thirty miles between the Vire and the Orne at the cost of 11,000 casualties of whom not more than 2,500 lost their lives.

With no reserves behind the thin beach defences and no heavy artillery to challenge the naval bombardment squadrons, Rommel had failed to smash the invasion on the beaches and by 9th June, despite an attack by XXI Panzer Division, the Allied bridgeheads had been safely consolidated. The previous year Churchill had expressed hopes for the liberation of France 'before the fall of autumn leaves'. The liberation had not come and the Germans scattered green paper leaves in French streets bearing the mocking inscription: 'I have fallen, Oh Churchill! Where are your soldiers?' They were here now. Rommel had insisted that the first twenty-four hours of the invasion would be decisive. They had been.

Science at War

Science has made a vital contribution to the defence of nations since the advent of gunpowder, but it took two world wars to make it vital to national survival. Just as a Chinese firework became an arbiter of power, the most obvious examples of how science was harnessed with devastating effect in the Second World War—radar, rockets, and the atom bomb—were forged from basic scientific discoveries made before the war began. The impact of science was due to the incentive the war provided for its technological exploitation; the greatest war ever fought produced a commensurate effort in the laboratories. But it was not as simple as that. To take the products of research, mass-produce them and transfer them to the battlefield required as much a political as a scientific insight, and it was here the Allies had the edge. The Allies developed, in varying degrees, a new climate of co-operation between scientists and servicemen at all levels and a comparable co-operation between science and industry. Nazi Germany on the other hand, for all the political debt it owed to technology, failed to realize where science and politics parted company.

The story of science and the Second World War is of how effectively the brilliance and invention of the individual was realized in the field. Allied victory in the scientific war was dictated by superior organization at this stage, providing speedy answers to the most simple and the most complex of problems. The basic situation has been outlined. To every advance the enemy made counter measures had to be devised, tested, and mass-produced and this called for the greatest flexibility and constant operational liaison. For each new weapon, teams of operators had to be quickly trained, and their knowledge—together with the unfamiliar new weapons—had to be passed on to millions. New theatres of war brought new challenges, whether it was malaria in New Guinea, or wrecked harbours in France —and a rapid answer had to be found in every case.

The war years themselves produced massive challenges to which massive research programmes were one answer; but the basic discoveries, often the work of an individual starved of resources, which allowed the development of an atom bomb, radar, the jet engine and the rocket, had been made before 1939. German scientists, drawing on the lessons of 1914-18 when Germany's war-machine had been run on a siege economy, had invested much effort in material science. Germany not only had a healthy synthetic rubber industry but a plastics and hydrogenated petrol programme based on coal. These plants became primary targets in the USAAF precision bombing offensive. The same was true in metallurgy. When I.G. Farben scientists first produced magnesium alloys for aircraft construction and engine castings they made a technological gap which British and American scientists launched crash programmes to close.

Before the war, however, Great Britain alone had taken the trouble to organize cadres of scientists to be ready to assist the services. This is ironic when one considers how much the political climate of appeasement in Britain and France during German re-armament was born of a popular fear of the scientific unknown. The prospects of strategic bombing, the distortedly high estimates of deaths per 'bomb tonnage' and the vision of aeroplanes raining lethal gas on London or Paris sapped the will to prepare for war in the West. The popular press was full of death-rays; the film of H.G. Wells' *Shape of Things to Come* saw a Europe flattened by super-bombs and ravaged by germ warfare. And there had been a revolution in communications too. It had already altered the face of politics. Now the rival propagandists had, in mass broadcasting and the cinema, the instruments to instantly reach their populations. Marconi's idealistic hope that radio might go some way to averting the 'evils of war' was turned on its head in the Second World War.

Just as the major areas of research had been opened before the war, the war itself ended with a series of 'might have beens' precursing the age of the nuclear umbrella. Basic research on nerve gases had been implemented in the course of German insecticidal research before the war. By 1945, 'tabun', 'sarin' and 'soman' had been stockpiled by the Germans in vast quantities. Toxic gases had been used operationally by the Japanese in China; botulinum toxin, the deadliest agent of biological warfare, was under test in the United States in 1943. Long-range rocket bombardment

Top: Barnes Wallis—British bomb designer. He invented the bouncing bombs used to attack the Möhne, Sorpe, and Eder dams in the Dambuster raid. Centre: Sir Henry Tizard, chairman of the Aeronautical Research Committee from 1933 to 1942. The Tizard Committee was responsible for first developing radar in Britain. Bottom: Sir Alexander Fleming whose discovery, penicillin, was developed in America during the war and was used to treat sepsis of wounds which had caused huge loss of life in all previous wars

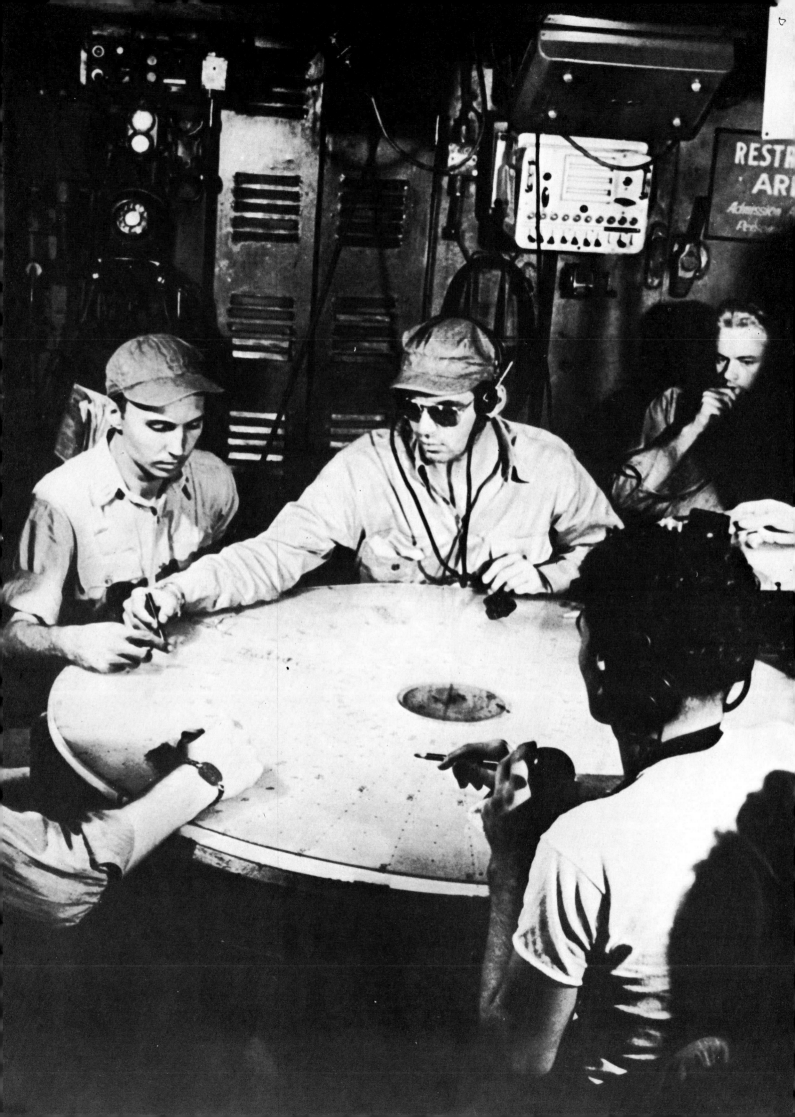

of London and Antwerp was carried out by the Germans in an attempt to reverse the tide of the war. The German A-9 rocket and the *Laffarenz-projekt*, on the drawing board in 1945, were the ideas from which the ICBM and the Polaris submarine were developed; Above all, the atom bomb had been dropped on two Japanese cities.

The developments in mathematical science, computing systems and instrumentation could ensure new accuracies and prediction of effects. Thus the delivery systems existed; the weapons of total destruction existed. The story of science and the Second World War, underwriting Allied victory, is not only the story of an arms race; it tells of how new weapons were used, and also why some new weapons were never used at all.

Even before 1936, Great Britain was aware that scientific research was a most integral part of national defence, faced as she was with the prospect of a massive hostile bombing force negating the two historic advantages in British defence—the Channel and the Royal Navy. In March 1935 the Tizard Committee on Air Defence discovered that the only instrumental aid for providing warning of the approach of hostile aircraft was the telescope. If there was any hope at all, it lay in Admiralty research into the possibilities of locating hostile ships and aircraft by their heat radiation, or the Air Defence Experimental Establishment's work on sound location. In the pre-Munich period, British air defence had rested on biplane fighters and immovable concrete sound-mirrors with a ten-mile range—and they were placed facing France, not Germany. By July 1939, however, an operative system of radio location was in existence.

By 1936, it had been realized in several countries that an aircraft reflects radio waves. Radar was in operation in Britain first, because the brilliance of the individual scientist was backed up by foresight and faith at the committee stage; the Treasury's release of funds through the initial efforts of A.P. Rowe and H.E. Wimperis at the Air Ministry, through the Tizard Committee led to the construction of a coastal radar chain with an ability to measure range and plot the position of hostile aircraft approaching Britain—to a

Left: The radar plotting room aboard a US aircraft-carrier in the Pacific. Working on information provided by radar, the men plot the positions of hostile and friendly surface vessels and aircraft. Above right: Painting by J. S. Baker of a train transporting V2s bombed by the RAF. Travelling at speeds up to 3,000 mph, V2 rockets were almost impossible to intercept, unlike their predecessors, the V1s, whose maximum speed was 400 mph.

range of 100 miles and more. British industry was becoming geared to the new technology, a pool of specialist operators had been established, and Fighter Command group headquarters and fighter stations linked early warning by high-frequency radio-telephony to the eight-gun 350 mph monoplane designs of Camm and Mitchell —the Hurricane and the Spitfire.

The operative lessons of radar research had a wider relevance. A.P. Rowe's Telecommunications Research Establishment at Bawdsey developed a system of operational liaison between scientists and services which allowed prototype testing in action and post-design, in which parties of scientists were sent to squadrons actually using the new radar equipment to find out just how well (or indeed badly) it worked. Operational Research—the subjection of military operations to quantitative analysis —largely began in the British Air Ministry, though it was later brought to a high pitch of perfection by the Americans. It came into being through the need to improve the technique of interception by radar direction, a problem which the Germans failed to satisfactorily resolve until comparatively late in the war. The demands made by such militarized technology on manpower justified the compilation of that central register of qualified men devised by Professor Hill and Dr Goodeve in 1938. Two months before the war it contained the names of 5,000 scientists in 'reversed' occupations, thus separating the 'boffins' and operators—each to his alloted task. This made good sense, in direct contrast to the woeful German

experience of 1939 when academics were indiscriminately drafted to handle rifles in the infantry or to be sergeants in command of a signals platoon.

'The sleeping giant'

Scientific organization in the United States between the wars was not so pressured by the immediate prospects of national defence. Remembering that the American Expeditionary Force of 1917 had been given its aeroplanes, gas masks, steel helmets, tanks, even its automatic weapons by Britain and France, the wartime development of weapon science, other than production techniques, had little prominence. In 1939 America was the world's largest industrial producer. If its plant was not tuned to munitions production, the slack in the economy and the ample labour supply, both legacies of the Depression, made America both militarily and industrially a 'sleeping giant'. The war which began for America with the blip on an untrusted and primitive radar scanner above Ford Island ended with the dropping of the atom bomb from the stratosphere. Meanwhile, American technology had established its ability to overcome any problem of logistics and terrain—from the spotwelding of 'Liberty ships' to the massproduction of DDT and penicillin: above all, it had proved its ability to develop, test and implement new devices, new answers to new problems. Take as examples the whole range of amphibious vehicles designed for the Pacific Campaign, or the long-range bomber escort which arrived in quantity to affect materially a deteriorating military situation for which existing technology had until then proved inadequate.

The American scientific effort depended on the immediate assimilation of as much British material as possible and the avoidance of the mistakes of departmentalism and misdeployment of resources. In the summer of 1940, the British government approved the despatch of a scientific mission to the United States led by Sir Henry Tizard. The great research facilities and manufacturing power of the US overruled any security considerations. Due to this mission, 16 months before they entered the war, the Americans were in possession of the most important findings of British research to date: the Kerrison anti-aircraft gun predictor, solid-propellant rockets, the proximity fuse, asdic, RDX explosive, ship-borne radar and especially the cavity magnetron.

This last device allowed the second revolution in radar. Its transformation from an early-warning screen to an airborne, sea-borne, high- or low-level instrument of acute long-range perception depended on the generation of shorter radio wavelengths. Two devices seemed to have potential: the 'Klystron' developed by the Varian brothers at Stanford University, California, and an American invention of 1921—the magnetron itself. Two British scientists, Professor J.T. Randall and Dr H.A.H. Boot, applied a simple resonator principle to this last device, producing by February 1940 a wave-length of 9 cm at a power of 400 watts. The valve had made centimetric radar possible. Reducing redundant information echoing from the landscape, it closed a blind spot which prevented low-flying aircraft from escaping detection, and proved of vital importance in the Battle of the Atlantic and the strategic bombing of Germany.

The revelation of the cavity magnetron allowed American radar research to make a quantum jump forward. Karl T. Compton, chief of the Radar Division National Defence Research Committee, had long foreseen the importance of micro-waves. He appreciated the prediction of Sir Charles Wright that the side which developed power on the shortest wave-length would win the coming war. The Americans significantly put the project into a civilian laboratory, establishing a short-wave research laboratory at the Massachusetts Institute of Technology. American military research relied heavily on the resources of the universities and of industry. This was largely because the Office of Scientific Research and Development, established in 1940 under Vannevar Bush, felt itself to be pressed for time. The OSRD reported directly to President Roosevelt and received funds from Congress by direct appropriation, either administering them by negotiating contracts

with private or industrial laboratories.

The National Defence Research Committee's work was split into 19 divisions, each responsible for a particular area, such as radar or rocketry. The Committee for Medical Research was responsible—among other things—for the manufacture of penicillin and plasma. There were, however, organizational gulfs within the American scientific effort which went some way to impairing its efficiency. The Military Establishments, particularly the Army Service Forces under Lieutenant-General Sommervell, placed the army's semi-independent technical services under a single close control, but they never approached the degree of operational liaison current in Great Britain. Sommervell's sprawling empire included Quartermaster, Ordnance, Signal, Engineer, Medical, Chemical warfare and Transportation departments. Each department conducted research and development and placed contracts for procurements, functions which overlapped yet remained isolated from the sub-committees of the NDRC. And the sub-committees were themselves compartmentalized, relying on sheer weight of resources to produce results. The products of American science therefore —the Manhattan Project aside, unique in its scale, organization and funding—tended to have a distinct technological bias, characterized by the capacity for series development and volume production. The Americans excelled in such simple war-winning innovations as the amphibious truck, the DUKW, which allowed rapid turnaround at an invasion beachhead, the bazooka which could knock out a Tiger Tank, and the armoured bulldozer which cleared airstrips under fire in the Pacific island-hopping campaign.

Weapons of revenge

The German scientific effort during the Second World War was the one that most excited popular imagination. Certainly, the spectacle of long-range rocket bombardment, jet and rocket aircraft, Mach 10 wind tunnels, helicopters, assault rifles, infra-red devices, true 'submarines' running on hydrogen peroxide, influence warheads and nerve gases made it possible to imagine the most ingenious and deadly arsenal which science could put at man's disposal. Why, therefore, was the German scientific effort constantly baffled and rendered ineffective by the Allies? The ability of the Third Reich actually to produce new weapons capable of deciding the issues of war was not only greatly overestimated by its enemies (a misapprehension not without significance for the scientists who worked on America's atom bomb), but remains so by those who look only at the products of science—and forget the significance of their implementation. Germany's pro-

gramme of technological development was a programme characterized not by organization but by chaos.

The post-war investigation by the Allies showed that at the outbreak of war, the German leaders believed they could achieve final victory with the weapons they already had. In the crucial years of 1939–43, basic research on radar had been halted on Hitler's orders. German scientists had rejected centimetric radar as impractical until an H$_2$S set with its magnetron core was recovered from a crashed RAF night-bomber. No scientist was asked to advise effectively on the U-boat war until the end of 1943, and the advantage held by the Allies was by then so great there was no chance of reversing it. The most significant area of research, the Army's A-4 rocket project, capable of delivering a ton of high explosive at a 200-mile range, was advanced in preference to the development of the guided anti-aircraft missiles capable of blasting the four-engined Allied bombers out of the sky.

The *Enzian* and *Wasserfall* AA rocket programmes could, with coherent direction, have interdicted German airspace to the very bombers pounding all *Vergeltungswaffen* (the 'revenge weapons' V1, V2 and V3) installations. But coherent direction was lacking. Partisans of rival schemes fluttered about Hitler's court until a project was rejected or approved, given a highest priority stamp, millions of cubic tons of ferro-concrete allocated (this always found particular favour with the Führer) and labour mobilized. The *Führerprinzip* worked in two ways. A dubious project such as the Coender 'high-pressure pump gun' (the V3) was given a priority far beyond its proven ability, whereas a potentially vital development such as the Me 262 jet fighter was diverted by Hitler himself to a highly unsuitable bomber role, against the pleadings of Luftwaffe experts. During the war there was not one single German agency, let alone one individual, which controlled the vast number of overlapping projects. Only the intervention of a powerful political initiative could ensure the durability of a research programme. The increasing infiltration by the SS into the Army's rocket project and its transfer from Peenemunde to Blizna in Poland shows how completely the political monoliths inside the Third Reich intervened in weapons programmes without imposing the coherence that a 'totalitarian system' may presuppose.

In these ways the undesirable brilliance of individual German scientists was cauterized and grotesquely framed in the Aryan vision of science which denounced Einstein's relativity theory as being Jewish, and saw medical experiments on concentration camp prisoners as legitimate. The division of scientific effort between the universities, industry, the Wehrmacht and the SS was never reconciled. Reflecting the National Socialist emphasis on practical technology rather than pure science with its *Untermensch* tinge, it was the engineer who could command attention and funds and who was amply rewarded and cosseted by the state—such men as Ferdinand Porsche, designer of the Volkswagen and Tiger tank, Wernher von Braun, the 'interplanetary travel enthusiast' and guiding light of the German rocket programme, or Kurt Tank, designer of the Fw 190 fighter. This emphasis on the engineer coupled with the Nazi distrust of the natural scientist had, long before 1939, already prejudiced their efforts in the field of nuclear technology.

There was never a 'race' for the ultimate deterrent, the atom bomb; the Germans

never got near it. Apart from the efforts of the Allied sabotage offensive, the manufacture of heavy water at the Rjukan plant in Norway had never taken place in anything approaching industrial quantities. Germany's uranium production came to a dead halt with the bombing of the Degussa plant in 1943. However, German atomic science was already foredoomed by the usual disadvantages of poor organization and inadequate recognition by the Reich leadership. Another contributory factor to their slow development in this field was the absence of those physicists driven into exile by Nazi racial and ideological policies, such men as Einstein, Born, Peirils, and Haber, and the Italian refugees from Fascism—Fermi, Pontecorvo and Gullicini. Again, the Germans had insufficient technical equipment, machine tools, telemetry and computers for so vast a project. And finally, in contrast to the rocket lobby who had managed to overcome Hitler's initial indifference by their sheer enthusiasm and got their 'V-weapons'—if not a means to land on the moon—the atomic scientists themselves did little to overcome the authorities' incomprehension of the importance of such research and technical development. Only Göring at the Air Ministry, an agency which proved consistently fecund in its research programmes, saw its potential—but too late. The last V-2, the ideal delivery system for atomic warfare, had already been launched, while a German nuclear reactor, let alone a bomb, had never been tested.

The key to victory

The American atom bomb was, however, not destined for Germany. A highly complex technological war waged by America, Britain and Russia had already defeated the Third Reich. The lesson of that war, in the terms of operational experience, was that finely balanced scientific ingenuity needed political and military scope to use it; it had to ensure the right weapon was in the right place at the right time. But however subtle the 'secret war' may have been, it was often a simple technological factor that swung the outcome of a battle. The elegance of the Allied anti-submarine effort

Above: The indicator of the ASV (air to surface vessel radar) Mark II. Operational from 1940, this meter equipment enabled bombers to detect and home on surfaced U-boats. Left: Laying a supply pipe-line across the English Channel. Code-named PLUTO, the Pipe-Line-Under-The-Ocean carried fuel from England to France for the Allied forces in Western Europe. Although not functioning until forty-one days after D-Day, in the final stages of the war PLUTO was capable of delivering a million gallons of fuel a day

in the Atlantic for example, using High-Frequency direction finding, H₂S airborne radar and ahead-throwing weapons might have been negated had *Schnörkel*-equipped U-boats appeared earlier. Similarly, the RAF night-bombing offensive had by 1944 exhausted all the technical subtleties in its armoury. Oboe and Gee, its navigational aids, H₂S and 'Window', the anti-radar device which showered metal foil into the beams of the German electronic defences, had been rendered largely ineffective by German electronic counter-intelligence and new night-fighter tactics. However, the appearance of the P-51 Mustang long-range escort fighter equipped with droptanks in the day-time skies over Germany gave the USAAF bombing effort an absolute advantage. Similarly, the great battle on Germany's Eastern Front was materially turned in 1942 by the appearance of the Russian T-34 tank, with its sloped armour, 75-mm gun, and high standard of durability. It made obsolete the bulk of Germany's tank and anti-tank arsenal at a stroke. Chronologically, at least, jets, rockets, perhaps even the bomb itself were an afterthought in the story of science and the Second World War, the prototypes heralding an unfought new age of warfare. Where the scientist, technologists, doctors and engineers held the key to victory was in providing devices as simple yet as subtle as a tank that could swim up a beach, an engine filter that might resist the dust of the desert and a spray that would kill malarial mosquitoes. The fact that the German scientific war effort failed to produce the mundane but effective weapons in preference to the spectacular is a factor that largely contributed to the Allied victory in the Second World War. And just as important, war experience had made it apparent that science itself had a vital role to play not only on the battlefield, but in maintaining the social fabric of both war and peace.

7 WAR AT THE TOP

The Strains of Alliance

The surprising thing is not that the Grand Alliance of Great Britain, the United States, and the Soviet Union began to fall apart as soon as Nazi German forces surrendered in May 1945. The surprising thing is that it lasted as long as it did. All the cards were stacked against it. There had been the thirty-year-old feud between Soviet Communism and British liberal democracy, Soviet mistrust of British appeasement policies in the 1930's, and British revulsion against the Nazi-Soviet Pact which had made war inevitable in 1939. Russia had unsatisfied territorial claims in Eastern Europe and the Far East, whereas Great Britain had entered the war in 1939, in part at least, to defend an East European state against aggression, and the United States had a traditional aversion for territorial changes without the consent of the people concerned. In relations between Great Britain and America, there was suspicion on the American side, symbolized in the person of President Roosevelt, that Great Britain was once more using a war for the liberation of mankind in order to shore up the British Empire, on the British side that Americans intoxicated themselves with high-flown language while misunderstanding political realities. In relations between America and Russia, there was the deep-seated fear and mistrust of the capitalist giant on the Soviet side; on the American, ignorance of Russia's security requirements in Eastern Europe, quickly followed by repugnance when these became known.

What held the Big Three together was

Left: The Big Three at Yalta, February 1945. Churchill, Roosevelt and Stalin

the common struggle against Germany and her allies in Europe; Anglo-American dependence on the continuing exhaustion of German forces by the Red Army on the Eastern Front and on a Soviet entry into the war against Japan after Germany's defeat; Soviet reliance on aid from the Western powers and Stalin's wish not to alienate President Roosevelt while Soviet paramountcy in Eastern Europe was still being established; and the genuine belief among the three allies that conflict between them in the post-war world could, without exaggeration, tear the world apart.

Inter-Allied differences arising from the actual conduct of military operations and the terms and manner of the enemy's surrender were inextricably linked with the wider political issues of the war. This was especially true for Churchill and Stalin owing to the long experience of both their countries of European wars and politics. Churchill was keen to reach an understanding with Stalin about Russia's post-war territorial claims in Europe almost as soon as Germany invaded Russia on 22nd June 1941, while Russia was still dependent on Western military aid, rather than later when she might be able to dictate an East European settlement from the basis of her own strength. Stalin, too, sought Western consent to Soviet territorial claims while the struggle on the Eastern Front wavered to and fro. Roosevelt, however, with a more doctrinaire distinction between war and peace, clung to Germany's overthrow as the prime object: territorial issues should await the peace conference. Hence it was owing to American influence that territorial agreements

were not included in the twenty-year Anglo-Soviet treaty signed on 26th May 1942 and that Churchill's argument was not accepted, when German resistance was collapsing in the spring of 1945, that Anglo-American forces should strike as deep as possible into Eastern Europe in order to limit Soviet freedom to prescribe the post-war settlement there.

Nevertheless, the military struggle left its mark, psychologically at least, on the later development of political differences. The first and major military discord concerned the opening of a second front in Europe by the two Western powers. Stalin, with Nazi forces rolling deep into Russia in 1941, called insistently for an attack on Germany from the west, insinuating that Great Britain and America were afraid of taking on German might and suspecting that they were hoping to see Nazism and Communism destroy one another while keeping their own strength intact. The United States was keener on attacking Western Europe than Great Britain was. As early as 11th June 1942, following the visit of the Soviet foreign minister Molotov to Washington, the White House stated, more definitively than Churchill wished, that understanding was reached 'with regard to the urgent tasks of creating a second front in Europe in 1942'.

Bitter feelings

This intention was revised at the Anglo-American summit meeting in Casablanca in January 1943, when the decision was reached to attack Sicily. Stalin conveyed his bitter feelings about this to Roosevelt on 15th March 1943 and again on 11th June, when he condemned the decision to attack Italy and charged his allies with bad faith.

Another source of East-West conflict over the actual waging of the war was the British decision in July 1942 temporarily to suspend convoys of supplies to Russia's northern ports owing to losses inflicted by German aircraft and submarines. Again there followed Soviet charges of British faint-heartedness countered by Churchill's indignant defence of British seamen.

A further military controversy with strong political overtones which sprang up between Russia and the West concerned the conditions and manner of the enemy surrender. The question was how the three Allies were to be represented at the surrender of enemy forces and on the control commissions to administer conquered enemy territory. The general principle was adopted that each ally should be responsible for receiving surrender offers on fronts on which its own forces were mainly engaged, but the Italian surrender in 1943, because of the special nature of the case, raised special problems.

Stalin had already complained about not being kept informed about political affairs in North Africa, where a regime under the French admiral, Darlan, was installed by British and American forces, to be succeeded by General Giraud after Darlan's assassination in December 1942. In August 1943 Stalin first objected to not being informed about the Italian offer to surrender and then demanded a say in the Italian settlement; these differences became critical at the three-power foreign ministers' conference in Moscow in October 1943. From this dispute emerged a three-power advisory council for Italy, but it was evident that the Soviet representative on this would have as little real say as the British and American representatives on the control commissions created for the four ex-enemy states of Bulgaria, Finland, Hungary, and Rumania, which the Red Army subdued. This was in accord with the famous 'spheres of influence' agreement reached by Churchill at his Moscow meeting with Stalin in October 1944, when Rumania was ceded to ninety per cent and Bulgaria to seventy-five per cent Soviet influence and Greece to ninety per cent British, with Yugoslavia and Hungary shared equally between Russia and Great Britain. Roosevelt never accepted this kind of bargain over the fate of nations and clung to the idea that, as in the Atlantic Charter of August 1941, the wishes of the people should be the principal factor in deciding their political fate.

Anglo-American co-operation in settling military as well as political issues of the alliance was naturally more intimate than that between the two Western powers and Russia. Geographical situation, ideological

affinities, cultural and sentimental bonds, together with the peculiar relationship which sprang up between Churchill and Roosevelt, on one side, and Soviet secretiveness, on the other, had much to do with this. All told, Churchill had five major private meetings with Roosevelt during the war with Germany—at Placentia Bay, Newfoundland, in August 1941; in Casablanca in January 1943; in Washington (the 'Trident' Conference) in May 1943; in Quebec (the 'Quadrant' Conference) in August 1943; in Cairo in November and December 1943, where they also met Generalissimo Chiang Kai-shek; and again in Quebec in September 1944. The two also met briefly at Malta in February 1945 before the Yalta Conference. Churchill only went twice to the Soviet Union alone, once in August 1942 and again in October 1944. Roosevelt never saw Stalin alone except for short exchanges during the three-power Tehran and Yalta meetings in November 1943 and February 1945, though he vainly proposed a two-power meeting in May 1943. The Big Three met together only three times: in Tehran in November 1943, Yalta in February 1945 and Potsdam—where the United States was represented by President Truman, Roosevelt having died on 12th April—in July and August 1945.

The comparative rarity of tripartite talks was largely due to Stalin's unwillingness to leave Russia while personally directing military operations. At the same time, Churchill did his utmost to ensure that Roosevelt and Stalin did not get too close together for fear that this might be at Great Britain's expense, while Roosevelt often shunned Churchill's private approaches lest Stalin suspect that they were 'ganging up' against him. In addition to heads-of-government meetings, the foreign ministers of the three powers held an important conference in Moscow in October 1943 and all three states were represented at the Dumbarton Oaks and San Francisco Conferences of August-October 1944 and April-June 1945 respectively for finalizing agreement on the United Nations Charter.

The first inter-Allied political difference emerged over the Atlantic Charter signed by Churchill and Roosevelt on 12th August 1941. Churchill himself dissented in the House of Commons on 9th September 1941 from the Rooseveltian conception of the charter when he insisted that Article 3, asserting the rights of all peoples to choose the form of government under which they live, could not apply to the British Empire. Later, at the Yalta Conference, he protested 'Never! Never! Never!' against a Soviet-American wish that all dependent territories be placed under international trusteeship. The Russians, on the other hand, who had not been consulted

about the Atlantic Charter though they adhered to it, wished to reach an agreement with their allies about Article 2—'no territorial changes that do not accord with the freely expressed wishes of the peoples concerned'—so as to legalize their territorial acquisitions in 1939-1940 during the operation of the Nazi-Soviet Pact of 1939. When the British foreign secretary Anthony Eden visited Moscow in December 1941 Stalin pressed for immediate incorporation into the Soviet Union of the three Baltic states, Soviet acquisitions from Finland as a result of the Winter War of 1939-40, eastern Poland as far as the Curzon Line, and Bessarabia. Stalin promised in return Soviet support for the acquisition of British military bases in western Europe.

Great Britain was not hostile to these demands but had reservations about the Soviet claim to Lwów which, in Churchill's, though not Stalin's, view lay west of the Curzon Line. Churchill was more interested then, as he remained throughout the war, in the independence of the Polish political regime to be left in the new Polish territory, which was to include former German territory in the west as compensation for the area of eastern Poland to be ceded to the USSR. The United States, however, was hostile and not until Eden visited Washington in March 1943 did the Americans express their agreement to Soviet territorial demands. Even so, at the tripartite foreign ministers' conference in Moscow in October 1943 the United States was still standing out for plebiscites in eastern Poland and the Baltic states. When the Big Three met at Tehran in November 1943, however, agreement was reached on the main lines of the territorial settlement in Eastern Europe and, in very broad outline, of a Polish settlement, too.

The Big Three meet
Some progress had also been achieved on three other major questions before the Yalta Conference in February 1945. First, with regard to the post-war treatment of Germany, differences arose between Churchill and Roosevelt at their Quebec meeting in August 1943. Roosevelt favoured the dismemberment of Germany into weak provinces, a policy his spokesman pursued at the foreign ministers' conference in October, while the British delegation was cautious, mindful of the consequences of creating an economic and power vacuum in the heart of Europe. At Tehran in November 1943, the first Big Three meeting, no decisions were reached about post-war Germany; Roosevelt again advocated its division into five separate states, whereas Churchill called merely for the splitting of Prussia and the south German states from the rest of Germany and the organization of the

latter as part of a larger Danubian federation. Stalin opposed this as a threat to Russia. By the time Churchill and Roosevelt met for their second Quebec conference in September 1944 British views had moved a shade nearer the tougher American attitude. Both leaders tentatively accepted the notorious Morgenthau Plan which involved the destruction of German industry and the conversion of the country into a weak pastoralized state. But the Morgenthau Plan was no sooner adopted than it was dropped. The two Western leaders went to their Yalta encounter with Stalin with only the vaguest ideas about the post-war treatment of Germany. They wanted time to think out a policy.

Secondly, ideas moved forward on the post-war settlement in the Far East. When Churchill and Roosevelt met Chiang Kai-shek in Cairo in November 1943, they agreed that Japan should be stripped of all the Pacific islands which it had seized or occupied since 1914, and that all the territories Japan had taken from China, such as Manchuria, Formosa, and the Pescadores, should be restored; Korea, ruled by Japan since 1910, was to be free and independent. Then, at the Tehran Conference a month later, Stalin made clear that if, after Germany's defeat, the Soviet Union took part in the Far Eastern war, she would expect her reward in the form at least of access to a warm-water

port in the Pacific, the southern half of Sakhalin, and the Kuriles.

As for the third of these issues, progress towards the shaping of a future world security organization, Eden had listened in Washington in March 1943 to the view of Roosevelt that it should be dominated by America, Great Britain, China, and Russia. Roosevelt then believed, unlike Churchill, that France was incapable of playing the role of a world leader; not until 26th August, two months after the Allied landing in northern France, was General Eisenhower authorized to accept General de Gaulle's Committee of National Liberation as the de facto authority in France. In Quebec in August 1943 Churchill and Roosevelt agreed that the new world organization must be based on the principle of sovereign equality and that the Soviet Union must be a dominant member after Germany's defeat. The agreed intent to form a world security organization was further elaborated at the three-power foreign ministers' meeting in Moscow in October 1943, when the two basic principles were laid down: firstly, that the organization, founded on the concept of sovereign equality and open to all 'peace-loving' states, should be formed 'at the earliest practicable date'; and, secondly, that, 'pending the re-establishment of law and order and the inauguration of a system of general security,' they – the Big Three – would 'consult with one another and as occasion requires with other members of the United Nations with a view to joint action on behalf of the community of nations'. The broad framework of the world

security organization was drawn up at the Dumbarton Oaks Conference in October 1944 but four major questions still remained to be answered by the Big Three: the principle of representation for the great powers; the rules governing enforcement action by the new organization; the powers of the General Assembly representing all member-states; and the position of France.

The meeting of Churchill, Roosevelt, and Stalin at Yalta in the Crimea (4th-11th February 1945) represented the high tide of Allied unity. But this was largely due to the exhilaration arising from the imminent total German collapse and because many key questions were glossed over by fair-sounding compromises which reality destroyed in the following months before the Potsdam meeting in July and August. On the position of France, Stalin – and to a lesser extent Roosevelt – remained hostile notwithstanding the signature of a Franco-Soviet mutual assistance pact on 10th December 1944. It was chiefly due to Churchill's pressure that France was granted an occupation zone in defeated Germany, to be formed out of the proposed British and American zones, and invited to be a fourth member of the Allied Control Council for Germany. On Germany itself, it was agreed that supreme authority in the country would pass to the three and that its exercise would include the 'complete disarmament, demilitarization, and dismemberment of Germany'. But agreement was reached neither then nor afterwards on how uniformity was to be attained in the government of the occupation zones, the borders of which were being worked out by

'I like waiting' — German cartoon of 1943 mocks Churchill who was not present at private talks between Stalin and Roosevelt during the Tehran Conference

a three-power European Advisory Commission sitting in London, or how, if ever, independent German political life was to be revived.

On the vexed question of reparations, the general principles were laid down that removals were to take place from the national wealth of Germany within two years of the end of the war so as to destroy its military potential; that there should be annual deliveries of goods from current production in Germany 'for a period to be fixed'; and that German labour should be used in the reconstruction of war-devastated lands. A detailed plan to implement these principles was to be drawn up by a three-power Allied Reparations Commission sitting in Moscow, though this was never able to reconcile the conflict between the Soviet determination to milk Germany dry in order to make up Russia's war losses and British and American reluctance to pump assistance into western Germany to keep life going there while reparations went out on the other side to Russia. However, in the teeth of British resistance, Stalin secured in the Yalta accords the phrase that the Reparations Commission 'should take in its initial studies as a basis for discussion the suggestion of the Soviet government that the total sum of reparations . . . should be twenty billion dollars and that fifty per cent should go to the USSR'. Was this a definite commitment to

that sum split in that ratio? Russia later said it was. Britain and America denied it.

Then came the crucial accord over Poland. Stalin's achievement at Yalta, the fruit of Russia's overwhelming military presence in Poland, was to secure Churchill's and Roosevelt's agreement to take the 'Provisional Government now functioning in Poland' — that is, the handpicked Communist group based on Soviet patronage in Lublin — as the core of a reorganized regime with the inclusion of 'democratic' leaders from Poland and Poles abroad. This reorganization was to be effected by a three-power commission in Moscow, the Lublin regime, and other Poles, including the exiled leaders in London. The new Provisional Government of National Unity was pledged to 'the holding of free and unfettered elections as soon as possible on the basis of universal suffrage and secret ballots'. As to Poland's new boundaries, the eastern frontier would follow the Curzon Line 'with digressions from it in some regions of five to eight kilometres in favour of Poland' which would receive in recompense 'substantial accessions of territory' from Germany in the north and west.

It is hard to know whether Churchill or Roosevelt really believed that the new Polish government would ever be anything but a projection of the Soviet state, or that Western and Soviet differences over the definition of 'democracy' could ever render meaningful the Declaration on Liberated Europe which the three also signed at Yalta. This committed them to European reconstruction by processes which would enable the liberated peoples 'to destroy the last vestiges of Nazism and Fascism and to create democratic conditions of their own choice'. Two months later Russia arrested fifteen of the sixteen Polish resistance leaders who had gone to Moscow to discuss the agreed broadening of the Lublin regime and on 21st April concluded a treaty of alliance with a virtually unmodified Lublin administration, now recognized as the provisional government of Poland. Meanwhile, on 6th March a Soviet-nominated government had been installed in Soviet-occupied Rumania. The most Churchill and Roosevelt could claim was that they had secured certain paper pledges from Stalin which could later be used in the war of words as East and West went their separate ways. But the brutal facts were that Russia exercised dominant military control in Eastern Europe and was determined that never again would that region act as a corridor through which German forces could march into Russia.

Had differences not developed between the three Allies over the future regimes in Germany and Eastern Europe, the Yalta accords on the post-war United Nations Organization might have fared better. All

three agreed that the five permanent members of the proposed Security Council — Great Britain, China, France, the Soviet Union, and the United States — should be unanimous when enforcement action to keep the peace was envisaged and that parties to a dispute, including the great powers, should refrain from voting when pacific means of settlement were under discussion. But Stalin's reluctance to allow the Security Council even to inquire into an issue in which enforcement might have to be resorted to, except on the basis of great-power unanimity, foreshadowed later East-West conflict over the organization's right of intervention to maintain peace.

The same applies to the secret Yalta accords on the Far East, disclosed only after Roosevelt's death, to which Great Britain was little more than an observer. Stalin demanded as Russia's price for entering the war against Japan recognition of the status-quo in Outer Mongolia, South Sakhalin, the Kuriles, a lease of the Manchurian naval base, Port Arthur, and participation in the Manchurian railway to Dairen, and the internationalization of Dairen. Roosevelt undertook to secure China's agreement to this deal. But it was struck before the power of the atomic bomb to secure a quick Japanese surrender was known and when Mao Tse-tung's Communists were far from securing their final victories in China. It was only later, when Stalin cashed his Yalta cheque after two weeks' fighting against the Japanese in Manchuria and helped the Chinese Communists with arms, that the Yalta accords on the Far East became the symbol of appeasement in America.

The break-up of the alliance

In the interval between Yalta and Potsdam unity between East and West followed a downward path. The surrender of German forces in May destroyed the most vital bond between them; the Reparations Commission in Moscow made no progress; the Lublin regime, undiluted by non-Communist elements of any significance, became for Russia the Polish government and was recognized, because they had no alternative, by Great Britain and America in July; Communism was entrenched in Rumania and the Greek government was barely able to keep afloat during the Communist disturbances supported by Tito's Yugoslavia. By the time the Potsdam meeting convened in July to hammer out methods of securing four-power agree-

Right: 1 Molotov, after his arrival in Great Britain in May 1942 to discuss the Anglo-Soviet alliance. 2 Painting by Charles Pears of British Arctic convoy. 3 Soviet troops in Manchuria after Russia's attack on the Japanese

1 ◁

2 ▷

3 ▽

ment on the treatment of Germany and to finalize the accords on the new East European territorial arrangements, it was clear that ideological differences, together with fear on both sides about the future balance of power in Europe, would result in little more than agreements to differ all along the line. When President Truman was notified at Potsdam that the atomic bomb worked, some of his advisers, notably George Marshall, urged him to use it as a threat to compel Stalin to respect his pledges of self-determination in Eastern Europe. Whether American opinion would have tolerated this is doubtful, but the fact that the proposal was made testifies to the extent to which the rift had grown.

On 29th April Churchill had written his famous letter to Stalin summing up his feelings on relations between the Allies. 'There is not much comfort,' he wrote, 'in looking into a future where you and the countries you dominate plus the Communist parties in many other states are all drawn up on one side and those who rallied to the English-speaking nations and their associates are on the other. It is quite obvious that their quarrel would tear the world to pieces and all of us leading men on either side who had anything to do with that would be shamed before history.'

With the advent of the détente in East-West relations since about 1962, Western historians, especially in the United States, have revised their views on the origins of this celebrated international rift. More attention is now paid to the weakened Soviet condition in 1945 and the unlikelihood of any Soviet attack, as was feared after Potsdam, on Western Europe; to the natural Soviet fears of a German revival; and to a great power's inevitable demand to have a friendly sphere of influence adjacent to its borders. Moreover, the East-West rift did not, as Churchill feared, 'tear the world to pieces'; it led to a hard-headed recognition on both sides of the suicidal character of armed conflict in the nuclear age. Above all, though Eastern Europe has been denied the freedoms promised at Yalta, as the tragic Czechoslovak experience shows, the de facto division of Europe which sprang from the great-power discords of that time led, paradoxically, to greater order in Europe than it had seen since the 20th century began.

Above: Roosevelt and Churchill with Chiang Kai-shek and Madame Chiang in Cairo, November 1943. Centre: Truman (left) Churchill (centre) and Stalin (right) in conference at Potsdam, 1945. Below: The Big Three, now Attlee, Truman and Stalin, at Potsdam, July 1945. Roosevelt had died on the 12th April, Churchill lost the British general election during the conference

Roosevelt and Stalin

The Japanese attack on the American naval base at Pearl Harbour which brought the United States into the Second World War put a sudden end to a long period in which the United States under the leadership of President Roosevelt had increasingly involved itself in measures directed towards sustaining the countries at war with Germany and Italy in Europe, and with Japan in the Far East. Some American writers observing this undoubtedly un-neutral course, have seen President Roosevelt as deliberately contriving a situation which should leave the United States no option but to go to war. It has even been hinted that the warnings that were available as to the proposed Japanese onslaught were deliberately concealed so as to make the provocation more deadly. The latter charge can be dismissed; the former contains an element of truth in the sense that the United States was putting curbs on Japan's forward march and that it was always likely that a point would come at which Japan would prefer to put the issue to the test of force.

The ambiguity about Roosevelt's intentions and hopes in the pre-Pearl Harbour period is not an isolated problem. Throughout his career as President his objectives and policies were subject to divergent interpretations, and it is not surprising that his allies as well as his enemies did not always find them easy to fathom. In foreign as well as in domestic affairs, Roosevelt eschewed binding commitments and clear-cut positions. Among his own advisers he gave his confidences fully to no-one, and preferred to make use of several channels for making his wishes known and his desires felt. His approach to each subject was primarily that of the politician—concerned with the total effect of his actions upon the situation and in particular upon his position with the American electorate rather than with individual goals.

It is hard to say that he had a definite philosophy of foreign affairs or a fully thought out view of where America's interests lay. He had come into politics as a follower of Woodrow Wilson and had campaigned for the League of Nations. But during the decade in which he was out of national politics—through his illness and later his absorption in New York state affairs—he had come to accept the general tenets of the prevalent isolationism. Roosevelt's return to the national arena had

placed him among those who believed that economic recovery, the nation's prime need, could best be attained by action on the home front, rather than through attempts to rebuild the tattered structure of international credit and finance. Much of the early New Deal was isolationist in spirit and Roosevelt found little to quarrel with in this attitude.

He had, it is true, been concerned both with the Japanese encroachments upon China from 1931 onwards and with the increasing aggressiveness of Nazi Germany and Fascist Italy, and his recognition of the Soviet government in 1933 was in response to developments in the Far East as well as to the hope that a market in Russia for American business might provide an important way out of the Great Depression. By 1937 Roosevelt was warning the American people that their own lot would not be comfortable in a world where aggression was allowed to go unchallenged. But the lack of response was enough to prevent him following these warnings up with any suggestions for concrete action which might conceivably involve the United States in political commitments.

After the outbreak of war in Europe, he had managed to get the neutrality laws relaxed and through the device of Lend-Lease to make the United States in his own words, 'the arsenal of democracy'. But it was only the submission of France and the possibility of the British fleet falling into German hands that galvanized him into more positive action directed towards sustaining the British war effort. And his policies in this respect were still justified—as during his successful campaign for re-election in the autumn of 1940—by the argument that they would help keep America out of war. After Hitler's attack on Russia in June 1941, Roosevelt had extended material aid to the Soviet government as well. To do this it was necessary to face the strong anti-Communist sentiment still powerful in the United States, and enhanced by the failure of relations to live up to the expectations placed on the 1933 agreement as well as by the activities of the American Communist Party and its sympathizers, particularly after the Nazi-Soviet Pact.

For this reason, although from the summer of 1941 the United States was a non-belligerent associate of both Great Britain and the Soviet Union and from December 1941 their partner, relations between these three great powers were neither simple nor symmetrical. Roosevelt now had to deal not with American politicians, most of whom were no match for him

Roosevelt—he placed great reliance on personal contact with Stalin, believing he was open to amicable persuasion

War at the Top

in political skills and none of whom could command equal popular support, but with two veteran statesmen, Josef Stalin and Winston Churchill, each the unquestioned leader of a major power and each with ideas of his own about the nature of the contest and its desirable outcome. From 1941 until Roosevelt's death in April 1945, two interconnected problems monopolized his energies – the waging of war against the Axis and the laying of the foundations of a permanent peace.

While Stalin, like Churchill, was deeply involved in the day-to-day running of the military campaigns and in the detailed problems of supply, Roosevelt was prepared to delegate his powers to a much greater extent, particularly on the military side where his professional advisers played a more independent role than did their British and Russian counterparts. The main strategic decision to concentrate upon the defeat of Germany before embarking on the final overthrow of the Japanese was implicit in American thinking before the United States entered the war, and was confirmed over naval opposition afterwards. Most of the other strategic decisions followed from this one.

Roosevelt was thus somewhat freer than his allies to consider the political consequences of the war, and what America's aims would be in an ultimate settlement. On the other hand, he suffered from two limitations upon his freedom of action. In the first place, the American military took the view that there was no direct connection between the course taken by the campaigns and the position of the armies at the end of hostilities and an ultimate settlement. Moreover they strenuously objected to any suggestion that political as well as military considerations should enter into decisions respecting actual operations. In the second place, there was always the nagging possibility that the Russians if too hard pressed might make a separate peace – and the Nazi-Soviet Pact was there to dispel any claim that differences of ideology might make this impossible. And this meant that in any dispute with the Soviet Union there was always some reluctance to push the matter to extremes. Nor did this only affect policy in Europe where until the summer of 1944, it was the Soviet Union that was still engaging by far the largest part of Germany's military might. The toll of the island-hopping campaigns in the Pacific convinced the Americans that Russian help would be required if the Japanese were to be defeated in their Manchurian vassal-empire and in the Japanese home

Stalin – to him the war was another round in the conflict between the 'imperialist' and Communist halves of the world

islands. Even the small group privy to the secret could not rely upon the atomic weapon coming in time or being effective enough to preclude the necessity of a sea-borne invasion, so it was still necessary to keep the Soviet Union in line.

A further handicap, of lesser though not negligible significance, was that Roosevelt had public opinion to contend with (as of course did Churchill) while Stalin did not, and once the Americans and the Russians became allies, it was necessary to persuade American opinion that the Russians were no longer the Communist bogey-men of earlier years but Russian patriots only concerned with the defence of their fatherland. Pro-Soviet propaganda was thus given a free hand and prospered by it to the extent that Roosevelt himself became its victim, in that he did not perceive fully that the Russians made no distinction between the military and the political and that the war they were fighting, defensive though it might be in immediate origin, was nothing more in their eyes than another round in the inevitable conflict between the 'Communist' and the 'imperialist' halves of the world. Nor, believing this, could the Russians take seriously the Americans' protestations of political neutrality in respect of other countries. When any military decision was taken which did not suit their book, they assumed that it showed that their allies were still hankering after a compromise peace and had no real interest in relieving the Russian front.

The relations between Roosevelt and his principal allies were thus curiously paradoxical. Outwardly the intimacy was far greater between the Americans and the British than between either and the Russians. Their service and supply personnel worked in relations of mutual confidence and at many levels; the personal rapport that developed between Roosevelt and Churchill through personal encounters and continuous correspondence was paralleled lower down. The British had no hesitation about admitting their indebtedness to the Americans or their hopes that the partnership would be prolonged into the peace. They were prepared, in order to get the necessary results, to transfer to North America the work on atomic weapons which had made its first crucial strides on British soil.

On the Russian side everything was different. Help was asked for, and even demanded, but no accounting was given and no information as to Russia's own plans and resources was ever proffered; the Russian people were insulated as far as possible from the knowledge of the American (and British) contributions to their defence. Roosevelt and Stalin met only twice. Nevertheless, it was the American

belief that fundamentally Americans and Russians were fighting for the same ends and looking forward to the same kind of post-war world while the British were interested in objectives which were alien or antipathetic to American opinion. It was for a long time Roosevelt's clear desire not to do anything which could suggest that he and Churchill were making plans from which Stalin was excluded, and his clear belief that Stalin would be open to the kind of amicable persuasion that had been so successful an instrument of his domestic policy.

Roosevelt's illusions

The principal reasons why Roosevelt cherished such illusions—illusions encouraged by his highly unsuitable and poorly qualified ambassador in Moscow, Joseph E. Davies—could be found in three very abstract ideas which figured largely in Roosevelt's thinking but which had quite a different meaning from the ones that the Russians attached to them. In the first place he believed that the British —and Churchill in particular—were 'imperialist' and that both the Russians and the Americans were 'anti-imperialist'. That is to say he was worried lest Churchill try to influence the grand strategy of the war in ways which would be conducive to the defence of Britain's imperial possessions, or the recovery of those that had been lost, to the detriment of a more rapid overall victory. He did not perceive that the Russians attached quite another meaning to anti-imperialism and were by no means averse to using their power to spread the bounds of the Communist empire. In the second place, Roosevelt believed that Americans and Russians both stood for 'democratic' government while the British hankered after preserving or restoring monarchies and other non-democratic forms of government for instance in Italy and Greece. It was only towards the very end of his life, when Russian intentions in Poland could no longer be overlooked, that Roosevelt came to understand the interpretation that Stalin put upon democracy. Finally, Roosevelt shared the antipathy of his former leader Woodrow Wilson for the notion of the balance of power, imagining that the post-war world could be managed by an amalgam of the wartime Grand Alliance with the principle of national self-determination and the equality of states, the whole given institutional form in what became the United Nations Organization. He was thus averse to any consideration in advance of how the peace settlement could be assured of sufficient support against future revisionism. And this again separated him from Churchill, since, while the Russians could accept with equanimity Roosevelt's assumption that

once victory was won, American forces would rapidly be withdrawn from Europe, Churchill had to consider how British security could be safeguarded in such circumstances.

The practical consequences of the last of these attitudes revealed themselves particularly in respect of two other countries, China and France. Roosevelt believed that once Japan had been defeated China would become a great and friendly power deserving of a permanent seat in the Security Council of the United Nations, and was influenced in his assessment of the Asian scene by Chinese opinion. Churchill was much more sceptical about the Chinese regime and its future. He, again, was very conscious of Britain's need for a restored and strengthened France as an essential component of the new Europe. Having early decided that General de Gaulle and his movement was the most likely vehicle for France's recovery of her independence, Churchill gave the de Gaulle movement a considerable degree of material and moral support. Roosevelt on the other hand first took longer to despair of the Vichy government and then, after the liberation of North Africa, did his best to avoid handing over the political reins there to de Gaulle. Later on he tried to avoid installing de Gaulle's authority in France itself and to plan for some form of temporary Allied military occupation until the French could choose their own form of government. At both stages the strength of de Gaulle's position was such that Roosevelt's objectives were frustrated. Finally, Roosevelt and Stalin were at one in minimizing France's importance and in being unwilling to allow the de Gaulle government to share in the occupation and control of Germany and it was left to Churchill to make the running in favour of France's claims—this time successfully, partly perhaps because of a temporary Franco-Russian rapprochement.

Fundamentally—though the personal antipathy of Roosevelt and of his narrow and limited secretary of state, Cordell Hull, for de Gaulle had something to do with it— the point was that Roosevelt believed that France's major role in world politics was at an end and was indifferent to France's claims. He was also hostile to the continuation of France's overseas empire and his successor, in conjunction with the Chinese, was able to hold up the re-imposition of French authority in Indo-China after the Japanese defeat. Churchill did not hold these opinions but realized the extent to which Great Britain depended upon American goodwill and could never afford ultimately to defy the Americans for the sake of the French. Thus while the British were in fact doing what they could for de Gaulle, they gave the French the impression that they were wholly committed to the same attitude as the Americans—and this helped to foster de Gaulle's strong feelings about the 'Anglo-Saxons'.

For although Roosevelt played down the role of power in the post-war world so long as the war lasted, he was very ready to use American power to make sure that he got his way. But this realism could go the other way as well. His desire to see the Russians enter the war against Japan gave them the means of extracting concessions from the Americans at China's expense. In fact the Americans did not need Russian aid; the atomic bomb was enough. And the Russians did not need bribing to enter the war in the Far East since they had their own territorial and political aims to fulfil, nor did they require anyone's permission to do so. For the Russians it was never the same war as the one Roosevelt thought he was fighting.

But it would be a mistake to try to view the history of wartime diplomacy and policy-making in terms of 'Cold War' origins as is sometimes done. The lines of conflict between the Soviet regime and the West had been defined between 1917 and 1919 and had not changed in essentials. What happened during the period between 1941 and 1945 was a partial suspension of the conflict because of the mortal danger in which the Soviet Union found itself and because of the greater immediacy for the Western powers of the threat from Nazi Germany. For most of the war Roosevelt like his allies had to concentrate on the planning and winning of the campaigns against the immediate enemy. It is only in retrospect that one can see how the unresolved issues in the Soviet Union's relations with the rest of the world had their effects upon what was done.

The Americans were slower than the British in pledging support to the Soviet Union after Hitler's attack in June 1941 and shared British scepticism as to the ability of the Russians to carry out a prolonged resistance. But the visit of Roosevelt's confidant Harry Hopkins to Moscow set in train the process of supplying the Russians out of the now rapidly increasing war production of American industry.

The main issue was the Russian demand for a 'second front' against Germany: that is to say a landing as soon as possible on the mainland of Europe by Anglo-American forces so as to draw off part of the German land forces from the Russian front. This pressure began with a letter from Stalin to Churchill on 18th July 1941 and it was against Great Britain that the main pressure was directed. It was clear, however, that any such landings would have to involve American forces and the American military were indeed convinced that this strategy would be the most effective way of defeating Germany quite irrespective

of Russian needs. They were suspicious that Churchill's unwillingness to press forward with this policy and his interest in alternatives were due to an excessive concern about possible losses, and to a nostalgia for the 'indirect approach' exemplified in the Gallipoli operation of the First World War. On the other hand, in contrast to the Russians, the Americans were fully aware of the immense difficulties of making an amphibious assault on a heavily defended coastline and were unwilling to attempt such a thing until all the technical preparations had been made. Meanwhile they came round to relying for the time being upon the strategic air offensive against Germany itself and upon the Mediterranean operations which began in November 1942.

Uncertain alliance

The degree to which the Russian war was still considered as something separate is illustrated by the absence of the Russians from the meeting between Roosevelt and Churchill at Placentia Bay, Newfoundland, in August 1941 at which the policy to be adopted towards Japan was discussed and at which the Atlantic Charter, with its promise of joint action after the war in the setting up of a new and more peaceful world system was promulgated. It remained the case that relations with Japan with which Great Britain and the United States were at war from December 1941 was something from which the Russians deliberately held aloof, since they were unwilling to add Japan to the number of their enemies before they came in to seize their share of the spoils of Japan's defeat in August 1945. The Grand Alliance which was embodied in the United Nations Declaration of 1st January 1942 was thus of necessity ambiguous about the enemy against which it was directed.

Subsequently relations between Roosevelt and his principal two allies were for some time carried on on a triangular basis by means of bilateral discussions. And this may partly explain the ambiguities about the promises to invade Europe made in the summer of 1942. When it came to the North Africa landings which the Russians had perforce to accept as a substitute, the political issues of the future began to show themselves. In North Africa, the Americans took the lead, first in making a deal with the Vichy commander Admiral Darlan, and subsequently in endeavouring to promote General Giraud in preference to General de Gaulle and who had the support of the British and of the French resistance movement including the Communist elements and so might be expected to commend himself to the Russians.

An attempt was made to clear up the political and military difficulties in the

Mediterranean theatre in a meeting between Roosevelt and Churchill at Casablanca in January 1943. Stalin, who was invited, declared himself unable to leave Russia. It was here that the principle of 'unconditional surrender' was agreed upon; and Stalin later approved it.

In fact the phrase was not a very meaningful one since the important thing was the decisions that would be taken in handling the problems of the liberated territories and ultimately those of Germany, Italy, and Japan. Roosevelt was opposed in theory to the division of spheres of influence between the victors; but in practice there was no real alternative. The Soviet Union did not take part in the negotiations leading to the surrender of Italy, and its ultimate reappearance in October 1943 as an Allied co-belligerent; and the Russians were given after protest only a formal share in the running of Italian affairs. Events were to follow the same course in Greece where Great Britain, by agreement with the Russians, took the lead; and on their side, the Russians were ultimately to exclude all Western influence from the rest of Eastern Europe.

This was the reality against which one had to measure the work of the tripartite conferences which were the focus of the last phase of the conflict: the meeting of the three foreign ministers at Moscow in October 1943 and between the leaders themselves at Tehran in November-December 1943 and Yalta in February 1945. The Americans were too concerned to secure Russian co-operation in the setting up of a world security organization which was agreed upon in principle at the Moscow conference and in getting agreement on general principles for co-operation in the handling of a defeated Germany to worry overmuch about the precise nature of the political settlements arrived at. It was the loose diplomacy of this period and the refusal of the Americans to entertain the doubts which Churchill now began to express about Russia's future intentions, or to let the military operations take such doubts into account, that were typical of these final stages of the war in Europe. And it was in these circumstances that the ambiguous agreement over Berlin and access to it was allowed to go forward with all the future problems that this entailed.

But it would be an error to think that had Roosevelt lived there would have been a very different attitude towards relations with Russia from that which developed under President Truman. Towards the end of his life, the Russians' behaviour, particularly in respect of Poland, was already causing Roosevelt deep anxiety and had he lived the same decisions as fell to be made by Truman would almost certainly have been made by him.

Poland's Agony

Meeting at Tehran, in late November 1943, the Big Three, Stalin, Roosevelt, and Churchill, tackled one of the great political problems of the Second World War, that of Poland. In reality there were two problems: what should be the frontiers of the new Polish state, and what government should take charge of it after the war. In two after-dinner talks the Big Three amicably settled the first problem. Poland's frontier

Members of the Polish Home Army with Soviet troops in Sandomierz after the capture of the town by the Red Army

War at the Top

in the east was to be the so-called Curzon Line with some minor corrections in favour of Poland. For the territory in the east lost to the USSR Poland would get generous compensation at Germany's expense: much of East Prussia, Danzig, Pomerania, and Silesia as far west as the Oder and Neisse rivers. On the other problem the Big Three made less progress. They agreed that they wanted post-war Poland to be strong, independent, democratic, and friendly to the Soviet Union. Their conceptions of the kind of government best adapted to secure that end differed, but they did not want to spoil the harmony of the conference by airing their differences at that stage.

Great Britain and the United States recognized the Polish government-in-exile in London and the leaders of the two countries wanted it to be the basis of the future government of Poland. Churchill evidently thought that he could, in exchange for his backing of the Curzon Line, get Stalin to accept the London Poles as the dominant element of the new government. This was only possible if the London Poles quickly accepted the frontiers laid down at Tehran and made some concessions of a minor kind. Though he failed in his aim, Churchill remained convinced to the end that he could and would have succeeded if the Polish politicians had been realistic and co-operative.

In his dealings with the exile government Churchill could not expect any help from the US President: quite the opposite. Roosevelt made it plain at Tehran that he had to conceal his acceptance of the Curzon Line until after the presidential election of November 1944.

He was extremely worried that the large Polish minority in America which had voted for him solidly in the past, might in anger switch to the Republicans and possibly cause his defeat. While the governments of Great Britain and the USSR, without disclosing the Big Three agreement on the subject, soon afterwards openly declared that the Curzon Line was a fair basis for a settlement, Roosevelt remained publicly uncommitted, and indeed managed to create the impression that he kept an open mind on the issue. The official American line was that frontiers ought to be settled by agreement between the countries concerned or, failing such agreement, at the peace conference, as part of a general post-war settlement. Admittedly hints were dropped to the Polish government in London that the Americans could not support them against Churchill and that they ought to come to terms with the Russians. But when Roosevelt finally agreed to talk to the Polish Premier in Washington (in June 1944) he evaded answering the question where he stood on the Curzon Line issue.

This ambiguous attitude of Roosevelt gave the London Poles false hope that he might perhaps support them at the peace conference, and tended to stiffen their opposition to a more immediate settlement.

Massacre at Katyn

The USSR had broken off diplomatic relations with the exile government in April 1943, taking strong offence at the latter's demand for an International Red Cross investigation into the massacre of Polish army officers at Katyn. (In April 1943 German troops in occupied Russia claimed to have found a mass grave in Katyn Wood near Smolensk, in which the bodies of several thousand Polish army officers, who had been taken prisoner by the Russians in 1939, were buried.) As one necessary condition for resuming relations Stalin demanded a public endorsement of the Soviet claim that it had been a German atrocity—an unpalatable demand for the Poles who strongly suspected the Russians. Further, Stalin wanted at least the most rabid anti-Soviet individuals to leave the London government—a wish for which Churchill and Roosevelt had strong sympathy. Stalin alleged that the London-controlled resistance movement did not fight the Germans enough and that it sometimes liquidated Soviet partisans. He also complained of the unrepresentative character of the exile government, and mentioned Polish 'democratic organizations' in Great Britain, the USA, the USSR, and the underground in Poland, which were not included in the London coalition. As if to underline the Soviet claim, a National Council of the Homeland was set up secretly in Warsaw by the Communist Polish Workers' Party at the end of 1943. It was said to unite various progressive groups outside the London camp, and the military units under its control formed the People's Army. But it was the acceptance of the Curzon Line which was the paramount condition for resuming relations. Churchill at any rate was confident that the minor obstacles could all be overcome once the stumbling block which the Curzon Line represented was out of the way.

After returning to England from Tehran Eden and then Churchill personally got to work on the London Poles. They wanted the Poles to accept the Curzon Line (as Churchill once put it), not grudgingly, but with enthusiasm, as a just and reasonable frontier, which would be the foundation of lasting Polish-Soviet friendship. But to the great chagrin of the British leaders the Poles would not do it, though they resorted to evasions and delays rather than reject the demand outright. They queried details of the new frontiers in the east and the west. They suggested resuming diplomatic

relations with the Soviet government before negotiating frontiers. They proposed a temporary Soviet occupation of the pre-war eastern borderland of Poland leaving the permanent frontier to be settled after the war. They insisted on talks with Roosevelt before deciding, and so on. They readily agreed to intensify partisan and sabotage operations against the Germans by the Home Army—the military resistance movement under their control—and to get them to collaborate with the advancing Red Army. The one Soviet demand they did reject flatly was the purge of anti-Soviet politicians, indignantly branding it as an unwarranted interference with a sovereign government. More than six months of continuous British pressure did not succeed in inducing the London Poles seriously to try and come to terms with the Russians.

The chief architect and outstanding personality of the exile government, who had combined the offices of Prime Minister and Commander-in-Chief of the Polish Armed Forces, was General Władysław Sikorski. Churchill greatly respected him as a statesman and a realist, and was deeply sorry when he died in a plane crash off Gibraltar in July 1943. Sikorski was succeeded as Prime Minister by the Peasant Party leader Stanisław Mikołajczyk whose authority was not of the same order as Sikorski's. Mikołajczyk stood to the left of most of his cabinet colleagues and believed in the need to reach accommodation with the Soviet Union. But he doubted his ability to persuade them to accept any serious political sacrifices. His opponents, who feared and distrusted him, included two ministers (General Kukiel and Kot) and Sikorski's successor as commander-in-chief, General Kazimierz Sosnkowski. They were the men whom the Russians wanted particularly to see dropped from the government.

Poles of all political leanings tended to see their country as an innocent victim of aggression and the most persecuted nation in Europe. The thought of additional, territorial sacrifices was to most of them morally repugnant. The Poles' traditional enmity towards Russia was reinforced by the feeling that Stalin had joined in Hitler's aggression against Poland in 1939. Most London Poles strongly suspected that the Curzon Line was not the limit of Stalin's ambition, and that his ultimate aim was to control Poland through a subservient government. If any territorial concessions had to be made to the USSR, they ought to be coupled with cast-iron guarantees that within the new frontiers Poland would remain truly free and independent. Neither Churchill nor Roosevelt saw the need for, or the possibility of, such guarantees from a gallant ally whose

'Katyn—heaven under the earth.' A German poster accuses the Russians of the Katyn massacre. The Russians made a counter-accusation; but they were unable to substantiate the charge at Nuremberg, and it is widely believed that the Russians were responsible

third world war. Poland's territorial integrity seemed to him an excellent ground on which the West ought to make a stand and thus nip Soviet expansion in the bud. Sosnkowski's views, which Churchill privately denounced as mad, were shared by many high-ranking Polish officers. They were particularly prevalent in General Anders' Polish Corps. The corps had been formed in Russia and its members had experienced the Soviet occupation of eastern Poland, deportation, and captivity.

Mikołajczyk's problem of reaching an understanding with the Russians was further complicated by the necessity to take the views of the underground into account. The London government and the resistance leaders kept in close touch through radio and couriers, and no important action in Poland or abroad was undertaken without consultation between them. The leaders of the resistance movement were on the whole even more intransigent towards the Soviet Union than were the average politicians in London. In this respect there was little difference between the high command of the Home Army and the civilian underground authorities which included representatives of the major pre-war political parties—National Democrats, Labour (Christian Democrats), Peasants, and Socialists. The high command of the Home Army, consisting of Generals Bór-Komorowski, Pełczyński, and Okulicki, shared the background and the ideology of their army colleagues abroad. To all of them the 1939 frontier was sacrosanct and territorial concessions to the Russians unthinkable. Mikołajczyk did not exaggerate when he told Churchill that his government might find itself repudiated by the underground if it agreed to the Curzon Line too easily. Churchill appreciated Mikołajczyk's difficulty and agreed to sound out Stalin about postponing the whole frontier issue till the end of the war, but Stalin remained adamant.

While Churchill battled against the immobility of the London Poles the rapid advance of the Red Army on the Eastern Front raised an acute practical problem for the non-Communist underground. What was to be their attitude to the Soviet forces after they crossed the 1939 Soviet-Polish frontier, which they did in March 1944? A long prepared plan, sanctioned by the London government, provided for the situation and it was put into effect in the Volhynia region and also tried out in the cities of Lwów and Wilno. The Polish partisans rose against the Germans when the front arrived and co-operated with the Red Army. At the same time they revealed their loyalty to the London government as the legitimate authority over the territory. The outcome of the operation, known as 'Tempest' from its code name,

friendship both men wished to cultivate. Finally, the government-in-exile underestimated Soviet strength and ability to beat Germany without Western aid. Hence they over-estimated the amount of pressure that Churchill and Roosevelt could bring to bear on Stalin.

The Polish suspicion of Russia took an extreme form in the mind of General

Sosnkowski. He saw Russia, because of her militant Communist ideology, not as a genuine ally, but as the second greatest enemy of both Poland and the West, aiming at the conquest of Europe in the wake of Germany's defeat. If Russia were not checked soon, while she was still relatively weak, her ambition would inevitably lead to a clash with the Western powers and a

*Left: Stanisław Mikołajczyk (centre) at a meeting of the Polish government-in-exile in London, October 1944. **Right:** The end of the Warsaw Rising. General Bór-Komorowski of the Polish Home Army surrenders to the Germans. 200,000 Poles lost their lives in Warsaw*

was predictable. The Russians welcomed Polish assistance during the fighting, but afterwards the partisans were ordered to lay down their arms and to join 1st Polish Division of General Berling on the Soviet side. Resistance to the order was suppressed by executions and arrests. For a time all attempts at large-scale Polish struggle against the Germans ceased, and the military and civilian authorities stayed underground or left the Russian-occupied territory.

Mikołajczyk as well as Churchill had hoped that a gesture towards military collaboration might soften Stalin's attitude to the London government, but the political demonstration which accompanied the fighting clearly provoked Russian hostility. Mikołajczyk then decided on a personal approach to Stalin. It had been recommended to him long ago by the Czechoslovak President-in-exile Beneš who had reached an agreement with Stalin and established the kind of friendly relationship with Moscow which the British were hoping the Poles might achieve. Roosevelt and Churchill gave their blessing to the venture, and though Stalin seemed lukewarm he agreed to receive Mikołajczyk at the end of July. But the visit was preceded by an event which was clearly calculated to weaken Mikołajczyk's position. On 22nd July 1944 a Committee of National Liberation, sponsored by the Communist-dominated National Council of the Homeland, was set up in the first indisputably Polish city occupied by the Soviet army. The so-called Lublin Committee claimed to be a coalition of genuinely democratic and patriotic forces, which wished to be friendly to the Soviet Union, accepted the Curzon Line, and were agreed on far-reaching social and economic reforms. It was promptly recognized by the Soviet government as the only lawful

authority in Poland, and the Soviet-armed forces were instructed to co-operate only with its representatives.

The Warsaw Rising

Before Mikołajczyk's departure for Moscow the London government had sanctioned the proposal of the resistance leaders that Operation Tempest be attempted in Warsaw. The Home Army command and the government delegate in the underground were to be guided by the local military situation (the nearness of the Soviet army, the collapse of German defence, etc.) and were given discretion to decide when and whether to stage an uprising. There was some division on the issue in London. General Sosnkowski feared the military and political risks of a rising which might, as had happened east of the Curzon Line, simply provoke Soviet hostility and reprisals. Mikołajczyk, on the other hand, welcomed it. A successful military and political demonstration in the capital could have great prestige value and strengthen his hand against Stalin in the coming talks. By chance the outbreak of the rising in Warsaw exactly coincided with Mikołajczyk's arrival in Moscow.

Till the middle of July General Bór-Komorowski and his colleagues in the Home Army command viewed the situation rather pessimistically. They were conscious of the difficulty of conducting military operations in a city with a million inhabitants. The Home Army in Warsaw was poorly armed and lacked the heavy equipment necessary to capture fortified buildings. The flower of the Home Army was in fact in the provinces and could not be transferred to the capital. But their attitude changed suddenly when the thrust of the Red Army towards Warsaw caused a panic evacuation of German civilians. At the same time the invasion of France and

the attempt on Hitler's life suggested the possibility of an imminent total collapse of the German military machine. The uprising was triggered off by a rumour, unchecked and almost immediately disproved, that the Russians were in strength on the eastern outskirts of the city. In fact the Germans had sufficient reserves of troops and armour to close a temporary gap in their defences and to hold a large bridgehead east of Warsaw for several weeks. The inescapable conclusion is that the military leaders gambled on the chance, uncertain though it was, that the Russians would soon enter Warsaw and drive out the Germans, if the Poles had not managed to do so by themselves. Not to take the chance was to lose perhaps the last opportunity of demonstrating to the Russians, fellow Poles, and the world the existence and heroism of the free resistance movement. The alternative was to let the Russians and the 'Soviet agents' of the Lublin Liberation Committee take over the country without protest.

The rising began on 1st August at 1700. Badly led and badly prepared it was doomed from the start. The Home Army could only throw 2,500 armed men into action, against 15,000 or so heavily armed Germans stationed in the city. The crucial assaults of the first three days failed to capture more than a limited area of the city; afterwards, though the insurgents' strength grew, the Germans brought in reinforcements much faster. The German forces were a motley collection of policemen, gendarmes, punitive battalions, and Russian deserters, and their atrocities inspired fanatical resistance in the Poles. But the Germans were also able to use bombers, tanks, mortars, and artillery, against which the rebels were quite helpless and which inflicted terrible losses on the civilian population. When regular Ger-

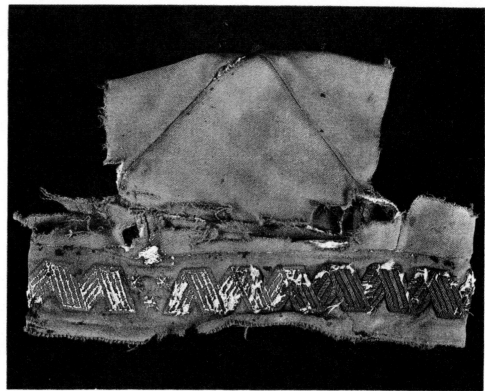

*Left: Poland, pre- and post-war. **Right:** Part of Sikorski's cap found in his wrecked aircraft. He opposed any frontier changes, and it has been suggested, without any evidence — most recently by Hochhuth in his play 'Soldiers' — that Churchill engineered his death*

man troops, withdrawn from the eastern bank of the Vistula, reinforced the others, the Home Army's resistance quickly collapsed though its last detachments were only captured on 3rd October. It is estimated that about 200,000 people—nine-tenths of them civilians—lost their lives in Warsaw. The bombardment, the fires, and the systematic demolition of undamaged buildings afterwards, reduced the city to rubble. Precious historical monuments, museums, art collections, libraries and archives, besides vast quantities of private property, perished in the rising. Altogether the losses may have amounted to as much as seventy per cent of the national wealth.

The Russians, who were taken completely by surprise, denounced the rising as a folly and a political act against them, and would have nothing to do with it. Because of heavy German reinforcements the Red Army only managed to reach Warsaw's suburbs on the east bank of the Vistula in the middle of September. Some attempts to cross the river were made by small Polish detachments under Soviet command but proved futile. Having begged Stalin for help in vain, Mikołajczyk returned to London and pressed Churchill and Roosevelt to intervene. Stalin had denied the use of Russian airfields to British and American planes with supplies for Warsaw. As a result regular help from the West could only be on a very small scale, and it was only after several weeks' delay that Stalin agreed to the landing of one large American mission behind Soviet lines after dropping supplies over Warsaw. Churchill raged at Stalin's callousness in private and proposed strongarm methods and reprisals to Roosevelt. But the American President vetoed anything which might spoil their relations with Stalin. The rising wrecked any chance there was of Mikołajczyk's

getting frontier concessions from Stalin. On the question of a government Stalin made it clear that there would have to be a coalition with the Lublin Committee. Its representatives met the London Premier in Moscow, but the two sides failed to reach agreement.

Poland's last chance

Churchill accepted the idea of a coalition as inevitable, but still hoped that he could secure for the London Poles at least a half share in the new government. They themselves, however, were prepared to offer the Polish Workers' Party one-fifth of ministerial posts and to make only moderate territorial concessions in the east. A conference of representatives from London and Lublin met in Moscow in October; Stalin, Molotov, Churchill, and Eden also attended some sessions. The London Poles once more provoked Churchill's fury by refusing to accept the Curzon Line even at that stage while Stalin would not contemplate anything except parity for the Lublin element. Churchill saw the Moscow conference as the last chance to obtain reasonable terms for the London Poles and could not grasp why they were so abominably short-sighted. The Polish delegation then returned to London to consult with the rest of the government. After further delays, caused by the Poles' obsession with adequate guarantees, the settlement worked out in Moscow was rejected by the government-in-exile. At this Mikołajczyk resigned and after a good deal of hesitation and entreaties from the British, agreed some time later to enter a coalition with the Communists as leader of the Peasant Party.

The machinery to set up the new government was worked out by the Big Three at Yalta in February 1945, but it took months of consultations and bargaining before its

composition was finally settled. Being in effective control of Poland the Russians were naturally able to press the case of their Lublin protégés very strongly. Their unwillingness to compromise and ruthlessness towards non-Communist elements filled Churchill with anger and apprehension for the future of the alliance. A characteristic Russian action was the arrest and trial for anti-Soviet activities of sixteen prominent leaders of the London underground while negotiations were in progress. The 'Provisional Government of National Unity', which the three powers recognized as the government of Poland in July 1945 was a victory for Stalin and for the Polish Workers' Party and its allies. They had fourteen out of twenty-one cabinet posts and all the key positions. Western leaders still hoped that a free election in the near future would enable Mikołajczyk to acquire the dominant position they had failed to secure him in the Provisional Government.

One more thing remained to be done: fixing the details of the western frontier of the new Polish state. This was done at Potsdam and produced some unexpected but unsuccessful opposition of Churchill to the western Neisse section of the frontier. But harmony was reached once more and all of the German territory east of the Neisse and the Oder, including Stettin, but excluding the Königsberg area of East Prussia, was put under Polish administration pending the formal ratification of the decision by the peace conference. The Polish problem was finally solved, at least in so far as it ceased to preoccupy the big powers. But it is clear that the solution fell rather short of the objective of establishing the independent and democratic Poland Churchill, Roosevelt, and Stalin agreed on during their conference in Tehran.

The July Plot

The July Plot is so called because on 20th July 1944 Colonel Claus von Stauffenberg succeeded in putting a time-bomb, with its fuse set, in the room where that morning Hitler was holding his daily conference on the military situation. The place was the Führer's HQ at Rastenburg in East Prussia, and the time was the moment when Stauffenberg entered the room in the company of Field-Marshal Keitel, shortly after 12.30 p.m. Stauffenberg was able to participate in this top-level, and top-security, meeting because some months earlier he had been appointed chief of staff to General Fromm, C-in-C of the Reserve Army, and Hitler on 20th July wanted to hear the latest facts and figures on the availability of reserve divisions to stem the onrush of the Russian armies then at a distance of about fifty miles from Rastenburg. As Keitel and Stauffenberg entered the room, the field-marshal briefly interrupted General Heusinger in his report on the Eastern Front to present Stauffenberg to Hitler. After that, Heusinger resumed, and Stauffenberg, telling Keitel that he had to make an urgent telephone call to his office in Berlin, placed his brief-case, in which the live bomb was hidden, against the heavy wooden support beneath the table on the side nearest Hitler and left the room. The bomb exploded ten minutes later. It failed to kill Hitler. Not only this—Stauffenberg's co-conspirators in Berlin totally failed to take advantage of the three hours during which Hitler's headquarters was shut off from the outside world to initiate their carefully planned rebellion. It was a disaster of the first magnitude, and it led to a purge in which barbarism by the Nazis toward their fellow Germans reached new heights. The failure was one in which ineptness, weakness, and plain bad luck all played their part.

Yet this German resistance group was apparently a formidable one. As in the course of the war the movement's basis widened and broadened, its members came to regard themselves, with much justification, as the only legitimate alternative to the Nazi government, as the German opposition. It needs no special elaboration to say that while in the countries of the liberal West, opposition had always been an essential part of the ordinary processes of government, in Nazi Germany opposition was equivalent to treason. The anti-Nazi opposition, therefore, was only able to work, plan, scheme and plot under conditions of the most acute personal danger.

Who were 'the German opposition'? At the centre stood the group formed early in the war by Helmuth von Moltke. This is usually called the Kreisau circle after the Moltke estate in Silesia where, once in 1942 and twice in 1943, Moltke assembled a numerous and steadily growing group of anti-Nazis to thrash out with them the details of the programme which the first post-Hitler government was to present to the world. The result of these meetings was that a considerable degree of unity on fundamental questions of social, economic, religious, and foreign policy was reached. Two items from the programme in particular will show how eminently practical and limited in aim their programme was. The provision for the punishment of war criminals envisaged the passing of retro-active legislation for the punishment 'by death or imprisonment' of all those who had offended against 'divine, international, and positive law'—a concept not basically different from the Allied Control Council Law of 1945 which convened the International Military Tribunal at Nuremberg. Secondly, at the final Kreisau meeting of 9th August 1943, agreement was reached regarding the men who, after a successful coup against Hitler, would head the administrations of the German regions after the take-over from Nazi officials.

Towards a new Germany

Kreisau was a power-house of ideas, political energies, and well-aimed projects. Moltke, without any doubt the most single-minded, incisive, and inspiring person among them all, did not regard the work of the opposition as only that of a government-making agency. He felt that the true alternative to the Hitler system must be concerned with generating a real, vital force capable of a break-through in Germany's moral and ethical regeneration. That he dedicated himself to such lofty aims does not mean that he became lost in idealistic generalities. He was a man of law both by training and conviction; in the war he worked as a consultant in international law in German counter-intelligence, the famous Abwehr, under Wilhelm Canaris and Hans Oster. With the help of these two sophisticated masters in political camouflage, Moltke was able to forestall Nazi crimes by warning, often just in time, the intended victims. In Norway, Holland, Belgium, and northern France he established a working contact with local resistance movements and was able to act against the taking of hostages, the illegal detention of patriots, and the massacre of Jews.

Göring (left) with Luftwaffe aides inspects the shattered conference room at Hitler's Rastenburg headquarters after the explosion of Stauffenberg's bomb

During visits to neutral countries, such as to Turkey in 1943, he made a number of attempts to establish contact with enemy diplomats and governments, but here he was doomed to bitter disappointment. One of the weaknesses of his position was that as a convinced 'Westerner' he worked out several plans for his group to end the war in the West alone while the front in the East was, for the time being, to be held. Again, although in Turkey in 1943 he had declared himself ready, after a passionate argument, to accept unconditional surrender on behalf of the post-Hitler government, his further suggestions, such as to fake an air-crash and by this means get a fully authorized negotiator into England to finalize the terms of co-operation between the Allies and the opposition before or after the invasion of France, were still coloured with a patent 'Western only' tinge which to him was psychologically understandable (his mother was Scottish-South African), but tactically dangerous. He made further approaches to the British and American governments from Stockholm, even though he was denied all support by neutral Sweden's foreign minister. The only reply from the West was a stony silence. Whatever views were held in Downing Street and Washington of the value and reliability of the opposition within the Reich, Western governments were not prepared to enter into negotiations which might arouse Russian suspicions of a separate peace between Germany and the West.

Another difficulty in Moltke's position was that until late in 1943, he was unmovably opposed to the idea of Hitler's assassination. Arrest and put him on trial, yes, but murder him, no. Not only did he think, and often say, that people like themselves were simply the wrong men to plan and carry out an assassination attempt— 'we are all amateurs and would only bungle it', he once said with tragic truth—but to him all murder was wrong. 'Why are we opposed to National Socialism?' he once asked a friend. 'Surely because it has turned wrong-doing into a system? And we must not set out on a new beginning, on our work of renewal, by doing wrong

Left: 1 Beck. He was allowed to commit suicide when General Fromm, who knew of the conspiracy, determined to cover his tracks by eliminating the leaders.
2 Stauffenberg, Fromm had him shot.
3 Freisler (centre), the vindictive president of the People's Court, opens proceedings against the surviving leaders. He went on sentencing purge victims until a bomb fell directly on the courtroom in February 1945 and killed him.
4 Moltke, the leader of the Kreisau circle, gives evidence. He was executed

ourselves.' Yet after returning from his disillusioning trip to Turkey he told General von Falkenhausen in Brussels in September: 'Despite all our scruples, we really have no choice but to eliminate Hitler physically.'

Moltke's arrest

Count von Moltke was arrested in January 1944 and taken to Ravensbrück, though his detention there was very mild. No one had denounced him, but a friend had given his name away under torture. It soon became clear that the police knew nothing of the Kreisau work, a remarkable state of affairs in view of the fact that the Kreisauers met not only in distant Silesia, but in a garage in Berlin, in apartments of friends considered safe, and in other people's country houses. His friends generally assumed that his arrest had been part of the operation the Nazi security services had lately mounted against the Abwehr where Moltke was still employed. (Both Oster and Canaris had been dismissed.)

As stated earlier, the Kreisau circle formed the centre of the German opposition and was its most energetic core. It was, of course, not the only group working against Hitler. We might briefly mention the group of predominantly older people round Karl Gördeler and General Ludwig Beck who, while being the Kreisauers' equals in straightness of mind and conscience, were less resilient and less capable of accepting the Kreisau notions of a new social system dedicated to ethical socialism. Gördeler himself, a somewhat austere traditionalist of considerable personal authority and kindly paternalism, displayed throughout the tensest years a deplorably deficient sense of security. Yet Gördeler was an asset for he was close to Beck, a former Chief of Staff of the Army and Germany's most acute military theorist since Karl von Clausewitz. Through Beck, even in retirement a universally respected figure, it was hoped to obtain the co-operation in the intended coup from army commanders on the Western and Eastern Fronts. Although Yorck von Wartenburg, a Kreisauer in the civil service, called Gördeler an 'arch-

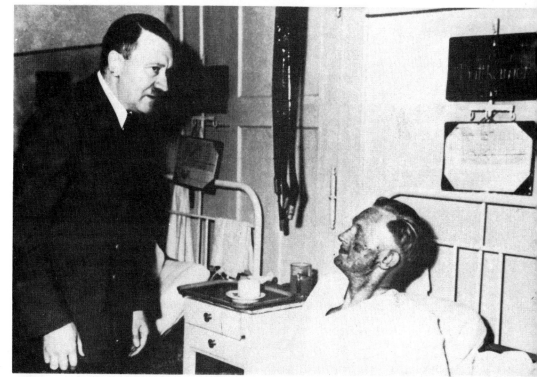

Top: Field-Marshal von Witzleben, who was to have been Army C-in-C after Hitler was dead, is hustled into court. Utterly broken, he had to keep hitching up his trousers because the police had deprived him of belt and braces. 'You dirty old man!' Freisler shouted, 'why do you keep fiddling with your trousers?'
Centre: Hitler speaks to Admiral Puttkammer who was injured when the time-bomb went off. **Bottom:** *Bormann (left), Hitler, and Jodl (with bandaged head) shortly after the abortive July Plot*

reactionary' and Moltke described his suggestions as a 'Kerensky solution', the Kreisau circle, especially after Moltke's arrest, agreed to make Gördeler with his administrative expertise the first head of government after the coup d'état, while placing next to him the Social Democrat Julius Leber, one of the giants of the opposition, as minister of the interior. The foundations of this compromise seemed a little tenuous, but then it was meant to cover merely the first period of transition. It could not be denied that by early 1943 Gördeler was as keen as most Kreisauers on a speedy launching of the coup d'état.

Previous attempts on Hitler's life
Hitler had already survived several assassination attempts. In the words of Alan Bullock, Hitler had 'the devil's own luck – a not inappropriate phrase'. Major attempts were in brief as follows:

▷ Borisov, 4th August 1941: Army Group Centre. The staff of this Army Group, which was under the command of Field-Marshal von Bock, was honeycombed with conspirators determined to arrest Hitler and have him put on trial. Leading lights were Major-General von Tresckow and his aide, Lieutenant von Schlabrendorff. Bock refused his support, unless the arrest succeeded. When he finally appeared, Hitler surprised the plotters by a massive bodyguard hedging in his every movement, and no plotter could get anywhere near him. The importance of this failure was that the same conspirators now realized that physical assassination was the only way to remove Hitler.

▷ Smolensk, 13th March 1943: again at HQ of Army Group Centre, now under the command of Field-Marshal von Kluge; Tresckow and Schlabrendorff were still there. Hitler's visit was announced as imminent, Canaris and other Abwehr officers personally brought plastic bombs and time-fuses to Smolensk. Like Bock, Kluge refused support, so Tresckow and Schlabrendorff placed bombs in two brandy bottles, wrapped them up in brown paper and just before Hitler's departure, asked Colonel Brandt, a member of the Führer's entourage, to deliver the bottles to a friend at Rastenburg. Brandt amiably agreed. The fuses were set for half an hour after take-off which meant that the Führer's aircraft was expected to blow up over Minsk. At Berlin and Smolensk plotters sat by the telephone breathlessly waiting for an announcement or signal. Soon it became known that the Führer had touched down safely at Rastenburg. With outstanding sang-froid Schlabrendorff next travelled to the Führer's HQ to retrieve the brandy bottles from the unsuspecting Brandt to whom he handed two genuine bottles instead, and then, on the train to Berlin,

dismantled his bombs which were of English manufacture, procured by Canaris. One theory as to why the bombs failed to explode is that the aircraft was flying too high for the fuse to work.

▷ Berlin, 21st March 1943: nothing daunted, Major-General von Tresckow organized a new attempt on Hitler's life. The opportunity was provided by Hitler's presence at a Heroes' Memorial Day celebration at the Armoury in Unter den Linden, Berlin. On this occasion, Colonel von Gersdorff was inside the Armoury building with two bombs in the pockets of his great-coat which required ten minutes for the fuse to work. Hitler's visit had been announced as to last thirty minutes, but he stayed for only eight. There was no time to set the fuse.

▷ Zossen, near Berlin, November 1943: throughout this month Hitler was always about to inspect a new great-coat for the army in Russia, but he cancelled the inspection at the last moment time and again. A young officer, Axel von dem Bussche, had agreed, on the pretext of modelling the great-coat before the Führer, to put a bomb into each pocket, ignite them, and blow up himself and the Führer. The day was finally fixed for late November; on the day before, Bussche was given his overcoat and his bombs. That night the whole storehouse of great-coats was burned down in an air-raid. The inspection was cancelled.

Stauffenberg joins the plotters
The opposition, at all events, was not deterred. Stauffenberg, in finally taking their bomb into the Führer's conference, acted as a lone vanguard of the opposition to which one of the few active generals, who was also an active conspirator, Friedrich Olbricht, as well as Beck, Moltke, Yorck von Wartenburg, and others had won him over a year earlier. He had been sounded discreetly in 1942 and had replied: 'No, we must win the war first. Things like this are not permissible in a war, especially a war against the Bolsheviks. But when we return home we shall know how to deal with the brown pest.' As he lay in hospital recovering from the grave injuries he had received in North Africa – the man who wanted to kill Hitler had only one eye and one arm, and had to set the fuse with an instrument like small pincers attached to the three remaining fingers of his left hand – members of the Kreisau circle came and talked to him and by the time he began his office work as Chief of Staff of the Reserve Army, the opposition had no more radiant, determined combatant in its ranks than this poetry-loving south German aristocrat.

He joined the others at a time when after years of disappointment and frustration morale was low. Oster and Canaris had

been replaced by SS intelligence men; Moltke was locked up; the Allies, committed to the 'unconditional surrender' formula, ignored the existence of the German opposition, and many became deeply affected by a sense of isolation, hopelessness, and despair. D-Day established the Allied armies in France; the Russians stood in East Prussia. Stauffenberg sent a friend to Tresckow: was it still worth going ahead? 'The assassination must be attempted at any cost,' came the reply. 'We must prove to the world and to future generations that the men of the German opposition movement dared to take the decisive step, and to hazard their lives on it. Nothing else matters.' Stauffenberg agreed and prepared himself.

The events immediately prior to Stauffenberg's brief appearance at Rastenburg show that Hitler's unnatural luck held while the actions of the opposition were blighted and ruined by a similarly inexplicable mixture of bad luck and the amateurish inefficiency which Moltke had prophesied:

▷ 11th July 1944, Berchtesgaden: Stauffenberg and Haeften went to Obersalzberg for a conference with Hitler. As on 20th July, a bomb was hidden in Stauffenberg's brief-case, but the fuse was not set because apart from Hitler no other top Nazis like Himmler and Göring were present. The attempt was therefore abandoned.

▷ 15th July 1944, Rastenburg: the Führer's HQ was now back in East Prussia; Göring and Himmler were both present. Hitler was called out of the room at the precise moment when Stauffenberg began setting the fuse, and did not return.

▷ 17th July 1944, a road near Rommel's HQ, northern France: Rommel, whose proposal for an armistice Hitler had rejected, was now determined to act on his own and bring about peace in the West by personal action. But Rommel's staff car was shot up by low-flying RAF aircraft and his driver was killed; Rommel was severely injured and put out of action for months.

The fateful day
While on that day of climax, 20th July 1944, Stauffenberg waited outside the conference room for the explosion, Heusinger's oral report continued within. Presently, Hitler and the officers next to him moved closer to the map spread out on the table. Colonel Brandt, the innocent carrier of the brandy bottles in 1943, spotted Stauffenberg's brief-case on the Führer's side of the table support and, in case it inconvenienced Hitler, obligingly placed it on the other side of the support. A few moments later came the explosion. Brandt himself, and two officers standing on Hitler's right were killed right away, as was a stenographer. Another two officers

Below: The room in Plötzensee prison where the first eight of those condemned after the plot were killed (some 5,000 died in the subsequent purge). One by one the eight were stripped to the waist and strung up by a noose of piano wire on the meathooks at the far end. On Hitler's orders, a film was made of their death agonies, but it was never found. The room remains as a memorial

were severely wounded, while others, further away from the bomb in this flimsily constructed room with its wide-open windows, received only slight injuries. The latter included Hitler.

Stauffenberg, having heard and seen the explosion, flew back to Berlin in the firm conviction that Hitler was dead. For something like five hours the rebels occupied and sealed off the governmental nerve-centre of Berlin. Yet it soon became clear that while the programme, directives, and men in command of Germany's first post-Nazi government were all ready to begin, the actual details of a full-scale coup d'état, which was the task of the military leadership, had not been worked out at all. When news came through in the evening that the Führer lived, all collapsed. The conspiracy did rather better in Paris where

the Wehrmacht governor of France, Karl Heinrich von Stülpnagel, managed to get the whole of the SS and SD leadership locked up in a French prison. He then went to the Commander-in-Chief of the Army, none other than Kluge, late of Army Group Centre, and asked him to act against the Nazi high command and make peace. In the end Kluge said: 'I would if only the swine were dead.'

They paid with their lives

In Berlin, Nazi authority was restored by dusk. One or two of the leaders of the conspiracy, including Beck, committed suicide. Stauffenberg was executed by firing squad in the courtyard of the War Ministry and so was spared torture, degradation, public trial under the obscene and fanatical Judge Freisler, and execution by

slow strangulation suspended from a meathook. This was the fate of his friends, of most of the Kreisau circle, and of many others who had been concerned only on the periphery. It was to be the fate of von Moltke since under Gestapo torture the Kreisau secrets at last came out.

The men wiped out by the final orgy of Nazi murder and revenge, which went far beyond anything even the Nazis had so far achieved outside concentration camps, all had in common one thing: that in decreasing hopefulness and mounting despair they wanted to prepare themselves and others for a world in which decency, political and racial tolerance, and a sense of belonging together should be the aim. For this they suffered through many years of sustained effort and finally paid with their lives for the sins of others.

VERDUNKELUNG

8 THE DEFEAT OF THE AXIS

The Bombing of Germany

At the outset of the war in September 1939 Bomber Command went into action with such stringent instructions to avoid causing civilian casualties that there was even doubt about the advisability of attacking German warships at their bases in case civilian dock staff should be on or near them. Less than three years later, in May 1942, Bomber Command launched a thousand bombers against the centre of Cologne. In late July and early August 1943 about 40,000 German civilians were killed in a series of Bomber Command operations against Hamburg. In February 1945 even greater casualties were caused by a catastrophic attack on Dresden.

In September 1939 Bomber Command was small in size, inadequate in equipment, and defective in technique. For operations against Germany it could muster about 280 aircraft. Bomber Command was not only much smaller than the corresponding German force but it was also equipped with less reliable high explosive bombs than the German equivalents. In addition, Bomber Command, surprisingly, had no proper system of navigation.

By the end of the war Bomber Command could regularly despatch more than 1,500 aircraft on a single operation. More than a thousand of these were four-engined Lancasters which, with their great range, their huge bomb loads of up to ten tons, and their remarkable durability, were, as heavy bombers, internationally in a class of their own. Of the rest, some 200 were Mosquitoes which, owing to their performance, had a versatility perhaps exceeding that of any

Left: German black-out poster

other aircraft which saw service in the Second World War. The bombs available ranged from the 4lb incendiary which chiefly accounted for the firestorms in Hamburg and Dresden, to the 22,000lb Grandslam designed by Dr Barnes Wallis which, with the smaller version, the 12,000lb Tallboy, brought down the Bielefeld viaduct.

Nor was this the whole, or even in terms of numbers of aircraft the greater part, of the bomber forces which, in the last year of the war, could be brought to bear upon Germany. Other than Great Britain, the United States was the only power which before the war had evolved a doctrine of strategic bombing and during it had worked up a force to carry it out. This working up began in 1942 when US 8th Air Force, having established bases in the United Kingdom for its B-17 Flying Fortresses and B-24 Liberators, both of which were four-engined bombers, began experimental daylight operations against targets in France and other parts of German-occupied Europe. In January 1943 these operations were extended to Germany but it was not until the end of the year that 8th Air Force had enough bombers to mount regular operations from 600 to 700 strong.

Meanwhile, another US bomber force, the 15th, was formed on Italian bases and in January 1944 these two formations were placed under unified command to compose the United States Strategic Air Forces in Europe. By June 1944 the American bomber forces so combined could despatch more than 1,500 aircraft on operations in a single day. Thus, within two years of their initial bombing attacks in August 1942

involving only a dozen aircraft, the Americans were ranging over all Europe from England and Italy in greater strength than RAF Bomber Command.

Because their aircraft carried lighter loads than the British, the Americans were in the last year of the war still inferior to the British in bombing power. All the same, American 8th and 15th Air Forces were in some other respects more significant fighting formations than Bomber Command. In particular, the Americans made a more important contribution to the winning of command of the air than the British, and command of the air was decisive in making bombing a really effective and ultimately conclusive way of waging war.

This paradox arose from the different bombing policies which the two forces followed. In the last three years of peace, when the bombing offensive was planned, and in the first year of the war, when it began to be attempted, the main idea of the British was the selection of key points in the German war machine such as power stations, oil plants, railway junctions and marshalling yards, dams, and other sensitive points destruction of which would impede or even dislocate the German war effort. This policy, to be effective, depended upon accurate intelligence since the whole idea of 'key point' attack would only work if the target really was a key point. It also depended upon a high degree of bombing accuracy and destructiveness.

Marching with this selective key point theory was another which owed its origin not only to its own merit but also, perhaps, to a fear in anticipation that key point bombing might be hard to realize in prac-

tice. It was that bombing, even if it lacked the accuracy and destructiveness to dispose effectively of key points, might, through its moral effect upon the people who lived and worked in their neighbourhood, nevertheless achieve important and possibly even decisive effects upon the enemy's capacity to continue the war. After all, the bombing of London in June 1917 by a mere handful of primitive Gothas had caused a panic. The merit of this idea was that it could seemingly be realized with a considerable bombing inaccuracy, such as for example would be produced in night operations, and by a force lacking the power to destroy major installations like concrete dams. The difficulty was that it might be considered improper to attack towns rather than installations and there had, indeed, been a furore about the bombing of people rather than things in the Spanish Civil War.

By Christmas 1939 Bomber Command had sufficient experience of war to know that it could not carry on major operations against Germany in daylight. The reason was simply that an aircraft able to go the distance and carry a worthwhile load of bombs could not achieve the performance to survive in combat with an enemy fighter which could do its work with a much smaller load and duration. By the autumn of 1941, Bomber Command had proved photographically that oil plants and even large railway marshalling yards were much too small to be found and hit in night operations against defended areas.

Area attack on major cities

Thus, at the end of 1941, Bomber Command was presented with the alternatives of being withdrawn from its strategic offensive against Germany or of concentrating upon much larger targets. At a time when British arms on land and at sea were defeated almost upon appearance, at a time when the Germans were advancing rapidly into the heart of Russia, and the Japanese, having struck down the American fleet at Pearl Harbour, were on the verge of the conquest of an empire, it is not to be wondered at that the British, despite some disagreement in their inner councils, refused to put Bomber Command into voluntary liquidation. Instead the policy of area attack upon major German cities was instituted as the prime one to be followed.

Though this did not initiate area bomb-

Above: Veteran Lancaster bomber about to make its 100th operational trip, May 1944. The base commander watches as the ground crew write a message on an 8,000-lb bomb to be loaded on the aircraft
Left: Flares illuminate German V1 flying bomb launching site for RAF Halifax bomber, July 1944. V1s killed some 6,000 people, mainly in London

ROTTERDAM
PARIJS - ANTWERPEN

C'est l'Angleterre qui a jeté les premières bombes le 12 janvier 1940 sur la population civile

ing, which had already been practised both by the British and the Germans, it did make it the main theme of the Bomber Command offensive, which it remained for the duration of the war. From this, and in particular from an important directive of February 1942, there flowed the great offensive of 1942-45 embracing the Battles of the Ruhr, Hamburg, and Berlin.

This was not wanton or indiscriminate bombing. It was an organized attempt to destroy German military power, which nothing else seemed able to check, through the systematic destruction of its greatest industrial and administrative centres. But to be effective, area bombing had to be concentrated, sustained, and very heavy. In the Thousand Bomber attack upon Cologne in 1942 only about 400 Germans were killed and this attack was only made possible by calling into action the whole front line of Bomber Command and the whole of its operational training organization as well. Clearly Bomber Command had to be greatly expanded and its operations had to be made much more concentrated.

This latter requirement found expression in the creation of the Pathfinder Force and accompanying techniques and equipment ranging from marker bombs to radar devices for navigation and target finding. By these means more and more bombers were brought over smaller and smaller areas in shorter and shorter times and in 1943 Bomber Command became more and more able to 'rub out' towns. These greater concentrations of bombers which emitted more and more radar emanations and pyrotechnics, however, offered the German night-fighter force easier targets for interception and the bombing offensive at night became a grim race between the destruction of towns by Bomber Command and the destruction of Bomber Command by the German night-fighter force.

In the summer of 1943 when the Battle of Hamburg was over, Albert Speer, the German minister for armament and war production, thought that six more blows on that scale would end the war. In the four and a half months of the Battle of Berlin from November 1943 to March 1944, Bomber Command lost the equivalent of the whole of its front line, mostly to German fighters, and it became obvious that a continuing offensive on that scale would end, not the war, but Bomber Command.

The Allied bombing of enemy cities gave the Germans good material for propaganda. Between 1939 and 1945 nearly 600,000 German civilians were killed in bombing raids. The total British civilian losses for the same period were 65,000. **Above:** *Posters issued in Holland and Belgium stress civilian suffering.* **Right:** *Germans salvage belongings after an air raid*

The Defeat of the Axis

As the fortunes of Bomber Command and the German night-fighter force see-sawed with each tactical shift and technical innovation, the constant factor was the inability of Bomber Command to deal directly with its scourge. Lancasters could not fight Junkers 88s or even Messerschmitt 110s. Their only hope was to dodge them. Nor could they bomb their airfields and factories. The area bombing offensive, for all its destructive and terrifying powers, could only achieve incidental or indirect effects against 'key' targets. Whatever else it may have done in diverting German effort and pinning it down, area bombing up to March 1944 had not resulted in a significant reduction in essential German war production nor had it prevented the German armed forces from continuing their operations in Russia and Italy or against Bomber Command itself.

The Americans had expected as much. They had refused to be diverted by British warnings from their plan of daylight precision attacks against selected key point targets. Throughout 1942, however, they had not felt strong enough in numbers to carry their determination into operational effect over Germany. In 1943 they began to do so. Believing that night area bombing was a blunt and ineffective tactic and possessing aircraft unsuitable for and crews untrained in night-flying, they massed their Flying Fortresses and Liberators in tight highly-disciplined formations and operated at very high altitudes. At high altitude they hoped to escape the worst of the flak and in their formations they hoped to bring such concentrated fire-power to bear that the formations would successfully fight their way to and from their targets in daylight.

One difficulty was that at altitude over Germany the bombers often found themselves over dense cloud so that the best they could do was to deliver approximate or area attacks. Another was that the formations were regularly shot to pieces by the German fighters. The Americans therefore gave higher priority to bombing Germany's aircraft industry. But the aircraft industry in Germany was divided into small units, well dispersed, and often at extreme range from England. So the Americans were given no alternative to the policy of seeking to make a dangerous and difficult task possible by undertaking a more dangerous and more difficult one. The result was disaster. Two-thirds of a force despatched to Schweinfurt on 14th October 1943 was destroyed or damaged. Within six days and from four attacks the Americans lost 138 bombers.

This was comparable to, and indeed, even more decisive than the fate which at that time was approaching Bomber Command in the Battle of Berlin and in incurring it the Americans had done much less damage to Germany than the British had achieved. So in the winter of 1943-44 it seemed that the strategic air attack on Germany had been a costly failure. The indications, however, were misleading. The break-through in the air was imminent and the heavy bombers of Great Britain and America were on the verge of achievements which were not only important but decisive for the war.

The reasons for this, one of the most extraordinary and abrupt changes in military fortune in the Second World War, are chiefly to be found in three singular developments: first, the introduction of an effective long-range fighter, secondly, the advance of Allied armies across France, and thirdly, the development by Bomber Command of heavy precision-bombing techniques.

After Schweinfurt, the Americans realized that their survival depended upon the introduction of a machine with the range of a bomber and the performance of a fighter. The answer was found in the hybrid P-51 Mustang, a North American aircraft with a Rolls Royce engine and hitherto chiefly in service with the RAF, which, with droppable long-range tanks, was rushed into action with US 8th Air Force from December 1943. By March 1944, it had developed the capacity to fight over Berlin from British bases. Moreover, it could take on any German fighter in service on at least equal and, in most respects, superior terms. These aircraft swept into action in such force – 14,000 were produced before the end of the war – and to such effect that the day-fighter force of Germany in the air was rapidly smashed and the way opened for a major resumption of the daylight bombing offensive. From February 1944 onwards 8th and 15th Air Forces seized their opportunity with growing confidence and rapidly diminishing casualties. The command of the daylight air over Germany and German Europe passed from the Germans to the Americans. In May 1944, the Americans began an offensive against German synthetic oil production.

To prepare for the invasion
During this period, Bomber Command still had to face severe casualties in maintaining what it could of the area offensive against Germany and in conducting a night precision offensive against the French railway system. The latter was to open the way for the invasion of Europe by the American and British armies. And it did. So accurate and so destructive were these Bomber Command attacks that the Germans lost the sovereign advantage which had previously made ideas of invasion academic, namely, an efficient interior system of communications which would enable them rapidly to concentrate a superior force against whatever invasion areas were selected.

The Bomber Command attacks, however, did even more than that. They showed the way to heavy precision bombing. They were the link between the vast destructive power which the needs of the area offensive had demanded and generated and the almost surgical accuracy of the Möhne Dam raid of May 1943. In June 1944, Bomber Command began to reinforce the American attacks on German oil plants. By September the Germans were confronted with an oil crisis so serious that they were compelled to restrict flying and the Allied air superiority became even more pronounced. As the armies advanced towards the German frontier, greatly aided by this superiority, the Germans lost the forward bases of their fighter defences and the Allied bomber forces were able to push their radar transmitters nearer the German targets upon which a greater and more and more accurate rain of bombs therefore descended.

Differences of opinion as to the best targets, together with weather and tactical considerations, divided the aim of the bombers between support of the armies, the oil offensive, the destruction of communications, naval bombing, and the continuing area offensive. But in late 1944 and early 1945, the huge destructive power of bombing was liberated by the attainment of command of the air. The great German synthetic oil plants were ruined beyond repair and the oil crisis became a famine. The communications system of Germany was rendered chaotic and eventually unworkable to the point where administration began to break down.

As the German armies retreated from the East and the West, they fell back not upon a heartland but upon a national disintegration which proved incapable of mounting even an underground resistance. The British and American bombers played a vital role in assisting the advance of the armies. They also produced a situation in the interior of Germany which guaranteed the collapse of the war machine.

The surviving paradox of the final triumph of strategic bombing is this: if the British had not adopted the policy of night area bombing, which in itself produced disappointing results, it is difficult to see how the power of heavy destruction of 1944-45 could have been generated. If the Americans had not persisted with the policy of daylight self-defending formation-bombing tactics, which produced poor results and terrible casualties, it is hard to see how command of the air could have been won. It was, in the last resort, the combination of command of the air and very heavy bombing which made a critical contribution to Germany's defeat.

From Normandy to the Baltic

The Allied liberation-invasion of Normandy, in June 1944, was the most dramatic and decisive event of the Second World War. The cross-sea move of the Anglo-American expeditionary force, based on England, had been delayed by bad weather. It was launched when the wind was still strong enough to make the move hazardous—but also unlikely. General Eisenhower's decision to take the risk was not only justified by the outcome of the Normandy invasion but contributed to its surprise effect.

The Allied landings were made on the morning of 6th June in the Bay of the Seine between Caen and Cherbourg and were immediately preceded by the moonlight dropping of strong airborne forces close to the two flanks. The invasion was prepared by a sustained air offensive of unparalleled intensity, which had been particularly directed against the enemy's communications, with the aim of paralysing his power of moving up reserves.

Although many factors had pointed to this sector as the probable scene, the Germans were caught off their balance—with most of their reserves posted east of the Seine. That was due partly to the ingenuity of the plans for misleading them, and partly

Troops of Cheshire Regiment land on east bank of the Rhine during opening phase of 21st Army Group's drive across the Rhine towards the heart of the Ruhr, March 1945

to an obstinate preconception that the Allies would come not only direct across the Channel but by the shortest route. The effect of this miscalculation was made fatal by the action of the Allied air forces in breaking the bridges over the Seine.

By deductions drawn from the lay-out of the Anglo-American forces in England prior to the invasion, and contrary to the views of his military staff, Hitler had, in March, begun to suspect that the Allies would land in Normandy. Rommel, who was put in charge of the forces on the north coast, came to the same view. But Runstedt, who was commander-in-chief in the West, counted on the Allies landing in the narrower part of the Channel between Dieppe and Calais. That conviction was due not only to the Allies' past fondness for maximum air cover, and the effect of their present deception plans, but even more to his reasoning that such a line was theoretically the right line since it was the shortest line to their objective. That was a characteristic calculation of strategic orthodoxy. Significantly, it did not credit the Allied command with a preference for the unexpected, nor even with an inclination to avoid the most strongly defended approach.

The invaders' actual plan secured more than the avoidance of the best prepared defences. In choosing the Normandy route, the Allied command operated on a line which alternatively threatened the important ports of Le Havre and Cherbourg and was able to keep the Germans in doubt until the last moment as to which was the objective. When they came to realize that Cherbourg was the main objective, the Seine had become a partition wall dividing their forces, and they could only move their reserves to the critical point by a wide detour. The movement was lengthened by the continued interference of the Allied air forces. Moreover, when the reinforcements reached the battle-area, they tended to arrive in the sector farthest from Cherbourg—the Caen sector. The British lodgement here became, not only a menace in itself, but a shield for the development of the American operations farther west, in the Cotentin Peninsula. That double effect and alternative threat had a vital influence on the success of the invasion as a whole.

The vast armada achieved the sea-passage without interference, and the beaches were captured more easily than had been expected, except where the American left wing landed, east of the Vire Estuary. Yet the margin between success and frustration, in driving the bridgehead deep enough, was narrower than appeared. The invaders did not succeed in gaining control of the keys to Caen and Cherbourg. Fortunately, the wide frontage of the attack became a vital factor in redeeming the chances.

Dutch SS poster predicts end of European culture from brutalized US 'liberators'

The Germans' natural concentration on preserving these keys on either flank left them weak in the space between them. A quick exploitation of the intermediate landings near Arromanches carried the British into Bayeux, and by the end of the week the expansion of this penetration gave the Allies a bridgehead nearly forty miles broad and five to twelve miles deep between the Orne and the Vire. They had also secured another, though smaller, bridgehead on the east side of the Cotentin Peninsula. On the 12th, the Americans pinched out the intermediate keypoint of Carentan, so that a continuous bridgehead of over sixty miles span was secured.

General Montgomery, who was in executive command of the invading forces as a whole, under Eisenhower, could now develop his offensive moves more fully.

The second week brought a marked expansion of the bridgehead on the western flank. Here American 1st Army developed a drive across the waist of the Cotentin Peninsula, while British 2nd Army on the eastern flank continued to absorb the bulk of the German reinforcements by its pressure around Caen.

In the third week, having cut off Cherbourg, the Americans wheeled up the peninsula and drove into the port from the rear. Cherbourg was captured on 27th June, though not before the port itself had been made temporarily unusable. Around Caen, British thrusts were baffled by the enemy's skilful defensive tactics in country favourable to a flexible defence, but their threat continued to distract the German command's free use of its reserves.

Under cover of this pressure, the build-up of the invading forces proceeded at a remarkably rapid rate. It was aided by the development of artificial harbours, which mitigated the interference of the weather and also contributed to surprise – by upsetting the enemy's calculations.

July was a month of tough fighting in Normandy, with little to show for the effort except heavy casualties. But the Germans could not afford such a drain as well as the Allies could, and behind the almost static battle-front the Allied resources were continually growing.

On 3rd July American 1st Army, having regrouped after the capture of Cherbourg, began an attempted break-out push southward towards the base-line of the peninsula. But the attackers were still short of room for manoeuvre, and progress was slow. On the 8th, General Dempsey's British 2nd Army penetrated into Caen, but was blocked at the crossings of the Orne. Successive flanking thrusts were also parried. On the 18th a more ambitious stroke, Operation Goodwood, was attempted – when a phalanx of three armoured divisions, one behind the other, was launched from a bridgehead north-east of Caen – through a narrow gap created by a terrific air bombardment by 2,000 aircraft on a three-mile frontage – and drove across the rear of the Caen defences. A break-through was momentarily in sight, but the Germans were quick in swinging a screen of tanks and anti-tank guns across the path. After that missed opportunity, fresh British and Canadian attacks made little headway. But they kept the enemy's attention, and best troops, fixed in the Caen sector. Seven of the eight Panzer divisions were drawn there.

At the western end of the Normandy bridgehead, the American forces under General Bradley advanced their front five to eight miles during the first three weeks of July. Meantime, General Patton's American 3rd Army had been transported from England to Normandy, in readiness for a bigger thrust.

Operation Cobra

Operation Cobra was launched on 25th July, initially by six divisions on a four-mile frontage, and was preceded by an air bombardment even heavier than in Operation Goodwood. The ground was so thickly cratered that it aided the sparse and dazed defenders in putting a brake on the American drive. On the first two days only five miles was covered but then the breach was widened, and progress quickened – towards the southwest corner of the peninsula. The decisive break-out took place on 31st July. It was helped by a sudden switch of the weight of British 2nd Army from east of the Orne to the central sector south of Bayeux, for an attack near Caumont, the previous day. While the enemy were reinforcing this danger-point with such troops as they could spare from Caen the Americans forced the lock of the door at Avranches, near the west coast of the Cotentin Peninsula.

Pouring through the gap, Patton's tanks surged southward and then westward, quickly flooding most of Brittany. Then they turned eastward and swept through the country north of the Loire, towards Le Mans and Chartres. The cramped seventy-mile front of the bridgehead had been immediately converted into a potential 400-mile front. Space was too wide for the enemy's available forces to impose any effective check on the advance, which repeatedly by-passed any of the road-centres where they attempted a stand.

The one danger to this expanding torrent was that the enemy might bring off a counter-thrust to cut the Avranches bottleneck, through which supplies had to be maintained. On Hitler's insistence, the Germans attempted such a stroke on the night of 6th August, switching four Panzer divisions westwards for the purpose. The approach, chosen by Hitler on the map at his remote headquarters in the east, was too direct, and thus ran head-on into the Americans' flank shield. Once checked, the attack was disrupted by the swift intervention of the Allied air forces. And when the thrust failed, it turned in a fatal way for the Germans – by drawing their weight westward just as the American armoured forces were sweeping eastward behind their rear. The American left wing wheeled north to Argentan, to combine in a pincer move with General Crerar's Canadian 1st Army, pushing down from Caen upon Falaise. Although the pincers did not close in time to cut off completely the two armies within their embrace, 50,000 prisoners were taken and 10,000 corpses found on the battlefield, while all the divisions which got away were badly mauled. Their vehicles were even worse hit than their men by the continuous air-bombing they suffered in an ever-narrowing space. The Germans' losses in the 'Falaise Pocket' left them without the forces or movement resources to meet the Allies' continued easterly sweep to the Seine, and past the Seine.

The rapidity of this wide flanking manoeuvre, and its speedy effect in causing a general collapse of the German position in France, forestalled the need of the further lever that was inserted by the landing of General Patch's American (and French) 7th Army in southern France on 15th August. The invasion was a 'walk-in', as the Germans had been forced to denude the Riviera coast of all but a mere four divisions, of inferior quality. The subsequent advance inland and up the Rhône Valley was mainly a supply problem, rather than a tactical problem. Marseilles was occupied on the 23rd, while a drive through the mountains reached Grenoble the same day.

On the 19th, the French Forces of the Interior had started a rising in Paris, and although their situation was critical for some days, the scales were turned in their favour by the arrival of Allied armoured forces in the city on the 25th. Meantime Patton's army was racing towards the Marne, north-east of Paris.

The next important development was an exploiting thrust by British 2nd Army, which crossed the Seine east of Rouen, to trap the remnants of German VII Army, which were still opposing Canadian 1st Army west of Rouen. Dempsey's spearheads reached Amiens early on the 31st, having covered seventy miles from the Seine in two days and a night. Crossing the Somme, they then drove on swiftly past Arras and Lille to the Belgian frontier – behind the back of German XV Army on the Pas de Calais coast. To the east, Hodges' American 1st Army had also leapt forward to the Belgian frontier near Hirson.

Farther east, Patton's army made an even more dazzling drive through Champagne and past Verdun, to the Moselle between Metz and Thionville, close to the frontier of Germany. And although it had begun to lose impetus through the difficulty of maintaining adequate petrol supplies and its armoured spearheads were halted by lack of petrol, its strategic importance was increasing daily. For Patton's army was hardly eighty miles from the Rhine. When they received sufficient fuel to resume their advance, opposition was stiffening. Patton's thrust had produced a decisive issue in the Battle of France, but the supply position checked it from deciding the Battle for Germany in the same breath. The strategic law of overstretch re-asserted itself, to impose a postponement. On this sector it proved a long one, as Patton became drawn into a direct approach to Metz, and then into a protracted close-quarter battle for that famous fortress-city to the forfeit of the prospects of a by-passing manoeuvre.

In the early days of September the pace grew fastest on the left wing, and it was

The Defeat of the Axis

thither that a bid for early victory was now transferred. British armoured columns entered Brussels on the 3rd, Antwerp on the 4th, and then penetrated into Holland. By this great manoeuvre, Montgomery had cut off the Germans' remaining troops in Normandy and the Pas de Calais – their principal force in the West. American 1st Army occupied Namur and crossed the Meuse at Dinant and Givet.

German recovery
At this crisis the executive command of the German forces in the West was taken over by General Model, who had gained the reputation on the Russian front of being able 'to scrape up reserves from nowhere'. He now performed that miracle on a bigger scale. On any normal calculation it appeared that the Germans, of whom more than half a million had been captured in the drive through France, had no chance of scraping up reserves to hold their 500-mile frontier from Switzerland to the North Sea. But in the event they achieved an amazing rally which prolonged the war for eight months.

In this recovery they were greatly helped by the Allies' supply difficulties, which reduced the first onset to a lightweight charge that could be checked by a hastily improvised defence, and then curtailed the build-up of the Allied armies for a powerful attack. In part, the supply difficulties were due to the length of the Allies' own advance. In part, they were due to the Germans' strategy in leaving garrisons behind to hold the French ports. The fact that the Allies were thus denied the use of Dunkirk, Calais, Boulogne, and Le Havre, as well as the big ports in Brittany, became a powerful indirect brake on the Allies' offensive. Although the Allies had captured the still greater port of Antwerp in good condition, the enemy kept a tenacious grip of the estuary of the Schelde, and thus prevented the Allies making use of the port.

Before the break-out from Normandy, their supplies had to be carried less than twenty miles from the base in order to replenish the striking forces. They now had to be carried nearly 300 miles. The burden was thrown almost entirely on the Allies' motor transport, as the French railway network had been destroyed by previous air attacks. The bombing that had been so useful in paralysing the German countermeasures against the invasion became a boomerang when the Allies needed to maintain the momentum of their pursuit.

In mid-September a bold attempt was made to loosen the stiffening resistance by dropping three airborne divisions behind the German right flank in Holland, to clear the way for a fresh drive by British 2nd Army up to and over the lower Rhine. By dropping the airborne forces in successive layers over a sixty-mile belt of country behind the German front a foothold was gained on all four of the strategic stepping-stones needed to cross the interval – the passage of the Wilhelmina Canal at Eindhoven, of the Meuse at Grave, of the Waal and Lek (the two branches of the Rhine), at Nijmegen and Arnhem respectively. Three of these four stepping-stones were secured and passed. But a stumble at the third forfeited the chance of securing the fourth in face of the Germans' speedy reaction.

This check led to the frustration of the overland thrust and the sacrifice of 1st Airborne Division at Arnhem. But the possibility of outflanking the Rhine defence-line was a strategic prize that justified the stake and the exceptional boldness of dropping airborne forces so far behind the front. 1st Airborne Division maintained its isolated position at Arnhem for ten days instead of the two that were reckoned as the maximum to be expected. But the chances of success were lessened by the way that the descent of the airborne forces at these four successive points, in a straight line, signposted all too clearly the direction of 2nd Army's thrust.

The obviousness of the aim simplified the opponent's problem in concentrating his available reserves to hold the final stepping-stone, and to overthrow the British airborne forces there, before the leading troops of 2nd Army arrived to relieve them. The nature of the Dutch countryside with its 'canalized' routes, also helped the defenders in obstructing the advance, while there was a lack of wider moves to mask the directness of the approach and to distract the defender.

After the failure of the Arnhem gamble, the prospect of early victory faded. The Allies were thrown back on the necessity of building up their resources along the frontiers of Germany for a massive offensive of a deliberate kind. The build-up was bound to take time, but the Allied command increased its own handicap by concentrating, first, on an attempt to force the Aachen gateway into Germany, rather than on clearing the shores of the Schelde to open up a fresh supply route. The American advance on Aachen developed into a too direct approach, and its progress was repeatedly checked.

Along the rest of the Western Front the efforts of the Allied armies during September and October 1944 amounted to little more than nibbling. Meantime the German defence was being continuously reinforced – with such reserves as could be scraped from elsewhere, with freshly raised forces, and with the troops which had managed to make their way back from France. The German build-up along the front was progressing faster than that of the Allies, despite Germany's great inferiority of material resources. The Schelde Estuary was not cleared of the enemy until early in November.

In mid-November a general offensive was launched by all six Allied armies on the Western Front. It brought disappointingly small results, at heavy cost; and continued efforts merely exhausted the attackers.

Allied differences
There had been a difference of view between the American and British commanders as to the basic pattern of this offensive. The British advocated a concentrated blow, whereas the Americans chose to test the German defences over a very wide front. After the offensive had ended in failure, the British naturally criticized the plan for its dispersion of effort. But closer analysis of the operations suggests that a more fundamental fault was its obviousness. Although the offensive was wide in the sense of being distributed among several armies, it was narrowly concentrated within each army's sector. In each case the offensive effort travelled along the line where the defender would be inclined to expect it. For the attacks were directed against the natural gateways into Germany. Moreover, the main attacks were made in flat country that easily became water-logged in winter.

In mid-December the Germans gave the Allied armies, and peoples, a shock by launching a counter-offensive. They had been able to hold the Allied autumn offensive and slow it down to a crawl without having to engage their own mobile reserves. So from the time when the chances of an American break-through waned, the risk of a serious German riposte might have become apparent – and the more so, in view of the knowledge that the Germans had withdrawn many of their Panzer divisions from the line during the October lull, to re-equip them with fresh tanks. But the Allies' expectations of early victory tended to blind them to the possibility of any counter-stroke, so that this profited by unexpectedness in that respect.

The German command also profited by treating the problem of suitable ground in a way very different from their opponents.

*The liberation of France. **Top:** Civilians kick and jeer at German soldiers in Paris. As the Allied forces approached the city, resistance to the occupiers came out into the open. **Centre:** Jeering townsfolk escort a woman collaborator, marked by her shaved head, out of a village near Cherbourg after that area's liberation in July 1944. **Bottom:** Crowds greet General de Gaulle as he walks down the Champs Elysées from the Arc de Triomphe on 26th August 1944, the day after Paris's liberation*

Dropping forces behind the front at Arnhem, September 1944, was part of a bold plan to outflank the Rhine defence-line. The gamble failed and hope for an early victory faded. **Left:** *British Horsa glider used to land troops.* **Right:** *American paratrooper at Arnhem*

They chose for the site of their counter-offensive the hilly and wooded country of the Ardennes. Being generally regarded as difficult country, a large scale offensive there was likely to be unexpected by orthodox opponents. At the same time, the thick woods provided concealment for the massing of forces, while the high ground offered drier ground for the manoeuvre of tanks. Thus the Germans might hope to score both ways.

Their chief danger was from the speedy interference of Allied air-power. Model summed up the problem thus: 'Enemy No. 1 is the hostile air force which, because of its absolute superiority, tries to destroy our spearheads of attack and our artillery through fighter-bomber attacks and bomb carpets, and to render movement in the rear impossible.' So the Germans launched their stroke when the meteorological forecast promised them a natural cloak, and for the first three days mist and rain kept the Allied air forces on the ground. Thus even bad weather was converted into an advantage.

High stakes on limited funds

The Germans needed all the advantage that they could possibly secure. They were playing for high stakes on very limited funds. The striking force comprised V and VI Panzer Armies, to which had been given the bulk of the tanks that could be scraped together.

An awkward feature of the Ardennes from an offensive point of view was the way that the high ground was intersected with deep valleys, where the through roads became bottle-necks. At these points a tank advance was liable to be blocked. The German command might have forestalled this risk by using parachute troops to seize these strategic defiles. But they had allowed this specialist arm to dwindle and its technique to become rusty since the coup that captured Crete in May 1941. Only a few handfuls were used.

The aim of the counter-offensive was far-reaching—to break through to Antwerp by an indirect move, cut off the British army group from the American as well as from its supplies, and then crush the former while isolated. V Panzer Army, now led by Manteuffel, was to break through the American front in the Ardennes, swerve westward, then wheel north across the Meuse, past Namur to Antwerp. As it advanced, it was to build up a defensive flank-barricade to shut off interference from the American armies farther south. VI Panzer Army, under an SS commander, Sepp Dietrich, was to thrust north-west on an oblique line, past Liège to Antwerp, creating a strategic barrier astride the rear of the British and the more northerly American armies.

Aided by its surprise, the German counter-offensive made menacing progress in the opening days, creating alarm and confusion on the Allied side. The deepest thrust was made by Manteuffel's V Panzer Army. But time and opportunities were lost through fuel shortages, resulting from wintry weather and growing Allied air-pressure, and the drive fell short of the Meuse, though it came ominously close to it at some points. In that frustration much

was due to the way in which outflanked American detachments held on to several of the most important bottle-necks in the Ardennes, as well as to the speed with which Montgomery, who had taken charge of the situation on the northern flank, swung his reserves southward to forestall the enemy at the crossings of the Meuse.

In the next phase, when the Allied armies had concentrated their strength and attempted to pinch off the great wedge driven into their front, the Germans carried out a skilful withdrawal that brought them out of the potential trap. Judged on its own account, the German counter-offensive had been a profitable operation, for even though it fell short of the objectives, it had upset the Allies' preparations and inflicted much damage at a cost that was not excessive for the effect—except in the later phase, when Hitler hindered the withdrawal.

But viewed in relation to the whole situation, this counter-offensive had been a fatal operation. During the course of it, the Germans had expended more of their strength than they could afford in their straitened circumstances. That expenditure forfeited the chance of maintaining any prolonged resistance to a resumed Allied offensive. It brought home to the German troops their incapacity to turn the scales, and thereby undermined such hopes for victory as they might have retained.

Since the summer of 1944 the main Russian front had been stationary along a line past Warsaw through the middle of Poland. But in mid-January 1945 the Russian

American column delayed whilst moving up to meet the German retaliation in the Ardennes, December 1944. The German counter-offensive inflicted some damage but it cost the Germans the chance of maintaining any prolonged resistance to a resumed Allied advance

armies launched another and greater offensive, making longer bounds than ever before. By the end of the month they reached the Oder, barely fifty miles from Berlin, but were there checked for a time.

A new Anglo-American offensive

Early in February 1945, Eisenhower launched another offensive by the Anglo-American armies, aimed to trap and destroy the German armies west of the Rhine before they could withdraw across it. The opening attack was made by Canadian (and British) 1st Army on the left wing, wheeling up the west bank of the Rhine to develop a flanking leverage on the German forces that faced American 9th and 1st Armies west of Cologne. But the delay caused by the enemy's Ardennes stroke meant the attack was not delivered until the frozen ground had been softened by a thaw. This helped the Germans' resistance. They improved their dangerous situation by blowing up the dams on the River Roer, thus delaying for a fortnight the American attack over that waterline. Even then it met tough opposition. As a result the Americans did not enter Cologne until 5th March. The Germans had gained time to evacuate their depleted forces, and much of their equipment, over the Rhine.

But the Germans had been led to throw a high proportion of their strength into the effort to check the Allied left wing. The consequent weakness of their own left wing created an opportunity for American 1st and 3rd Armies. The right of 1st Army broke through to the Rhine at Bonn, and a detachment was able to seize by surprise

an intact bridge over the Rhine at Remagen. Eisenhower did not immediately exploit this unexpected opening, which would have involved a switch of his reserves and a considerable readjustment of his plans for the next, and decisive, stage of the campaign. But the Remagen threat served as a useful distraction to the Germans' scanty reserve.

A bigger advantage was gained by 3rd Army's breakthrough in the Eifel (the German continuation of the Ardennes). 4th Armoured Division—once again the spearhead as in the break-out from Normandy—dashed through to the Rhine at Koblenz. Patton then wheeled his forces southward, over the lower Moselle into the Palatinate and swept up the west bank of the Rhine across the rear of the forces that were opposing Patch's 7th Army. By this stroke he cut them off from the Rhine, and secured a huge bag of prisoners, while gaining for himself an unopposed crossing of the Rhine when he turned eastward again. This crossing was achieved on the night of the 22nd, between Mainz and Worms, and was quickly exploited by a deep advance into northern Bavaria. That unhinged the Germans' whole front, and forestalled the much-discussed possibility that the enemy might attempt a general withdrawal into their reputed mountain stronghold in the south.

Assault on the Rhine

On the night of the 23rd the planned assault on the Rhine was carried out, far downstream near the Dutch frontier, by Montgomery's 21st Army Group. The great

river was crossed at four points during the night, and in the morning two airborne divisions were dropped beyond it, to loosen the opposition facing the newly gained bridgeheads. The Germans' resistance began to crumble everywhere, and this crumbling was soon to develop into a general collapse.

When the British advance developed, much the most serious hindrance came from the heaps of rubble created by the excessive bombing efforts of the Allied air forces, which had thereby blocked the routes of advance far more effectively than the enemy could. For the dominant desire of the Germans now, both troops and people, was to see the British and American armies sweep eastward as rapidly as possible to reach Berlin and occupy as much of the country as possible before the Russians overcame the Oder line. Few of them were inclined to assist Hitler's purpose of obstruction by self-destruction.

Early in March Zhukov had enlarged his bridgehead over the Oder, but did not succeed in breaking out. Russian progress on the far flanks continued, and Vienna was entered early in April. Meanwhile the German front in the West had collapsed, and the Allied armies there were driving eastward from the Rhine with little opposition. They reached the Elbe, sixty miles from Berlin, on 11th April. Here they halted.

On the 16th, Zhukov resumed the offensive in conjunction with Konev, who forced the crossings of the Neisse. This time the Russians burst out of their bridgeheads, and within a week were driving into the

suburbs of Berlin—where Hitler chose to remain for the final battle. By the 25th the city had been completely isolated by the encircling armies of Zhukov and Konev, and on the 27th Konev's forces joined hands with the Americans on the Elbe. But in Berlin itself desperate street by street resistance was put up by the Germans, and was not completely overcome until the war itself ended, after Hitler's suicide on 30th April, with Germany's unconditional surrender.

In Montgomery's 21st Army Group the advance across the Elbe by British 2nd Army began in the early hours of 29th April. It was led by 8th Corps, employing DD (swimming) tanks, while the infantry were conveyed in amphibian vehicles, as in the crossing of the Rhine. On its right it was also aided by US 18th Airborne Corps (of three divisions) operating on the ground, which crossed the Elbe on the 30th. Progress now became swift, and on 2nd May British 6th Airborne Division, also operating on the ground, meeting no opposition, occupied Wismar on the Baltic coast after a forty mile drive. (A few hours after its arrival Russian tanks appeared and made contact with the British troops.) British 11th Armoured Division entered the city of Lübeck, on the Baltic, without opposition, after an exploiting drive of thirty miles. The American troops on its right likewise made rapid progress. Meanwhile, British 12th Corps had passed through 8th Corps' bridgehead with the task of capturing Hamburg, but the German garrison commander came out to surrender the city, and the British troops entered it without opposition on 3rd May.

The war in Europe came to an end officially at midnight on 8th May 1945, but in reality that was merely the final formal recognition of a finish which had taken place piecemeal during the course of the previous week.

Left: 1 German soldier during the Ardennes counter-offensive. 2 Moment of weariness for US soldier in Bastogne, Belgium, one of the vital bottlenecks which held out against the German assault. Bastogne was weakly defended until the US 101st Airborne Division ('the Screaming Eagles') raced in from Reims one day ahead of the Germans. On 22nd December the German commander demanded surrender. McAuliffe, commanding the 101st, replied with just one word: 'Nuts!' 3 Painting by Canadian Alex Colville of infantry near Nijmegen, Holland Right: 1 Poster issued by SS in Belgium depicts profit-hungry Roosevelt riding to prosperity in war, exploiting efforts of Churchill and Stalin. 2 The vice tightens. Map shows the armies of the Allies advancing into Germany

1 △ 2 ▽

New Guinea and the Philippines

'The President of the United States ordered me to break through the Japanese lines and proceed from Corregidor to Australia for the purpose, as I understand it, of organizing the American offensive against Japan, a primary object of which is the recovery of the Philippines. I came through and I shall return.' So spoke General Douglas MacArthur on his arrival in Australia in March 1942 to assume command of the meagre Allied forces in the Southwest Pacific. At the beginning of American participation in the war, Roosevelt and Churchill had agreed that the Pacific area, including Australia, should be under American command—with the Middle East and India remaining under British control, and Europe and the Atlantic coming under joint Anglo-American direction. The command in the Pacific was further divided between MacArthur's Southwest Pacific Command and the Central Pacific Command of Admiral Chester Nimitz. Each was in control of the land, sea and air forces in his zone except that Nimitz had, in addition, the direction of the amphibious operations in his rival's command.

For almost 40 years the American Navy had expected war with Japan and, now that war had finally come, was determined that the Navy was to have the pre-eminent role in the Pacific. Nimitz and the Naval Chiefs of Staff headed by Admiral Ernest King did not want any naval forces under Army command and hence decided to launch a purely naval campaign west from their big base at Hawaii towards Japan, while the commander in the Southwest Pacific was to stay on the defensive. MacArthur, however, was too strong a personality and his ideas about the way to defeat Japan were too firm for him to accept this role, and he launched his own campaign north from Australia towards Japan. Having been driven out of the Philippines by force of arms, MacArthur felt strongly that the only way for the United States to regain control of the islands was by the same means, otherwise she would never be able to reassert her pre-war authority.

MacArthur believed that the Western Allies, having been defeated so disastrously by the Asians, must prove their superiority again, a factor he felt it was folly not to take into consideration when planning the Pacific strategy against Japan. For MacArthur the only road to Tokyo which took account of American interests in Asia lay through the Philippines.

Thus Nimitz and MacArthur were to compete against each other to see which of them could defeat Japan first. Fond of this sort of confrontation, Roosevelt approved the divided command in the hope of using the natural rivalry between the Army and Navy to produce faster results. MacArthur thought it was incredible that the Navy could allow inter-service rivalry to determine the course of the war and later wrote, 'Of all the faulty decisions of the war, perhaps the most inexpressible one was the failure to unify the command in the Pacific.' Through the insistence of Admiral King, however, the commands of Nimitz and MacArthur remained separate throughout the war, despite a general realization in Washington that this was not the best of arrangements.

MacArthur was indeed a controversial figure. He had been in conflict with Roosevelt since before the war and remained so throughout. The politics and personalities of the two men were in total contrast. The situation was exacerbated by the fact that MacArthur was a thoroughgoing conservative whom some Republicans on the home front promoted as a candidate for the presidency against Roosevelt. MacArthur was also in conflict with Army Chief of Staff George Marshall and the Army establishment on a number of issues, but mainly over the 'Europe first' policy against which MacArthur repeatedly protested. This conflict was perhaps less serious as the Army was glad to have a strong and popular figure like MacArthur, however much it itself disliked him, to uphold its role in the Pacific against the pretensions of the Navy.

When MacArthur arrived in Australia, he found his new command short of manpower, poorly equipped and quite deficient in air power. He also found Australian morale shattered by the Allied *débâcle* in Asia and especially by the fall of Singapore, which had been regarded by Australians as the keystone of their security; hence his first task was to infuse the Australians with an offensive spirit and his own sense of confidence. New Guinea was to be the first priority, as it was from there

Left: Painting of American marines landing on Bougainville in the Solomon Islands, 1st November 1943 by W. F. Draper. Right: An American transport, its decks crammed with supplies, including petrol and trucks, heads for Cape Gloucester in New Britain where Allied forces landed on 26th December 1943. Rabaul, the key Japanese base on New Britain, was virtually encircled and isolated by thrusts through the Solomons and Bismarck Archipelago

that the Japanese were threatening
Australia, which was the main American
base in the South Pacific. To make Australia
secure the Japanese would have to be
evicted from New Guinea. Since a large part
of New Guinea was Australian territory
a strong offensive there would do wonders
for Australian morale; it was as important
to the Australians to reconquer New
Guinea by force of arms as it was to Mac-
Arthur to re-occupy the Philippines

the same aggressively convincing manner.

In organizing his staff, however, Mac-
Arthur refused to appoint Australian and
Dutch officers to senior positions and indeed
brought most of his senior officers with him
from the Philippines. It was not until
General George Kennedy took command of
the air forces in the Southwest Pacific that
his breezy ebullience unlimbered Mac-
Arthur's stiff personality and brought him
out of this close circle of intimates and into

closer and warmer contact with the remainder of his subordinates, hence also
closer to current information and intelligence. MacArthur soon developed a highly
efficient team which played a major role in
his coming success. A further invaluable
asset for MacArthur was the discovery of
Commander Long of the Australian armed
forces, organizer of the superb intelligence
network of coastwatchers whose information made the difference in many opera-

tions. Within three months of his arrival, MacArthur was able to start on the road back to the Philippines.

The pressure of their original offensive launched in December 1941 had carried the Japanese forces to the chain of coral islands to the north of Australia but energy had flagged when the islands were only half occupied. The Japanese held the Solomons but the object of their next offensive was the remainder – New Hebrides, New Caledonia and Port Moresby in Papua. It was with this in view that men and ships were first concentrated for a seaborne move against Port Moresby. This expedition was turned back in the carrier action of 5th-8th May in the Coral Sea, the first fought entirely by airplanes and in which the ships of the opposing forces never sighted each other. A month later a powerful Japanese thrust across the central Pacific was turned into smashing defeat by Admiral Nimitz's ships

58/59 Australian Infantry Battalion storm Japanese strong-point ('Old Vickers') on Bobdubi Ridge, Salamaua, New Guinea, 28th July 1943. Painting by Ivor Hele

at Midway, after which Japanese attention again shifted to the Southwest Pacific. Suffering from what a Japanese admiral later called 'victory disease', and against all the dictates of sound strategy, the Japanese laid plans to enlarge their already

The Defeat of the Axis

over-extended position. The new Eighth Fleet under Admiral Mikawa was to spearhead a fresh advance from Rabaul with its newly enlarged airfields with the object of seizing the islands of Tulagi and Guadalcanal in the Solomons, and Port Moresby, the latter to be attacked by land over the Owen Stanley Mountain Range. By these moves the Japanese sought to gain mastery of the Coral Sea.

'Don't come back alive'

Having already broken the Japanese codes before the war, the Joint Chiefs of Staff were aware of the Japanese plan and formulated 'Operation Watchtower' to counter it. The goal of Watchtower was to remove the Bismarck Archipelago as a barrier to the recovery of the Philippines and to an assault on Japan itself. MacArthur was to seize the Solomons and the north-east coast of New Guinea, followed by the big Japanese base at Rabaul on New Britain and adjacent positions in and around New Guinea and New Ireland. This was the origin of what came to be known as the 'island-hopping campaign'. The Japanese had just occupied Tulagi and Guadalcanal, whence their bombers could menace the entire Allied position in the Southwest Pacific, so in August Operation Watchtower began with a Marine assault on both islands. In a hard-fought campaign from August 1942 to February 1943, American troops finally ousted the Japanese after seven major naval engagements and at least ten pitched land battles.

MacArthur began the campaign to clear Papua and New Guinea by increasing the garrison of Port Moresby which ultimately attained the strength of 55,000 American and Australian troops. The Japanese move over the Owen Stanley Range was, however, pushing back the Australian forces while on 25th August 2,000 Japanese marines made a landing near Milne Bay airstrip. The Australian defenders managed to hold for ten days and then began to push the enemy back, but a lengthy contest ensued. About the same time, the Japanese advance over the Owen Stanley Range was halted. The Japanese High Command then decided to de-emphasize the Papuan campaign and throw all their resources into the struggle for Guadalcanal. The Papuan campaign was being waged with considerable acrimony on the Allied side. MacArthur was not satisfied with Australian progress and considered these troops inferior to his Americans, yet his Americans were also coming in for some cogent criticism from the Australians, criticism which MacArthur knew had more than a little truth to it.

In October a new all-out offensive was launched, but progress was still slow. Finally MacArthur put General Robert Eichelberger in command, ordering him to take Buna, admittedly a tough nut to crack, or 'don't come back alive'. Leading his American and Australian troops through a stinking malarial jungle and reinforced by a fresh Australian brigade, Eichelberger did take Buna and successfully concluded the Papuan campaign by mid-January. But by 4th January it was already known that the Japanese command had decided to abandon both Papua and Guadalcanal, since by then control of air and sea had passed to the Allies and it was no longer possible to supply and reinforce the troops there.

With the victories in Papua and Guadalcanal, the offensive in the Southwest Pacific had definitely passed to the Allies. MacArthur was now arguing with his superiors in Washington, and not increasing his popularity in the process, that the best route to Japan lay along the 'New Guinea-Mindanao Axis'. Nimitz and the Navy argued cogently that a route through the Gilbert, Marshall, Caroline and Mariana Islands was not only shorter but necessary to protect the New Guinea-Mindanao Axis from air attacks staged from these islands. Thus the Nimitz-MacArthur race continued, although MacArthur now had greater resources as increased supplies and equipment flowed to his command. He was also aided by the appointment in October 1942 of Admiral William F. Halsey as commander of the naval forces in the Southwest Pacific. Like MacArthur, Halsey had a well deserved reputation for leadership, confidence and aggressiveness.

MacArthur now turned his attention to the rest of New Guinea and his main objective of Rabaul in New Britain. As first steps, the undefended Trobriand Islands, Finschhafen and Nassau Bay, were occupied. The Air Force sent a massive hundred-plane raid against Wewak, the principal Japanese base in New Guinea, while paratroops seized the Japanese airstrip at Nadzab in a daring attack. Australian forces took Lae and Salamaua. Finally in October 1943, another hard-fought and lengthy campaign was launched against Bougainville, a large island in the Solomons whose possession was necessary for the coming attack on Rabaul. The Bougainville fighting dragged on until March 1944. MacArthur was closing in on Rabaul but it was becoming apparent that island-hopping was too costly in time, hence 'leap-frogging' was substituted. This meant bypassing the stronger Japanese positions, sealing them off by air and sea and leaving them to 'wither on the vine' or as one of the more baseball-minded members of MacArthur's staff put it, 'hitting 'em where they ain't'. The Quadrant Conference at Quebec in August 1943 directed MacArthur and Halsey to bypass Rabaul and occupy Kavieng in New Ireland and the Admiralty Islands instead. This was surely a wise decision as Rabaul contained 100,000 defenders under a tough and resourceful general with ample supplies left from expeditions which had come to nought. An assault on Rabaul would have delayed the Allied advance by many months. So the occupation of the Admiralties was begun in February 1944 and completed in April. With the fall of Bougainville to the south, Rabaul was now sealed off and left to 'die on the vine'.

MacArthur now planned to leap-frog the 50,000-strong Japanese garrison at Wewak and in four operations arrive at the northwest point of New Guinea. Supported by Halsey's Seventh Fleet, MacArthur's forces pushed rapidly along the New Guinea coast in a series of amphibious operations. Wakde, Biak, Noemfoor and Sansapoor all fell to troops from a flotilla of 215 assorted LST's and LCT's, Biak being a particularly tough fight because the Japanese had prepared a skilled defence in depth. On 30th July, the capture of Sansapoor completed Allied control of New Guinea and was the last stop on that island on MacArthur's road back to the Philippines. There were still mopping-up operations and many bypassed Japanese troops to be watched, but now MacArthur could look across the Celebes Sea towards Mindanao.

The strategy question was still unresolved at this point. The Naval Chief of Staff, Admiral Ernest King, led the Navy school of thought which wanted to bypass the Philippines, invade Formosa and set up a base on the Chinese mainland or in the Ryukyu Islands for the final assault on Japan. MacArthur's position was based on the liberation of the Philippines and use of Luzon as a base for the final assault. Loyal Luzon could be sealed off by Allied air and sea power far more successfully than hostile Formosa which Japan could easily reinforce from the Chinese mainland. He also insisted that the United States had a compelling moral duty to liberate the Philippines which had been nourishing the Filipino resistance movement, and where the troops he had left in 1942 were still imprisoned. At a conference at Pearl Harbour in July, MacArthur converted Nimitz and Roosevelt to his 'Leyte then Luzon' strategy which was then formalized by the Joint Chiefs of Staff. MacArthur and Nimitz were to continue their advances and converge on Leyte in December. But then the fast carrier forces of Halsey, spearheaded by the new Essex class carriers, demonstrated graphically Japan's great weakness in air power, so the date of the Leyte assault was moved forward two months to 20th October.

By way of preparation, Morotai and Saipan were seized as staging air bases against Leyte. The action at Saipan brought about a massive air battle in which the

Japanese lost 300 irreplaceable planes and pilots—the 'great Marianas turkey shoot' as American pilots called it. On 12th-15th October Allied Task Force 38 knocked out a further 500 planes based on Formosa, leaving Japan denuded of her naval air force. A powerful fleet was detached from the Central Pacific Command to assist Halsey in protecting MacArthur's 700 transports and auxiliaries carrying 174,000 troops. These forces landed on schedule the morning of 20th October in the Gulf of Leyte in the central Philippines.

The Japanese High Command chose to regard the Leyte operation as a major crisis. If the enemy succeeded in occupying the Philippines, the supply lines of Japan would be fatally obstructed. The High Command decided that the issue of the war hung on its ability to defend the Philippines, so it gathered its Navy to turn the American threat into a Japanese victory with one decisive blow. Now that Japan's naval air force had been virtually eliminated, however, the attack would have to rely on the battleship fleet led by the awesome *Yamato* whose 18-inch guns made it the most powerful ship afloat. The Japanese were also well supplied with cruisers and destroyers, but these would go into battle alongside the capital ships without air cover and with no way of striking at the enemy other than with gunfire and torpedoes. The Japanese Chief of Naval Staff, Admiral Soemu Toyoda, devised a complex plan to use a decoy force to draw off MacArthur's protective fleet of battleships and carriers under Halsey, after which two strong fleets would move in and attack the American forces while they were unprotected and in the highly vulnerable process of disembarkation. Toyoda counted on his forces making unimpeded contact with the enemy, free from air attack, and destroying the American transports and army by sheer gun power. Thus Toyoda laid his plans for what was to become the largest sea battle in history, a battle which if successful would have had the impact of a second Pearl Harbour and kept Japan in the war for at least another year.

On 23rd October the battle opened on a successful note for Toyoda as Halsey withdrew his entire force to chase the decoy force and never did get into serious action with his powerful fleet, a fact for which he was subsequently heavily criticized. The smaller Japanese attack force, led by two battleships supported by cruisers and destroyers, was ambushed by the remnants of the American fleet under Admiral Kinkaid in a hot night action from which only

Right: *End of a Kamikaze off the Philippines, June 1945. Under the guns of an American carrier a suicide bomber is transformed into a fireball*

one Japanese destroyer escaped. Spearheaded by five battleships, the larger Japanese attack force appeared soon after but bumped into a weak force of American escort carriers and a few destroyers. These delayed the Japanese for hours with a heroic fight while reinforcements were mustered. After learning of the annihilation of his sister force, the Japanese commander withdrew as he was coming under heavier air attack and was uncertain of the strength of his opposition. The decoy force escaped completely. The Battle of Leyte Gulf was the final action of the war for the Japanese Navy, which was so heavily battered that it was reduced to an auxiliary role. The great naval lesson of Leyte Gulf was that battleships without air cover are helpless in a modern sea battle; Toyoda's plan was defeated mainly by Japan's lack of planes and to a lesser extent by bad intelligence and a lack of co-ordination among his commanders.

As it was, Halsey had left MacArthur dangerously exposed and, had the Japanese decided to press home their second attack, the lack of co-ordination between the Navy and Army surely would have resulted in the stunning disaster for the Allies envisaged by Admiral Toyoda. In the event, however, the assault on Leyte was successful and after the first wave was ashore, MacArthur followed with Sergio Osmena, now President of the Philippines after the death of Manuel Quezon. Standing on the beach, MacArthur made the broadcast to the people of the Philippines for which he had been waiting two and a half years: 'People of the Philippines, I have returned. By the grace of Almighty God, our forces stand again on Philippine soil—soil consecrated by the blood of our two peoples.' The broadcast made a tremendous impact on the Philippines, and there on the beach MacArthur scribbled a note to Roosevelt urging him to grant immediate independence to the islands.

Although Japan had suffered a shattering defeat on the sea at Leyte Gulf, there were still 60,000 Japanese troops on Leyte under the tough and determined command of General Yamashita. Ever since their defeats in Papua and Guadalcanal, the Japanese had followed a policy of selling their territory as dearly as possible and Yamashita continued to do so on Leyte. MacArthur was forced to commit a quarter of a million troops to its capture. Progress was slow as American troops, largely conscripts, tended to bog down in the jungle and relied on artillery fire power to clear the way. When the battle for Leyte was over, the Japanese had lost an estimated 48,000 killed, as against 3,500 for the Allies.

Back to Corregidor

The strategy debate had continued right up to the assault on Leyte. MacArthur wanted to land on Luzon as soon as possible while Nimitz was still arguing for Formosa. Admiral King was all for bypassing Luzon in favour of Japan itself. By mid-September the others had come around to MacArthur's point of view, except for the adamant Admiral King. MacArthur informed the Joint Chiefs of Staff that he could land on Luzon on 20th December, and finally on 3rd October received a directive to do so. At the same time, Nimitz was ordered to attack Iwo Jima in January 1945 and Okinawa in March, so the two-pronged assault leading to Japan was to continue. MacArthur was understandably relieved at the final demise of the Formosa plan as it made little sense to attack in the direction of ally China rather than enemy Japan. The order to land on Luzon also meant that now he had authority to liberate all of the Philippines instead of only parts of them. It was a job he relished as he intended to eradicate all traces of the Japanese presence.

As the Japanese had done three years before, MacArthur decided to land on Luzon at Lingayen Gulf. With Halsey and the Third Fleet for cover, he would, after landing at Lingayen, secure both banks of the Agno River and then thrust southwards towards Manila. He was operating on the assumption, soon proved correct, that Yamashita would defend the Cagayan River and the Sierra Madre Mountains in northern Luzon to the end. The heavy fighting on Leyte, however, delayed the landing until 9th January. The Japanese offered little opposition to the landings, but their retreat north was slow and tedious. The fighting around Clarke Field, the major air base in the islands, was especially fierce. On 3rd February American troops entered Manila and after two weeks of hard fighting had secured control of the city, though Japanese diehards continued to hold out in the old quarter until March 3rd. Under MacArthur's personal supervision, XIV Corps sealed off the Bataan Peninsula at the end of January while XI Corps landed at Subig Bay, the major naval base on Luzon. The island fortress of Corregidor, last

Right: Top: Two highly romanticized views of the Pacific war. 1 'Fighter in the Sky' by Tom Lea. A grimly determined American pilot in combat with Japanese Zeros. On 19th June 1944, 891 American aircraft shot down 330 aircraft out of a 430-strong Japanese force. It was dubbed 'the Marianas turkey shoot'. 2 In a painting by T. Ishikawa American and Japanese carrier-borne aircraft duel over the south Pacific. 3 Chinese unloading ammunition from Dakotas at Kweilin in south China painted by Samuel D. Smith. The aircraft supplied the American 14th Air Force based there

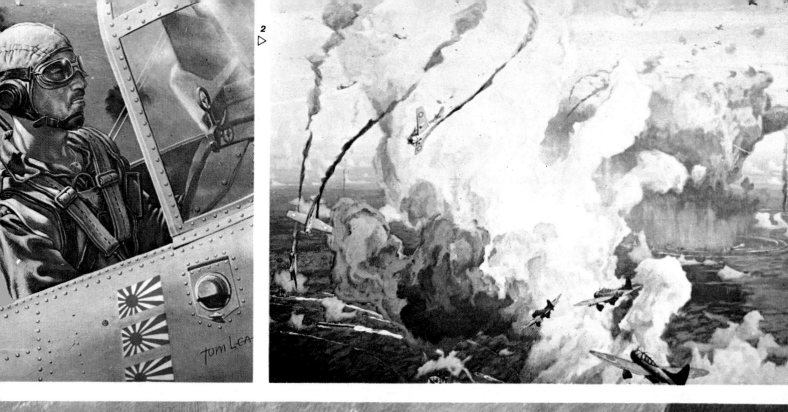

The Defeat of the Axis

American position to surrender in 1942, took weeks to capture as it was defended almost to the last man, only 26 of its 5,000-man garrison, being taken prisoner.

These were highly emotional days for MacArthur who had been enthusiastically welcomed by the Filipinos and who was now reconquering territory which he had been unsuccessful in defending in 1942. As the prison camps were liberated, the ragged, half-starved inmates wept at the sight of him and came running to touch him. These were the men for whom he had felt so strong a need to return. On 27th February MacArthur reintroduced constitutional government and insisted on the Philippine Commonwealth having the same autonomy as it had before the war.

The main objectives on Luzon had now been taken, but it remained to deal with Yamashita in the north. By April the sea route through the Visayas had been cleared while by June, under strong American pressure, Yamashita's 40,000 men had been reduced to several fiercely defended pockets in central Luzon and its north-east coast. When Japan capitulated in August, there were still about 50,000 Japanese holding out on Luzon. The Japanese defence had been admirably resolute, stalling the Ameri-

can re-occupation for months, and requiring large numbers of troops. Luzon in fact became the largest land campaign of the Pacific theatre, involving 15 American divisions and substantial numbers of Filipino troops as well. This was the most difficult and stubborn jungle fighting that MacArthur's troops had seen since Papua and Guadalcanal, with the Japanese soldier at his defensive best. The Allied task on Luzon was made easier, however, by the strong Filipino guerrilla movement which provided valuable intelligence and harassed the retreating Japanese.

MacArthur and his staff had been planning the re-occupation of the Netherlands East Indies and the invasion of the Japanese home islands when the use of the atomic bomb by President Truman removed the latter need. The last operations of the South-west Pacific Command were the despatch of some Australian units to Borneo.

The road from New Guinea to the Philippines had been a long and hard fought trip, usually against superior enemy forces. In New Guinea, MacArthur had had to overcome the arts of the Japanese in defensive warfare in territory favourable to the defenders, yet he had inflicted enormous losses in manpower on them. In the Papuan

campaign, for example, 13,000 of 20,000 Japanese participants were killed as against 3,000 Allied losses. In the Philippines, MacArthur faced a similar situation, except that he had far greater forces at his disposal during that campaign. As he once told Roosevelt, 'The days of frontal attack should be over. Modern infantry weapons are too deadly.... Good commanders do not turn in heavy losses.' MacArthur's battles were won by sheer artistry, by bringing his usually inferior force to bear on the enemy in places and at times when his opponent was off balance, so that his attack could succeed with minimum loss. Rather than assaulting the Japanese fortresses like Wewak and Rabaul directly, MacArthur's tactic was to envelop them by attacking their lines of communication until they were isolated and 'died on the vine'. MacArthur later wrote that this tactic was 'the ideal method for success by inferior in number but faster-moving forces . . . I determined that such a plan of action was the sole chance of fulfilling my mission.' By contrast the island-hopping campaign in the Central Pacific by Nimitz relied much more on simply overwhelming the enemy with a superior force, often resulting in appallingly high casualties.

The Pacific Island-Hopping Campaign

The achievements of the Imperial Japanese Navy between Pearl Harbour and the Battle of Midway rank as one of the classic campaigns of naval history. Following Admiral Yamamoto's meticulous strategic plan, Japanese naval air power knocked out the United States' surface fleet, and their ground, sea and air forces, and then bundled the British, Dutch and Americans out of the East Indies, the Philippines and Malaya in a matter of weeks.

The resulting 'island chain' of forward bases was intended to act as a defensive perimeter to protect the new Japanese conquests from any Allied counter-stroke. That counter-stroke was sure to come, for despite their humiliating losses the Allies had not been totally disabled. The American aircraft carriers were still untouched and, despite the loss of Singapore, the British could still muster troops and warships to defend both Australia and India.

The problem for the Japanese was that their impressive victories had not given them the secure perimeter that they needed. They wanted bases in the Indian Ocean if they were to keep the British from making a counter-attack and they needed New Guinea if they were to pose a serious threat to Australia. To meet this latter threat the US Navy took over responsibility for the Southwest Pacific, and it was in this theatre that the first big battle between the Japanese and American carriers took place. The Battle of the Coral Sea, 5th-9th May 1942, was in the material sense no more than a draw, but it checkmated the Japanese attempt to gain control of the Coral Sea and to capture Port Moresby in New Guinea.

The next move by the Japanese was an attack on the Aleutians and an attempted invasion of Midway Island, which they knew to be the 'sentry for Hawaii'. The Battle of Midway which ensued gave the Japanese a fleet action, but not the kind that they wanted. The opposing aircraft carriers struck at one another over a distance of 200 miles. As mentioned in an earlier chapter, losses in ships and aircraft were heavy on both sides, but by the early hours of 5th June 1942, after 24 hours of bitter fighting, it was clear to the Japanese that they had lost their chance of taking Midway.

Midway was the end of the Japanese Navy's dominance in the Pacific, for the ships and aircrew were never fully replaced, whereas the American losses were replaced many times over. Nor was the counter-attack long in coming, but the question was, where to strike? Although there were two schools of thought about how to defeat the Japanese in the Pacific, there was fortunately total agreement that the Solomon

Islands in the Southwest Pacific were to be the objective. This was because the area dominated New Guinea and Australia, and once in Allied hands it would make a good springboard for further operations, while removing the threat of a Japanese invasion of Australia. The Japanese, however, with the same advantages to themselves in mind, drew up their own plans to capture the Solomons. As a result they were moving powerful forces into the area at the same time as the Americans.

Death before surrender

The American landing on Guadalcanal, one of the largest of the southern group of the Solomons, and a simultaneous landing on the lesser island of Tulagi, were bitterly opposed by their Japanese garrisons. After a day of fierce fighting, however, all the major objectives were taken and by 8th August 1942 everything seemed to be going according to plan. Only one disquieting feature came to light: the defenders of Tulagi had been prepared to fight to the last man rather than surrender.

The Japanese naval commander at Rabaul, who been reinforced for a landing in the same area, was able to launch a rapid counter-attack. A cruiser squadron under Admiral Mikawa was sent to destroy the landing forces, and this group of five heavy and two light cruisers inflicted a severe defeat on the Allied naval forces in the Battle of Savo Island. In a disastrous night action the Australian *Canberra* and the American *Quincy*, *Vincennes* and *Astoria* were sunk without being able to reply. Mikawa does not seem to have grasped how close he had come to destroying the entire expedition, and just when he should have pressed on to attack the transports he retired rapidly.

Between August and December 1942 the battle over the Solomons raged, both on land and sea. The US Marines were locked in a struggle to the death with an enemy better trained and equipped to cope with the enervating heat and jungle conditions, who fought with fanatic courage for every yard of ground. At sea the fighting was less intense on a personal scale, but still distinguished by a ferocity unequalled any-

Right: Architect of the attack on Pearl Harbour: Admiral Yamamoto, C-in-C Combined Fleet. Left: A painting of Kamikaze suicide pilots by S. Awata. The Japanese first resorted to the use of these fliers, who dived their explosive-laden aircraft on to American warships, in January 1945 in the Philippines. Kamikaze or 'Divine Wind' was a reference to the typhoon that destroyed an invading Mongol armada in 1281

where else during the war. By day American air and sea power gave them control of the vital 'Slot', as the waters between the north-eastern and south-western islands were known; at night the Japanese had virtually a free hand to run in supplies, land men, or even bombard shore positions.

Fortunately the Allies had radar, and this gave them a chance in the night actions, but even so their forces were roughly handled during this period. After the Battle of Santa Cruz on 26th October the US Navy was left with only one damaged carrier, the *Enterprise*, although luckily she was able to fight on. In an action on the night of 14th

November the battleship *South Dakota* was badly knocked about, but the Japanese battleship *Kirishima* was sunk. This must be accounted the first Allied victory of the campaign, but just over a fortnight later a force of five cruisers was defeated by only eight Japanese destroyers, which sank the USS *Northampton* and damaged three others. Eventually the Allies were able to clear the 'Slot', and early in 1943 the Japanese defenders of Guadalcanal were evacuated.

As the remaining Japanese forces in the eastern part of New Guinea had been driven out by the end of December 1942, the way

was now clear for the prosecution of Admiral Nimitz's drive across the Pacific. As we know, the Army under General MacArthur wanted to recapture the Philippines, whereas the Navy wanted to strike with its far-ranging aircraft-carrier task forces straight across the Pacific to the heart of Japan. In the event, both strategic

Allied forces – largely American, but including Australian units in the south-west Pacific – bound towards Japan in an island-hopping campaign which began with landings on Guadalcanal on 7th August 1942 and ended in June 1945 on Okinawa

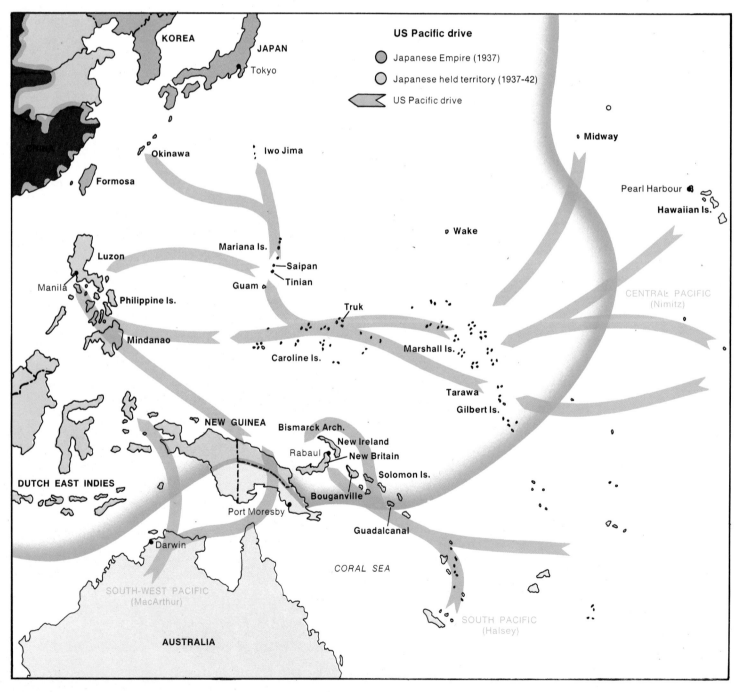

plans were followed to some extent, but the logic of the naval plan seems to have been both simpler and more economical. No matter how many Japanese garrisons were scattered across the Pacific, the Japanese mercantile marine was nowhere near adequate to keep them supplied.

On 29th March 1943 new directives were issued by the US Chiefs of Staff to the Army and Navy to clear the Solomons of Japanese forces and to attack New Britain. In February a small force of 9,000 men had captured the small Russell Islands, just north of Guadalcanal, and had shown how successful surprise attacks could be. Accordingly, assaults were planned against New Georgia and the Trobriand Islands, and the first moves were made to expel the Japanese from the Aleutians.

By the middle of 1943 the losses of the Guadalcanal campaign had been made good, and the new forces were better trained and equipped than those of a year before. The strategic aim was to break through the so-called Bismarck Barrier of island bases in the Bismarck Archipelago. To distract and bluff the Japanese about the main direction of the thrust, Admiral Nimitz was ordered to launch an offensive against the Marshall and Caroline Islands well to the north. The main Japanese fleet base was at Truk in the Carolines, and it was here that the weight of American carrier air-strikes would fall.

Against such an array of strength the Japanese could do little. Like the Germans all over Europe, they were trying to hold an impossibly large number of strongpoints. A new Combined Fleet under Admiral Koga at Truk was hoping to defend a perimeter stretching from the Aleutians down to the Andaman Islands in the Indian Ocean, but even that plan collapsed. Late in June 1943 nearly the whole of the Combined Fleet was withdrawn to protect the homeland against a fancied threat from Russia. The underlying reason for this was a chronic shortage of trained aircrew, carrier pilots who had been lost in the Coral Sea and Midway battles, or frittered away in attacks on heavily defended bases in the Solomons.

Although the Combined Fleet was allowed to return to Truk in July, some of its carriers still lacked crews for their aircraft. When the combined thrust from Nimitz at Pearl Harbour, and Halsey and MacArthur from the Solomons, began at the end of June 1943 they were ill equipped to cope. First came a successful move against the north-western coast of New Guinea, then came the landings in New Britain. The New Guinea landings were timed to coincide with Halsey's landing in New Georgia, so that the Allies now had six airfields around the southern Solomons to enable them to give air cover to all their ground forces.

Nimitz strikes

As the Japanese were now reduced to relying on sending their striking forces a distance of 400 miles from Rabaul, there was little they could do. But their ships still showed outstanding ability in fighting night actions, and once again the night battles raged in the 'Slot'. In two costly actions in July and August they showed that their night-fighting skill was only just matched by radar, and even then the slightest error by their opponents was punished heavily. Only after a year of fighting around the Solomons was there any sign of the Japanese weakening.

The first true example of 'island-hopping' came in August 1943, when Admiral Halsey switched from an attack planned against Kolombangara Island to one against Vella Lavella. This latter island was not only closer to Rabaul, but its possession also made the capture of Kolombangara redundant. Accordingly, a combined Allied amphibious force took Vella Lavella, and although the garrison took six weeks to capitulate, it proved an easier target than the original objective.

From Vella Lavella Halsey moved on to Bougainville, and although this large island north of New Guinea was strongly defended, the central part around Empress Augusta Bay promised an easier landing. It caught the Japanese on the wrong foot, with their Combined Fleet watching for a thrust by Nimitz against the Marshall Islands. For the whole of October 1943, therefore, Halsey's forces had no attacks from enemy carrier aircraft. Even when land-based aircraft attacked in November, the American carriers proved that they could stand up to them better than anyone had believed possible. Indeed, until then the risk had been thought unacceptable.

Nimitz was preparing to strike at the Marshalls, but he was aiming first at the Gilbert Islands. To gauge what this means in the context of the vast areas of the Pacific, it must be remembered that Pearl Harbour was over 2,000 miles from the west coast of the United States, and the same distance from the Gilbert and Marshall Islands; the Solomons were 3,000 miles from the Australian bases, and over 9,000 miles from the United States, and yet forces were fed, ammunitioned and maintained.

The islands attacked by Admiral Nimitz were Tarawa and Makin, as the Chiefs of Staff had decided that their garrisons dominated the Marshalls. At his disposal he had a fleet of battleships and aircraft carriers almost equal to the pre-war strength of the US Navy and, despite the presence at Truk of the giant battleships *Yamato* and *Musashi*, Admiral Koga was badly outclassed. Therefore there was almost no Japanese naval activity when Makin and Tarawa were attacked, but the

5,000 defenders of Tarawa inflicted 3,000 casualties on the Americans before they could be subdued; only 150 prisoners surrendered.

To the soldiers and marines who fought their way from Guadalcanal to Tarawa the whole campaign must have seemed a futile sacrifice of lives to wrest a string of useless coral atolls from the Japanese, but this was not the case. What was unfolding was a planned advance across the Pacific towards the Japanese homeland. The way was now clear for an even greater offensive in 1944.

The Japanese had decided late in 1943 to do what they should have done a year earlier; they drew up a more modest defensive perimeter, running from the Mariana Islands through Truk and Rabaul down to northern New Guinea and Timor. Behind this line they planned to deliver counter-attacks on the Allies, but they nevertheless allowed garrisons to remain outside the perimeter with a view to tying down and harassing the enemy.

The American assault on the Marshalls showed great boldness. On 31st January 1944, 40,000 troops landed on Kwajalein and Majuro, right in the heart of the islands. With small losses they took their objectives, and bases for heavy bombers were immediately set up. The larger islands were left alone, and although they remained in Japanese hands until the end of the war, their garrisons were almost annihilated by disease and starvation. Not all garrisons could be bypassed like this, but from now on the rule was to outflank and starve out isolated islands and bypass obstinate garrisons.

Following a highly successful carrier strike against the Marianas in February, the decision was made to leap-frog Truk and go straight on to land in the Marianas. This chain of islands in the central Pacific contains four whose names stand out: Saipan, Tinian, Rota and Guam. In a three-day air battle the carrier pilots of Admiral Mitscher's Fast Carrier Task Force destroyed the defending air forces in the famous 'Marianas turkey shoot'. This time the landings prodded the Japanese fleet into action, and the Battle of the Philippine Sea was the result. Again Japanese losses were heavy, particularly among their dwindling reserve of carrier pilots, and three more carriers had been sunk.

This highly mobile campaign was yielding ever better results, not only in terms of Japanese losses, but also in growing American skill in the techniques of shore bombardment and inter-service co-operation. The invasion of the Philippines reflected the skill developed in two years' constant campaigning. There was also the bonus of the great Battle of Leyte Gulf in October 1944, in which the Imperial Japanese Navy made its last attempt to defeat the Ameri-

cans in open battle, and was destroyed as an effective fighting force.

Epic on Iwo Jima

The last phase came in April 1945, when large forces attacked Okinawa, only 800 miles south of the Japanese mainland. It was needed as a forward base to assemble shipping for the eventual assault on Japan itself, and also as a bomber base. At the same time, it was decided to seize the little island of Iwo Jima, somewhat closer to Japan, to eliminate its fighter aircraft which were causing bomber casualties, and also to provide an emergency landing strip for damaged B-29s on their homeward run. As there were not enough ships to carry out both landings simultaneously, Iwo Jima was chosen as the first objective in the hope that it would prove the easier.

The epic of Iwo Jima was remarkable for the ferocity of the fighting on both sides. Despite a crushing bombardment from the naval forces, the defenders emerged from their underground bunkers and fought with such tenacity that the Americans suffered 21,000 casualties; that figure was only 1,000 less than the casualties inflicted on the Japanese. By comparison the landing on Okinawa was less costly, but this time the naval forces were heavily punished by Kamikaze attacks—suicidal dives by aircraft onto ships, which frequently turned them into a flaming shambles.

The fall of Okinawa on 21st June 1945, after nearly three months of fighting, marked the end of the island-hopping campaign. From the rebuilt airstrips bombers could now fly round-the-clock raids against Japanese cities, and carrier task forces were close enough to maintain a complete blockade of Japan. Operations continued against outlying garrisons, particularly in Borneo, and carrier aircraft methodi-

Above: Rather death than dishonour: a dead Japanese soldier lies in the sand of Namur islet, Kwajalein, in the Marshalls after squeezing the trigger of his rifle with his foot. Although Namur received a heavy preliminary bombardment, marines who assaulted the islet met stiff resistance from an intricate system of blockhouses. Left: US marine on Guadalcanal in the Solomons. Although landings on the island were unopposed, the Japanese soon reacted violently, and for nine months Guadalcanal was the scene of bitter battles.
Right: 1 Incendiary bombs rain from the bellies of American B-29s over Yokohama, Japan, May 1945. Forty per cent of the built-up area of more than sixty Japanese cities and towns was destroyed in these incendiary raids. 2 Kobe receives its third incendiary bomb raid on 5th June 1945. 3 View of railway yards near Osaka after American air raid

1 ◁
2 ▷

3 ▽

cally eliminated the surviving units of the Japanese Navy. Without fuel for ships or aircraft the Japanese were now helpless, and the end was a matter of time.

On 26th July the Allies issued the Potsdam Declaration, which stipulated unconditional surrender for the Japanese armed forces, though not for the Emperor or his government. It was hoped that this formula would allow the Japanese to 'save face', but when no clear reply was received the Allies set in motion plans for the final destruction of the country. The choice lay between the atomic bomb, terrible but costing no Allied soldiers' lives, or a gigantic invasion of the land, with the likelihood of one million casualties.

The choice of the bomb was inevitable, but in strictly military terms it was not necessary. The three-year campaign waged across the Pacific by the US Navy had brought Japan to its knees, and by July 1945 the mainland was 'besieged' by naval forces which enjoyed almost complete immunity. Battleships were shelling industrial targets in daylight, and air strikes could hit whenever and wherever they chose. It is hard to see how much longer the Japanese military authorities could have maintained any defence in the face of starvation and the collapse of civilian morale caused by a truly horrific scale of air raids.

The island-hopping campaign was primarily an exercise in sea power, both in attack and defence. It could only be waged by highly mobile task forces of aircraft carriers, supported by tankers and supply ships. Conversely it could only have worked against a maritime empire, for it was the deadly onslaught against the Japanese supply lines which made it so hard for them to launch any counter-attacks. But it also needed the fullest inter-service co-operation, and the land-based air forces and ground troops were all vital to the victory.

Left: Top: Marines burn out Japanese resistance with a flame-thrower, Guam, July 1944. Centre: Marines hug the beach after landing on Iwo Jima in the Bonin Islands, 19th February 1945. During the month that it took to break organized resistance on the formidably fortified island the Americans suffered 26,000 casualties of whom 6,800 were killed and when all resistance ceased on 26th March the 21,000-man garrison had been virtually annihilated. By the end of the war emergency landings had been made on the island by 2,251 B-29s which might otherwise have been forced to ditch in the Pacific. Bottom: Jubilant marines with a souvenir of war, Leyte Island, Philippines, December 1944. Right: Ecstatic Allied prisoners-of-war at a camp near Yokohama celebrate their liberation by American forces, August 1945

The Russians Reach Berlin

The last year of the Second World War was a year of decisive battles, the results of which affected the fate of many peoples. The thunder of the battles of the winter of 1943-44 died away and summer drew near. The belligerents surveyed the lessons of the campaign just over and began working on new plans. The Germans had much to think about, for the time when the course of the war on the Eastern Front was decided by Hitler's HQ and the German General Staff was past. The initiative now lay exclusively in the hands of the Soviet armed forces.

'We cannot win the war by military means,' wrote Jodl to Hitler in February 1944. A number of other German generals and statesmen shared his view, and there were serious grounds for holding it. Germany had failed in every military campaign from the hard-fought Battle of Stalingrad on suffering heavy losses. The country's economy was finding increasing difficulty in coping with the demands of war. The July Plot to assassinate Hitler was a reflection of Germany's worsening situation. The political, economic, and military superiority of the USSR over the Third Reich was obvious by summer 1944.

In 1944 the Soviet Union achieved great new successes in economic development and consequently a mighty advance in war production: 29,000 tanks and self-propelled guns, over 40,000 aircraft, and about 122,000 pieces of artillery. The Soviet rear ensured the supply to the front of an ever-increasing quantity of trains loaded with arms, equipment, and food. There was also an improvement in the quality of the guns, tanks, and aircraft produced, and new types of weapons, equipment, and shells made their appearance. All this led to an increase in the striking-power and mobility of the Red Army.

It should be mentioned that the war production of Germany and her allies also increased down to the second half of 1944. In the summer of that year German output of armaments and military equipment reached its highest level for the entire war. Yet the Nazi leaders were unable to raise their war economy to the level attained by the economy of the USSR and they were incapable of replacing the losses suffered by the German forces on the Soviet-German front. Then in the autumn of 1944 there was a serious decline in German war production. The chief cause of this

The end of Hitler's Thousand-Year Reich, Berlin, May 1945. Russian soldiers hoist the Red Flag above the Brandenburg Gate

decline was the victorious advance of the Red Army, which deprived Germany of numerous sources of strategic raw materials. The ever-increasing shortage of labour also had a considerable effect.

By the summer of 1944 Germany's position had become hopeless. This was the result not only of the decisions taken by Roosevelt, Churchill, and Stalin at the Tehran Conference of November 1943 but also of the Allied invasion of northern France. This huge, well-organized landing operation evoked a feeling of satisfaction in the Soviet Union but unfortunately the slow pace of the Allied advance failed for a long time to confirm the hopes aroused by the operation.

Meanwhile in the occupied countries of Europe popular liberation movements developed on a wider scale, and in the countries of the Nazi coalition—Finland, Rumania, Hungary—anti-war feeling and the desire to end association with Germany increased.

Military plans

Despite its heavy losses in previous campaigns, the German army was still, at the beginning of June 1944, strong in numbers and well-equipped. On the Soviet-German front it maintained, including the armies of Germany's allies, 228 divisions and 23 brigades, with over 4,000,000 men, 49,000 guns and mortars, 5,250 tanks and assault guns, and about 2,800 aircraft. In the West, in France, Belgium, and Holland, the Germans had at this time only 61 divisions.

The fundamental idea of the German plan for the further conduct of the war was set out in a report by Field-Marshal Keitel at a conference at Sonthofen on 5th May 1944. It was to employ the bulk of Germany's forces to maintain the defence of the Eastern Front while using the remainder to resist invasion from the West. The great hope of the Germans was to prolong the war and bring about a split between the Allies.

To make his defence line firmer Hitler had already ordered, in March 1944, that a system of fortresses and strong-points be constructed on the Eastern Front. He thus hoped to 'pin down as many Soviet troops as possible'. The generals appointed to command these fortresses were men who could be relied upon, it was considered, to hold them to the end, even if they should be surrounded. 'Only the army group commander personally may, with my approval, remove a fortress commander from his post and assign him to other tasks,' said the order.

The Defeat of the Axis

At the start of the summer offensive the Red Army's operational forces amounted to 6,425,000 men, with 92,500 guns and mortars, 7,750 tanks, and over 13,400 aircraft. The plan for the Soviet offensive envisaged the delivering of a sequence of powerful blows in different directions aimed at routing the enemy's principal groupings on Soviet territory, and the transferring of military operations on to enemy territory. The main blow was being prepared for the centre of the Soviet-German front, in Belorussia and the western regions of the Ukraine.

Stalin told Churchill about the plans of the Soviet Supreme Command for the summer of 1944. 'The summer offensive of the Soviet forces, organized in accordance with the agreement made at the Tehran Conference, will begin in the middle of June on one of the important sectors of the front,' he wrote on 6th June. 'Our general offensive will be developed in stages by the successive involvement of the armies in offensive operations. At the end of June and during July, offensive operations will be transformed into a general offensive by the Soviet forces.'

In their estimate of the intentions of the Soviet Supreme Command the Nazi leadership committed an irrevocable mistake. At a conference of Eastern Front army commanders in May 1944 Keitel reported: 'Given our information on the regrouping of the enemy forces and the overall military and political situation, it must be reckoned that the Russians will probably concentrate their main forces on the southern sector of the front. They are not now in a position to give battle in several main directions at the same time.' This false assumption by the German General Staff was skilfully exploited by the Soviet Supreme Command.

The summer offensive begins

The task of beginning the summer offensive of 1944 fell to the forces on the Karelian and Leningrad fronts, commanded by Generals Meretskov and Govorov. Despite the strong fortifications confronting them, and the forested, marshy, lake-covered terrain, unfavourable to offensive

February 1945: Soviet infantry march through Kraków, the ancient former capital of Poland

operations, the forces of these fronts made considerable progress on the Karelian Isthmus and in Karelia. Field-Marshal Schörner's Army Group North was forced back to the Finnish Frontier, suffering heavy losses and abandoning the towns of Vyborg and Petrozavodsk. The Kirov railway and the White Sea-Baltic canal, of great importance as transport arteries, were cleared of German troops. Influenced by these military developments, Finland's President Riuti, one of Germany's most fervent supporters, resigned his office. On 4th September Finland broke off relations with Germany, and, although German troops continued to hold positions in the north of Finland, a fortnight later an armistice agreement was signed between the Finnish and Soviet governments.

The offensive in Karelia was in full swing when the Red Army began operations on the central sector of the Soviet-German front. On 23rd and 24th June, 1st Baltic front and the three Belorussian fronts, commanded by Generals Bagramyan, Chernyakhovsky, Zakharov, and Rokossovsky, began their offensive. This offensive in Belorussia was disastrous for the Germans. Army Group Centre, commanded by General Busch, was routed. Large concentrations of German forces were surrounded and destroyed before Vitebsk and Bobruysk, to the east of Minsk, and around Brest Litovsk and Wilno. On 17th July 57,000 German prisoners-of-war captured in the Soviet offensive were marched round Moscow's ring road. The Belorussian Republic, a considerable part of Poland, most of Lithuania, and part of Latvia were liberated from German occupation. Soviet forces reached the frontiers of East Prussia and the Rivers Narew and Vistula. Favourable conditions had been created for the final liberation of Poland and the invasion of Germany but the offensive potential of the Soviet forces operating in this direction was for the time being exhausted.

The tragic events which occurred in Warsaw can still be keenly felt. Polish reactionary circles irresponsibly encouraged the inhabitants of the city to launch an ill-prepared uprising without prior agreement with the Soviet military command. The result was the killing by the Germans of many thousands of people and the complete destruction of Warsaw.

The success of the Belorussian offensive facilitated the Red Army's operations elsewhere. To the north, in the middle of July, 2nd and 3rd Baltic fronts went over to the offensive, and by the end of August liberated a substantial part of the Baltic region. To the south, 1st Ukrainian front, commanded by Marshal Konev inflicted a major defeat on General Harpe's Army Group North Ukraine. Konev's forces reached the banks of the Vistula and the foothills of the Carpathians. Almost the whole of the Soviet Ukraine and the south-eastern parts of Poland were now freed. A large bridgehead was established on the far side of the Vistula in the region of Sandomierz, and this, together with the bridgeheads to the south of Warsaw conquered by Rokossovsky's forces, created favourable conditions for a further advance westward. The total losses of the German armies on the Eastern Front between 1st June and 31st August were, according to German figures, some 917,000 men. German losses in the West in the same period came to 294,000 men.

Offensive in the south

The German command believed in the summer of 1944 that the Red Army had its hands full with operations against Army Groups North and Centre and that consequently a big offensive against Army Group South Ukraine was 'improbable' in the near future. They were mistaken.

Early in the morning of 20th August, 2nd and 3rd Ukrainian fronts, under Generals Malinovsky and Tolbukhin, began a powerful new offensive on the southern wing of the Soviet front in the region of Jassy and Kishinev. On the fifth day of the offensive Soviet forces surrounded the main forces of Army Group South Ukraine. The total losses suffered by Army Group South Ukraine exceeded half a million men. Between 20th August and 3rd September alone the Soviet forces took 208,000 prisoners including twenty-one generals.

Malinovsky's forces went on, by the end of September, to liberate almost the whole of Rumania and reach the frontiers of Hungary and Yugoslavia. During the next three months they continued to strike blows at Army Group South, freed the northern part of Transylvania, took Debreczen, crossed the Tisza on a wide front, and opened the road to Budapest.

Meanwhile Tolbukhin's forces cleared the northern Dobruja and crossed the Bulgarian border. By the end of September Bulgaria had been completely cleared of German troops. Then, together with the People's Liberation Army of Yugoslavia, Tolbukhin's troops liberated the eastern part of Yugoslavia.

The liberation of the Ukrainian areas of Transcarpathia was also completed in this period. By the end of October, 4th Ukrainian front under General Petrov had cleared the Germans from the towns of Mukačevo and Užhorod.

The end of October saw the start of the Budapest operation and on 26th December troops under Malinovsky and Tolbukhin encircled the 188,000 enemy troops in the Hungarian capital. The subsequent warding off of the enemy's several attempts to relieve the besieged troops went on until their eventual destruction by Soviet forces in mid-February 1945.

These operations in the south were distinguished by their speed, flexibility, and great scope. One operation led to another without any lengthy pauses for the preparation of a new advance. The Red Army showed great ability in surrounding and destroying large forces of the enemy in a wide variety of circumstances—in open country, in large cities, along the seashore. There was skilful co-operation between the fronts and the air arm, the Black Sea Fleet, the Danube Flotilla, and the Soviet anti-aircraft defences.

The successful offensive of the Red Army on the southern wing of the Soviet-German front brought the people of South-Eastern Europe liberation from Nazi rule and enabled them to re-establish their independence. Anti-Nazi governments came to power in Rumania on 24th August and Bulgaria on 8th September. In Hungary the Provisional National Assembly, opened in Debreczen in the second half of December, elected a new government, so giving legislative form to the overthrow of the fascist regime. Under their new governments these countries did not merely cease to fight on Germany's side, they declared war against their former ally and their troops fought alongside those of the Red Army.

The strategic situation on the Soviet-German front continued to improve. Soviet forces entered the eastern part of Czechoslovakia, and took up suitable positions for advancing further into Czechoslovakia, Austria, and southern Germany.

Successes in the north

The successes achieved on the central sector of the front and on the southern wing made it possible to undertake the final liberation of Soviet territory in the Baltic region and within the Arctic Circle.

On 14th September the forces of 3rd, 2nd, and 1st Baltic fronts, commanded by Generals Maslennikov, Yeremenko, and Bagramyan, moved into action to liberate Riga, while the troops of the Leningrad front, commanded by Marshal Govorov, aided by the Baltic Fleet, struck at Tallinn. Soon the flag of free Estonia was raised on Tallinn's ancient tower of Toompea. On 15th October Soviet forces drove the German forces out of Riga, and by the end of October all Latvia had been freed.

The operations in the Baltic region resulted in the rout of a large strategic grouping of enemy forces, the release of a large number of Soviet forces for other tasks, and the capture of naval bases for the Baltic Fleet. The Red Army reached the Baltic Sea along a wide front.

On the northern flank of the Soviet-

The Defeat of the Axis

German front the troops of 14th Karelian front, commanded by General Meretskov, with the help of the Northern Fleet, commanded by Admiral Golovko, spent three weeks of October 1944 in smashing German XX Mountain Army and liberating the Petsamo region. Soviet forces entered Norway and began the liberation of that country from the Nazis.

The year 1945 had begun. The Red Army had been victorious on all fronts and the Anglo-American forces had also had considerable success, driving the Germans out of northern Italy, France, and Belgium. Germany was being squeezed between two fronts, east and west. The Soviet General Staff saw the strategic situation as one in which Germany could be completely crushed in the very near future. 'Essentially, the Soviet army and the Anglo-American forces had won positions from which they could proceed to a decisive offensive against Germany's vital centres,' wrote General Shtemenko, former head of the Operations Department of the Soviet General Staff. 'It was now a matter of making a final vigorous thrust and finishing off the enemy in a short time.'

The Nazi leaders still had no intention, however, of acknowledging their defeat. They were still striving to prolong the war, to bring about a split between the Allies, and to make a separate peace with the West. The greater part of the Wehrmacht was concentrated on the Soviet-German front. Here there were over 179 German and 16 Hungarian divisions. These forces amounted to over 3,000,000 men, 28,000 guns and mortars, about 4,000 tanks and assault guns, and 2,000 aircraft. Between the Vistula and the Oder the Germans had equipped seven defence lines, which it was hoped would halt the Soviet advance. At this time 107 German divisions were fighting in the West against the forces of Great Britain and the United States.

'Fanaticization' of the struggle

To strengthen the resistance put up by their forces on German soil, the German command issued an order for the 'fanaticization' of the struggle. 'In the zone of military operations,' said this order, 'our fight must be carried on with the utmost stubbornness, and every able-bodied man must be used to the fullest extent. Every bunker, every quarter of every German town, and every German village must be turned into a fortress where either the enemy will be drained of blood or the garrison will perish in hand-to-hand fighting and be buried under the ruins. There can

German soldiers captured by the Russians. The signpost, in Russian, points forty-two kilometres to Berlin

The Russians Reach Berlin

be no alternative but defence of one's position or annihilation.'

The Red Army's operational forces at this time were very strong, amounting to about 6,000,000 men, with 91,400 guns and mortars, about 11,000 tanks and self-propelled artillery mountings, and 14,500 aircraft.

So as to break the German's resistance once and for all and force them to surrender, the Soviet Supreme Command decided to destroy the largest concentrations of German troops and finish the war victoriously along with the Allied armies. The main blow was to fall on Berlin. At the Yalta Conference, held in February 1945, Roosevelt, Churchill, and Stalin agreed on and planned in detail 'the timing, scale, and co-ordination of fresh and even more powerful blows to be struck at the heart of Germany . . . from east, west, north and south.'

The Red Army's offensive in the final campaign was planned for 20th January 1945, but at the request of the British Prime Minister, in connection with the setbacks suffered by the Allied forces in the Ardennes, it was brought forward by eight days. Simultaneously, five fronts struck at the enemy along a line 750 miles long, stretching from the Baltic Sea to the Carpathians. After the first breakthroughs, large tank formations rushed deep into the rear of the enemy defence.

On 17th February the British Prime Minister sent congratulations to Moscow on the gigantic offensive that had begun. It was followed next day by a message from President Roosevelt who wrote that the heroic feats of the Soviet soldiers and the efficiency they had already shown in their offensive gave grounds for hoping that the Allied forces would soon be winning victories on all fronts.

The successes achieved were indeed tremendous. The Germans were defeated in East Prussia and Pomerania. On the main line of the offensive Soviet troops reached the Oder at the beginning of February. In March they cleared the enemy from the whole of the right bank of the Oder and widened their bridgehead on its western bank in the Küstrin area. The Baltic ports of Danzig and Gdynia were also liberated in March, and Soviet troops south of the Carpathians repulsed a German offensive near Lake Balaton.

It is sometimes asked whether the Rus-

Top: Street fighting in Berlin, April 1945. Red Army machine-gun emplacement. Centre: Marshal Zhukov, the conqueror of Berlin, on the steps of the Reichstag. Russian soldiers have scratched their names on the columns. Bottom: Eastern Front meets Western Front, April 1945

The Defeat of the Axis

'Death to the German invaders!' Soviet poster of 1945. The Red Army thrusts at the heart of Nazi Germany — Berlin

sians could not have taken Berlin by storm immediately after their arrival on the banks of the Oder in February 1945. Careful analysis shows that they could not. In their impetuous advance westward the fronts had left their rear services lagging behind and the troops were experiencing shortages of munitions and fuel. 1st Belorussian front was greatly weakened by its previous advance of more than 250 miles and the main forces of the front had been sent to the north where, as Keitel said after the war, the German High Command intended 'to launch a counter-offensive against the forces advancing on Berlin, utilizing for this purpose the Pomeranian bridgehead'. In addition the Germans were reinforcing their already considerable forces between the Vistula and the Oder, and concentrating new forces on Hungarian territory, hoping to thrust Tolbukhin's troops back across the Danube. To have attempted to capture Berlin by storm in such circumstances as these would have been highly dangerous. By eliminating the danger on the flanks and by making thorough preparations for the advance on Berlin, the Russians were able to ensure that the operation, when it came, was really crushing.

The struggle for Berlin

The Red Army went on to occupy East Prussia and Pomerania, to liberate Poland and a substantial part of Czechoslovakia, to complete the liberation of Hungary, and to enter Austria. The powerful Soviet offensive forced the German command in January 1945 to send against it the bulk of the forces which had been until then

fighting the Allied troops in the Ardennes. In February and March the Anglo-American forces pushed the enemy back to the Rhine and seized a number of bridgeheads on its east bank.

Berlin was now the Red Army's next objective. The Germans were ready to defend their capital 'to the last man and the last bullet'. One million men had been concentrated in the Berlin sector, with 10,400 guns and mortars, 1,500 tanks and assault guns and 3,300 aircraft. The Berlin garrison amounted to more than 200,000 men. The defence consisted of an outer belt of minefields, outer and inner defence zones, and the defended area itself. The underground railway and the network of drains were to be used for defending the city. Railway and road bridges, and other large installations were prepared for demolition in the event of Soviet troops getting through. Blocks of flats and reinforced concrete structures were transformed into fortified strong points. An order by General Reimann, the commandant of Berlin, demanded that every quarter of the city be defended at all costs, and likewise every house, every storey, every fence, and every shell-hole. 'The struggle for Berlin can decide the outcome of the war,' was the watchword inspiring the defenders of Germany's capital.

The Soviet Supreme Command assigned 2nd and 1st Belorussian fronts and 1st Ukrainian front, commanded by Marshals Rokossovsky, Zhukov, and Konev, to take part in the historic battle for the German capital. These fronts numbered 2,500,000 men, with more than 42,000 guns and mortars, over 6,200 tanks and self-propelled guns, and 8,300 aircraft.

Not long before the operation began — on 12 April 1945 — President Roosevelt died. The death of the leader of one of the Allied states was viewed by the Nazis as the possible start of a new political situation. But such hopes were vain. On 16th April the Russians began their massive assault on Berlin.

Tens of thousands of guns and mortars began a mighty barrage just before dawn. After this artillery preparation assault troops, supported by aircraft, moved to the attack. A fierce conflict developed. Despite the stubborn resistance put up by the Germans, the Oder-Neisse defence line was broken and attempts to hold lines behind this one also ended in failure. On the night of 21st April Soviet troops broke into the outskirts of Berlin. Bloody battles took place in the streets of the city. On 25th April the armies of Zhukov and Konev linked up to the west of Berlin and completed the encirclement of the city. On the same day one of Konev's divisions encountered forward units of American 1st Army in the Torgau area, an event marked by

mutual greetings and firm handshakes. The day before, German IX Army had been surrounded to the south-east of Berlin. By a decisive blow from the Soviet divisions the opposing German forces were surrounded and cut into two parts, each of which was then destroyed separately.

On 30th April Soviet soldiers broke into the Reichstag building and on the same day Hitler killed himself. As the hour of reckoning drew near, his close assistants fled in all directions, like rats from a sinking ship. Only two days earlier Hitler's fellow dictator Mussolini had been arrested and shot by Italian partisans who had discovered him attempting to flee.

Berlin falls

On the morning of 1st May, the Red Flag was hoisted over the statuary which rises above the columns of the main entrance to the Reichstag building. This was a banner proclaiming that the road to peace, freedom, independence, and social progress had been opened. On 2nd May the German garrison of Berlin headed by General Weidling surrendered. On 8th May at Karlshorst plenipotentiaries of the German High Command, headed by Keitel, signed a document of unconditional surrender in the presence of representatives of the USSR, Great Britain, the USA, and France. The war in Europe had ended in complete victory for the Allies.

The German people had paid dearly for Hitler's crimes. Germany's total losses in the Second World War amounted to 13,600,000 men of whom ten million fell on the Soviet-German front. During the war the Soviet armed forces destroyed or took prisoner more than 500 German divisions and 100 divisions of Germany's satellites. On the Soviet-German front Germany lost the bulk of her artillery and tanks, seventy-five per cent of her aircraft, and 1,600 warships and transport vessels. The Allied forces defeated 176 enemy divisions in Western Europe, North Africa, and Italy.

The Russians reached Berlin after overcoming very grave ordeals and winning many battles on a grand scale. It took them 1,418 days to reach the German capital and win victory. It was a thorny path, demanding unprecedented efforts and enormous sacrifices. Out of the total of fifty million people killed in the Second World War, twenty million were Soviet citizens, and of these about fifty per cent were civilians and prisoners-of-war, killed or tortured to death on occupied Soviet territory.

The fall of Berlin and the arrival of the Allied armies on the Elbe showed the inexhaustible possibilities possessed by the United Nations when their efforts are directed in common toward the attainment of just aims.

The Fall of the Dictators

During the evening of Sunday, 29th April 1945, the short-wave receiver in Adolf Hitler's underground shelter in Berlin— the 'bunker'—picked up a broadcast from Radio Stockholm reporting the death of Benito Mussolini, struck down the previous day near Milan by Italian partisans. A few minutes later the text of the broadcast was shown to Hitler. It was in this way that the Führer learned of the death of the Duce, the man he had never ceased to admire. When he read this report, Adolf Hitler's decision had already been taken. Next day he would join his old comrade, in death.

On 17th April Mussolini had left his villa at Salò, near Gargnano, on the shore of Lake Garda. Abandoning Rachele, his wife, he had decided to go to Milan. After Otto Skorzeny had rescued the Duce from captivity on the Gran Sasso in September 1943, Mussolini was still full of hope. When he met Hitler after his escape, the latter had confided in him that secret weapons were about to change the course of the war. But then the Allies had landed in Normandy. The Russian advance had become a flood. In Italy the Americans, British, and French had crossed the Apennines and turned Kesselring's retreat into a rout. For Mussolini as for so many others the hour had struck for an end to illusions. Physically he was now no more than a shadow of himself. When his mistress Claretta Petacci rejoined him beside Lake Garda she found him, as she said later, *'flacco, debilitato, svagato'*—weakened, debilitated, ravaged. In fact Mussolini suffered from a stomach ulcer which his grave worries had considerably aggravated.

When, on 17th April, Mussolini decided to leave for Milan, the neo-Fascist governmental institutions set up after his escape no longer existed except in theory. The Committee of National Liberation had decreed that the Fascist leaders could be executed without trial.

Mussolini as the ill, ageing head of the puppet Salò Republic just before his final flight in April 1945

Everything that Mussolini did at this stage shows that he realized he was no longer able to control his fate. He said: 'I am close to the end . . . I await the epilogue of this tragedy in which I no longer have a part to play. I made a mistake, and I shall pay for it, if my life can still serve as payment.'

On 21st April news of the capture of Bologna reached Milan; on the 23rd the fall of Parma was reported. Mussolini's entourage asked the Germans for an aeroplane, in order to enable the Duce to escape to Spain. Mussolini himself had not been consulted on the matter. In any case, the occupying authorities refused to provide the aeroplane.

On the morning of the 24th Mussolini received his last message from Hitler. It told that the Soviet forces had entered Berlin. That same day Gian-Riccardo Cella, an industrialist, asked to meet Mussolini. When he was in the Duce's presence, Cella revealed that he was a member of the Committee of National Liberation. He wished to spare Milan the horrors of civil war. Since the defeat of Fascism was an accomplished fact, why should not Mussolini hand over his powers to the resistance? Mussolini replied calmly that it was an interesting proposal. He required, however, to be given guarantees for himself, his people, his entourage. During the afternoon Cella reported to the committee on his interview with Mussolini and its outcome. The committee proposed to Mussolini a meeting on the following day, at 5 pm, at the residence of the Archbishop of Milan, Cardinal Schuster. Mussolini agreed. 'At this moment,' we are told by those who had dealings with him then, 'he showed no irritability, only great fatigue.'

'The Germans have betrayed us'

Next day, at the time arranged, the meeting took place. It lasted an hour. With Cardinal Schuster as chairman, Mussolini, Marshal Graziani, the Fascist ministers Barracu and Zerbino, and the prefect of Milan, Bassi, faced General Cadorna, the advocates Marazza and Arpesani, and the engineer, Lombardi. Mussolini asked what guarantee could be given to Fascists who surrendered, and to himself. The reply was: 'The ordinary guarantees given to prisoners-of-war.' Mussolini then asked in whose name the undertaking would be given and was told: 'In the name of the Committee of National Liberation and of the Allies.'

It was proposed that the Duce spend the night at the Archbishop's house. There he would be regarded as a prisoner-of-war and kept in hiding until the Allies arrived. Marshal Graziani broke in roughly: 'We will not make an agreement behind the

The bodies of Mussolini and Claretta Petacci strung up in Milan. Mussolini's face was horribly distorted, but many were struck by Claretta's look of peace

Germans' backs, because fidelity to an ally is a sign of honour and justifies our attitude in the past.'

General Cadorna replied ironically: 'This concern for the Germans seems misplaced. They have been negotiating with us for a long time now, behind your backs.' Cardinal Schuster confirmed this, producing evidence of secret negotiations carried on between the Wehrmacht and the Italian resistance. Mussolini stood up, flushed with anger, and shouted: 'They have always treated us like dogs, and in the end they have betrayed us!'

Turning towards the members of the committee, he said, more calmly: 'Very well. I accept all your conditions. First of all, though, I want to see the Germans . . . I mean to throw this premeditated treason in the face of these people who, for so many years, have been calling us traitors. As soon as I have done that I shall come back here and sign whatever you want.' Then he left, saying that he would be back in an hour. When he went out the time was 7.15 pm.

He did not return. When he got back to the prefecture of Milan he encountered the German general in command there. He went straight up to him and insulted him: the Germans were, he said, 'traitors and cheats'. After that, he appears to have been called on by Milan's prefect of police, who implored him vehemently not to go back to the Archbishop's house. The prefect of police did not believe that the Committee of National Liberation was in a

position to honour its promises. Mussolini would not be handed over to the Allies but to a people's tribunal, and everyone knew what that would mean. Perhaps this explains why Mussolini did not return to the Archbishop's house. Perhaps he had never intended to do so. What is certain is that on 25th April 1945, at 8 pm, Mussolini had given up the idea of negotiating with the resistance. At that hour he left Milan in his open Alfa-Romeo, escorted by a line of cars occupied by panic-stricken Fascist dignitaries. The column was preceded by a German detachment made up of ten cars and two armoured cars, together with an Italian detachment. In one of the private cars was Claretta Petacci, Mussolini's mistress. The rear of the column was brought up by trucks loaded with fifty-six suitcases, large and small, containing state papers and the Republic's 'treasury' – amounting to two thousand million present-day lire or about a million pounds. As the column emerged on to the Como motorway, explosions rent the air. The first battles between partisans and Fascists had begun in the suburbs of Milan.

At 9 pm the column arrived at the prefecture of Como where Mussolini stayed seven hours. During the night he wrote a last letter to his wife: 'Here I am, on the last lap of my life, at the last page of my book.' He told her he was going to make for the Valtellina with some Fascist partisans. He advised his wife and children to try to get to Switzerland, or else to give themselves up to the Allies. 'I ask your forgiveness for all the harm I have done you without wishing to. But you know that you are the only woman I have really loved.' A little later that night, Mussolini managed to contact Rachele by telephone. 'There is no-one left. I am alone . . . Rachele, you will start a new life, but I must follow my destiny.'

At dawn the column set off again, now much reduced. In front was the German car occupied by Lieutenant Birzer, entrusted with Mussolini's 'security'. Then came Mussolini's own car, followed by an SS van and a car belonging to the SD (Security and Intelligence Service of the SS). The Duce was obviously now a mere prisoner – the prisoner of his former allies. Apparently Mussolini did not know where he was going. That evening they halted at Menaggio, not yet having left Lake Como. There it was that Claretta found Mussolini again, after having done everything she could to rejoin him. Next day they continued their journey. Mussolini said no more about the Valtellina redoubt. The Fascist partisans whom he had summoned to his side for this 'last stand' had failed to turn up – another disappointment. And so they drove on northward, towards the Swiss frontier. Though the Swiss had announced officially that they would not allow Mussolini to enter their country, it seems likely that the Duce wished to attempt this as a last resort. In the previous few days he had several times remarked: 'I am a Freeman of the city of Lausanne.'

After leaving Menaggio the column met up, by chance, with a German Luftwaffe convoy going north – about twenty trucks – and decided to merge with it. Towards noon, just before reaching the village of Dongo, the column came to a halt, its way suddenly blocked by barricades. The partisans of 52nd Garibaldi Brigade were stopping the convoy. The partisan leaders came forward. Their names were Bellini Della Stelle, nicknamed Pedro, and Costatina Lazzari, who preferred to be called Bill. They explained that they had been ordered to let the Germans through but to stop the Italian Fascists escaping. Accordingly they had to check the cars and trucks. The German major agreed to this inspection. The partisans made Claretta Petacci and her brother Marcello get out of the car they were in. They examined the first two trucks but found nothing of interest. In the third, amid a seated group of six German soldiers, the partisans noticed a man crumpled up against the driver's cabin, wearing a Wehrmacht sergeant-major's greatcoat. A young German lieutenant explained: 'He's drunk.'

Mussolini's flight is checked

Two partisans, Ortelli and Peralli, then noticed that the man was wearing boots of good-quality leather, and also that he had sun-glasses on, although the sun was not shining. They ordered him to get out. He obeyed, jumping to the ground. Someone removed his glasses. There was a cry of astonishment: it was Mussolini.

They took him to the municipal offices. The villagers gathered round, amazed, unable to believe their eyes. Calmly, Mussolini drank a cup of coffee. He was asked questions about the war and about his government, and he replied to them. He was coping with the situation, very much at his ease. That evening he was taken to the customs-officers' barracks at Germasino. It was raining. At 11 pm, after eating a meal, Mussolini lay down on a camp bed which had been prepared for him. He was not left to sleep for long. Shortly after 1 am on the morning of 28th April he was awakened. Apparently the resistance leaders feared intervention by the partisans of the extreme Left and had therefore decided to take Mussolini to the residence of the industrialist Cademartori, four miles from Como, on the lake shore. Concealed in this place of refuge the Duce would be safe until the Americans arrived. At 1.35 am a car drove away with Pedro and his prisoner. As it left the village of

Cover of post-war novelette about Mussolini and Claretta. Their affair preserved an aura of romance despite the violent reaction against Fascism

Dongo this car passed another one, containing Claretta Petacci. Once more, Benito and Claretta had found each other; they were not to be separated again. During the night major decisions had been taken in Milan. The Committee of National Liberation, which had hitherto favoured turning the Duce over to the Americans, had changed its mind. Cadorna tells us: 'I imagined the consequences for Italy of the capture of Mussolini by the Allies and the spectacular trial that would inevitably ensue, which would become a trial of Italy's political life during the past twenty years – whereas silence was now needed regarding facts and circumstances in which it would be hard to distinguish between the responsibility of the nation and that of its leader. . . In any case, I would never of my own free will have undertaken to arrange for Mussolini to be handed over to the Allies, to be judged and executed by foreigners.'

A certain Walter Audisio, a Communist partisan who used the name 'Colonel Valerio', came to see Cadorna. He told him that he had instructions to 'go and find Mussolini and execute him'. It seems clear that the general did nothing to hinder this 'mission'. He even dictated a document which looked like a grant of full power.

Valerio set off at once, at full speed, along the Como road. Pedro has told how, as he was driving towards Como with Mussolini, he heard a sound of shooting. On the advice of one of his companions, Captain Neri, he decided to take Mussolini and Claretta Petacci into the house of a peasant

patriot at Bolzanigo, above Azzano. There it was, in this little isolated house, in a tiny room with whitewashed walls, scantily furnished with a double bed, a dressing-table with a washbasin, and some straw-bottomed chairs, that Mussolini and his mistress spent the rest of the night, and also the morning and the first part of the afternoon of the day. At mid-day their peasant hosts, the De Maria family, gave them polenta with milk, and some bread and sausage, which the prisoners ate in silence. There was water to drink.

At 4 pm, a civilian in a raincoat, accompanied by two men in khaki uniform, burst into the room. It was Colonel Valerio. He told Mussolini he had come to release him. The Duce's eyes at first showed great amazement, then lit up with joy: 'I will give you an empire!'

Claretta dressed hurriedly and Mussolini put on his greatcoat. They left the house and got into a black Fiat 1100, which set off towards Lake Como. The driver, who had been conscripted for the job by Valerio, later told Bandini: 'I could see the couple in the driving mirror. They were sitting close together, their heads touching. Mussolini was pale, the lady seemed calm. They didn't appear to me to be particularly frightened.'

The car stopped before the gate of the Villa Belmonte, one of those fine residences of which there are so many along the shores of Lake Como. Valerio said to Mussolini and Claretta: 'Get out.' He pushed them towards a low wall two yards away. He spoke a few words very quickly, talking of an order and a sentence of death. 'Mussolini did not stir, it was as though his thoughts were elsewhere,' the driver recalls, 'but Claretta suddenly showed great energy. She clung to Mussolini and looked from Valerio to him and back again. "No, you can't, you can't do that!" Her expression was terribly strained, her voice was shaky, her eyes were wild. In a dry tense voice Valerio exclaimed: "Get out of the way or I'll shoot you as well." But Claretta remained pressed against Mussolini as if she had not heard.'

Valerio pulled the trigger of his weapon. It failed to go off. One of the other partisans handed him his sub-machine-gun. Mussolini clutched his greatcoat, opened it and said in a loud voice: 'Aim at my breast.'

'At that very moment,' the driver tells us, 'Claretta was standing on Mussolini's left, partly protecting him. Valerio fired the fatal burst – I think there was only one, continuous burst. The first to be shot was Claretta, who fell to the ground with a dull thud. She neither screamed nor groaned; and I had the impression that she had fallen before the bullets hit her. Mussolini fell almost immediately after her, but his fall was hindered by the wall, against which he slid slowly to the ground. He was in a bent position, his right shoulder against the wall, and he reached the ground as though sitting down on his legs as they folded under him, almost squatting. . . . Mussolini's throat rattled for several seconds, sepulchrally, and this affected me deeply. He seemed to be breathing hard. Valerio pulled out his revolver, went forward, checked where Mussolini's heart was, and fired a coup de grâce. Mussolini's body gave a last convulsion and then moved no more.'

A little later, Valerio presided at Dongo over the execution of fifteen Fascist army officers who had been arrested along with Mussolini. The bodies of Mussolini and Claretta were added to the fifteen bodies thrown on to a truck. Next day all seventeen were taken to a yard in front of a garage at a corner of the Piazza Loreto in Milan. A noose was pulled tight around Mussolini's feet and he was hoisted up to the roof of the garage porch, so that his head hung six feet above the ground. Beside him they hung Claretta, also by the feet. Then a great silence fell on the jeering crowd. 'It was as if,' said a man who was there, 'we had all in those few seconds shared in the realization that there had been a time when we would have given his dead body the honours due to a hero, and the prayers worthy of a saint.'

Death of Adolf Hitler

All that now remained of Hitler's empire was a narrow corridor in the middle of Germany and a few pockets of resistance in the south. On 16th April 1945, at 5 am, Marshal Zhukov's offensive had begun, with the Soviet forces attacking on a front nearly 250 miles long. The Battle of Berlin had begun; it was to end on 2nd May, at 3 pm, with the city's fall.

Adolf Hitler had lived through this battle under fifteen yards of concrete, in his underground shelter in the Reich Chancellery. Berlin was dying. Crushed beneath bombs and shells, the city was burning down. Who could doubt, in this situation, that the defeat of the Third Reich was inevitable? It was no longer anything but a matter of days, or even of hours. The extraordinary feature of this unprecedented tragedy was, however, that one man in Berlin did still believe a Nazi victory to be possible. That man was Adolf Hitler.

In these days Captain Gerhardt Boldt, General Guderian's aide-de-camp, was taken aback by the wretched physical state of the Führer. 'His head sways slightly. His left arm hangs down as if paralysed, the hand trembling all the time. His eyes shine in an indescribable way, suggesting almost inhuman anguish. His face and the pockets under his eyes show how tired he

is, and how exhausted. He moves like an old man.' Hitler's hair was now almost white, and he walked with a stoop.

On 20th April he celebrated his fifty-sixth birthday. This was the last official ceremony of the Third Reich. The dignitaries came to the bunker to offer their good wishes to the dictator: Göring, Himmler, Goebbels, Ribbentrop, Bormann, Arthur Axmann, leader of the Hitler Youth, Admiral Dönitz, Field-Marshal Keitel, General Krebs, and General Karl Koller, Chief of Staff of the Air Force. We must picture these visitors lined up in the concrete central corridor, and Hitler walking down the line, shaking their hands and thanking them. The survivors of the occasion have recorded how their hearts were wrung by the sight of this tattered remnant of a human being. But that did not stop propaganda minister Goebbels from proclaiming on the radio: 'I can assure you that the Führer is in the best of health. As always, he is at the head of his troops, bringing them encouragement and inspiration.'

Himmler had come from his headquarters in the north, Göring from his in the south. These two men had only one thing in common: they both knew all was lost. There was only one hope, that a separate peace might be made with the Western Allies. Himmler was already preparing through Count Bernadotte, of the Swedish royal family, to negotiate on his own behalf. That day he dared, for the first time, to implore Hitler to stop the fighting. Hitler refused. Himmler then urged him at last to leave Berlin. Hitler again refused, reiterating his confidence in victory. In his view the Soviet forces had taken a risk in attacking Berlin. It was still possible to defeat them outside the city. On the morning of 21st April, Hitler ordered an offensive to be launched. General Steiner of the SS would take command of some of the troops defending Berlin and attack in the suburbs of the city. This attack by XI Army would sound the knell of the Soviet adventure. Next day at 3 pm, when the routine military conference began, the Führer immediately asked for news of XI Army. No-one spoke. 'I demand a reply! Has Steiner attacked?' General Krebs did not dare reply. It was General Jodl who spoke up. The fragments of units stationed in Berlin were so disorganized that it had not been possible to bring them together into a single force. XI Army had remained a fantasy, a dream in the brain of Adolf Hitler alone. Worse still, in order to create Steiner's army, units had been withdrawn from the front north of Berlin, and the Russians, finding themselves facing abandoned positions, had immediately attacked there. As Jodl was speaking, the Soviet troops were entering Berlin.

Then Hitler burst into one of those frightful rages that terrified those around him: 'I have been betrayed by the SS! This is something I should never have expected! By the SS!'

He went on shouting for a long time, denouncing everybody and everything. All the same, he had not yet accepted defeat. During the night of 22nd-23rd April he sent Keitel to see General Wenck, commanding XII Army, located fifty miles west of Berlin. Wenck was an excellent general. Keitel told him Hitler's orders – to march at once on Berlin and relieve the capital. This was in fact, Hitler's last idea. In the next few days he was to follow on the map the advance of Wenck's army, declaring himself confident that Wenck, in a lightning counter-offensive, would drive back 'the Asiatic invader'.

What did Wenck's army really amount to? Made up of remnants of various formations, reinforced by boys of the Hitler Youth and veterans of the First World War – the Volkssturm – it dragged itself along broken roads to obey Hitler's command. At a point ten miles south of Potsdam Wenck's force linked up with General Busse's 40,000 men, who were as worn out as they were and had no ammunition left. Frenzied orders kept coming from the bunker. Wenck's army was called upon to attack forthwith. In the midst of such a catastrophic situation, orders like this took on a sinister, nightmarish quality. Busse and Wenck put their heads together. These soldiers, who had up to that moment always been slaves to discipline, decided for the first time in their lives to disobey orders. A man who gave such orders at such a moment was no longer worthy to be the leader of the German people. Wenck and Busse resolved to fall back and lead their men towards the American lines, so as to spare them the fate of being taken prisoner by the Russians.

The strong concrete revetment of the bunker protected its inmates from bombs and shells. Those fifteen yards of concrete seem to have cut them off from reality as well. In the central corridor of the bunker Hitler presided every day over a general staff meeting. One door, to the left, led to the series of six rooms which constituted the quarters of Hitler and Eva Braun, the discreet partner of his days of glory, and now of misfortune.

'My orders are that Berlin be relieved at once. Where is Heinrici? What is Wenck's army up to? What is happening to XI Army? When are Wenck and Busse going to link up?' This was the message that Keitel received from Hitler: a message woven out of anguish. And, naturally, Keitel gave back no answer. After further demands, the answer so intensely awaited was given, at about 8 pm on the 28th. It did not bear Keitel's signature—he was obviously terrified. It merely reported, in very few words, that Wenck's army had ceased to exist.

Eye-witnesses tell us that when Hitler read this message he said nothing, but withdrew into his room. The Soviet forces were now only a few hundred yards from the Chancellery. And only now did Adolf Hitler concede his defeat. During that evening of 28th April Hitler told his orderly officer Heinz Linge that he was going to marry Eva Braun—to marry her before he died. Goebbels was instructed to summon to the Chancellery an official competent to solemnize the marriage. Extremely scared, the registrar Walter Wagner arrived at the bunker not knowing what he was expected to do. On 29th April, about half past midnight, he married Adolf Hitler to Eva Braun. Stammering, he asked the Führer to state whether he was of Aryan extraction. With complete seriousness the Führer replied that he was, as also did Eva Braun. When they had exchanged their vows, they each signed the register. The bride began by writing 'Eva B. .', then struck out the B and wrote: 'Eva Hitler née Braun.'

Hitler and Eva Braun. He rewarded her empty-headed devotion by marrying her, on the last day of his life. She had no desire to survive him and they died together

In the next few hours Hitler dictated his last will. There was not the slightest self-examination or conflict of conscience. He had always been right, only he had seen clearly. 'It is false,' he declared in this will, 'that I wanted or that anyone in Germany wanted war in 1939. The war was sought and provoked exclusively by international politicians belonging to the Jewish race or working for the Jews. The numerous offers that I made to disarm are there to testify before posterity that responsibility for the war cannot be ascribed to me. I said often enough, after the First World War, that I had no desire at all to fight Great Britain. Nor did I want war with the United States. In times to come the ruins of our cities will keep alive hatred for those who bear the real responsibility for our martyrdom: the agents of international Jewry.'

The dictation of this will was briefly interrupted for a reception to be held, at which Hitler and Eva received the congratulations on the occasion of their marriage, of those who had remained loyal to them to the last. When saying goodbye, Hitler remarked suddenly: 'National Socialism is dead. We have lost the game. All that remains is for us to die worthily.'

Heinz Linge reports that he spoke 'in a calm and steady voice'. When Hitler withdrew to his quarters, everyone felt sure that they would never see him alive again.

However, 29th April passed without Hitler seeming to have varied his usual routine in any way. At noon he held, just as on any other day, a conference on the military situation. He held another one at 10 pm, when the Soviet troops were only 300 yards from the Chancellery.

On 30th April, at 2 am, Hitler received, at his own request, all the women who were in the bunker—secretaries, cooks, and chambermaids. He wished while still alive to hear their condolences on his death. Then he went back into his own quarters.

Adolf Hitler's last day had begun. At 10 am according to Linge's account, Hitler came out of his room wearing a new uniform decorated with his gold Party badge, his Iron Cross, and his medal for wounds received in the First World War. At his command, Linge asked the telephone switchboard for the latest news. When he returned to the Führer's side he reported: 'All resistance has ceased nearly everywhere. The Russian vice gripping Berlin is unbreakable. The Russians will be here tomorrow, at the latest.'

The leader of the Hitler Youth, Axmann, broke in vehemently: 'I still have 200 Hitler Youth and a tank. Let us try to get you out of here.' Hitler refused with a shake of his head, and mumbled: 'No, no, it's useless. I must die.'

Linge records that the Führer lunched with Eva Braun: 'they had a frugal meal,

*Fallen hero: Norwegian SS newspaper of
5th May relays Hamburg radio's announcement of 1st May that 'Hitler, fighting
to the last breath against Bolshevism,
fell for Germany in his operational
headquarters in the Reich Chancellery'*

for we were short of provisions.' Once
again, farewells were said to the most
faithful comrades. Standing before Frau
Goebbels, Hitler showed emotion. He had
just learned that she and her husband had
decided to kill themselves, together with
their six children. Hitler unpinned his
gold Party badge and fastened it on Frau
Goebbels's dress, kissing her as he did
so.

Then Hitler and his wife went to their
quarters. 'I had left in there, as I had
been ordered,' states Linge, 'two revolvers
which I had loaded myself. One was a
Walther PP 7.65-mm, as used by the police.
The other, of smaller calibre, a 6.35-mm,
was for Eva Braun to use, or to take the
place of the other weapon should it not
work properly. Suddenly we heard a shot.
It was about 3.35 pm. There was no second
shot, and when I felt sure about this,
approximately a quarter of an hour later,
I went into the Führer's quarters. He was
sitting on the couch. He had fired a 7.65
bullet into his right temple – not into his
mouth, as has often been said. The revolver
had fallen at his feet and his blood had
poured onto the carpet. Beside him, half-
lying on the couch, was his wife: she had
preferred to take poison.'

Hitler had asked that his body and that
of Eva be burned. He did not want them
to become playthings for the Soviet soldiers. On Bormann's instructions, Erich
Kempka, head of the transport service of
the Chancellery, had managed with difficulty, to get together 180 litres of petrol.

Bormann, Dr Stumpfegger, the doctor of
the bunker, Linge, Kempka, and Günsche,
the Führer's aide-de-camp, climbed the
thirty-nine steps that led up to the armoured door of the bunker carrying the two
bodies and went out into the garden. They
found themselves amid a storm of fire and
steel. Never before, perhaps, had the bombardment been so heavy. At every moment
the ground was ploughed up by shell
splinters. Hastily they laid the bodies
down, three metres from the door. Kempka,
helped by Linge, poured the petrol over
the bodies, can by can. Linge set fire to
them, using a paper towel soaked in petrol.

An hour later it was possible to ascertain
that the bodies had not burned at all well.
The petrol had been absorbed mainly by
the wrappings and the earth. Accordingly,
Linge, so he says, gave an order for the
bodies to be buried in a bomb crater near
the place where they had tried to burn
them, and this was duly done.

Many disputes have arisen over the actual
circumstances of the Führer's death. There
has been an attempt to create a 'mystery
of Hitler's end'. Some sensational newspapers published articles after the war was
over trying to prove that Hitler had
succeeded in escaping from Berlin at the
last moment. It must be said that the
Soviet authorities did much to confer
credibility on these legends. On 9th June
1945, during a press conference in Berlin,
Marshal Zhukov, the Soviet commander-in-
chief, said, regarding Hitler's death: 'The
circumstances are very mysterious. We
have not identified Hitler's body. I can say
nothing for certain about his fate. He may
have got away from Berlin by air at the
last moment. The state of the runway
would have made that possible.'

Then Colonel-General Berzarin, military
commandant of Berlin, spoke: 'We have
found several bodies, among which one
may be Hitler's, but we cannot state
definitely that he is dead. I think Hitler
is hiding somewhere in Europe, probably
in Franco's Spain.'

On 26th May 1945 Stalin told Harry
Hopkins, the US envoy, that, in his
opinion, 'Bormann, Goebbels, Hitler, and
probably Krebs got away and went underground'. On 6th June Stalin repeated to
Hopkins that 'he was convinced that Hitler
was alive'. On 17th July the Soviet leader
said at the Potsdam conference that he
believed Hitler to be alive, 'probably in
Spain or the Argentine'.

These statements did not reflect reality
in any way. When these Soviet spokesmen
gave them utterance the remains of Hitler
and Eva Braun had long been found.
Professor Trevor-Roper has suggested that
this was on Stalin's direct orders to
prevent any chance of Hitler's death being
interpreted as heroic and thus acting as a

cult round which a revival of Nazism could
flourish. It was only very recently – in
1968 – that the Russians decided to pub-
lish their material on the subject. A Soviet
historian and journalist, Lev Bezymensky,
has published a book entitled *The Death of
Adolf Hitler*. He quotes all the records
of the investigations, exhumations, and
autopsies carried out. On 4th May 1945
Lieutenant-Colonel Klimenko, head of
the counter-espionage unit of the Red
Army's 79 Corps, found the bodies of Hitler
and Eva Braun buried in a shellhole in the
garden of the Chancellery.

Identification and autopsy

Subsequently, the bodies were shown
to German prisoners and formally identified. The jaw of Hitler's body, which was
intact, corresponded very exactly to the
mouth-chart drawn by the Führer's own
dentists. The autopsy made possible the
discovery of traces of cyanide. 'No sign of
a wound or of fatal disease was found in
this body, which had been badly distorted
by fire. The presence of fragments of a
crushed glass phial in the mouth, as in
the mouths of the other bodies, the pronounced smell of bitter almonds given
off the body, and the forensic-medical
examination of the internal organs, in
which cyanide was found, all permit the
commission to conclude that, in this case,
death was due to poisoning with cyanide.'
These were the actual words of the report
completed on 8th May 1945.

This is a revelation of great significance. The survivors of the bunker,
notably Günsche and Linge, asserted that
Hitler had killed himself with a revolver
bullet. It is odd, however, that Günsche
spoke of the right temple and Linge of
the left, while other accounts, collected
by Trevor-Roper, indicate the mouth as
the target of the fatal shot. The Soviet
autopsy report puts an end to all these
legends. Hitler died by cyanide poisoning.

It should be mentioned that the Soviet
investigators gave particular attention
to the statements of Major-General-SS
Mohnke. According to him, Hitler had
indeed swallowed the cyanide, but Linge
was assigned the responsibility of giving
him the coup de grâce when he came into
the room. Another German prisoner in
Soviet hands, Major-General-SS Ratten-
huber, confirmed Mohnke's testimony.

In spite of everything said to the contrary, the doctors who carried out the
autopsy maintain their view. Over twenty
years later, Dr Shkaravisky, who presided
over the 1945 autopsy, told Lev Bezymensky: 'The fact of poisoning is irre-
futable. Whatever may be said nowadays,
our commission found no trace of a bullet
on 8th May 1945. Hitler poisoned himself.'

Victory in Burma

Even before Singapore fell on 15th February 1942, the Japanese XV Army under General Iida had crossed the Burma frontier from Siam and pushed beyond the river Sittang. Opposing him he found 1st Burma Division and 17th Indian Division and, as he had expected after the Japanese experience in Malaya, these kept retreating whenever his columns made hooks through the jungle to get behind them. There would be no major battle, he anticipated, until he reached the capital, Rangoon. In fact, when he reached here on 8th March it was to discover to his amazement that the city had been abandoned; and he knew that his campaign had virtually been won.

From the British viewpoint, the war in the Far East had been developing like an ugly dream. The Empire seemed to be falling apart. And now in the spring of 1942, with Malaya and the impregnable bastion of Singapore lost to the enemy, the loss of Burma had to be faced also. In Burma, General Sir Harold Alexander took over as General Officer Commanding Burma, soon to be joined by Lieutenant-General William Slim, of the Indian Army, as General Officer Commanding 'Burcorps', as the land forces were now designated. But even these two soldiers of proven ability could not halt the retreat; by 23rd March the last of the RAF units had been forced to retire to India, and Japanese X Air Brigade dominated the sky; by the end of March it became evident that the defensive line on the Irrawaddy could not be held; and on 26th April Alexander decided that Burma was lost and his main object must be the defence of India. A few months later he returned to Europe.

It must be mentioned that not only British and Indian troops took part in the opening battles for Burma. Under the American Lieutenant-General Joe Stilwell, Chinese 5th Army marched south and fought a spirited action near Toungoo. Prickly and temperamental, though not without military talent, Stilwell wielded his Chinese forces effectively, but, denied air cover – like the British and Indians of Burcorps – was forced to retreat back to China. Here he reorganized and later on was to take part in the advance from the north in 1944 which reopened the Burma

Above left: Japanese invasion, December 1941 to May 1942. Left: Allied reconquest February 1944 to August 1945. Starting with the defeat of the Japanese 'March on Delhi', the Burma campaign was fought in some of the most difficult conditions in the world, showing in the end that Commonwealth troops could beat the Japanese in jungle warfare

road, the vital supply line to China.

Japan's immediate object in going to war in December 1941 had been to break out of the stranglehold which the United States was maintaining over her supplies of raw material. Her declared political object was to set up a Greater East Asia Co-Prosperity Sphere, dominated by herself and comprising the Philippine Islands, the Netherlands East Indies, and Malaya. Burma was to be captured for strategic reasons, to form a protective flank for the conquered areas, and also as a source of vital supplies, especially oil and rice. The long-term consequences of occupying a country contiguous with India do not seem to have been thought out in any detail; but there was a facile assumption on the part of some generals that with Malaya and Burma gone the British would have as much as they could do to hold down the Indian nationalist movements. Even if the Indian Army should remain loyal, they did not consider it a force of any great consequence.

The field of battle

But what lay between Burma and India? Here it is necessary to enter into some geographical details, for without them the campaigns may appear somewhat incomprehensible. They were, in fact, incomprehensible at the time, even to the Combined Chiefs of Staff, who on one occasion asked why the fighting should be characterized by so many battalion and company actions. Briefly then, Burma occupies about a quarter of a million square miles, and if placed on the map of Europe would cover Belgium and France together. To the west, east, and north it is flanked by great mountain barriers, largely covered by thick jungle. On the west (towards India) the mountains run 600 miles from the Himalayas to the sea in a succession of chains some 200 miles across. Within these ranges lie the small countries of Assam and Manipur, at this time forming part of British India. Linked to this barrier, and running parallel to the coast, lie the Arakan Yomas; they separate Burma proper from the coastal regions. To the east lie more ranges, forming the borders with China, Yunnan, and Siam. As the mountains run from north to south, so do Burma's great rivers, the Irrawaddy (with its tributary the Chindwin), the Sittang, and the Salween. Even in 1941 these remained great highways of communication, for away from the large cities roads were few, and there was only one main railway line from north to south. Burma is not solidly covered with jungles, as the popular imagination sees it; large areas of

The Defeat of the Axis

the central plain are, in fact, devoted to cultivation of rice. To the south, however, the Pegu Yomas, a wooded range of hills, lie between the Arakan Yomas and the Karen Hills.

The climate of Burma runs to extremes. In the plains the heat can be almost unbearable and in the hills the rainfall often exceeds 200 inches. In Assam 800 inches have been known. The heat and the damp encourage blood-sucking leeches and all manner of insects which sting or bite or infect; and malaria, scrub typhus, dysentery, and even cholera are endemic. Away from the towns, Burma is an uncomfortable country to live in, and it is hell to fight in, especially during the monsoon. By the end the troops would be called upon to endure no less than three monsoons.

The British had completed their annexation of Burma in 1885 and since that date generations of civil servants and soldiers had laboured to bring the benefits of civilization. To their efforts the Burmese, an independent and highly xenophobic race, reacted with indifference. The only loyalty towards the British, as the Japanese invasion would show, developed among the hill tribes, especially the Karens and Kachins. In 1937 the British government separated the administration of Burma from that of India, and the country received a measure of self-government. This, however, did not satisfy certain political groups who announced their intention to fight for freedom. Some of their leaders even visited Japan to enlist support. While these political moves were developing, the British tried to make up their minds how Burma should be defended, and who should be responsible. As she lay between India and Malaya, it was felt at Westminster that her defence should come under the Commander-in-Chief Far East. But in Delhi another view prevailed; as Burma lay on the north-east frontier of India, it was argued, GHQ Delhi should take over her defence. Despite many conferences, no agreement was reached, and the whole matter was given a low priority. Even in August 1940, the chiefs of staff recorded their opinion that the Japanese invasion of Burma remained a threat too remote for serious consideration. Only with the fall of Singapore did reality assert itself, and by then it was far too late.

When Slim's bedraggled forces retreated over the border from Burma in the summer of 1942, most of them made for Imphal, the capital of Manipur, which lies some 2,600 feet up in the mountain barrier, to the south of Assam. The town itself lies on a plain, known as the Imphal Plain, which extends forty miles by twenty and originally formed the bed of a lake. It is a fertile area, growing all manner of fruit and crops and is inhabited by the Mani-

puris, a clean, prosperous people, with a love of song and dancing. Slim's men had little but the clothes they marched in and their weapons; and they were bitter with defeat. They had made the longest retreat in British military history, over difficult terrain, and during the last stages, through the monsoon. Their only blessing was that since the Chindwin there had been no pursuit. Slim has said 'the Japanese army seemed as little prepared as we were to advance in the monsoon and we might reasonably look forward to a breathing space. . . .' In fact, Colonel Hayashi, a staff officer, was already arguing that Imphal should be captured before the British could organize it as their forward base, but though his views found favour in Tokyo, Iida wanted to rest his division. For the moment the frontier seemed safe, and for the rest of 1942 the Chindwin saw nothing but patrol activity.

1943 was a year of frustration. Quite obviously, before any lost territory could be regained, a new army must be built up; and before this army could advance, communications (both road and rail) would have to be improved, forward airfields would have to be built, and a considerable stock-pile of war supplies achieved. Also, there were some formidable medical problems to be solved, for doctors examining the troops of Burcorps as they filtered back to India were horrified at their condition. Malaria and amoebic dysentery had taken an enormous toll, and had in fact caused a hundred times more casualties than the enemy. Equally important was the question of morale, for with their rapid conquests the Japanese began to take on the role of supermen. Could British and Indian troops ever defeat them in jungle warfare? Could their tactics be countered successfully? These matters were discussed at every level, and a good deal of uninformed nonsense was talked. One man, however, was convinced that given proper training, good leadership, and effective air cover, the Anglo-Indian forces could win. He was General Slim.

For the moment he did not have the chance to put his ideas into practice. The campaign in the jungles of the Arakan in early 1943, though launched by part of 15th Corps, which he commanded, was directed by his superiors in Eastern Army. It proved abortive and costly, and tactically

it achieved nothing. However, it did demonstrate convincingly that the long chain of command, running from GHQ Delhi via Eastern Army to the battle front, was quite impractical. A new command structure and new leaders were needed.

Before this change came about there took place a minor operation which must be mentioned: Major-General Orde Wingate's first Chindit operation, which took place in February and March 1943 ('Chindits' was the name given to his jungle groups). Wingate was a strange unorthodox soldier of great intellectual power, and for some time had been preaching the gospel of what he called 'long range penetration'. Briefly he planned that his brigade, specially organized into columns, should march into enemy territory, disrupt communications, gather intelligence, and be ready to take any opportunity to damage plant

Three of the men who forged the Allied victory in Burma. 1 Major-General Orde Wingate (right), a strange, unorthodox soldier, he hit the Japanese behind their own lines. 2 Lieutenant-General Joe Stilwell, 'a prickly American, not without military talent'. 3 Lieutenant-General Sir William Slim—his genius broke the Japanese onslaught

and installations. The guerrilla columns would have no line of communications, but would be supplied from the air. Wavell's original intention was to co-ordinate the operations with an advance by the Chinese American forces from the north, but when this was cancelled, Wingate was still able to persuade him that the LRP operation, was worthwhile. In fact, it achieved very little in military terms, but the publicity it gained was enormous. The fact that 3,000 men could operate hundreds of miles behind the enemy lines and the vast majority get back, gave the Allied armies a tremendous boost. In terms of morale alone, the gamble had paid off.

It was in August 1943 at the first Quebec

3

Conference that the new command structure was created. It was called South-East Asia Command and its task was to take over the conduct of the war in this theatre. The supreme commander was to be Admiral Lord Louis Mountbatten, and under him would be three commanders-in-chief for the three services. All British Commonwealth land forces in the war zone would come under Sir George Giffard's 11th Army Group and the strike force on the Burma borders would be designated 14th Army, under General Slim. The rapidity and extent of the changes brought about by these new commanders was remarkable. At Imphal 4th Corps under Scoones built up a vast forward base and patrolled forward to the Chindwin, and in the Arakan 15th Corps under Christison prepared for a new offensive. But the rail link from India, cut by the Brahmaputra River, was still inadequate and limited the build-up. From the Brahmaputra it ran to the railhead at Dimapur, where a supply base had been set up and from here supplies had to be loaded on to trucks for the hundred-mile journey through the mountains, via

Kohima and Maram to Imphal. Never had a front presented such logistical problems, and as Mountbatten saw at once, his only hope of maintaining the troops already in Assam and the Arakan, let alone building up an effective strike force, lay in air supply. One of his many preoccupations now and throughout the campaigns to come, would be borrowing transport aircraft.

The Japanese had also improved their command structure. Based on Rangoon, the Burma Area Army Headquarters was formed, with a cautious general called Kawabe as its commander. Under Kawabe came Hanaya's XXVIII Army in the Arakan, Renya Mutaguchi's XV Army in central Burma, and various formations facing Stilwell and the Chinese in the north, which were later to be incorporated into Honda's XXXIII Army. Kawabe was cautious, but Mutaguchi was completely his opposite: thrusting, ambitious, and ruthless. A defensive role was not to his taste, and by the early autumn of 1943 he was urging his superiors to launch an offensive against Imphal. This, he believed, would prevent an Allied counter-offensive, and would cause the Indian people to rise in rebellion. Privately, he saw no reason why the Japanese should not keep advancing till they reached the plains of India; and he even had daydreams (as he confessed later) 'of riding through Delhi on a white horse'.

After a good deal of argument his plan was accepted, though the objectives were limited to 'the strategic areas near Imphal and in north-east India'. The plan was that Hanaya should attack in the Arakan, forcing Slim to commit his reserves; and when these had been committed, Mutaguchi should advance on Imphal and Kohima. Kohima was a strong tactical position north of Imphal, on the road to Dimapur; and once this had been captured, Imphal itself would be cut off. In three weeks, Mutaguchi hoped, his troops would break through the mountain barrier and come streaming down on to the Imphal plain. And the British front would automatically collapse.

By January 1944 the British had got wind of the coming offensive and Slim, following Mountbatten's personal directions, made his plans accordingly. When it came under attack in the Arakan, 15th Corps would not retreat, but stay where it was, supplied by air drops. Two divisions of 4th Corps, then in forward positions towards the Chindwin, would retreat back to the Imphal Plain and fight the battle on its perimeter. Slim, it must be mentioned, had already made a great impression on his new army; officers and men alike realized that at long last they had the commander they needed.

The 'March on Delhi'

The Japanese offensive in the Arakan was launched on 4th February, led by Lieutenant-General Sakurai of LV Division. Soon he had moved round the flank of the leading divisions of 15th Corps and mounted a series of ferocious attacks from the jungle. 15th Corps held firm, as Slim had planned, but he was forced to commit his reserve, 5th Indian Division. Receiving the news, Mutaguchi launched his army over the Chindwin on 15th March and the 'March on Delhi' had begun. What he did not realize was that Mountbatten would be able to call on new formations from India, notably 2nd British Division which was soon moving by road and rail to Dimapur. But Mutaguchi was also able to spring a surprise: Sato's XXXI Division was heading across the mountains towards Kohima and making rapid progress.

(It may be mentioned here that Mutaguchi was advised by Tazoe, the Commander of III Air Division, to postpone his advance till he had dealt with Wingate who had now mounted a second and more ambitious campaign. But he refused, a decision he would live to regret.)

The twin battles at Kohima and Imphal raged from March to June and were undoubtedly the decisive battles of the Burma campaign. The territory was thick and mountainous; the slopes were steep and once the monsoon set in, the conditions under which the troops were asked to fight became a nightmare of rain and mud. By mid-April Sato had taken all but the central ridge of Kohima and the garrison was nearing exhaustion. Stopford's 33rd Corps, moving up the road from Dimapur, were having to fight every inch of the way over terrain which presented appalling difficulties. From the start it was obvious that the battle for Kohima would be a long one. Meanwhile, Scoones's forward divisions had been caught on their way back from the Chindwin and Cowan's 17th was having to break through a series of road blocks. The order to retreat had been given too late; and the battle was starting untidily.

However, Cowan was an excellent soldier; he not only got his divisions back to the Imphal Plain, but dealt his opponent Yanagida such a savage blow that the latter lost faith in the campaign and was later dismissed. By mid-April Scoones's 4th Corps was concentrated and ready for the concerted attack to come. Meanwhile Mountbatten had received confirmation that ninety-nine transport aircraft would be lent him from Mediterranean Command, and with these Imphal could be supplied.

Though he remained confident, Mutaguchi was unable to capture Imphal in three weeks as promised; and on 23rd April he learned that at Kohima General

The Defeat of the Axis

Sato had gone over to the defensive. From now on events swung against Japan and though Mutaguchi moved forward to take command in the field, he could do nothing to prevent this. On 1st June Sato began retreating from Kohima against orders, hotly pursued by 33rd Corps. On 22nd June, the road to Imphal was opened and supplies and reinforcements poured in; from a beleaguered fortress, Imphal was transformed into a base for offensive operations. For Mutaguchi and the Japanese, disaster followed disaster. Sakurai's men had already come back defeated in the Arakan; and now the remnants of the XI Army streamed back towards the Chindwin, thousands dying from disease and starvation (Mutaguchi's ramshackle line of communications had collapsed) and attacked from the air by the RAF. This was the greatest disaster suffered so far by any Japanese army in the field.

Though the monsoon was now at its height, swamping roads and jungle alike, Mountbatten took the decision to fight on; and such was the morale of 14th Army that the troops responded. Rapidly the Japanese were pushed back over the Chindwin, and then hounded towards the Irrawaddy. Once his armies had debouched from the jungle, Slim planned to deploy his tanks on the central plain, where they could operate to maximum effect. The days of 'thrashing around in jungles', as Churchill had described the early operations in the Arakan, would be over.

It was in the early months of 1945 that the battle for central Burma developed. Slim, whose army now included West African and East African formations, apart from his veteran Indian and British divisions, now struck at Kimura (Kawabe's successor) who was defending the Irrawaddy line. In February Slim secured bridgeheads south of Mandalay, then captured Meiktila, to the south-east. In this swift and carefully prepared move, Slim had tricked Kimura, who now found his communications with Rangoon cut off, and his armies isolated from each other. Honda, whose XXXIII Army had been retreating before a combined offensive by Stilwell's forces and the Chinese, was rushed to take command at Meiktila. But though he threw in his forces in a series of ferocious actions it was to no avail. The remnants of his army were forced to retreat to the southeast, with XV Army on its right flank being rapidly cut to pieces.

The race was now on for Rangoon, and Slim's forces moved south in two great columns, Stopford's 33rd Corps down the Irrawaddy valley, and to the east, 4th Corps (now under Messervy) along the Toungoo/Pegu railway route. Slim decided that the enemy would not be able to hold him on both routes but, because of transport problems, had to concentrate his main thrust on the left. This route was the shorter of the two and, if Messervy's thrust was successful, vast numbers of Japanese would be cut off from their escape routes to the Sittang. Though, as the days of April went by, his advance gained momentum, Slim was in a difficult position. His land communications now stretched over a thousand miles, and could not survive the monsoon which was due in May. Somehow Rangoon must be taken before it broke. Fortunately, as he knew, an amphibious hook was being mounted from Akyab, now in Allied hands, and from Ramree, an island on the Burma coast, and if this were successful his task would be considerably eased.

Naturally, however, each division in 14th Army wanted to be the first to enter Rangoon, and none wanted this honour more dearly than Cowan's 17th Division, the only formation still in action which had taken part in the retreat back in 1942. Japanese XV Army was now little more than a rabble retreating through the Shan States and Honda's XXXIII Army, now desperately trying to reach the Sittang estuary, was being carved to fragments by Cowan's armoured columns. Town after town fell in rapid succession, and by 25th April Toungoo airfield had been secured. The fall of Rangoon could not be far away.

Decisive victory

In fact, it fell on 3rd May and the race was won by the troops on the seaborne landing, who were soon able to link up with their comrades coming from the north. The capital was found to be unoccupied. Now began the last phase of the Burma campaign. 15,000 men, the remnants of Sakurai's XXVIII Army, were trapped in the Irrawaddy valley and the Pegu Yomas to the east of it. Their only alternatives were to strike east or starve, and action could not long be delayed. On 11th May small parties began feeling their way forward, but found no escape route. Slim had ordered 4th Corps to cover the tracks leading from the Pegu Yomas, and 33rd Corps to clear the Irrawaddy Valley; he was determined that not one enemy soldier should escape. Though cornered, the Japanese still fought with their accustomed ferocity and time and again brought their mortars into action with great effect. On 3rd July Honda made a diversionary attack on Waw, hoping to help Sakurai by thinning Slim's line in the centre, but the attack petered out in the paddy fields. The monsoon had begun at the beginning of May and was unusually heavy. By July the Japanese were trying to slip round the flanks of the 14th Army positions in

small groups but even those who reached the banks of the Irrawaddy found themselves hounded night and day. As to those who tried to cross, Slim has recorded: 'They were surprised as they launched their rafts, shot as they swam and drifted across on logs, or swept away by the rapid current to drown.' Many who survived the passage of the Irrawaddy were cut down further east or drowned in the Sittang. In July 11,500 bodies were counted. And on 4th August no more Japanese came. There were none left to come. The Burma campaign was over.

How is one to sum up this extraordinary and unique episode of war in the 20th century? How was it that the Japanese won the first two rounds, but lost the third so decisively? Undoubtedly the weight of armament and manpower that Great Britain was able to summon from her Indian empire was an important factor; and the seizure of complete air superiority was vital. Moreover, from the spring of 1944 the British, Indian, and Gurkha soldiers were able to demonstrate that man for man they could outfight their enemy, and by the end their morale was superb. But troops are no good without the right leaders, and in Mountbatten and Slim, SEAC had two of the finest leaders ever produced by Great Britain. Arriving in India, Mountbatten had to overcome not only massive prejudice and inertia, but administrative and logistical problems of immense complexity; yet he succeeded through sheer professional ability, character, and integrity. As for Slim, he may be regarded by history as the greatest English general since Marlborough. Under him 14th Army was forged into a striking force of immense power. Quiet and courteous in manner, resolute but never too proud to take advice, even from private soldiers, he grew in stature as each month went by. And his vision, his prophecies, and his tactical plan were vindicated, for he gained one of the most complete and decisive victories in military history, destroying three entire armies in the field.

Of the Japanese it can be said that no soldiers ever fought harder or at greater sacrifice. Every unit fought to the last man; and, except for a few individuals, surrender was unknown throughout the whole campaign. Though restricted by the rigidity of Samurai code, the Japanese generals were men of considerable skill and energy. Mutaguchi came within an inch of success in the 'March on Delhi'; Sakurai made a great impression in the Arakan; and Honda was superb, even in defeat. If one has to select a single factor which swayed the balance it is Slim. The fury of the Japanese onslaught in 1944 was broken by his genius. And what came afterwards was inevitable.

The Bomb

The history of the birth of the atomic bomb has something to offer everyone. To the nuclear physicist, it is a tale of scientific research on an unprecedented scale, completed successfully in spite of appalling handicaps imposed by secrecy and wartime shortages of men and materials. To the engineer it is an epic of technological enterprise, in which 1,400 million dollars worth of productive resources were staked on four largely untested industrial processes, each one of which came perilously close to failure. To the political historian, it is a saga of machinations in the corridors of power, set against a backcloth of international hostility and suspicion. To the moral philosopher it is a study in conflicts of loyalty—the competing claims made upon a scientist or politician by his own instincts and ambitions, his

The fateful mushroom cloud billows up over the Japanese city of Nagasaki. It was here that the second atomic bomb was dropped on 9th August 1945

friends, his country, and mankind. To the man in the street it is like other stories of war – a drama at once thrilling and disgusting which is played by an enormous cast, with characters ranging from the most dedicated patriot to the most perfidious secret agent.

How do nuclear weapons work? The basic facts of nuclear physics had been established by 1940. To explain briefly, the nuclei of atoms consist of a mixture of protons and neutrons. The number of protons can be anything from one to 101 and this number determines the chemical element of the atom. Thus hydrogen nuclei have one proton, iron 26, uranium 92, and plutonium 94. The number of neutrons is variable, and nuclei differing only in the number of neutrons are called 'isotopes'. Thus there are three known isotopes of hydrogen with zero, one, and two neutrons, known colloquially as hydrogen, deuterium, and tritium respectively, and fourteen isotopes of uranium, of which the most abundant on earth are U^{235} and U^{238} with, respectively, 143 and 146 neutrons. The existence of these isotopes, and the non-existence of other isotopes with different numbers of neutrons, is a consequence of the rather peculiar laws governing the forces which hold nuclei together. Roughly speaking, protons and neutrons attract each other strongly when very close together and otherwise ignore or (in the case of protons) repel each other. Nature has had some difficulty in building stable units with this rather uncompromising material, and it turns out that the only viable combinations are those in which the nucleus has more neutrons than protons, but not many more. The most stable nucleus is that of iron (with 26 protons and 32 neutrons), and as a rule any nuclear reaction (that is a re-arrangement of protons and neutrons to form a new nucleus or nuclei) which leads to a nucleus in which the number of protons is closer to 26 than previously, results in a release of nuclear energy. Consequently one can obtain nuclear energy either by fusing together two nuclei which are much lighter than iron (for example, deuterium and tritium which both have one proton) or by fissioning (splitting into two roughly equal halves) nuclei which are much heavier than iron (for example, uranium 235 which has 92 protons). The hydrogen bomb is based on the former option, the atomic bomb on the latter.

Fortunately for the stability of the material world, both fusion and fission only occur under exceptional circumstances. Fusion only occurs when nuclei collide very violently, and until recently the temperature required (around 100 million degrees Centigrade) could only be reached on earth with the help of an atomic bomb.

Fission, on the other hand, is an exceptional phenomenon only because the universe is many millions of years old, and during its evolution most of the nuclei capable of spontaneous fission have already done so, and the few that are left (for example radium) fission so slowly as to be useless as sources of energy. However, since certain heavy nuclei are only just stable, the addition of one more neutron is sufficient to tip them over the edge. The uranium isotope U^{235} and plutonium are examples of this. Since each fission releases two or more neutrons, it is possible to induce a chain reaction: a first neutron is captured by a heavy nucleus which fissions, releasing two neutrons which are captured by two more nuclei and so on.

Such a chain reaction can be thought of as a population explosion in neutrons, and it leads to the enormously rapid release of nuclear energy which occurs in every atomic explosion. However, like all population explosions, it depends upon maintaining a 'reproduction rate' of more than one neutron per neutron captured. Two adverse factors can prevent this. First, if the lump of material containing the fissile nuclei is too small, too many neutrons can escape from its surface, rather than undergo capture by other nuclei within it and thus lead to fission. Second, if the nucleus which captures a neutron is of the wrong kind, it may not undergo fission at all, or not fast enough. The first factor is not crucial – it simply shows that the lump of material must exceed a certain critical size, and atomic bombs are in practice ignited by bringing together two lumps of uranium, each slightly less than the critical size. However, the second factor is crucial, for uranium 238 is not fissile. Thus even a fairly small proportion of U^{238} in a lump of U^{235} is sufficient to prevent an explosive chain reaction from occurring within it. In fact, natural uranium consists of 99·3% of U^{238} and a mere 0·7% of U^{235}, so before U^{235} can be used as a nuclear explosive it is necessary to separate it from a much larger quantity of U^{238}. The other fissile material, plutonium, does not exist in nature at all; however, if one bombards U^{238} with *slow* neutrons (obtained by passing fast neutrons through a 'moderator' made of heavy water or graphite in a nuclear reactor) it slowly becomes transmuted into plutonium which can then be separated off and used as an explosive. The first option (U^{235}) was used in the bomb exploded at Hiroshima, the second at Nagasaki.

Virtually all the physical ideas described above were familiar to the nuclear physicists of all nations by September 1939, and it is hardly surprising that every scientifically advanced country took steps to explore the military potential of nuclear energy.

But progress in the various countries concerned was very uneven. In France nearly all work stopped with the German occupation and most of the principal nuclear physicists fled to England (and later transferred to Canada), including two who were to make a considerable impact, Halban and Kowarski. In the Soviet Union the Academy of Sciences formed a 'special committee on the uranium problem', but its plans were frustrated by the German invasion which led to the evacuation of the bulk of Soviet industry and research establishments beyond the Urals. This delayed their nuclear programme until the end of 1942, by which time they were already receiving regular communications about the British and American work from their agent Klaus Fuchs. But it seems they did not give high priority to producing their own bomb until 1945.

In Germany, work was impeded from the outset by the loss of many of the most gifted nuclear physicists during the anti-Jewish purges of the academic community immediately before the war, and by factional disputes among those who remained. Nevertheless, by mid 1940 a powerful group of physicists, including Bothe, Weizsäcker, and Heisenberg, had set up a research institute in Berlin which was given the code name 'The Virus House'. Until about 1942 their work was at a level roughly comparable with that of America. However, in April 1942, an Anglo-Norwegian sabotage team wrecked the heavy water plant at Rjukan, upon which their programme heavily depended, and from then on their fortunes declined. Nevertheless, the possibility of an imminent German weapon continued to serve as a spur to Allied physicists until the discovery of Weizsäcker's papers in Strasbourg (captured in 1944) revealed how far behind they then were.

In Great Britain, most of the nation's scientists were initially occupied in other war work and in the early months the nuclear effort depended largely upon refugees who were prevented by their nationality from being incorporated into secret military projects! Nevertheless, during the early years, Great Britain made most of the main contributions to nuclear weapons development. The first serious indication that it was possible to build an atomic bomb was given in February 1940 by Professors Peierls and Frisch, then working at Birmingham University. In their outstanding *Memorandum* (which has since been published) they set out in three pages the main problems in designing a bomb, and the possible solutions. They pointed out for the first time that it was vital to separate U^{235} from U^{238} and indicated a method by which this could be done – 'thermal diffusion'. They calculated the 'critical mass' of U^{235} and obtained a figure of 600 grams, an answer which was subsequently revised upwards to nine kilograms as more accurate nuclear measurements were made. The resulting explosion, they estimated, would be equivalent to about 1,000 tons of TNT, and they commented on the lethal effects of the radiation which would be produced.

With the stimulus provided by the Peierls-Frisch memorandum, research on isotope separation was given steadily increasing support during 1940, chiefly under the direction of Professor Simon at Oxford University. By the end of the year it was clear that a different separation process—gaseous diffusion—was better than thermal diffusion and that a plant capable of separating enough U^{235} for a bomb would cost over five million pounds and would require materials for its construction which only considerable research and development effort could produce. In the meantime, the French physicists Halban and Kowarski, who had joined Cambridge University, had shown that a slow chain reaction could be maintained in natural uranium, producing plutonium, provided that heavy water was used to moderate the speed of the neutrons, and their colleagues Bretscher and Feather suggested that the plutonium could indeed be used as a nuclear explosive. Finally, at Birmingham University, Oliphant was working on a third technique for separating isotopes—the electromagnetic method. However, neither this approach nor the Cambridge plutonium approach appeared very hopeful at this stage, and when the Maud Committee (set up by the Air Ministry to investigate nuclear weapons) finally reported in mid-1941, it came down in favour of the gaseous diffusion method.

By this stage, it was clear to most British scientists that the larger scale work which was now required could only be carried out in America where the necessary productive resources were still available. Until 1942, the American effort had been less intense, and less successful, than the British; indeed they had repeatedly pressed for closer co-operation with Britain. By the summer of 1942, however, as a result of the impact of Pearl Harbour and the strongly favourable report by the Maud Committee on the feasibility of nuclear weapons, the American effort had at last acquired momentum. Their programme, which for security reasons was known as the 'Manhattan Project', was now put under the control of the army, in the person of the formidable General Groves, and expenditure which had hitherto been measured in thousands of dollars was now to be measured in millions. The timing of this major expansion was such that Great Britain graciously consented to co-operate with

America in a development programme at precisely the moment when the American scientific leaders Conant and Bush had decided they were no longer dependent upon British help. The resulting breakdown in co-operation was a disastrous episode in Anglo-American relations, and the resentment and suspicion on both sides were only slowly removed even after the quarrel had been officially resolved by direct discussions between Churchill and Roosevelt which led to the Quebec agreement in August 1943. In the meantime, work progressed in America on all the approaches described above—gaseous diffusion isotope separation under Urey and Dunning at Columbia University, electromagnetic separation under Lawrence at California, thermal diffusion separation under Abelson at Anacostia, and plutonium breeding with slow neutrons under Fermi at Chicago. The fluctuating fortunes of these four approaches were the despair of General Groves and his scientific advisers. The gaseous diffusion method required the manufacture of literally acres of 'membrane'—thin metal sheets with millions of fine holes in them through which uranium hexafluoride gas diffused—and the construction of a vast industrial plant consuming enough electricity to supply a large city. This plant, at Oak Ridge, Tennessee, was largely completed (at a cost of 280 million dollars) by July 1944 but technological difficulties with the 'membrane' were still proving so formidable that there was a serious possibility that the entire investment would be wasted. The electromagnetic method depended on scaling up a delicate laboratory instrument to industrial dimensions. The electromagnet used in Lawrence's early experiments had measured a few inches across: in the electromagnetic separation plant (also at Oak Ridge) it was a massive 122 feet long and 15 feet high with electrical windings made of 86,000 tons of pure silver, borrowed from the Treasury bullion reserves for the purpose. Here again there were repeated setbacks: the plant began to operate in February 1944, but by July it was clear that there was no hope of relying upon this method alone to produce enough U^{235} before the end of the war. The thermal diffusion process proved useless as a means of enriching U^{235} by a large amount, though good for small improvements. Finally there was the plutonium approach, which appeared very hopeful after the success of Fermi's first experimental pile, built in Chicago in December 1942. This pile, which was the brilliant forerunner of all subsequent nuclear reactors, led to the construction of several enormous plutonium breeding reactors at Hanford on the Columbia river. The first of these was set into action by Fermi in September 1944, but

within a few hours it shut itself down, as a result of a totally unexpected 'nuclear poisoning' phenomenon.

In the end, all four approaches were used. The thermal diffusion method was used to raise the U^{235} content of uranium from 0.7% to 0.9%. This slightly enriched material was then fed into the gaseous diffusion plant, which took it up to about 20% U^{235}, and finally the electromagnetic plant was used to produce material with over 90% U^{235}. As a result, enough U^{235} for a weapon was available by August 1945 at a total cost of about 1,000 million dollars. Plutonium production proved more difficult to plan, since the amount required to produce a weapon remained uncertain until the last minute, and there were doubts at one stage whether it could be made to work at all. For this reason, it was decided to test a plutonium weapon as soon as enough became available. This test was carried out in the Alamogordo desert in New Mexico on 17th July 1945, under the scientific direction of J.Robert Oppenheimer, the physicist who was responsible for the top secret weapon design laboratory at Los Alamos. The explosion, which comfortably exceeded the calculations of the theoreticians, had an impact which was not to be measured only in kilotons equivalent of TNT. For a number of the scientists who witnessed the test, the horror of the experience convinced them that the weapon must never be used against men. However the majority (at least of the senior scientists whose voices carried weight in government circles) had no serious doubts that nuclear weapons should be used against Japan if by so doing the war could be shortened. In spite of strenuous protests by Szilard and other leading scientists, the final decision to use it was taken by Truman, with the concurrence of Churchill, and the bombs were dropped on Hiroshima on 6th August and on Nagasaki on 9th August. The Japanese Emperor communicated his decision to surrender on the 10th. How events would have developed if the bombs had not been dropped is one of the great unresolvable uncertainties of history. A strong though not watertight case can be made that the Japanese would shortly have surrendered in any case, without further major bloodshed. At a different level it has been argued that the use of the weapons then has given them the credibility upon which their role as deterrents to world warfare now depends. It is impossible to be certain about such imponderables: what is certain is that the events of August 1945 initiated a debate about the morality and efficacy of these weapons of destruction which will continue at least until general and complete disarmament has become a practicable means of ordering human affairs.

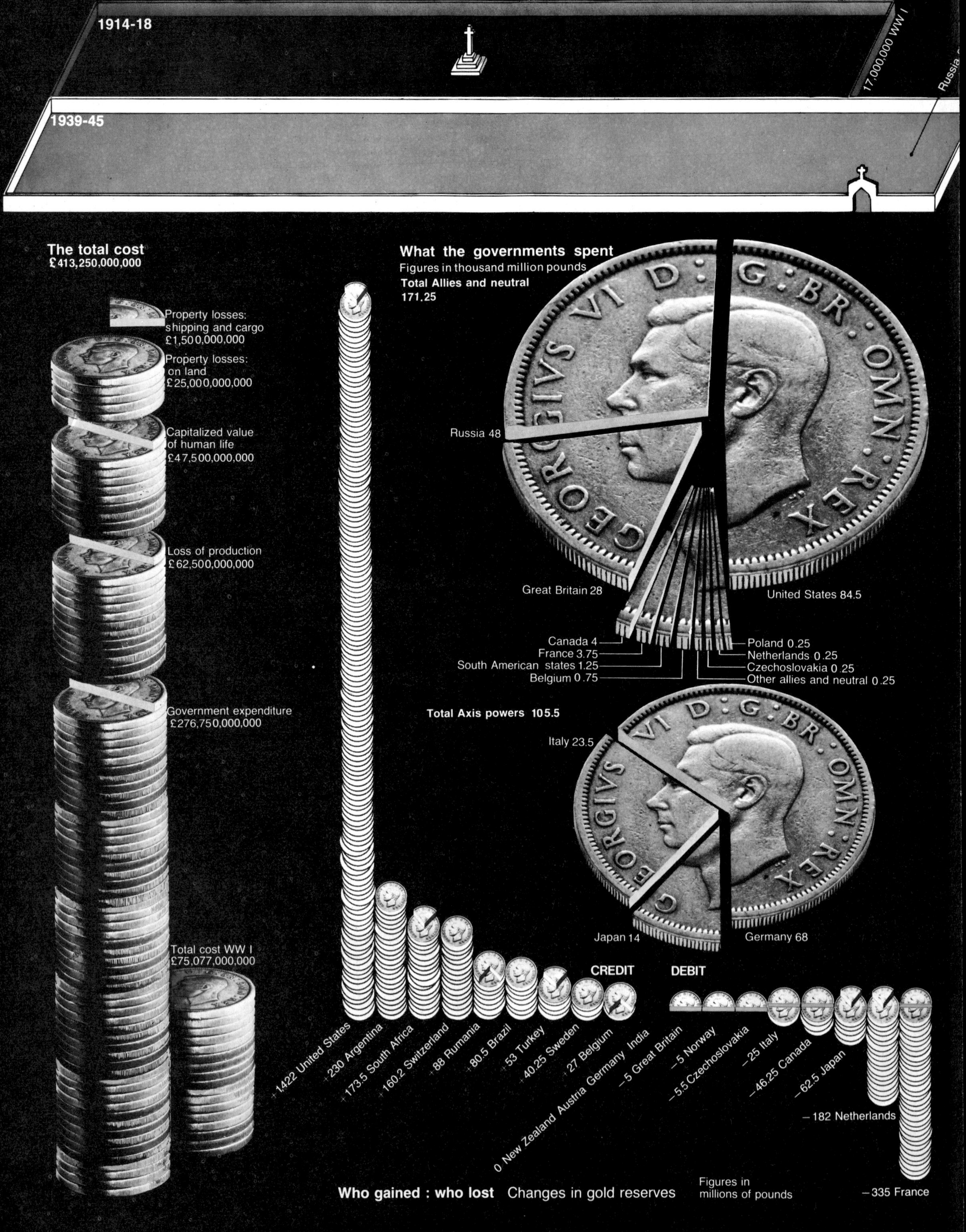

1914-18
17,000,000 WW I
Russia
1939-45
The total cost
£413,250,000,000
Property losses: shipping and cargo £1,500,000,000
Property losses: on land £25,000,000,000
Capitalized value of human life £47,500,000,000
Loss of production £62,500,000,000
Government expenditure £276,750,000,000
Total cost WW I £75,077,000,000
What the governments spent
Figures in thousand million pounds
Total Allies and neutral 171.25
Russia 48
Great Britain 28
United States 84.5
Canada 4
France 3.75
South American states 1.25
Belgium 0.75
Poland 0.25
Netherlands 0.25
Czechoslovakia 0.25
Other allies and neutral 0.25
Total Axis powers 105.5
Italy 23.5
Japan 14
Germany 68
CREDIT
DEBIT
+1,422 United States
+230 Argentina
+173.5 South Africa
+160.2 Switzerland
+88 Rumania
+80.5 Brazil
+53 Turkey
+40.25 Sweden
+27 Belgium
0 New Zealand Austria Germany India
−5 Great Britain
−5 Norway
−5.5 Czechoslovakia
−25 Italy
−46.25 Canada
−62.5 Japan
−182 Netherlands
−335 France
Who gained : who lost Changes in gold reserves
Figures in millions of pounds

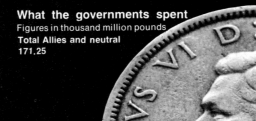

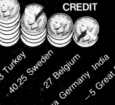

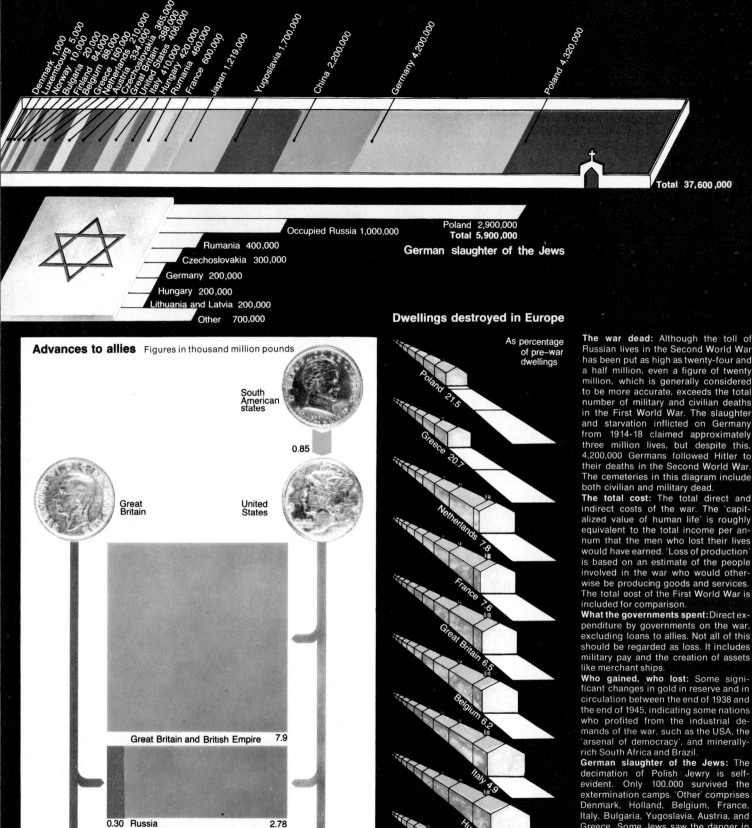

Denmark 1,000
Luxembourg 5,000
Norway 10,000
Bulgaria 20,000
Finland 84,000
Belgium 88,000
Greece 160,000
Netherlands 210,000
Austria 334,000
Czechoslovakia 365,000
Great Britain 388,000
United States 406,000
Italy 410,000
Hungary 420,000
Rumania 460,000
France 600,000
Japan 1,219,000
Yugoslavia 1,700,000
China 2,200,000
Germany 4,200,000
Poland 4,320,000

Total 37,600,000

Occupied Russia 1,000,000
Poland 2,900,000
Total 5,900,000
Rumania 400,000
Czechoslovakia 300,000
Germany 200,000
Hungary 200,000
Lithuania and Latvia 200,000
Other 700,000

German slaughter of the Jews

Dwellings destroyed in Europe

As percentage of pre–war dwellings

Poland 21.5
Greece 20.7
Netherlands 7.8
France 7.6
Great Britain 6.5
Belgium 6.2
Italy 4.9
Hungary 3.9
Norway 3.6
Czechoslovakia 3.4

Advances to allies   Figures in thousand million pounds

South American states

0.85

Great Britain

United States

Great Britain and British Empire   7.9

0.30   Russia   2.78

0.30   France   0.11

1.2   USA

China   0.40

0.1   Other countries   0.40

The war dead: Although the toll of Russian lives in the Second World War has been put as high as twenty-four and a half million, even a figure of twenty million, which is generally considered to be more accurate, exceeds the total number of military and civilian deaths in the First World War. The slaughter and starvation inflicted on Germany from 1914-18 claimed approximately three million lives, but despite this, 4,200,000 Germans followed Hitler to their deaths in the Second World War. The cemeteries in this diagram include both civilian and military dead.

The total cost: The total direct and indirect costs of the war. The 'capitalized value of human life' is roughly equivalent to the total income per annum that the men who lost their lives would have earned. 'Loss of production' is based on an estimate of the people involved in the war who would otherwise be producing goods and services. The total cost of the First World War is included for comparison.

What the governments spent: Direct expenditure by governments on the war, excluding loans to allies. Not all of this should be regarded as loss. It includes military pay and the creation of assets like merchant ships.

Who gained, who lost: Some significant changes in gold in reserve and in circulation between the end of 1938 and the end of 1945, indicating some nations who profited from the industrial demands of the war, such as the USA, the 'arsenal of democracy', and minerally-rich South Africa and Brazil.

German slaughter of the Jews: The decimation of Polish Jewry is self-evident. Only 100,000 survived the extermination camps. 'Other' comprises Denmark, Holland, Belgium, France, Italy, Bulgaria, Yugoslavia, Austria, and Greece. Some Jews saw the danger in time: 280,000 left Europe for the United States, South America, Great Britain, and Japan from 1933-40.

Advances to allies: Loans by the United States and Great Britain to their allies. British advances to the United States were termed 'reciprocal aid' and consisted of raw materials.

Dwellings destroyed in Europe: For some countries—including Russia and Germany—there are no exact figures. Rough estimates put the dwellings destroyed or damaged in these areas at about 7,500,000.

Index

Index

Acknowledgments

This book has been compiled from material contained in the *History of the 20th Century* partwork published by BPC Publishing Ltd. Pictures were obtained from the following sources: Archiv Gerstenberg; Associated Press; Australian War Memorial, Canberra; Herman Axelbank; AZ-Archiv, Vienna; Barnaby's Picture Library; Alexander Bernfes Archives; Black Star; Bundesarchiv, Koblenz; Camera Press; Central Press; Chicago Daily News; V. Chochola, Prague; Editions Rencontre; Fox Photos; Anne Frank Foundation, Amsterdam; Coll. C. Golding; William Green; Historical Research Unit; Robert Hunt Library; Imperial War Museum; Institute of Social History, Amsterdam; Keystone Press; Keystone, Tokyo; Kladderadatsch; Library of Congress; M.B.Linke, Warsaw; Magnum Photos; Magnum Photos (Robert Capa); Moro, Rome; Musée Royal de l'Armée, Brussels; Museo di Via Tasso, Rome; National Gallery of Canada; National Maritime Museum; Novosti; Pictorial Press; Planet News; Paul Popper; Press Association; Radio Times Hulton Picture Library; Science Museum, London; Search Ltd; Signal; Sikorski Museum, London (Chris Barket): Simplicissimus; SPB, Prague; Sudd-Verlag; Time-Life Inc; Topix; Ullstein; Ullstein (Rohnert); United Press International; US Air Force; US Army Dept; US Army Photo Dept; US Defence Dept; US Navy Dept; Westminster Library; World Wide Photos.

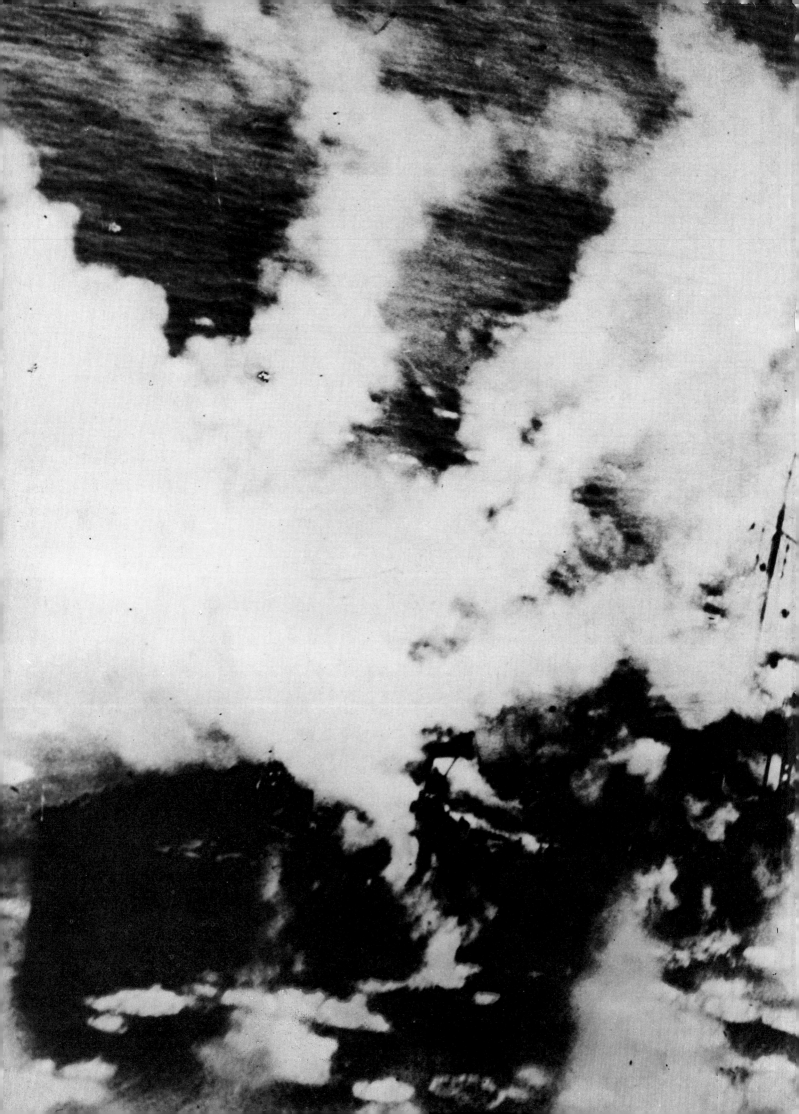